New Context

Teacher's Manual

Cornelsen

New Context Teacher's Manual

Im Auftrag des Verlags herausgegeben von
Prof. Hellmut Schwarz, Mannheim

Erarbeitet von
Dr. Jana Schubert, Leipzig; Sabine Tudan, Erfurt; Dr. Jens-Peter Green, Oldenburg;
Angela Ringel-Eichinger, Bietigheim-Bissingen; Hellmut Schwarz, Mannheim;
Mervyn Whittaker, Bad Dürkheim; sowie
Barbara Derkow Disselbeck und Allen J. Woppert

Verlagsredaktion
Michael R. Ferguson (Projektleitung), Dr. Marion Kiffe (verantwortlich),
Neil Porter, Marc Proulx

Umschlag
Knut Waisznor

Layoutkonzept
Gisela Hoffmann

Technische Umsetzung
Ludwig Niethammer, Berlin

Weitere Bestandteile des Lehrwerks
Student's Book: Bestellnummer 310450
Workbook: 310477
Listening Comprehension Doppel-CD: 310485
Video: 310493
DVD: 360148

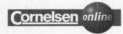 http://www.cornelsen.de

1. Auflage   Druck 6 5 4 3   Jahr 08 07 06 05

© 2003 Cornelsen Verlag, Berlin

Druck: CS-Druck CornelsenStürtz, Berlin

ISBN 3-464-31046-9

Bestellnummer 310469

Gedruckt auf Recyclingpapier, hergestellt aus 100 % Altpapier.

INHALTSVERZEICHNIS

Allgemeine Grundlagen

New Context ist ein kombiniertes Lese- und Arbeitsbuch und entspricht damit den Forderungen neuerer (Rahmen-) Lehrpläne und Bildungsstandards, die neben dem Erwerb von soziokulturellem Wissen die Schulung von Kompetenzen in das Zentrum des Lernprozesses rücken.

Im Vergleich zu traditionellen Oberstufenlesebüchern, die vorwiegend landeskundlich orientierte Textsammlungen mit angeschlossenen Frageapparaten darstellten, zeichnet sich *New Context* durch eine Reihe von Innovationen aus:

– Zusätzlich zu den herkömmlichen Themen mit soziologisch-politischem und historischem Schwerpunkt (z.B. Kapitel 8, „The UK – Redefining a Nation?"; Kapitel 9, „We the People") werden auf die Entwicklungsstufe von Jugendlichen zugeschnittene und somit diskursfördernde Themen (z.B. Kapitel 10, „Who Am I?"; Kapitel 11, „Moving Out") aufgenommen. Andere Kapitel haben propädeutische Funktion im Hinblick auf die bevorstehende Studien- und Berufswahl (z.B. Kapitel 3, „Science and Technology"; Kapitel 5, „A Global Marketplace").

– Das Training von *skills*, sowohl der vier *basic skills* als auch von *study skills*, und damit die Ausbildung von Methodenkompetenz steht zumindest gleichrangig neben dem Erwerb von Sachkompetenz und ist in die Bearbeitung der Themen integriert.

– Ein besonderer Akzent im Rahmen der Kompetenzschulung ruht auf dem Sprachtraining, das auch auf der Oberstufe das Fundament des Unterrichts bilden und daher intensiv betrieben werden sollte. Es wird – mit Schwerpunkt auf der Lexik- und der Stilebene – in die Arbeit mit praktisch allen Texten einbezogen, hat seine spezifische Ausprägung im Bereich des *everyday English* (vgl. die „Getting Along In English"-Seite in jedem Kapitel) und vernachlässigt ebenso wenig die Wiederholung und Fehlerprophylaxe in der Grammatik (vgl. die „Watch Your Language"-Seite in jedem Kapitel).

Die Adressaten von *New Context* sind S der Oberstufe, die dieses Buch ab Jahrgangsstufe bzw. Klasse 11 bis zum Abitur benutzen können, und zwar aufgrund der (im *Teacher's Manual* ausgewiesenen) Differenzierung der Texte nach Schwierigkeitsgrad auf allen Niveaustufen bzw. in allen Kurstypen.

Ein zentrales Ziel der Arbeit mit *New Context* stellt die Entwicklung der **Lernerautonomie** dar: Die S werden durch die Aufgabengestaltung zunehmend vom lehrer- zum selbstgesteuerten Lernen geführt und erwerben damit eine immer größer werdende Lernkompetenz, die sich auch in der Beteiligung an der Textauswahl niederschlagen sollte. Sie manifestiert sich besonders in der **Selbstevaluation** der S, die mit der „Introduction" und den dort bereitgestellten „Self-assessment Sheets" beginnt und kontinuierlich bis zum Abitur wiederholt werden sollte.

Nach wie vor spielt der sachgemäße **Umgang mit Texten** unterschiedlichster Art eine zentrale Rolle: Die S lernen, Sachtexte und fiktionale Texte hörend und lesend zu erschließen sowie angemessene Analysetechniken anzuwenden (auch mit Hilfe der „Skills Pages" und des „Glossary"). Ebenso wichtig wie der rezeptive ist der produktive Ansatz: In den Aufgaben zu nahezu jedem Text werden die S aufgefordert und angeleitet, selbst Texte zu verfassen – häufig mit einer kreativen Komponente. Das gilt ebenso für den ausgeprägten Bereich der Bild- und Filmbetrachtung: Die *viewing skills* münden fast immer in eine produktive Sprech- oder Schreibaufgabe .

Ziel ist aber nicht nur das fertige „Produkt", sondern auch der **Lernprozess**, der zu ihm hinführt. Viele Aufgaben sind daher als *research* oder *project tasks* formuliert und veranlassen die S, in Partner- oder Gruppenarbeit zu kooperieren, mithin auch soziale Kompetenzen zu entwickeln.

Lernen mit *New Context* vollzieht sich nicht einseitig kognitiv, sondern **ganzheitlich**: Texte und Aufgaben sprechen unterschiedliche Sinne an, evozieren Empathie und affektive Zuwendung. Bei ihrer Auswahl wurde die motivatorische Zielsetzung besonders hoch gewichtet.

Die Bestandteile von *New Context*

Schülerbuch (SB): s.u.

Teacher's Manual (TM): s.u.

***Workbook*:** Das *Workbook* enthält zusätzliche Aufgaben zur Sprach- und Textarbeit sowie zum *skills*-Training. Ein Lösungsheft ermöglicht das eigenverantwortliche Arbeiten der S. Auch die „Self-assessment Sheets" dienen der Selbstkontrolle.

Doppel-CD: Die zwei CDs umfassen eine Auswahl an Texten aus dem SB sowie weitere Hörmaterialien, auf die im SB jeweils verwiesen wird (z.B. alle Hörtexte aus den „Getting Along in English"-Seiten).

Video/DVD: Video und DVD präsentieren Auszüge aus Filmen und TV-Sendungen zu den einzelnen Kapiteln des SB, das differenzierte Aufgaben dazu anbietet.

New Context Online (www.cornelsen-teachweb.de/co/newcontext): Dieser Service umfasst folgende Angebote, die – bis auf die Klausurvorschläge – kostenfrei sind:

– alle Kopiervorlagen aus dem TM und zusätzliche Arbeitsblätter.

– zu jedem Kapitel eine Zusammenstellung des „Active Vocabulary" und des „Topic Vocabulary" (s.u.) zum Kopieren und Bearbeiten für die individuelle Lerngruppe.

– die Transkripte aller Hörtexte sowie TV- und Filmauszüge, die auf CD bzw. Video/DVD zu finden sind.

– Klausurvorschläge: Es werden zu jedem Kapitel zwei Klausurtexte angeboten. Aufgrund der unterschiedlichen Leistungsmessformen in den einzelnen Bundesländern werden zu jedem Klausurtext zwei auf die Anforderungen verschiedener Bundesländer zugeschnittene Aufgabenapparate angeboten. Hinzu kommen Vorschläge für neuere, kreative bzw. prozessorientierte Leistungsmessformen. Die Klausuren können von L an die Bedürfnisse ihrer Lerngruppe angepasst werden. Der Zugriff erfolgt über die Cornelsen-Kundennummer der L.

Unterrichtssoftware: Sie enthält neuartige Aufgabenformen zu den Themen, Fertigkeitsbereichen und sprachlichen Anforderungen des SB, die mediengerecht aufbereitet werden.

Der Aufbau des Schülerbuchs

Das SB besteht aus folgenden Teilen:

– einer **„Introduction"**: Sie enthält einen fiktionalen Langtext und einen kürzeren Sachtext mit zugeordneten Aufgaben, die diagnostische Funktion haben (auch in Verbindung mit den „Self-assessment Sheets") und ein gemeinsames Fundament für die beginnende Oberstufenarbeit legen sollen.

– **elf Kapiteln**, denen jeweils ein Thema zugrunde liegt und die in beliebiger Reihenfolge behandelt werden können. Allerdings wird durch die im SB gewählte Anordnung eine mögliche Chronologie vorgeschlagen. Alle Kapitel enthalten die gleichen „Bausteine", die jedoch unterschiedlich positioniert und flexibel einsetzbar sind. Lediglich das „Lead-in" (immer am Anfang des Kapitels) und „Watch Your Language" (jeweils am Ende) haben ihren festen Ort.

Daneben ist es möglich, durch die kapitelübergreifende Zusammenstellung von Texten mit thematischen, textsorten- oder autorenbezogenen Schwerpunkten neue Unterrichtsreihen zu entwickeln (vgl. hierzu auch die Übersicht über Textsorten, Themen und Autoren unten).

– **„Skills Pages"**, auf denen 29 unterschiedliche *skills*, also Fertigkeiten, Methodenelemente und Lernstrategien, auf Englisch definiert und erläutert werden. Sie sind durch ein Verweissystem mit der „Introduction" und den elf Kapiteln verwoben.

– einem **„Glossary"**, in dem 150 zentrale literarische Termini – auf die ebenfalls aus den Texten heraus Bezug genommen wird – erklärt werden. Sie sind in einer alphabetischen Liste (S. 270) übersichtlich zusammengestellt.

Der Aufbau der Kapitel des SB

Jedes der elf Kapitel hat folgende Bestandteile:

– **„Lead-in"**: Alle Kapitel beginnen mit einem – häufig bildgesteuerten – zweiseitigen Einführungsteil. Dieser sollte am Anfang behandelt werden, da er in wichtige Aspekte des Themas einführt und die lernpsychologisch unverzichtbare Verbindung zu den Erfahrungen und dem Umfeld der S herstellt. Daneben reaktiviert er zentralen Wortschatz und vermittelt neue, auf das Thema bezogene Lexik. Bereits hier werden erste Hinweise auf die „Skills Pages" und das „Glossary" gegeben.

– **„Sections"** mit Texten und Aufgaben: Jedes Kapitel besteht aus mehreren thematisch bestimmten, nummerierten *sections* mit authentischen Texten und einer Palette von Aufgaben. Die Fülle an Texten und Aufgaben bedingt, dass nicht alle Kapitel komplett unterrichtet werden können, sondern von L – nach Möglichkeit unter Mitwirkung der S – eine Auswahl getroffen werden muss. Dies erweist sich auch deshalb als sinnvoll, da der nötige Freiraum zum Einsatz von Ganzschriften bzw. selbst gefundenen Texten geschaffen werden muss.

Die Texte decken eine große Bandbreite von Textsorten ab: Neben klassischen Lesetexten finden sich Gemälde und Fotos sowie (auf CD bzw. Video/DVD) auditive und audiovisuelle Texte. So wird dem erweiterten Textbegriff Rechnung getragen.

Die Aufgaben sind sowohl kognitiv-analytisch als auch kreativ-produktionsorientiert bzw. handlungsorientiert angelegt. Sie werden nur selten als Fragen, sondern zumeist als *tasks* (mit spezifischen „Operatoren" wie *collect/describe/ explain/compare/discuss*) präsentiert. Einfache Verständnisfragen werden dagegen fast völlig ausgespart (diese werden aber zu einigen Texten im TM angeboten). Zahlreiche Aufgaben legen andere Sozialformen als den traditionellen Frontalunterricht nahe. So werden regelmäßig Vorschläge für Rollenspiele, Projekte, Partner- und Gruppenarbeit gemacht, um den S mehr Eigenverantwortung für ihren Lernprozess zu übertragen, soziale Kompetenzen zu fördern und unterschiedlichen Lernertypen gerecht zu werden.

Lexikalische Hilfen für die Bearbeitung einzelner Aufgaben werden durchgehend in der Rubrik „Useful Words and Phrases" bereitgestellt.

In der Randspalte finden sich Annotationen, „Trouble Spots" und Verweise auf die „Skills Pages" bzw. das „Glossary", die von den S zunehmend selbstständig einbezogen werden sollten.

– **„Context Box"**: In jedem Kapitel werden die authentischen Haupttexte durch eine lexikorientierte „Context Box" ergänzt. Sie enthält zwar auch wichtige Informationen zum Thema des Kapitels oder einem zentralen Teilaspekt, unterscheidet sich aber deutlich von der „Info-Box" früherer Lehrwerke, die eher faktenorientiert und enzyklopädisch angelegt war. Im Text der neuentwickelten „Context Box" wurde die Zahl der Fakten dagegen auf ein für deutsche Lerner realistisches Maß zurückgeschraubt zugunsten eines großen Angebots an themenbezogenem Vokabular, das zumeist in hochfrequenten Kollokationen (und blau hervorgehoben) präsentiert wird. Ebenfalls neu sind abschließende Aufgaben, die dazu beitragen, sowohl den Wortschatz als auch den Inhalt zu festigen.

– **„Getting Along in English"**: In Oberstufenlesebüchern wurde traditionell auf die Übung des *everyday English* verzichtet. In *New Context* ist dieses Defizit in mehrfacher Hinsicht beseitigt:
  Auf den „Getting Along in English"-Seiten des SB werden die S mit Alltagssituationen wie einem Arztbesuch, einer Essenseinladung oder Urlaubsvorbereitungen konfrontiert. Häufig hören sie dazu von der CD Musterdialoge mit englischen Muttersprachlern unterschiedlicher regionaler Herkunft. Dabei schulen sie nicht nur ihre rezeptiven und produktiven Fertigkeiten und (re)aktivieren die nötigen Sprachmittel, sondern erwerben auch interkulturelle Handlungsfähigkeit – ein wesentliches Ziel von *New Context*.

– **„Watch Your Language"**: Die Abschlussseite eines jeden Kapitels, die allerdings bereits in den Unterricht mit den *sections* einbezogen werden kann, ist ausschließlich der sprachlich-stilistischen Arbeit gewidmet. In der Regel überprüfen die S eingangs ihre sprachliche Kompetenz im Hinblick auf ausgewählte, besonders fehlerträchtige Bereiche der englischen Grammatik und punktuell auch des Wortschatzes. Nach diesem diagnostischen Teil wiederholen sie die relevanten Grammatik-Paragraphen und vertiefen ihr Wissen und ihre Sprachbewusstheit. Den Abschluss bilden Übungen, um – in Verbindung mit dem *Workbook* und der Unterrichtssoftware – die Anwendungssicherheit der S zu erhöhen.

Das *Teacher's Manual*

Das TM wurde mit über 400 Seiten Umfang im Format DIN A4 sehr aufwändig gestaltet, um den L möglichst vielfältige Hilfen anbieten zu können. Zur leichteren Handhabung liegt es gelocht und perforiert vor; die Übersichtlichkeit wird durch die blaue Farbe erhöht.

Jedes Kapitel des TM enthält folgende Elemente (vgl. z.B. S. 39, 45 und 189):

– ein **„Didaktisches Inhaltsverzeichnis"**

– eine **Textbox**, in der zur schnellen Information für jeden Text Quelle, Thema, Länge, Schwierigkeitsgrad („basic" und/oder „advanced") übersichtsartig angegeben sind.

– Lernvokabular (**„Active Vocabulary"**): Zu jedem Text werden ausgewählte Wörter oder Kollokationen angegeben (ca. 10–20 pro Text), die die S lernen, d.h. in ihren produktiven Wortschatz integrieren sollen. Ausgenommen davon ist die „Context Box", deren blau hervorgehobener Wortschatz dem Lernvokabular der anderen Seiten entspricht. Auch für das „Lead-in" mit seinem den Wortschatz reaktivierenden und strukturierenden Schwerpunkt sowie für die „Getting Along in English"- und „Watch Your Language"-Seiten wurde auf eine separate Ausweisung des Lernwortschatzes verzichtet.

– **„Didaktisch-methodische Hinweise"** zu allen Themen, Kapitelteilen, Texten, Bildern, Hörpassagen und Videoauszügen. Im Anschluss an die Ausführungen zur Auswahl und Zielsetzung werden lediglich knappe methodische Vorschläge gemacht, da die Vorgehensweise in der Regel in die Aufgabenstellung im SB integriert ist.

- **„Unterrichtstipps"**, die spezielle methodische Einzelhinweise (z.B. zum Einstieg) geben.

- **„Info"** mit weiterführenden Informationen zu Themen, Autoren, Begriffen usw. Sie stellen ein bewusst weit gespanntes Angebot für L bzw. auch für die Projektarbeit der S dar.

- Vorschläge zur **„Differenzierung"** und **Zusatzaufgaben**. Diese umfassen auch Arbeitsaufträge zur Sprachmittlung (Mediation), z.B. Zusammenfassungen und Auswertungen englischsprachiger Textvorlagen in der Muttersprache. Für die Zusatzaufgaben, bei denen die S Textstellen übersetzen sollen, werden online Lösungsvorschläge angeboten.

- **„Lösungshinweise"**: Sie werden auf Englisch zu allen geschlossenen oder halb-offenen Aufgaben gegeben, gelegentlich mit Tafelbildern. Die Schülerantworten werden je nach Leistungsvermögen der Lerngruppe variieren. Die Formulierungen in den Lösungshinweisen stellen deshalb keinen Erwartungshorizont dar, der in jeder Unterrichtssituation zu erreichen ist. Sie sind vielmehr Maximallösungen, von denen in schwächeren Lerngruppen – v.a. sprachlich – deutliche Abstriche zu machen sind. Auf der Grundlage der Lösungshinweise können Tafelbilder entwickelt werden, die dem jeweiligen Leistungsstand der S entsprechen.

- **„Kopiervorlagen"**
  - mit zusätzlichen Unterrichtsideen oder Zusatzinformationen
  - mit dem Lernvokabular „Active Vocabulary" (vgl. S. 430)
  - mit dem „Topic Vocabulary": Sie enthalten möglichst umfassenden, strukturierten Wortschatz zum Kernthema jedes Kapitels, der – anders als das „Active Vocabulary" – nicht notwendigerweise aus den Texten des SB stammt. Diese KVs sind als Arbeitsblätter zu verstehen, mit deren Hilfe die S aktive Wortschatzarbeit betreiben, indem sie deutsche oder englische Erläuterungen zu den Begriffen oder wichtige Kollokationen zusammenstellen. Da es zu den Themen Vereinigtes Königreich (Kapitel 8) und USA (Kapitel 9) schwer möglich ist, eine umfassende Sammlung von Vokabular anzubieten, entfallen die KVs für diese Kapitel.

- **Transkripte** der auditiven bzw. audiovisuellen Texte auf CD bzw. Video/DVD

- Verweise auf das *Workbook*

- **Symbole** zur schnellen Orientierung:

    `CD`

    `VIDEO`   auch für die DVD

        für Partnerarbeit

    ❖   für Gruppenarbeit

    ☞   für Dinge, die bei der Organisation des Unterrichts rechtzeitig bedacht werden müssen, oder für Warnhinweise

Eine Auswahl von Textformen, Themen und Autoren in New Context

Text forms
– Adverts: pp. 39, 44, 108, 122, 130, 195

– Speeches: pp. 144, 145, 169, 173

– Poems: pp. 26, 43, 74, 77, 131, 166, 198, 207

– Short stories: pp. 8, 47, 60, 80, 128, 186, 217

– Fable: p. 111

– Excerpts from novels: pp. 31, 120, 125, 135, 146, 165, 174, 202, 204, 214

– Excerpts from dramas: pp. 78, 92, 154, 190

– Songs: pp. 37, 41, 64, 77, 104, 167, 193

– Statistics/figures: pp. 28–29, 150, 153, 170, 213

Visuals
– Paintings/drawings: pp. 21, 43, 75, 76, 124, 151, 155, 168

– Photos: pp. 26–27, 36–37, 43, 55, 137–139, 142–143, 200

– Cartoons: pp. 24, 68, 82, 87, 88, 91, 107, 118

Video material
pp. 33, 64, 88, 117, 132, 134, 137–139, 156, 182, 191, 215

Listening material
– Listening only texts: pp. 14, 24, 34, 37, 41, 64, 65, 77, 78, 79, 100, 101, 119, 135, 140, 145, 149, 166, 177, 182, 192, 193, 194, 201, 216

– Texts in SB on the CDs: pp. 43, 77, 80, 198, 207

Topics
– *Economy: Chapter 5;* pp. 39, 85, 115, 120, 152, 157, 160B, 168, 170, 174, 182

– *Education / growing up: Introduction, Chapters 1, 2, 10 and 11;* pp. 78, 80, 83, 124, 146, 167D, 178

– *Nature and the environment: Chapter 4;* pp. 154, 155, 166, 180, 182C

– *Immigration:* pp. 102, 144, 145, 146, 151, 152, 160, 166B, 167C, 168, 174, 175, 207, 217

– *Ethnic minorities:* pp. 122 (ad), 135, 144, 145, 146, 151, 152, 168, 170, 173, 174, 175, 186, 189, 190, 191

– *Globalization:* pp. 38, 47, 101, 115, 116, 118, 158, 161, 171, 172, 182C

– *The English language:* pp. 101, 161, 192, 193

– *War and peace:* Chapter 7; pp. 47, 60, 64, 69, 111, 160, 171, 207

– *Australia:* p. 8

– *Ireland:* p. 217

Authors

Douglas Adams: p. 56
Maya Angelou: p. 198
Paul Auster: p. 165
Julian Barnes: pp. 125, 156
T. Coraghessan Boyle: p. 174
Ray Bradbury: p. 60
Billy Bragg: p. 104
Bill Bryson: p. 180
Melvin Burgess: p. 204
George W. Bush: p. 169
Robin Cook: p. 144
Queen Elizabeth II: p. 145
Niall Ferguson: p. 158
Milton and Rose Friedman: p. 102
Robert Frost: p. 198
Ernest Hemingway: pp. 127, 128
Jesse Jackson: p. 173

James Joyce: p. 217
Paul Krugman: p. 85
Philip Larkin: p. 26
Emma Lazarus: p. 166
Laurie Lee: p. 202
Katherine Lee Bates: p. 166
Tom Lehrer: p. 64
Alan J. Lerner: p. 193
Andrea Levy: p. 214
John McCrae: p. 131
Arthur Miller: p. 92
Willy Russell: p. 78
Carl Sandburg: p. 131
William Shakespeare: pp. 43, 77, 132–134, 154
Zadie Smith: p. 146
James Thurber: p. 111
William Butler Yeats: p. 77

Abkürzungen	
S	Schüler/innen
L	Lehrer/in
CEG	*Cornelsen English Grammar* (Best-Nr. 63100)
OALD	*Oxford Advanced Learner's Dictionary*, 6. Auflage 2000 (Best.-Nr. 115429)
SB	*Student's Book*
TM	*Teacher's Manual*
WB	*Workbook*
KV	Kopiervorlage
OHP	*Overhead Projector*
AE	*American English*
BE	*British English*
AustrE	*Australian English*
CanE	*Canadian English*
IrE	*Irish English*
v	*verb*
adj	*adjective*
n	*noun*

Zu Beginn der Oberstufe kommen in der Klasse 11 bzw. den neu gegründeten Kursen S mit den unterschiedlichsten Kenntnissen und Fähigkeiten, mit verschiedenen Vorerfahrungen und Motivationen zusammen. Das Einstiegskapitel in *New Context* hat daher zweierlei Funktionen: die Schaffung gemeinsamer Grundlagen für die Arbeit mit fiktionalen wie nicht-fiktionalen Texten und die Selbstevaluation der S. Die Überschrift des Kapitels – „Finding Myself" – spiegelt so nicht nur die Inhalte der beiden Texte wider (das Erwachsenwerden), sondern auch die Funktion des Kapitels: eine Art *finding oneself* im Hinblick auf die eigene Position im Spracherwerbsprozess.

Didaktisches Inhaltsverzeichnis

SB, p.	Title	TM, p.	Text form	Topic	Skills and activities
8	**Land/scape** Nadia Wheatley Sections ix–xi: CD1, track 1	13	short story	son–father relationship	skimming; speculating about the continuation of a story; working with imagery; extensive reading; listening comprehension; examining a coming-of-age story; writing an account of a family trip; self-assessment
18	**Young, Talented and Rebellious** Marie-Anne Sapsted	19	feature story	teenagers rebelling against high-pressure parents	discussing with a partner; listening and correcting a partner's mistakes; analysing the difference between a fictional and literary text; writing a text for a school magazine; self-assessment

Selbstevaluation mit Hilfe von *self-assessment sheets*

Die Evaluation des Kenntnisstands der S ist besonders in Klasse 11 bzw. am Anfang der Kursstufe von Bedeutung, da hieraus Schlussfolgerungen für die weitere Arbeit gezogen werden können. Wenn die S diese Einschätzung selbst vornehmen, wird ihre Reflexionsfähigkeit geschult und sie werden motiviert, zielgerichtet und eigenverantwortlich an der Beseitigung der festgestellten Defizite und am Ausbau ihrer Stärken zu arbeiten. Es ist davon auszugehen, dass vor der ersten Selbstevaluation ein Bewusstsein für und ein Interesse an der Untersuchung eigener Lernprozesse geschaffen werden muss. Den S sollte deutlich gemacht werden, dass die Selbstevaluation keine Form der Leistungsüberprüfung darstellt, sondern im Wesentlichen zwei Zielen dient:

1. das eigene Lernen in den Blick zu nehmen, um die Lernkompetenz zu verbessern und die Arbeit an der individuellen Lernersprache eigenständig gestalten zu können,
2. gemeinsam mit L das Lernen in der Lerngruppe nach deren Bedürfnissen zu planen.

Um die Selbsteinschätzung der S zu strukturieren, werden Selbstevaluationsbögen (*self-assessment sheets*) verwendet. Diese Bögen befinden sich im WB (vgl. S. 79) sowie als Kopiervorlagen im TM (vgl. S. 21). Hier bewerten die S anhand kleinschrittiger Fragen ihre Fähigkeiten in allen Bereichen der Sprachverwendung: Lesen und Hören, Sprechen, Schreiben und Diskutieren, Sicherheit in Grammatik und Wortschatz. Damit die S beim ersten *self-assessment* eine Basis für diese Selbsteinschätzung haben, beziehen sich einige der Evaluationsbögen auf konkrete Texte und dazugehörige Aufgaben. Ein anderer Teil der Evaluationsbögen ist hingegen so angelegt, dass sie die Fähigkeiten der S textunabhängig überprüfen und deshalb in regelmäßigen Abständen (z.B. am Ende jedes Schulhalbjahres) eingesetzt und mit dem vorigen Evaluationsbogen verglichen werden können (vgl. die Möglichkeiten für Einträge auf den rechten Seiten). Am Ende jedes *self-assessments* bekommen die S die Gelegenheit, einen „Plan of action" zu erstellen, in dem sie festlegen, wie sie ihre diagnostizierten Defizite bekämpfen wollen.

Die Arbeit mit den *self-assessment sheets* ist fakultativ. Die Evaluationsbögen können daher den Bedürfnissen der Lerngruppe angepasst werden, z.B. indem sie in größeren Zeitabschnitten bearbeitet oder indem einzelne Abschnitte ausgelassen werden.

Vor der Lektüre der Kurzgeschichte „Land/scape" (vgl. SB, S. 8) beantworten die S die Fragen in Teil I der Evaluationsbögen. Dabei sollte ihnen die Funktion des *self-assessments* deutlich gemacht werden (s.o.). Teile II bis IV werden im Anschluss an einzelne Abschnitte der beiden Texte der „Introduction" bearbeitet (das SB verweist an den entsprechenden Stellen auf die Evaluationsbögen). Der Hörverstehenstext für Teil III befindet sich auf CD1, *track* 1; ein Transkript befindet sich auf S. 37. Dabei muss darauf geachtet werden, dass die S nach Bearbeitung der Aufgaben im Buch ihre Ergebnisse vergleichen, bevor sie die *self-assessment sheets* bearbeiten, damit sie eine Grundlage für die Einschätzung ihrer Fähigkeiten haben. Teile V–VI sind unabhängig von den Texten und können zu beliebigen Zeiten eingesetzt und wiederholt werden, damit die S ihre sprachliche Weiterentwicklung dokumentieren und beobachten können. Insbesondere erhalten sie dann Aufschluss darüber, ob ihr in Teil VII entworfener *plan of action* wirkungsvoll war oder ob er ggf. angepasst werden muss.

Die S füllen ihre Evaluationsbögen in Einzelarbeit aus, dann werden die Ergebnisse in der gesamten Lerngruppe diskutiert. Stärken und Schwächen der Gruppe werden festgehalten und weitere Schritte zur Übung und Vertiefung vereinbart. Eine zweite Möglichkeit, die Evaluationsbögen auszuwerten, besteht darin, sie anonym ausfüllen zu lassen und dann einzusammeln. Nach ihrer Auswertung können gemeinsam mit den S die wichtigsten Ergebnisse für die Lerngruppe festgehalten und erörtert werden. Haben die S ein Portfolio angelegt, können die *self-assessment sheets* darin integriert werden.

Die folgende Übersicht stellt die inhaltlichen Schwerpunkte der Evaluationsbögen, ihren Bezug zu den Texten sowie die Abfolge von Textbearbeitung und Evaluation dar:

Text	Aufgaben	Assessment sheet, Teil	Evaluierte Bereiche
–	–	I	*experience of learning English; general assessment*
„Land/scape", *sections* i–iii, (vgl. SB, S. 8–14)	Nr. 1–4 (vgl. SB, S. 14; TM, S. 15)	II	*reading comprehension; working with the tasks; classroom discussion*
„Land/scape", *sections* ix–xi, (vgl. CD1, *track* 1)	Nr. 5–9 (vgl. SB, S. 14–15; TM, S. 17)	III	*listening comprehension; working with the tasks; classroom discussion*
„Land/scape", *sections* xiv–xvi (vgl. SB, S. 15–17) „Young, Talented and Rebellious" (vgl. SB, S. 18–19)	Nr. 16 (vgl. SB, S. 17; TM, S. 18) Nr. 1–7 (vgl. SB, S. 19; TM, S. 19)	IV	*partner discussion; writing; general assessment of working with the introduction*
–	–	V	*the four skills*
–	–	VI	*correctness and comprehension*
–	–	VII	*(plan of action)*

SB, S. 8 **A Land/scape** Nadia Wheatley

Source:	*The Night Tolkien Died* (1994)
Topic:	Son-father relationship
Text form:	Short story (extract)
Language variety:	AustE
Number of words:	3442 (printed text); 1067 (listening)
Level:	Basic/advanced
Skills/activities:	Skimming; speculating about the continuation of a story, working with imagery, extensive reading, listening comprehension, examining a coming-of-age story, writing an account of a family trip, self-assessment

Lern-
vokabular

Active vocabulary: 'Land/scape' (p. 8)

dread sth. (l. 8), spend time together (l. 9), have an opinion on sth. (l. 13), have different opinions (l. 17), expect more of sb. (ll. 39–40), keep on doing sth. (l. 34), actually (l. 42), polite (l. 77), be busy doing sth. (l. 92), for that matter (l. 94), embarrassing (l. 112), make an effort to do sth. (l. 126), control yourself (l. 126), lose your temper (l. 127), challenge (l. 131), right on cue (l. 158), defiant (l. 167), possession (l. 168), avoid sth. (l. 185), lose courage (l. 224), live up to sth. (l. 243), fit in (l. 248)

Didaktisch-
methodische
Hinweise

Diese Kurzgeschichte handelt von einer Annäherung in einem schwierigen Vater-Sohn-Verhältnis, bei der die Veränderung der gegenseitigen Wahrnehmung, das Entstehen gegenseitigen Respekts und die Abstimmung über schulische und berufliche Ziele des Jungen eine entscheidende Rolle spielen. Damit stellt dieser Text einen Konflikt dar, wie er vielen S aus ihrem Leben vertraut sein sollte. Wegen ihrer Länge mag diese Geschichte einigen S zunächst als schwieriger Text erscheinen, doch durch ihre schülernahe Thematik, das exotische *setting* und die einfache Sprache sollte sie das Interesse der S wecken und halten können, zumal sie in Abschnitten und mit unterschiedlichen Aufgabentypen behandelt wird.

Der Text und die dazu gehörigen Aufgaben stellen die Basis des *self-assessments* dar, das die S zu Beginn der Oberstufenarbeit durchführen sollten. Wichtig ist dabei, dass die S nach der Bearbeitung der Aufgaben im SB ihre Ergebnisse vergleichen, um auf dieser Basis dann in dem jeweiligen Abschnitt der *self-assessment sheets* ihre Leistung zu bewerten.

Als Einstiegskapitel bietet die „Introduction" den S zudem die Gelegenheit, sich mit dem Anhang des Buches vertraut zu machen, damit sie in den folgenden Kapiteln selbstständig damit arbeiten können.

Der erste Verweis auf die „Skills Pages" im Anhang findet sich vor dem Text, wenn die S aufgefordert werden, „Section i" von „Land/scape" kursorisch zu lesen *(skimming)* (vgl. SB, S. 8). Da diese Fertigkeit für den Umgang mit Texten auch außerhalb der Schule wichtig ist, erscheint es sinnvoll, ihm einige Zeit zu widmen, damit die S lernen, dass sie besonders bei einem längeren Text nicht jedes Wort verstehen müssen, um ihm die wichtigsten Informationen zu entnehmen. Aus diesem Grund wurden bei „Land/scape" nur wenige Wörter annotiert.

Auch auf das Glossar (SB, S. 255–270) wird an mehreren Stellen verwiesen (vgl. SB, S. 14, 17, 18, 19). Die entsprechenden Einträge sollten mit den S durchgearbeitet werden, damit die S später selbstständig mit dem „Glossary" umgehen können. Für eine tiefer gehende Analyse der short story können die folgenden Einträge von Nutzen sein, die Beispiele aus der Kurzgeschichte „Land/scape" enthalten: „third-person narrator" (S. 259), „mode of presentation" (S. 259–260), „character and characterization" (S. 260), „action and plot" (S. 261), „atmosphere" (S. 262), „setting" (S. 262), „informal style" (S. 266), „enumeration" (S. 267–268), „simile" (S. 268), „personification" (S. 268), „rhetorical question" (S. 269).

Unterrichts-tipps

Je nach Leistungsstärke der S können die *sections* des Textes zusammen oder in kürzeren Abschnitten gelesen werden. Aufgabe 1 (vgl. SB, S. 14) bietet sich für ein Unterrichtsgespräch an, während Aufgaben 2–4 zunächst in Stillarbeit (oder als Hausaufgabe) bearbeitet und anschließend in Partner- oder Kleingruppenarbeit verglichen werden. Dann werden die Ergebnisse in der Klasse besprochen, bevor die Schüler das *self-assessment sheet* ausfüllen.

Nach dem *listening* (vgl. SB, S. 14–15) werden Aufgaben 5–7 im Unterrichtsgespräch besprochen. Aufgabe 8 könnte in einem Kugellagerverfahren (vgl. S. 429) diskutiert werden, bei dem in der ersten Runde 8a, in der zweiten 8b im Vordergrund steht. Anschließend bearbeiten die S die entsprechenden Teile der Evaluationsbögen.
Auch die Ergebnisse der Schreibaufgabe (*task* 16) können in Gruppen verglichen werden: Unter Berücksichtigung des *skills* „The Stages of Writing" (vgl. SB, S. 244) fertigen S eine *rough copy* an, tauschen ihre Texte aus, korrigieren sie gegenseitig und fertigen dann eine *neat copy* an, bevor sie den entsprechenden Evaluationsbogen ausfüllen.

Diese Kurzgeschichte bietet sich an, um die S Wortfelder aus dem Text herausziehen zu lassen. Es finden sich viele Beispiele für 'words of movement', 'words for introducing speech or involving speech' und 'words for looking', die zumindest den rezeptiven Wortschatz der S vergrößern können. Gegebenenfalls können die S nur ein oder zwei dieser Wortfelder suchen bzw. die Suche arbeitsteilig durchführen. Da die 'words of movement' sich v.a. in zwei Abschnitten befinden, kann die Suche auf Z. 152–154 und Z. 170–203 beschränkt werden.

<u>Words of movement</u>: 'potter around' (l. 56), 'arrive at (a place)' (l. 65), 'bush-walking' (ll. 152–153), '(go) hiking' (l. 153), 'climb sth.' (l. 153), 'clamber up' (ll. 153, 178), 'plunge down into sth.' (l. 154), 'stride on' (ll. 170–171), 'flounder' (l. 171), 'thrust on ahead' (l. 179), 'push your way through sth.' (l. 181), 'reach sth.' (l. 184), 'spurt ahead' (l. 188), 'be lost' (l. 191), 'get your bearings' (l. 201), 'pop into sth.' (l. 203), 'potter about' (l. 263), 'head to/towards (a place)' (ll. 264, 266).

<u>Words for introducing speech or involving speech</u>: 'add sth.' (ll. 76, 127), 'say sth.' (ll. 26, etc.), 'yell sth.' (l. 83), 'waste your breath' (ll. 47, 238), 'snap' (l. 121), 'explain sth. to sb.' (ll. 101, 122), 'splutter (out)' (ll. 168, 239), 'inquire' (l. 188), 'tell sb. sth.' (ll. 211), 'ask sb. (about) sth.' (ll. 48, 222), 'murmur' (l. 244), 'call sb. sth.' (l. 255), 'joke' (l. 272), 'agree' (l. 291).

<u>Words for looking</u>: 'gawp' (l. 89), 'glance at sb./sth.' (l. 163), 'gaze' (l. 200), 'scan sth.' (l. 270), 'glance over sth.' (l. 297).

Info

Nadia Wheatley (born 1949) began writing fiction in 1976, after completing postgraduate work in Australian history. Her published work includes picture books, novels for children, short stories, as well as works of history and criticism. She has also written for television and the theatre.
Her novels for teenagers include *Dancing in the Anzac Deli* (1985), *The House That Was Eureka* (1986), *Vigil* (2000) and *A Banner Bold* (2000).

Land Rights (l. 14): The rights of the indigenous people in Australia (usually referred to as Aboriginals and Torres Strait Islanders) has always been controversial. Until recently, all unclaimed Australian land was considered to be Crown land, but in the 1970s courts started to recognize the rights of indigenous people over certain areas of land that were not used or claimed by any other groups.

Info

The Mabo decision (l. 14): In 1982, Edward Koiki Mabo, together with four other Torres Strait Islanders, started proceedings in the High Court of Australia against the state of Queensland. They asserted the rights of their families to particular tracts of land on the Murray Islands. In 1992, a decision was handed down which became the most important decision of the courts for indigenous peoples in Australia's colonial history. In the Mabo decision, the High Court recognized the right to possession and occupation of their lands by indigenous peoples according to their laws and customs. The significance of the decision is in the recognition that native title was a pre-existing right, inherent to indigenous peoples by virtue of their distinct identity as first owners and occupiers of the land and their continuing system of law. Native title was not a grant from the colonial government nor was it dependent upon the government for its existence. The judgement did not confine itself to the Murray Islands specifically. Rather, the High Court declared the law applicable to indigenous people throughout Australia.

Nuclear energy (l. 14): Australia mines approximately one quarter of the world's uranium. As such it is one of the most important exporters to countries using nuclear power. With abundant and cheap coal, Australia has, however, not built any nuclear reactors for the production of its own electricity.

Woodchipping (l. 14): Woodchipping is the use of by-products of sawing as well as the felling of old trees in Australia to produce cheap woodchips for use in industry and for heating. It is controversial, as woodchipping usually involves the destruction of large areas of Australian native forests.

American military involvement in the Gulf (l. 15): This is a reference to the American involvement in the Persian Gulf following the invasion of Kuwait by Iraq in 1991. Since that time Americans have had a strong presence in the Gulf region and are stationed in various countries like Qatar and Saudi Arabia. Australia has always been one of the staunchest supporters of American foreign policy, and sent troops to help the Americans during the Korean and Vietnam Wars as well as the first Gulf War and strongly supported the American invasion of Iraq in 2003.

School uniforms (l. 15): As in Britain, school uniforms are obligatory for students in Australia who have to attend school, but there has been much discussion about the need for students to wear school uniforms.

The republic (l. 16): The British monarch is still the head of state of Australia, which has for some time been considered an anachronism by many Australians. In 1999, a referendum was held in which the Australian people were asked if they wished to become a republic. As most people were dissatisfied about the terms under which a new president would be elected, the referendum was rejected, even though the majority of people seem to wish to break the ties with the British monarchy.

Compulsory enrolment in the cadets (l. 16): Australia is the only English-speaking country which enforces service in the cadets (school corps which teaches military training) for all youngsters, as everyone must be ready to serve in the army in times of war.

Lösungs-
hinweise

1 'Escape', 'seascape', 'moonscape' and 'scapegoat' might be mentioned.
The punctuation of the title makes the reader aware of other words which contain the syllable 'scape'. Especially the idea of an 'escape' has some relevance for the text: both Tony's and Ant's escape into the landscape, where they discover more about each other and escape from the views that they hold of each other, which have hindered their relationship. Thus it also sets the tone for the literal/figurative subtitles (cf. task 4 below). The author might also be putting emphasis on the photographic elements of

the story; often Ant sees himself and his situation from the outside like looking at a 'landscape' and perhaps by separating 'scape' the author is emphasizing the aspect of a frame or photo still when Ant looks at himself, the general situation, his relationship with his father, etc. (cf. ll. 78–82).

2 The relationship seems to be quite tense. Ant feels pressurized due to his father's excellence at school (cf. ll. 36–41). There is no emotional closeness between the two of them. Ant does not want to follow in his father's footsteps (cf. ll. 172–173). He feels very uncertain and self-conscious in the presence of his father, and feels he has to hide part of himself when they are together (cf. ll. 150–152). He does not look forward to spending five days with him and hopes the holiday will pass quickly (cf. ll. 53–56).
His father, on the other hand, does not seem to know much about Ant's real interests, his strengths and weaknesses (cf. ll. 47–49).
Information in the text that explains the relationship: Tony left the family five years beforehand and since then there seems to have been little contact between Tony and Ant, as these five days are the longest period of time the two will have spent together during those five years (cf. ll. 8–9). Tony went to the same school as Ant and was excellent at sport and academic subjects, while Ant is more interested in creative subjects. While Ant's teachers expect the same from him, Ant feels unable to live up to those expectations (cf. ll. 24–31). Tony seems to enjoy the outdoors, while Ant is more an indoors person (cf. ll. 55–60).

 3 Auf die Frage, wie sich die Beziehung zwischen Ant und seinem Vater weiterentwickelt, gibt es individuell verschiedene Antworten, keine richtige oder falsche Lösung. Die S sollten aber dazu angehalten werden, ihre Überlegungen am Text zu belegen, um nicht in freies Spekulieren zu verfallen. So weisen die S genaue Textkenntnis und Wissen über die Charaktere und ihre Beziehung nach. Da die Erwartungen der S in Aufgabe 10 wieder aufgenommen werden, sollten die S ihre Überlegungen schriftlich festhalten.

Hints at distance and tension:
'Ant was dreading the thought of five days with this father' (l. 8), 'And he knew his father would have different opinions' (ll. 16–17), 'Don't stand there gawping' (l. 90), 'How on earth did you manage that?' (l. 121), 'Ant said nothing' (l. 122), 'His father seemed to interpret this as some sort of challenge' (ll. 130–131), 'Didn't his father remember anything?' (l. 205).

Hints at understanding and closeness:
'Despite himself, Ant grinned ... He and Tony used to pretend that Antarctica belonged to Ant' (ll. 69–73), 'Ant, however, was able to see his father making an effort to control himself' (ll. 126), 'He glanced at his father: cameras were respectable, weren't they?' (l. 163), 'He thrust on ahead to the next hill, so Ant could get his shot' (ll. 179–180).

4 In the Wilds:
Literal meaning: an area of a country far from towns or cities, where few people live.
Figurative meaning: people can have wild, mixed up feelings, which can be very strong positive or negative feelings. At the beginning Ant has a lot of wild feelings. 'In the Wilds' can also imply that someone is lost and is uncertain of how to find his or her way.

His father's footsteps:
Literal meaning: the marks his father's feet leave in the sand.
Figurative meaning: Do as someone else does, follow the same path as somebody else, have the same lifestyle as someone else; all things Ant does not want to do.

CD **5** Aufgaben 5–8 sind *listening comprehension*-Aufgaben. Der Hörtext befindet sich auf CD1, *track* 1; ein Transkript S. 37.
Möglicherweise muss der Text mehrmals vorgespielt werden; auf Wortschatzhilfen sollte aber verzichtet werden, um eine authentische Hörverstehenssituation zu schaffen. Aufgrund des erhöhten Schwierigkeitsgrades des Hörverstehens dienen die Aufgaben der Verständnisüberprüfung; erst Aufgabe 9 fordert Textanalyse.

The cave inspires religious feelings in Ant, of the earth creating the earth. He feels awe at the bigness and smallness coming together. He is overwhelmed by the power of nature, and feels that creation is still taking place around him. This results in a feeling of well-being.

CD **6** When the lights go out, Ant thinks about all the ways he knows to describe black, e.g. 'pitch black', 'ebony'. He enjoys the darkness and is fascinated by the depth of the colour as well as its density, and the complete lack of tones.

CD **7** Tony has a panic attack since he suffers from claustrophobia. He is unable to breathe properly so he starts to hyperventilate and is unable to move.

CD **8** **a** When they are outside the cave again, Ant remembers an incident when his father saved his life, pulling him out of the channel at Nambucca Heads. It makes him aware of the fact that his father did take him on a holiday when he was younger.

b Perhaps the fact that his father is in trouble and scared brings back the memory of his father helping him when he was in danger.

CD **9** Since Ant remembers the holiday with his father it occurs to him that he might have forgotten other things which his father did for him. He realizes that he was really worried about his father and that he cares for him more than he realized. Furthermore, he admits to himself that he does not know Tony very well (i.e. it's not only the father who does not know the son, as Ant had supposed earlier in the story). Since Ant helps his father, they get emotionally closer to each other. His father is seen to be a weaker, more human person by suffering from claustrophobia and is no longer the strong person without failings in whose shadow Ant must live.

10 Individual answers.

11 Before Tony went to that school, his father had been a student there too, and Tony had the same problem of having to live up to expectations from the teachers. Ant thinks that it is different since his grandfather and his father are good at the same things, whereas Ant is interested in completely different things.

12 **a** At the end of the story Ant has a more relaxed relationship to his father, they have got closer to each other. Ant opens himself up, speaks about his problems and his father listens to him, accepts his wish to change school and shows understanding for him.

b At the beginning, Ant wanted to go back home as quickly as possible (cf. ll. 53–55). Now at the end he is happy to accept his father's offer to spend a bit more time together (cf. ll. 283–291). He dares to bring up the problems he has, even though his mother warned him not to do so (cf. ll. 233–251).
At the beginning he thought his father might not respect his interest in art (cf. ll. 150–152), at the end he is drawing his sketches while sitting next to his father, who thinks they are good (cf. ll. 297–299).

At the beginning the atmosphere between the two of them is quite tense, towards the end it becomes more friendly, with Ant calling Tony 'dad' (l. 255) and speaking his mind jokingly without worrying about his father's reactions (cf. ll. 272–276).

At the end they respect and like each other and seem to be willing to improve their relationship.

13 It is a coming-of-age story as Ant, an adolescent, starts to change his view of his relationship to his father as well as his view of himself. Throughout the story he becomes more self-confident, e.g. he states what he really wants to do and stops hiding his real interests. He becomes aware of the fact that he has misjudged his father.

14 Ant's creative side is contrasted with his father's desire for them to go camping, which is a sign of the gulf between the two (cf. ll. 55–60). His passion for colours is in direct contrast to what he thinks his father enjoys (cf. ll. 143–154), which in the end is shown to be false (especially 'plunging down caves', l. 154). He gives in to his fear of his father's reaction towards him as a possible 'wimp' by taking out a camera rather than his sketchpad (cf. ll. 159–160). Yet even this turns to disaster, as Ant feels that Tony is responsible for the final photo, and that it is no longer his photo (cf. l. 187). Once the relationship has improved, Ant feels able to take out his sketchpad, thereby indicating he has freed himself from the false notions he had of his father and from his own fears.

15 The weather seems to reflect Ant's mood and the father-son relationship. When he goes camping with his father – an activity he obviously does not like very much – it is drizzling. Due to the rain, which prevents him from seeing properly, he destroys the tent. To make things worse, just at that moment it starts to pour down heavily (cf. ll. 84–120). The miserable, wet weather is an image of the miserable relationship between the two.

When he wants to take a picture of the sea, the sun is never in the right position so all his efforts are in vain (cf. ll. 178–187).

Towards the end of the story when his relationship with his father is improving, the wind is described as 'dropping' (cf. l. 256), while the storm has 'blown itself out' (l. 256). At the end the sky is described as 'getting bigger' (l. 294).

16 Individual answers.

B Young, Talented and Rebellious Anne-Marie Sapsted

Source:	*The Sunday Telegraph*, 16 February, 2002
Topic:	Teenagers rebelling against high-pressure parents
Text form:	Feature story
Language variety:	BE
Number of words:	579
Level:	Basic/advanced
Skills/activities:	Discussing with a partner, listening and correcting a partner's mistakes, analysing the difference between a fictional and literary text, writing a text for a school magazine, self-assessment

Lern-
vokabular

Active vocabulary: 'Young, Talented and Rebellious' (p. 18)

excel in sth. (l.1), refuse to do sth. (ll. 3, 12), stick to sth. (l. 4), grasp the opportunities before you (ll. 5–6), regret sth. (l. 7), get a degree (l. 10), A-level results (l. 10), turn your back on sth. (l. 18), go along with sth. (ll. 20–21), end up (l. 21), give sth. up (l. 26), leave sth. too late (l. 27), cope with sth. (l. 32), take advantage of sth. (l. 44)

Didaktisch-
methodische
Hinweise

Nachdem die S die Kurzgeschichte „Land/scape" gelesen haben, begegnen sie hier einem kurzen Zeitungsartikel zur gleichen Thematik, der Selbstfindung Jugendlicher. Der Textsorte entsprechend wird das Thema völlig anders als in der Kurzgeschichte gestaltet: anhand einiger Beispiele wird in die Problematik rebellierender Jugendlicher eingeführt, die nicht den von ihren Eltern gewünschten Bildungsweg einschlagen wollen. Schließlich berichten Wissenschaftler von ihren Forschungsergebnissen über den weiteren Lebensweg solcher Jugendlicher.

Nach dem literarischen begegnen die S hier einem nicht-fiktionalen Text. Neben der Verständnissicherung dienen die Aufgaben v.a. der Benennung von Gemeinsamkeiten und Unterschieden fiktionaler und nicht-fiktionaler Texte, so dass die S für die Besonderheiten der beiden Textarten sensibilisiert werden.

Unterrichts-
tipps

Der Einstieg in die Textarbeit kann erfolgen, indem die S anhand der Überschrift des Texts über sein Thema und die Textsorte spekulieren. Bei Aufgaben 1–6 ist darauf zu achten, dass sie, wie im SB vorgesehen, zunächst in Partnerarbeit besprochen werden, da die S in den *self-assessment sheets* ihre Fähigkeit einschätzen sollen, Gespräche in der Fremdsprache zu führen.

Lösungs-
hinweise
◆◆

1 Possible answers:

<u>Yes.</u> A university degree is very valuable when it comes to finding a good and well-paid job. Actors are rarely lucky enough to find a job, and many are unemployed. Moreover, you are dependent on people's taste and on contacts with directors and other people in the film business more than on talent.

<u>No.</u> It is important for young people to do what they want to do. By making your own mistakes, you find out who you are and cannot blame others for what goes wrong. Doing something adventurous and different can result in a successful career and a happy life.

◆◆ **2** Freeman believes that gifted teenagers turn their backs on education because they need to be rebellious, especially if their parents are trying to push them in a particular direction.

Coleman believes that rebellion is part of the process of an individual developing his or her own identity. He considers it to be a healthy process, as some adolescents have the feeling that they must do something completely different from their parents, just to define themselves as being different people. With so much choice around, however, it can be difficult for young people to know in what direction they should go, and this fear of choice might also lead to depression and mental health problems.

◆◆ **3** Freeman's advice to parents is that they have to learn to let go. Some parents try to live their lives through their children because they did not have so many opportunities when they were younger. She advises parents to talk to their children about their plans. They should avoid anything that makes their children feel under pressure. In some cases they might need to send their children to professional counselling.

◆◆ **4** Both Ant's and Alexandria's stories deal with the perceptions young people have of what is expected from them by their parents, with the problem of how parents try to influence their children's education and way of living and how young people try to escape from their parents' influence.

◆◆ **5** Possible answers:
Text B gives greater insight into how parents think because it gives concrete facts based on scientific research (cf. ll. 15–23, 28–40). Since a feature story uses direct quotes and relies on first-hand reporting it is only natural that such a text gives more information about the topic it is dealing with. A short story, on the other hand, is a fictional work and usually deals with the thoughts and experiences of a character.

Text A gives the greater insight as it gives more effective and personal insights. It is only slowly that we see that Tony is not the one-dimensional father that Ant thought he was. So we see a more detailed account of a parent–child relationship. At the same time we are never really shown Tony's thoughts, so we only understand him from one perspective, that of the child who feels aggrieved.

◆◆ **6** Individual answers.

7 Individual answers.

Assessing Your Level in English

Name: _____

I Learning English so far

1 Where and how have you learned English so far?
(Tick [√] all the answers that apply.)

- ▪ in the classroom
- ▪ doing homework
- ▪ listening to songs
- ▪ listening to the radio
- ▪ other: _____

- ▪ watching films
- ▪ reading books or magazines
- ▪ speaking to foreigners
- ▪ watching TV

_____

_____

_____

2 These are the areas I feel comfortable and confident in when I use English:

_____

_____

_____

_____

_____

3 These are the areas I think I need to work on:

_____

_____

_____

_____

_____

II Working with the First Part of 'Land/scape' (cf. pp. 8–14)

1 I found the first part of the story

- ▪ enjoyable because
  - ▪ I was curious to see how it would develop.
  - ▪ I could identify with the main character.
  - ▪ I felt it was easy to understand and pleasant to read.

- ▪ not enjoyable because
  - ▪ it was too difficult to understand.
  - ▪ the subject did not interest me.
  - ▪ it was too long.
  - ▪ I don't like reading very much anyway.

- ▪ other: _____

2 I found the vocabulary used in the story

- ▪ easy to understand and I did not need to look up many words.
- ▪ okay, but I needed to look up quite a lot of words.
- ▪ difficult, so I really could not follow the story.
- ▪ other: _____

3 I found the sentences in the story

- ▪ relatively simple and easy to understand.
- ▪ tricky, but I was able to follow the story.
- ▪ too long and complicated.
- ▪ other: _____

4 I found tasks 1–4 on p. 14

- ▪ easy to answer.
- ▪ useful, as they made me think about the story more.
- ▪ too difficult to answer without help from the teacher.
- ▪ other: _____

5 During the classroom discussion

- ▪ I joined in a lot.
- ▪ I joined in when I knew what I wanted to say.
- ▪ I was unable to express my ideas clearly.
- ▪ I felt uncomfortable talking in English in front of others.
- ▪ other: _____

III Working with the Second Part of 'Land/scape' (cf. p. 14–15)

1 While listening to the text

▪ I found it easy to understand what was going on.

▪ I could understand the gist of what was happening.

▪ I understood very little of what was going on.

▪ other: _____

2 My main difficulty with the story was the fact that

▪ the vocabulary was difficult to understand.

▪ the speaker was difficult to understand.

▪ the sentences were very long and complicated.

▪ the speaker spoke too quickly.

▪ other: _____

3 The tasks 5–9 on pp. 14–15 were

▪ easy to answer.

▪ useful, as they made me think about the story more.

▪ too difficult to answer without help from the teacher.

▪ other: _____

4 During the classroom discussion

▪ I joined in a lot.

▪ I joined in when I knew what I wanted to say.

▪ I was unable to express my ideas clearly.

▪ I felt uncomfortable talking in English in front of others.

▪ other: _____

IV Working with the Final Part of 'Land/scape' and with 'Young, Talented and Rebellious' (cf. pp. 15–19)

In tasks 1–6 on p. 19 you and a partner discussed the tasks alternately and then together.

1 When I was talking,

- ◼ I found it easy to express what I wanted to say.
- ◼ I felt uncomfortable speaking in English.
- ◼ I used words from the text to express what I wanted to say.
- ◼ I used my own words when dealing with the tasks.
- ◼ I found my partner's comments useful.

2 When I was listening,

- ◼ I found it easy to understand what my partner was talking about.
- ◼ I just listened to what my partner said until he or she was finished.
- ◼ I made it clear to my partner that I understood him or her and asked questions if I didn't.

You have probably written two short texts – an account of a family trip (p. 17, task 16) and a feature story for your school magazine (p. 19, task 7). Now fill in the questionnaire. (You may tick more than one item):

1 How did you prepare for the actual writing?

- ◼ I wrote down a number of ideas.
- ◼ I organized my ideas to give my text a meaningful structure.
- ◼ I didn't prepare at all, but just started writing immediately.
- ◼ other: _____

2 How did you structure your thoughts?

- ◼ I thought about individual paragraphs, giving each one a title.
- ◼ I created a mind map.
- ◼ I relied on my imagination during the writing process.
- ◼ I did not structure my ideas.
- ◼ other: _____

3 Did you think about possible readers of your texts while preparing or writing?

- ◼ Yes, I tried to consider what they might expect.
- ◼ No, I didn't think about possible readers.
- ◼ Partly, but I was more interested in writing for me.

4 Where did you get the words you used in your text?

☐ I knew most of the words already.

☐ My teacher provided me with new words.

☐ I used my German-English dictionary.

☐ I used my monolingual dictionary.

☐ I asked my teacher or friends for words I was unsure about or wanted to use.

5 How did you move from one idea to the next in your text?

☐ Each idea was given a new paragraph.

☐ I used quite a number of connectors (e.g. 'firstly', 'therefore', 'on the one hand ..., on the other ...') to move from one idea to the next.

☐ I didn't always know which connectors to use and when to use them.

☐ I don't really feel comfortable using connectors, so I left them out.

☐ I didn't feel that connectors were needed in my texts.

Looking back on the work on the Introduction, I would say my main strengths were:

_____

_____

_____

_____

My main weaknesses were: _____

_____

_____

_____

V The Four Skills

1 Reading

a I enjoy reading in English and don't really consider it to be hard work.

■ true   ■ mostly true   ■ not true

It depends: ....

b I can understand letters and e-mails that deal with everyday matters and feelings.

■ true   ■ mostly true   ■ not true

It depends: ....

c I can follow a story with little or no difficulty.

■ true   ■ mostly true   ■ not true

It depends: ....

d I can understand articles and reports that deal with current events and issues and
I can recognize the writer's viewpoint.

■ true   ■ mostly true   ■ not true

It depends: ....

e I can analyse things I have read for style and literary devices.

■ true   ■ mostly true   ■ not true

It depends: ....

	End of the first term				End of the second term				End of the third term			
	true	mostly true	not true	improved? +/-	true	mostly true	not true	improved? +/-	true	mostly true	not true	improved? +/-
	▪	▪	▪	—	▪	▪	▪	—	▪	▪	▪	—
●	▪	▪	▪	—	▪	▪	▪	—	▪	▪	▪	—
	▪	▪	▪	—	▪	▪	▪	—	▪	▪	▪	—
	▪	▪	▪	—	▪	▪	▪	—	▪	▪	▪	—
●	▪	▪	▪	—	▪	▪	▪	—	▪	▪	▪	—

2 Speaking

a I can talk about myself, my home and my school with no difficulty.

■ true   ■ mostly true   ■ not true

It depends: _____

b I can talk about current events with little or no preparation.

■ true   ■ mostly true   ■ not true

It depends: _____

c I can express my opinion and give reasons for it.

■ true   ■ mostly true   ■ not true

It depends: _____

d I can summarize the contents of stories, newspaper articles, films, etc.

■ true   ■ mostly true   ■ not true

It depends: _____

e My pronunciation in English is clear and easy to understand.

■ true   ■ mostly true   ■ not true

It depends: _____

	End of the first term				End of the second term				End of the third term			
	true	mostly true	not true	improved? +/-	true	mostly true	not true	improved? +/-	true	mostly true	not true	improved? +/-
	■	■	■	__	■	■	■	__	■	■	■	__
●	■	■	■	__	■	■	■	__	■	■	■	__
	■	■	■	__	■	■	■	__	■	■	■	__
	■	■	■	__	■	■	■	__	■	■	■	__
●	■	■	■	__	■	■	■	__	■	■	■	__

3 Listening

a I can follow classroom discussions without any problem.

☐ true   ☐ mostly true   ☐ not true

It depends: ....

b I can understand normal conversation about everyday matters.

☐ true   ☐ mostly true   ☐ not true

It depends: ....

c I can understand the news on the radio and television and pick out the most important information.

☐ true   ☐ mostly true   ☐ not true

It depends: ....

d I can understand song lyrics.

☐ true   ☐ mostly true   ☐ not true

It depends: ....

d I can understand different varieties of English (e.g. Received Pronunciation, Northern English, American English, Australian English.)

☐ true   ☐ mostly true   ☐ not true

It depends: ....

	End of the first term				End of the second term				End of the third term			
	true	mostly true	not true	improved? +/-	true	mostly true	not true	improved? +/-	true	mostly true	not true	improved? +/-
	▪	▪	▪	__	▪	▪	▪	__	▪	▪	▪	__
●	▪	▪	▪	__	▪	▪	▪	__	▪	▪	▪	__
	▪	▪	▪	__	▪	▪	▪	__	▪	▪	▪	__
	▪	▪	▪	__	▪	▪	▪	__	▪	▪	▪	__
●	▪	▪	▪	__	▪	▪	▪	__	▪	▪	▪	__

4 Writing

a I can write personal e-mails and letters without difficulty.

■ true ■ mostly true ■ not true

It depends: ....

b I can write well-structured texts about things I know and care about.

■ true ■ mostly true ■ not true

It depends: ....

c I can present information in an essay or report, analysing different standpoints and giving reasons for my own standpoint.

■ true ■ mostly true ■ not true

It depends: ....

d I can write stories and/or poems in clear English and make them interesting to read.

■ true ■ mostly true ■ not true

It depends: ....

	End of the first term				End of the second term				End of the third term			
	true	mostly true	not true	improved? +/-	true	mostly true	not true	improved? +/-	true	mostly true	not true	improved? +/-
	■	■	■	__	■	■	■	__	■	■	■	__
	■	■	■	__	■	■	■	__	■	■	■	__
	■	■	■	__	■	■	■	__	■	■	■	__
	■	■	■	__	■	■	■	__	■	■	■	__

VI Correctness and Comprehension

1 Grammar

a I make very few grammatical mistakes when I'm speaking or writing English, and my mistakes don't lead to misunderstandings.

■ true   ■ mostly true   ■ not true

b I often make mistakes although I know the rules.

■ true   ■ mostly true   ■ not true

c I know how to find the correct forms in my grammar book, etc. when I'm not sure of them.

■ true   ■ mostly true   ■ not true

d I don't have problems with grammatical structures when I read a text.

■ true   ■ mostly true   ■ not true

2 Vocabulary

a I choose the right words, and my mistakes don't lead to misunderstandings.

■ true   ■ mostly true   ■ not true

b If I can't think of a word, I can describe what I mean so that other people can understand me.

■ true   ■ mostly true   ■ not true

c I know how to find words that I need in my dictionary, etc.

■ true   ■ mostly true   ■ not true

d I can understand most of the words used in texts or guess their meaning from the context.

■ true   ■ mostly true   ■ not true

	End of the first term				End of the second term				End of the third term			
	true	mostly true	not true	improved? +/-	true	mostly true	not true	improved? +/-	true	mostly true	not true	improved? +/-
	▪	▪	▪	__	▪	▪	▪	__	▪	▪	▪	__
●	▪	▪	▪	__	▪	▪	▪	__	▪	▪	▪	__
	▪	▪	▪	__	▪	▪	▪	__	▪	▪	▪	__
	▪	▪	▪	__	▪	▪	▪	__	▪	▪	▪	__
●	▪	▪	▪	__	▪	▪	▪	__	▪	▪	▪	__
	▪	▪	▪	__	▪	▪	▪	__	▪	▪	▪	__
	▪	▪	▪	__	▪	▪	▪	__	▪	▪	▪	__
	▪	▪	▪	__	▪	▪	▪	__	▪	▪	▪	__

VII Plan of Action

I have identified these areas of weakness and intend to do the following to improve my English in those areas:

Reading: _____

Plan: I will try to _____

_____

_____

Speaking: _____

Plan: I will try to _____

_____

_____

Listening: _____

Plan: I will try to _____

_____

_____

Grammar: _____

Plan: I will try to _____

_____

_____

Vocabulary: _____

Plan: I will try to _____

_____

_____

Land/scape

SB, p. 14 ### Section ix: Inside

A bell rang, and a uniformed ranger led the way to a door in the wall.

Ant and his father found themselves at the front of the queue as the ranger ushered the group through the door and down a flight of extremely steep limestone steps. Though this stairwell was floodlit, it was very narrow; with the forty or so other tourists pushing down behind, it did feel as if there was no way back, if you should happen to have second thoughts.

Ant found himself remembering the story of Alice tumbling down the rabbit hole. There was a giddying feeling about this rapid descent.

And then the stairs opened out into a vast cavern, and all that Ant was aware of was a sense of the earth that overcame him.

Though there was Chapel every morning at school, Ant had never felt religious; now he did. But the awe he felt was not at *God* making the earth, but at the *earth* making the earth: it was a sense of bigness and smallness coming together, as Ant became aware of how each and every drop of calcium carbonate was part of this creation process: and it was a sense of combination of oldness and newness, for if this creation had been happening since the very beginning, it was happening still, all around Ant, at this very second. Stalactites were building unseen ...

All of this produced in Ant such a feeling of wellbeing that he didn't mind the comments of the other tourists around him – 'Look, darling, it's just like Disneyland!' ... 'Oooh, that's a cute one!' ... 'Here's one that looks like a rocket!' – who seemed to regard the cave just as something put there for their amusement. Tony, of course, wasn't saying any of this stuff; indeed, Ant hadn't heard him say anything since they'd been down here.

'I'll turn the lights out now,' the ranger announced, 'so that you can experience the darkness. Even on a moonless night,' he explained, 'there is always some light in the sky, and your eyes adapt to it. But down here, there is a complete absence of light. Ready?'

'*Ooooooooooo!*' gasped the crowd as the lights went off.

Pitch – Ant thought, running through the ways he knew to describe black – pitch black, jet black, inky black, ebony, black as coal, black as a crow, but nothing in his experience was black as a cave.

He revelled in it, and it wasn't just the depth of colour that was extraordinary to him – it was the density, the complete lack of tones. With no light, there was no shadow. Was this what the colour field painters had been aiming at: pure colour?

Again Ant was aware of the tourists around him: the darkness seemed to make them feel a need for comedy, for they were giggling and cracking pathetic jokes.

'*Ooooookie spooooookies ...*' said the voice of a grown woman.

And then a man cut in abruptly: 'What's that noise?'

'The Monster from the Deep,' the first joker replied.

'No, I'm serious,' the man said.

'Yeah, just listen ...' said another voice, sounding alarmed.

They all hushed then, and Ant could hear what they meant: there was a terrible sound of breathing, of short loud rasping breaths, as if some huge creature was in the cave with them, ready to pounce.

'*Quick!*' someone yelled. '*Turn on the lights!*'

But it seemed to take a while for the ranger to reach the switch, and during that time the monstrous panting seemed to Ant to get closer and louder.

'*Ahhhhh!*' there was a collective sigh of relief as light flooded the cavern. And then they were all staring around apprehensively.

What was it?

Where was it?

It was Ant who realised. The monster was his father.

Section x: Shrinking

Tony stood as if frozen beside a pillar of golden limestone, his face whitish-green and covered (Ant could see) with a film of sweat. The loud breathing was still going on, getting faster and faster. It was clear that Tony was breathing too fast to take in enough oxygen.

'He's hyperventilating,' Ant heard someone say. 'Get him out of here!'

As the ranger gently took Tony's arm, he started to shake his head wildly back and forth. *'I can't, I can't,'* he seemed to be saying between huge breaths and – as if against his will – his tall body began to hunch, and now Ant's father became smaller and smaller, shrinking down in front of the stalactite pillar until he was curling at its base like a child.

'Is he always claustrophobic like this?' the ranger asked Ant.

'I don't know,' Ant said, and then found himself admitting, 'I don't know him very well.'

'C'mon, mate ...' The ranger bent over the frightened body. 'You really do have to let us help you.'

The ranger and Ant managed to lift Tony to his feet, then slung his arms around their shoulders and struggled their way up the shaft steps and onto the rim of the earth.

Section xi: Outside

Tony sat on the bench outside the exit door. He seemed to be concentrating very hard as his breathing changed over from the hysterical panting to something a little slower, a little deeper.

He was still shivering however.

Ant took his parka off, wrapped it around Tony's shoulders, then found himself rubbing up and down Tony's back in long, firm strokes.

Click.

Ant's mind saw this picture, and then imposed over it – or maybe under it – an almost identical picture of a tall thin bloke comforting a sobbing child.

Dad-and-me. That time I got caught in the channel at Nambucca Heads, and he swam in and pulled me out, and he rubbed my back and made me better, and he didn't go crook at me even though he'd told me there was a bad rip today and I was to stay in the camping ground.

Click.

So he did take me on a holiday at least once before, Ant realised. He took me camping. He saved my life. What other nice things did he do that I've forgotten?

'Here you go, mate.' The ranger handed Tony a cup of tea. 'Lots of sugar in it. That'll fix you up in no time.'

'Thanks,' Tony said. He looked at Ant. 'Both of you.'

Mit dem Titel dieses Kapitels wird an die gleichnamige US-amerikanische *sitcom* erinnert (1971–1983), in der am Beispiel des bigotten, rassistischen New Yorkers Archie Bunker die konservative Mittelschicht der USA ironisiert wird. Sicher hat das dort entworfene Familienbild nur noch wenig Relevanz für heutige S, doch die Familie kann auch heute als primäre Sozialisationsinstanz unserer Gesellschaft angesehen werden. Wie in der Shell Studie von 2002 (www.shell-jugendstudie.de • 1.8.03) nachzulesen ist, misst ein großer Teil der Jugendlichen der Familie eine große Bedeutung bei. So wohnt die Mehrheit der Jugendlichen noch bei ihrer Familie und geht davon aus, dass man Familie zum Glücklichsein braucht. Gleichzeitig ist aber auch zu beobachten, dass klassische Familienstrukturen auf dem Rückzug sind und neue entstehen: Stichwörter wie „Patchwork-Familie", allein erziehende Eltern, homosexuelle Paare mit Kindern verdeutlichen dies.

In diesem Spannungsfeld steht das erste Kapitel des Buches mit Texten zu den Themen Familienbegriff, Verhältnis zwischen Eltern und Kindern, Leben in der Familie und veränderte Familienstrukturen. Die S begegnen einer Vielzahl verschiedener Materialien und Textformen: Neben einem Gemälde finden sie einen Artikel aus einer Jugendzeitschrift, ein Gedicht, einen Romanauszug und einen Sachtext; die S analysieren ein Diagramm und eine Tabelle, sie hören ein Rundfunkinterview und sehen einen Auszug aus einer *sitcom*. Auch die Aufgaben sind sehr vielfältig: Bildanalyse, *information gap activity*, (Weiter)Schreiben einer Geschichte und eines Gedichts, Analyse von Diagrammen und Tabellen usw. Durch diese Textsorten- und Aufgabenvielfalt in Verbindung mit dem schülernahen Thema eignet sich dieses Kapitel besonders als Einstieg in die oberstufengemäße Textarbeit.

Didaktisches Inhaltsverzeichnis

SB, p.	Title	TM, p.	Text form	Topic	Skills and activities
20	**Lead-in**	40	headlines painting	family life	mind mapping; describing, analysing a painting; writing a text based on a headline
22	**The Trouble with Mother**	42	magazine article	teenager dealing with an over-protective mother	summarizing the text; information gap activity; listening and asking questions; writing an ending to a story; working with language register; role play
24	Sex Columnist CD1, track 2		radio interview	mother-daughter relationship	listening comprehension
26	**This Be the Verse** Philip Larkin	45	poem	influence of parents on children	analysing poetry; relating photos to a text; writing a (stanza of a) poem
28	**Households and Families: 1990 and 2000**	46	text and diagrams	changes in households and families in USA in recent years	comparing different methods of presenting information, analysing diagrams; class discussion
30	**Context Box**	49	–	changing families	working with words
31	**Giving Thanks** Laurie Halse Anderson	51	novel (extract)	family's failed attempt to celebrate Thanksgiving	comparing a text and a painting; analysing humour; changing the narrative perspective of a text
33	**Taking Responsibility** Video/DVD	54	sitcom (extract)	family behaviour patterns	analysing a sitcom
34	**Getting Along in English** CD1, tracks 3–9	55	–	invitation to a meal	–
35	**Watch Your Language**	57	–	prepositions	–

Lead-in

Der Einstieg in dieses Kapitel erfolgt über fiktive Zeitungsüberschriften, die verschiedene Aspekte des Themas Familie widerspiegeln, insbesondere die Veränderungen der
Familienstrukturen in den letzten Jahrzehnten. Anschließend betrachten die S ein
Gemälde des amerikanischen Malers Norman Rockwell, das ein traditionelles Familienbild entwirft (Großfamilie, klassische Rollenverteilung, gemeinsames Begehen
eines festlichen Anlasses). Diese provokante Gegenüberstellung konträrer Familien-
bilder sollte den S viele Redeanlässe bieten. Der schülerorientierte Schwerpunkt der
Aufgaben ermöglicht es den S, sich ihrer eigenen Vorstellung von Familie bewusst zu

→ WB, ex. 2 werden und dieses Bild kreativ umsetzen.

Info

Norman Rockwell (1894–1978) received his first assignments as an illustrator when he
was still in his teens. When he was 22 he was commissioned to create a cover for *The
Saturday Evening Post*, America's most popular magazine at the time. For the next 47
years he was associated with this magazine. During this time his pictures reflected the
development of American society – the invention of radio and television, auto-mobile
and airplane travel.
During World War II Rockwell felt inspired by Roosevelt's 1941 State of the Union Address,
in which the President laid out four essential human freedoms: 'freedom of speech and
expression', 'freedom of every person to worship God in his own way', 'freedom from
want' and 'freedom from fear'. Rockwell brought the President's words to life in his four
paintings based on these four freedoms (www.nrm.org/exhibits/current/four-
freedoms.html · 1.8.03). With these paintings he encouraged his fellow Americans to
buy War Bonds (i.e. money lent to the government on low terms of interest during a war).
Rockwell is seen by many Americans as an American icon. One reason for this is the fact
that his paintings bring to life core values of American society which, in modern
society, seem to have been forgotten. Rockwell is loved for having recreated the
American way of life in his paintings. He has painted the portrait of a nation, its daily
life, thus providing millions with inspiration.
When he was 70, Rockwell started working for *Look* magazine and painted pictures
addressing the Civil Rights struggle, which came as a surprise for people used to his
uncontroversial subject matters.
In the 1970s he left his works and the contents of his studio to a museum in his home
town of Stockbridge, Massachusetts.

1 **a** Vgl. die Kopiervorlage auf S. 59.
Möglicherweise werden auch Wörter genannt, die von *family* abgeleitet sind, z.B. *be
familiar with sb./sth.*, *familiarity (breeds contempt).*

b Individual answers.

→ WB, ex. 1 ▢ *Describe the picture in detail.*
The subject of the picture is a family gathered around a table to share a meal. At the
head of the table is the grandfather, who is centered in the picture. His wife is slightly
below him, suggesting that the man is the head of the household. All the other family
members frame the picture. The fact that they are all looking at different members of
the family links the group. The atmosphere is relaxed and cheerful, but also a little
solemn: the family members look happy; the grandfather seems proud and solemn and
the grandmother is concentrating on placing the turkey on the table. The turkey is in
the middle of the picture, and is just above the table, which reinforces the fact that the
family is gathered together to eat. The table is laid out perfectly and nothing is out of
place. The cutlery and crockery are all pale in colour so that the people and food come

across more clearly. The man in the bottom right-hand corner is looking at the painter, which gives the painting a photographic touch, as if the painter is taking a quick photograph, rather than painting an intricate picture.

2 **a** Rockwell's image of 'the family' is of a happy family where everybody gets on well with everyone else. Everyone is smiling and happy. The different generations enjoy being together, but the oldest family members are still the most important (both are standing, while everyone else is seated). The gender roles are conventional, with the woman wearing an apron and doing the cooking, while the man carves the turkey.
Lots of things help give the painting its atmosphere: the colours are warm and homely; the wallpaper and curtains make you feel the house is really a home – well looked after and nice to be in; the smiles on the faces of the table convey happiness, delight at being together and excitement about the meal. The serious expressions on the old couple's faces show that they want the meal to be a success. The hairstyles and clothes show that the picture is from another era.

What occasion do you think Rockwell has captured in his painting? Give reasons for your answer.
It could be either Christmas or Thanksgiving. As there are no Christmas decorations, it seems more likely to be Thanksgiving. This is the day when American families traditionally come together to celebrate American values and family life. They normally eat turkey. (Cf. the information about *Thanksgiving* on p. 52.)

b Possible answer:
The grandmother: 'I hope the turkey tastes nice – and that everyone enjoys the meal. Today is so important for dear Tom: he always worries so much about Thanksgiving, he always wants everything to be just perfect. Dear Tom, he's so pleased that all the children have managed to come and bring the grandchildren, three of them now. Dear little Lucy, she's his favourite with that sweet smile and that golden hair. 'Mary,' he said to me, 'I want young Lucy to sit next to me. She makes me feel young again!' I know just what he means: it's as if the sun has come out when she arrives.

 3 Bevor die S ihren Artikel verfassen, müssen folgende Fragen geklärt werden: Wodurch zeichnen sich die erwähnten journalistischen Textsorten aus? (vgl. hierzu das Glossar, SB, S. 262). Wo kann ich ein entsprechendes Beispiel finden? (z.B. in anderen Kapiteln des Buches, im Internet, englischen Zeitungen usw.). Nachdem die S die Artikel
→ *WB, ex. 6* verfasst haben, können diese in der Klasse aufgehängt und verglichen werden.

Mother abandons baby: divorced woman, lost job, worried about money, baby cries a lot, lack of sleep, depressed, cannot manage, wants baby to have a good home, leaves it in a hospital.
Single parent families on the increase: in the past, the family unit consisted of mother, father and children; children need both parents; far more divorces than 20 years ago; society is more relaxed; no need to marry; women can manage on their own; women earn good money; childcare and nursery schools mean women can go out to work.
More fathers take paternity leave: fathers can look after small children just as well as mothers; fathers are more patient; fathers need to get to know their children; if both parents work, why shouldn't the father take time off work?
Unmarried couples can adopt: rules for adoption very strict; the new home must be safe, comfortable, caring; no reason why a couple who live together but are not married cannot provide a home like that; in some countries the law allows unmarried couples to adopt.
Designer baby born to childless couple: scientists help people without children/who cannot have children; should scientists interfere with nature?; people who want children and were unable to have them are delighted when the baby arrives.
Pop star marries childhood sweetheart: they went to school together, he used to carry

her books, then he went to London and became famous, never forgot her, they were married in the church at the end of the road where they grew up.

a–d Individual answers.

4 **a–b** Individual answers.

SB, S. 22 # 1 The Trouble with Mother

Source:	*Jackie*, 15 June 1991
Topic:	Tense relationship between a daughter and her mother
Text form:	Magazine article
Language variety:	BE
Number of words:	Partner A: 443; Partner B: 542
Level:	Basic/advanced
Skills/activities:	Summarizing the text, information gap activity, listening and asking questions, working with language register, role play

Lern-vokabular

Active vocabulary: 'The Trouble with Mother' (pp. 22, 25)

partner A, p. 22: be pretty strict (l. 1), be unbearable (l. 4), have some privacy (l. 5), I can't help feeling jealous (l. 20), worry (l. 25), not mind sth. (l. 25), reassure sb. (l. 27)
partner B, p. 25: call sb. sth. (l. 4), accuse sb. of doing sth. (l. 6), argue back (l. 7), embarrassing (l. 9), concerned (l. 12), watch sb.'s every move (ll. 12–13), quiz sb. about sth. (l. 16), be embarrassed by sb./sth. (l. 18), get on well with sb. (l. 32), constant questions/accusations (ll. 33–34), take sth. the wrong way (l. 36)
tasks: appropriate, comfortable

Didaktisch-methodische Hinweise

Dieser Text ermöglicht den S einen leichten Einstieg in die Textarbeit des Kapitels. Die Erzählerin des Texts ist etwa gleichaltrig mit den S und berichtet in einem leicht verständlichen Englisch über die Spannungen zwischen ihr und ihrer Mutter, die in der Wahrnehmung des Mädchens zu viel Kontrolle ausübt. Auch wenn die S die Intensität des Konflikts vielleicht nicht aus eigenem Erleben kennen, werden ihnen sicher seine Gegenstände vertraut sein. Das hier entworfene Familienbild steht in einem starken Kontrast zur Harmonie, die im Bild Rockwells im „Lead-in" ausgedrückt wird (vgl. SB, S. 21; TM, S. 40).
Die Textpräsentation erfolgt im Rahmen einer *information gap activity* in zwei Textabschnitten. Damit schulen die S ihre Fähigkeit, Inhalte zusammenzufassen, sie verständlich darzustellen und ggf. durch Nachfragen ihr Textverständnis zu sichern. Individuelle Lesarten des Textes und der Problematik selbst bringen die S zum Ausdruck, wenn sie den Text zu Ende schreiben oder ein Rollenspiel durchführen (Aufgaben 2 und 5).

Unterrichts-tipps

Als Einstieg in die Textarbeit kann die folgende *pre-reading*-Aufgabe dienen:

⬭ *What topics do you and your parents disagree or argue about?*
Es ist auch denkbar, dass die S ihre Vorstellung einzelner Situationen in Standbildern darstellen, nachdem sie Aufgabe 1 bearbeitet haben (vgl. *freeze frames*, S. 429).

Lösungs-hinweise
◆◆

1 **a–b** Partner A: The daughter says that her mother has always been very strict, but that this has not been a problem for her until recently. She says she no longer has any privacy at home . This is due to her sister Suzanne. Suzanne moved in with her boyfriend a few months beforehand, even though her parents were against it. So now her mother has lost all trust in her other daughter, too. As an example of her mother's extreme watchfulness the daughter gives an incident in a disco. She had told her mother all about her plans, who she was going with and when and how she was getting home. Partner B: After the disco had finished, the narrator went for some chips with some friends. Her mother came by and saw her in a chip shop and accused her in front of all her friends of lying about the disco. There have also been cases when the mother calls her daughter's friends' houses when she says she is going there. The narrator no longer likes to take friends home with her because her mother asks too many questions, and she cannot even mention a boy's name without her mother interrogating her. The worst thing her mother did was to open her mail and withhold letters from her sister. The daughter would like to have a good relationship with her mother, but now she tries to avoid telling her mother anything.

→ WB, ex. 3

 2 Vor dem Schreiben sollten die S sich Gedanken darüber machen, welche Gesichtspunkte bei der Weiterführung der Geschichte zu beachten sind, z.B. *perspective (first-person narrator); style (chatty, similar to the way you would tell a friend about your problems); logic (storyline must be continued logically).* Das Ende des Texts befindet sich auf S. 60.

3 Form:
- First-person narrator: makes identification between the girl and the reader easier;
- chatty style, similar to the way you would tell a friend about your problems;
- informal language: 'Mum' used to refer to mother, use of emphatic 'do' (p. 22, l. 6), 'anyway' (p. 22, l. 17) used to continue the narration, use of short forms;
- exaggeration: 'went mad' (p. 22, l. 9), 'waiting for an explosion' (p. 22, l. 16), 'she dragged me off home', (p. 25, ll. 7–8), 'quizzed endlessly' (p. 25, l. 16), 'the third degree (p. 25, l. 17), 'constant questions and accusations' (p. 25, ll. 33–34);
- frequent change of tenses: simple past when recounting things that happened, present perfect when discussing what has been going on, simple present when making general statements.

Content: The personal nature of the text (trouble with her mother, her sister moving out, her father's attempts to help her) give the reader the feeling that he or she is listening to a friend talking about her problems. The narrator's use of detailed examples makes it all seem very plausible. Some readers' own experience of parental behaviour (or that of people they know) may lend credibility to the account, even if it is a little exaggerated.

 4 a Vor Bearbeitung der Frage sollten die S Merkmale des *informal English* benennen.

- Short forms: 'Mum's always had ...' (p. 22, l. 2), '... where we're going, who we're seeing ...' (p. 22, l. 3).
- Informal words and phrases: 'things got pretty tense' (p. 22, l. 16), 'Mum went mad' (p. 22, l. 9), 'Mum and Dad reckoned ...' (p. 22, l. 13), 'Suzanne was dead against rushing things' (p. 22, l. 14), 'pretty tense' (p. 22, l. 16), 'row' (p. 22, l. 17), 'stuff like that' (p. 22, ll. 24–25), 'a crowd of mates' (p. 22, l. 26), 'a girl's night out' (p. 22, ll. 26–27), 'eyed up the talent' (p. 22, l. 30), 'what on earth' (p. 25, l. 8), 'accidentally-on-purpose' (p. 25, l. 10), 'bumping into me' (p. 25, l. 10).

b Possible answers:
'got pretty tense' > became quite tense
'went mad' > became very angry/annoyed
'reckoned' > thought/believed/felt
'was dead against rushing things' > did not want to rush anything / was totally against rushing things
'pretty tense' > relatively tense
'row' > quarrel

'stuff like that' > things like that /similar things
'a crowd of mates' > a group of friends
'a girl's night out' > an evening with some of my girlfriends
'eyed up the talent' > flirted with some of the boys
'what on earth' > what exactly
'accidentally-on-purpose' > in a way that seems accidental but is not
'bumping into me' > meeting me by accident
The more formal versions would be appropriate to a newspaper or magazine for adults, especially straight reporting (which is generally also written in the third person).

5 Für Hinweise zum Umgang mit *role plays* vgl. S. 428.

6 Dieser Hörtext befindet sich auf CD1, *track* 2; das Transkript auf S. 64. Die Aufgaben sind so angelegt, dass die S beim *listening* zielgerichtet auf einzelne Details achten. Bei leistungsschwächeren Kursen kann es sinnvoll sein, die folgenden Wörter zu semantisieren:

yearbook: book that is produced by the senior class in a high school and contains photographs of students and details of school activities
wind up: end up
spin on sth.: way of presenting sth. (esp. news or information)
'Sex and the City': TV show about a woman who writes about the sex lives of herself and her friends in New York City
sample: example of sth.
like (AE infml): used when you are introducing an example or direct speech
ruminate: think deeply
school (AE): college, unversity
Journalism/English major: student studying journalism/English as their principal subject
step up to the plate (AE): (from baseball) take a big step forward to do sth. important

a Kaley is a 19-year-old girl who studies at the University of Wisconsin. She is from Naperville (which is close to Chicago). She writes a sex column for the university newspaper.

b
– She got the job because a good friend suggested she write for the university paper. She wrote a few articles that had something to do with sex, which were liked by the newspaper staff, and then they asked her to do a sex column.
– Her mother is not very comfortable with her daughter's job. She was at first surprised, but she now seems to accept what her daughter does. If she were very uncomfortable, it is unlikely that she would even have appeared on the phone-in show. Very often she stumbles over words, as if she is a little embarrassed to talk about the subject. Obviously, there are certain things that they can talk to each other about (e.g. the pill and being responsible), but other subjects like masturbation are too embarrassing for Cindy. One can argue that the relationship has improved, as Cindy seems to respect her daughter's decision to write about sex, even if they themselves will be careful in approaching the subject.

c It is when a girl has spent the night with someone and has to go back to her room wearing the same clothes as the night before, but with her make-up looking bad.

7 Diese Aufgabe kann als schriftliche Hausaufgabe bearbeitet werden. Für eine Besprechung in der Klasse eignen sich Verfahren wie *pyramiding, fish bowl* oder *double circle* (vgl. S. 428–429).

Individual answers.

2 **This Be the Verse** Philip Larkin

Source:	*High Windows*, 1974
Topic:	The destructive influence of parents on their children
Text form:	Poem
Language variety:	BE
Number of words:	83
Level:	Basic/advanced
Skills/activities:	Analysing poetry, relating photos to a text, writing (a stanza of) a poem

Didaktisch-methodische Hinweise

Die S begegnen hier einem Gedicht eines der beliebtesten englischen Dichter des letzten Jahrhunderts, das in Großbritannien wegen seiner direkten Sprache und der provokativen Aussage sehr bekannt ist. Es beschreibt drastisch den vermeintlich schädlichen Einfluss von Eltern auf ihre Kinder und zieht daraus die Schlussfolgerung, dass Jugendliche so früh wie möglich aus dem Elternhaus ausbrechen und keine eigenen Kinder haben sollten. Die Aufgaben zielen v.a. auf eine kritische, persönliche Auseinandersetzung mit dem provokativen Rat, den dieses Gedicht gibt (vgl. auch die Zusatzaufgabe unten).

Die ergänzenden Fotos mit Familienszenen aus unterschiedlichen Zeiten, die unterschiedliche Ideale und Werte implizieren, ermöglichen einen Blick auf Eltern-Kind-Beziehungen in historischer Perspektive.

Unterrichts-tipps

→ *WB, ex. 5*

Das Gedicht hat ein recht regelmäßiges jambisches Metrum, so dass es sich gut für einen Einstieg in das laute Vortragen von Gedichten eignet. Die S lesen den Text zunächst in Einzelarbeit still, bevor sie in Dreiergruppen das laute Vorlesen üben. Beim Vortrag vor der Klasse liest jeder S eine Strophe.

Info

Philip Larkin (1922–1985) was born in Coventry on 9 August, 1922. Larkin attended King Henry VIII Grammar School, where he regularly contributed to the school magazine. He then studied at Oxford, graduating with First Class Honours in English in 1943. Larkin was initially influenced by the works of Auden, Lawrence and Yeats. His first poem, 'Ultimatum', was published in 1940.

He failed to get into the civil service, and so instead became a librarian. Since 1955 he began working in the library at Hull University. He lived in Hull until his death, never marrying or having children.

Although he wrote a few novels, e.g. *Jill* (1946) and *A Girl in Winter* (1947), it was as a poet that he gained his reputation. In 1951 he privately published the collection *XX Poems*. His reputation as one of the leading modern British poets was established by his collection *The Less Deceived* (1955). His other collections of poems, *The Whitsun Weddings* (1964) and *High Windows* (1974), were also well received.

Lösungs-hinweise

1 The speaker's advice is to leave home and not to have children, because however you bring them up, you will have a destructive influence on them.

2 Possible answers:

I agree: Parents usually want their children to be like them or to make them as they would like them to be, so they try to make them act and think and dress as the parents wish, even if this is not in the interests of the child. Children need and want to be different and cannot be happy if they are unable to create their own identity. But every generation keeps trying to do it.

I don't agree: I think parents usually want the best for their children. They want their kids to have a better time than they did, to have more money, more fun, and to be more successful. So they try to teach them not to make the same mistakes, not to have the same faults. So, they are actually helping and not messing up the children.

⬭ *How seriously do you think you should take the advice given in the poem? What do you think was the intention of the poet?*
Possible answer:
Larkin's statement may seem logical at first sight: you can only break this never-ending circle of parents having a destructive effect on their children, who then do the same to their children, by not having children. However, the consequence of following the advice would be resignation and, ultimately, the end of humanity. Larkin probably wanted to make readers aware of the circle. His poem might result in children viewing their parents' mistakes with more leniency. No matter how well-meaning you are as a parent, you will always hand down some negative emotions and values to your children, which may have a negative influence on them.

3 **a** The rhyme scheme is: a b a b c d c d e f e f (alternate rhyme). The metre is iambic (an unstressed followed by a stressed syllable). The combination of the rhyme scheme and the metre makes the poem sound light-hearted, which forms a stark contrast to the taboo words and its depressing message.

b The phrase 'fuck up' (l.1), which is then repeated in l. 5, comes as a surprise, as one does not expect taboo language in a poem. The fact that it is the only instance of taboo language in the poem reinforces the shock. It seems as if a lot of emphasis is being put on this single phrasal verb, which contains the (intentionally and provocatively) simplistic message of the poem.

4 **a** Als Erweiterung dieser Aufgabe können die S gebeten werden, selbst Fotos mitzubringen, die das Gedicht illustrieren.

In all three photos we can see parents with their children. In the first photo a father is going hunting with his teenage son. In the second photo we see a young, hippy, anti-authoritarian couple, lounging around with their children. The third photo is very old (it was probably taken around 1900) and shows a family dressed up and walking in a park.
In all three photos parents are handing down their values to their children. The parents very strongly determine their children's lifestyle. Of course, it is not possible to say whether the children have been messed up, but one can speculate as to whether this might not be the case. The fact that a conservative hunting family is contrasted with a hippy family indicates that no matter what parents do, they are going to have a strong influence on their children. The photo from the 19th century also implies that this has been going on forever.

b Individual answers.

SB, S. 28 **3 Households and Families: 1990 and 2000**

Source:	Report by the US Census Bureau, 2001
Topic:	Information on households in the USA
Text form:	Report/pie-chart/table
Language variety:	AE
Level:	Advanced
Skills/activities:	Comparing different methods of presenting information, analysing diagrams, discussing sth. in class

Active vocabulary: 'Households and Families: 1990 and 2000' (p. 28)

grow by sth.(l. 1), increase (l. 2), the vast majority of sth. (l. 7), be related to sb. (l. 8), the average (family) size (ll. 16–17), decrease (l. 17), over (a period of time) (l. 17), decline (l. 18), respectively (l. 18), downward trend (l. 18)

Didaktisch-methodische Hinweise

In den Materialien dieser *section* wird „Familie" bzw. „household" als statistische Größe behandelt: Die Diagramme sowie der Text stellen Informationen über die Zusammensetzung amerikanischer Haushalte in den Jahren 1990 und 2000 dar.

Der sichere Umgang mit solchen Gebrauchstexten ist von entscheidender Bedeutung, da die S in ihrem Alltag wie auch in ihrer späteren Arbeitswelt immer wieder mit Statistiken konfrontiert werden. Unterrichtliches Ziel ist die Befähigung zum Umgang mit Statistiken in englischer Sprache. Die S entnehmen Informationen, vergleichen die Effektivität verschiedener Darstellungsformen und setzen graphisch präsentierte Informationen in geschriebenen Text um. Schließlich nutzen sie die so gewonnenen Informationen für eine Diskussion.

Unterrichts-tipps

Die Bearbeitung dieser Materialien im Unterricht ist anspruchsvoll: Allein die Menge unterschiedlichster Zahlen und wenig vertraute statistische Begriffe wie z.B. die Bezeichnung einer Einzelperson als „nonfamily" werden bei vielen S Verständnisschwierigkeiten hervorrufen. Einige S mögen auch auf scheinbare Unstimmigkeiten zwischen den Angaben des Textes und der Diagramme hinweisen. Z.B. nennt der Text für „one person, nonfamily" im Jahr 2000 die Zahl 27,2, während es in den Diagrammen 25,8 ist. Ursache hierfür ist, dass übersehen wurde, dass der Text mit absoluten Zahlen, die Diagramme hingegen mit Prozentzahlen arbeiten. „Table 1" enthält allerdings tatsächlich eine Unstimmigkeit: Die Kategorie „Unmarried partner households" müsste eigentlich als Unterkategorie zu „Nonfamily households – Two or more people" dargestellt werden.

Um das Verständnis zu erleichtern, sollten unbedingt einige demographische Fachbegriffe semantisiert werden:

A household (cf. l. 1) is a person or group of people who occupy a housing unit (e.g. a house, flat, mobile home, etc.). The householder is the person in whose name the housing unit is owned, rented or occupied.

A family household (cf. l. 3) consists of a householder and one or more people living together in the household who are related to the householder by birth, marriage or adoption. Such a household may, of course, also contain people unrelated to the householder.

A nonfamily household (cf. l. 11) consists of a person living alone or a householder who shares the home with people who are not related to him or her, e.g. friends or an unmarried partner.

Nachdem die S die drei Materialien durchgearbeitet haben, kann das Textverständnis überprüft werden, indem die S der „Table 1" (SB, S. 29) eine weitere Zeile hinzufügen und die absoluten Zahlen aus dem Text den Prozentzahlen der Tabelle zuordnen. Auf diese Weise durchschauen sie auch den Aufbau der Tabelle:

91,947,410	105,480,101	51.7	23.5	12.2	7.2	4.2	2.1	25.8	6.1	5.2	3.7	2.59	3.14
		54.5 m		12.9 m		4.4 m		27.2 m	6.5 m				

(Die erste Zeile dieser Tabelle enthält die Ziffern aus „Table 1", die letzte die Zahlen, die die S eintragen sollen).

Kopiervorlage

Eine weitere Möglichkeit, das Textverständnis zu prüfen, ist die KV „True or false?" (vgl. S. 61). Hier finden die S verschiedene statistische Aussagen, die sie auf der Basis der Materialien überprüfen und ggf. korrigieren sollen. Die S können dabei arbeitsteilig in Dreiergruppen arbeiten: Jeweils ein S ist für Text, Tabelle bzw. Diagramm verantwortlich und überprüft sein Material auf Informationen zu der zu beurteilenden Aussage.

Die Lösungen sind:

1 False: 6.1 percent (figure 1; table 1).
2 False: 2.59 (text, l. 17; table 1).
3 True (text, ll. 22–23; figure 1).
4 False: 3.7 percent (table 1).
5 True (text, ll. 13–14).
6 False: It rose to 105, 480, 101 (table 1).
7 True (figure 1).
8 False: 3.7 percent of all households (table 1).
9 False: Family households consist of 3.14 people on average (text, l. 17; table 1).

→ *WB, ex. 4*   10 True (text, ll. 7–9; figure 1; table 1).

Lösungs-
hinweise   **1** Die S bearbeiten diese Aufgabe in Einzelarbeit, bevor die Ergebnisse zusammengetragen werden. Diese Aufgabe fordert eine intensive Auseinandersetzung mit dem Text und den Statistiken. Die S müssen alle Informationen verstehen und miteinander vergleichen, um die für sie persönlich interessantesten oder überraschendsten Fakten herauszufinden. Dies mag um so schwieriger erscheinen, als sich die Verhältnisse zwischen 1990 und 2000 nur geringfügig gewandelt haben.

Possible answers:
What surprised me was the large number (4.4 million) of households headed by a man with no wife. This means either that there are a lot of widowed men or that more men are seeking and winning custody of their children following a divorce than was previously the case.
What interested me was the fact that the trend towards people living together without being married increased only slightly. It is unclear whether they are living together as a couple or whether they are friends just sharing a flat. I would have expected more people living together.

2 – Presenting exact numbers: primarily in the form of a table, but also as a text;
– presenting facts for quick comparison: pie charts;
– explaining and interpreting facts: text.
Pie charts, the most user-friendly for a quick impression of relations between numbers, are also the most limited as to what they can present: they are not normally able to transport exact numbers, and they do not explain the reasons behind trends or relationships.

3 a Bei der Sammlung dieser Wendungen sollten die S auf zwei Varianten hingewiesen werden: Während es im AE heißt „the number ... grew (...) since 1990" (l. 1), lautet der Satz im BE „the number ... has grown (...) since 1990". Der Text verwendet die Kollokation „the number of ... increased 15 percent" (l. 2); gebräuchlicher ist allerdings die Verwendung von „increased by 15 percent".

'the number of (households) grew by (over 13 million) since (1990)' (l. 1)
' the number of (households) increased (15 percent)' (l. 2)
'from (91.9 million) in (1990) to (105.5 million) in (2000)' (ll. 2–3)
'increased faster' (l. 5)
'increases in (the number of households) since (1990) (l. 15)
'decreased over the decade' (l. 17)
'declines' (l. 18)
'continue the downward trends in ...' (l. 18)
'increased in (the last 10 years) from (50.7 million) to (54.5 million)' (ll. 20–22)
'down from (55 percent) in (1990)' (l. 23)
'the (numbers/the percentage share) increased slightly from (1990) to (2000)' (ll. 24–25)

b 'the vast majority' (l. 7);
'almost three times the number' (ll. 10–11);

'predominated' (l. 12);
'more than four times as common as ...' (ll. 12–13)

c Example:

Between 1990 and 2000, the share of nonfamily households increased by slightly more than 2 points, from 29.8 percent to 31.9 percent. The increase in one-person households was a bit greater than in nonfamily households with two or more people: they went up by 1.2 points and 0.9 points respectively, although considering the difference in size between the two groups, the increase in the latter could be considered more significant. Altogether one can see that in 2000 more people are living alone or living with a partner or person to whom they are not married than in 1990.

The 10-year period showed a downward trend in family households, which decreased from 70.2 percent to 68.1 percent. The biggest decline was in the number of married-couple households while families with either a single male or female householder increased. Married-couple households still represent a majority of households, and there were more than three times as many family as nonfamily households in 2000.

❖　**4**　Diese Aufgabe stellt eine Vorbereitung auf *debating* dar (vgl. SB, S. 252), das in späteren Kapiteln eingeübt wird (z.B. SB, S. 116, Aufgabe 3b).

⬭　*Find corresponding information about Germany and present it in the way you find most suitable.*

Informationen hierzu können die S durch Arbeit mit einer Internet-Suchmaschine finden. Hilfreich sind z.B. die Internetseiten des Statistischen Bundesamts (www.destatis.de) oder des Bundesministeriums für Familie, Senioren, Frauen und Jugend (www.bmfsfj.de).

SB, S. 30　## Context Box

Didaktisch-methodische Hinweise　Die „Context Box" behandelt die Veränderungen, die der Familienbegriffs in den letzten Jahrzehnten erfahren hat. Als Einstieg in die Arbeit mit der „Context Box" können die Bilder und die Bildunterschriften dienen:

⬭　*Look at the pictures and translate the captions into German.*

Nuclear family = *Kernfamilie*; extended family = *Großfamilie*; gay parents = *schwule Eltern*.

⬭　*Explain the social and historical background of the pictures, saying when and where these types of families can/could be found.*

Nuclear families were especially characteristic of European and North American societies after the Second World War, when mortality rates dropped and social benefits such as pensions meant that parents no longer had to rely upon their children to look after them. The nuclear family still exists in the West, but with the increase in divorce, the decrease in childbirth and the decision of many single people not to get married, it is no longer the predominant type of household.

Extended families are especially frequent in less developed societies where families care a lot more for each other and take on responsibility for each other. In Western societies many immigrant communities are made up of extended families.

Gay parents are few and far between and exist only in certain Western countries, as it is difficult for gay men to adopt children. Lesbians have more opportunity to raise children as they are able to give birth.

Lösungs-hinweise　**1**　a Die Ergebnisse dieser Aufgabe können genutzt werden, um eine Diskussion über Gemeinsamkeiten und Unterschiede sowie (subjektiv empfundene) Vor- und Nachteile von *traditional families* und *new kinds of families* zu initiieren (vgl. hierzu auch die Zusatzaufgabe unten).

<u>Traditional families:</u> nuclear families, natural, adopted, break up, separate, divorce, support, breadwinner, homemaker, look after sb., double income, childcare, family unit, extended family, bring sb. up, family values.

<u>New kinds of families:</u> natural, adopted, one-parent families, break up, separate, divorce, support, breadwinner, stay single, look after sb., double income, childcare, family unit, extended family, bring sb. up, family values, gay couple, surrogate mother, test-tube baby, clone.

The lists overlap, which may indicate that the differences between so-called 'traditional families' and 'new kinds of families' are relatively superficial and concern the structure rather than the substance of family life. For example, gay parents or single parents will bring up children and look after them and care for them in much the same way as families consisting of a father and mother.

b Possible answers:

adopt (v), adopted (adj), adoptive (adj), adoption (n);

separate (v), separated (adj), separately (adj), separation (n);

divorce (v), divorced (adj), divorce (n), divorcé/divorcee (n);

support (v), supportive (adj), support (n) (used also attributely, e.g. support group), supporter (n);

surrogate (adj), surrogate (n), surrogacy (n);

clone (v), clone (n), cloning (n).

c–d Individual answers.

⬭ *Write down or discuss the advantages and disadvantages of the following forms of family: a) nuclear family, b) single-parent family, c) gay parents, d) extended family.*

a) <u>Advantages of a nuclear family</u>: cosy, secure, if one parent is ill or away the other is still around; you do not have to explain anything to other people, as it is 'normal'; if both parents work, the family has more money; there are some things that are easier to talk to a mother about and some that are easier to talk to a father about. It is good for children to have role models from both sexes.

<u>Disadvantages of a nuclear family</u>: there are always two adults against you; parents expect you to do lots of stuff together; one of your parents is almost always around, etc. Some families might have entrenched gender roles, which do not serve as a good model.

b) <u>Advantages of a single-parent family (single parent)</u>: you can build up a stronger relationship with one parent; you can both be quite independent, without a guilty conscience, because each needs a break from the other.

<u>Advantages of a single-parent family (divorced)</u>: You can have two homes, two rooms; you can get lots more treats from both, because they feel guilty / because they want you to enjoy being with them more; you travel more often since you go on holidays with both of them. Life might be more peaceful once the parents have divorced.

<u>Disadvantages of a single-parent family (single parent)</u>: You mainly get the views of your mother or your father; the parent might not have enough time for the children and be more irritable due to more pressure. Usually single-parent families have less money. Boys, especially, might miss a male role model in their life.

<u>Disadvantages of a single-parent family (divorced)</u>: You might lose contact with the parent who you do not live with. In that case you have all the disadvantages listed in the case of a single parent. Even if you spend time going between two parents, you might feel disoriented and rootless, with no real home.

c) <u>Advantages of gay parents</u>: two mothers or fathers are just as good as one mother and one father; it is nice to be different; there may be fewer quarrels between gay couples about role division; it makes you stronger, more tolerant and less bound by convention.

<u>Disadvantages of gay parents</u>: Other children might bully you or say cruel things; you could never really be like other kids, you would always wonder what it would be like to have a mother and a father instead of two mothers or two fathers.

d) <u>Advantages of extended families</u>: There is always someone to take care of you or to talk to about problems. There is less tension than in single-parent or nuclear families, as the parents also have time for themselves. You learn more about wider social contact, especially across the generations.

<u>Disadvantages of extended families:</u> You are part of a clan that watches your every movement, so it is difficult to break free from the family influence.

Differenzierung ⬭ Die folgende Aufgabe ist insbesondere für den LK geeignet und sollte mit Hilfe des Internets gelöst werden. Die Verwendung deutschsprachiger Informationen fördert die Entwicklung der Fähigkeit zur Sprachmittlung.

With a partner choose one of the following topics (or one of your own choosing): surrogacy, divorce rates, adoption of children by gay couples.

One of you research the topic for Germany, the other for another country. Try to find out about numbers, the legal situation, changes in recent years, methods, etc. Together make notes on your findings and present a comparison of the two countries in class.

⬭ *Write a comment on the following topic: Gay and lesbian couples living in an officially registered partnership (*eingetragene Lebenspartnerschaft*) should have the same rights as married couples.*

SB, S. 31 # 4 Family Life

A Giving Thanks Laurie Halse Anderson

Source:	*Speak*, 1999 (Section: 'Second Marking Period'; Chapter: 'Giving Thanks')
Topic:	Family stress at Thanksgiving
Text form:	Novel (extract)
Language variety:	AE
Number of words:	1155
Level:	Basic/advanced
Skills/activities:	Comparing a text and a picture, analysing humour, changing the narrative perspective of a text

Lern-vokabular **Active vocabulary: 'Giving Thanks' (p. 31)**

save sb. from sth. (l. 2), turn into sth. (l. 4), set a goal for sb./sth. (l. 9), beg sb. to do sth. (l. 12), plead with sb. to do sth. (ll. 12–13), suggest sth. (l. 20), be impressed (by sth.) (l. 23), mean sth. to sb. (l. 24), obligation (ll. 24–25), have nothing in common (l. 26), do a better job (l. 66), grade (l. 72), bury sth. (l. 88)

Didaktisch-methodische Hinweise Dieser Romanausschnitt beschreibt die Vorbereitungen auf das *Thanksgiving dinner* einer amerikanischen Familie, bei der die Erwartungen an dieses Fest und das tatsächliche Geschehen sehr weit auseinander liegen. Der Text stellt damit einen starken Kontrast zu dem traditionellen Bild von *Thanksgiving* dar, wie es Rockwell entworfen hat (vgl. SB, S. 21).

Auch wenn der Text aufgrund seines alltagsnahen Themas einfach erscheinen mag, stellt seine häufig informelle oder dem *slang* entstammende Sprache eine Hürde dar. Vor allem werden den S beim oberflächlichen Lesen viele witzige, ironische Stellen entgehen. Deshalb wird mit den Aufgaben 2 und 4 ein Schwerpunkt auf die Entschlüsselung des Humors dieser Geschichte gelegt.

Unterrichts-tipps Vor der Lektüre sollten kurz der geschichtliche Hintergrund und der Stellenwert des *Thanksgiving* in der amerikanischen Gesellschaft wiederholt werden (s. u.), auch da Aufgabe 3 sich auf das Rockwell-Gemälde „Freedom from Want" (vgl. SB, S. 21) im „Lead-in" bezieht.

Kopiervorlage
→ *WB, ex. 7*

Bei leistungsschwächeren S kann der Text in drei Abschnitten (Z. 1–31; 32–49; 50–Ende) präsentiert werden, bei leistungsstärkeren im Ganzen. Zur Sicherung des Inhalts dient die KV auf S. 61, bei der die S eine „Series of Catastrophes" vervollständigen. Eine Lösung für diese KV befindet sich auf S. 62. Es ist ebenfalls denkbar, die S einzelne Szenen in Standbilder umsetzen zu lassen (vgl. *freeze frames*, S. 429).

Darüber hinaus bietet es sich an, Wörter aus dem Wortfeld *meals and cooking* zu sammeln: „order (food)" (l. 3), „live on sth." (ll. 7–8), „peel potatoes" (l. 19), „a frozen turkey" (l. 19), „have sth. for dinner" (ll. 20–21), „cook sth." (l. 23), „pour sb. sth." (l. 33), „drink sth." (l. 33), „pot of boiling water" (l. 46), „boil sth." (l. 46), „thaw sth." (l. 58), „a slice of turkey" (l. 61)

Info

Laurie Halse [hɔːls] *Anderson* (born 1961) grew up in Syracuse, New York. She started writing news-paper columns, stories and letters when she was still a child. She graduated from Georgetown University with a degree in Languages and Linguistics. She started her writing career writing for her local newspaper and later the *Philadelphia Inquirer*. She has published picture books and novels for teenagers and children.

Speak (1999) is about a teenage girl, Melinda, who gets raped at a party the summer before she starts high school. Totally shocked, she calls the police, who break up the party. Since Melinda does not even tell her best friends what happened to her, everyone turns against her for ruining the party. By the time school starts, she is totally alone and miserable. She withdraws more and more, hardly talking to anybody and neglecting school. When the same boy who raped her at the party attacks her again she fights back and regains her self-confidence.

Thanksgiving: In September 1620, 102 Pilgrims left England for America. The Pilgrims were a group of Protestants who questioned the beliefs and structures of the Church of England. As they felt unable to worship freely in England, they sailed to northern Virginia, but due to a storm they landed in Plymouth (in the present-day state of Massachusetts) and remained there. The Pilgrims' first winter was very difficult. It was too late to grow many crops or to build a sufficient number of houses. So they suffered from the cold and lack of food, and half of them died. The following spring the Iroquois ['ɪrəkwɔɪ] Indians taught them how to grow corn and shared their knowledge of hunting, fishing and farming. The harvest in October was very successful and the Pilgrims harvested corn, barley, pumpkins and beans. They decided to have a feast and invited their Indian neighbours. In the following years, the original colonists celebrated the autumn harvest with a feast of thanksgiving. To this day, Thanksgiving dinner almost always includes some of the foods served at the first feast: roast turkey, cranberry sauce, potatoes and pumpkin pie. In 1863 President Abraham Lincoln appointed a national day of thanksgiving, the fourth Thursday in November. Traditionally, it is the day when most families in the USA get together for a large meal.

*Lösungs-
hinweise*

1 The mother wants to be a successful retailer, so she works very hard, especially during the period before Christmas, which is the most important shopping season of the year. But she also wants to be a good mother who cares for her family. She thinks that to be this, she has to cook a big turkey for Thanksgiving, like millions of other American mothers. Her family would not mind eating something simpler, but she feels that cooking for Thanksgiving is proof that they are still a happy family. And so, every year, the conflict between work and home turns into a crisis on Thanksgiving. It is this conflict between expectations and reality that is the theme of the extract.

2 Ein kreativer Einstieg in diese Aufgabe könnte darin bestehen, die S den kurzen Dialog zwischen Vater und Tochter szenisch darstellen zu lassen.

The writer has written a dialogue, but here the cue 'Me' indicates that the narrator should be saying something, but the line is left empty, indicating that she does not say anything. It is a way of showing that the narrator participates actively but refuses to comment. One could say that it represents resignation, desperation, depression, exasperation, etc.

3 Rockwell's picture shows the perfect Thanksgiving meal. The whole family is round the table, looking happy, the turkey looks perfectly cooked, the grandmother, who obviously has been doing the cooking, looks calm.
By contrast, the scene at the end of the extract is of an exhausted, frustrated father, an absent mother who failed to cook anything and a child who is just as happy to eat a pizza from a delivery company as a turkey. It is a picture of a nuclear family under stress.

4 The writer introduces humour into the story by:
– allowing it to be told from the <u>point of view</u> of the daughter, who is not really involved in the whole affair. She is like an observer watching from the outside, commenting on her parents' behaviour, her mother stressed out by work and her father trying hard to be a good father;
– <u>exaggeration</u>: 'strung-out retail junkie' (ll. 4–5), 'If she doesn't sell a billion shirts and twelve million belts ..., the world will end' (ll. 6–7); 'We beg her not to. We plead with her, send her anonymous notes' (ll. 12–13), 'Dad stumbles downstairs' (ll. 29–30), etc.
– <u>contrast</u>: 'The Pilgrims gave thanks at Thanksgiving ... I give thanks at Thanksgiving ...' (ll. 1–3) – in neither case is the reason for giving thanks what one expects. The informal 'sorry butts' (l. 2) contrasts with the solemn atmosphere of Thanksgiving. The daughter's relief at her mother going out to work and her father ordering pizza contrast with Thanksgiving traditions.
– <u>amusing images</u>: 'swearing like a rap star' (l. 8), 'it's like watching someone caught in an electric fence, twitching and squirming and very stuck' (l. 11), 'a ten-pound turkey iceberg. A turkeyberg' (ll. 34–35), 'like a rope tying her to the stake' (l. 45), 'a pot of glue' (l. 80).

5 <u>Example: ll. 14–28:</u> Mellie goes to bed at 10 p.m. the night before Thanksgiving. Her mother is pounding at her laptop on the dining-room table. When Mellie comes down Thanksgiving morning, she's still there. The thought goes through Mellie's head that her mother probably hasn't been to bed.
The mother looks up at her daughter in her robe and bunny slippers. 'Oh, damn,' she says. 'The turkey.'
Mellie peels the potatoes while the mother gives the frozen turkey a hot bath. The windows fog up, separating them from the outside. Mellie wants to suggest that they have something else for dinner, spaghetti maybe, or sandwiches, but she knows her mother wouldn't take the suggestion the right way. Her mother hacks at the guts of the turkey with an ice pick to get out the bag of body parts. The daughter is impressed. Last year the mother cooked the bird with the bag inside.
Mellie thinks that cooking Thanksgiving dinner means something to her mother, as she sees it as a holy obligation, part of what makes her a wife and mother. The family doesn't talk much and has nothing in common, but the daughter suspects the mother believes that if she cooks a proper Thanksgiving dinner, it means they'll all be a family for one more year. 'Kodak logic', thinks the daughter. 'Only in film commercials does stuff like that work.'
<u>Effect:</u> The story becomes more ordinary, plodding. Some of the humour is lost. The voice of the narrator needs to be heard to make it work.
It also becomes difficult to keep the two female characters apart – you have to keep adding 'the mother' and 'the daughter' or 'Mellie'.

6 It's the same every Thanksgiving: it drives me nuts. At least there's football on TV which I'd enjoy watching if my darling daughter didn't dance around the room blocking out the screen just as they score. 'Get out of the way, Mellie!'

And now the wife's on the phone again – that's the third time they've called from the store. Haven't they ever heard of a family holiday? The telephone cord is all twisted around her – she looks as if she'd been tied to the stake. Perhaps if she were to burn, it would be better for the rest of us.

And what is that boiling in the kitchen? I think I had better go and help.

No, I don't believe it: She's boiling the frozen turkey! What's she mouthing ...? Too big for the microwave. Well, Mellie is doing the right thing there, filling up with doughnuts – I don't think there'll be anything else to eat for quite a while. Ugh, phone call over ...

'What the heck are you doing?'

'I'm trying to thaw the chicken. What do you think?'

'It'll take hours to thaw that way!'

'Well, I'm sorry, but it's too big for the microwave.'

'Well, honey, I was thinking it might be better to get a take-out. I mean, you've got all this work and then the cooking, too.'

'Think I can't manage the household, huh?'

'No, no, I don't think that. But that bird is gonna take hours to thaw.'

'So, are you in a hurry?'

'No, of course not. Say, why don't I chop the bird up – like that it'll thaw more quickly.'

'But it won't look like a traditional turkey.'

'No, but it'll taste like one, won't it? And we'll manage to eat it this Thanksgiving instead of next Thanksgiving. Come on, that way you'll have less ...'

'I don't believe it, the goddam phone again. Well, if you think you can do any better, go ahead.'

'Right. I'll take it out of the water. Ouch! It's hot! Where's the oven mitt?'

My wife points distractedly in some general direction.

'Right. Now, where's the hatchet? Good. Here goes.'

I feel like a fool carrying this darn bird across the back yard. But I'll show her I can do it better. Hell, this bird is tough. Damn, they're both watching. But I'll get this right. There
→ WB, ex. 8   you go.

SB, S. 33   **B Taking Responsibility**

VIDEO

Source:	*My Family*, 2000 (Series 1: Episode 1)
Topic:	Everyday family problems
Text form:	TV sitcom (extract)
Language variety:	BE
Length:	5:35 mins
Level:	Basic
Skills/activities:	Examining typical family behaviour, viewing skills

Didaktisch-methodische Hinweise

In diesem Auszug aus der *sitcom My Family* werden alltägliche Eltern-Kind-Probleme dargestellt – Situationen, die den meisten S bekannt sein werden und die sie wiedererkennen sollten: Streit über ausgeliehene und defekte Geräte, Missverständnisse bei der Terminplanung, Streit über das Essen.

Unterrichts-tipps

Die S sollten bereits vor dem ersten Sehen der Ausschnitte (vgl. Video/DVD und die Transkripte auf S. 66) die erste Aufgabe lesen, damit sie ihre Aufmerksamkeit auf die entsprechenden Aspekte lenken können. Da die meisten Jugendlichen *sitcoms* kennen, aber möglicherweise nicht genau definieren können, was deren Merkmale sind, sollten sie vor Aufgabe 2 das Glossar konsultieren (vgl. SB, S. 257). Im Zusammenhang mit diesem Auszug könnte die Frage besprochen werden, warum britische Serien in Deutschland seltener ausgestrahlt werden oder weniger bekannt sind als amerikanische. Als Gründe für die Popularität amerikanischer Serien könnten der amerikanische Humor genannt werden, der vielleicht leichter zugänglich ist als der britische. Auch ist die Marktmacht amerikanischer Sender größer (vgl. auch SB, S. 115).

Gegebenenfalls können vor dem ersten Sehen folgende Vokabeln semantisiert werden:

submergible: able to go under the surface of water
gas fitter: person who fixes gas pipes, etc.
tank top: type of ugly pullover without sleeves
toad-in-the-hole: English dish consisting of batter (= *Teig*) and sausage
en vacances: (French) on holiday

Lösungs-vorschläge **VIDEO**

1 Die Auszüge befinden sich auf dem Video / der DVD; die Transkripte auf S. 66.

– Stressed mother in charge of three children preparing breakfast; mother orders children around; mother gives typical response to children who are looking for lost things ('Where were they when you last had them?'); has to cook, but is not very good at it; tells children to have more responsibility.
– Children ignore their mother ('Whatever it was, I wasn't listening'), ask their mother where things are, buy a pet without saying, insult mother's cooking, try to persuade parents to do what they want by twisting truth, by flattery, by playing on their fears; mock their father, ignore him when he complains about his day at work; children mock each other (e.g. Nick shaking his hands when greeting sister).
– Parents expect argument when a problem arises.
– Father disapproves of his daughter's nail polish, tries to reject son's request to use his laptop, arrives late from work, seems to have little time for his family.

VIDEO **2** Canned laughter; actors deliver lines at each other rather than talking normally; joking all the time (e.g. 'it's just hole', 'toad en vacances', 'it [the rabbit] needs to go in for a bit longer'); witty replies to each other ('we don't want to kill it on its first day', 'keep trying'); understatement ('I need more than hints'); play on words ('a rebel with a rabbit' rather than 'a rebel without a cause'); contrast (e.g. girl on the Internet turning out to be an older gas fitter from northern England); situational comedy (e.g. mother tearing up recipe, boy walking in front of mother with a rabbit, mother introducing her family to her husband).

SB, S. 34 # Getting Along in English

Didaktisch-methodische Hinweise Diese *section* bereitet die S auf eine Essenseinladung bei einer Familie in Großbritannien oder den USA vor. Als Basis dienen zwei Dialogreihen, die eine formelle Dinnereinladung in England, ein zwangloses Abendessen bei Eltern einer Freundin in England und ein Barbecue in den USA zum Thema haben.
Die folgende Tabelle stellt die Inhalte und ihre Position auf CD1 dar (vgl. auch die Transkripte auf S. 68):

Track	Topic	First set of dialogues	Track	Topic	Second set of dialogues
3	invitation	formal dinner, England	6	actual meeting	formal dinner, England
4	invitation	informal dinner, England	7	actual meeting	informal dinner, England
5	invitation	informal barbecue, USA	8	actual meeting	informal barbecue, USA
			9	telephone call	formal dinner, England

Ziel ist es, die S für interkulturelle Unterschiede hinsichtlich Pünktlichkeit und sonstiger Verhaltensnormen zu sensibilisieren. Sie üben auch, wie man in formellen und informellen Situationen eine Unterhaltung führt.

Als Einstieg dienen die Fragen im SB, die von den S stichpunktartig schriftlich beantwortet werden sollen, so dass sie sich nach Bearbeitung der section ihren Lernfortschritt verdeutlichen können. Diese Fragen können für die S auch eine Strukturierungshilfe für die Themen sein, zu denen sie *useful phrases* notieren sollen.

Lösungshinweise

CD

1 Die Dialoge befinden sich auf CD 1, *track* 3–5; die Transkripte auf S. 68. Die S hören, wie in den drei beschriebenen Situationen die Einladung ausgesprochen und angenommen wird.

Possible answers:
Useful phrases:
Formal English invitation: That's very kind of you. / I would love to come. / At what time? / I look forward to it. / Thank you very much for the invitation.
Informal English invitation: That would be great. / What time? / What can I bring? / Please thank (your mum and dad). / I look forward to (Saturday).
Informal American invitation: What time should I come? / Great. I'll be there! / Can I bring anything?
Different customs: Formal English invitation: you are expected to come a bit earlier than dinner is served so that you can have a drink with the hosts first.
Informal English invitation: one should never come early or on the dot, but neither too late (between 10 and 15 minutes after the time given is usually acceptable).
Informal American invitation: barbecues are afternoon affairs. Quite often everybody brings some food like starters, salads or dessert.

2 a Die Sammlung dieser möglichen Fragen und Gesprächsthemen bildet die Grundlage für Aufgabe 4. Die S sollten besonders darauf hingewiesen werden, dass es als unhöflich empfunden wird, Kritik an einem Land oder seiner Bräuche zu äußern, und seien es vermeintlich harmlose Dinge wie der Ärger über unpünktliche Busse.

Possible questions your host might ask you:
How long have you been here?
How long are you going to stay?
What part of Germany do you come from?
Tell us something about your family.
What do your parents do for a living?
Have you already had the chance to see anything around here?

b Individual answers.

CD

3 Die Dialoge befinden sich auf CD1, *track* 6–9; die Transkripte auf S. 69. Auf *tracks* 6–8 sind die Gespräche zu finden, die während des Essens stattfinden. *Track* 9 enthält den Abschluss der formellen Dinnereinladung: der Anruf, mit dem sich der Gast beim Gastgeber bedankt.
Da viele der *useful phrases,* die die S hier sammeln, sowohl in formellen als auch in informellen Situationen verwendet werden können, bietet es sich an, sie von den S in einer Übersicht mit folgenden Überschriften zusammenstellen zu lassen:
– How to accept an invitation
– What to say at the table
– How to ask where the toilet is
– What to say when you want to leave
– How to thank somebody for the invitation the following day.

Useful phrases (formal): Thank you so much for inviting me. / A beer would be fine, thank you. / This is delicious. / Would you like some more potatoes? / Could you please pass me the broccoli? / It was a wonderful meal. / Excuse me, where is the toilet? / I didn't realize how late it was. I think I should go now. / It has been a delightful evening. I wanted to thank you for having me to dinner.

<u>Useful phrases (informal):</u> I brought a little gift. / This (Irish stew) is one of the best things I've eaten. / Well, it has been a lovely evening, but I think I should be going. Informal American: Hello, I'm Suzy. / Nice to meet you all. / Everybody is so friendly. / I prefer (it) well done.

<u>Different customs:</u> not arriving too early; a drink before dinner; after dinner (including coffee or tea) the evening might be over but you can stay longer if asked to do so; American barbecues are very relaxed events.

4 Die S greifen auf ihre Ideensammlung aus Aufgabe 2 zurück und erstellen in Gruppen (je zwei Gäste und zwei Gastgeber) Dialoge. Sie sollten besonders darauf achten, dass unverfängliche Themen besprochen werden, dass die Gäste auf alle Fragen ehrlich, aber vor allen Dingen höflich antworten und dass sie selbst Fragen stellen (vgl. auch SB, S. 177). Wichtig ist auch zu bedenken, dass die Gastgeber i. A. keine langen Ausführungen zu einem Thema erwarten, es sei denn, sie fragen nach.
Bei der Auswertung der Dialoge könnten folgende Kriterien eine Rolle spielen: Freundlichkeit des Gastes, Angemessenheit der gewählten Themen, Interesse am Gastgeber.

CD **5** Zur Vorbereitung dieser Aufgabe kann ggf. *track* 9 noch einmal gespielt werden (vgl. auch das Transkript auf S. 72).
In den USA und GB spielen auch sogenannte '*thank you' cards* eine wichtige Rolle. Es ist eine Möglichkeit, seinen Dank und seine Wertschätzung nach einem gelungenen Abend oder zu anderen Gelegenheiten auszudrücken, und ist in den USA wie in Großbritannien sehr beliebt. Als Hausaufgabe könnten die S folgende Aufgabe be-arbeiten:

Imagine you were invited to dinner by your English friend's parents. Write a 'thank you' card to them.
Dear Mr and Mrs X,
I would like to thank you again for the lovely evening the other night at your house. The food was wonderful and the company excellent, and I really enjoyed myself. I hope to meet up again with you soon.
Yours,

Imagine you are asked by an American or a British person staying in your country about customs when invited to dinner. What advice would you give them?

SB, S. 35 # Watch Your Language

*Didaktisch-
methodische
Hinweise*
→ *WB, ex. 9*
Schwerpunkt dieser *section* ist die korrekte Verwendung von Präpositionen – ein Bereich, in dem Fehlerprävention deshalb so schwierig ist, weil es keine grammatischen Regeln gibt, die die S internalisieren könnten. Die S müssen sich stattdessen die Verbindung z.B. von Verb und Präposition als lexikalische Einheit einprägen.

*Lösungs-
hinweise*
1
a – typical of
– mother just doesn't trust
– discuss their problems
– being too sensitive;
– she needn't / doesn't have to be
– strict
– speak to a counsellor
– explain to them
– agree with each other

b – 'typical of': dictionary under 'typical'
- 'mother doesn't': *CEG* §3c (Index under 'negatives: form/word order' or 'negatives: statements' or '*do*: auxiliary' or '*do*: to form negatives'); *CEG* §74 (Index under '*do*: to form negatives')
- 'discuss sth.': dictionary under 'discuss'
- 'sensible/sensitive': dictionary under 'sensible' will at least show that this is the wrong choice of word, although the *OALD* also has a box comparing 'sensible' and 'sensitive', alternatively the student will have to use a bilingual dictionary
- 'she doesn't have to be / needn't be': *CEG* §40 (Index under '*have/have to*': substitute form of 'must')
- 'strong/strict': dictionary under 'strong' will show that this is the wrong choice of word, but a bilingual dictionary might be more help
- 'speak to a counsellor': dictionary under 'speak' – also note the helpful box comparing 'talk' and 'speak' in the *OALD*, which says that 'When a noun follows *speak*, it must be a language: He speaks Italian'.
- 'explain to them': dictionary under 'explain'; *CEG* §20d (Index under 'explain sth. to sb.')
- 'agree with each other': dictionary under 'agree'

2 The students need to practise negation and perhaps modals. Preposition and word choice errors due to interference with the native language are more difficult to tackle systematically. Lists of common mistakes specifically for German learners might be useful, but the student should also learn to be more conscious of language when reading and listening to English: all the expressions the student misused are quite common, and the student is likely to have encountered them many times.

3

a 1 typical of
2 a symbol of
3 a poem by Larkin
4 on television/TV
5 on the radio
6 at the cinema

b 1 You agree with sb. on sth.: 'We can agree on that at least. / We cannot agree with you.'
2 Thinking of sth. is sudden, as when sth. occurs to you; thinking about is a deliberate act, involving conscious thought over a period of time: 'I was just thinking of you. / I was thinking about where to go for summer.'
3 Looking at sth. means you can see it; looking for sth. means you are trying to find it: 'I was looking at that man walking by. / Every morning I have to look for my keys.'
4 Asking about sth. means trying to get information about that thing; asking for sth. means requesting or trying to get that thing: 'We could ask the tourist office about the opening times. / There's somebody on the phone asking for you.'

c 1 Tomorrow we are going to talk about / discuss adoption by gays / gay people.
2 If I ask my brother, he'll do anything for me.
3 Do you have a good relationship with your parents?
4 My father's friends rely/depend on him quite a bit.
5 We agree on one thing: family is important.

Topic Vocabulary: 'Family'

Family Members
relative
relation
wife
husband
parent(s)
mother
father
sister
brother
half-sister/brother
sibling
twin(s)
child
daughter
son
stepmother
stepfather
stepsister
stepbrother
stepdaughter
stepson
in-laws
mother-in-law
father-in-law
sister-in-law
brother-in-law
daughter-in-law
son-in-law
aunt
uncle
niece
nephew
cousin
grandmother
grandfather
grandchild
granddaughter
grandson
great-grandmother
great-grandfather

Near-Family
godparent(s)
godmother
godfather
goddaughter
godson

Family Structures
a married couple
a couple
nuclear family
one-/single-parent
 family
a childless couple
an adopted child
natural/adoptive parents
extended family
an only child
gay/same-sex couple
gay/same-sex
 partnership
be related to sb.

Planning a Family
family planning
adopt a child
be adopted
surrogate mother
artificial insemination
sperm bank
test-tube baby
clone a human being

Parents and Children
bring sb. up
raise sb.
look after sb.
take care of sb.
support sb.
educate sb.
have good/bad
 relations with sb.
have a good/bad
 relationship (with sb.)
get on well with sb.
be strict with sb./
 about sth.
lay down the law
allow sb. to do sth.
check up on sb.
obey sb.
(dis)obedience
rebel against sb.
obey/break rules

Providing for a Family
support your family
 (financially)
main breadwinner
homemaker
single/double income
pay maintenance (to sb.)
childcare (support)

Living Together/Apart
live together
move in with sb.
be engaged to sb. / to get
 married
fiancé
fiancée
get married
be married
start a family
be happily/
 unhappily married
divorce sb.
get divorced
be divorced
separate (from sb.)
be separated
break up (with sb.)
live by yourself
live alone
stay/remain single
bachelor
widow
widower
live at home
live under one roof
leave home

SB, p. 23
Task 2
(cf. TM, p. 43)

The Trouble with Mother

Here is the last part of the text.

Talking about it might seem the obvious answer and I have tried but all she says is that as long as I'm not hiding anything then I've got nothing to worry about. But that's not the point, is it? Sometimes she's nice for a few days and I think things are finally getting better until I find another letter opened or I discover things have been moved about in

5 my room.

In a way I can see what's made her like this but I think it's wrong and just wish she could understand that too. I'm sure Mum would hate it if someone wanted to know everything that went on in her life – why then, can't she extend a bit of trust to me and mine?

10 Maybe things will get easier as I get older or once she starts getting over what happened with my sister, I don't know. All I know right now is that I'm getting punished for something that I haven't done. I can only hope that things get better as time goes on but whether they will is anyone's guess ...

SB, p. 28
(cf. TM, p. 47)

Households and Families

True or False?

Read through the following statements, then look at the text, figure 1 and table 1 on pp. 28–29 again and say whether they are true or false. If they are false, correct them. Support your answer by saying from which source you took the information.

1. In 2000, 6.1 million households were nonfamily households with two or more people.

    ■ True   ■ False

    Source: _____

2. In 2000, the average number of people per household was 2.63.

    ■ True   ■ False

    Source: _____

3. The percentage of married-couple households decreased between 1990 and 2000.

    ■ True   ■ False

    Source: _____

4. The percentage of multigenerational households was 3.7 million in 2000.

    ■ True   ■ False

    Source: _____

5. In 2000, 6.5 million households consisted of two or more people who were not related to each other.

    ■ True   ■ False

    Source: _____

6. The total number of households decreased to 105,480,101 in 2000.

    ■ True   ■ False

    Source: _____

7. The percentage of families with a male householder was 4.2 percent in 2000.

    ■ True   ■ False

    Source: _____

8. 3.7 percent of nonfamily households were multigenerational households in 2000.

    ■ True   ■ False

    Source: _____

9. 3.14 percent of households in 2000 were family households.

    ■ True   ■ False

    Source: _____

10. Most family households consisted of a married couple in 2000.

    ■ True   ■ False

    Source: _____

SB, p. 31
(cf. TM, p. 52)

Family Life

A Series of Catastrophes

Thanksgiving at the narrator's house could be described as a series of catastrophes. Below, you can find a list containing some of the things that go wrong. Add the rest.

■ The mother works the night before Thanksgiving, forgetting ——————— .

■ ————————————————————————
————————————————————————

■ ————————————————————————
————————————————————————

■ ————————————————————————
————————————————————————

■ The mother's store calls (second time).

■ ————————————————————————
————————————————————————

■ ————————————————————————
————————————————————————

■ ————————————————————————
————————————————————————

■ ————————————————————————
————————————————————————

■ The father tries to ——————————————— .

■ ————————————————————————
————————————————————————

■ ————————————————————————
————————————————————————

■ ————————————————————————
————————————————————————

■ The father ——————————————————— .

SB, p. 31
(cf. TM, p. 52)

A Series of Catastrophes

Lösungsvorschlag

The mother works the night before Thanksgiving, forgetting to thaw the turkey.

The mother hacks at the guts of the turkey with an ice pick.

The mother's store calls (first time).

The mother tries to thaw the turkey in the sink.

The mother's store calls (second time).

The mother's store calls (third time).

The mother tries to thaw the turkey in boiling water.

The mother and father argue.

The mother's store calls (fourth time).

The father tries to chop the turkey with a hatchet.

The father washes the meat with detergent as it got dirty.

There is smoke in the kitchen, a glass breaks.

The father's turkey soup looks like glue, because father added too much thickener.

The father orders pizza.

The father buries the soup in the garden.

CD ## Sex Columnist

SB, S. 24	*Interviewer:*	You and your mom are on separate phones at your house.
Task 6	*Kaley:*	Yeah.
	Interviewer:	And, Kaley, how old are you?
	Kaley:	I'm 19.
	Interviewer:	19. Went to high school locally, here?
	Kaley:	Uh, yeah, at Naperville Central.
	Interviewer:	Naperville Central and, um, and then you headed off. Did you do any writing in high school?
	Kaley:	I worked on the yearbook and I also did a little bit for the newspaper.
	Interviewer:	OK.
	Kaley:	And ... I just ... I've always liked to write, so ...
	Interviewer:	So you get up to the University of Wisconsin and you see an opportunity to write for the paper up there, right?
	Kaley:	Yeah, actually one of my best friends ... um ... has worked on it for a long time and she got me into it.
	Interviewer:	How do you wind up getting the job as the sex columnist, for the *Badger Herald*?
	Kaley:	Well, I was a news reporter earlier in the year and I'd actually done two articles that were sex-related and they liked my spin on it, you know, I kinda joked about it and made it a little more interesting ...
	Interviewer:	Uh hmm ...
	Kaley:	And they kind of joked around about, you know, *Sex and the City* and maybe me being the sex columnist, and then they asked me to write up a sample column one time and I wrote up about 800 words and brought it in to an editor-in-chief and he liked it, so ...
	Interviewer:	What was the sample column about?
	Kaley:	Um, it was just kind of an introduction. Just talking about ... kind of ... the point of the column, how it wasn't going to be like question and answer or advice really, it was just kind of ruminating ...
	Interviewer:	Topical.
	Kaley:	Yeah.
	Interviewer:	Right. Now, Cindy ...
	Cindy:	Yes.
	Interviewer:	Cindy Mills, the mom. Um ... at what point do you find out that this is the direction that Kaley's heading?
	Cindy:	You know, she went off to school and ... not even being a Journalism major or an English major, so it came as a suprise to me when she, uh, when she told me, that was early in the fall, I guess in September. You know, I never would have thought she had any interest in doing a column. I know she was leaning towards writing stories and that kind of thing, but it took me by surprise, you know, because it didn't seem like Kaley at the time, you know.
	Interviewer:	What was ..., Kaley, what was the atmosphere at your home? Did you and your mom feel comfortable discussing sex through your high-school years, or were you pretty typical that you just: 'Mommm!'
	Kaley:	Yeah, we don't really ... we still don't really, I mean ...
	Cindy:	To be honest, I don't read the ... I read the first couple of columns, but, you know, it's the kind of thing you don't ... I know it's not about Kaley personally, necessarily, but it's still, you know, not quite ...
	Interviewer:	You can dream, can't you, Cindy?
	Cindy:	What was that?
	Interviewer:	I said, you can dream, can't you?
	Cindy:	Yeah. Well, a lot of it ... you know ...
	Interviewer:	Well, I mean, this has to come up. Kaley ...

Kaley:	Yes?
Interviewer:	... stop me if I'm wrong: Have you had sex?
Kaley:	Yes, and she does know about that.
Cindy:	That was not a suprise.
Interviewer:	OK. You do know that Kaley is no longer a virgin.
Cindy:	Right. Kaley's been, you know, um, boy-crazy since she was 15 ... had several serious boyfriends. So that part was no suprise.
Interviewer:	So, did you guys ever have the 'responsibility' conversation?
Cindy:	We, I think we have. Before ... particularly before she went to college about ... say like going on the pill and that kind of thing, you know.
Interviewer:	Kaley, do you recall that? Do you recall your mom sitting you down and having the conversation?
Kaley:	Yeah, 'cause I actually brought up I wanted to go on the pill. I'd wanted to go on it for a while. But, I mean, we never even really, we never really could even say 'sex' around each other. Now that I ... since I've been a sex columnist she's gotten a little ... we've gotten a little more comfortable but I've always been a lot more open about that kind of thing.
Interviewer:	You more open than she has?
Cindy:	Yes, I would say that.
Kaley:	Yeah, definitely.
Interviewer:	OK.
Cindy:	It's probably a generational thing, but ...
Interviewer:	Kaley, what column ... tell us the topics of some of the columns you've written for the *Badger Herald*.
Kaley:	Um, well ...
Interviewer:	I have in front of me, um, about music and sex ...
Kaley:	Yeah.
Interviewer:	... about how helpful that is sometimes.
Kaley:	Yeah.
Interviewer:	And one about women taking responsibility, um, women need to step up to the plates.
Kaley:	Yes.
Interviewer:	Um ... and what else do I have here? What are some of the other topics?
Kaley:	Uh, well, one of my favourite ones was on 'the walk of shame'.
Interviewer:	And what's that?
Kaley:	Um, it's when, uh, it's a pretty popular term around college campuses, uh, when you stay over at someone's place unexpectedly on like a Friday or Saturday night, and then you have to walk home the next day in your clothes ...
Interviewer:	... in the same outfit.
Kaley:	Yeah, in the clothes you went out in ... and your make-up not quite so pretty as maybe when you left.
Interviewer:	Uh huh.
Kaley:	And yeah, it's 'the walk of shame' back across campus.
Interviewer:	Cindy, had you been familiar with that term before you read it in Kaley's column?
Cindy:	Actually that's one of the few that I read, and, no, I was not familiar with it.
Interviewer:	Kaley, is there anything that you hesitate to write about because you don't want your mom to read it?
Kaley:	Yes, definitely.
Interviewer:	Like what?
Kaley:	Well, I guess, ... more risqué topics like probably like masturbation or, you know ...

Cindy:	I'm hiding my face.
Interviewer:	Now, that's not something you two ever talked about?
Cindy:	No, definitely not.
Interviewer:	No, it just seems ... just seems, what a perfect way to, I mean what an opening to have these conversations, and yet it's so fascinating that, Cindy, you're still much more uncomfortable with it than Kaley is.
Cindy:	Definitely so.
Interviewer:	Wow, Kaley, do you think that's the case with most of your friends?
Kaley:	Uh ... yeah ... pretty much. Everybody I know, my friends, are all sort of like: 'Does your mom read it?' And I'm like: 'I told her to stop.'

VIDEO **Taking Responsibility**

SB, p. 33

(Breakfast time, in the kitchen.)

Susan:	Toast. Jenny, what have I told you about painting your nails at the table?
Janey:	Whatever it was, I wasn't listening.
Michael:	Mum, where are my football boots?
Susan:	Where were they when you last had them?
Michael:	On my feet.
Susan:	So wise so young, they say, do not live long.
Michael:	What?
Susan:	I am not your slave. Nick! Breakfast!
Ben:	Congratulations. You've woken up every Nick in the world.
Susan:	Except one.
Ben:	Ah! Purple. Um, that's nice. That gives you that great fingers-slammed-in-the-car-door look.
Janey:	Mazda or BMW?
Susan:	Off!
Janey:	Hi, Nick.
Nick:	Hi, Janey. Dad?
Ben:	No.
Nick:	What?
Ben:	I'm anticipating your next question. It begins with 'can I have'.
Nick:	Wrong. It begins with 'can you lend'.
Ben:	Funny – they both end with 'no'.
Nick:	Just want to borrow your new laptop.
Ben:	I gave you the old laptop.
Nick:	It doesn't work.
Ben:	Neither do you. You're compatible.
Nick:	Why do you always give me things that are broken?
Ben:	Because you always break them.
Nick:	I didn't break it. Just got a little damp.
Ben:	Nick, portable does not mean submergible.
Nick:	It didn't say that in the instructions.
Susan:	How do you know? You didn't read the instructions.
Nick:	I didn't want to get the pages wet.
Ben:	I think I'm going to quit while I'm ahead.
Susan:	So, shall I book the restaurant before or after the film?
Ben:	What ... you didn't tell me we had plans tonight.
Susan:	I left that note on the fridge, I got Bridget to put it in her appointment book and I wrote it in lipstick on the bathroom mirror.
Ben:	I need more than hints, Susan.
Susan:	I hope my next husband has your sense of humour.

Ben:	Look, Mr Unsworth broke a tooth. The only time he could come in was this evening after work. So why don't we go out tomorrow night?
Susan:	All right.
Ben:	Excuse me?
Susan:	I said, 'all right'.
Nick:	Stop it, Susan, stop laying the guilt trip on me, OK? OK? If I let Unsworth down again, he'll go somewhere else.
Susan:	All I said was 'all right'.
Nick:	There you go again, you see, you can't stop it, can you? It's just guilt, guilt, guilt. It's unbearable. I mean, you know, you must be really upset.
Susan:	Ben, I understand. I am not upset.
Michael:	Mum, football boots?
Susan:	Didn't you hear me? Take some responsibility for yourself.
Ben:	Hey, why are you angry with him and not angry with me?
Susan:	Because with him there's still a point.
Ben:	Oh, right. Good, good. Good luck, Michael.
Nick:	Mum, you know, you're really too good for him.
Susan:	I know, and you still can't borrow the laptop.
	If you really need a computer, why don't you borrow Michael's?
Nick:	'Cause it's ... sort of personal.
Susan:	You're not chatting up girls on the Internet again?
Ben:	What do you mean 'again'? What, you've done this kind of thing before?
Nick:	Yeah, and it worked really well. Talia, her name was. This 19-year-old cellist from Prague. We had a really deep and rewarding e-relationship going.
Susan:	Until Talia turned out to be a 48-year-old gas fitter called Stewart from Sunderland.
Nick:	All right. So he was a man. It meant a lot to me while it lasted.
Ben:	You know when parents say they'll love you no matter what? They're lying.

(Later, in the kitchen.)

Michael:	Hello.
Susan:	Hello. What is that?
Michael:	It's a rabbit.
Susan:	I can see it's a rabbit. But what is it?
Michael:	Well, I wanted a rabbit so I bought a rabbit.
Susan:	But you didn't ask our permission.
Michael:	Well, I'm rebelling.
Susan:	A rebel with a rabbit.
Michael:	You told me to take more responsibility.
Susan:	I say a lot of things: I told your father he looked good in a tank top.
Michael:	Well, this is a symbol of my independence.
Susan:	That's nice, dear. Take it back to the shop.
Michael:	If you make me take it back, I'll never believe anything you say again. I'll become aimless and remote, and my school work will suffer.
Janey:	He'll become another Nick.
Susan:	Welcome to your new home. Just keep it away from the food.
Janey:	Yeah, we don't want to kill it on its first day.

(Later, at the dinner table.)

Susan:	Janey, stop admiring your teeth and eat something.
Janey:	Mel says you've got to love yourself before others can love you.
Nick:	Well, keep trying.

Janey:	What is this?
Susan:	Toad-in-the-hole, but we don't have any sausages.
Janey:	So it's just 'hole'?
Susan:	It's not just 'hole', it's French, its *toad-en-vacances*.
Ben:	Hello.
Susan:	Good evening. Nice to meet you. My name is Susan Harper and these are your children: Janey, Nick and Michael.
Janey:	Hello.
Ben:	All right, all right. I'm late. But it's the only time some of these people can come in. And don't ask me what sort of day I've had. OK, I'll tell you anyway. In a word: bloody awful.
Nick:	That's two words.
Ben:	And I've got another two words for you. Do I get dinner?
Nick:	That's four words.
Susan:	It's in the kitchen.
Ben:	Oh, it's in the kitchen. Any specific location?
Susan:	On the counter.
Ben:	Ah! I think it needs to go in for a bit longer.

CD

Getting Along in English

SB, p. 34
Task 1

Dialogue 1

Mrs Brown:	Good morning, Klaus. How are you?
Klaus:	Fine, thanks. And you?
Mrs Brown:	Couldn't be better. By the way, we were just wondering, you've been working at the firm for a week now and we thought it would be nice to get together outside of the office. My husband and I talked about it last night and wondered whether you would like to come to dinner at our house on Friday.
Klaus:	Oh, thank you very much, Mrs Brown. That's very kind of you. I would love to come. At what time?
Mrs Brown:	Seven for seven thirty?
Klaus:	Er ... I'm sorry, does that mean seven or half past seven?
Mrs Brown:	It means any time after seven, but a bit before seven thirty. The idea is that one has time for a drink before sitting down to eat at half past seven.
Klaus:	Oh, I see. Well, I look forward to it. Thank you very much for the invitation, Mrs Brown. Oh – by the way – what can I bring?
Mrs Brown:	Oh, you don't have to bring anything.
Klaus:	At home in Germany you always bring something.
Mrs Brown:	No, really. You don't have to.
(Fade out and in.)	
Klaus:	John, Mrs Brown has invited me to dinner. What should I take with me?
John:	I don't know. Perhaps you could take a bottle.
Klaus:	A bottle? A bottle of what?
John:	Wine, of course.
Klaus:	In Germany I would normally take some flowers.
John:	Well, take some flowers then. I bet her old man never gives her any. She'll probably be really pleased.

Dialogue 2

Sally:	Hi, Max! Mum and Dad asked if you'd like to come and have dinner with us this Saturday.
Max:	That would be great. What time?
Sally:	Oh, around half past seven.
Max:	I should be there at half past seven. Fine.
Sally:	Max, this is England, not Germany. Around half past seven means don't come before half past seven, don't come on the dot of half past seven, but come at about twenty minutes to eight, OK?
Max:	OK! And what can I bring? Flowers for your mother?
Sally:	You don't have to bring anything, but you will anyway, I suppose – you continentals are so polite!
Max:	We are, aren't we. But maybe I'll bring some chocolates – the flower shops here don't put the flowers together as nicely as at home.
Sally:	Did I say polite?!
Max:	Sorry. Anyway, please thank your mum and dad. I look forward to Saturday.

Dialogue 3

Bobby:	Hi, Susi. We're having some people over for a barbecue on Saturday. My mom thought you might wanna join us.
Susi:	Yeah, I'd love to. What time should I come?
Bobby:	It's just a barbecue, so come any time you want.
Susi:	Oh. Well, would seven be OK?
Bobby:	Actually, that's kinda late. Dad'll fire up the charcoal around four, so any time between then and 5:30 would be good.
Susi:	Great. I'll be there! Can I bring anything?
Bobby:	Oh, lots of people will be bringing dishes, so there'll be plenty of food. But if you want to bring something from Germany, I'm sure everybody'd get a kick out of it.
Susi:	Sure, OK. I was thinking of something for the hostess?
Bobby:	Oh no, that's not necessary. This is just an informal kind of thing.
Susi:	Fine then. I'll bring a *gugelhopf.*
Bobby:	Right, sounds interesting ...

SB, p. 24
Task 3

Dialogue 1

Mr Brown:	Good evening, you must be Klaus. Do come in.
Klaus:	Good evening, Mr Brown. Thank you so much for inviting me.
Mrs Brown:	Good evening, Klaus. I'm glad you could follow my directions.
Klaus:	Yes, thank you, Mrs Brown, they were quite clear. Er ...
Mrs Brown:	Oh, are those for me?
Klaus:	Yes, just a few flowers.
Mrs Brown:	You really didn't need to bring anything. Well, how lovely, freesias are my favourites! Look, George. Thank you so much, Klaus. I'll just go and put them in water.
Mr Brown:	Now, Klaus, how about a drink? We've got sherry, beer, wine, gin, whiskey, or would you prefer something non-alcoholic like fruit juice or tonic water?
Klaus:	Oh, thank you. A beer would be fine, thank you.
Mr Brown:	Here you go. So, how are you liking the job?
Klaus:	Oh, it's really interesting. And all my colleagues are very kind to me.
Mr Brown:	Well, that's good to hear. Had you been to England before?

Klaus:	Yes, I did a school exchange and my parents sent me to a summer school in Brighton one year.
Mr Brown:	Ah! Well, that explains your good English. We're not so good at foreign languages in this country, you know.
Klaus:	Oh, I think the English are very modest. I have seen British journalists and historians interviewed on German television and they spoke German very well.
Mr Brown:	But you look around at work and you probably won't find one person who can put a German sentence together.
Klaus:	Well, you'd be surprised. Mr Johnson's secretary ...
Mrs Brown:	You can come through to the dining room! Dinner is served.
Mr Brown:	Come on then – oh, and, er, bring your drink with you, Klaus.
(Fade out and in.)	
Klaus:	This is delicious, Mrs Brown.
Mrs Brown:	Oh, I'm so glad you like it. Would you like some more potatoes?
Klaus:	Yes, please. Would you like some more, Mr Brown?
Mr Brown:	Er, no thank you, but I'll pass them on. Here, dear ...
Klaus:	Er ... could you pass me the broccoli, please?
Mr Brown:	Of course ... I am sorry, here you are.
Klaus:	Thank you. Mrs Brown, can I pass you the broccoli?
Mrs Brown:	Yes, I think I will have a little more, thank you.
Mr Brown:	So, what do you think of Ealing, Klaus?
Klaus:	I like it very much, Mr Brown. It's so green and pretty, you can't really believe you're in London.
Mrs Brown:	What's it like where you come from, in Dresden?
Klaus:	Oh, it's beautiful. They call our city the Florence on the Elbe – the River Elbe runs through ...
(Fade out and in.)	
Mrs Brown:	Let me take your coffee cup, Klaus.
Klaus:	Oh, thank you. It was a wonderful meal, Mrs Brown.
Mrs Brown:	Well, thank you.
Klaus:	Er ... excuse me, but where's the toilet?
Mr Brown:	You go up the stairs and it's the first door on the right.
Klaus:	Thank you.
(Fade out and in.)	
Klaus:	I didn't realise how late it was. I think I should go.
Mrs Brown:	Oh, must you really?
Klaus:	Well, my landlady doesn't like it if I get in too late. Thank you so much, it has been a delightful evening ...

Dialogue 2

Mr Smith:	Hello! Are you Max?
Max:	Yes, I'm Max. Good evening, Mr Smith.
Mr Smith:	Well come on in. This is my wife, and Sally you already know!
Mrs Smith:	Hello, Max. So you found us all right?
Max:	Yes, thank you. Er, I brought you a little gift.
Mrs Smith:	Oh, you didn't need to do that. Mmm, Belgian chocolates! My favourites! Thank you so much. We'll have them after dinner.
Max:	Well, I wanted to say thank you for the invitation.
Mr Smith:	Wait till after the dinner!
Mrs Smith:	Well, talking of dinner, I'd better get back to the kitchen or we'll be eating at midnight!
Sally:	I'll come and help, Mum.
Mr Smith:	Sit down, Max, sit down. Tell us a bit about yourself. Where in Germany do you come from?

Max:	I come from Leipzig; it's in one of the eastern states.
Mr Smith:	Oh, very nice. Isn't that where they have the book fair?
Max:	Yes, that's right. It's a famous book fair, quite interesting. The city itself is quite pleasant but the countryside here is more beautiful than around Leipzig.
Mr Smith:	And the beer in Germany's not bad, either, eh?! Seriously, though, have you had time to travel around a bit since you've been here?
Max:	Yes, a bit. I've been to Cambridge for a day – that was beautiful. We don't really have anything like that in Germany ...
Sally:	Dinner's ready!
(Fade out and in.)	
Max:	It's really delicious, Mrs Smith.
Mrs Smith:	Well, tuck in then ... er ... just help yourself to more if you want it .
Mr Smith:	And you can pass me the potatoes while you're at it. Thanks.
Mrs Smith:	Is the food very different in Germany, Max?
Max:	Well, there's a lot of sausage and a lot of pork ... I like our food, but this Irish stew is one of the best things I've eaten.
Mr Smith:	Don't overdo it, Max, or she'll be expecting compliments from us, too. More juice?
(Fade out and in.)	
Mrs Smith:	Well, if everyone's finished, we could go back to the sitting room. Oh, and Max, if you want the loo, it's the second door on the right.
Max:	Thanks, Mrs Smith.
Mr Smith:	I expect you go to bed quite early in Germany, don't you? You have to start work much earlier than we do.
Max:	Yes, we do. My parents are always in bed by 10.30.
Mrs Smith:	Oh dear! We're night birds by comparison! Never in bed before midnight!
(Fade out and in.)	
Max:	Well, it's been a lovely evening, but I think I should be going. There's a bus I can catch at 10.25.
Mr Smith:	Nonsense! They're showing a *Star Trek* special tonight. Stay and watch and then I'll run you home in the car.
Max:	Well ...
Mrs Smith:	Oh, go on, don't be so polite!
Max:	OK. I'd love to stay. Thank you.

Dialogue 3

Steve:	We're here! Come around back!
Susi:	Er ... hello ... I'm Susi.
Steve:	And that must be the *gugelhopf*. Bobby's been telling us about this thing you'd be bringing.
Susi:	Yes, this is it.
Jackie:	Nice to meet you, Susi. Don't let their teasing bother you. Just put the cake down on the table with the other food. I'm Jackie, by the way – Bobby's mom. The guy at the grill is Steve, my husband.
Steve:	If you want anything barbecued, just ask me – I'm the master chef. Just introduce yourself to the others – they don't bite. Oh, and if you need the bathroom, just go in the back door – it's the first room on your right.
Susi:	OK, thanks. Nice to meet you all.
Bobby:	Want a coke, Susi?
Susi:	Yes, thanks.
Jackie:	Come and sit down, Susi. So, tell me, how do you like it here?
Susi:	Oh, it's great. Everybody is so friendly.

Steve:	Susi, how do you like your steaks?
Susi:	Um ...?
Jackie:	Do you like the meat well done or rare – you know, a bit bloody.
Susi:	Oh, I prefer it well done, please.
Steve:	Right! So, how do you like the US of A, Susi?
Susi:	Mrs Stine just asked me and I said how friendly everybody is. And everything is so relaxed.
Steve:	Yup! Nothing I hate more than a coat and tie on the weekend. Anyone want a rare steak? Bobby?
Bobby:	Yeah, sure.
Steve:	Sorry, Susi, for well done you have to wait a little.
Susi:	Oh, that's fine. There's so much food here, I never get a chance to get really hungry!

(Fade out and in.)

Susi:	It's been a lovely evening, but I think I should be getting back now.
Steve:	Are you in a dorm on Central Avenue?
Susi:	Yes, I am.
Jackie:	Well, Bobby'll run you back. Take the jeep, Bobby, the Roadster's just about out of gas.
Bobby:	OK. Thanks, Mom. Come on, Susi.
Susi:	Well, thank you again. The food was great and it's been so nice.
Jackie:	It's nice that you could come.
Steve:	Goodbye!

Dialogue 4

Mr Brown:	564093.
Klaus:	Mr Brown?
Mr Brown:	Yes? Who is this, please?
Klaus:	It's Klaus Schmitz. I do hope I'm not disturbing you. I wanted to thank you and your wife for dinner last night.
Mr Brown:	Oh, Klaus! You'd better speak to the wife. Hold on a minute, please.
Mrs Brown:	Klaus?
Klaus:	Yes, good afternoon, Mrs Brown. I hope I'm not disturbing you. I wanted to thank you for having me to dinner last night. The meal was delicious.
Mrs Brown:	Well, thank you. How nice of you to call. Oh, and your flowers are looking lovely.
Klaus:	I am glad. Well, thank you again. See you on Monday.
Mrs Brown:	Right. Have a nice weekend. And thank you for calling. Goodbye, Klaus.
Klaus:	Goodbye, Mrs Brown.

Dieses Kapitel nähert sich dem Thema Jugendkultur aus verschiedenen Blickwinkeln:
– *Section 1*, „This Thing Called Youth Culture", betrachtet Jugendkultur aus historischer Perspektive und versucht eine Begriffsbestimmung;
– *Section 2*, „My Music", befasst sich mit einem der Lieblingsthemen vieler Jugendlicher, der Musik.
– *Section 3*, „How I See Me, How I See You", behandelt das Thema Schönheitsideale, das zunehmend Jungen wie Mädchen beschäftigt.
– *Section 4*, „The Morning After", zeigt, wie Jugendzeitschriften die Folgen des Alkoholmissbrauchs behandeln.
– *Section 5*, „Y2K.CHATRM43" enthält eine Kurzgeschichte, in der die Problematik persönlicher Nähe in der virtuellen Realität behandelt wird.
Die Texte bieten den Jugendlichen Identifizierungsmöglichkeiten und schaffen vielfältige Kommunikationsanlässe, um über vergangene und gegenwärtige Trends und die damit verbundenen Chancen und Risiken zu sprechen. Die Textauswahl ist durch ein breites Textsortenspektrum und den Einbezug historischer Materialien gekennzeichnet: Neben Texten aus Jugendzeitschriften finden sich ein soziologisch orientierter Zeitungstext, ein Shakespeare-Gedicht, eine lange Kurzgeschichte sowie zwei Popsongs.

→ *WB, ex. 8*

Didaktisches Inhaltsverzeichnis

SB, p.	Title	TM, p.	Text form	Topic	Skills and activities
36	**Lead-in**	74	photos	youth culture	doing a brainstorming; describing photos; speculating about a photo
37	Everybody's Free (...) CD1, track 10	75	song		listening; analysing the tone of a text
38	**This Thing Called 'Youth Culture'**	77	essay	the emergence of youth culture	writing a summary; writing a letter to the editor
39	**Context Box**	79	–	young people as consumers	working with vocabulary; writing an essay
40	**I'm Britain's Top Teen DJ**	80	feature story	a teenage DJ	working with language register; discussing a topic; writing an article
41	**Two Generations of Pop** Whiter Shade of Pale Because I Got High CD1, tracks 11 and 12	82	songs	drug-induced hallucinations the harmful effects of drugs	comparing songs; writing a review of a favourite song; creating a radio programme
42	**Diet-crazy Girls ... and Boys** Cahal Milmo	84	news story	teenage obsession with appearance	writing a summary; doing a mind map; analysing a picture/advert;
43	**Sonnet 130** William Shakespeare	85	poem	the description of a lover	analysing poetry; examining concepts of beauty
44	**Sex After Drinking**	87	advert	the dangers of getting pregnant when drunk	analysing an advert; working with vocabulary
45	**Doctor Sarah Brewer Says ...**	89	advice column	the dangers of alcohol	comparing two texts; designing a leaflet
46	**Getting Along in English**	91		using chat and e-mail	writing an e-mail
47	**Y2K.CHATRM43** Alden R. Carter	91	short story	discovering the value of the real world and the virtual world	analysing the development of a story; giving one's opinion; writing e-mails;
53	**Watch Your Language**	94		comparisons	–

Lead-in

Im „Lead-in" werden die S dazu angeregt, ihr Verständnis des Begriffs *youth culture* zu präzisieren. Sie betrachten Fotos, die einen Querschnitt durch Jugendbewegungen der letzten Hälfte des letzten Jahrhunderts darstellen, und stellen durch Vergleich fest, welche Aspekte zur Jugendkultur gehören. Dadurch und durch das Brainstorming in Aufgabe 1 findet eine Vorentlastung von Text 1 „This Thing Called 'Youth Culture'" statt. Im Anschluss begegnen die S in einem Song einer für Jugendliche sicher sehr charakteristischen Situation: Ein Erwachsener gibt (hier nicht ganz ernst gemeinte) Ratschläge zur Lebensgestaltung. Da im Unterricht Fotos und Lied nacheinander besprochen werden, werden sie auch im Folgenden getrennt behandelt.

Fotos

Die Fotos stellen verschiedene Aspekte der Jugendkultur dar (zu den einzelnen Motiven vgl. den Lösungsvorschlag zu Aufgabe 2b). Gemeinsames Merkmal ist in den meisten Fällen ein exzentrisches, sich von der Erwachsenenwelt distanzierendes oder sie provozierendes Verhalten. Lediglich dem linken Bild auf S. 37 fehlt dieses Moment. Die Betrachtung der Bilder soll Anlass sein, über eben dieses Gemeinsame der Jugendkulturen nachzudenken; die S sollen aber auch die eigene Jugendkultur in der Tradition vieler anderer vorher sehen. Sollten die S einige Fotos altmodisch oder fremd finden, sollte mit ihnen reflektiert werden, wie ihre heutige Jugendkultur möglicherweise in der Zukunft wahrgenommen wird, auch von ihnen selbst.

1 Dieses Brainstorming sollte bei geschlossenen Büchern bearbeitet werden, um eine Beeinflussung durch die Fotos auszuschließen. Die Lösung sollte auf einer gesonderten Seite angefertigt werden, die die S während der Arbeit an diesem Kapitel ständig aktualisieren. Es empfehlen sich regelmäßige Übungsphasen, die die S selbst gestalten können, z.B. durch die Erstellung von kurzen Lückentexten, Wortfamilien usw.

Vgl. die KV „Topic Vocabulary: 'Youth Culture'" auf S. 96.

2 a Bei dieser Aufgabe sollen die S auch die Position der Bilder auf der Seite korrekt beschreiben. Zur Semantisierung können die Begriffe aus dem Kasten im SB an die entsprechende Stelle der Tafel geschrieben werden. Ebenso kann es erforderlich sein, Wortmaterial für den Ausdruck von Unsicherheit und Hypothesen zur Verfügung zu stellen: *I think/I guess, If you ask me, ..., I wonder/assume/suppose that ..., The photo could/might show ..., I'm (not) sure ..., but I would say that ..., perhaps, probably.*

Possible answers:
– I think that the bottom left-hand photo shows a bunch of young people trying to fit themselves into a telephone box. They are laughing, so I guess it's some kind of bet or gag. Possible titles: Cramming into a telephone booth / Getting closer.
– The guy in the photo in the top left-hand corner is dressed like a punk, but he seems to be playing a double bass. Punks were quite common in the 1970s and 1980s, but you still see some today. So you can't really say when the photo was taken. Possible titles: The new and the old / Punk bassist / Beethoven goes punk.
– I guess the photo in the middle row on the left shows a scene from some kind of parade – maybe a carnival or a techno group, or perhaps a love parade. Possible titles: At the Love Parade / Fun in the open air.
– The photo in the middle row on the right shows some teenagers planting trees. Perhaps they are helping the community. Possible titles: Helping the community / Bringing nature back to town.
– I wonder if the top right-hand photo has something to do with fashion. The colours and the miniskirts remind me of the films made in the late 1960s and early 1970s. Their clothes look a bit old-fashioned, so I think the picture was taken a while ago. Possible titles: Colourful stockings / Psychedelic clothes / The swinging sixties.

- The photo at the <u>bottom right</u> looks like a bike gang in the UK (there's a double decker in the background). The photo seems to be old judging from the people standing behind the bikers. <u>Possible titles</u>: Loud and Heavy / Bikers' Parade.

 b Im Folgenden werden die Entstehungszeiten und -orte der Fotos genannt; von den S soll allerdings nur eine ungefähre Einordnung verlangt werden.

- <u>Bottom left-hand photo (p. 36)</u>: Phone booth stuffing, California, 1959, a craze among students. It shows that young people are keen to do strange and pointless things that test their abilities and also involve group work; at the time there was also an element of competition involved in phone booth packing (e.g. who could break the record).
- <u>Top left-hand photo (p. 36)</u>: A punk playing music, London, possibly 1980s, but probably more modern (the double bass gives it an ironic twist). It shows that young people want to look different and to rebel a little.
- <u>Large photo on the right (p. 36)</u>: A techno parade, Berlin, 2001. It shows that music and partying play a big role in the lives of young people. The costumes reveal the desire to look different and be creative.
- <u>Photo on the left (p. 37)</u>: Volunteerism, USA, 1980s–present-day. Helping the community and others is considered an important value among young people (here, environmental awareness seems to be involved).
- <u>Top right-hand photo (p. 37)</u>: Mary Quant, fashion designer, London, 1968 (responsible for the miniskirt and the first to target teenagers as fashion consumers). The desire to look different and dress colourfully are the main aspects.
- <u>Bottom right-hand photo (p. 37)</u>: Rockers/Bikers, London, 1971. The desire to be different and somewhat threatening has often been a part of youth culture.

<u>Possible chronological order:</u> 1 phone booth packing, 2 Rockers, 3 Mary Quant, 4 the punk, 5 volunteerism, 6 techno parade.

c <u>The aspects which are the same:</u> The youngsters seem very involved in and committed to what they are doing, so a sort of idealism unites the pictures. Apart from the volunteers, all the youngsters tend to be dressed and behave in a way that is in contrast to middle-class, adult norms and values. So most of them seem to be distancing themselves from grown-ups to a certain extent in order to find their own identity.
<u>The aspects which are different:</u> The situation in each case; some have to do with fashion, others less so; some are more female-oriented, e.g the picture of Mary Quant, while some are more male-oriented, e.g. the bikers; the photo of the telephone booth involves a craze.

⬭ *Choose a person in one of the pictures and write a speech bubble for him or her.*

3 Diese Aufgabe muss zu Hause vorbereitet werden. Da die mitgebrachten Bilder u.U. zu klein sind, um sie allen S zu präsentieren, können die S diese Aufgabe in einem Kugellager (vgl. S. 429) besprechen. So wird auch der Redeanteil aller S erhöht.

Individual answers.

SB, S. 37 **Everybody's Free (to Wear Sunscreen)** Baz Luhrmann

Source:	*Everybody's Free (to Wear Sunscreen)*, 1999
Topic:	Advice to youngsters
Text form:	Song
Language variety:	AE
Length:	5:05 min
Level:	Basic
Skills/activities:	Listening, analysing the tone of a text

In diesem Lied (vgl. CD1, *track* 10, und das Transkript auf S. 99) werden von einer erwachsenen Stimme Ratschläge zur Lebensführung gegeben; die Situation erinnert an die Begrüßung neuer Studierender an der Universität. Hier jedoch verbinden sich ernst gemeinte mit ironischen, philosophische mit banalen Ratschlägen. Die S, für die es sicher nichts Ungewöhnliches ist, Ratschläge zu erhalten, werden durch die sonderbare Zusammenstellung von Ratschlägen mit einer weniger vertrauten Situation konfrontiert, die sie genau hinhören lassen wird. Die S diskutieren im Anschluss, inwieweit Ratschläge an die jüngere Generation generell berechtigt und vielleicht sogar wünschenswert sind und welche Empfehlungen des Songs sie im Einzelnen für sinnvoll halten.

Unterrichts-
tipps

Vor dem ersten Hören könnte L die folgende Frage stellen:

⬭ *Adults like to pass on their experience and views to the younger generation. Write down three pieces of advice you have heard from either your parents, your grandparents or your teacher.*

Don't waste your time with useless things like shopping, hanging out with your friends, etc.; Get good marks at school; Make sure you are always home when we tell you; Don't smoke / take drugs / drink; Wear decent clothes.

L notiert etwa zehn dieser Ratschläge und verdeckt sie, während das Lied gespielt wird. Nach Bearbeitung der Aufgabe 1 vergleichen die S ihre Ratschläge mit denen des Liedes. Erste Reaktionen auf das Lied können mit folgender Frage eingefangen werden:

⬭ *Who do you think the person talking is and what might be the situation?*

Info

Mary Schmich is a columnist for the *Chicago Tribune*. She wrote the text as part of a column in June 1997, in which she imagined what advice she would give in a commencement address. It was picked up and e-mailed around the world. Baz Luhrmann, an Australian film director and producer (*William Shakespeare's Romeo and Juliet, Moulin Rouge*) liked it and set the words (spoken by the actor Lee Perry) to music.

Lösungs-
hinweise
Kopiervorlage
`CD`

4 **a** Vgl. CD1, *track* 10, und das Transkript auf S. 99.
Die S sollten zunächst das Lied ein Mal gehört haben, bevor das Arbeitsblatt ausgeteilt wird (vgl. die KV „Recommendations", S. 97). Da die Liste der Ratschläge auf dem Arbeitsblatt recht lang ist, sollte den S Zeit gegeben werden, es in Ruhe zu lesen, bevor sie den Song ein zweites Mal hören. Durch den Vergleich der Ratschläge im Lied mit denjenigen, die sie zu Beginn der Stunde gesammelt haben, sollten die S die Doppelbödigkeit und Ironie des Lieds erkennen (vgl. Aufgabe 4b). Die folgenden Ratschläge werden im Lied gegeben: 1, 2, 3, 5, 6, 7, 9, 11, 12, 13, 15, 16, 18, 19, 20, 22, 23, 26, 27, 28, 29, 30.

Differenzierung

In schwächeren Kursen kann es sinnvoll sein, statt des Arbeitsblatts ein Transkript des Songs auszuteilen (vgl. S. 99), bei dem L einzelne Wörter mit Tipp-Ex abgedeckt und durch Nummern ersetzt hat. Die ausgelassenen Wörter erscheinen in einer Wortleiste am Rand des Arbeitsblatts. L spielt das Lied abschnittweise vor, die S finden das fehlende Wort in der Liste und ordnen ihm die entsprechende Nummer zu.

b The opening about using sunscreen seems to be a joke: The speaker appears to be making a fairly formal speech (cf. 'ladies and gentlemen') but then says 'use sunscreen', which is unexpected and comes across as somewhat banal. The speaker does not seem to take his advice very seriously: his advice is based on his 'meandering experience'. Other phrases also indicate a lightness in tone: 'worrying is as effective as trying to solve an algebra equation by trying to chew gum'. Yet this lightness of tone does not mean that all his advice is nonsense; he only wants to lighten his tone and leaves it up to the listener to decide which recommendations to follow.

⬭ *Why do you think the speaker dispenses his advice in this way?*

By using a humorous tone the speaker does not come across as moralizing, unlike many adults who give young people advice. Therefore young people might be more likely to listen to the words – and may in the end be more inclined to take notice of them – than if the speaker were lecturing them seriously.

❖ **c** Diese Aufgabe kann in Kleingruppen besprochen werden.

Individual answers.

❖ **d** Diese Aufgabe kann im Kugellagerverfahren (vgl. S. 429) bearbeitet werden.

Individual answers.

SB, S. 38 **1 This Thing Called 'Youth Culture'** Katie Milestone

Source:	*Guardian*, 18 November, 1999
Topic:	The emergence of youth culture
Text form:	essay
Language variety:	BE
Number of words:	350
Level:	Basic/advanced
Skills/activities:	Writing a summary, writing a letter to the editor

Lern-vokabular

Active vocabulary: 'This Thing Called "Youth Culture"' (p. 38)

emergence (l. 1), phenomenon (l. 2), leisure time (l. 2), rite of passage (l. 5), provoke a response (ll. 10–11), contradictory (l. 10), a defining moment (l. 15), inspire sth. (l. 15), impact (l. 18), lead the way (l. 22), slow down (l. 27), distinct (l. 28), contemporary (l. 30), dull (l. 30) *tasks:* contain sth., make a point, relate to sth.

Didaktisch-methodische Hinweise

Dieser Text untersucht das Phänomen *youth culture* aus historischer und soziologischer Perspektive. Die S erfahren, dass sich Jugendkulturen aus bestimmten gesellschaftlichen Situationen heraus entwickeln und damit verändern. Ihre Ausprägungen können ganz unterschiedlicher Art sein: Gewaltbereitschaft, Konsumorientierung, Amerikanisierung werden zu unterschiedlichen Zeiten als Merkmale von Jugendkultur genannt. So systematisiert und ergänzt der Text die Impressionen, die die S im „Lead-in" gewonnen haben.

Unterrichts-tipps

Der Text kann ohne größere Vorbereitung gelesen werden, da die S durch das „Lead-in" auf das Thema eingestimmt sind und durch die erste Aufgabe eine detaillierte Verständnissicherung erfolgt.

Info

Rock 'n' Roll (l. 13) is a type of popular music played with electric guitars, drums, etc., which first appeared in the USA in the 1950s. It developed from blues, jazz and country-and-western music. It was performed by musicians such as Bill Haley, Elvis Presley, Chuck Berry and Buddy Holly.

Bill Haley (1925–1981) (l. 14) was one of the first US singers to make rock 'n' roll popular. He played in the group 'The Comets'. Among his best known songs are 'Shake, Rattle and Roll' and 'Rock Around the Clock'. The latter song was used in the film *Blackboard Jungle* (1955), which was about an unruly inner-city school, and became an international hit.

Info

Teds (l. 20) (from 'Teddy Boys') took their name from the clothes they wore, which were supposedly derived from Edwardian England (Ted is the shortened form of Edward). They wore long jackets with velvet collars, drainpipe trousers, brightly coloured socks and shoes with thick rubber soles; their hairstyle was swept upwards and backwards. They were a reaction to the austerity of working-class England of the 1950s and soon earned a reputation for violence. They tended to listen to rock 'n' roll, and continued to exist until well into the 1980s.

Mods (l. 20) (from 'modern style of dressing') emerged in the 1960s in England. They listened to soul music, wore smart clothes, had short, neat hair and were above all famous for their scooters (= small motorcycles). They attracted a lot of attention for the fights they got involved in at seaside towns on bank holidays. The mod culture was probably best captured in a film made about them in 1979 called *Quadrophenia*.

Skinheads (l. 20) first appeared in Britain in the 1960s but had their heyday in the 1970s. They were young people, usually men, with shaved heads, who wore braces and heavy boots, especially Doc Martens. They were known for their violent behaviour and their support for right-wing political groups such as the British National Party. Skinheads still exist today.

Punks (l. 21) (also called 'punk rockers') followed punk fashion, e.g. Mohican hairstyles, torn jeans and T-shirts and safety pins through the lips, and listened to punk music. They became popular, especially in Britain, in the late 1970s, with groups such as 'The Sex Pistols' and 'The Clash'. Punk music was usually loud, fast and violent, and expressed their anger at society.

Lösungs-hinweise

1 **a**
Paragraph 1: Key sentence: 'The emergence ... phenomenon' (ll. 1–2).
Possible titles: How 'Youth Culture' emerged in the 20th century / The emergence of 'Youth Culture' / 'Youth Culture': reasons for its emergence.
Paragraph 2: Key sentences: 'British post-war ... rock 'n' roll.' (ll. 12–14); 'But the impact ... punks.' (ll. 21–23)
Possible title: British Youth Culture: a response to American popular culture / The impact and variety of British Youth Culture.
Paragraph 2: Key sentences: 'By the late 70s ... oriented.' (ll. 25–26); 'In fact ... teenager' (ll. 28–29).
Possible title: Everyone's a teenager now.

b An example of a summary:
'Youth Culture' emerged in the 20th century, due to a change in lifestyles. Previously, adolescence had not been considered a separate category between childhood and adulthood, but now it was.
People reacted to it differently. Many feared it was an example of vibrant young American culture based around Rock 'n' Roll taking over British culture, but actually British youth developed their own particular forms of subcultures.
Youth cultures became increasingly analysed, and soon revivals of subcultures took place, while the violent aspects of youth life disappeared. The strange thing that happened was that everyone started behaving like a teenager, and real youngsters were viewed as being uninteresting.

2 Individual answers.

3 **a** The first statement: The point of a youth subculture is to be separated from the main, adult culture. If an adult sociologist understands a youth culture, it is no longer separate, private, and so no longer has any real point for young people. The fact that in the statement the word 'understood' is in quotation marks shows perhaps that the writer does not think sociologists really understand youth cultures or rather that they understand it in an intellectual way, without any feeling for what it really represents. <u>The second statement:</u> Because nowadays most grown-ups have experienced 'youth culture', they compare the innovative and even occasionally violent subcultures of their youth with the teenagers of today, who are living in the legacy of what earlier generations started. As parents and children often wear the same type of clothes, parents are unable to see their children doing anything really innovative.

b Individual answers.

⬭ *What youth cultures do you notice in your school or town? Describe in detail the different clothes, appearance and music tastes these subcultures make use of to define membership of the subculture.*

→ WB, ex. 1, 2, 3, 4

SB, S. 39

Context Box

Didaktisch-methodische Hinweise

Heutigen Jugendlichen wird sicher nicht bewusst sein, dass Werbung speziell für junge Leute ein relativ neues Phänomen ist. Die „Context Box" betrachtet daher Jugend aus einer für die S neuen, nämlich einer ökonomischen Perspektive: Sie bietet einen Überblick darüber, wie Jugendliche nach dem zweiten Weltkrieg als eigenständige Konsumentengruppe entdeckt wurden. Die Industrie sprach diese neue Zielgruppe gezielt durch Werbemaßnahmen an und entwickelte Trends, die viele Jugendliche aufnahmen. Gleichermaßen reagierte die Industrie auf Trends unter den Jugendlichen und versuchte, eigene Produkte an diese Trends zu koppeln. Eine Anbindung an das Kapitel „A Global Marketplace" (vgl. SB, S. 90) ist denkbar.
Die Aufgaben zielen v.a. auf die Umwälzung des Vokabulars und auf die Beschreibung komplexer Zusammenhänge im Hinblick auf die Vermarktung von Konsumprodukten für Jugendliche, wobei die S auch ihr Weltwissen einbeziehen müssen.

Unterrichts-tipps

Die Einstimmung kann über folgende Befragung der S erfolgen:

⬭ *Sum up briefly your shopping habits. Compare your results in small groups.*

Kopiervorlage

Alternativ kann die KV „My Shopping Habits" (vgl. S. 98) eingesetzt werden, in der die S ihre Kaufgewohnheiten darstellen. Um zu vermeiden, dass die S der Klasse zu persönliche Informationen über tatsächliche Käufe preisgeben, sollten ggf. nur die Antworten auf „Why do you buy what you buy and where you buy it?" besprochen werden. Die KV kann auch die Basis einer anonymen Befragung sein, die die S auswerten und deren Ergebnisse sie grafisch präsentieren:

⬭ *What things influence you to buy a product? How many people in your class are influenced by each thing? Make a list showing the five strongest influences on the class, starting with the strongest influence.*

Lösungs-hinweise

1 **a** Um das Verständnis der Wörter zu überprüfen, können die S in zwei arbeitsteiligen Gruppen Erläuterungen, Paraphrasen oder ggf. Übersetzungen jeweils zur Hälfte der Begriffe zusammenstellen. Diese Definitionen werden nach Überprüfung durch L der anderen Gruppe präsentiert, die dann das entsprechende Wort aus dem Text nennt.

Individual answers.

❖❖ **b** Bevor die S diese Aufgabe bearbeiten, können in den „Skills Pages" die Abschnitte zu *writing skills* nachgelesen werden. Die Überprüfung kann in Partnerarbeit erfolgen.

Individual answers.

2 This statement ties in very well with the information in the Context Box, as it is clear that manufacturers – or, in this case, film producers – quite deliberately target teenagers, to the extent of putting characters into stories so that teenagers see themselves and their way of life reflected in those stories. The Context Box goes a bit further still, though, claiming that manufacturers of certain goods actually make the teenagers feel they need those goods rather than just offering them to them.

→ WB, ex. 1, 4

SB, S. 40

2 My Music

Da die meisten Jugendlichen sich für Musik interessieren und viele Trends der Jugendkultur entweder die Musik beeinflusst haben oder von ihr beeinflusst wurden, ist diesem Thema eine *section* gewidmet. Hier lesen die S über die Lebensgeschichte eines Gleichaltrigen, der ein bekannter DJ wurde, und hören zwei zu verschiedenen Zeiten entstandene Lieder, bevor sie über ihre eigene Lieblingsmusik reden.

SB, S. 40

A I'm Britain's Top Teen DJ

Source:	*Sugar*, March 2002
Topic:	A teenage DJ
Text form:	Feature story
Language variety:	BE
Number of words:	600
Level:	Basic/advanced
Skills/activities:	Working with language register, discussing a topic, writing an article for a teenage magazine

Lern-vokabular

Active vocabulary: 'I'm Britain's Top Teen DJ' (p. 40)

honest, keen, be over the moon, get used to sth., have a laugh (1st column);
dedicated to sth., have a chat, down to earth, wish sb. luck (2nd column);
in the meantime, ambition (3rd column)

Didaktisch-methodische Hinweise

In diesem Artikel aus einer Jugendzeitschrift berichtet ein Jugendlicher über sein Hobby als DJ und reflektiert über seinen Sieg bei einem DJ-Wettbewerb für Jugendliche. Dieser Erfahrungsbericht stellt für die die S eine Anregung dar, ihre eigenen Erfolgserlebnisse und Hoffnungen auf einer selbst gestalteten Seite einer Jugendzeitschrift darzustellen. Der Text verwendet eine sehr jugendnahe Sprache; eine Aufgabe besteht daher darin, Elemente der *informal speech* oder des *slang* zu identifizieren. Die S setzen sich kritisch mit den Meinungen des DJs und eines Journalisten auseinander.

Unterrichts-tipps

Zur Einstimmung auf den Text kann die folgende Frage dienen:

Have you ever thought of turning a hobby into a profession? If so, have you taken concrete steps to realizing your dream?

Trotz des jugendnahen Themas kann der Text aufgrund seiner umgangssprachlichen bzw. *slang*-Lexik Schwierigkeiten bereiten. Zudem wird der Wortschatz aus dem Bereich Musik weniger musikinteressierten S nicht vertraut sein. Die S sollten daher den Text still lesen (leistungsschwächere in Abschnitten) und in Partnerarbeit versuchen, Verständnisprobleme zu lösen. Der musikbezogene Wortschatz sollte (möglichst nach Bearbeitung von Aufgabe 3) gesammelt werden, da er bei der letzten Aufgabe und für das im „Lead-in" begonnene Mind-Map von Nutzen sein kann. Diese Wörter sind:
1st paragraph: decks, record, mixer, amp, speaker, headphones, mixing, beat;
2nd paragraph: disco;
3rd paragraph: DJ, gig, tape, funky, house;
4th paragraph: club;
5th paragraph: eJay music, turntable.

Info

Carl Cox (born 1962) has been one of Britain's leading DJs since the 'Summer of Love' of 1988, which saw the start of rave music and the club scene in Britain. Born of Barbadian parents in Manchester, Cox is now one of the leading international DJs who does venues throughout the world, including Ibiza and the Love Parade in Berlin.

Boy George (born 1961) came to international attention as the singer-songwriter for the group 'Culture Club' (1982–1986). His flamboyant clothes, make-up and androgenous appearance made him one of the most distinctive singers of the 1980s. For a while he went solo, but was never very successful, so he started working as a DJ in the English club scene, where he made a name for himself.

Lösungs-hinweise

1 He entered the 'Young UK DJ of the Year' competition and won.

2 Hier ist ein arbeitsteiliges Verfahren möglich, bei dem einige S Belege für Joes Bescheidenheit, andere wiederum Belege für großes Selbstbewusstsein finden.

Joe is <u>relatively modest</u>: 'To be honest, mixing came quite naturally to me' (1st paragraph); 'it was hardly professional' (2nd paragraph); 'I was over the moon, but I knew I'd have to stay calm' (4th paragraph); 'I just kept on practising' (4th paragraph); 'I got quite nervous' (5th paragraph); 'alongside the real DJ-ing masters like Carl' (7th paragraph); 'I'm happy just working toward my ambition' (7th paragraph).
Joe is <u>not so modest</u>: 'I thought I had a chance of doing well 'cause I'm so dedicated' (5th paragraph); 'I had a quick chat and he said how impressed he was with me' (6th paragraph); 'When I found out I had won, I wasn't too shocked as I think I'm good at what I do' (6th paragraph); 'I love it and it shows!' (6th paragraph); 'I gave the crowd what they wanted and everyone went bananas' (6th paragraph).

3 Für die S ist es nicht einfach, in einer fremden Sprache das Register eines Wortes zu bestimmen. Sie sollten hier mit einem einsprachigen Wörterbuch arbeiten.

spin-tastic (journalistic slang, not from Joe);
1st paragraph: amp (infml), pretty (infml);
2nd paragraph: get the whole dance thing (sl), be over the moon (infml), I guess (infml);
5th paragraph: 'cause (infml), loads (infml);
6th paragraph: go bananas (sl).
The use of informal and slang words (together with the very straightforward language) make the text sound both cool and chatty. You feel Joe is talking directly to you.

❖ **4** Diese Aufgabe kann nach individueller Vorbereitung auch in einem *fish bowl* (vgl. S. 428) bearbeitet werden. Um Stereotypisierungen zu vermeiden, sollten von den S Begründungen und Beispiele eingefordert werden.

Individual answers.

5 Vor der Bearbeitung können die S auf die Einträge unter „Non-fictional Texts" im Glossar (vgl. SB, S. 262) verwiesen werden. Ihre Ergebnisse können in der Klasse ausgehängt bzw. an eine Partnerschule verschickt werden, die etwas Ähnliches erstellt und zurücksendet.

Individual answers.

B Two Generations of Pop

`CD`

'Whiter Shade of Pale'

Source:	*Procol Harum*, 1967; group: Procol Harum
Topic:	Drug-induced hallucinations
Text form:	Song
Language variety:	BE
Length:	4 min
Level:	Basic/advanced

'Because I Got High'

Source:	*The Good Times*, 2001; group: Afroman
Topic:	The harmful effects of drugs
Text form:	Song
Language variety:	AE
Length:	3:18 min
Level:	Basic/advanced
Skills/activities:	Comparing songs, writing a review of a favourite song, creating a radio station's programme

Didaktisch-
methodische
Hinweise

Da die Mehrzahl der S regelmäßig Musik hört, sind sie in der Regel über neue Trends gut informiert. In dieser *section* geht es zunächst darum, Abstand zur heutigen Musik zu bekommen. Die S hören ein Lied aus den 60er Jahren und vergleichen es mit einem aus dem Jahr 2001 (vgl. CD1, *tracks* 11 und 12; und die Transkripte auf S. 100–101). Die Songs wurden ausgewählt, weil sie das gleiche Thema (die Auswirkungen des Drogen-konsums) auf unterschiedliche Weise behandeln und die musikalische Gestaltung sehr differiert. Während „Whiter Shade of Pale" wie in einem *stream of consciousness* Visionen auflistet, die der Sänger während eines Drogenrauschs hat, beschreibt der Sänger von „Because I Got High", wie er durch Drogen die Kontrolle über alle Bereiche seines Lebens verliert. Im Vordergrund der Besprechung sollten (dem Inhalt der *section* entsprechend) die musikalischen Elemente stehen; grundsätzlich denkbar ist aller-dings auch eine Vertiefung des Themas und eine Verknüpfung mit *section* 4 „The Morning After", SB, S. 44 und TM, S. 87). Im Anschluss beschreiben die S ihre persön-lichen musikalischen Präferenzen, wenn sie über ihren Musikgeschmack sprechen bzw. eine Radiomusiksendung vorbereiten.

Unterrichts-
tipps

Als Einstieg können die folgenden Fragen dienen:

⬭ *What do you think are the themes and issues which songs of today deal with?*

⬭ *Would you say that pop songs from earlier generations also dealt with the same themes and issues?*

⬭ *What might have been different in earlier eras?*

Insbesondere bei „Whiter Shade of Pale" muss mit einigen Verständnisproblemen ge-rechnet werden, die zum einen aus unbekannter Lexik resultieren, zum anderen aus der Zusammenhanglosigkeit der dargestellten Visionen. Es empfiehlt sich daher, mit „Because I Got High" zu beginnen und das Verständnis zu sichern, bevor die S mit „Whit-er Shade of Pale" konfrontiert werden. Folgende Wörter sollten semantisiert werden:

fandango: a Spanish dance
turn cartwheels: Rad schlagen
the miller told his tale: probably a reference to *The Canterbury Tales*, a medieval collection of stories told by different people, e.g. a miller who tells a crude tale about a woman cheating on her husband
vestal virgin: a priestess who tended the state cult of Vesta, the goddess of the hearth, in ancient Rome

Die S beschreiben mit Hilfe des Transkripts die Bilder dieses Lieds und ihren Mangel an Kohärenz. Im Rückgriff auf ihre Kenntnis des ersten Lied sollten sie Drogenkonsum als Ursache des assoziativen Charakters des Lieds identifizieren können .

Lösungs-hinweise

1 Die Songs befinden sich auf CD1, *tracks* 11 und 12; die Transkripte auf S. 100–101.

<u>What they have in common:</u> They seem to be dealing with drugs.

<u>What is different:</u> 'Whiter Shade of Pale' sounds as if the speaker is having hallucinations, as it is very unclear what he is referring to. The song seems to be about images rather than issues. The singer does not talk directly about drugs, rather the song seems to have been composed as a reaction to drugs. He seems, however, to be enjoying the experience. The song takes itself seriously.

In 'Because I Got High' the speaker is talking about being high all the time. The singer talks directly about how drugs make him incapable of doing anything. The tone is light-hearted, despite the subject.

2 'Whiter Shade of Pale' is quite gentle with a beautiful, haunting melody that sweeps the listener away. 'Because I Got High' is a reggae song; it relies more on the rhythm than on the tune.

There are still beautiful, melodic songs today, just as there are drugs, but it seems as if the music that is based around the drug culture today is faster (e.g. techno). While 'Whiter Shade of Pale' was part of the music that revolutionized the music of the 1960s, nowadays it is hip hop and techno that are both innovative and controversial; melodic songs seem to cater more to the taste of the general public. Today, just as in the past, there is still the feeling that musicians are trying to experiment and make new music.

3 **a–b** Individual answers.

4 Diese Aufgabe beinhaltet die Erstellung verschiedener Textsorten. Während der Planung sollten die Art der Beiträge, ihre Inhalte, Dauer, technische Voraussetzungen, Verfasser und Moderatoren schriftlich festgelegt werden. Sollte die Radiosendung bewertet werden, sind zuvor mit den S Kriterien zu entwickeln (z.B. Inhalt, sprachliche Umsetzung, Präsentation, entsprechend der Textsorte eingesetzte Effekte, Übergänge usw.). Dafür sollten ausreichend Zeit eingeplant und die technischen Voraussetzungen geklärt werden.

Individual answers.

SB, S. 42 # 3 How I See Me, How I See You

Schönheitsideale haben Menschen zu allen Zeiten beschäftigt. Die Annäherung an diese Ideale versprach Bewunderung und soziale Anerkennung und nicht selten auch berufliche Vorteile. Daran hat sich bis heute kaum etwas geändert; gleichzeitig nimmt die Zahl psychischer Störungen wie Magersucht zu und betrifft heute immer mehr auch Jungen und Männer. In dieser *section* werden Schönheitsideale kritisch hinterfragt. Ein aktueller Zeitungsartikel beschreibt die zerstörerischen Auswirkungen des Schlankheitswahns bei Jugendlichen. Anhand eines Sonetts von Shakespeare und Bildern von Schönheiten aus verschiedenen Jahrhunderten wird eine historische Perspektive aufgezeigt und deutlich gemacht, dass Schönheitsideale sich wandeln und gerade die Abweichung vom herrschenden Schönheitsideal eine Person interessant machen kann.

A Diet-crazy Girls ... and Boys Cahal Milmo

Source:	*The Independent*, 16 October 2000
Topic:	Teenage obsession with appearance
Text form:	News report
Language variety:	BE
Length:	338
Number of words:	Basic/advanced
Skills/activities:	Writing a summary, doing a mind map, analysing a picture/advert, working with language

Lern-
vokabular

Active vocabulary: 'Diet-crazy Girls ... and Boys' (p. 42)

diet (ll. 3, 27), self-esteem (l. 2), concern about sth. (l. 2), survey (l. 4), lose weight (l. 6), appearance (l. 8), skip sth. (l. 10), desire (l. 13), anxiety (l. 14), shape (l. 18), be aware of sth. (l. 19), make sb. comfortable with sth. (ll. 20–21), health campaigner (l. 22), encourage sb. to do sth. (l. 23), be sceptical about sb./sth. (l. 23), exercise (l. 27), question sth. (l. 28)

Didaktisch-
methodische
Hinweise

Der Artikel referiert die Ergebnisse einer Studie, die bei britischen Jugendlichen eine überkritische Einschätzung ihres Gewichts und gesundheitsschädliche Essgewohnheiten diagnostizierte. Ernährungswissenschaftler fordern deshalb bessere Aufklärung über Essstörungen und über die manipulierende Rolle der Medien. Damit behandelt der Text ein Thema, das viele der S betreffen wird. Bei seiner Besprechung wird aber jeder Bezug zu ihrer individuellen Situation vermieden; die S denken vielmehr über die Bedeutung dieses Themas für Jugendkultur im Allgemeinen nach und setzen sich kritisch mit dem in den Medien propagierten Schönheitsideal auseinander. Dieser Text kann auch im Zusammenhang mit dem Kapitel „Who am I?", insbesondere mit der *section* 4 A, behandelt werden.

Unterrichts-
tipps

Es empfiehlt sich, dem auf Fakten basierenden Text eine Einstiegsaufgabe voran zu stellen, die die S emotional auf das Thema einstimmt. L könnte Bilder von sehr schlanken Frauen bzw. muskulösen Männern zeigen, ggf. umrahmt von Männern bzw. Frauen, die sie bewundernd ansehen. Die folgenden Fragen könnten gestellt werden:

⬭ *Describe the pictures/adverts. What do they have in common? What is the message of the picture/adverts? Why do such adverts/pictures have a strong impact particularly on young people?*

→ WB, ex. 5

Lösungs-
hinweise

1 Die S sollten vor Bearbeitung der Aufgabe Richtlinien für Inhaltsangaben wiederholen, mit dem besonderen Hinweis auf den Umgang mit Beispielen und Zitaten.

British teenagers of both sexes worry about their weight although many do not need to. They are trying to conform to an 'ideal' image. The reason is often low self-esteem and anxiety about looks.
In Germany it is probably not very different. Lots of young people worry about their weight and want to wear clothes that only look good on thin people. Both British and German teenagers are heavily influenced by the mass media.

2 Health: health education, health campaigners, eat healthily, exercise, lose weight, watch your weight, etc.
Self-image: be/consider yourself overweight, anxiety about appearance, conform to an 'ideal shape', focus on your appearance, worry about your shape, etc.
Eating disorders: skip breakfast, be diet-crazy, miss/skip lunch/meals, go without food, (also: obesity, anorexia, bulimia), etc.

❖ **3** Diese Aufgabe kann als Hausaufgabe vorbereitet und dann in der Klasse im *fish bowl* (vgl. S. 428) diskutiert werden.

4 Individual answers.

❖ **5** Für die Besprechung eignet sich besonders das Kugellagerverfahren (vgl. S. 429).

⬭ *Translate ll. 1–12 into German.*

⬭ *Imagine you are writing an article on eating disorders for your school magazine. Report to your fellow editors in German about the contents of the article.*

SB, S. 43

B Sonnet 130   William Shakespeare

`CD`

Source:	*Complete Sonnets* (sonnets written in the 1590s; first printed in 1609)
Topic:	The description of a lover
Text form:	Poem
Language variety:	BE
Number of words:	123
Level:	Advanced
Skills/activities:	Analysing poetry, examining concepts of beauty

*Lern-
vokabular*

Active vocabulary: 'Sonnet 130' (p. 43)

tasks: characteristic features, stylistic device, apply to sth.

*Didaktisch-
methodische
Hinweise*

Shakespeare setzt sich in diesem Sonett mit dem Schönheitsideal seiner Zeit spöttisch auseinander, indem er – formal den Traditionen der Sonettdichter seiner Zeit folgend – seine Geliebte in allen Einzelheiten beschreibt, dabei aber deutlich macht, dass sie dem damaligen Schönheitsideal nicht im Geringsten entspricht. Seiner Liebe zu ihr tut das allerdings keinen Abbruch. Durch die Lektüre des Gedichts erhalten die S einen Einblick in das Schönheitsideal der Shakespearezeit und können einen unmittelbaren Vergleich mit heutigen Schönheitsvorstellungen anstellen. Zudem bietet ihnen Shakespeares Distanzierung von gängigen Normen eine Vorlage zur kritischen Auseinandersetzung mit dem Streben nach perfektem Aussehen (vgl. auch „Info").

*Unterrichts-
tipps*

Als Einstieg in das Thema empfehlen sich die Bilder auf S. 43, die Schönheitsideale verschiedener Zeiten abbilden: Die Gemälde zeigen Elisabeth I (Maler Nicholas Hilliard) bzw. Marilyn Monroe (Maler Andy Warhol), das Foto das Supermodel Naomi Campbell.

⬭ *Describe the three pictures on p. 43. What do they say about the ideal of female beauty through the ages?*

Women, more than men, have always been put on a pedestal for their beauty. Whereas in former times, white skin and high birth were highly valued, today beauty and thinness are highly valued in society. In each of the pictures, the woman is constrained to present some form of artificiality, e.g. the white skin and tight dress (and presumably red wig) of the queen, the dyed platinum blonde hair of the actress, and the thinness of the supermodel who walks down the catwalk in an unnatural way.

⬭ *Examine the paintings of Elizabeth I and Marilyn Monroe. What do they tell you about the women's role in society?*

The portrait of Elizabeth is a portrait of power and wealth, as seen through the jewels and embroidery, whereas the portrait of Monroe is the distorted image (cf. heavily made-up lips and eyebrows) of one of the icons of the 20th century, famous not so much for her talents but for her sex appeal and glamour.

Info

The *sonnet* was introduced to England in the first half of the 16th century by Sir Thomas Wyatt, who while on diplomatic service in Italy became acquainted with the sonnets of Petrarch. They were developed by the Earl of Surrey, whose 'English sonnet' (also called the 'Shakespeare sonnet') form of a b a b c d c d e f e f g g (as well as his blank verse) were later used by Shakespeare, who in his cycle of 154 sonnets became the master of the sonnet.

The 'I' in Shakespeare's sonnets has often been closely identified with Shakespeare himself. The first 126 sonnets were written to a young man, while 127 to 154 were addressed to a 'dark lady', who finally betrays the speaker by loving other men. Metaphors from the fields of trade, law and medicine can be found in Shakespeare's sonnets.

Sonnet 130 is an unusual tribute to the dark lady ('black' wires). In this sonnet Shakespeare makes fun of the conventional and traditional love sonnet. He rejects typical love metaphors – he does not compare his love to Venus, etc. The ordinary beauty and humanity of his lover are what is important to Shakespeare, and he deliberately uses typical love poetry metaphors against themselves. The references to objects of perfection are present, but they are there to illustrate that his lover is not as beautiful, or at least that her beauty needs no false metaphors. Shakespeare develops the theme of his lover's simplicity in the three quatrains and concludes the sonnet in the final couplet by proclaiming his love for his mistress despite her lack of adornment.

Lösungs-hinweise

1 **a** Beauty ideals of Shakespeare's time: bright, shiny eyes, white skin, dark red lips, golden hair, red cheeks, white breasts. She should smell nice, have a pleasant voice and walk lightly and gracefully.

b His portrait of his lover shows that she does not comply with the ideal of beauty of her time: her eyes are not bright, her lips pale, her breath does not smell pleasant. With these comparisons, Shakespeare is revealing the artificiality of traditional metaphors used to describe a woman, since they always refer to things which are not actually connected to a woman (sun, snow, coral, etc.). He also states that even though his love cannot be described as a beauty, she is something special for him.

2 He uses similes, e.g. 'are nothing like the sun' (l. 1) and metaphors ('no such roses see I in her cheeks', l. 6) but in an unusual way, by negating them. This leads to understatement and contrast. Through understatement Shakespeare makes the point that poets (and indeed most lovers) exaggerate when describing their beloved one. The contrast is achieved through the negation of the imagery (e.g. 'if snow ..., why then ...', l. 3). The effect builds up, but rather than the expected conclusion that his love does not amount to much, he then states that he is happy with his quite ordinary, imperfect lover. He thereby draws a portrait of a mortal woman while ridiculing the other poets of his time.

CD

3 Bei dieser Aufgabe kann die Hörversion des Sonetts präsentiert werden (vgl. CD1, *track* 13), damit sich die S besser auf den Klang konzentrieren können.

The rhyme scheme: a b a b c d c d e f e f g g.
Metre: iambic pentameter (iambic: a metrical foot of two syllables, the first unstressed and the second stressed; pentameter: a line consisting of five feet).
The quatrains all deal with aspects of her beauty, whereas the couplet presents a concluding thought. The fact that the couplet at the end of the sonnet breaks the pattern has the effect that you take more notice of the last two lines. In the couplet the speaker declares that even if he does not wish to compare his lady falsely, this does not prevent him from declaring that he loves her in a way that is 'rare', i.e. more than most lovers love their beloved.

4 **a** Shakespeare thinks his lover is beautiful, even if she does not fulfil the idea of perfection other poets see in their lovers.

b Each artist (painter or photographer) created a portrait of a beautiful woman. But the portraits are quite different – the women are very different in colouring, shape, use of make-up, etc. – as they were made in different times. We cannot even be sure how close to reality the portrait of Elizabeth I is. So, one can argue that beauty may be in the eye of the beholder, but each age has its own ideals of beauty.

c The article says that the media these days are encouraging young people to believe that to be beautiful you have to be thin. Schools should be teaching students that beauty/attractiveness do not conform to any rules. Even if you do not look like a model, someone will like the way you look.

⬭ *Do you agree with the saying in task 4?*

⬭ *Find one other sonnet from the Elizabethan time, written either by Shakespeare or by another poet, which deals with a woman's beauty and present it to the class. You might want to illustrate it and put all the poems on display.*

SB, S. 44 **4   The Morning After**

Jugendkultur wird oft mit Alkoholkonsum assoziiert. Diese *section* thematisiert den übermäßigen Alkoholkonsum Jugendlicher auf Partys und seine möglichen Folgen. Bei der Behandlung der Texte liegt der Schwerpunkt aber nicht auf der Vermittlung von Fakten, da diese den S ohnehin bekannt sein dürften, sondern auf der Beurteilung der Effektivität zweier Texte, die ihre Leser vor den Folgen des Alkohols warnen wollen. Die S betreiben also Medienkritik und erweitern ihr Wissen über mediale Darstellungsformen. Als Transferleistung entwerfen sie ein Merkblatt zur Drogenprävention und diskutieren ihre Entwürfe in der Gruppe.

Unterrichts-
tipps Da beide Texte kurz sind, können sie in unmittelbarer Folge gelesen und bearbeitet werden. Als Einstieg in die Thematik ist eine Umfrage über das Verhalten bei Partys denkbar, bei der gleichzeitig ein Teil der Lexik semantisiert wird, die im Laufe der Arbeit zu einem Wortfeld vervollständigt werden soll. Bei der Befragung ist Fingerspitzengefühl vonnöten, da die S nicht unbedingt bereit sein werden, ihr Privatleben zum Gegenstand des Unterrichts zu machen. Die Anonymität der Umfrage sollte also unbedingt gewährleistet sein. Möglicherweise sollte sie auf andere Gleichaltrige ausgeweitet werden. Folgende Fragen können gestellt werden:

⬭ *What kind of parties do you like to go to? Who usually goes with you? What do you eat/drink there? Would you tolerate other people consuming drugs in front of you? What might be unpleasant aftermaths/effects of drinking too much alcohol or taking drugs?*

SB, S. 44 **A Sex After Drinking**

Source:	*J-17*, December 2001
Topic:	The dangers of getting pregnant when drunk
Text form:	Advert
Language variety:	BE
Number of words:	163
Level:	Basic/advanced
Skills/activities:	Analysing an advert, working with vocabulary

Active vocabulary: 'Sex After Drinking' (p. 44)

hangover, throb, there's nothing like ... to ..., unwanted pregnancy, sober sb. up, regret sth., mix sth. with sth. else, contraception, confidential
tasks: get one's message across, be implied in sth., double meaning

Diese Anzeige wurde 2001 in einer Kampagne gegen *teenage pregnancies* eingesetzt, einem in Großbritannien viel häufigeren Problem als in Deutschland (vgl. „Info"). Bild und Text sollten die Jugendlichen ansprechen, da der Ton witzig und nicht belehrend ist. Die Aufgaben zielen v.a. darauf, die Wirkung der Anzeige und ihre Gestaltung zu beschreiben (vgl. auch die AIDA-Formel, SB, S. 122 und TM, S. 222). Da sie mit vielen Wortspielen arbeitet, werden die S angeleitet, diese zu erkennen und verstehen.

Die Präsentation des Textes kann über eine Folie mit der ewas vergrößerten Anzeige erfolgen, bei der die einzelnen Abschnitte mit Post-its abgedeckt sind und Schritt für Schritt aufgedeckt werden. Die S überlegen bei jedem Schritt, worum es in dieser Anzeige gehen könnte.

Info

Teenage pregnancies: Britain has the highest rate of teenage pregnancies in western Europe. It is twice that of Germany, three times higher than in France and six times that of the Netherlands. While the rest of the continent has seen dramatic falls in teenage parenthood since the early 1980s, the UK has long been the exception with a high rate which has remained static since the late 1970s. Each year, around 56,000 babies are born to teenage mothers in Britain with nearly 8000 conceived by girls under 16 and 2200 by under-14-year-olds. Among the reasons given for the high rate of pregnancies are: poverty, poor educational opportunities, the fact of being the child of a teenage mother, and lack of work opportunities. Women in deprived areas are six times more likely to get pregnant by the age of 20 than those in the most affluent areas of Britain. Studies reveal that most teenage mothers do not plan their pregnancies.

1 Possible answers:

The girl and baby, who are both depicted in vivid colours, looking at each other with big round eyes, which indicate surprise on both sides; the hand-written heading; the word 'sex' written white on black.

It seems to be addressing only girls, as the picture shows a girl. Girls are more likely to be reading teen magazines. The use of the word 'nurse' shows again that girls are being targeted – the consequence of an unwanted pregnancy concerns girls more than boys. However, boys might feel that they are being targeted too, as the girl in the picture is naked, which is likely to attract the boys' attention. The text on the right, however, addresses teenage boys and girls.

2

- The large, hand-written sentence top left is short and to the point.
- The picture of the helpless-looking girl with big round eyes and the surprised-looking baby illustrates the situation the advert is warning about.
- The question: 'Sex – Are you thinking about it enough?' is provocative as normally it is said that people think too much about sex.
- The humorous exaggerations, e.g. 'Your breath could kill a buffalo at forty feet' in addition to the puns (cf. task 3) give the text a light-hearted tone.
- The text describes a situation many youngsters may have experienced without sounding moralistic about it.
- The small drawings in the text give the text a light, cartoony impression.
- The typeface looks like handwriting.
- The advert is very colourful.

3 **a** Two meanings of 'nurse' are implied in the ad: 1 'to take care of an injury or an illness'; 2 '(of a woman or a female animal) to feed a baby with milk from the breast' (6th definition in the *OALD*).

The picture explains what it is that you might be nursing after having too much to drink: not just a hangover, but also a baby.

b 'Sober up': means to recover from a hangover but it also means to make you more serious about sth.

'Mix sex with alcohol' and 'cocktail': 'mixing' refers to combining two things, here sex and alcohol at the same time, while a 'cocktail' is literally a mixed drink, while it also has the meaning of being a 'mixture of two different substances, usually ones that do not mix together well'.

'Sex – Are you thinking about it enough?' refers to the idea of someone always thinking about sex (i.e. wanting to have sex), while here it means thinking about the consequences of having sex.

⊂⊃ *Imagine there were a similar campaign in Germany, and you were asked to translate the text into German. Think of some striking or amusing German expressions to transmit the message of the text – you will probably be unable to translate word by word.*

SB, S. 45 **B Doctor Sarah Brewer Says ...**

Source:	*Sugar*, May 2001
Topic:	The dangers of alcohol
Text form:	Advice column for teenagers
Language variety:	BE
Number of words:	245
Level:	Basic/advanced
Skills/activities:	Writing an outline, comparing two texts, designing a leaflet, presenting group work

Lern-
vokabular

Active vocabulary: 'Doctor Sarah Brewer Says ...' (p. 45)

excess (l. 1), addiction (l. 5), get pregnant (ll. 6–7), physical/mental abnormalities (ll. 10–11), take advantage of sth. (ll. 16–17), vomit (l. 30), be in (any) doubt (l. 32), seek advice (l. 33), treat sb. (l. 34), treatment (l. 35)
tasks: as compared to, discourage sb. from doing sth., provide information

Didaktisch-
methodische
Hinweise

Dieser Text thematisiert das Problem des Alkoholkonsums auf ganz andere Weise als die Anzeige. Sachlich listet er die Gefahren und Folgen von Alkoholexzessen auf und gibt klare Handlungsanweisungen, wie Jugendliche ihren Alkoholkonsum in Grenzen halten und wie sie mit Freunden umgehen sollten, die zu viel trinken. Der Text bietet eine gute Gelegenheit, ein *advice column* zu analysieren, indem die S das Layout und vor allem die Sprache des Textes analysieren und eine Gliederung schreiben.

Unterrichts-
tipps

Als Einstieg könnte ein kurzes Schülerreferat mit Diskussion über die gesetzlichen Vorschriften anderer Länder zum Alkoholkonsum Jugendlicher dienen.

Lösungs-
hinweise

1 **a** Text B is much more sober in its presentation:
- The black background is not interesting, unlike the green background with the triangle in the ad.
- There is a portrait of the doctor rather than the cartoon.
- The typeface used is normal as opposed to playful, and there are no little drawings or doodles to break it up.
- The language is more formal and contains a number of difficult words, whereas the ad does not.

– Whereas text B uses facts, the ad uses humour.
– Grammatically, Text B makes use of imperatives, *if*-clauses and the modal 'should'; the ad uses only two imperatives ('try not to mix' and 'phone Sexwise').
– The tone of Text B is preachy, which the ad is not.

b Drinking heavily can be dangerous for your health.

c

I   Results of excess alcohol intake:
   A   Raised blood pressure
   B   Death from abnormal heart rhythms
   C   Alcohol hepatitis
   D   Liver fibrosis
   E   Liver cirrhosis
   F   Addiction
   G   Reduced fertility
   H   Risks to unborn babies if pregnant

II Risks from binge drinking:
   A   Sudden death from abnormal heart rhythms
   B   Strain on the liver
   C   Being taken advantage of sexually
   D   Serious accidents

III Recommendations if a friend is drunk:
   A   Persuade them not to continue drinking
   B   Make them drink water and eat if possible
   C   Don't leave them alone:
         1 their blood glucose can fall dangerously low
         2 they can inhale vomit and die
   D Get medical advice if in doubt

IV Recommendations when drinking alcohol
   A   Drink in moderation
   B   Eat before drinking
   C   Alternate alcoholic and non-alcoholic drinks
   D   Don't drink and drive

V Legal matters
   A   Illegal to buy alcohol under 18
   B   Illegal to drink alcohol in public under 18

The outline is not that much shorter than the original text. This shows that the text is very dense, especially at the beginning, where it is little more than a mere listing of dangers. This is compounded by the fact that there are so many technical terms in the first paragraph.

2 Ad more effective:
– amusing and talks directly to teens at their level and in their own language;
– does not preach, so you are more likely to read the entire message.
Advice column more effective:
– contains real information, hard facts and practical advice;
– information is given by medical expert, which makes it more authoritative;
– more likely to have long-term effects, as it contains more hard facts, including a lot of scary information – maybe scarier than an unwanted pregnancy.

❖   ⬭ *In groups, look at all the health problems in the text associated with excess drinking. Find out more about them and present your findings to the class.*

→ WB, ex. 6   **3** Individual answers.

Getting Along in English

Die Kommunikation per Chat und E-Mail ist aus privaten wie aus beruflichen Lebens-
bereichen nicht mehr wegzudenken und erfreut sich besonders bei jungen Leuten
großer Beliebtheit. Dabei zeigt sich eine große Kreativität im Umgang mit der Sprache,
wie die vielen *emoticons* und die lange Liste von gebräuchlichen Abkürzungen
belegen. Die folgende Seite greift diese neuen Kommunikationsformen auf, knüpft an
bekannte Formen an und gibt einen kurzen Überblick über neue Abkürzungen. Nützliche Informationen zum Schreiben von E-Mails finden sich unter: www.webfoot.com/
advice/email.top.html · 1.8.03. Stichworte für online-Suche von *chat*-Verhaltensre-
geln sind: *chat conventions, chat etiquette, net etiquette.*

*Unterrichts-
tipps* Als Einstieg könnten die S überlegen, in welchen Situationen elektronische Kommunikationsmittel angemessen sind und wann eher nicht:
Used in private communication, business contacts, e-mail projects with partner
schools, advertising, sending greetings/photos, seeking information.
Not used for contracts or legal documents.

*Lösungs-
hinweise* **1** Die S sollten darauf hingewiesen werden, dass der Text präzise und kurz sein
sollte; z.B. kann eine Begründung für die Unterbrechung des Kurses entfallen.

Possible subject lines: 'Course interruption possible?'; 'Questions about my course'.
Start: 'Dear Sir or Madam'.
Finish: 'I look forward to hearing from you', then 'Yours faithfully' (BE) or 'Sincerely' (AE).

2 **a** Abbreviations and short forms:

brb = be right back;	thx = thanks;
prob = problem;	tho = though;
ur = you are/ you're (occasionally also 'Your');	cu = see you;
aug = August;	:-) = smile

b It would be said like this: 'R Davies at mail dot M T' (mt = Malta)

c Spelling: shortened forms.
Punctuation: only used to avoid lack of understanding (e.g. full stop to separate
sentences, question marks).
Grammar: At the beginning, Mark uses full sentences. Then he starts to leave out
pronouns (e.g. 'I') and verbs belonging to subject pronouns.

→ WB, ex. 5 **3** Individual answers.

5 **Y2K.CHATRM 43** Alden R. Carter

Source:	*Time Capsule*, 1999
Topic:	Discovering the value of the real and the virtual worlds
Text form:	Short story
Language variety:	AE
Number of words:	2701
Level:	Basic
Skills/activities:	Analysing the development of a story, giving one's opinion, writing an e-mail, discussing a topic

Active vocabulary: 'Y2K.CHATRM43' (p. 47)

dusk (l. 5), block (l. 6), depressing (l. 12), have got a point (l. 22), hit a nerve (l. 31), get sb.'s point (l. 33), addict (l. 45), irritate sb. (l. 50), junk (l. 54), catch on (l. 59), claim to be sth. (l. 65), ozone layer (l. 72), cure sth. (l. 73), peacekeeping (l. 92), civil war (l. 100), distraction (l. 111), hesitate (l. 139), foot the bill (ll. 144–145), lose your temper (ll. 157–158), wonder (l. 201), give sth. a try (l. 211), for a change (l. 217)
tasks: predictability, keep in touch, exchange e-mails

Didaktisch-methodische Hinweise

Viele Jugendliche verbringen heute einen großen Teil ihrer Freizeit mit elektronischen Medien. Längst haben sie eine eigenständige Webkultur entwickelt, deren Sprache und Regeln oft nur von Insidern zu verstehen sind. Während sie das Internet v.a. zum Zweck der Unterhaltung nutzen, steht gelegentlich aber auch die ernsthafte Suche nach einem Verständnis ihrer Zeit und nach Kontakt mit Gleichgesinnten im Vordergrund. Diesen Gedanken greift die vorliegende Kurzgeschichte auf und folgt zwei Teenagern, die sich schon seit langer Zeit kennen, sich allerdings erst durch das Internet näher kommen. Damit bietet sie eine Grundlage für eine Diskussion über die Rolle des Internets für den Einzelnen als Kommunikationsmittel. Einige S werden Schwierigkeiten mit dem Satz in Z. 45–46 haben. L sollte ihn folgendermaßen vervollständigen: 'I just dig the Web and have done so since the first time I had a computer powerful enough to really cruise.'

Unterrichts-tipps

Als Alternative zur *pre-reading*-Aufgabe im SB kann L eine Diskussion über die Nutzung des Internets durch die S anregen (z.B. Häufigkeit, Dauer, Zweck der Nutzung). Eine weitere Möglichkeit wäre es, die S nach der Bedeutung des Titels zu fragen und ihre Erwartungen an die Kurzgeschichte formulieren zu lassen. Die S werden schnell erschließen, dass „CHATRM" *chat room* heißt und „43" seine Nummer ist. Problematischer könnte „Y2K" sein, die Abkürzung für das Jahr 2000 („Y" = *year*, „2K" = *2000*; cf. „K" = *kilo*).

Es bietet sich an, die S aus dem Text Wörter aus dem Wortfeld „Computer" sammeln zu lassen:

Wordfield *Computers*: 'turn off a computer' (l. 1), 'cyberspace' (l. 2), 'electronic' (l. 3), 'chat room' (l. 26), 'the Web' (l. 35), 'newsgroup' (l. 47), 'cybersurfer' (l. 48), 'flame sb.' (l. 52), 'log-in' (l. 63), 'fake' (l. 65), 'cyberpunk' (l. 68), 'chatmaster' (l. 82), 'log on to sth.' (l. 87), 'server' (l. 87), 'keyboard' (l. 109), 'type' (l. 111), 'log into sth.' (l. 122), 'put a computer to sleep' (ll. 166–167), 'log on' (l. 181), 'host sth.' (l. 215).

Eine *while-reading*-Aufgabe könnte darin bestehen, den S vor der Lektüre eine Liste mit Stichwörtern auszuteilen, die sie im Verlauf der Textpräsentation in die richtige Reihenfolge bringen.

☐ *Arrange the following keywords about the text in a suitable way:*
Adrien, Joel, computer, chat room, Jill, the future, Sonja, homework, the Web, landmine, solve problems, webdict, Y2K.CHATRM43, users from thirty countries, rules, nightly subjects, chatmaster, international peacekeeping, Vlad, Fred, little brother, Art, discussions.

Possible answer:

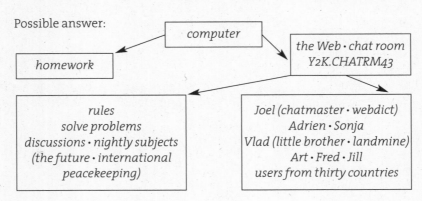

→ WB, ex. 7

Info

Alden R. Carter (born 1947) is an award-winning author of novels, history books for teenagers and picture books for children and young adults. His novels include *Sheila's Dying* (1987), *Up Country* (1989), *Between a Rock and a Hard Place* (1995) and *Crescent Moon* (1999). A former naval officer and teacher, Alden R. Carter lives in Wisconsin, where he and his family are keen enthusiasts of hiking, canoeing, cycling and baseball.

Lösungs-hinweise

● *Pre-reading:* Individual answers.

1 Joel's opening statement that he is 'supposed to turn off [his] computer and go outside to enjoy a beautiful autumn evening' (ll. 1–2) comes true in the end. He has learned that the real world is more important than cyberspace. Moreover, the relationship between Joel and Adrien has changed: they have gone from being 'just friends and neighbors for just about forever' (l. 8) to a possibly romantic relationship.

2 She thinks he is spending too much time on the Internet and not enough talking with 'real people' (l. 27), and that he practically lives on the Web (cf. ll. 34–35), and she is worried that he is getting depressed. Before, he used to be in a band and do things. She goes into the chatroom for various reasons. She says that she wanted to 'keep an eye on' him (l. 195), but it also seems that she secretly wanted to express her views, that she did find the idea behind the chatroom important. There is the possibility that she also had strong feelings for him (which was why she was angry that he was not with real people, i.e. her) and that in this way she could be close to him.

3 Her English improves once Vlad logs in (cf. l. 121 onwards).
There might be various reasons:
- She simply forgets to continue to write bad English.
- She is genuinely concerned about Vlad's brother, so feels unable to express genuine emotion in a false language.
- She is talking about serious subjects, while at the beginning she is talking about trivial matters.

4 A love story: The story starts and finishes with Adrien and Joel. They are clearly the most important characters, and it is their relationship that develops in the story from mere friendship to a beginning romance. They see each other through different eyes at the end.
A coming-of-age story: The narrator matures in the course of the story. He recognizes that, though his chatroom is an important platform, it is not going to solve any of the world's problems and so it should not consume all his time. He learns to appreciate the real world, as opposed to cyberspace. And at the same time he discovers a new emotion: love.

5 Individual answers.

6 Individual answers.

7 Individual answers.

◯ *Look at the chat again (cf. ll. 108–146). Rewrite all the sentences in 'good' English.*
L. 108: Hey kids. I'm here. Do you want to hear some news?
L. 112: Do you have a new pair of skis, Sonja?
L. 113: No, that was last week's news.
L. 114: Do you have a new boyfriend?
L. 115: Oh, they come and go. I don't worry about that.
L. 116: Is Sven history then? / Have you and Sven broken up?

L. 117: No, he's still here. As are Erik and John.

L. 118: How many do you keep at once?

L. 119: I don't count.

L. 123: Hi, everyone. I'm sorry I was away for three days. My little brother was hurt by a land mine exploding. He lost his right leg and foot. The other leg is getting better. He is in hospital. Sorry, things are not so good here.

L. 127: Hey, sorry, Vlad. I hope he comes through ok.

L. 129: Yeah. Sorry, Vlad. That's tough.

L. 130: Tell him we are thinking of him, ok?

L. 131: Sorry, Vlad. Lousy land mines. We ought to talk about them some night, Joel.

L. 134: Sorry, Vlady. Really, really sorry. Give him our love. And Joel, I'm sorry I got everyone talking about navels and things like that. Tell us the big question again.

L. 137: International peacekeeping. When is it justified? Who should do it? How much force is ok/acceptable? You go first, Sonja.

L. 144: The problem is that it always seems like the U.S. sends the troops and foots the bill.

L. 146: Italians help sometimes. In Africa we do a lot with no help.

⬭ *What do you think is more important: grammatical (and lexical) correctness or being easily understood?*

⬭ *The narrator says he 'wasn't sure how this next part was going to sound' (ll. 222–223). What do you think he means by this?*

The narrator was worried that he was going to sound sentimental. He was worried that he might sound somewhat strange or corny.

⬭ *Describe the narrator's motives for starting his chat room and evaluate the group's success.*

– He wanted to feel that he was doing something useful about the problems in the world. He also felt a need to talk about serious issues with other teenagers.

– The group seems to be quite successful because there are a number of regular chatters who keep coming back. They have found a place where they can discuss the larger issues that concern them all. Also, they are introduced to different views and philosophies from different cultures and backgrounds. They learn to work with discipline (e.g. sticking to Joel's rules) and accept differing viewpoints (cf. Jill and Art, who disagree on the UN but do not lose their tempers).

⬭ *Translate ll. 1–15 into German.*

SB, S. 53

Watch Your Language

*Didaktisch-
methodische
Hinweise*
→ *WB, ex. 9*

Grammatischer Schwerpunkt dieser *section* sind Vergleiche; der zu korrigierende Text enthält aber auch Fehler aus anderen grammatischen Bereichen. Auch wenn S bei einfachen Vergleichen vielleicht wenig Fehler machen, stellen die unregelmäßigen Formen auch in den höheren Klassen immer noch eine häufige Fehlerquelle dar.

*Lösungs-
hinweise*

1 a

1 Too <u>many</u> old (better: older) people think our music is not as good <u>as</u> their music (better: theirs) was.

2 It's <u>worse</u> to diet all the time <u>than</u> to live with a few extra pounds.

3 The <u>worst</u> thing about _ advertising is that it always <u>tells</u> us what to wear.

4 <u>According to</u> the study, spending too much time on the Internet is not <u>as/so</u> bad as people think.

5 I <u>think</u> it's <u>less</u> important what people think than how you feel about yourself.

b

1 'many people': *CEG* §219b (Index under '*much*', '*many*', '*as … as*')
  'not as good as their music': *CEG* §200 (Index under 'comparison: with adjective')

2 'worse … than': *CEG* §198 (Index under '*bad:* comparative and superlative', '*worse, worst*', 'adjective: comparative and superlative', 'comparative and superlative: of the adjective'); *OALD* under '*worse*', '*bad*'

3 'worst': *CEG* §198 (Index under '*worse, worst*', '*bad:* comparative and superlative')
  'the advertising': *CEG* §183a (Index under 'abstract noun: use of *the*', '*the*: with abstract nouns'); *OALD* under 'advertising' (cf. examples)
  'tells': CEG §64a (Index under 'simple present: form'), *CEG* §74 (Index under 'simple present')

4 'According to': 'after' in *OALD* would confirm that the choice of words is incorrect; if the student cannot remember 'according to', he/she will need a bilingual dictionary
  'not as/so bad as': *CEG* §200 (Index under 'comparison: with adjective')

5 'think': 'mean' in *OALD* would confirm that the choice of word is incorrect; if the student cannot remember 'think' as the correct rendering of *meinen*, he/she will need a bilingual dictionary
  'less important': *CEG* § 219f (Index under '*little:* comparative and superlative'

2 Comparison of adjectives; the use/non-use of the definite article with concrete and abstract nouns; quantifiers (e.g. *much/many*); third person singular present simple –*s*.

3 Individual answers.

Topic Vocabulary: 'Youth Culture'

Young People
youth
youths (= young men)
youngster
adolescence
adolescent
teenager
teenage (adj.)

Leisure Time
free/spare time
go out
go clubbing
club
go to a concert/gig
venue
pub
party
go shopping
listen to music
drink
have fun
chill out
hang out
at home
be/feel relaxed

Music Styles
pop
rock
house
techno
hip hop
grunge
punk
gothic

Youth as a Consumer Group
pocket money
have a weekend job
consume sth.
spending power
major force in the market
wield power
dominate the market
designer label
target of marketing
  campaigns
buy into sth.
satisfy new needs

Conformism/ Individuality
peer pressure
group mentality
the in-crowd
conform to sth.
outsider
individual
be different

Self-Image
self-esteem
concern about your image
feel good/bad about
  yourself
misunderstood

Appearance
looks
trendy
attention-grabbing
normal
slender
thin
anorexic
overweight
blemish-free
acne
spots
diet
go/be on a diet
go without food
miss/skip meals
lose weight
gain weight
eat healthily
exercise
do sport
go to the gym
do aerobics
muscular

Social Involvement
idealistic
help others
volunteer
community service
join an organization
change the world
be environmentally
  aware
get involved in sth.
be committed to sth.

Drugs and Alcohol
get drunk
have a hangover
take drugs
drug/alcohol abuse
become addicted to sth.

Love/Sexuality
have a girl-/boyfriend
have a relationship
be in love (with sb.)
be crazy about sb.
be attracted to sb.
go on a date
have a date with sb.
pick sb. up
have a one-track mind
have a one-night stand
have (unprotected) sex
pick up / get a sexually
  transmitted disease /
  STD
get/become pregnant
cheat on sb.

Communication
computer
virtual reality
the real world
e-mail
send an attachment
digital camera/photo
(on) the Internet
be/go online
have access to the
Internet
download sth.
chat
chat room
play computer games
mobile phone (BE) /
  cell phone (AE)
text message sb.
send a text message

SB, p. 37
Task 4
(cf. TM, p. 76)

Everybody's Free (to Wear Sunscreen)

Recommendations

Carefully read through the following recommendations. Then listen to the song once more and tick off (√) all the recommendations that are mentioned in the song.

1   Enjoy your youth.

2   Don't worry about the future.

3   Do one thing every day that scares you.

4   Scare somebody once a day.

5   Sing, floss, stretch, travel and use sunscreen.

6   Don't hurt or play with someone else's feelings.

7   Don't hang around people who hurt or play with your feelings.

8   Be jealous of your lover.

9   Don't waste your time with jealousy.

10   Remember insults and forget compliments.

11   Remember compliments and forget insults.

12   Keep love letters and throw away old bank statements.

13   Don't feel guilty if you never really know what you want to do in life.

14   Plan what you want to do with your life by the time you are 22.

15   Don't congratulate or berate yourself too much.

16   Make sure you eat lots of calcium.

17   Get married and then get divorced.

18   Enjoy your body and dance a lot.

19   Always read directions.

20   Don't read beauty magazines.

21   Don't get ugly or fat.

22   Have a good relationship with your parents and your brothers and sisters.

23   Hold on to a few precious friends while realizing that friendships come and go.

24   Work hard to bridge gaps.

25   Settle down in either New York City or northern California.

26   Live once in New York City and once in northern California.

27   Accept certain truths and that life is not perfect.

28   Depend upon yourself.

29   Leave your hair alone, otherwise it will turn into a mess.

30   Listen to people's advice but be careful about always accepting it.

SB, p. 39
(cf. TM, p. 79)

Context Box   My Shopping Habits

Reflect on your shopping habits and then fill in the following table.

Products/items	Do the products have a designer name?	Why do you buy these products?	Where do you by them?	Why do you buy them there?
Clothes, e.g. … …				
Accessories, e.g. … …				
Sports gear, e.g. … …				
Electronic goods, e.g. … …				
Cosmetics, e.g. … …				
Food, e.g. … …				

Everybody's Free (to Wear Sunscreen)   Baz Luhrmann

SB, p. 37   Ladies and gentlemen of the class of '99: wear sunscreen. If I could offer you only one tip for the future, sunscreen would be it. The long term benefits of sunscreen have been proved by scientists, whereas the rest of my advice has no basis more reliable than my own meandering experience. I will dispense this advice now.

Enjoy the power and beauty of your youth. Never mind, you will not understand the power and beauty of your youth until they've faded. But trust me, in 20 years you will look back at photos of yourself and recall in a way you can't grasp now, how much possibility lay before you and how fabulous you really looked. You are not as fat as you imagine.

Don't worry about the future or worry, but know that worrying is as effective as trying to solve an algebra equation by chewing bubble gum. The real troubles in your life are apt to be things that never crossed your worried mind. The kind that blindsides you at 4 p.m. on some idle Tuesday.

Do one thing every day that scares you.

Sing.

Don't be reckless with other people's hearts, don't put up with people who are reckless with yours.

Floss.

Don't waste your time on jealousy. Sometimes you're ahead, sometimes you're behind. The race is long and in the end, it's only with yourself.

Remember compliments you receive, forget the insults. If you succeed in doing this, tell me how. Keep your old love letters, throw away your old bank statements.

Stretch.

Don't feel guilty if you don't know what you want to do with your life. The most interesting people I know didn't know at 22 what they wanted to do with their lives; some of the most interesting 40-year-olds I know still don't. Get plenty of calcium. Be kind to your knees, you'll miss them when they're gone.

Maybe you'll marry, maybe you won't. Maybe you'll have children, maybe you won't. Maybe you'll divorce at 40, maybe you'll dance the 'Funky Chicken' on your 75th wedding anniversary. Whatever you do, don't congratulate yourself too much or berate yourself either. Your choices are half chance. So are everybody else's.

Enjoy your body. Use it every way you can. Don't be afraid of it or what other people think of it. It's the greatest instrument you'll ever own.

Dance. Even if you have nowhere to do it but in your own living room.

Read the directions even if you don't follow them.

Do not read beauty magazines, they will only make you feel ugly.

Get to know your parents. You never know when they'll be gone for good.

Be nice to your siblings. They are your best link to your past and the people most likely to stick with you in the future.

Understand that friends come and go. But with a precious few, you should hold on.

Work hard to bridge the gaps in geography and lifestyle, for the older you get, the more you need the people you knew when you were young.

Live in New York City once, but leave before it makes you hard. Live in northern California once, but leave before it makes you soft.

Travel.

Accept certain inalienable truths: prices will rise, politicians will philander, you too will get old and when you do, you'll fantasize that when you were young, prices were reasonable, politicians were noble and children respected their elders. Respect your elders.

Don't expect anyone else to support you. Maybe you have a trust fund, maybe you'll have a wealthy spouse, but you never know when either one might run out.

Don't mess too much with your hair or by the time you're 40, it will look 85.

Be careful whose advice you buy, but be patient with those who supply it. Advice is a form of nostalgia. Dispensing it is a way of fishing the past from the disposal, wiping it off, painting over the ugly parts and recycling it for more than it's worth.
But trust me on the sunscreen.

(Words: © Mary Schmich, *Chicago Tribune*)

CD   **Whiter Shade of Pale**   Procol Harum

SB, p. 41   We skipped the light fandango
Turned cartwheels 'cross the floor
I was feeling kinda seasick
But the crowd called out for more
The room was humming harder
As the ceiling flew away
When we called out for another drink
The waiter brought a tray

And so it was that later
As the miller told his tale
That her face, at first just ghostly,
Turned a whiter shade of pale

She said, 'There is no reason
And the truth is plain to see.'
But I wandered through my playing cards
And would not let her be
One of sixteen vestal virgins
Who were leaving for the coast
And although my eyes were open
They might just as well've been closed.

And so it was that later
As the miller told his tale
That her face, at first just ghostly,
Turned a whiter shade of pale.

(Music and lyrics by Gary Brooker and Keith Reid; © Onward Music Ltd.)

Because I Got High   Afroman

SB, p. 41

(Roll another.)
I was gonna clean my room until I got high;
I was gonna get up and find the broom but then I got high;
my room is still messed up and I know why.
(Why, man?)
Yeah heh, 'cause I got high, because I got high, because I got high.

I was gonna go to class before I got high;
(Come on, y'all. Check it out.)
I coulda cheated and I coulda passed but I got high;
I'm taking it next semester and I know why.
(Why, man?)
Yeah heh, 'cause I got high, because I got high, because I got high.

(Go to the next, go to the next, go to the next)
I was gonna go to court before I got high;
I was gonna pay my child support but then I got high;
(No, you weren't.)
They took my whole paycheck and I know why.
(Why, man?)
Yeah heh, 'cause I got high, because I got high, because I got high.

I wasn't gonna run from the cops but I was high;
(I'm serious, man.)
I was gonna pull right over and stop but I was high;
Now I'm a paraplegic and I know why.
(Why, man?)
Yeah heh, 'cause I got high, because I got high, because I got high.

I was gonna make love to you but then I got high;
(I'm serious.)
I was gonna eat your _ too but then I got high;
Now I'm _ and I know why.
Yeah, heh, 'cause I got high, because I got high, because I got high.

I messed up my entire life because I got high;
I lost my kids and wife because I got high;
Now I'm sleeping on the sidewalk and I know why.
(Why, man?)
Yeah heh, 'cause I got high, because I got high, because I got high.

I'm gonna stop singing this song because I'm high;
I'm singing this whole thing wrong because I'm high
And if I don't sell one copy, I'll know why.
(Why, man?)
Yeah heh, cause I'm high, 'cause I'm high, 'cause I'm high.

(Written and produced by Joseph 'Afroman' Foreman;

Multimedia und Datenhighway, Transrapid und Biotechnologie, intelligente Waffen und das Klonschaf Dolly – zu Beginn des 21. Jahrhunderts scheinen die Möglichkeiten der modernen Forschung fast unbegrenzt. Gleichzeitig stellt sich immer wieder die Frage nach den Grenzen des Fortschritts und der Freiheit von Wissenschaft und Forschung. Dieses Kapitel spricht zentrale Kontroversen um diese Frage an und fordert die S auf, Position zu beziehen. Folgende Themen stehen dabei im Vordergrund:

– *Section 1*, „Who's Boss?", behandelt das Verhältnis von Mensch und Maschine.
– *Section 2*, „Genie in the Bottle", diskutiert die Verantwortung der Wissenschaft.
– *Section 3*, „How Things Work", fordert die S heraus, die Darstellung komplexer technischer Vorgänge zu verstehen.
– *Section 4*, „Can Science Save Us from Ourselves?", diskutiert den Nutzen der Gentechnologie.

Die naturwissenschaftliche Orientierung dieses Kapitels legt es nahe, auch im Hinblick auf die Sprachkompetenz der S einen naturwissenschaftlichen Schwerpunkt zu legen und so Grundlagen der Fachsprache Englisch zu vermitteln. Deshalb werden in vielen Aufgaben fachsprachlicher Wortschatz und Strukturen vermittelt (z.B. „Lead-in", S. 54, Aufgabe 1b; *section* 3, S. 67, Aufgaben 3 und 4).

→ *WB, ex. 7*

Didaktisches Inhaltsverzeichnis

SB, p.	Title	TM, p.	Text form	Topic	Skills and activities
54	**Lead-in**	103	photos	science and technology	describing pictures; working with vocabulary; doing research; giving a presentation
56	**From Calculator to Typewriter** Douglas Adams	106	newspaper article	development of the computer and its usefulness	writing a summary; writing a report / feature article
58	**Remote Control** Dave Barry	107	newspaper column	dealing with sophisticated household appliances	analysing the writer's attitude; identifying stylistic devices; comparing two texts; discussing a pro/con topic; writing a dialogue
60	**The Flying Machine** Ray Bradbury	110	short story	the tension between technological advancement and moral responsibility	summarizing; analysing imagery; giving one's opinion
64	**Oppenheimer** Video/DVD	113	documentary drama serial		examining the difference between two programmes;
64	**Wernher von Braun** Tom Lehrer CD1, track 14	115	song	a famous scientist's disregard for his own moral responsibility	listening comprehension; writing an essay
65	**Getting Along in English**	117	–	going to the doctor	listening comprehension; writing a short dialogue
66	**How Things Work**	118	magazine article	how a hydrogen car works	doing an information gap activity; understanding scientific descriptions; working with technical illustrations
69	**Context Box**	120	–	science, technology and controversy	working with vocabulary; translating; doing research; giving a presentation
70	**Can Science Save Us from Ourselves?** Natasha Walter	122	newspaper article	stem-cell research and people's expectations of science	paraphrasing words/phrases; doing research; writing a leaflet
73	**Watch Your Language**	125	–	participle constructions	

Lead-in

Der Einstieg in das Thema dieses Kapitels erfolgt über Abbildungen aus verschiedenen Wissenschaftsbereichen und über die Porträts berühmter Wissenschaftler. Die Arbeit mit den Abbildungen verlangt von den S präzise Bildbeschreibungen und eine Zuordnung zu verschiedenen wissenschaftlichen Disziplinen. Dadurch erweitern bzw. festigen sie ihren Wortschatz im Hinblick auf Lagebeschreibungen sowie genaue Form- und Farbangaben; darüber hinaus werden Bezeichnungen wissenschaftlicher Disziplinen bereitgestellt. Weitere Schwerpunkte sind die Erarbeitung einer Präsentation über berühmte Forscherinnen und Forscher sowie eine kreative Schreibaufgabe zur Bedeutung von Wissenschaft und Technik.

Die S betrachten die Fotos auf S. 54–55 und beschreiben diese mit Hilfe der zur Verfügung gestellten Vokabeln. Nachdem Aussprache und Bedeutung der Wörter „triangular", „rectangular", „oval", „spherical", „square", „curved" und „straight" geklärt wurden, ordnen die S die Begriffe den folgenden Zeichnungen an der Tafel zu:

Die Bezeichnungen der *textures* stellen weniger von der Aussprache als möglicherweise von der Bedeutung her eine Schwierigkeit dar. Hier bietet es sich an, Gegenstände aus dem Klassenzimmer bzw. aus der unmittelbaren Umgebung der S zu umschreiben, um die Wörter vorzuentlasten, z.B. „A road with many holes is bumpy", „Your hands can get coarse from working in the garden a lot", „The rocks along the coast are often jagged, which means that they have sharp edges."

1 Im Folgenden finden sich ausführliche Beschreibungen der Bilder (für Bilder A, C und D stichwortartig). Sie dienen der Information der L; der Erwartungshorizont ist im Hinblick auf Detail und Umfang der Beschreibungen deutlich niedriger anzusiedeln.

Picture B shows a coloured circle (which is probably a sphere) on a black background. Towards the bottom of the sphere there is an irregularly-shaped patch of colour in a very dark blue. Around that there is another patch of colour, which is a lighter blue – it is shaped like a pear. This pear-shaped thing has a turquoise-coloured ring around it, and there is a yellow ring around that. The left-hand part of the yellow ring is more yellowish-green, and in the lower left part of the yellow ring there is a patch of red. The rest of the sphere is greenish-blue. Stretching out almost from the centre to the upper right of the sphere you can see an irregular shape that almost looks like a shadow. It is fairly narrow at the bottom and swerves to the right. As it gets closer to the edge of the sphere it gets gradually wider. It looks a bit like South America.

Picture A:
- an irregular pattern which seems to have a certain system;
- green and purple patches running from the lower left to the upper right;
- red lines of different widths run from the upper left to the lower right, some of them ending in pink cubes or squares;
- some of the red lines are not straight but they make 45° or 90° turns.

Picture C:
- a complicated structure consisting only of lines; the lines form two clusters: one in the upper right, one in the lower right moving towards the upper left;
- in the lower right: a circular structure containing three pairs of smaller circles and a cross stretching out from the middle of the circles;
- below the circular structure: rectangles of different shapes and sizes, some of them lying on top of the others at a 180° angle;
- from the outer circle to the upper left of the picture: five curved lines running parallel;

between the outer line on the left and the next line to the right there are two wavy lines ending in two circles;
- in the upper right: two squares with rounded edges, each of them containing a circle surrounded by four other circles; the inner circle on the left is thicker than the other;
- most of the elements of the clusters are linked to other elements by straight or curvy lines.

Picture D:
- in the middle: a rough purple surface with a sponge-like structure and yellowish bits;
- around/under it: a sort of brownish-orange rough surface;
- a soft transition from bright orange in the upper half to more brownish in the lower half;
- the upper half looks illuminated;
- at the bottom, finger-shaped structures stick out from the orange surface .

2   **a** The pictures show:
A the ozone hole over the Antarctic;
B a computer chip;
C the blueprint of a section of a(n Airbus) jet engine;
D an HIV infecting a T-cell.

b The photos represent:
A climatology, meteorology;
B electrical engineering / electronics;
C aeronautical engineering, drafting;
D medicine / medical research / immunology.

What occupations correspond to each of the fields of science and technology listed in the box? Explain what these people do.

❖ Durch diese Aufgabe, die die S ggf. mit Hilfe eines Wörterbuchs lösen, wird weiterer Wortschatz reaktiviert und systematisiert. Aus Zeitökonomie empfiehlt sich die Arbeit in Gruppen, die je vier der Begriffe bearbeiten.

aeronautics – aeronautic engineer: designs, produces and maintains all types of aircrafts;
astronomy – astronomer: studies the stars, space and the universe;
biology – biologist: studies living organisms such as plants and animals;
botany – botanist: studies plants;
chemistry – chemist: studies the structure of substances and the way they react with each other (it is also the name used for someone working in a shop selling medicine);
climatology – climatologist: studies the climate and changes and developments in the climate;
drafting – draughtsman/draftsman/-woman: draws mechanical plans to scale of things such as buildings, machinery and devices;
electronics – electronics engineer: designs, develops, tests and supervises the manufacture of electronic equipment;
engineering – engineer: designs, develops, tests and supervises the manufacture of engines, buildings, roads, communication systems, etc.
geography – geographer: studies the natural features of the earth's surface as well as humanity's relationship with them;
geology – geologist: studies rocks and the composition of the earth;
mathematics – mathematician: studies numbers, quantities, shapes and space and the interrelation between them;
mechanics – mechanic: maintains or operates all forms of machinery;
medicine – doctor: examines and treats people who are ill;
meteorology – meteorologist: studies the earth's atmosphere and changes and developments in the climate;

oceanography – oceanographer: studies all aspects of the world's seas;
physics – physicist: studies properties of matter and energy and the interrelationship between them;
zoology – zoologist: studies all aspects of animals.

c Als Denkanstoß kann der Verweis auf Kollokationen wie *scientific studies* oder *technological development* dienen.

Science involves the knowledge and understanding of natural phenomena.
Technology is the application of scientific knowledge to practical matters.

→ *WB, ex. 1*

3 Eine Aufgabe mit ähnlichem Anforderungsprofil, die alternativ behandelt werden kann, findet sich bei der „Context Box" (Aufgabe 3, vgl. SB, S. 69).

Differenzierung
♦♦ Bei leistungsschwächeren S wird es sinnvoll sein, einen Lösungsansatz für diese Aufgabe in Partnerarbeit zu entwickeln. Die S verständigen sich, wie sie diese Aufgabe angehen könnten und erstellen eine Gliederung, die ihre Vorgehensweise verdeutlicht. Ggf. kann L die Teilschritte vorgeben:

⬭ *In class, think of as many names of famous scientists or technicians as you can and what they are famous for.*

♦♦ ⬭ *With a partner, choose one of the scientists or technicians and find out as much as possible about them:*
  – *background, education;*
  – *what motivated them to work in their particular field;*
  – *their discoveries;*
  – *the effects of their discoveries.*

⬭ *Present your findings to the class in as interesting a way as possible.*

⬭ *As you listen to your classmates' presentations, start collecting useful words for talking about science and technology and arrange them in a way you find helpful.*

L kann auch folgende Wissenschaftler/innen vorschlagen:
– Gertrude Belle Elion (1918–1999), American pharmacologist
  (cf. www.infoplease.com/ce6/people/A0817086.html • 1.8.2003);
– Joseph Locke (1805–1860), famous railway engineer;
– Rosalind Franklin (1920–1958), physiologist;
– James Watt (1736–1819), inventor of the steam engine;
  (for Locke, Franklin and Watt cf. www.spartacus.schoolnet.co.uk/engineers.htm • 1.8.2003);
– Alexander Fleming (1881–1955), discoverer of penicillin;
– Edwin Hubble (1889–1953), astronomer;
  (cf. www.time.com/time/time100/scientist/index.html • 1.8.2003).

4 **a–b** Individual answers.

SB, S. 56 # 1 Who's Boss?

Das Verhältnis von Mensch und Maschine steht im Mittelpunkt dieser *section*. Die beiden Texte durchleuchten am Beispiel alltagsnaher Situationen und auf humorvolle Weise die Tücken des Fortschritts. Während der Mensch hofft, sich von Maschinen unangenehme oder gefährliche Arbeiten abnehmen zu lassen, folgt die Nutzung von Maschinen im Alltag häufig ganz eigenen Regeln. Der Schwerpunkt bei der Analyse liegt auf Sprache und Ton der Autoren. Eine persönliche Stellungnahme zum Inhalt der Texte bildet den Abschluss.

A From Calculator to Typewriter Douglas Adams

Source:	*Independent on Sunday*, 19 March, 2000
Topic:	Development of the computer and its usefulness
Text form:	Newspaper article
Language variety:	BE
Number of words:	476
Level:	Basic/advanced
Skills/activities:	Summary writing, writing a report / feature article

Lern-
vokabular

Active vocabulary: 'From Calculator to Typewriter' (p. 56)

screen (l. 5), chocolate bar (l. 6), disposable income (ll. 10–11), be of use to sb. (ll. 8–9), sophisticated (l. 18), stand for sth. (ll. 18–19), breakthrough (l. 20), short-sighted (l. 21), incomprehensible (l. 23), be familiar with sth. (l. 35), actually (l. 38), prevent sb. from doing sth. (l. 41)

Didaktisch-
methodische
Hinweise

Der Text setzt sich auf humorvolle Art und Weise mit der Entwicklung des Computers auseinander. Die S bekommen aus der subjektiven Perspektive des Autors einen Überblick über die Entwicklung des Computers, dessen zögerliche Akzeptanz für die Jugendlichen vielleicht überraschend sein wird. Bei der Behandlung des Texts stehen deshalb v.a. die Entwicklung alltäglicher Geräte sowie der humorvolle Ton dieses Texts im Vordergrund.

Unterrichts-
tipps

Die S werden durch die *pre-reading*-Aufgabe im SB auf den Inhalt des Texts eingestimmt. Sie lesen ihn still und notieren die *key words*, mit deren Hilfe sie die Entwicklungsschritte des Computers wiedergeben können.

Info

Douglas Adams (1952–2001) was born in Cambridge, England. He attended Cambridge University, where he studied English literature. He wrote his most famous book *The Hitchhiker's Guide to the Galaxy* originally as a radio series in 1978. Following its publication as a book he wrote four sequels, *The Restaurant at the End of the Universe* (1980), *Life, The Universe and Everything* (1982), *So Long and Thanks for all the Fish* (1984) and *Mostly Harmless* (1992).

Lösungs-
hinweise

⬛ *Pre-reading*: Judging from the illustrations (on p. 56, photos of an old-fashioned-looking installation and old computers; on p. 57, photos of more modern electronic appliances) the text is going to be a text dealing with historical technological developments, especially concerning the computer. The words to watch out for are probably the names of different technological devices (e.g. calculators, typewriters, computers) or developments.

1 Um das Textverständnis zu sichern, fassen die S seinen Inhalt zunächst mündlich zusammen. Vor der Bearbeitung der Aufgabe sollten die S kurz die wesentlichen Merkmale einer guten Zusammenfassung nennen bzw. den entsprechenden Abschnitt der „Skills Pages" lesen. Die Zusammenfassung kann zu Hause verschriftlicht werden.

In his article Adams reflects on the changing function of the computer. He remembers the first computer he saw – it was enormous with a tiny screen. As he thought of it as a complicated adding machine, he could not imagine what use it could be to a writer. But then came the breakthrough: it converted numbers to letters and became, in his view, an elaborate typewriter. Next came pixels: Adams thought of it at this stage as a TV with a typewriter attached. He sees the latest development – the world wide web – as being a sort of brochure.

But his conclusion is that the computer is none of the things he has mentioned – it is a modelling device that allows us to model anything. We interpret it as being a typewriter, etc., because we know what these things are in the real world. He urges the reader to go beyond just interpreting the computer as a device to do things we already do and try to use it to do things we cannot do in the real world.

2 Vor der Beantwortung der Aufgabe erscheint eine Wiederholung des Terminus *tone* sinnvoll (vgl. das „Glossary", SB, S. 265).

The tone of the article is humorous. Adams talks of the breakthrough in computing – letting numbers stand for letters (cf. ll. 18–19) – but when he then says that this new machine is a typewriter (cf. l. 22), he is poking fun at this development (typewriters had been around for decades, so it would hardly have been a breakthrough). Similarly, the result of inventing pixels is described by Adams as a 'television' with a typewriter in front of it (cf. l. 29). When he describes the latest stage of development as a 'brochure', a fairly dull medium, he uses a number of adjectives which express motion, activity, modernity, and thereby creates a stark contrast to 'brochure' (cf. ll. 32–33).

He also pokes fun when he talks about how 'www' takes longer to say than 'world wide web' (ll. 30–31).

Further indicators of his humorous, playful tone are his exclamation 'Bingo' (l. 20), descriptions that do not seem serious, e.g. 'numbers, which were now flying round inside these machines at insane speeds' (ll. 25–26) and the seemingly disrespectful label 'the damn thing' (l. 36) used for the computer.

3 The computer belongs to both computer science and computer engineering as well as information technology and electrical engineering.

4 Für Anregungen vgl. die Auflistung von Haushaltsgeräten bei der ersten Zusatzaufgabe zu Text B (vgl. S. 108).

Individual answers.

SB, S. 58 **B Remote Control**   Dave Barry

Source:	*Washington Post*, 15 March, 2000
Topic:	Dealing with sophisticated household appliances
Text form:	Newspaper column
Language variety:	AE
Number of words:	842
Level:	Basic/advanced
Skills/activities:	Analysing the writer's attitude, identifying stylistic devices, comparing two texts, discussing a pro/con topic, writing a dialogue

Lern-vokabular **Active vocabulary: 'Remote Control' (p. 58)**

remote control (title), manufacturer (l. 2), consumer (l. 2), drive sb. insane (l. 2), turn sth. on (l. 6), with all due respect (l. 9), sense sth. (l. 19), a foolproof system (l. 22), determine sth. (l. 22), feature (l. 34), operate sth. (l. 40), at random (l. 50)

Didaktisch-methodische Hinweise Dieser Text knüpft durch Thema und Darstellungsform an den Text „From Calculator to Typewriter" an (SB, S. 56): Er beschäftigt sich auf ironische Art mit technischen Haushaltsgeräten, die eigentlich das Leben erleichtern sollten, die aber aufgrund ihrer immer komplizierter werdenden Funktionen kaum noch zu bedienen sind. Um einen Vergleich der beiden Texte im Hinblick auf die Effektivität ihrer Gestaltung vorzubereiten, liegen Schwerpunkte der Textbehandlung auf der Beschreibung der Haltung des Autors und auf seiner Sprache, insbesondere der Stilmittel, die dem Text seinen satirischen Ton verleihen.

Unterrichts-
tipps

Als *pre-reading activity* bietet es sich an, die S alle technischen Geräte nennen zu lassen, die sie zu Hause haben. So wird der entsprechende Wortschatz aktiviert und den S wird bewusst, wie viele dieser Geräte sie tagtäglich nutzen. Anschließend beschreiben die S, wie gut sie diese Geräte bedienen können und welche Neuentwicklungen sie sich wünschen.

⬭ *Name all the appliances you have at home.*
TV, VCR (also: video recorder, video, video cassette player/recorder), DVD player, telephone, answerphone / answering machine, computer, printer, scanner, blender, mixer, food processor, toaster, refrigerator, freezer, microwave (oven), dishwasher, washing machine, tumble dryer, waffle iron, electric cooker, electric kettle, steam iron, electric tin opener, vacuum cleaner.

⬭ *Are you and your parents familiar with all the functions of your appliances?*

⬭ *In the future coffee machines will all have timers and vacuum cleaners will clean the floor by themselves. Can you imagine any other functions modern appliances may have in the future?*

Differenzierung

Der ironische Ton des Textes, die Häufung von Adjektiven und teilweise sehr lange Sätze (vgl. z.B. Z. 55–58, Z.60–65) können in schwächeren Kursen zu Schwierigkeiten bei der Textrezeption führen. Da die Aufgaben zum Text v.a. Analyse- und Transfer-funktion haben, bietet es sich bei leistungsschwächeren Kursen an, zusätzliche Verständnisfragen bearbeiten zu lassen.

⬭ *What smart appliances does the writer mention?*
A dishwasher that can be turned on from the office, a refrigerator that knows when all the milk is gone and a bathroom scale that transmits your weight to the gym.

⬭ *What smart appliances does the writer suggest would be useful?*
Barry proposes a dishwasher that reminds people to put their dirty dishes in it and a refrigerator that prevents people from eating too much.

⬭ *Why is Barry against smart appliances?*
The exaggerated picture Barry draws of smart appliances indicates that in his view manufacturers develop new technologies that may look impressive, but are of no value in our everyday lives. He states that people usually do not know how to use all the features modern appliances have. He is afraid that one day appliances will get so complicated that nobody will be able to use them any more.

Es bietet sich an, die S aus dem Text Wörter und Kollokationen zum Bereich *household* heraussuchen zu lassen:
Wordfield *household*: 'turn on the dishwasher' (l. 6), 'refrigerator' (l. 7), 'be out of sth.' (l. 7), 'bathroom scale(s)' (l. 7), 'load a dishwasher' (l. 11), 'start a dishwasher' (l. 14), 'flush the toilet' (l. 16), 'dirty dishes' (l. 19), 'kitchen counter' (l. 19), 'put dishes in the dishwasher' (l. 20), '(operate a) telephone' (ll. 36, 40), 'operate a TV' (l. 40), 'remote control' (l. 41), 'watch TV' (l. 45), 'turn the TV on' (l. 49), 'record a TV show' (l. 52), 'furniture' (l. 68), 'microwave oven' (l. 71)

Info

Dave Barry (born 1947) has been a humour columnist for the *Miami Herald* since 1983. His column appears in more than 500 newspapers in the USA and abroad. In 1988 he won the Pulitzer Prize for Commentary. He has also written 24 books.

1 Bei dieser Frage ist es wichtig, dass die S erkennen, dass Barry seine Kritik an den Produzenten durch starke Übertreibungen illustriert.

Barry is very critical of appliance manufacturers and their technical developments. He ridicules them, accusing them of 'smoking crack' (l. 10) when they devise new technical gadgets because he considers their ideas unnecessary and impractical (cf. ll. 10–12, ll. 21–23, 26–31). He paints a humorously exaggerated picture of the world of the future with smart appliances, making it clear how absurd the plans of appliance manufacturers seem to him (cf. ll. 13–16). According to Barry, appliances are already too complicated (cf. ll. 32–35, 51–52).

2 Die Berechtigung von Barrys Kritik können die S überprüfen, wenn L eine Gebrauchsanweisung mitbringt und auszugsweise mit den S liest. Nach Möglichkeit sollte das entsprechende Gerät zur Verfügung stehen, damit der Nutzen der Gebrauchsanweisung überprüft werden kann (z.B. CD-Player oder Videorekorder der Schule).

Barry criticizes owner's manuals for
– not explaining labels clearly (cf. ll. 45–46);
– not making clear how to use all the features of an appliance (cf. ll. 45–49);
– being indispensable for even the most trivial operations such as turning on the TV (cf. ll. 48–49);
– being complicated and badly written, because they use technical jargon and complex language that is incomprehensible to ordinary people (cf. ll. 60–62).

3 Die S sollten zuerst die Formulierungen sammeln, die dem Text seinen humorvollen Ton verleihen, und diese schließlich gruppieren. So sollte es ihnen leichter fallen, anschließend das jeweilige Stilmittel zu benennen.

– Contrast between seemingly serious beginning of first sentence ('Recently the *Washington Post* ...', l. 2) and its absurd ending ('... plan to drive consumers insane', l. 2);
– ridicule and abuse of appliance manufacturers ('... have been smoking crack', ll. 9–10; 'Are they nuts?', l. 26);
– exaggeration: his imaginary dialogue (cf. ll. 13–16); the number of buttons on his remote controls (cf. ll. 36–38; 45–46);
– absurd suggestions and speculations (cf. ll. 17–20, 22–25; 27–31)
– invention of nonsense words (cf. ll. 62–64);
– use of language you would find somewhere else (e.g. in a mathematics textbook) in an inappropriate context (cf. ll. 64–65);
– alternation between slang and colloquial language ('the wazooty', ll. 40–41; 'nuts', l. 26) and formal language ('with all due respect', l. 9);
– abuse of politicians as an aside (cf. ll. 67–68).

4 Individual answers.

5 Adams thinks man is the boss: he stresses instances where man consciously changed and improved the machine according to his wishes (cf. ll. 34–36, 39–41). He also appeals at the end to use a leap of imagination to do more things with computers. However, when Adams describes his own naivety as to the use of a computer, one might conclude that man is definitely not the boss (cf. ll. 12–14).
Barry's position is clearer: he fears that machines are threatening to become the bosses because they may be able to transmit personal information without our knowledge (cf. ll. 26–31) and because they are too complicated to operate (cf. ll. 33–35). Yet, the real power behind the machines is in the hands of the manufacturers, who develop appliances according to their own ideas (cf. ll 3–5). Hence Barry's call at the end of his article for people to protest to the appliance manufacturers (cf. ll. 68–71).

→ WB, ex. 2

6 **a** Example of smart appliances: an iron which irons the laundry itself; washing machine which transports the laundry to the tumble dryer.

b Individual answers.

◯ *Write a letter to an appliance manufacturer complaining about the development of so-called smart appliances.*

◯ *Write a letter to Dave Barry in reaction to his article. You might either agree with his point of view and add some of your own negative experiences with modern appliances or you might disagree with him, explaining your vision of smart appliances.*

SB, S. 60

2 Genie in the Bottle

In dieser *section* steht die Frage nach der Verantwortung für die Ergebnisse wissenschaftlicher Forschung im Vordergrund. Am Beispiel der fiktiven Figuren aus der Kurzgeschichte „The Flying Machine" und der realen und umstrittenen Wissenschaftler Oppenheimer und von Braun diskutieren die S die Frage, inwieweit Forschung frei sein oder beschränkt werden sollte. Die S werden hier mit einer für die Menschheit zentralen ethischen Problemstellung konfrontiert, so dass auch ein erzieherischer Aspekt in den Vordergründ rückt. Die Problematik wird anhand verschiedener Materialien dargestellt (Kurzgeschichte, Auszug aus einem Dokumentarfilm und einem *drama serial*, politisches Lied), so dass die S die Gestaltungs- und Wirkungsweisen der verschiedenen Medien vergleichen können.

SB, S. 60

A The Flying Machine Ray Bradbury

Source:	*The Golden Apples of the Sun and Other Stories*, 1957
Topic:	The tension between technological advancement and moral responsibility
Text form:	Short story
Language variety:	AE
Number of words:	1742
Level:	Basic/advanced
Skills/activities:	Summarizing, analysing imagery, giving one's opinion

Lern-
vokabular

Active vocabulary: 'The Flying Machine' (p. 60)

harvest (l. 2), miracle (l. 7), prepare yourself for sth. (l. 23), at last (l. 25), thoughtful (l. 26), wave to sb. (l. 38), splendid (l. 40), protect sb. from sb./sth. (l. 42), preserve peace (ll. 42–43), clumsy (l. 55), seize sb. (l. 79), bewildered (l. 81), wind sth. up (l. 90), plead (l. 100), wonder (l. 109), spare sb. (l. 112)

Didaktisch-
methodische
Hinweise

Diese Kurzgeschichte spielt im Jahr 400 n. Chr. und handelt von der Reaktion eines chinesischen Kaisers auf die Erfindung einer Flugmaschine. Der Kaiser veranlasst die Hinrichtung des Erfinders, denn er fürchtet die Freiheit und Schönheit, die durch die Maschine erlebbar gemacht werden können, und die Bedrohung durch Invasoren aus der Luft. „The Flying Machine" ist eine Art Science-Fiction-Geschichte. Zwar spielt die Handlung nicht, wie in der klassischen Science Fiction, in der Zukunft, und es werden keine Szenarien entworfen, in welche Richtungen sich bereits abzeichnende technologische Entwicklungen gehen könnten, doch es finden sich Science-Fiction-Elemente:

das Thema Forschung und gesellschaftliche Reaktionen auf Forschungs-ergebnisse sowie das spekulative Moment (hier in die Vergangenheit gerichtet: Wie könnte die Gesellschaft auf eine Erfidung reagiert haben, die für uns heute alltäglich ist?).

Die Kurzgeschichte ist ein Beispiel politisch engagierter Literatur: Sie diskutiert die Frage, ob Erfindungen, die auch zum Schaden der Menschheit eingesetzt werden können, verhindert werden sollten. Den S wird so nicht nur ein affektiver Zugang zu diesen Themen ermöglicht, sie erleben auch, wie im Medium Literatur politische Themen behandelt werden.

Unterrichts-tipps

Der Text kann von leistungsstärkeren S zu Hause vorbereitet werden; leistungsschwächere sollten ihn in Abschnitten lesen (z.B. Z. 1–44; 45–87; 88–124).

Vor Beantwortung der Aufgabe 1 kann durch die folgende Zusatzaufgabe eine inhaltliche Sicherung stattfinden:

⬭ *Complete the following sentences with the help of the text.*
1 *The servant was very excited because ...* (... he had seen a man flying; cf. l. 14)
2 *The Emperor did not believe him because ...* (... it was not likely to be true; cf. ll. 21–22)
3 *The Emperor wanted to know whether anyone else had seen the flying man because ...* (... he did not want the invention to fall into the wrong hands; cf. ll. 117–119)
4 *The flying man's wife did not know anything about the machine because ...* (... she would have considered her husband crazy; cf. l. 69)
5 *The Emperor had the man killed because ...* (... he was afraid that others might misuse such an invention to threaten China; cf. ll. 121–123)

Info

Ray Douglas Bradbury (born 1920) is a US science-fiction author and winner of many literary awards. He grew up in Illinois and California during the Great Depression. He worked as a journalist for magazines before becoming a science-fiction writer. He is acclaimed for his powerful themes which combine social commentary and fantastical settings featuring futuristic societies. One of his most famous works, which has also been filmed, is *Fahrenheit 451* (1953). It tells of a society in the future which prohibits the possession of books. Opponents of this ban confront the problem by learning literary classics by heart. Another famous story, *The Martian Chronicles* (1950) deals with the colonization of Mars by humans and shows the ways in which people come to terms with completely unfamiliar environments.

The Great Wall of China is a fortification system that runs for 2400 km, mostly along the southern edge of the Mongolian plain. It is an amalgamation of many walls built in ancient times to protect China from northern nomads. The first unified wall was built in the 3rd century BC. The wall's present form dates largely from the Ming dynasty (1368–1644). It is about 7.6 m in height and is 4.6–9.1 m thick at the base, sloping to 3.7 m at the top. Guard stations and watchtowers are placed at regular intervals. Despite the wall, however, both the Mongols and Manchurians were able to invade China due to the weakness of the country's government.

Lösungs-hinweise

1 The servant of a Chinese Emperor in AD 400 sees a man flying in the sky and points him out to his master. The Emperor has the man brought to him and asks him what he has done. He replies that he has flown in the sky, but the Emperor says that the flyer does not really know what he has done. He has the flying machine destroyed and the flyer executed and threatens the witnesses with death if they ever say a word about the incident to anyone.

2 Individual answers.

→ WB, ex. 3 **3** The Emperor says he has created his machine, his little mechanical world, in order to make birds sing, forests murmur, people walk – i.e. his aim is narrow and clearly defined. The flier says that with his machine he has been able to find beauty, to smell and see the sea and to feel free – i.e. his experience of flying has been broad, filled with feelings. The Emperor argues that the flyer has not understood the consequences of his creation – another man may come along and use the flying machine for different purposes than just to experience the beauty of flying. One purpose might be to use the flying apparatus to attack his country from outside. But the experience of flying itself may be considered a danger, too: people see the world from a different angle, they leave the confinements of everyday life behind and experience freedom. And so, by executing the flier, the Emperor hopes that the flying machine will never be known or used again and the status quo will be preserved.

4 **a** The story is not only about the events described. It is also about:
- the search for beauty (cf. ll. 63–64, ll. 100–111);
- the dangers of the idea of freedom (i.e. what freedom could destroy): 'neither too happy nor too sad' (l. 3), 'which had protected ... and preserved peace ...' (ll. 42–43); cf. ll. 113–119, ll. 139–141;
- the purpose of inventions (cf. ll. 56–60, ll. 83–85, ll. 92–99);
- the desire to halt progress/change (cf. ll. 39–44, ll. 83–85, ll. 113–115, ll. 139–141).

→ WB, ex. 4 **b** Hier empfiehlt sich eine Vorentlastung der Begriffe *image* und *simile*. Je nachdem, ob den S diese Begriffe bereits vertraut sind oder nicht, bietet sich entweder eine Wiederholung mit Hilfe des „Glossary" (vgl. SB, S. 268) oder eine Einführung anhand von Beispielen aus dem Text an.

- 'a dragon in the heavens with a man in its mouth' (ll. 17–18): This conjures up a very vivid picture, which induces both the feeling that the machine (the dragon) is dangerous (because it breathes fire) and also that it is bigger and more powerful than we are (because it carries the man in its mouth, as if about to swallow him up);
- 'he was soaring all about like the largest bird in a universe of birds, like a new dragon in a land of ancient dragons' (ll. 34–35): Again this is a vivid picture of flying; in the case of the bird, although we associate birds with flying free, the size of the bird in the simile has something threatening about it; in the case of the dragons there is the idea of the dragon which is more developed than the old ones – therefore maybe even more threatening;
- 'that splendid snake of stones which writhed with majesty across the entire land' (ll. 40–41): The metaphor of the Great Wall of China is portrayed as something beautiful, but a little evil at the same time – the snake is a wonderful creature to watch, but is, at the same time, dangerous;
- 'the birdlike keel of the apparatus' (ll. 61–62): Yet another image that takes us to the world of birds, though here the mixed simile/metaphor – a 'keel' is normally in a boat – this leads us to think of birds that are not really birds and machines that are not really machines;
- 'And I have soared like a bird' (ll. 103–104): The word 'soared' in this simile implies that feeling of open skies and endless freedom – i.e. the flier has tasted freedom;
- 'Like ants?' (l. 110): The emperor suspects that that's what people look like from the sky, i.e. tiny, impersonal, not to mention vulnerable, squashable; the distance from people removes their human features;
- 'drop huge stones upon the Great Wall of China' (ll. 122–123): This can be understood literally but also as a metaphor for the destruction of China.

The two key images in the story are birds – representing freedom and man's power to soar, at least in imagination and creativity, and the Great Wall of China – representing boundaries, not only physical, but also to thought, research and imagination.

❖ **5** Diese Frage kann in einer *fishbowl discussion* (vgl. S. 428) beantwortet werden.

He was right to execute the flier because:
- the flier posed a threat to the Empire;
- the Emperor is responsible for the protection of his people;
- the flying man does not seem to be aware of possible consequences of his flying machine.

He was wrong to execute the flier because:
- progress cannot be stopped and so someone else is going to invent a similar machine;
- if you only accepted inventions/discoveries which can be used positively, we would still be living in caves;
- the Emperor acted in a very brutal, reckless way, and the life of one human being is still precious.

⬭ *Translate ll. 14–23 into German.*

SB, S. 64 **B Oppenheimer**

VIDEO

Documentary	
Source:	*The Day After Trinity*, 1980
Topic:	The use of the atomic bomb against Japan
Text form:	Documentary
Language variety:	AE
Length:	4:28 min
Level:	Basic/advanced
Drama Serial	
Source:	*Oppenheimer*, 1982
Topic:	Scientists concerned about the use of the atomic bomb
Text form:	Drama serial
Language variety:	AE
Length:	6:24 min
Level:	Basic/advanced
Skills/activities:	Listening comprehension, comparing information in two different sources

Didaktisch-methodische Hinweise

Nachdem die S in der Kurzgeschichte Bradburys den fiktionalen Charakteren des Kaisers und des Bauern mit der Flugmaschine begegnet sind, werden sie hier mit der Geschichte eines realen Menschen konfrontiert. Die beiden Videoauszüge stellen die Konfliktsituation dar, in der sich J. Robert Oppenheimer, der Erfinder der Atombombe, und seine Kollegen befanden: Die Entwicklung der Atombombe war zur Zeit des Krieges gegen Nazi-Deutschland forciert worden; nach dem Sieg der Alliierten stellte sich die Frage, ob und mit welcher Rechtfertigung das Programm weitergeführt werden sollte. Die S sehen Auszüge aus einem Dokumentarfilm und einem Fernsehfilm. Der Dokumentarfilm lässt Wissenschaftler aus dem Umfeld Oppenheimers zu Wort kommen, die über eigene und fremde Rechtfertigungen für die Fortsetzung des „Manhattan Projects" reflektieren. Im *drama serial* äußern Mitarbeiter Oppenheimers Bedenken an dem Projekt, die Oppenheimer zurückweist, indem er Regierungen und nicht Wissenschaftlern die Verantwortung für umstrittene Forschungsergebnisse zuweist.

Unterrichts-tipps

Die Ausschnitte befinden sich auf dem Video / der DVD, die Transkripte auf S. 128. Bevor die S die Videoausschnitte zum ersten Mal sehen, muss der historische Kontext der Auszüge bekannt sein. Die S müssen ein Überblickswissen insbesondere über die Atombombenforschung und die Person Oppenheimers haben. Die Bedeutung folgen-

113 CHAPTER THREE – SECTION 2

der Stichwörter und Namen, die im Zusammenhang mit der Atombombenforschung stehen, könnten die S z.B. in Referaten erläutern: J. Robert Oppenheimer, General Groves, Leo Szilard, President Eisen-hower, Robert Wilson, Edward Teller, Hiroshima, Trinity, Manhattan Project (vgl. „Info": „The atom bomb"). Ein interessanter Link zu Dokumenten, die im Zusammenhang mit der Atombombe stehen, ist:
www.dannen.com/decision/index.html • 1.8.03.
Vor Betrachtung des Videos müssen folgende Stichwörter geklärt werden:

The Day after Trinity:
Robert Wilson (1914–2000) was a physicist who worked on the Manhattan Project and designed the atomic bomb.
Frank Oppenheimer was J. Robert's brother and worked together with him at Los Alamos.
Freeman Dyson is an English-born physicist who worked under Oppenheimer in the late 1940s and was involved in developing manned spaceships, but not the atom bomb.
VE Day: Victory in Europe Day (8 May, 1945).

Oppenheimer:
Edward Teller was a physicist who worked on the Manhattan Project and later became known as the 'father of the hydrogen bomb'.
Chicago disease: many scientists working for the Manhattan Project at the University of Chicago, led by Leo Szilard, expressed their concerns about the use of the atomic bomb and signed a petition to President Roosevelt.
Trinity: the name given to the first test of the atom bomb (16 July, 1945).
Little Boy: the name of the atom bomb that was dropped on Hiroshima.
Secretary Stimpson: secretary of war under President Roosevelt, who set up the *Interim Committee* to consider the use of the atom bomb. It met with the scientific panel, consisting of Oppenheimer, Enrico Fermi, Ernest O. Lawrence and Arthur H. Compton, and decided to use the atomic bomb against Japan without warning.

Info

J. Robert Oppenheimer (1904–1967) (often called 'Oppie') was born to a Jewish family in New York City. He studied at Harvard and then later in England and Germany. Fluent in several languages, he was interested in poetry and literature as well as physics. The rise of fascism in Germany alerted him to the dangers inherent in the political changes that were taking place in Europe and made him become interested in left-wing politics. Indeed his wife, Kitty, was a member of the Communist Party. When it became clear in 1939 that the Germans were capable of splitting the atom, President Roosevelt set up the Manhattan Project in 1941 to commence work on an atomic bomb. In 1942, Oppenheimer was appointed director and set up a new research centre in Los Alamos, New Mexico, to which he summoned the best scientists at his disposal. By 1945, they had developed the first atomic bomb, which was then used to destroy the cities of Hiroshima and Nagasaki. After the war Oppenheimer initially opposed the development of the hydrogen bomb but under pressure from President Truman did start work on it. During the McCarthy period of anti-communist purges in the 1950s, Oppenheimer, due to his links with communists in the 1930s, lost his security clearance; he worked at Princeton University for the rest of his professional life.

Info

The atom bomb was developed due to the fear that Nazi Germany would develop the bomb first. In the first test (called 'Trinity') a bomb (referred to as 'The Gadget') was detonated on 16 July, 1945; bombs were then dropped on Hiroshima on 8 August and on Nagasaki on 9 August. There is still controversy as to whether it was necessary to drop the bombs on Japanese cities, especially because the Japanese at that time were unable to develop an atom bomb. Many felt that the bombs could have been exploded close to Japanese cities to show them the force that now lay at the Americans' disposal. The main argument was that the atomic bombs shortened the war and saved hundreds of thousands of American (and Japanese) lives, which would have been lost had the battle been taken to mainland Japan. The scientists involved in the work had mixed feelings about the bomb, and few celebrated its use.

Lösungs-
hinweise

VIDEO

1 Vgl. die Ausschnitte auf dem Video / der DVD und die Transkripte auf S. 128.

The <u>documentary</u> gives some brief background information, introduced by the presenter, but it focuses on the views of two people involved in the Manhattan Project. This way we see real people talking about and analysing the events (though obviously in hindsight). The third, speaker, Freeman Dyson, was not involved in the development of the bomb, but through his knowledge of Oppenheimer and his own scientific background, is able to give an interesting analysis of the events. The documentary probably offers better analysis of what happened and about people's attitudes to the bomb.
The <u>film</u> requires more background information, as the characters are obviously talking about things they know about. There is more drama and tension involved as Oppenheimer and the scientists are discussing their problems with the use of the bomb. The entire drama might be better watching, as sympathy is invoked with the characters.

2 Oppenheimer is different from the flier. In a sense he comes across as the servant of the 'Emperor' (who in this case would be the American president), following the orders given to him, irrespective of what the consequences are. He believes that scientists do not have moral responsibility, but rather elected politicians must take decisions. It seems unlikely that he would design something that was not required of him. However, in a way he is also similar to the flier since both do not think about the consequences of their inventions – the flyer, because of a certain naivety, which leaves him unaware of controversy his invention might provoke; Oppenheimer, because he does not consider himself responsible.

a *After the war, Oppenheimer said 'the physicists have known sin; and this is a knowledge which they cannot lose'. Explain what he meant.*

b *Imagine you were one of the scientists working at Los Alamos, and you heard this statement. Write a letter to Oppenheimer, expressing your agreement or disagreement with him*

SB, S. 64 ## C **Wernher von Braun** Tom Lehrer

CD

Source:	*That Was the Year that Was*, 1965
Topic:	A famous scientist's disregard for his own moral responsibility
Text form:	Song
Language variety:	AE
Length:	1:49 min
Level:	Basic/advanced
Skills/activities:	Listening comprehension, writing an essay

*Didaktisch-
methodische
Hinweise*

Dieser satirische Song wird als Hörtext präsentiert. Ziel ist neben der Schulung des Hörverständnisses, dass die S die Haltung des Sängers zum Wissenschaftler Wernher von Braun analysieren. Sie sollen die Aussagen, die Tom Lehrer über Wernher von Braun trifft, auch auf Text A „The Flying Machine" (vgl. SB, S. 60) anwenden. Das Lied dient der Auseinandersetzung mit der Frage, inwieweit Wissenschaftler für die Folgen ihrer Arbeit verantwortlich gemacht werden können oder sollen. Bei Interesse kann das Lied als Ausgangspunkt dienen, um sich intensiver mit dem Leben von Wernher von Braun oder anderen umstrittenen Wissenschaftlern auseinander zu setzen.

*Unterrichts-
tipps*

Obwohl der Text des Liedes gut zu verstehen ist, sollten vor dem Hören folgende Vokabeln semantisiert werden:

allegiance: support of or loyalty to a party, person, institution, etc. (cf. the pledge of allegiance in American schools);
expedience: action that is useful for a particular purpose, but not always fair;
frown: make a serious or worried expression by bringing your eyebrows closer together so that lines appear on your forehead;
renown: fame and respect because of sth. you have done that people admire;
gratitude: feeling of being grateful.

Das Lied (vgl. CD1, *track* 14, und das Transkript auf S. 130) kann zunächst als Hörtext präsentiert werden. Danach beantworten die S Aufgabe 1. Für eine intensivere Textarbeit empfiehlt es sich, den Text auf Folie oder als Kopie zu präsentieren. Zur Integration von Wortschatzarbeit können im Transkript einige Wörter ausgelassen werden, die die S beim Hören einsetzen, z.B.
1. Strophe: „nuclear nations", „know-how";
2. Strophe: „frown", „allegiance", „expedience";
   Refrain: „hypocritical", „apolitical";
3. Strophe: „rockets", „department";
4. Strophe: „attitude", „gratitude";
5. Strophe: „hero", „count backwards".

Info

Wernher von Braun (1912–1977) was a German scientist who developed ballistic missiles, first for the Nazis during the Second World War and later for the US Army. Inspired as a young boy by the writings of Jules Verne and H.G. Wells, von Braun developed a passion for space flight, which eventually led to a doctorate in aerospace engineering. During the war he helped the Nazis develop V-2s, high-speed ballistic missiles which were capable of carrying huge warheads to distant targets, and were used to bomb London. He was arrested by the SS, as he was more interested in producing rockets that would go into space. He was, however, quickly released, and foreseeing the inevitable victory of the Allies, von Braun organized the advance surrender of his team and their scientific plans to the Americans, following which, under Project Paperclip, they were moved first to Texas and finally to Alabama, where they continued their missile research, this time for the US Army. When NASA was established in 1960, von Braun became director of the Marshall Space Flight Centre. He has been accused by some of the reckless pursuit of scientific goals regardless of the moral and human costs. His German V-2 missiles, for example, were controversially manufactured at a forced labour factory.
(For more information on the controversy surrounding the development of the V2 rocket, cf. http://history.msfc.nasa.gov/vonbraun/bio.html • 1.8.2003)

*Lösungs-
hinweise*

CD

1 Vgl. CD1, *track* 14, und das Transkript auf S. 130.

Lehrer thinks von Braun is immoral and unethical because
– he does not care who he works for (cf. ll. 7–8);
– he does not object to being associated with the Nazis (cf. l. 9);
– he does not consider the consequences of his research (cf. l. 13).

2

Hypocritical: pretending to have moral standards or opinions that one does not really have.
Apolitical: not interested in politics, not thinking politics are important.
a) The Emperor sacrifices the joys and the freedom of flying in the interest of national security. He is not hypocritical, but honest about his motives.
b) Certainly 'apolitical' could apply to the flier – he does not see, or want to see, any further significance of his invention.

3 Individual answers.

SB, S. 65

Getting Along in English

*Didaktisch-
methodische
Hinweise*

Diese *section* soll die S auf einen Arztbesuch im englischsprachigen Ausland vorbereiten. Als Basis dienen drei Dialogreihen (vgl. CD1, *tracks* 15–26 und die Transkripte auf S. 131–134). In der ersten Dialogreihe stellen die Patienten Jill, Mr Martin, Miss Schmidt und Michael ihre Beschwerden dar; in der zweiten stellt der Arzt seine Diagnose und erläutert die Therapie. In der dritten Dialogreihe stellen die Patienten Fragen zur Therapie und zu den verschriebenen Medikamenten. Die S lernen die Bezeichnungen für häufig auftretende Krankheiten kennen, schulen ihr Hörverstehen, indem sie Dialoge zwischen Arzt und Patienten hören, und gestalten selbst einen Dialog beim Arzt, in dem sie das neue Wortmaterial umwälzen.

*Unterrichts-
tipps*

Die drei Dialogreihen beziehen sich aufeinander und sollten daher möglichst in einer Unterrichtseinheit besprochen werden. Als Einstieg in die Behandlung bieten sich die folgenden Fragen an: „Which of you has already had to see a doctor abroad? What was your experience of that situation?". Eine andere Möglichkeit ist der Einstieg über Realia, d.h. L bringt Dinge wie Tabletten, Fieberthermometer, Verbandsmaterial, Pflaster u.ä. mit und sammelt gemeinsam mit den S die englischen Bezeichnungen an der Tafel. Nachdem in Aufgabe 1 unabhängig von den Dialogen Wortmaterial zum Thema zusammengetragen wird, beziehen sich die Aufgaben 2 bis 4 auf die Dialoge.

*Lösungs-
hinweise*

Pre-reading: wordfield *illnesses*: hurt (sb./sth./oneself), injure (sb./sth./oneself), broken arm/leg/ankle, go to hospital, cold, ill, sick, operation, operate on sb., patient, temperature, penicillin, antibiotics, an infected wound, put bandages around the wound, surgeon, bacteria, etc.

1 Bei dieser Aufgabe sollte auch auf die korrekte Aussprache der Begriffe geachtet werden, die die S selbst mit Hilfe eines einsprachigen Wörterbuchs ermitteln können.

Individual answers.

CD

2 Die Dialoge befinden sich auf CD1, *tracks* 15–18; die Transkripte auf S. 131–132.
Dialogue 1: have a terrible cold, not seem to be able to get rid of it, have a runny nose, sneeze a lot, have a temperature, have headaches, itch.
Dialogue 2: hurt my ankle, (of pain) get worse, (of ankle) be quite swollen.
Dialogue 3: a cut on my hand, begin to throb, look a bit red.
Dialogue 4: keep getting awful stomach pains, hurt around here, symptoms like nausea, diarrhoea, feel sick.

3 Individual answers.

CD **4** **a** Die Dialoge befinden sich auf CD1, *tracks* 19–22; die Transkripte auf S. 132.

1 Hay fever is an allergy to pollens.
2 The nurse is going to strap up Mr Martin's ankle.
3 The informal word for injection is 'jab' (This is a BE term. The AE word is 'shot').
4 The doctor will send Michael for some tests .

CD **b** Die Dialoge befinden sich auf CD1, *tracks* 23–26; die Transkripte auf S. 133–134.

Individual answers.

c Individual answers.

SB, S. 66 # 3 How Things Work

Source:	*Newsweek*, 8 April, 2002
Topic:	How a hydrogen car works
Text form:	Magazine article
Language variety:	AE
Number of words:	325
Level:	Advanced
Skills/activities:	Understanding scientific descriptions, identifying and explaining grammatical forms, working with technical illustrations

Lern-
vokabular

Active vocabulary: 'How Things Work' (p. 66)

run out, give way to sth., run on sth., charge sth., oxygen, store sth., generate current, convert sth. into sth. else, receive a signal, power a car

Didaktisch-
methodische
Hinweise

Aktuelle Entwicklungen auf dem Gebiet der alternativen Energien und der Einsatz von elektronisch gesteuerten Ratten sind die Themen, auf deren Grundlage sich die S mit wissenschaftlich-technischen Texten auseinander setzen. Ziel ist – auch im Hinblick auf die Bedeutung des Englischen als Wissenschaftssprache – dass die S ihr Verständnis solcher Texte schulen. Die Besonderheit des vorliegenden Textes ist die Kombination von Illustrationen und Text (im eigentlichen Sinn); eine Darstellungsform, die sich häufig im (populär)wissenschaftlichen Bereich findet. Schwerpunkt der Textbehandlung ist vornehmlich die Rezeption dieser – zumindest in der Fremdsprache – wenig vertrauten Textform mit ihrem schwierigen technologiebezogenen Inhalt. Als grammatischer Schwerpunkt werden die für wissenschaftliche Texte typischen Partizipialkonstruktionen wiederholt und geübt (vg. auch „Watch Your Language", SB, S. 73). Hier bietet sich eine vorbereitende Hausaufgabe an.

Unterrichts-
tipps

Vor der Lektüre des Textes empfiehlt es sich, mit den S die Funktion der Illustrationen zu erörtern. So werden sie darauf aufmerksam gemacht, dass Text und Bilder sich gegenseitig ergänzen und bei Problemen des Textverständnisses die Illustrationen hinzugezogen werden können. Die S lesen den Text still. Damit sich keine fehlerhafte Aussprache einschleift, sollte die Aussprache einiger Vokabeln sichergestellt werden, die

Differenzierung

leistungsstärkere S auch selbstständig in einem einsprachigen Wörterbuch nachschlagen können:

'hydrogen' ['haɪdrədʒən], 'battery' ['bætri ☆ -təri], 'oxygen' ['ɒksɪdʒən ☆ 'ɑːk-], 'circuit' ['sɜːkɪt], 'molecule' ['mɒlɪkjuːl ☆ 'mɑːl-], 'hydrocarbons' [ˌhaɪdrə'kɑːbənz], 'methane' ['miːθeɪn].

Lösungs-hinweise ◆◆

1 Bevor sich die S in Aufgabe b mit einem Partner austauschen, müssen ihre Lösungen zu Aufgabe a korrigiert werden, damit bei der Partnerarbeit keine Verwirrung gestiftet wird. So können den S z.B. jeweils für A und B Kopien mit den Lösungen ausgeteilt werden. In leistungsstärkeren Gruppen ist auch denkbar, dass jeweils vier As bzw. Bs zusammenkommen, ihre Lösungen vergleichen und korrigieren.

Partner A's statements:
1 False. The fuel cell produces energy.
2 True.
3 False. In order to tell the difference, you have to look inside.
4 False. You fill the tank 'at the pump, just like a gas tank'.
5 True.
6 False. It is sent to the 'traction inverter module', which turns the wheels.

Partner B's statements:
1 False. It uses hydrogen to produce energy and water.
2 True.
3 False. The electrons pass through an external circuit, which produces the electric current for the car.
4 False. Extracting hydrogen from methane is cheaper.
5 True.
6 False. They already provide power for spacecraft and might even power whole cities in the future.

2 Benefits of the hydrogen-powered car:
– would reduce dependence on oil or petroleum, supplies of which are limited;
– would eliminate emissions which directly affect health;
– would eliminate emissions which contribute to global warming;
– would eliminate emissions which damage the ozone layer;
– could be cheaper to own and operate.
The losers would be oil companies and countries with large oil reserves.

→ WB, ex. 5

3 **a** Zur Vorbereitung dieser Aufgabe bietet sich eine kurze Wiederholung der Partizipial-Konstruktionen an, entweder durch eine vorbereitende Hausaufgabe oder durch Kurzvorträge.
Bei den hervorgehobenen grammatischen Formen handelt es sich um Partizipien, wie sie häufig in wissenschaftlichen Texten auftauchen. Durch sie können Sätze verkürzt und somit der für wissenschaftliche Texte übliche verknappte Stil erreicht werden. Besonders beim zweiten Satz bietet es sich an, diesen auch übersetzen zu lassen, um den S bewusst zu machen, dass ein Partizip in einem englischen Satz nicht automatisch mit einem Partizip im Deutschen wiedergegeben werden kann.
The first example contains a participle replacing a relative clause; the second contains a participle describing accompanying circumstances of an action (vgl. *CEG* §153c,d, §160):
'Hydrogen, pumped to the cell's negatively charged side, ...': past participle replacing a relative clause. It is a past participle because of the passive verb in the relative clause. The construction with a relative clause would be: 'Hydrogen, which is pumped ...'.
'A platinum membrane ... to the positive side, thus forcing them ...': past participle describing accompanying circumstances.

b Hydrogen is pumped to ... side, where it divides ...
Hydrogen, which is pumped ... side, divides ...
When hydrogen is pumped ... side, it divides ...
A platinum membrane ... side, which forces ...
A platinum membrane ... side, which are then forced ...
A platinum membrane ... side and forces ...
The construction can be used to shorten complex sentences, e.g. ones with relative clauses, and so it is more economical. Therefore it is often used in scientific texts, where a lot of information is given in a very dense manner. It can also be used to express the fact that two things are happening at the same time ('accompanying circumstances') or that one leads to another, which is useful for describing processes, and is common in scientific prose.

→ WB, ex. 6   **4** **a** I think rats might be controlled from afar by remote control. Scientists might transmit signals which cause the rats to do what the scientists want them to. The signals could, for example, cause the rats to feel pain or pleasure, which could then be used to guide them in a certain direction.

b Vor allem bei Beispielsatz a muss hier mit Verständnisproblemen der S gerechnet werden, die sich z.B. aus den zwei aufeinander folgenden „it" ergeben. Hier bietet sich u.U. eine Übersetzung des Teilsatzes an.

1 b, 2 c, 3 a, 4 d.

5 Individual answers.

SB, S. 69   # Context Box

Didaktisch-methodische Hinweise
Die „Context Box" skizziert das Verhältnis zwischen wissenschaftlicher Forschung und Gesellschaft aus historischer Sicht, um dann dieses Thema auch bezogen auf die Gegenwart zu diskutieren. Besonderes Gewicht kommt dabei der Frage nach der Verantwortung von Wissenschaftlern und der Ethik der Wissenschaft zu.
Die Aufgaben und das hervorgehobene Vokabular zielen auf die Formulierung komplexer Aussagen zu kontroversen wissenschaftlichen Forschungen bzw. Entdeckungen.

Unterrichtstipps
Zur Einstimmung auf die „Context Box" können die S über die Person Einsteins reflektieren oder den Titel der „Context Box" erläutern:

⬭ *What do you know about the scientist in this picture and his findings?*

⬭ *The caption implies that Einstein's formula lead to the deaths of tens of thousands of people. In your opinion, can a scientist be blamed for the results of his or her discoveries or inventions?*

⬭ *The title of this Context Box is: 'Science, Technology and Controversy'. In what areas can science and technology be controversial?*

Die folgenden Aufgaben dienen dem allgemeinen inhaltlichen Verständnis der „Context Box" und können vor den Aufgaben im SB gelöst werden.

⬭ *Decide whether the following statements are right or wrong and correct them if necessary.*
1 *Astronomy was the first science that developed because people have always tried to understand natural phenomena.*
(False: It was because people believed that the stars influence events on earth.)

2 *Galileo was burned at the stake because his findings contradicted the teachings of Catholic Church.*
(False: He was not executed, but he was forced by the Church to renounce his views.)

3 *Today there are no longer any controversies between researchers and the society they live in.*
(False: In some societies researchers are not allowed to publish their findings.)

4 *Today the science of genetics is causing the most controversy because it touches on moral and religious questions.*
(True)

5 *Scientists today feel responsible for how their findings are used.*
(False: Many scientists claim they are not responsible for what others do with their findings.)

6 *Einstein felt that concern for humanity and its fate must be the main purpose behind all technical developments.*
(True)

Lösungs-
hinweise

1

– Ideas conflict with widely held views (e.g. the earth revolving round the sun).
– Some societies are closed to certain kinds of knowledge (e.g. North Korea, some Islamic fundamentalist countries).
– Publication can lead to controversy (e.g. evolution, where debate continues to this day in the USA).
– Discoveries touch on the moral and religious views of society (e.g. genetic engineering).
– Discoveries might have unforeseen, undesirable consequences (e.g. discovery of minerals leading to strip-mining; Einstein's theory of relativity leading to the atomic bomb).
– Discoveries could be abused by oppressive regimes (e.g. aerodynamic research leading to the invention of the V2 rocket in Nazi Germany).

2 a Diese Aufgabe dient der Arbeit an neuer Lexik, bei der die S mit dem Wörterbuch arbeiten und ihre Wortbildungskenntnisse anwenden. Es ist sinnvoll, diese Aufgabe gemeinsam an der Tafel oder mit dem OHP auszuwerten, so dass alle S die entsprechenden Verben bzw. Substantive aller im Text hervorgehobenen Wörter schriftlich festhalten können. Um das Verständnis zu sichern, bietet es sich an, unbekannte Wörter zu semantisieren und ggf. zu übersetzen (z.B. „occurrence", „oppression", „endeavour", „blessing", „curse", „comprehend", „emerge", „reject", „accompany").

nouns	verbs	nouns	verbs
application	apply sth.	knowledge	know sth.
observation	observe sth.	experiment	experiment
researcher	research sth.	study	study sth.
discovery	discover sth.	life	live
destruction	destroy sth.	occurrence	occur
oppression	opppress sb.	concern	concern sb.
interest	interest sb.	endeavour	endeavour sth.
creation	create sth.	blessing	bless sb.
curse	curse sb.	discussion	discuss sth.
debate	debate sth.		
gain	gain	comprehension	comprehend
emergence	emerge	rejection	reject
publication	publish	discovery	discover
development	develop	expectation	expect
accompaniment	accompany		

b *sich auf jdn. auswirken:* 'affect sb.';
der Lauf der Dinge: 'the course of events';
zum Leidwesen von Wissenschaftlern: 'unfortunately for scientists';
Kontroverse erzeugen: 'spawn controversy';
jdn. zur Verantwortung ziehen: 'hold sb. responsible';
inwiefern: 'to what extent'.

c Individual answers.

3 Diese Aufgabe hat Projektcharakter und ist im Anforderungsprofil ähnlich der Aufgabe 2 aus dem „Lead-in". Es empfiehlt sich, nur eine dieser beiden Aufgaben bearbeiten zu lassen oder sie als Alternativaufgaben zu stellen.

SB, S. 70

4 Can Science Save Us from Ourselves? Natasha Walter

Source:	*Independent*, 28 February, 2002
Topic:	Stem-cell research and people's expectations of science
Text form:	Newspaper article
Language variety:	BE
Number of words:	1096
Level:	Advanced
Skills/activities:	Paraphrasing words/phrases, doing research, writing a leaflet

Lern-vokabular

Active vocabulary: 'Can Science Save Us from Ourselves?' (p. 70)

current (l. 5), predispose sb. to sth. (l. 9), perception of sth. (l. 11), outrun sb./sth. (l. 12), conceive (a child) (l. 17), fertility treatment (l. 18), failure rates (l. 19), in the forefront of sth. (l. 24), manipulate sth. (l. 25), suffer from sth. (l. 29), retirement (l. 32), curable (l. 32), ripe old age (l. 35), predictable (l. 42), a wide range of sth. (l. 48), show signs of sth. (l. 53), obesity (l. 54), incidence of sth. (l. 57), sexually transmitted diseases (l. 57), rise sharply (l. 59), packet of sth. (l. 69), take account of sth. (ll. 74–75)

Didaktisch-methodische Hinweise

Ausgehend von der Entscheidung des britischen Oberhauses im Jahr 2002, die Forschung mit embryonalen Stammzellen zu erlauben, stellt die Autorin die These auf, dass wir von wissenschaftlichem Fortschritt die zunehmende Beherrschung von Krankheiten erwarten, gleichzeitig aber durch unseren Lebensstil immer weniger zu deren Vermei- dung beitragen. Damit wirft der Text ein ganz anderes Licht auf die Problematik der Gentechnologie, da er die häufig diskutierten ethischen Fragen außen vor lässt. Er bietet eine provokante Diskussionsgrundlage für die Frage nach der Bedeutung der Gentechnologie und nach der Verantwortung, die wir persönlich für unsere Gesundheit haben.

Der Text ist sowohl inhaltlich als auch sprachlich anspruchsvoll. Dies resultiert zum einen aus seiner großen Fülle an Informationen aus verschiedenen Wissenschaftsbereichen, zum anderen aus der großen Zahl von Metaphern (z.B. „we strap ourselves into steel cages", Z. 66–67; „we ride a wave of urgent passion", Z. 68–69).

Unterrichts-tipps

Um den Text vorzuentlasten, empfiehlt sich die im SB abgedruckte *pre-reading*-Aufgabe. Eine alternative Herangehensweise könnte in dem Tafelanschrieb „Genetic engineering – blessing or curse for mankind?" bestehen, der als stummer Impuls die S dazu auffordert, ihr Vorwissen und ihre Meinung zum *genetic engineering* einzubringen und ihnen so die Einordnung der Sichtweise Walters erleichtert.

Die im SB abgedruckten Aufgaben zum Text haben v.a. Analyse- und Transfercharakter. Um zunächst das Textverständnis zu sichern, können die S Überschriften für Abschnitte des Texts finden. Auch die folgenden Inhaltsfragen können gestellt werden:

◯ *What decision was taken in the House of Lords?*
The House of Lords decided that scientists are allowed to carry out research with cells that have been taken from cloned human embryos (cf. ll. 4–5).

◯ *Find reasons why this decision, according to the writer, does not really surprise people.*
The writer mentions that recently there have been so many stories about 'designer babies' and genetic manipulation, including a story about a baby that was only conceived so that its genetic material could be used to rescue its brother and about another that was selected not to carry the gene responsible for Alzheimer's (cf. ll. 5–10).

◯ *In what respect has the public's perception 'outrun reality' (l. 12)?*
Many people believe that scientists are easily able to create designer babies, clone humans and help couples who cannot have a baby naturally without any difficulties. In reality all these things are still fairly difficult and have a high failure rate.

◯ *What expectations do people in the Western world have regarding scientific research?*
Life should be controllable (cf. ll. 27–28); babies should be perfect; nobody should suffer from diseases caused by genetic dysfunction (cf. l. 29); research should be used to fight disabilities (cf. ll. 30–31); old age should become curable (cf. ll. 31–32).

◯ *If science is making such great progress, why, according to Walter, will there still be no cure for some illnesses?*
There will be no cure for some illnesses because most of them do not depend on our genes but our lifestyle. We will suffer from high blood pressure, overweight and other illnesses which all occur because of the wrong food, too much alcohol, too little exercise and smoking.

Info

Stem-cell research: On 27 February, 2002, the House of Lords recommended that stem-cell research on embryos be allowed in the UK. This means that British scientists can create a limited number of human embryo clones under tight regulations. Stem cells, the body's master cells that have the potential to develop into any other type of cell in the body, can theoretically be used to repair damaged or defective tissue in the parent of the cloned cells and could be used to grow replacement livers or other organs for transplant without fear of rejection. They might also be used to create healthy nerve cells for people with Alzheimer's or Parkinson's disease.

The controversy arises because stem cells are obtained either from 'spare' human embryos or from cloned embryos. While reproductive cloning is banned, this form of cloning (called therapeutic cloning) is now legal in the United Kingdom and there are fears that this decision could result in reproductive cloning, in which identical copies of human beings are created. It is also controversial as an embryo cell will have its DNA removed and replaced with the genetic material from the tissue cell; in effect an embryo has been created in order to serve another purpose.

The Human Fertilisation and Embryology Authority is responsible for regulating the research and is only allowed to issue licences if the research is deemed 'necessary and desirable'. In most other countries, therapeutic cloning is still banned.

Info

Aldous Huxley (1894–1963) (ll. 2–3) was a British novelist and essayist who came from a renowned scientific and literary family. Originally intending to become a doctor, he was forced to change his plans due to an eye illness and instead studied literature at Oxford University. In his early fictional works, e.g. *Antic Hay* (1923), as well as in his essays he discusses social and philosophical issues, becoming increasingly wary of Western civilization. His best-known novel, *Brave New World* (1932), depicts a totalitarian society which seeks to create total human happiness by breeding different grades of humans for different societal roles and tasks, by conditioning individuals and by supplying a pleasure drug.

Stanley Kubrick (1928–1999) (l. 3) was a US film director who worked in a wide variety of film genres, among them science fiction (*2001: A Space Odyssey*, 1968), war films (*Full Metal Jacket*, 1980) and horror (*The Shining*, 1980). Many of his films were based on novels (e.g. Anthony Burgess's *A Clockwork Orange*, Stephen King's *The Shining*, Vladimir Nabokov's *Lolita*). Kubrick is renowned for his attention to detail and the detached pessimism visible especially in his science-fiction films.

Lösungs-hinweise
◆◆

▬▬ Die *pre-reading*-Aufgabe sollte schriftlich, ggf. in Partnerarbeit gelöst werden, damit diese Liste nach Lektüre des Textes mit den Aussagen der Autorin verglichen werden kann.

Possible answers:
Medical research: combat/treat illnesses (e.g. diabetes, cancer, AIDS); prevent babies being born with illnesses; enable organ transplants (e.g. liver, kidney, heart); invent cosmetics that prevent us from getting wrinkles; invent vaccines against fatal diseases; control epidemics;

Climatology: be able to forecast natural catastrophes; stop global warming; invent ways to stop deserts from spreading;
Technology: invent cars which run on environment-friendly fuels; develop renewable energies;

Agriculture: invent crops that are resistant to illnesses; find new food resources; invent machines that can harvest crops which are still harvested by hand.

1 Eating too much (cf. l. 54); eating the wrong food (cf. l. 56); not taking enough exercise (cf. l. 56); having unprotected sex (cf. l. 58); drinking too much alcohol (cf. ll. 59–60); smoking too much and at too young an age (cf. ll. 60–61); drunk driving (cf. ll. 66–67); driving too fast (cf. l. 67).
The students might add the following ideas: dangerous sports; drug abuse; no medical checkups or visits to the dentist.

2 Walter is sceptical of science and people's expectations of science. This can be seen in her irreverent tone: 'The Lords in their wisdom' (l. 3), 'scientists should be able to dabble in cells' (l. 4), 'scientists could already clone dozens of dinky copies of themselves' (ll. 13–14), 'If you buy into that dream' (l. 43), 'put their glittering achievements into perspective' (l. 85).
She also humorously overstates the case sometimes to make her point, e.g. ll. 31–32, 40–42, 74–76, 86–87.
She also makes a political comment by comparing the 'saving' of one baby in the USA with the deaths of babies in developing countries (cf. ll. 78–81).

3 Individual answers.

4 Gegebenenfalls kann den S anhand einiger Beispiele demonstriert werden, wie diese Aufgabe gelöst werden kann:

genetic material (l. 8): 'the information stored in the DNA';
Alzheimer's (l. 31): 'a disease that affects the brain, which no longer works properly';
combat disabilities (l. 30): 'fight against handicaps'.

5 Bei dieser gestalterischen Aufgabe müssen die S über Qualitätskriterien einer Broschüre nachdenken, damit sie Bewertungsmaßstäbe für die eigenen Broschüren haben. Eine solche Liste sollte vor der Erstellung der Schülerprodukte entwickelt und nach dem Vergleich der *leaflets* ggf. komplettiert werden.
Qualitätskriterien könnten sein:

1 Design:
- eye-catching front page;
- attractive layout;
- clear structure, perhaps with a list of contents at the beginning;
- suitable picture material.
2 Presentation of contents:
- interesting, well-researched contents;
- logical structure, clear presentation;
- references to further information on the subject (literature, Internet);
- list of sources, 'imprint'.

⬭ *Translate ll. 11–23 into German.*

SB, S. 73 # Watch Your Language

Didaktisch-methodische Hinweise Als Schwerpunktthema werden hier noch einmal die *participle constructions* in ihren verschiedenen Verwendungsmöglichkeiten geübt (*participles instead of relative clauses, participle expressing accompanying circumstances*; vgl. *section 3*, Aufgabe 3 und *CEG* §§153 c,d, 160). Die S müssen Partizipien erkennen, umformen und übersetzen. Weiterhin spielt der Gebrauch des *definite article* eine Rolle.

Lösungs-hinweise **1** **a**
- known
- left school
- at 15
- returned to school
- earning
- establishing
- held

b
- 'known': *CEG* §153c,d (Index under 'participle: instead of a relative clause') und *CEG* §153a (Index under 'participle: with a noun')
- 'left _ school': *CEG* §184a (Index under 'school: use of *the*')
- 'at 15': *OALD*, Appendix 3: Numbers (last square dot: To refer to a particular event you can use at/by/before ...')
- 'to _ school': *CEG* §184a (Index under 'school: use of *the*')
- 'earning': *CEG* §153c,d (Index under 'participle: instead of a relative clause') und *CEG* §153a (Index under 'participle: with a noun')
- 'establishing': *CEG* §153a (Index under 'participle: with a noun')
- 'held': *CEG* §160 (Index under 'participle: instead of an adverbial clause') und *CEG* §153a (Index under 'participle: with a noun')

2 The student mainly needs to study participle constructions, but also the use of the definite article. The best way to do this is with a grammar book.

→ WB, ex. 8 **3** **a** Both sentences contain participle clauses expressing accompanying circumstances (cf. *CEG* §160). In the first sentence, the participle construction and the main clause have the same subject (cf. *CEG* 162). The participle is a present participle and has an active meaning (cf. *CEG* §153a).
In the second sentence, the participle construction has its own subject, which is differerent from the main clause. It is a past participle and has a passive meaning (cf. *CEG* §153a).

b Die S setzen hier *present* bzw. *past participles* in Sätze ein. Da diese Sätze sprachlich anspruchsvoll sind, empfiehlt es sich, in leistungsschwächeren Kursen den S die Reihenfolge der Verben vorzugeben, so dass sie sich auf die richtige Verwendung der Partizipien konzentrieren können.

1 giving up
2 learning (having learned), urging
3 providing, known
4 frightened, advocating, drafted
5 ignored

c
1 Als/Nachdem Hitler Kanzler geworden war/wurde, gab Einstein seine deutsche Staatsbürgerschaft auf und verließ Deutschland.
2 Als Einstein erfuhr, dass Deutschland eine Atombombe entwickelte, schrieb er an Präsident Roosevelt und bat diesen eindringlich um Wachsamkeit und, wenn nötig, schnelles Handeln seitens der Vereinigten Staaten.
3 Einstein, ein Pazifist, veröffentlichte die allgemeine Relativitätstheorie und schuf damit die Grundlage für die tödlichsten Bomben, die die Menschheit kennt – die Atombombe und die Wasserstoffbombe.
   … die allgemeine Relativitätstheorie, womit / mit der er …
   … die tödlichsten der Menschheit bekannten Bomben …
4 Weil er befürchtete, dass die Atombombe noch einmal eingesetzt werden könnte, gab er eine Stellungnahme ab, in der er eine Weltregierung mit einer von den USA, Großbritannien und der Sowjetunion entworfenen Verfassung befürwortete.
   Aus Angst, die Atombombe könnte …
   … eine Weltregierung mit einer Verfassung befürwortete, die von den USA, Großbritannien und der Sowjetunion entworfen würde.
5 In seinem späteren Leben weitgehend ignoriert, setzte Einstein seine Forschungen bis zu seinem Tod in den USA im Jahr 1955 fort.
   In seinem späteren Leben wurde Einstein weitgehend ignoriert. Er setzte seine Forschungen bis zu seinem Tod in den USA im Jahr 1955 fort.

Topic Vocabulary: 'Science and Technology'

New Discoveries
advances in modern
  science
new/recent
  developments in science
  and technology
technological advances in
  computing/
  telecommunications
a scientific discovery
(scientific) research
observation and
  experiment
natural phenomena
scientist
researcher
research into sth.
inventor
discoverer
discovery
publish your findings (in
  a journal)

Weapons and the Nuclear World
nuclear
  physicist/scientist
nuclear/atom(ic)/
  hydrogen bomb
weapons of mass
  destruction
chemical/biological/
  nuclear weapons
nuclear power plant

The Space Race
space programme
send a rocket to the moon
  / into space
launch a rocket
spaceship
satellite picture
space shuttle
intelligent life on other
  planets

Computer Technology
computer
computer monitor/screen
computer chip
binary system
World Wide Web
on the Internet

Electrical Goods
appliance
device
features
remote control
instruction manual

Health
medicine
doctor
surgeon
health system
have (private) health /
  medical (AE) insurance
feel ill/sick/dizzy
have flu / a temperature /
  a cold
stomach ache
headache
presciption
prescribe
  tablets/medicine / a
  cream
medication
a medicine
have an injection / a jab
  against sth.
take antibiotics
advances in medical
  science / the world of
  medicine
traditional medicine
homeopathy
treatment
complaint
injury
diagnosis
cure
curable
disability
physical/mental illness
be allergic to sth.

Pregnancy
test-tube baby
sperm bank
artificial insemination
surrogate mother
foetus
abortion

The World of Genetics
genetics
genetically modified / GM
  produce/food
clone an animal / a
  human being
a clone
cloned human embryo
genetic manipulation
genes
have a gene that
  predisposes you to an
  illness / a disease
stem-cell research

Scientific Responsibility
ethics of science
centre of controversy
meaning of life
nature of life
further the cause of
  knowledge
be held responsible for
  sth.
foresee the consequences
  of sth.

Oppenheimer

VIDEO   **Extract from:** *The Day After Trinity*

SB, p. 64

Presenter: Across the Pacific the war raged on against Japan, but in the spring of '45 there was victory in Europe. The Nazis had never come close to building an atomic bomb. Germany surrendered. VE Day. Eisenhower returned triumphant.

Robert Wilson: I would like to think now that I, at the time of the German defeat, that I would have stopped, taken stock, thought it all over very carefully, and that I would have walked away from Los Alamos at that time. And I, in terms of all of my ... everything that I believe in, before and during and after the war, I cannot understand why I did not take ... make that act. On the other hand, it simply was not in the air. I do not know of a single instance of anyone who had made that suggestion or who did leave at the time. There might have been someone that I didn't know, but at the time, it just was not something that was part of our lives. Our life was directed to do one thing; it was as though we had been programmed to do that, and we, as automatons, were doing it.

Frank Oppenheimer: It is amazing how the technology tools trap one. I mean, they're so powerful. I was impressed, because most of the sort of fervour for developing the bomb came (from) kind of an anti-fascist fervour against Germany. But when VE Day came along, nobody slowed up one little bit. No one said, 'Ah well now, the main thing. It doesn't matter now.' We all kept working, and it wasn't because we understood the significance against Japan. It was because the machinery had caught us in the trap, and we were anxious to get this thing to go.

Robert Wilson: I organized a small meeting at our building. The title was 'The impact of the gadget on civilization'. Oppie tried to persuade me not to have it. I don't know quite why, but he certainly didn't try to dissuade me. On the other hand, I went ahead and did hold the meeting. And perhaps between 30 and 50 people came. Oppie came too, which added a certain ... always added tone to any meeting. We did discuss whether we should go on or not. And in the context of what was happening in the world. But, of course, it was called in the context that perhaps what we were doing was morally wrong. Particularly Oppie pointed out that it would be well that the world knew about the possibility of an atomic bomb rather than that something would be kept secret while the United Nations was being formed. On that basis, that logical basis, we all decided that that was right and that we ought to go back in the laboratory and work as hard as we could to demonstrate nuclear weapon before the ... and so that the United Nations would be set up in the awareness of this horrible thing to come.

Freeman Dyson: The Faustian bargain is when you sell your soul to the devil in exchange for knowledge and power. And that, of course, in a way is what Oppenheimer did, there's no doubt. He made this alliance with the United States Army in the person of General Groves, who gave him undreamed-of resources, huge armies of people and as much money as he could possibly spend in order to do physics on the grand scale in order to create this marvellous weapon. And it was a Faustian bargain if ever there was one. And, of course, we are still living with it ever since. When once you sell your soul to the devil then there's no going back on it.

Extract from: *Oppenheimer*

SB, p. 64	*Oppenheimer:*	Kitty?
	Scientist 1:	Hallo, Oppie.
	Scientist 2:	Mrs Oppenheimer just stepped out for a while. She said it'd be OK if we waited for you.
	Oppenheimer:	Is this a social call, or a delegation?
	Scientist 1:	We wanted to see you, Oppie. A number of us are concerned about the future.
	Scientist 2:	Are we really gonna hit the Japs with this thing?
	Oppenheimer:	Ah, this is what General Groves calls a Chicago disease.
	Scientist 2:	No, it isn't a Chicago. It's a lot of us here aren't happy.
	Scientist 1:	Have you read any of the reports from the metallurgy lab yet?
	Oppenheimer:	I've read them.
	Scientist 1:	What do you think?
	Oppenheimer:	I just got back from Trinity. Second trip this week.
	Scientist 2:	How's it looking?
	Oppenheimer:	Very good. Well, this bothers you too, Edward?
	Edward:	Very much.
	Oppenheimer:	All right, I've read the reports. I think their proposals on the international control of atomic energy are very interesting. I've made some proposals of my own on that subject, as you know.
	Scientist 1:	Yes, but what about the immediate question? How to use the bomb?
	Scientist 2:	Or whether to? Surely the two questions are linked. If we use the bomb, a weapon will be developed in secret without warning then we'll have no moral basis after the war to call for international control.
	Oppenheimer:	You know, I never heard any of these arguments when Germany was the target.
	Scientist 2:	Is that suprising?
	Oppenheimer:	No, I suppose not.
	Scientist 1:	Oh, Jesus, Oppie, we know the Japanese don't have any kind of atomic programme.
	Oppenheimer:	As a matter of a fact they do.
	Scientist 1:	Oh, come on!
	Oppenheimer:	But it hasn't gotten anywhere.
	Scientist 2:	We're very worried about this, Oppie.
	Scientist 1:	Look, the heart of it is there seems to be no intention to consult us on the use of the bomb.
	Oppenheimer:	Personally, I've never been able to see any sense in trying to decide whether or not to use the bomb till we knew if we had it, and we don't know that yet. We won't know until after Trinity.
	Scientist 1:	Well there's no doubt about the uranium. We know Little Boy will go.
	Oppenheimer:	I'm glad to hear that. Look, I think you may be exaggerating the kind of influence we have. Particularly with these reports and petitions. With all due respect for the people in Chicago, I don't think Washington pays very much attention to petitions. Now I can tell you this: Secretary Stimpson has asked that a scientific advisory panel meet with him soon to talk about these questions. I'm on it. Fermy's on it, Ernest Lawrence and Arthur Compton will be there from Chicago. Now that's where I think something can be accomplished, face to face, at the top.
	Edward:	And you'll be putting our case?

Oppenheimer:	I don't know what I'll say until I know what I'm asked. But, you all know me. We've worked together a long time, and I know your views. Don't you feel you can trust me?
Scientist 2:	Yes. We ought to have known you'd be with us; we shouldn't have troubled you.
Oppenheimer:	No, no, no. I'm very glad you came.
Scientist 2:	Well ...
Oppenheimer:	I think you have to accept the fact that this is not just a scientific decision. It's political and military.
Scientist 1:	But you will be going to Washington?
Oppenheimer:	Yes, I'll be there.
Scientist 2:	Well, that's good.
Scientist 1:	Thanks, Oppie. Night.
Edward:	I wanted to see you specially. I got this today from Leo Szillard. It's a petition. He thinks he might be able to get this one to Truman and it might be my name would add some weight.
Oppenheimer:	Yes, I think it certainly might.
Edward:	What do you think?
Oppenheimer:	What do you want me to tell you, Edward?
Edward:	I want your advice. It would mean a great deal to me to hear what my director has to say about this.
Oppenheimer:	Well, I'll tell you the truth. I think these people in Chicago are being naive. Are we really the only ones that see the important issues here? Are we the only ones that are specially qualified to judge? I think maybe these decisions belong in the hands of those that were elected to make them.
Edward:	So you don't think I should sign?
Oppenheimer:	I don't think scientists should get mixed up in politics.
Edward:	No. No. It's a terrible responsibility. Good night, Oppie.

CD **Wernher von Braun**

SB, p. 64 And what is it that put America in the forefront of the nuclear nations? And what is it that will make it possible to spend 20 billion dollars of your money to put some clown on the moon? Well, it was good old American know-how, that's what, as provided by good old Americans like Dr. Wernher von Braun.

Gather round while I sing you of Wernher von Braun,
A man whose allegiance is ruled by expedience.
Call him a Nazi, he won't even frown:
'Nazi, schmazi!'
Says Wernher von Braun.

Don't say that he's hypocritical.
Say rather that he's apolitical.
'Once rockets are up, who cares where they come down!
That's not my department,'
Says Wernher von Braun.

Some have harsh words for this man of renown
But some think our attitude should be one of gratitude,
Like the widows and cripples in old London town,
Who owe their large pensions
To Wernher von Braun.

You too may be a big hero,
Once you've learned to count backwards to zero:
'In German oder English, I know how to count down
Und I'm learning Chinese,'
Says Wernher von Braun.

© 1965, Tom Lehrer. Used by permission.

CD # Getting Along in English

SB, p. 65
Task 2
Dialogue 1

Doctor:	Hello, Jill. And what can I do for you this morning?
Jill:	Hello, Dr James. Well, I have a terrible cold and I don't seem to be able to get rid of it.
Doctor:	A cold? What symptoms do you have?
Jill:	Well, I have a runny nose and I sneeze a lot.
Doctor:	Have you had a temperature?
Jill:	Er ... no. No, I don't think so. But my eyes itch a lot.
Doctor:	And what about headaches: any headaches?
Jill:	No, no headaches, doctor.
Doctor:	Open your mouth and let's have a look at your throat.

Dialogue 2

Doctor:	Good afternoon, Mr Martin.
Mr Martin:	Good afternoon, doctor.
Doctor:	Well now, what seems to be the problem?
Mr Martin:	It's my right ankle, doctor. I was playing badminton last Thursday and I landed rather badly and hurt my ankle.
Doctor:	Last Thursday!
Mr Martin:	Yes, well I thought it would get better by itself. Oh, it hurt all right, but not so badly that I couldn't walk. So I just carried on.
Doctor:	And why have you come now?
Mr Martin:	Well, doctor, the pain is getting worse and the ankle is quite swollen.
Doctor:	Well, hop up onto the bed and let me take a look.

Dialogue 3

Doctor:	Good morning ... er, Miss Schmidt.
Miss Schmidt:	Good morning.
Doctor:	Are you on holiday here in Bristol?
Miss Schmidt:	No, I'm working as an au pair ... with the Bladon family.
Doctor:	Ah, the Bladons. Yes, of course. Well, how can I help you, Miss Schmidt?
Miss Schmidt:	Well, it's this cut, doctor ... here on my hand.
Doctor:	Oh dear, how did that happen?
Miss Schmidt:	I took the children to the park for a picnic and they got the fruit knife dirty. I was trying to clean it, but it slipped in my hand and this happened. I wouldn't have come to the surgery, but in the night it began to throb and it looks a bit red this morning.
Doctor:	Yes ... When did you last have a tetanus injection, Miss Schmidt?
Miss Schmidt:	Oh, a long time ago, I think.

Dialogue 4

Doctor:	Evening, Michael. We haven't seen you at the surgery for a while.
Michael:	No, I'm glad to say! Hi, doc.
Doctor:	And what brings you now?
Michael:	Well, it's probably nothing, but I keep getting these awful stomach pains.
Doctor:	Where does it hurt?
Michael:	Around here …
Doctor:	And how long have you been having the pains?
Michael:	Oh, for about the last four weeks.
Doctor:	And are there any other symptoms – nausea, diarrhoea?
Michael:	No diarrhoea, but I do sometimes feel a little nauseous.
Doctor:	Well, take off your shoes and T-shirt and lie down on the bed and I'll have a look at you.

SB, p. 65
Task 4a

Dialogue 1

Doctor:	Well, Jill, I can't see any signs of an infection. But I have an idea what the problem might be. Tell me, is there any time of day when your symptoms are particularly bad?
Jill:	It's funny you should ask that, doctor. I always wake up with a sneezing fit at around five o'clock in the morning.
Doctor:	Just as I thought. You're not suffering from a common cold, Jill, you've got hay fever.
Jill:	Hay fever?
Doctor:	Yes. It's an allergy to various pollens. And pollen is particularly active first thing in the morning. Now, what we'll have to do in the winter is test you to find out which pollens you're allergic to. But right now I can alleviate your symptoms with some very effective medication. I'll write you a prescription for pills and a nose spray. OK?

Dialogue 2

Doctor:	OK, Mr Martin, you can put your shoes and socks on again. There's nothing broken, I'm happy to say, but I think it's a nasty sprain. So, I'm going to send you to the nurse so that she can strap the ankle up properly. And when you get home you should keep your foot elevated – you know, up – as much as possible. Have you got any pain killers at home?
Mr Martin:	Yes, paracetamol, that sort of thing.
Doctor:	That should be fine. If the pain gets too bad, take a paracetamol. And whenever you can, take the weight off that ankle and put the foot up. OK?

Dialogue 3

Doctor:	Well, the cut doesn't need stitches, but I'm afraid it's definitely infected. Now, the first thing I want to do is give you a tetanus jab …
Miss Schmidt:	Jab?
Doctor:	Sorry, that's an injection. We need to give you a booster, an injection to renew your protection against tetanus. Then the nurse will dress the wound, she'll clean it and bandage it. And I'll prescribe some antibiotics. Do you have any allergies?
Miss Schmidt:	Yes, I'm allergic to penicillin.
Doctor:	Right. Take this to the chemist and start taking the pills right away. And I'd like to see you again tomorrow.

Dialogue 4

Doctor:	Right, Michael, you can get dressed again.
Michael:	Do you think it's anything serious, doc?
Doctor:	Probably not, but I'd like to keep an eye on you. I think it may be a rumbling appendix.
Michael:	A what?!
Doctor:	A rumbling appendix – that's an appendix that's hurting a bit, but isn't ready to be taken out. They usually settle down again pretty quickly. But, as I said, I'd like to keep an eye on you. If your symptoms haven't gone in a week, I'd like you to come back and then we'll have to organize some tests.

SB, p. 65
Task 4b

Dialogue 1

Jill:	What's in the pills? I mean, are they antibiotics?
Doctor:	No, no. They're antihistamines. No side effects.
Jill:	Don't they make you sleepy?
Doctor:	Not any more. They've improved them a lot over the last few years.
Jill:	And how often do I take the pills, doctor?
Doctor:	Once, when you get up in the morning. If the hay fever gets any worse, you can take another pill before going to bed.
Jill:	And what about the nose spray?
Doctor:	Three times a day.
Jill:	And what are the tests you were talking about?
Doctor:	Well, when the hay fever season is over, we can do some tests that tell us what exactly you're allergic to. And then we may be able to give you a course of injections that mean, over a couple of years, we may be able to cure you.
Jill:	Right. Well, thank you very much, doctor. Bye-bye.
Doctor:	Bye. Next patient, please.

Dialogue 2

Mr Martin:	How long do you think it will be till I can play badminton again, doctor?
Doctor:	Let's leave the ankle strapped up for a week, and then we'll see.
Mr Martin:	The thing is, I'm playing in a tournament at the end of the month. Do you think I'll be fit by then?
Doctor:	I'd be hopeful, but I can't give you any guarantees.
Mr Martin:	And while the ankle's strapped up, can I walk around normally?
Doctor:	It depends what 'normally' is. You should try and put as little strain on it as possible. Especially if you want to play in that tournament!
Mr Martin:	OK, doctor. I'll be good! Thank you.

Dialogue 3

Miss Schmidt:	I like to take as little medicine as possible, doctor. In Germany I go to a homeopathic doctor.
Doctor:	Well, I really must advise you most strongly to have the tetanus jab. And, I personally can only prescribe you these antibiotics as I'm not a homeopathist.
Miss Schmidt:	Do you know of a homeopathist?
Doctor:	If you ask my receptionist, she'll be able to help you there. But I must emphasize that there is an infection there and that something must be done about it quickly. These antibiotics don't have any known side effects, you know.
Miss Schmidt:	And how long would I have to take them?

Doctor:	You would have to take a full course – that's the whole packet: it lasts seven days.
Miss Schmidt:	What could happen if I don't take the pills?
Doctor:	The infection could spread – you might get blood poisoning. That's really serious.
Miss Schmidt:	OK, then I had better take the prescription. Thank you for your patience, doctor.

Dialogue 4

Michael:	If it is a … 'rumbling appendix', will I need an operation?
Doctor:	Well, you may need to have the appendix removed at some time.
Michael:	Is that a big operation?
Doctor:	It's a routine operation these days, but it would probably mean five days in hospital.
Michael:	And what tests would you do if the symptoms don't get better?
Doctor:	Well, I'd do some blood tests, and if we still didn't have an answer, I'd send you to the hospital for maybe an X-ray and a scan.
Michael:	Does a scan hurt?
Doctor:	No, not at all. It's a bit noisy, but it doesn't hurt.
Michael:	And what do I do if the pain gets worse now?
Doctor:	If the pain gets worse or you suffer any nausea, then you must come straight back to the surgery, OK? And if it's at night, go to the Accident and Emergency department of your nearest hospital.
Michael:	OK. Thanks, doctor.

Dieses Kapitel behandelt die Themen Natur und Umwelt. Dabei stehen nicht die häufig mit dem Begriff *Umwelt* verbundenen Themen wie Naturzerstörung, globale Umweltprobleme und Bemühungen um den Umweltschutz im Vordergrund. Vielmehr ist es zentrales Anliegen des Kapitels, den S die emotionale Bindung des Menschen an die Natur ins Bewusstsein zu rücken, aus der sich sinnvollerweise sein Interesse am Erhalt der Natur ergibt.

Das Kapitel ist folgendermaßen strukturiert:

– Section 1, „Where the Cricket Sings", bietet Beispiele für die Beziehung des Menschen zur Natur aus verschiedenen Genres und unterschiedlichen Epochen.

– Section 2, „What Happened during the Ice Storm", illustriert anhand einer Kurzgeschichte die Sensibilität junger Menschen im Umgang mit der Natur.

→ WB, ex. 9, 10

– Section 3, „Earth Awareness", betrachtet die Themen Umweltbewusstsein und ökologisches Engagement aus verschiedenen Perspektiven.

Didaktisches Inhaltsverzeichnis

SB, p.	Title	TM, p.	Text form	Topic	Skills and activities
74	Lead-in	136	poem drawing	humans and nature	analysing a poem; analysing a drawing; thinking up a title for a picture; comparing a poem and a picture
76	The Lake at Petworth J.M.W. Turner	139	painting	nature as depicted in art	describing and analysing a picture; presenting a landscape
77	The Lake Isle of Innisfree William Butler Yeats	140	poem	nature as a refuge from everyday stress	interpreting a poem; comparing a poem with a picture
77	It Was a Lover and His Lass William Shakespeare	142	song	lovers lying in a field in spring	interpreting a poem; comparing a song with a picture and a poem
78	Nice Places Willy Russell	143	drama	a young girl thinking about her surroundings	examining a character's feelings; analysing language; writing an informal letter
78	Country of Our Time CD1, track 29	144	radio documentary	various reflections on the importance of the environment for our well-being	listening to a radio programme; comparing views on the environment
79	Getting Along in English CD2, tracks 1–5	146	–	–	planning a trip; asking for information; making conversation
80	What Happened during the Ice Storm Jim Heynen	146	short story	the reaction of youngsters to animals in distress	summarizing a story; describing how one's senses reacted to a story; analysing images; analysing an author's style; doing a hot seating activity
82	Context Box	149	–	nature and the environment	working with vocabulary; writing a fact sheet
83	Too Much Trouble? Erin Jackson	149	essay	the problems involved in saving the planet	listing information from the text; explaining information; giving one's own opinion; doing research for a project
84	What Is 'Eden' about? Tony Kendle	151	brochure article	the Eden project	writing interview questions; doing research

85	Economists Are Also Environmentalists Paul Krugman	152	essay	why saving the environment is good for the economy	writing a summary; evaluating the effectiveness of an argument; doing a role play
87	Cartoons Dealing with the Environment	155	cartoon	environmental issues	describing a cartoon; doing an information gap activity
88	The Destruction of Habitats Video/DVD	155	documentary film	the destructive effect of humans on the habitats of other species	listening comprehension; identifying film elements
89	Watch Your Language	157	–	gerund and *to*-infinitive	

Lead-in

SB, S. 74

Didaktisch-methodische Hinweise

Das „Lead-in" besteht aus drei Teilen: der vorbereitenden Wortschatzarbeit, dem *shape poem* und der Radierung Magrittes. Sie dienen der Sensibilisierung der S für die Schönheit und Gefährdung der Natur und der lexikalischen Vorentlastung von Diskussionen zu Umweltthemen. Das *shape poem* beschreibt in hypothetischem Perspektivwechsel („If the Earth Were …") Einzigartigkeit und Schutzbedürftigkeit der Erde. Im Gegensatz dazu wirkt Magrittes Bild mit seinem Surrealismus (die Wurzel hält die Axt, die den Baum fällte) bedrückend und verstörend – ein Eindruck, der sich angesichts des gesunden Baumes auf dem Farbfoto darüber noch verstärkt.

Unterrichts-tipps

Als Einstieg in das „Lead-in" sollte Aufgabe 1 bearbeitet werden. Im Anschluss können von S oder L mitgebrachte Bilder über Natur und Umwelt als weitere Impulse für das in Aufgabe 2 geforderte Mind-Map fungieren. Es empfiehlt sich, die S hinsichtlich der Wortschatzkategorien zu steuern, da diese im Verlauf des Kapitels immer wieder aufgegriffen und erweitert werden sollen (vgl. Lösungshinweise).

→ *WB, ex. 2*

Lösungs-hinweise

1 **a** Skiing, snowmobiling, walking, trekking, snorkeling, bungee jumping, playing football, gardening, orienteering, diving, mountaineering, dunebuggying, cycling, skating, jogging, canoeing, sailing, rafting, etc.

b Possible answers:
Gardening: can add to diversity of plant life, leads to release of oxygen, can create biospheres for different animals, e.g. piling up leaves for hedgehogs to spend the winter; but it can also be harmful if one uses too many pesticides in the garden, thereby killing small animals.
Diving: brings in tourist revenue, which encourages authorities to take care of reefs, etc.; but it can also disturb marine life and destroy coral reefs if tourists insist on taking pieces of coral home.

c Individual answers.

 2 „Offene" Mind-Maps, die ständig ergänzt werden sollen, erfordern viel Platz, den die S vorher kaum abschätzen können. Daher werden Mind-Maps bei ihrer Erweiterung oft unübersichtlich oder unsauber. Für das hier im Unterricht entwickelte Mind-Map könnten als Hausaufgabe die jeweiligen Kategorien (z.B. *fauna, flora, climate, landscape, activities of animals, activities of people, global problems*) mit dem dazugehörigen Wortschatz auf Karteikarten oder Blätter übertragen und so fortgeführt werden.

Individual answers.

If the Earth   Joe Miller

Source:	*If the Earth were ...*, 1998
Topic:	The beauty of the planet Earth
Text form:	Poem
Language variety:	AE
Number of words:	192
Level:	Basic
Skills/activities:	Analysing a poem, comparing a poem with a picture

Lern-
vokabular

Active vocabulary: 'If the Earth' (p. 74)

diameter, marvel at sth., layer, creature, surface, sacred, heal sb./sth., gain knowledge

Didaktisch-
methodische
Hinweise

Das im Jahr 1975 geschriebene, sehr populäre Gedicht wurde erst 1998 veröffentlicht. Mit seiner einfachen Sprache und seiner leicht verständlichen und auf andere Lebensbereiche übertragbaren Aussage (durch Perspektivveränderung lasse sich das Wesentliche und Wertvolle eines Objekts, hier der Erde, leichter erkennen) bietet es einen leichten Einstieg in die Thematik. Die S werden aufgefordert, den im Gedicht vorgenommenen Perspektivwechsel nachzuvollziehen und sich die Schönheit der Erde vor Augen zu führen. Gleichzeitig veranlasst sie das Hypothetische („If") des Gedichts, den unausgesprochenen Gedanken fortzuführen und zu fragen, wie die Menschen die Erde tatsächlich betrachten und behandeln – eine Anspielung auf Respektlosigkeit und Naturzerstörung, die bei Magritte (s.u.) ihre Fortführung findet.

Unterrichts-
tipps

Sollte der Begriff *shape poem* den S nicht bekannt sein, kann er mit Hilfe des Glossars (SB, S. 256) eingeführt werden. Da das Gedicht keine größeren Hürden aufweist, kann nach der Lektüre mit der Bearbeitung der Aufgaben begonnen werden.

Lösungs-
hinweise

3   He probably wrote it as a shape poem so that the circular shape would reflect the shape of the earth. The poem's form reflects its subject.

4   **a**   The main themes of the poem are:
– the idea of the world as an object floating above a field (ll. 1–5);
– the geography of the earth (ll. 5–8);
– the atmosphere and climate (ll. 8–9);
– the animals on the surface and in the water (ll. 9–11);
– the reaction of the people to the earth (ll. 11–20).

b   The main image is of the earth as a ball. It may be considered a little banal, since the earth in fact has the shape of a ball and this is an observation hardly worth stating. The image may, however, be considered highly effective, since the poem is about how a change in perspective alters the appreciation of an object.

5   It is <u>a poem</u>, as it has strong imagery; it is divided into lines; it makes use of repetition (cf. opening and closing lines, 'people would ...', ll. 5, 7, 'the people would ...', ll. 9, 11), enumeration ('to pray ..., to be healed, to gain knowledge, to know beauty and to wonder ...', ll. 14–16).
It is <u>not a poem</u>, as it has no real rhymes; it consists simply of prose sentences divided randomly into lines in a shape.

Picture by René Magritte

Topic:	Nature's reaction to its destruction by humans
Text form:	Etching
Level:	Basic/advanced
Skills/activities	Describing an illustration, thinking up a title for a picture, comparing a poem with a picture

Didaktisch-methodische Hinweise

Magrittes Radierung „Les Travaux d'Alexandre" („The Labours of Alexander") stellt einen Baumstumpf dar. Der abgeholzte Baum scheint jedoch nicht tot zu sein, denn eine seiner Wurzeln hält offensichtlich die Axt fest, die ihn fällte. Es bleibt dem Betrachter offen, darüber zu spekulieren, was sie damit tun wird. Schlägt sie zurück als Rache an den Menschen, die den Baum abgeholzt haben? Verteidigt sie andere Bäume? Oder, noch surrealistischer, hat sich der Baum selbst umgebracht? Nachdem die S das Bild detailliert beschrieben haben, suchen sie nach einem geeigneten Titel und steigen so in eine Diskussion über seine Aussage ein.

Info

René Magritte (1898–1967) was a surrealist Belgian painter. Magritte developed a style in which he combined realism with irony and juxtaposition. His works often contain elaborate fantasies constructed around commonplace situations and frequently deal with human isolation.

Lösungs-hinweise

6 **a** The picture is a black-and-white etching. It shows a tree stump. The tree has apparently been recently chopped down because one can still see some wood chips around the stump. One of the roots of the tree is growing over an axe which is lying on the ground, as if holding it down.

b The actual title of the picture is 'Les Travaux d'Alexandre' ('The labours of Alexander').

7 Similar: Both deal with humanity's relationship with nature.
Different: The poem uses a positive image to get its point across: one of the earth in miniature, and how this would make people want to protect it; the picture shows the destructive effect of humans on the environment, and implies that nature will take revenge.

1 Where the Cricket Sings

Viele Menschen assoziieren Natur mit Ruhe, Frieden und Harmonie. Für andere ist sie der Inbegriff von Langeweile und Ereignislosigkeit. In dieser *section* begegnen die S vier unterschiedlichen Materialien, in denen ein vielschichtiges Naturbild entworfen wird: einem Gemälde und einem Gedicht aus dem 19. Jahrhundert, einem Lied aus einer Shakespeare-Komödie, Auszüge aus einem Drama und einer Radiosendung vom Ende des 20. Jahrhunderts. Turners Landschaftsbild schafft eine idyllische Abendatmosphäre. Yeats zeichnet die Natur als Ort der Erinnerung und Sehnsucht im Kontrast zur Stadt. Shakespeare besingt das einfache, sinnenfrohe Landleben im Kreislauf der Jahreszeiten. Russell thematisiert die unerfüllte Sehnsucht der unterprivilegierten Schichten in Ballungsräumen nach einem grünen Wohnumfeld. Der Auszug aus einer Radiosendung diskutiert die Begrünung großer städtischer Flächen.

→ WB, ex. 1, 3

A The Lake at Petworth   J.M.W. Turner

Topic:	Nature as depicted in art
Text form:	Painting
Level:	Basic/advanced
Skills/activities:	Describing and analysing a picture, presenting a landscape

*Lern-
vokabular*

Active vocabulary: 'The Lake at Petworth' (p. 76)

tasks: convey sth., achieve sth., artificial

*Didaktisch-
methodische
Hinweise*

Das hier abgebildete Gemälde von J.M.W. Turner soll die S dazu anregen, seine Natur-darstellung detailliert zu beschreiben und im nachfolgenden Projekt ihre individuellen Reaktionen auf einen selbst gewählten Ort darzustellen. Der didaktische Schwerpunkt dieser *section* liegt auf der Erweiterung des Wortschatzes im Hinblick auf Naturdarstel-lungen und durch Naturerlebnisse hervorgerufene Emotionen.

*Unterrichts-
tipps*

Da viele S zu dieser Thematik einen begrenzten Wortschatz haben, empfiehlt sich be-sonders die Arbeit mit den empfohlenen *skills*-Seiten und dem Wörterbuch.

Info

J(oseph) M(allord) W(illiam) Turner (1775–1851) was the foremost English romantic landscape painter and one of the founders of English watercolour painting. He received almost no general education, but by the time he was 18 he had his own studio and was making topographical drawings for magazines. By his early 20s the sale of his work was successful enough for him to be able to devote himself to the visionary interpretations of landscapes for which he became famous. In 1802, when he was only 27, Turner became a full member of the Royal Academy and began travelling widely in Europe. Turner studied the effects of sea and sky in every kind of weather. His paintings became increasingly abstract as he strove to portray light, space and the elementary forces of nature. Despite his success Turner lived a life of a recluse without any close friends except his father, with whom he lived for 30 years. Among his most famous paintings are 'The Burning of the Houses of Lords and Commons' (1835), 'The Fighting "Temeraire" tugged to her last berth to be broken up' (1838) and 'Rain, Steam and Speed' (1844). Many of his paintings can be seen in the Turner Collection at Tate Britain, London. To see more of his paintings online cf. www.ibiblio.org/wm/paint/auth/turner · 1.8.03.

The Lake at Petworth was painted during a stay at Petworth House in Sussex, the home of one of his patrons. Turner did several paintings of the garden and house. The garden was laid out by the famous landscape gardener 'Capability' Brown.

*Lösungs-
hinweise*

1   The painting shows a lake. Around the lake are trees and in the distance there seem to be hills. The sun, which is situated in the centre of the picture, is either just rising or just setting. The atmosphere is one of tranquility and natural harmony.
The artist achieves this effect by using very soft, gentle, warm colours and by making all the outlines very soft (e.g. the contours of trees and the shoreline are blurred); nothing is sharp and precise. The light from the sun is reflected in the nature and also seems soft and warm.

2   Individual answers

❖ ⬭ Die folgende Aufgabe kann in Kleingruppen bearbeitet werden, wenn die S kleinformatige Bilder mitbringen. So kann der Sprachumsatz aller S gesteigert werden.

Bring to class a favourite landscape painting (either as a poster or a postcard). Describe it in detail and explain the atmosphere the artist is trying to convey. Give information about the artist and the period as well.

❖ **3** Bei dieser Aufgabe sind folgende Verfahren denkbar: Die S arbeiten einzeln oder in Kleingruppen an ihrer Präsentation und stellen sie in Gruppen oder aber vor dem Plenum vor. Die S suchen zunächst einen Ort aus, zu dem sie eine emotionale Verbindung haben, z.B. einen Park, einen Sportplatz, das Schulumfeld, aber auch eine laute Straßenkreuzung, eine zubetonierte Einkaufsstraße usw. Von diesem Ort erfassen sie tabellarisch Fakten und Eindrücke, die sie ggf. mit Hilfe eines Wörterbuchs so genau wie möglich beschreiben. Dazu können sie Fotos, Skizzen oder Videoaufnahmen machen. Dieses Material nutzen sie für eine Präsentation (ein Plakat, eine Mappe, einen kurzen Videofilm bzw. eine Powerpoint-Präsentation). Sie beschreiben die Bilder bzw. das Videomaterial detailliert und drücken ihre persönliche Beziehung zu diesem Ort aus (die keinesfalls positiv sein muss). Besonders effektvoll wirkt die Präsentation, wenn sie mit passender Musik oder Geräuschen unterlegt wird. Abschließend erfolgt eine Auswertung, bei der sich andere S zu den gezeigten Orten äußern können. Die Plakate und Mappen können im Klassenraum ausgestellt werden.

SB, S. 77 **B The Lake Isle of Innisfree**   William Butler Yeats

CD

Source:	*The Rose*, 1893
Topic:	Nature as a refuge from everyday stress
Text form:	Poem
Language variety:	BE
Number of words:	132
Level:	Basic/advanced
Skills/activities:	Interpreting a poem, comparing a poem with a picture

Lern-vokabular

Active vocabulary: 'The Lake Isle of Innisfree' (p. 77)

hive (l. 3), veil (l. 6), glow (l. 7), shore (l. 10), pavement (l. 11)
tasks: support sth., quote, feature sth., reflect sth.

Didaktisch-methodische Hinweise

In diesem Gedicht von W. B. Yeats beschreibt das lyrische Ich einen *locus amoenus*, einen schön gelegenen Ort, an dem es Frieden sucht und sich Ruhe vor dem lauten Alltag erhofft. Allerdings wird dieser Ort nur in der Imagination als Ziel aller Wünsche heraufbeschworen. Natur erscheint als Ort der Sehnsucht, der im Alltag Kraft gibt. Auch wenn vielleicht nicht alle S den Wunsch nachvollziehen können, aus der Stadt in die Natur zu fliehen, werden sie Situationen kennen, in denen sie sich weit fort von dem Ort wünschen, an dem sie sich befinden. Die Zusatzaufgabe betont diesen persönlichen Aspekt. Strukturell ist das Gedicht ein gutes Beispiel für das Zusammenspiel von Inhalt und Form (hier dem Rhythmus). Die Abweichung des Sprechryhthmus vom Metrum in der jeweils ersten Hälfte der Zeilen illustriert den Wunsch des lyrischen Ich nach Aufbruch, während das ruhigere Versmaß in der zweiten Zeilenhälfte den erläuternden Anmerkungen angemessen ist (vgl. auch die Lösungshinweise zu Aufgabe 2 und „Info").

Unterrichts-tipps

Als Einstieg können die S das Foto auf der Seite betrachten und überlegen, welche Gründe jemand haben könnte, dort leben zu wollen. Danach spielt L das Gedicht (vgl. CD1, *track* 27) bei geschlossenen Büchern vor. Während die S beim ersten Hören nur versuchen, ein allgemeines Textverständnis zu erlangen, schreiben sie beim zweiten Hören Notizen zum Inhalt des Gedichts und bereiten so Aufgabe 1 vor. Für ein tieferes Textverständnis sollte der Text gelesen werden. Um den Effekt des Rhythmus als poetisches Stilmittel selbst zu erfahren, werden die S zum lauten Vortragen des Gedichts angeregt.

→ WB, ex. 4

Info

William Butler Yeats [jeɪts] (1865–1939) was born in Ireland but was brought up in London and only returned to live in Ireland in 1881, although the summers of his childhood were often spent in the west of Ireland. He studied at the Metropolitan School of Art in Dublin, where he became interested in mysticism, a subject that fascinated him for the rest of his life. In 1887 the family returned to London, and Yeats devoted himself to writing. At the heart of much of his poetry lies Ireland, its history, folklore and contemporary politics. In 1897 he met Lady Gregory, with whom he founded the Irish Literary Theatre. Yeats worked as a director of the theatre for the rest of his life, writing several plays for it. His most famous dramas were *Cathleen Houlihan* (1902) and *The Land of Heart's Desire* (1894). Although a convinced nationalist, Yeats deplored the intolerance of the national movement. He was appointed to the Irish Senate in 1922. In 1932 Yeats founded the Irish Academy of Letters and in 1933 he was briefly involved with the fascist Blueshirts in Dublin. He received the Nobel Prize for Literature in 1923. Yeats died in France.

'The Lake Isle of Innisfree' is one of his best-known early poems. It came to mind when he heard the tinkling sound of water from a fountain in a shop window in London. It expresses his memory of an islet in Lough Gill (cf. photo on p. 77), a lake near the town of Sligo in the west of Ireland He said it was 'my first lyric with anything in its rhythm of my own music'. It was published in his second book of poems, *The Rose* (1893). The poem is written mostly in hexameter, with six feet in each line, in a loosely iambic pattern. The last line of each of the four-line stanzas has only four stresses. The tranquil, hypnotic hexameter recreates a rhythmic pulse similar to the lapping of water (cf. l. 10). Each of the three stanzas has the same a b a b rhyme scheme. The simple imagery of the quiet life the speaker longs to lead makes the reader share the fantasy, until the penultimate line jolts the reader back to the reality of urban life (cf. l. 11).

Lösungs-
hinweise

1 The speaker seems to want a very simple life, alone and close to nature, where he can build his own simple house and grow his own food ('I will arise ... cabin build there', ll. 1–2; 'And I shall have some peace there', l. 5; 'I will arise ... deep heart's core', ll. 9–12).

2 Für diese Aufgabe bietet es sich an, das Gedicht noch einmal von CD vorzuspielen und die S zu bitten, besonders auf den Unterschied zwischen dem ersten und zweiten *Differenzierung* Teil der Zeilen zu achten. Wegen der Abweichungen von einem gleichmäßigen Versmaß sollte eine genaue Versmaßuntersuchung leistungsstarken S vorbehalten sein.

The most important aspect of the rhythm of the poem is the caesura [si'zjʊərə] (the pause in the line of verse). In most lines the first half, before the caesura, has a more urgent, hurried rhythm than the second half (cf. ll. 1–3, in each case the first half being busy and restless, the second half being slower, reflecting the desire for peace.)

3 Es sollte hierbei Wert darauf gelegt werden, dass die S ihre Meinung begründen.

Individual answers.

⬭ *Every day you wake up early and come to school – what place do you dream of to get away from school? Bring photos to the class which depict this place. Explain what this place offers you.*

C It Was a Lover and His Lass   William Shakespeare

Source:	*As You Like It*, 1600
Topic:	Lovers lying in the fields in spring
Text form:	Song
Language variety:	BE
Length:	1:45 min
Level:	Basic/advanced
Skills/activities:	Interpreting a poem, comparing a song with a picture and a poem

Didaktisch-methodische Hinweise

Der Song „It was a Lover and His Lass" (vgl. CD1, *track* 28 und das Transkript auf S. 161) ist Shakespeares Komödie *As You Like It* entnommen und ergänzt das in den ersten beiden Materialien dieser *section* entworfene Naturbild um einen weiteren Aspekt: das sinnenfrohe, ursprüngliche und im Einklang mit den Naturzyklen stehende Treiben der Landbevölkerung. Damit wird auch die Darstellung der Natur als Gegenpol zum ermüdenden Stadtleben mit seinen Intrigen sichtbar, die in Shakespeares Werken häufig zu beobachten ist.

Viele S haben eine distanzierte Ehrfurchtshaltung vor Shakespeare und können sich nicht auf die oft unbeschwerte Fröhlichkeit und Sinnenfreude einlassen, die man besonders in seinen Komödien findet. Daher empfiehlt es sich, mit den S die Einfachheit und Ursprünglichkeit von Thema und Struktur herauszuarbeiten (Wiederholungen von Ausrufen und Versen, Schlichtheit der Sprache und Eindimensionalität des dargestellten Verhaltens). Als Hörfassung dieses Lieds wurde die jazzige Version von Cleo Laine aus dem Jahr 1978 gewählt, um den S deutlich zu machen, dass auch alte Texte ein modernes Publikum ansprechen und immer wieder neu interpretiert werden können.

Unterrichts-tipps

Bevor die S das Lied zum ersten Mal hören, können sie durch folgende Fragen auf die Thematik eingestimmt werden:

○ *What do you associate with a sunny spring day?*
Spring flowers, warm temperatures, fresh air, trees producing buds, a cheerful mood, longer daylight, etc.

○ *Name some popular outdoor activities for a warm spring day.*
A bike tour, a boat trip, walking, playing football, skating, lying in the sun, etc.

Kopiervorlage

Es kann eine zweimalige Präsentation des Liedes erfolgen. Nachdem sich die S einen ersten Eindruck über Stimmung und Thematik des Songs verschafft haben, füllen sie während eines erneuten Hörens die KV „It Was a Lover and His Lass" (vgl. S. 160) zur detaillierten Texterfassung aus.

Info

Shakespeare and music: Music played an important role in Elizabethan life, as it was one of the few forms of entertainment. Many people were able to play instruments, even if they could not read music. Besides the sophisticated madrigals and church music, the streets of London would have echoed with folk music, ballads and love songs. In Shakespeare's native Warwickshire towns and villages would have been more used to folk music and dances. On the stage, too, music played an important role: there was a special musician's gallery above the stage and sometimes the music was played on the stage itself. Shakespeare's comedies are full of songs, which were often accompanied by the lute, while tragedies and histories would have had many fanfares of trumpets and drums. 'The Lover and His Lass' is one of the few songs by Shakespeare whose music, composed by Thomas Morley, has survived.

Info

Pastoral comedies: As You Like It is a pastoral comedy, in which rural life is idealized in contrast to the injustices of court life. As was typical of most pastoral drama, rural life is seen from the perspective of the city dweller, so that the country experience is used as a means of criticizing urban values. It features an interaction between urban sophistication and a simplified version of life away from the city. It suggests that the oppressions of the city can be remedied by a trip into the country's therapeutic woods and fields, and that a person's sense of balance and rightness can be restored by conversations with shepherds and shepherdesses living in uncorrupted harmony with nature. This type of restoration enables the characters to return to the city better people, capable of making the most of urban life. Shakespeare reminds the audience that life in the Forest of Arden, where part of *As You Like It* is set, is a temporary affair. The simplicity of the forest provides shelter from the strains of the court. But it also creates the need for urban sophistication – town and country need each other.

Lösungs-hinweise

CD

1   **a**   Vgl. CD1, *track* 28 und das Transkript auf S. 161.

b It is about two lovers in the countryside, lying in the fields and making love because life is short and it is there to be enjoyed.

2   What it has <u>in common with the picture</u>: Cheerful atmosphere (the sun makes the picture feel warm, just like the easy-going lyrics and music of the poem).
What it has <u>in common with the poem</u>: In both the poem and the song, there are birds which make sounds (the linnet's wings in the poem; the singing of the birds in the song). Also a strong emphasis in both on the role of nature.

What differences are there between the song and either the painting 'The Lake at Petworth' or the poem 'The Lake Isle of Innisfree'?
<u>The painting</u> is more an impression than a representation of nature. There are no people in the painting.

<u>The poem</u> is more thoughtful and pessimistic, as the speaker wants to escape (only scholars know that the Shakespeare song also represents a flight from city life).

In <u>the song</u> the lover and the lass go to the fields together; in the poem the speaker imagines a lonely place where there is no one but himself.

Look at the photo of the Isle of Innisfree on p. 77. What would you do if you were there for the day?

SB, S. 78   **D**   **Nice Places**   Willy Russell

Play extract	
Source:	*Our Day Out*, 1976
Topic:	A young girl thinking about her surroundings
Text form:	Drama
Language variety:	BE
Number of words:	134
Level:	Basic
Skills/activities:	Examining a character's feelings, analysing language, writing an informal letter

Country of Our Time	
Source:	*Country of Our Time*, BBC, 2003
Topic:	Various reflections on the importance of nature for our well-being
Text form:	Radio documentary
Language variety:	BE
Length:	2:55 min
Level:	Basic/advanced
Skills/activities:	Listening to a radio programme, comparing views on the environment

*Lern-
vokabular*

Active vocabulary: 'Nice Places' (p. 78)

sit next to sb. (l. 1), chop sth. down (l. 9)
tasks: based on sth., examine sth., background, advantage

*Didaktisch-
methodische
Hinweise*

Die täglichen Umwelterfahrungen vieler Menschen sind häufig geprägt von Lärm, infrastruktureller Vernachlässigung, Mangel an Grünflächen und Umweltproblemen. Russell stammt selbst aus solch einer Gegend in der Nähe von Liverpool und beschreibt in vielen seiner Stücke die Träume der einfachen Leute. Hier wünscht sich das Mädchen Carol, das in einem heruntergekommenen Viertel lebt, beim Anblick der schönen Landschaft während eines Schulausfluges, selbst einmal in einer Gegend wohnen zu können, in der es Gärten und Bäume gibt – schlicht „nice places", wie sie es nennt.

Anhand dieses Auszuges sollen die S über das Verhältnis Mensch und Natur in der heutigen Zeit nachdenken. Die Analyse der beiden Figuren unter dem Aspekt ihrer gesellschaftlichen Stellung bietet einen Ansatzpunkt, um die These zu diskutieren, dass nur privilegierte Schichten freien Zugang zur Natur haben.

Bei Aufgabe 4 hören die S einen Auszug aus einer Radiosendung der BBC (vgl. CD1, *track* 29 und das Transkript auf S. 161), in der ein Wissenschaftler und verschiedene Anwohner eines Waldstücks über die Rolle der Natur in ihrem unmittelbaren Umfeld sprechen. Einige der Sprecher haben den typischen Akzent der Midlands und sind deshalb möglicherweise für die S nicht leicht zu verstehen, so dass sie den Auszug ggf. mehrfach hören sollten.

*Unterrichts-
tipps*

❖

Als Einstieg in diese Sequenz kann L Bilder von verschiedenen Häusern in unterschiedlichen Wohnumfeldern mitbringen. Empfehlenswert sind Bilder aus dem englischsprachigen Raum, um zugleich landeskundliches Wissen zu wiederholen und zu vermeiden, dass das Umfeld einzelner S zur Diskussion steht. Die S besprechen in Gruppen, welche Wohnmöglichkeit sie für sich, z.B. für eine Wohngemeinschaft, auswählen würden und halten die Gründe für diese Entscheidung fest. Diese Gründe werden nach Bearbeitung der Aufgabe 1 mit Carols Empfindungen verglichen. Als Impulse könnten folgende Wörter vorgegeben werden:

Kind of house: (semi-)detached house, flat (AE: apartment), council house
Location: city/town centre, village, suburb, in the country, council estate, nice/rough/deprived area, green environment
Infrastructure: good facilities for shopping, recreation and education, industrial estates, public transportation etc.
People living there: middle class, working class, agricultural workers
Surroundings: gardens, trees, concrete and bricks
Atmosphere: depressing, welcoming, busy, hectic, calm, relaxed

Bevor die S Aufgabe 4 bearbeiten, sollten die folgenden Wörter semantisiert werden:

urban: of or belonging to a town
boost: thing that helps or encourages sth.

commute: travel to work by car or train, etc.
get bogged down in sth.: get too involved in sth.
jargon: language used by experts on a subject
stroke: Schlaganfall
club together: get together and give money for sth.
woodpecker: Specht
be proposed to: be asked by sb. to marry him or her
Brueghel = Pieter Brueghel the Elder (1525–1569): Flemish Renaissance painter

Info

Willy Russell (born 1947) was born in Whiston near Liverpool. He grew up in a working-class family. At fifteen he left school with little idea of what he wanted to do. Dismayed at the prospect of factory work, he drifted into hairdressing, where after five years he eventually had his own salon. On days that were not busy he would write sketches, poems and songs. He then decided to become a student, and managed to get his school leaving qualifications, after which he trained as a teacher and studied drama. While at teaching college he began writing plays. His plays proved successful, with *Educating Rita* (1980) being made into a film. The play *Our Day Out* was first shown on BBC2 TV. It tells the story of some underprivileged schoolchildren who are taken on a day's outing by their teachers. Despite its humour and celebration of the joys and agonies of growing up, it shows that for many of the children a bleak future awaits them.

Lösungs-hinweise

1 Carol does not like the area she lives in. By comparison with what she wishes, one can gather that she lives in a place similar to the one they are driving through ('horrible', l. 2). She hates the dirt and the fact that there are no trees and gardens where she lives. She dreams of having a 'nice place' when she grows up.

2 **a** Carol makes grammatical mistakes ('I like them nice places', l. 4, 'them places', l. 6; use of personal pronoun instead of possessive determiner); she uses slang ('thingy', l. 4, 'telly', l. 6, 'bommy night', l. 9); she is unable to express what she means clearly, hence she uses lots of words that are imprecise ('thingy', l. 4, 'an' that', l. 4, 'them places', l. 6). Mrs Kay, on the other hand, speaks standard English.

b Together with her description of where she lives, Carol's language reveals that she comes from an uneducated background; she says she needs to learn how to read (cf. l. 11). This would probably mean that her parents have unskilled jobs – in a factory or a shop – or might even be unemployed. Probably the family tend to watch a lot of television.
On the other hand, Mrs Kay, as a teacher, would certainly have been to college or university. She probably reads a lot and it is likely that her parents at least valued education, even if they did not have the chance to get as far as their daughter.

3 Individual answers.

CD

4 Vgl. CD1, *track* 29 und das Transkript auf S. 162. Um sich leichter über den Inhalt verständigen zu können, könnte L die Namen der Sprecher an die Tafel schreiben.

a Both Carol and Gloria William were brought up in industrial cities. Carol's dream is to live somewhere nice with trees and gardens; Gloria has achieved this dream ('it was my goal as a child to come up here and live. And when I eventually achieved that [...], I thought I'd come to heaven.'). They both were aware even as children that one's environment is important for one's well-being.

b A pleasant environment boosts our health and happiness, makes us feel good, reduces stress levels, improves the air we breathe, brings us peace, makes us feel relaxed.

Getting Along in English

In dieser *section* trainieren die S am Beispiel eines Ausflugs in den australischen Regenwald, an der Reisende aus verschiedenen Ländern teilnehmen, ihre interkulturelle Kommunikationsfähigkeit. Die S schulen ihr Hörverstehen unterschiedlicher regionaler Akzente (australisch, amerikanisch, britisch) und lernen, höflich Fragen zu stellen, sich bei jemandem zu bedanken, zu einer Unterhaltung eine kurze Geschichte beizutragen bzw. auf eine solche zu reagieren.

*Unterrichts-
tipps*
Die Dialoge befinden sich auf CD1, *tracks* 30–32, die Transkripte auf S. 163–165. Da die Aufgaben eine thematische Einheit bilden, sollten zumindest Aufgaben 1–2 innerhalb einer Unterrichtsstunde bearbeitet werden. Als Hausaufgabe kann das neue Vokabular geübt werden, das die S bei Aufgabe 5 anwenden sollen.

*Lösungs-
hinweise*
1 Possible things to enquire about: Type of tours, price, what forms of payment are accepted, how long the tours last, what one needs to bring along.
Expressions that make requests and questions sound more polite: 'We were wondering if ...', 'Excuse me, but ...', 'I'm sorry, but ...', 'I'm afraid I ...', 'You don't happen to ...', 'Do you happen to ...?'.

`CD` **2** Der Dialog befindet sich auf CD1, *track* 30, das Transkript auf S. 163.

a–b Individual answers.

`CD` **3** Der Dialog befindet sich auf CD1, *track* 31, das Transkript auf S. 164.

a–b Individual answers.

`CD` **4** Der Dialog befindet sich auf CD1, *track* 32, das Transkript auf S. 165.

Thanking somebody: 'I don't know how we can thank you enough', 'thank you so much', 'thank you very much', 'thanks'.
Intensifiers: 'very', 'absolutely', 'truly'.

5 Individual answers.

2 What Happened during the Ice Storm Jim Heynen

Source:	*The One-Room Schoolhouse*, 1993
Topic:	The reaction of youngsters to animals in distress
Text form:	Short story
Language variety:	AE
Number of words:	289
Level:	Basic/advanced
Skills/activities:	Summarizing a story, describing how one's senses reacted to a story, analysing images, analysing an author's style, doing a hot seating activity

Active vocabulary: 'What Happened during the Ice Storm' (p. 80)

branch (l. 3), glisten (l. 3), livestock (l. 4), barn (l. 4), ditch (l. 7), huddle (l. 12), expect sb. to do sth. (l. 19), pounce on sb./sth. (l. 19), yell (l. 19), barbed-wire fence (ll. 20–21), seed (l. 21), yolk (l. 22), layer (l. 27), shell (l. 30), soak through sth. (l. 32)
tasks: cover sth., reveal sth., behave

Didaktisch-methodische Hinweise

Diese Kurzgeschichte beschreibt, wie wilde Fasane – von einem plötzlichen Schneesturm mit Eisregen überrascht – unweit einer Farm hilflos mit zugefrorenen Augen im Schnee verharren. Damit sind sie leichte Beute für die Bauern. Auch eine Gruppe von Jungen nähert sich den Tieren. Von ihrer Hilflosigkeit berührt, breiten sie jedoch ihre warmen Jacken über die Vögel und laufen zur Farm zurück. Auf sensible und symbolträchtige Weise illustriert diese Episode, wie Jugendliche Mitgefühl und Verantwortung für schwache Kreaturen zeigen und sich vom Verhalten der Erwachsenen distanzieren. Damit wird hier ein ganz anderes Verhältnis von Natur und Mensch dargestellt als in den anderen Texten: Hier ist die Natur, das Wetter, feindlich und lebensbedrohend, während die Jungen positiv, nämlich schützend und gütig und nicht als störende Eindringlinge geschildert werden.

Unterrichts-tipps

Diese Geschichte zeichnet sich durch eine atmosphärisch dichte Darstellungsweise aus, die die S als Leser Kälte und Feindseligkeit der Natur nachempfinden lassen wird. Damit die Sinne der S tatsächlich angesprochen werden, ist der Hinweis in der Einleitung zu beachten, dass die S die Augen schließen und sich die Szene im Detail vorstellen sollen. Eine besondere Wirkung kann der Text entfalten, wenn er von CD vorgespielt wird (vgl. CD1, *track* 33). Da er sprachlich wie inhaltlich einfach ist, sollten die S keine Probleme haben, Aufgabe 1 nach ein- oder mehrmaligem Hören zu lösen.

Der Geschichte ist eine besondere Spannung zu eigen, da lange nicht vorhersehbar ist, was die Jungen wirklich tun werden. Deshalb kann nach Zeile 25 oder nach „Then one of the boys said, ..." (Z. 26) eine Zäsur gesetzt und über den Fortgang spekuliert werden. Weiterhin sollten die S auch das in Aufgabe 2 (vgl. SB, S. 74) begonnene Mind-Map durch Wortmaterial aus diesem Text ergänzen, da sehr viele Wörter aus dem Bereich „Landschaft und Tiere" bzw. „Umwelt" stammen:

Climate/weather: 'ice storm' (title), 'winter' (l. 1), 'freezing rain' (l. 1), 'ice' (l. 2), 'snow' (l. 10), 'icy rain' (l. 13).

Fauna: 'livestock' (l. 4), 'animal' (l. 5), 'pheasant' (l. 5), 'wing' (l. 11), 'yolk' (l. 22), '(egg) white' (l. 22–23), 'unborn bird' (l. 23), 'hen' (l. 31), 'cock' (l. 32).

Flora: 'tree branch' (ll. 2–3), 'stem of grass' (l. 21), 'grass seed' (l. 21).

Human landscape: 'barn' (l. 4), 'gravel road' (l. 6), 'roadside ditch' (l. 7), 'barbed-wire fence' (ll. 20–21), 'fence post' (l. 21), 'slippery field' (l. 33).

Activities: 'harvest sth.' (l. 6), 'slide your feet along' (l. 9), 'break the ice' (l. 10).

Info

Jim Heynen was born and raised on a farm in northwest Iowa in the last county in the state to get electricity, and attended one of the last one-room schoolhouses in the state before going on to high school in Hull, Iowa. He studied English Renaissance Literature at the University of Iowa. After teaching at the University of Michigan, he went to graduate school at the University of Oregon, where he studied creative writing. Heynen has written poems, novels, non-fiction and short stories. His most important collection of short stories, *The One-Room Schoolhouse*, was published in 1993. Concentrating on young adolescent boys in the rural Midwest of several decades ago, it contains over 100 stories, in which Heynes displays his mastery of rural wisdom, speech and behaviour. Other publications include *The Man Who Kept Cigars in His Cap* (1979), *Being Youngest* (1997) and *The Boys' House* (2001).

Lösungs-hinweise

1 Antworten sind auf verschiedenen Abstraktionsniveaus möglich. Der Erwartungshorizont ist im Wesentlichen eine Zusammenfassung; denkbar wäre auch eine Antwort mit den Stichworten *compassion, responsibility towards animals* o.ä.

The story is about a group of boys who go out in the fields to hunt pheasants, which due to the freezing rain have been blinded and are unable to move. When the boys see the helpless creatures, they take off their coats and cover the birds with them.

→ WB, ex. 5

2 **a** Da die S nach dem Lesen oder Hören der Geschichte über ihre Gefühle und Assoziationen berichten sollen, empfiehlt es sich, sie in einer Nachbearbeitungsphase Notizen machen zu lassen. Es könnte hilfreich sein, die Struktur der folgenden Tabelle an die Tafel zu schreiben, die die S ausfüllen. Einige Beispiele sind angegeben:

I saw	I heard	I felt	I smelled	I tasted
lots of snow	the rain as	the cold of the	fresh air	the cold on my
shiny, glistening	it hit the ice	icy day		tongue
branches	cracking ice			

b <u>Sense of sight:</u> 'How beautiful! ... shine with ice' (ll. 1–2), 'tree branches glistened like glass' (ll. 2–3), 'Ice thickened ... blurred' (ll. 3–4), 'their eyes froze shut' (l. 5), 'dark spots along a fence' (l. 8), 'how easy it was to see them' (ll. 11–12), 'slow puffs of steam ... little white puffs' (ll. 13–14), 'blindfolded with ice' (l. 15), 'Things around them ... covered with ice too' (ll. 20–25), 'the thin layer of ice splintering in flakes' (ll. 26–27), 'gray', 'brown' (l. 31), 'blurry lights of the house' (l. 34).

<u>Sense of hearing:</u> 'broke like glass' (l. 3), 'ice-skating down the gravel-roads' (l. 6), 'The boys slid their feet along slowly' (l. 9), 'breath ... puffs' (ll. 13–14), 'to yell Bang!' (l. 19), 'dripping' (l. 20), 'one of the boys said, Shh' (l. 26), 'the thin layer of ice splintering' (ll. 26–27).

<u>Sense of feeling:</u> 'freezing' (ll. 1, 2, 8); 'covered with ice' (ll. 24–25), 'the inside of the coat was dry and warm' (l. 28), 'the boys felt the rain soaking through their shirts and freezing' (ll. 32–33), 'the ice clinging to their skin' (ll. 33–34).

<u>Sense of smell:</u> (no explicit images)

<u>Sense of taste:</u> (no explicit images)
The author depicts a winter landscape, which especially through the senses of sight, hearing and feeling makes the reader able to imagine the landscape and be a part of it. The sensations are limited to ones which most people are familiar with (mostly related to feelings of cold), so the reader may well experience more sensations than the ones explicitly mentioned in the story by fleshing out the story and setting in his or her mind.

3 The author reveals little about the setting. The story takes place in a rural farming community (the only job mentioned is that of the farmers). The reader learns nothing about the boys, neither their names nor ages, nor indeed how many there are. The vagueness in some ways makes the reader feel as if the story is dealing with people and places which he or she already knows, thus drawing him or her into the story. At the same time, it leaves much to the imagination, allowing the reader to complete the story with images of his or her own. The setting and the characters are largely formed then by the reader's own imagination, making him or her partly the creator of the story.

4 Sollten die *interviewer* Hilfestellung zur Formulierung der Fragen benötigen, könnte L einige Anregungen geben, z.B. „What is winter like where you live?", „How did you feel when you were out in the cold?", „Why did you decide to help the pheasants?", „What were you thinking as you went home?", „Did you tell your parents what you did? If so, how did they react?" Alternativ können die Männer aus der Geschichte befragt werden.

Translate ll. 1–12 into German.

Context Box

Schwerpunkte der „Context Box" sind Naturzerstörung, globale Umweltprobleme sowie die Versuche, ihnen entgegenzusteuern. Sie gibt Beispiele für den weltweiten Raubbau an der Natur, aber auch dafür, dass Umweltschutz für viele Menschen eine Selbstverständlichkeit geworden ist. Dennoch besteht auf globaler Ebene großer Handlungsbedarf.

Methodisch eignet sich der Einsatz der „Context Box" im Zusammenhang mit dem „Lead-in", da die S dort bereits eine Themenliste bzw. ein Mind-Map angelegt haben. Sollte die „Context Box" zu einem späteren Zeitpunkt eingesetzt werden, können die Begriffe aus dem „Lead-in" aufgegriffen und erweitert werden.

Unterrichts-
tipps

Der Einstieg kann über die Karikatur erfolgen: Die S beschreiben das dort skizzierte Verhältnis des Menschen zur Natur und nennen weitere Beispiele für eine solche Haltung. Als Überleitung zu Text 3C (vgl. SB, S. 85) oder als Transferaufgabe eignet sich folgende Frage:

→ *WB, ex. 6*

⬭ *Do you think there should be taxes on products that are harmful to the environment?*

Lösungs-
hinweise

1 Individual answers.

2 Living in harmony with nature means: eating wild animals which have been hunted in their own environment, but eating little meat so as not to drive the animals to extinction; gathering plants rather than developing agriculture; not destroying the woodlands or natural landscapes; living in small settlements rather than cities.

3 Individual answers.

3 Earth Awareness

Anhand fünf verschiedener Texte setzen sich die S in dieser *section* mit dem Thema Umweltbewusstsein auseinander und bringen individuelle Sichtweisen ein. Inhaltliche Schwerpunkte sind die nachlassende Bereitschaft, für den Umweltschutz Unannehmlichkeiten auf sich zu nehmen, ein Öko-Projekt und die Vereinbarkeit ökologischen und ökonomischen Denkens. Neben Lesetexten finden sich ein Auszug aus einem Dokumentarfilm, ein Text als Einstieg in eine Internetrecherche und

→ *WB, ex. 8*

Karikaturen, die in einer *information gap activity* bearbeitet werden.

A Too Much Trouble? Erin Jackson

Source:	*Envirozine Online Magazine*, ca. 2002
Topic:	The problems involved in saving the planet
Text form:	Essay
Language variety:	CanE
Number of words:	566
Level:	Basic
Skills/activities:	Listing information from the text, explaining information, giving one's opinion, doing research for a project

Active vocabulary: 'Too Much Trouble?' (p. 83)

become apathetic (l. 8), perform sth. (l. 9), deal with sth. (l. 9), car-pooling (l. 10), recycling (l. 10), be passionate about sth. (l. 10), environmental awareness (l. 13), deplorable (l. 24), passion (l. 26), convenience (l. 28), abandon sth. (l. 32), craving for sth. (l. 37), evident (l. 37), dependence on sth. (ll. 37–38), replace sth. (l. 39), consumerism (l. 41), resources (l. 45)
tasks: loss, take up an interest, consist of sth.

Didaktisch-
methodische
Hinweise

Auch wenn viele Menschen von sich sagen, dass sie Umweltschutz für eine wichtige Sache halten, ist dennoch festzustellen, dass in den letzten Jahren umweltbewusstes Verhalten abnimmt und Menschen sich wieder dazu bekennen, selbst nichts für den Umweltschutz zu tun. Es fehlt oft die Bereitschaft, für Umweltschutz auf Bequemlichkeit oder Konsum zu verzichten, auch wenn auf der Ebene der Politik umweltfreundliche Entscheidungen und Gesetze verlangt werden. In diesem Text beschreibt eine 20-jährige kanadische Studentin aus ihrer Sicht, wie sich die Einstellung zum Umweltschutz verändert hat. Da sie auf Belehrungen oder Vorwürfe verzichtet und sachlich die Werteverlagerung vom Umweltschutz zu Bequemlichkeit darstellt, in der sich viele S wiedererkennen werden, sind die S sicher eher bereit, sich mit dem Text auseinander zu setzen.

Unterrichts-
tipps

Als Einstieg in das Thema bieten sich folgende Fragen an:

What do you understand by 'Earth awareness'? What would you expect from a text with that title?

Do you and your family live an environmentally aware life?

What would you say are some of the problems involved in living in an environmentally friendly way?

Lösungs-
hinweise

1 **a** Erin and her friends did the following: they recycled, compacted cans, flattened boxes, cleaned up the schoolyard, made posters, sang songs about the environment, encouraged others.

b <u>Recycling:</u> This means collecting glass bottles as well as plastics and paper and taking them to bottle banks or recycling bins; from there they are taken to special factories where they are treated in such a way that the materials can be used again.
<u>Compact cans:</u> This means pressing cans together so that they become flat; this saves storage capacity in bins used for collecting tins; therefore the bins do not need to be emptied so often, which saves petrol and thus protects the environment.
<u>Flatten boxes:</u> cf. 'compact cans', above.
<u>Clean the schoolyard:</u> A clean schoolyard looks nicer and gives people pride in their environment. At the same time, toxic substances like nicotine cannot get into the soil.

2 **a** Convenience has become more important than environmental protection, consumerism is more important than caring.

b Possible answers:
It might be considered uncool to take your lunch to school in a box; environmentally friendly products cost more; cleaning a yoghurt cartoon is a hassle; travelling by bike instead of by car or taking bottles to the bottle bank etc. may take up too much time.

c Individual answers.

❖ **3** Zur Vorbereitung auf das Projekt können die S ein Interview mit Julia Butterfly Hill lesen (vgl. http://greenmuseum.org/generic_content.php?ct_id=54 · 1.8.2003). Die S sollten dieses Thema nicht allgemein, sondern auf ihr Umfeld bezogen bearbeiten. Sie können recherchieren, wie in ihrer Stadt oder Gemeinde die „five Rs" beachtet werden, welche Umweltgruppen es gibt usw. In diesem Zusammenhang können sie auch das Sprachmitteln üben (hier das Zusammenfassen deutscher Texte auf Englisch).

◯ *Consumerism is a major factor in the degradation of the earth. Huge amounts of the earth's resources are being used up to produce the things we buy, many of which get thrown away when something 'new' comes along. Discuss ideas how this vicious circle might be interrupted.*

◯ *Translate ll. 5–17 into German.*

SB, S. 84   ## B What Is 'Eden' about?   Tony Kendle

Source:	*Eden, the Guide*, 2001
Topic:	The Eden project
Text form:	Brochure article
Language variety:	BE
Number of words:	123
Level:	Basic
Skills/activities:	Writing interview questions, doing research

Lern-vokabular

Active vocabulary: 'What Is "Eden" about?' (p. 8)

symbol of (l. 1), mankind (l. 1), rejection (l. 2), conservation policy (l. 2), keep sb. out of sth. (l. 4), live in harmony with nature (l. 6), destruction (l. 6), a beneficial effect (l. 7), challenges lie ahead (l. 7), meet a challenge (l. 8)

Didaktisch-methodische Hinweise

Dieser kurze Textauszug dient als Anstoß zu einer Recherche zum *Eden Project*. Was *Eden* konkret ist, welche Aufgaben, Ziele und Organisationsstrukturen es hat, sollen die S selbst mit Hilfe des Internets herausfinden, nachdem sie auf der Grundlage des Texts Fragen formuliert haben. Durch diese *section* wird ihre Fähigkeit geschult, systematisch zu einem Thema zu recherchieren, und so ein Beitrag zum wissenschaftspropädeutischen Arbeiten geleistet: Die S legen fest, welche Fragen sie für klärungsbedürftig halten, bevor sie einer Quelle gezielt Informationen entnehmen. Es ist denkbar, diesen Rechercheauftrag um die Darstellung der Ergebnisse zu erweitern und so die Präsentationsfähigkeit der S zu schulen.
Als Einstieg könnten die S Assoziationen zum Begriff *Eden* sammeln.

Info

The Eden Project is a set of large greenhouses (called 'biomes') containing plants from around the world. Situated east of St. Austell, near Plymouth, it houses more than 100,000 plants. Since many of these are tropical plants, the Eden Project is home to the world's largest greenhouse called the 'Humid Tropics Biome'. One of Eden's aims is to make plants interesting to ordinary people, to inform people about the relationship between humans and plants and explain what importance plants have for us. The Project is owned by The Eden Charitable Trust. More information on the Eden Project can be found at www.edenproject.com · 1.8.03.

Lösungs-hinweise

1 **a–b** Individual answers.

◯ *Design a leaflet that could be handed out to visitors of the Eden Project.*

◯ *In German, write a paragraph on the Eden Project for a German tourist guide to Cornwall.*

C Economists Are Also Environmentalists   Paul Krugman

Source:	*The Accidental Theorist and Other Dispatches from the Dismal Science*, 1989
Topic:	Why saving the environment is good for the economy
Text form:	Essay
Language variety:	AE
Number of words:	123
Level:	Advanced
Skills/activities:	Writing a summary, evaluating the effectiveness of an argument, doing a role play

Lern-vokabular

Active vocabulary: 'Economists Are Also Environmentalists' (p. 85)

enthusiastic (l. 1), well-educated (ll. 2–3), well-off (l. 3), sentimental (l. 4), favo(u)r sth. (l. 10), incentive (l. 18), a tax on sth. (l. 18), tend to do sth. (l. 24), discourage sb. from doing sth. (l. 28), revenue from sth. (l. 29), income tax (l. 31), reduction in sth. (l. 33), aside from sth. (ll. 35–36), the general consensus (l. 39), on balance (l. 39), so what? (l. 41), leisure time (l. 44), agree on sth. (l. 46), cuddly (l. 47)
tasks: affect sth., convice sb. of sth.

Didaktisch-methodische Hinweise

Mit diesem Text wird das Thema Ökologie um einen weiteren Aspekt ergänzt, nämlich um die Frage nach dem Verhältnis von Ökonomie und Ökologie. Der vorliegende Text eines führenden US-Wirtschaftsexperten widerlegt die These, dass umweltbewusstes Verhalten mit höheren Kosten verbunden sein muss. Der Autor plädiert für die Einführung einer Umweltsteuer. Damit wird eine Brücke zu ökonomischen Betrachtungsweisen geschlagen, die im Kapitel „A Global Marketplace?" (vgl. SB, S. 90) vertieft werden. Der Text kann zusammen mit *section* 4 behandelt werden, in der der Nutzen staatlicher Eingriffe in die Wirtschaft z.B. durch Steuern diskutiert wird (vgl. SB, S. 102).

Unterrichts-tipps

Der Text ist sprachlich wie inhaltlich anspruchsvoll. Seine sprachliche Schwierigkeit liegt v.a. in der großen Anzahl von Fachtermini aus dem ökonomischen Bereich begründet. Der überwiegende Teil dieser Vokabeln wird in den Annotationen erläutert; ggf. sollten die folgenden Wörter semantisiert werden: „predispose sb." (l. 9), „incentive" (l. 18), „induce" (l. 19), „other things being equal" (l. 23). Eine Definition von *gross domestic product* kann ebenfalls hilfreich sein: „the market value of all final goods and services produced within a country in a given period of time" (N.G. Mankiw, *Essentials of Economics*, Fort Worth, 2001, S. 330). Um das Textverständnis zu sichern, entwerfen die S ein Flussdiagramm, das die Kausalkette in Z. 17–24 verdeutlicht.

Info

Paul Krugman (born 1953) is a professor of Economics at Princeton University. A popular columnist, he writes regularly for the *New York Times*.

'*People who know the price of everything and the value of nothing*' (l. 12): This is a quote from Oscar Wilde's play *Lady Windemere's Fan*; it was Lord Darlington's definition of a cynic.

Lösungs-hinweise

⬛ *Pre-reading: OALD* definitions:
Lifestyle: the way in which a person or a group of people lives and works;
in text: 'pretty well-off' (l. 3), 'I bring bags and bottles to the recycling center in my gas-guzzling sports utility vehicle' (ll. 5–6), 'drive cleaner cars' (l. 19), 'avoid driving altogether' (ll. 19–20), 'second car' (l. 21).

Taxation: money that has to be paid as taxes;
in text: 'pollution taxes' (l. 17), 'tax reduces the incentives to work, save and invest' (l. 18), 'taxes …will … reduce overall monetary output' (ll. 23–24), 'about a third of GDP passes through [government] hands' (ll. 27–28), 'revenue from any new taxes on pollution could be used to reduce other taxes' (ll. 29–30).

Payoff: an advantage or a reward from sth. you have done;
in text: 'tax on exhaust emissions from cars will … lower the payoff to earning extra money' (ll. 18–20), 'people will not have to work as hard as they would have' (l. 22), 'reduce other taxes, such as Social Security contributions or the income tax' (ll. 30–31), 'a rise in consumption of nonmarket goods like clean air and leisure time' (ll. 43–44).

1 They are well-educated and well-off and Americans like that are usually sentimental about the environment, and therefore believe in environmental protection. The argument goes that taxing fuel will not lower GDP substantially, but will result in a healthy environment, which is what people want anyway.

2 **a** Taxes mean that extra money you might earn goes to the government and therefore you have less money for buying things. However, taxes in the hands of the government are used for financing other areas of the economy and for paying employees of the state.

b Krugman justifies a pollution tax by explaining that if a new tax is levied on pollution other existing taxes can be lowered, so that in the end the GDP would stay the same or even rise.

3 Key sentences:
Paragraph 1: 'Economists are … enthusiastic environmentalists'.

Paragraph 2: 'upper-middle class Americans are sentimental about protecting the environment as long as it does not impinge on their lifestyle' and 'standard economic theory predisposes … to favor strong environmental protection.'

Paragraph 3: 'everyone knows that economists … believe that whatever free markets do must be right'.

Paragraph 5: 'pollution taxes will reduce GDP' and 'people will not work as hard as they would have without the tax'.

Paragraph 6: 'taxes on pollution could be used to reduce other taxes'.

Paragraph 7: 'on balance consensus is that pollution tax would be more likely to reduce GDP'.

Paragraph 8: 'getting the price of the environment right means a rise in … nonmarket goods like clean air and leisure time'.

Paragraph 9: 'Can 2,500 economists be wrong?'

Summary:
The writer's thesis is that economists are also environmentalists.
He claims that economists are upper-middle class Americans who care about the environment and who realize that protecting the environment makes economic sense. He looks at the effect of protecting the environment on the gross domestic product. Pollution taxes would reduce the GDP, as there would be less desire to make more money. People would drive less or have fewer cars, so there would be less money spent and therefore a lower GDP.
But if there were more taxes in the government's hands, then other taxes could be reduced, which would mean that there is the same amount of money in the hands of people. According to an argument called the 'double dividend' debate, which the writer does not explain, pollution taxes would reduce the GDP slightly.

But GDP is not the only way to measure a nation's well-being and one must take nonmarket goods like clean air and leisure time into account.

4 The writer makes use of questions to anticipate the queries the reader might have. He shows that he has considered all the arguments before putting pen to paper. The writer also introduces the common view of economists as being incapable of knowing the value of anything and of just believing that free markets will regulate everything. This enables him to dismiss prejudices against economists, but it also allows for the fact that there is truth in the prejudice, so if economists really do believe in protecting the environment, then there are good economic reasons for this.
He uses simple, rather informal language, so that the reader feels he or she can understand economic theory, rather than being talked down to by an expert. Yet at the same time the writer uses terms from the world of economics to show that his arguments have been carefully thought through.

❖ **5** Zum Rollenspiel vgl. auch S. 428. In einem ersten Schritt bereiten die S in Kleingruppen *role cards* vor, d.h. alle S, die eine Person vertreten, sammeln gemeinsam in einem Brainstorming Ideen, wie diese Person in der Diskussion auftreten wird. Danach gehen die S in die gemischten Gruppen, in denen die Vertreter aller Personen diskutieren. Vor Beginn der Arbeit sollten die S sich darüber verständigen, welches Ergebnis erwartet wird, d.h., ob die Diskussionsrunde zu einer Lösung kommen muss (bei der auch Kompromisse möglich sind) oder ob eine Vertagung möglich ist.

The role cards might include some of the following ideas:
Town councillor: has to welcome everybody, has to explain the issue and the plan of the town; has to try to lead the discussion in such a way that a solution can be found.

Local shopkeeper: is in favour of the housing project since more inhabitants mean more turnover for him or her; as a consequence he or she will pay more tax to the town which is, of course, good for the town.

Homeless person: is in favour of the project, as he or she feels that he might be able to afford a flat in the new housing estate; generally he or she has the feeling that all those environmentalists are more interested in animals and plants than in fellow human beings; he or she is fed up with living in a shelter.

Teenage environmentalist: wants the environment to be protected, and believes a biotope is necessary not only for the environment, but to teach children about nature, plants, animals, etc.

Mother of a small child: is against the housing project since she thinks it might encourage hooligans, as poorer people have criminal tendencies; she wants to keep the wood for walking with her child, as it is a safe place without traffic where children can play; she feels the town council is only interested in making money.

Birdwatcher: claims the wood is a biotope for lots of birds; they will become extinct if the wood is destroyed; the wood is the only place where he can enjoy his hobby; the town council should try to find a different space for the city people.

⬭ *Translate ll. 1–14 into German.*

SB, S. 87 **D Cartoons Dealing with the Environment**

Source:	p. 87: *The New Yorker*, 1999; p. 88: *The New Yorker*, 1989
Topic:	Environmental issues
Text form:	Cartoon
Language variety:	AE
Number of words:	123
Level:	Basic/advanced
Skills/activities:	Describing a cartoon, doing an information gap activity

Didaktisch-methodische Hinweise

Auf humorvolle, doch nicht weniger kontroverse Art stellen die beiden Karikaturen ihre Wahrnehmung der Beziehung von Mensch und Umwelt dar. Bei der Behandlung der Karikaturen stehen Bildbeschreibung und die Auswahl einer geeigneten Bildunterschrift im Vordergrund. Über das Angebot im SB hinausgehend sollten die S die Aussage der Karikaturen beschreiben, d.h. die Kritik an einer zu späten Reaktion auf Umweltprobleme und an nationalstaatlichem Denken. Anschließend können die S entscheiden, welche der Karikaturen sie lustiger, interessanter bzw. wirksamer finden.

Lösungs-hinweise

Partner A:

1 **a** Four politicians are sitting in armchairs in an office in Washington, D.C. To the right of the desk an American flag is hanging from a pole. The room is flooded, and the politicians' feet are in water. The Capitol and the Washington Memorial are visible through the window; both are half-submerged in water. A boat with two rowers can also be seen.

b The correct caption for Partner A's cartoon is No. 3.

Partner B:

1 **a** A car is driving along a road. Clouds and trees are visible. The area where the car is coming from is dark, while the area into which the car is going is light. The car is in the middle of this divide. Just beside the road is a sign saying 'State Line'.

b The correct caption for Partner B's cartoon is No. 3.

Explain the message of each of the cartoons.

Cartoon on p. 87: The cartoonist is showing how politicians react too late to environmental problems. It is only when the world's disasters affect the politicians directly do they start to take the problem seriously.

Cartoon on p. 88: It implies that the approach to environmental problems must be a global one, because pollution crosses borders.

SB, S. 88 **E The Destruction of Habitats**

VIDEO

Source:	*State of the Planet*, 2000
Topic:	The destructive effect of humans on the habitats of other species
Text form:	Documentary film
Language variety:	BE
Length:	2:58 min
Level:	Basic/advanced
Skills/activities:	Listening comprehension, identifying film element

Während in *section* 3A als Grund für Naturzerstörungen und Umweltsünden v.a. die Bequemlichkeit des Menschen genannt wurde, wird von vielen sicher seine vermeintlich aggressive, böse und rücksichtslose Natur dafür verantwortlich gemacht. Als letzter Text dieser *section* wird ein kurzer Auszug aus einem Dokumentarfilm des bekannten englischen Naturwissenschaftlers und Filmemachers David Attenborough gezeigt, in dem diese These widerlegt und vielmehr begründet wird, warum die Tendenz des Menschen, die Umwelt seinen Bedürfnissen anzupassen, über Jahrtausende sein Überleben und die Ausweitung seines Lebensraums gesichert hat. Die Aufgaben zielen auf eine Auseinandersetzung mit dieser Thematik und – durch die Bewusstmachung ausgewählter Filmtechniken – auf die Medienkompetenz der S.

Unterrichts-tipps Differenzierung

Als Vorbereitung auf den Inhalt des Films (vgl. Video/DVD und das Transkript auf S. 165) bearbeiten die S die *pre-viewing*-Aufgabe und diskutieren sie ggf. in Gruppen. Bei weniger leistungsstarken S ist es sinnvoll, nach dem ersten Sehen des Videos zunächst durch Aufgabe 2 das Verständnis zu sichern, bevor mit Aufgabe 1 ein Bezug zur *pre-reading*-Aufgabe hergestellt wird. Bei leistungsstärkeren S kann möglicherweise auf eine detaillierte Verständnissicherung verzichtet und nur Aufgabe 1 gelöst werden. S, die wenig Erfahrung mit der Videoanalyse haben, sollten die entsprechende Seite der „Skills Pages" (SB, S. 227) durcharbeiten, bevor sie den Film ein weiteres Mal sehen und Aufgabe 3 lösen.

Info

Sir David Attenborough (born 1926) joined the BBC in 1952, where he worked especially in natural science programming. In 1969 he was appointed Director of Programmes with editorial responsibility for both of the BBC's television networks. In 1973, he resigned to return to programme-making. Since then he has made numerous documentaries and is perhaps the most recognized and mostly highly regarded presenter on British television. An estimated 500 million people worldwide watched his series *Life on Earth* (1979). His brother is the feature film director, producer and actor, Sir Richard Attenborough.

Lösungs-hinweise

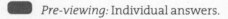 *Pre-viewing:* Individual answers.

VIDEO **1** Individual answers.

VIDEO **2** **a** Humans have destroyed the environment because:
- humans have had to survive by destroying the wilderness;
- the human population expands rapidly due to its capabilities;
- it needs to gain security, which it does by controlling and altering nature.

b It is natural to dominate the environment in order to survive. It is difficult to use moral judgements when examining this issue since what used to be valued as a sign of human capability is today discredited as disrespectful and reckless domination.

c The modern industrialized and technological society has made humans too effective at altering and ultimately destroying entire habitats.

VIDEO **3**

- Shots of nature are interspersed with interviews with a scientist; this gives weight to the documentary.

- Loud dramatic music emphasizes that something important is being dealt with.

- Woodland view is shown before a cut to straight lines of bushes or plants grown in agricultural areas: shows the changes man has made.

- The film is shot in fast motion when the film makers want to emphasize how fast technology is moving forward.

- Shots of satellite pictures of the earth are cut between shots of grain moving from one area (harvesting) to another (bag of grain landing with a bang), which shows that humans have made the globe into a small village.

- Camera panning away from the highway in a circular motion is attractive while showing the mess that humans create.

- The shots of a city at night reveals how humans have stamped their presence on nature, leaving little space for anything else.

- The shot showing lights on the planet imply that the earth is overpopulated.

- The uncommented and interspersed shots of old deserted civilizations imply that bad management leads to the collapse of civilization.

- The shot of the sun setting over the mountains and of the barren landscape reinforces the image of humans fighting against nature.

SB, S. 89

Watch Your Language

Didaktisch-methodische Hinweise

Schwerpunkt dieser *section* ist die Verwendung von Gerundium und *to*-Infinitiv. Die S machen in diesem Bereich häufig interferenzbedingte Fehler: Sie benutzen den Infinitiv an Stelle des Gerundiums, da letzteres im Deutschen nicht existiert. Noch schwieriger ist es für sie, die semantischen Unterschiede zu erfassen, die zwischen der Verwendung eines Infinitivs bzw. eines Gerundiums nach demselben Verb bestehen (z.B. *stop doing sth.* und *stop to do sth.*).

Lösungs-hinweise

1 **a/b**
- 'people's': *CEG* §179a (Index under 'possessive form')
- 'found that': *CEG* §304d△ (Index under 'comma')
- 'mind separating': CEG §139a (Index under '*mind:* + gerund', 'gerund: used as object after certain verbs')
- 'if': CEG §251d△ (Index under '*when:* conjunction')
- 'stop doing': CEG §139c (Index under '*stop* + gerund or *to*-infinitive')
- 'true of saving': CEG §141 (Index under 'gerund after adjective + preposition)
- 'if': CEG §251d△ (Index under '*when:* conjunction')
- 'turning off': CEG §138 (Index under 'gerund: used as subject')
- 'starting slowly': CEG §138 (Index under 'gerund: used as subject')
- 'remember to do': CEG §139c (Index under '*remember:* + gerund or *to*-infinitive', 'gerund: or *to*-infinitive after certain verbs', 'infinitive: *to*-infinitive: or gerund after certain verbs'); dictionary under 'remember' (cf. *OALD* under meaning 4)
- 'forget to do': CEG §139c (Index under '*forget:* + gerund or *to*-infinitive', 'gerund: or *to*-infinitive after certain verbs', 'infinitive: *to*-infinitive: or gerund after certain verbs'); dictionary under 'forget' (cf. *OALD* under meanings 1 and 2)
- 'educating': CEG §138 (Index under 'gerund: used as subject')
- about conserving': CEG §144 (Index under 'gerund: after prepositions', 'prepositions: + gerund'

2 The student needs to study and practise the difference between 'if' and 'when' and the gerund vs. the *to*-infinitive.

3 **a**

1 cleaning, doing
2 seeing
3 to save; to fit / fitting
4 to do, saving
5 to remember, collecting / to collect
6 living

b Possible answers:

1 Please remember to take the rubbish out when you leave.
  I cannot remember saying that. Are you sure?

2 My secretary forgot to book my flight, so I shall have to go by train.
  I'll never forget seeing her reaction when I asked her to marry me.

3 My classmate went on to become prime minister.
  My brother did not sleep but went on studying all night.

4 When I study, I stop to have a cup of tea every few hours.
  I must stop drinking so much coffee; it keeps me up all night.

c Aufgrund der grundsätzlichen Schwierigkeit des Übersetzens ist diese Aufgabe nur für leistungsstärkere S geeignet. Möglicherweise kann die Einschränkung gegeben werden, nur die Verbpaare und ihre Übersetzungen aus 3b zu verwenden. Bei besonders leistungsstarken S können auch Verben wie *lieben, hassen* usw. verwendet werden, nach deren englischen Äquivalenten das Gerundium wie der *to*-Infinitiv stehen können (vgl. *CEG* §139b).

Possible answers:
Es tut mir so Leid, ich habe schon wieder vergessen, deine Blumen zu gießen.
'I'm so sorry. I forgot to water your plants again.'

Ich will wirklich aufhören zu rauchen.
'I really want to stop smoking.'

Er konnte sich nicht erinnern, jemals einen so blöden Film gesehen zu haben.
'He couldn't remember seeing such a crap film.'

Sie vermisst es wirklich, mit ihren Freunden auszugehen.

→ WB, ex. 7 'She really misses going out with her friends.'

Topic Vocabulary: 'Nature and the Environment'

Planet Earth
the planet
the Earth
the world
nature
wildlife
fauna
flora
crop
irrigation
surroundings
landscape
seascape
desert
tropical forests
oxygen-giving

Climate Changes
climate change
global warming
greenhouse effect
greenhouse gas
fossil fuels
carbon dioxide
eliminate greenhouse gases
depletion of the ozone layer
destroy the ozone layer
hole in the ozone layer
flooding (of low-lying areas)
freak storm

Destruction of the Environment
destroy the environment
ecologically harmful
contribute to sth.
deforestation
chop sth. down
destroy (tropical) rainforests
pollute the air/water
waste product
consume fuel
exhaust fumes/emissions
emissions of sth.
air pollution
landfill
municipal / toxic waste dump
soil erosion
desertification
drought
malnutrition
famine
a species becomes/is extinct
extinction of a species
threatened/endangered species

Environmental Awareness
live in harmony with nature
live a simple life
feel relaxed
reduce stress levels
a sustainable lifestyle
environmentalist
environmental group
eco-warrior
(raise) environmental awareness
environmental protection
protect the environment
levy/impose a tax on pollution
an environmentally friendly product
environmentally sound
save the planet
separate rubbish (BE) = (AE) garbage
collect glas/plastic bottles
recycling programmes
recycle sth.
re-use sth.
reduce sth.
save fuel (BE) = (AE) gas
natural resources
conservation
conserve resources
reduce pollution
strict environmental protection law

SB, p. 77
Task 1a
(cf. TM, p. 142)

It Was a Lover and His Lass

Listen to the song on the CD and then fill in the gaps.

1   It was a _____ and his lass,

With a hey, and a ho, and a hey nonino,

That o'er the green _____ did pass

In the _____ time, the _____ time, the only pretty ring time,

5   When _____ do sing, hey ding a ding, ding:

Sweet lovers love the _____ .

Between the acres of the _____ ,

With a hey, ho, hey nonino,

These pretty _____ folks would lie,

10   In the _____ time, the _____ time, the only pretty ring time,

When _____ do sing, hey ding a ding, ding:

Sweet lovers love the _____ .

This carol they began that _____ ,

With a hey, ho, hey nonino,

15   How that a life was but a _____

In _____ time, the _____ time, the only pretty ring time,

When _____ do sing, hey ding a ding, ding:

Sweet lovers love the _____ .

And therefore take the _____ time

20   With a hey, and a ho, and a hey nonino;

For _____ is crowned with the prime

In the _____ time, the _____ time, the only pretty ring time,

When _____ do sing, hey ding a ding, ding:

Sweet lovers love the _____ .

CD **It Was a Lover and His Lass** William Shakespeare

SB, p. 77
Task 1a

It was a lover and his lass,
With a hey, and a ho, and a hey nonino,
That o'er the green cornfield did pass
In the spring time, the spring time, the only pretty ring time,
When birds do sing, hey ding a ding, ding:
Sweet lovers love the spring.

Between the acres of the rye,
With a hey, ho, hey nonino,
These pretty country folks would lie,
In the spring time, the spring time, the only pretty ring time,
When birds do sing, hey ding a ding, ding:
Sweet lovers love the spring.

This carol they began that hour,
With a hey, ho, hey nonino,
How that a life was but a flower
In the spring time, the spring time, the only pretty ring time,
When birds do sing, hey ding a ding, ding:
Sweet lovers love the spring.

And therefore take the present time
With a hey, ho, hey nonino;
For love is crownéd with the prime
In the spring time, the spring time, the only pretty ring time,
When birds do sing, hey ding a ding, ding:
Sweet lovers love the spring.

Nice Places

SB, p. 78
Task 4 **Country of Our Time**

Presenter:	We need to restore nature to the heart of the economy, which is why I'm sitting here in my own urban front garden. Because there's no better place to start than in the towns and cities where so many of us live and work. And I want to follow a hunch, that the urban green spaces close to home are not just important for wildlife, but they're a very real boost to our own health and happiness.
Roger Ulrich:	The general conclusions, scientifically, are in accord with traditional beliefs held in widely different cultures, whether it's Britain or other Western countries or even Asian countries, and that is that looking at nature somehow makes us feel good. We found that if people commuted to work, other things being equal, going through nature, especially in contrast to the urban environment without nature, they were measurably less stressed, as evidenced in blood pressure, for example.
Presenter:	That's the scientist talking, and the evidence is very convincing. Thanks to researchers like Roger Ulrich from A&M University in Texas, we now have proof that easy access to wildlife where we live and work relieves our stress, improves the air we breathe. But before we get too bogged down in technicalities and jargon, let's just listen to what these people think about their urban green space: Warley Woods, in Smethwick, deep in the industrial West Midlands.
Gloria William:	My name is Gloria William. I live over the road. I spend an average of five to six hours a day in the woods, now I'm in retirement. And it's my sanctuary, it's my think tank, it's everything that brings peace. My husband's had a serious stroke, so I need this now more than ever.
Marion Blockley:	I'm Marion Blockley and I'm the Restoration Project Manager for Warley Woods. People clubbed together to save this space, lots of individuals bought individual shares of the site to protect it from development. It is so essential here, we're only a mile or so away from the busiest motorway intersection in the country, and there are spotted woodpeckers, you can hear the birds' song. It is a haven for the people of Smethwick and Barewood.
Gloria William:	When I was a child, I lived in the deep area of Smethwick, the industrial area, and it was my goal as a child to come up here and live. And when I eventually achieved that, 21 years ago, I thought I'd come to heaven.
Marion Blockley:	People were proposed to here. When the abbey was demolished, they took pieces of the abbey away to put in their gardens, so it's a part of their identity, their sense of 'this is where we belong, this is what Barewood means to us', and at any season ... I mean in winter, this site covered in snow is like a Brueghel landscape, it's absolutely teeming with people. It is the centre for the toboganning ... it's fabulous, and people love it to bits.
Gloria William:	I can come out dreading, full of pain. An hour walking round here and I feel relaxed, ready to go back and start again.

Getting Along in English

SB, S. 79
Task 2a

Bruce:	G'day. How can I help you?
Phil:	Good morning. We've just arrived in Brisbane and we'd like to enquire about booking tickets for one of your tours.
Max:	One of our teachers came to Australia last year. He did a tour with you. Mr Green from Pimlico, in London.
Bruce:	Oh, I remember him – Jim Green. Yeah, he was keen on cricket, right?
Phil:	That's him!
Bruce:	Nice bloke, Jim. Right then. Well, what we do is one-day tours into the rainforest.
Max:	We thought we might like to spend a few days in the rainforest. Do you have longer tours?
Bruce:	Sorry, mate, they're all one-day tours. But we do a different tour each day of the week – so you could go on several different tours to see different parts of the forest.
Phil:	But there would be no possibility of spending a night in the rainforest with your tour company?
Bruce:	No. And in fact there are very few places where you can stay. We want to make sure that the rainforest we still have survives!
Max:	I see. Well, the best days for us would be Thursday and Friday of this week. What could you offer us?
Bruce:	Well on Thursday we do my favourite tour. It goes to the Glasshouse Mountains and Kondalilla Falls National Park.
Phil:	And could you please tell us when that tour leaves?
Bruce:	All our tours leave at 8 am.
Phil:	And where do we have to come?
Bruce:	You don't have to come at all – we pick you up from wherever you're staying.
Phil:	I beg your pardon?
Bruce:	We pick you up from the address you give us when you book.
Max:	Erm, excuse me, but is there an extra charge for that?
Bruce:	No extra charge!
Phil:	Well, that's great. And how much does the tour cost?
Bruce:	55 Australian dollars, no hidden extras. For that we pick you up, drive you to the National Park, taking in some wonderful scenery on the way, and then do a guided walk with you.
Max:	And how long is the walk?
Bruce:	About five kilometers.
Max:	So what time do you usually get back to Brisbane?
Bruce:	Around six o'clock in the evening.
Phil:	I hope you don't mind me asking, but who are the guides on your tours?
Bruce:	Of course I don't mind you asking. All our tours are led by a very interesting and knowledgeable guide who is a great nature enthusiast and will be able to tell you lots about the plant and animal life in the rainforest. In fact, they're all led by Bruce ... that's me, by the way!
Max:	You're Bruce?!
Bruce:	Yup!
Phil:	Well, we're very pleased to meet you.
Bruce:	Likewise. Now, do you want to take our brochure away and think about it?
Max:	No, I don't think so. I think we want to book, don't we, Phil?
Phil:	Yes, indeed. Two tickets for Thursday, please.
Max:	Oh, what will we need to bring with us? Do you have a list?
Bruce:	You need a hat, sunscreen, camera, swimmers, ...
Phil:	Excuse me interrupting, but what are 'swimmers'?
Bruce:	Sorry, a bit of Aussie there! Swimmers are what you call swimming trunks.

Phil:	Ah, thank you.
Max:	Do we need anything else, Bruce? Er, is it all right if I call you Bruce?
Bruce:	Sure thing. And you are …?
Max:	My name's Max and this is Phil.
Bruce:	Well, Max and Phil, you're also going to need a water bottle – filled with water – some lunch and good walking shoes.
Phil:	So you don't provide lunch, is that right?
Bruce:	Yeah, that's right. We've found it's better that way – everyone brings what they like. Now, any more questions?
Phil:	Well, yes, if you don't mind. What transport do you use?
Bruce:	My trusty minibus. The seats are comfortable and … it's air-conditioned!
Max:	And how many people usually come on these tours?
Bruce:	It's a maximum of ten. Let me see … on Thursday there are three people booked already.
Phil:	There is one more thing: what kind of weather should we expect? Sun, I suppose, because of the sunscreen? But might it rain? Does it ever get cold?
Bruce:	It certainly won't get cold – it's more like a sauna some days! Now rain, well, that's another matter entirely …

SB, p. 79	*Bruce:*	Hi there, Phil, Max! Got everything?
Task 3a	*Max:*	Hello, Bruce. Yes, I think we've got everything we need.
	Bruce:	Well, climb in and meet the others. Introduce yourselves, will you, while I get us through the traffic and out to the rainforest.
	Phil:	Hello. My name's Phil …
	Max:	… and I'm Max.
	Ute:	Hello, I'm Ute. I'm from Germany. Where are you two from?
	Phil:	Hello, Ute. We're from England.
	Jenny:	Hi, you guys. My name's Jenny and I'm from Colorado, USA. This is my husband, Larry, and this is our daughter, Lara.
	Max:	Hi, nice to meet you.
	Larry:	Hi. Whereabouts in England do you come from?
	Phil:	We're from London.
	Lara:	Gee, that's a cool place.
	Bruce:	Well, it's around now I like to feel that you're all really getting to know each other. Now, anyone who comes on a rainforest walking tour is a bit of an adventurer, right?
	All:	Right!
	Bruce:	So, why don't we all while away the first part of the journey by each telling a travel story. I'm sure you've all got lots … but just one will do! Lara, why don't you start?
	Lara:	OK, sure. Erm … yeah, I know. It was when I was quite small and we went on vacation in Mexico. We stayed in this really cool place in the middle of the jungle. And when I went to bed, one of the maids said to me: 'Be sure to shake out your shoes in the morning'. Gee, I went to bed real excited, because I thought there was maybe something like the Mexican tooth fairy going to come in the night. So, next morning I couldn't wait to shake out my shoes: nothing. OK, I thought, maybe you have to be good and patient all day, and then you get the surprise. So, next morning, I shook out my shoes again: nothing. The next night was going to be our last night in that place. I was quite angry at this tooth fairy or whatever, not showing up, but I thought I'd give it one last try. So when I woke up, I leaned over the edge of the bed and picked up my shoes and shook them and the next thing I knew my dad was screaming: 'Don't move, honey, stay where you are!' And guess what had fallen out of my shoe and was crawling around the floor by my bed. A humongous scorpion!
	All:	Ugh!
	Phil:	How old were you, Lara?

Lara:	Oh, about eight, I guess.	
Phil:	Well! You started travelling early!	
Jenny:	Kids travel much younger these days. I think that's really good. I hadn't been anywhere outside the States until I was 25, and then it was for a family affair – a wedding in Chester. Do you know it, Max?	
Max:	No, I don't.	
Ute:	But I do! When I started learning English, our English schoolbook was set in Chester and our teacher took us there on a class trip. It's very beautiful ...	

SB, p. 79   *Bruce:*   OK, guys, back to the city, I'm afraid. Time to get into the bus and go.

Task 4   *Jenny:*   Bruce, I don't know how we can thank you enough. This has been a very special day.

Larry: Yeah, absolutely terrific, Bruce. We've learned so much ...

Lara: ... and not just about the rainforest and the environment. You sort of learn something about yourself out here, don't you?

Max: Lara's right. It's been truly amazing, Bruce. Thank you so much.

Ute: It was wonderful: very informative but at the same time most enjoyable. Thank you very much, Bruce.

Larry: And such a nice bunch of people. How do you manage that?

Bruce: Ah. Well, that's just luck! You get some quite nice groups and you get some very nice groups and you lot belong in the last category!

Phil: I agree with Bruce – I've enjoyed meeting you all very much. But the star is Bruce. Thanks, Bruce.

Bruce: Well, you're wrong there, Phil. The star is our beautiful rainforest!

VIDEO **The Destruction of Habitats**

SB, p. 88   *David Attenborough:*   The destruction of habitats is doing more damage to bio-diversity around the world than any other human activity. As our population increases and as we cover more of the earth's surface with our buildings and our cultivated fields, we will inevitably lose more wild habitat.

The damage we have inflicted on the world's environments has led many to question whether the human species is deliberately destructive.

Edward Wilson is a biologist who's made a special study of the effect of human behaviour on the rest of life.

Edward Wilson: I think it would be a grave injustice to speak of the human species as in some sense evil. Even though we are destroying the environment so efficiently at the present time. Basically that's not our intent. It never was. It was very natural, in fact it was necessary for survival for the ancestral human beings to throw everything they had against the wilderness in an attempt to conquer it, to utilize it. That is the nature of humankind, to expand the population, to gain security, to control, to alter. And for millions of years that paid off without undue damage. But then what happened was, as we developed a modern, industrial capacity, then the techno-scientific capacity to eliminate entire habitats quickly and efficiently, we succeeded too well, and at long last we broke nature. And now almost too late we're waking up to the fact that we've overdone it and we're destroying the very foundation in the environment on which humanity was built.

Dieses Kapitel befasst sich mit verschiedenen Aspekten des Themas Wirtschaft. Dabei geht es nicht darum, betriebs- oder volkswirtschaftliche Fachkenntnisse in englischer Sprache zu vermitteln. Vielmehr sollen die S – entsprechend der Zielsetzung des Fremdsprachenunterrichts auch an allgemein bildenden Schulen – anhand nicht-fachsprachlicher Texte elementare wirtschaftliche Zusammenhänge versprachlichen lernen.

Aus Gründen der Motivation und der Konkretisierung stehen zunächst Menschen und ihre Erfahrungen im Vordergrund, bevor auf einer abstrakteren Ebene das Verhältnis von Staat und Wirtschaft sowie Entwicklungstendenzen in einer zunehmend globalisierten Wirtschaft thematisiert werden:

– *Section 1*, „Business is Business", illustriert anhand eines Auszugs aus Arthur Millers *Death of a Salesman* den Konflikt zwischen Menschlichkeit und betriebswirtschaftlichen Bedingungen.

– *Section 2*, „Down and Out – and Up?", befasst sich mit dem Thema Armut v.a. in Industrieländern und diskutiert den Weg in die Selbstständigkeit als Ausweg aus ihr.

– *Section 3*, „As Basic as the Screwdriver", untersucht die Bedeutung des Englischen als internationaler Wirtschaftssprache.

– *Section 4*, „Freedom and Opportunity", kontrastiert amerikanische und europäische, neoliberale und sozialstaatliche Vorstellungen des Verhältnisses von Politik und Wirtschaft.

Dem inhaltlichen Schwerpunkt des Kapitels entsprechend, dominieren hier nicht-fiktionale Texte (vgl. aber den Dramenauszug in *section* 1 und das politische Lied in *section* 4). Sie haben unterschiedliche Schwierigkeitsgrade, so dass für leistungsschwächere wie -stärkere S angemessenes Material zu finden ist.

→ *WB, ex. 3*

Didaktisches Inhaltsverzeichnis

SB, p.	Title	TM, p.	Text form	Topic	Skills and activities
90	Lead-in	167	photos cartoon	the economic system	working with vocabulary; describing somebody's role in the economy; analysing a cartoon
92	**Business Is Business** Arthur Miller	169	drama (extract)	a conflict between an employer and an employee	analysing a conflict; explaining images; analysing tragedy; doing a role play
95	**Poverty Is Relative** Mari Marcel Thekaekara	173	article	poverty in Scotland (and India)	analysing poverty; comparing one's own views on sth. with those of sb. else
96	**I Have to Keep the Hot Water for the Kids** Bob Holman	174	diary extract	personal experience of poverty	analysing a text; supporting a view with evidence from a text; doing research; drawing up a fictional budget
97	**Starting Your Own Business**	175	fictionalized case studies	the experience of two people who want to become self-employed	working with vocabulary; describing a person's situation; discussing a topic; doing research; writing an e-mail
99	**Context Box**	178	–	the global economy	examining globalization
100	**Getting Along in English**	180	–	going shopping	listening comprehension; doing a role play
101	**As Basic as the Screwdriver** Stephen Baker et al.	181	feature story	English as the international language of business	analysing the global role of English

101	Interviews with Braj Kachru and David Crystal CD1, track 37	183	radio interviews	the worldwide spread of English	listening comprehension; analysing metaphors; identifying reasons for the spread of English
102	**Political and Economic Freedom** Milton and Rose Friedman	184	extract from a non-fiction book	the importance of freedom for economic development	examining American history; comparing two viewpoints; writing a summary
103	**The Fair Society** Will Hutton	187	extract from a non-fiction book	the role of government in regulating social affairs	comparing two texts; giving one's own opinion; discussing a topic
104	**NPWA** Billy Bragg and the Blokes	189	song	criticism of the consequences of globalization	listening comprehension; giving one's opinion; writing a summary
105	**Watch Your language**	191	–	definite article collocations	writing a speech

SB, S. 90

Lead-in

Didaktisch-methodische Hinweise

Die S begegnen hier fünf Figuren, die für ausgewählte Akteure im Wirtschaftsgeschehen stehen, und beschreiben grundlegende wirtschaftliche Zusammenhänge:

Bild 1: Der Börsenmakler steht für die Finanzmärkte. Aktionäre erwerben Anteile an Unternehmen in der Hoffnung auf Teilhabe an deren Gewinn; sie übernehmen damit aber auch Anteile an den Unternehmensrisiken. Soziale und ökologische Anliegen und die ökonomischen Interessen der Aktionäre stehen häufig in einem Spannungsverhältnis zu einander (vgl. auch „Context Box", SB, S. 99).

Bild 2: Handelsvertreter und Apotheker repräsentieren Unternehmen (Groß- und Einzelhandel), die Waren kaufen und verkaufen (vgl. auch die Figur des Handlungsreisenden in „Business Is Business", SB, S. 92).

Bild 3: Die Jugendlichen verkörpern die Haushalte, die Waren (hier: Kleidung) und Dienstleistungen kaufen und konsumieren (vgl. auch „Getting Along in English" mit dem Schwerpunkt Einkaufs- bzw. Verkaufsgespräch, SB, S. 100).

Bild 4 und 5: Demonstranten und Plantagenarbeiter stehen für Arbeitnehmer, die ihre Arbeitskraft unter den existierenden Marktbedingungen „verkaufen" (müssen). Die Forderung, der Demonstranten, Rover zu verstaatlichen, wirft die Frage nach dem Verhältnis von Staat und Wirtschaft auf (vgl. „Context Box", SB, S. 99, und „Freedom and Opportunity", SB, S. 102).

Die Boxen mit Wortmaterial bieten den S eine Basis für die weitere Arbeit mit dem Kapitel. L kann besonders auf die Bedeutungsunterschiede zwischen *salary* und *wages* und auf die Kollokation *work for a firm* hinweisen.

Anschließend beschreiben die S anhand der Karikatur den Interessenskonflikt zwischen Arbeitnehmern, die am Erhalt ihres Arbeitsplatzes interessiert sind, und Aktionären, die Kostensenkung anstreben. Die Bilder und die Karikatur bieten auch Anknüpfungspunkte für Fragen nach sozialer Gerechtigkeit.

Lösungs-hinweise

1 **a** – –

b An die Sammelphase kann sich eine Bewusstmachung zur Wortbildung anschließen, z.B. die Suffixe *-er* und *-or* für *agents*, *-ion*, *-ation* und *-ment* für *actions*.

verb	**adjective**	**noun (agent)**	**noun (action)**
purchase	–	purchaser	purchase/purchasing
consume	–	consumer	consumption
distribute	distributive/ distributional	distributor	distribution

exploit	exploitative/ exploitive (AE)	exploiter	exploitation
invest	–	investor	investment
represent	representative	rep(resentative)	representation
sell	–	seller salesperson salesman/-woman	sale
trade	–	trader	trade

c 1–B: A stockbroker's job is to buy and sell shares (stakes in the ownership of an enterprise) on the stockmarket. He or she trades these shares on behalf of shareholders. The rise and fall of share prices depends mainly on the profitability of the company concerned. A skilful stockbroker will follow economic trends and anticipate booms and slumps. Shares also react to changes in the exchange rate of world currencies and a stockbroker should be able to take advantage of currency exchange rates to make money for his or her client.

2–A: A sales rep(resentative) is responsible for selling a company's merchandise to retailers and distributors. His or her aim is to secure contracts for his or her company's goods. A rep will try to receive as many orders for the goods and services as possible. This creates profits for the firm and secures him or her a good reputation. He or she usually travels a lot, advising customers on new products and distributing samples. 3–C: The customer purchases or buys something at a retail outlet such as a shop. One speaks of the customer as a consumer, as he or she consumes the product or service offered by a business. As a target group, customers are generally influenced by advertising, which encourages them to spend money on the product being advertised. Where there is no direct need for a product, advertising will often try to create a demand for it. New products and services are constantly being put on the market.

4–E: Employees sell their labour to a firm in exchange for wages. Most people are employees, as they need to earn a living. Receiving a salary is often a comfortable way of earning money and most people will at some stage work for a firm, which can be large or small. Nowadays, many firms are under pressure to close down unprofitable areas and cut down on labour costs to avoid becoming unprofitable. Firms need to invest in people and machinery. If a firm is making a loss, it might seek to cut wages and labour costs, leaving some of their workforce redundant. The firm might then be faced with its employees going on strike. If a person is unemployed, he or she usually lives on benefits, especially if he or she needs to support a family. Others attempt to make a living by becoming self-employed.

5–D: Plantation workers form a large part of the working force in many developing countries. The primary sectors of agriculture and mining are still vital to the economies of third-world countries, where there is still a lot of cheap labour. Therefore products are cheaper to produce for the world market. As workers have fewer rights, however, they are easier to exploit. Since developing countries need to import things like manufactured products, they depend on exports to avoid falling too deeply in debt. Their exports are mostly raw materials, which are processed elsewhere. The price on the world market of their raw materials is considerably lower than those of industrialized nations, which makes them competitive, but it also means that the population is forced to live continually in poverty. If the price of raw materials slumps or a drought destroys crops, these countries then have to rely on richer countries to give them aid.

→ WB, ex. 1

2 Example: Teenage consumers and workers in a third-world country. Teenagers enjoy shopping for affordable clothes. For the clothes to be affordable, they are often made in developing countries. So money teenagers spend can provide employment for workers in poorer areas of the world. This might, however, lead to unemployment in the teenagers' own countries, while not improving the conditions in the developing countries, as western companies will be involved as middlemen and reap most of the profits, while the workers work for low wages in poor conditions. So if consumers inform themselves about the labels and who is behind them, they can use their spending power selectively to encourage manufacturers to provide a fairer deal for their employees.

3 Possible answer:

On Monday the dollar note was lying in the till of a 7–11 in Chicago. A secretary got it as change when paying for some sweets and drinks. On her way to work the next morning she was feeling generous, so she gave it to a busker who was playing the saxophone in a subway station. The busker immediately took it to his local bar and used it to pay for his beer. The bartender was a shady figure in the underworld who needed to pay large amounts of money in cash, so on Wednesday the dollar bill was given to his boss, who took it to the Bahamas with 49,999 others in a briefcase. On Thursday, it was among a bundle of dollar notes given to a tall blonde, who wouldn't stop kissing the boss when she saw him waving the money at her. The next morning, she exchanged the bundle of notes for a pair of bridal shoes, because she was going to get married to her cousin Louis in July. When on Saturday morning an American tourist bought new shoelaces in the shoe shop, he got the dollar note as change. On Sunday, he flew back to Chicago. Having been away for two weeks, he decided to fill his fridge and stopped at the nearest 7–11. Paying for his food he returned the dollar note to the till where its journey started.

→ WB, ex. 9 **4** The cartoon shows a scene in an office. An employee is sitting at his computer in his cubicle staring in surprise at the screen, with his hands raised off the keyboard in dismay. On the screen there is a message saying: 'You're laid off'. An older colleague pops his head in and reacts to the message with a rather cynical comment. The older man sympathizes with his younger colleague, saying that it is hard to lose your job, but reminds him that as a shareholder of the company that is firing him, he should be happy: obviously, the company is improving its profitability by cutting its workforce, and that means that share prices will go up, so shareholders will be better off.
The cartoon is drawing attention to the absurdity of an economic process that creates unemployment in the name of profit; the average employee will, of course, take little comfort from the fact that the shares have risen at the cost of his job, as the losses incurred from becoming unemployed are not outweighed by the gains one makes as a shareholder.

SB, S. 92 # 1 Business Is Business Arthur Miller

Source:	*Death of a Salesman*, 1949 (from: Act II)
Topic:	A conflict between an employer and an employee
Text form:	Drama (extract)
Language variety:	AE
Number of words:	1298
Level:	Basic/advanced
Skills/activities:	Analysing a conflict, explaining images, analysing tragedy, doing a role play

Lern-vokabular

Active vocabulary: 'Business Is Business' (p. 92)

$65 a week (l. 19), frankly (l. 21), ask a favour of sb. (l. 25), appreciate sth. (l. 30), desperately (l. 38), admit sth. (l. 39), streak (l. 48), self-reliance (l. 48), make a living (l. 55), career (l. 56), funeral (l. 62), comradeship (l. 65), gratitude (l. 65), pull yourself together (l. 88), fire sb. (l. 96), give sb. a hand (l. 102), false pride (l. 104), cripple (l. 110), stop by (l. 115)

Didaktisch-
methodische
Hinweise

Dieser Auszug aus Millers Drama stellt den Wertewandel in der Geschäftswelt dar: Der alternde Vertreter Willy Loman bittet seinen jungen Chef Howard darum, in den Innendienst versetzt zu werden, da das Reisen ihn zu sehr anstrengt. Er appelliert an Howard, Rücksicht zu nehmen und Willys langjährige Verbundenheit mit der Firma, insbesondere mit Howards Vater zu bedenken. Howard hingegen hat die Profitabilität seiner Firma vor Augen und sieht aufgrund Willys nachlassender Leistungsfähigkeit keine Möglichkeit, ihm einen Posten zu bieten.

Bei der Behandlung des dargestellten Konflikts muss eine Schwarzweiß-Zeichnung der Figuren (kalter, unmenschlicher, junger Arbeitgeber gegen familienorientierten, ausgebrannten, älteren Arbeitnehmer) vermieden werden. Die S müssen die Zwänge erkennen, in denen beide Figuren stecken. Anschließend können sie exemplarisch Lösungsansätze für den Umgang mit älteren Arbeitnehmern in einer sozialen Marktwirtschaft entwickeln und damit bereits die Diskussion über neoliberale und sozialstaatliche Gesellschaftsmodelle vorbereiten (vgl. SB, S. 99 und S. 102). Auch Will Huttons Vision einer gerechten Gesellschaft, in der der Staat z.B. durch Kündigungsschutzvorschriften aktiv zwischen den Sozialpartnern vermittelt (vgl. SB, S. 103, Z. 1–3), können hier bereits angerissen werden.

Unter literarischen Gesichtspunkten wird anhand des Dramenauszugs die Frage nach den Merkmalen des Tragischen aufgeworfen. Wesentlich ist dabei die Einsicht, dass Willy auch aufgrund seiner Wertvorstellungen paradoxerweise seinen eigenen Untergang verursacht. Da es sich bei diesem Text um einen Dramenauszug handelt, sollten die S ihm nicht nur als schriftliche „Partitur" begegnen. Sie können ihn z.B. als Filmszene erleben (bei www.lingua-video.com erhältlich) oder selbst als Theaterszene oder in einem *playreading* gestalten. Bei Interesse kann das Drama als Lektüre behandelt oder im Rahmen eines Referats vorgestellt werden.

Unterrichts-
tipps

Als Einstieg in die Lektüre wären folgende Aufgaben denkbar:

◯ *'Business is Business' – When might you hear this phrase? What does it mean?*
This phrase might be used when social, emotional, moral or ethical considerations interfere with strictly economic interests. It means that business has its own norms and rules, which may differ from societal norms in general.

◯ *Read ll. 1–10. How do you think Howard is likely to respond to Willy's request? What points are the two men likely to make?*

Die S lesen den Text still. Nach Z. 67 bietet sich erneut ein Punkt zum Einhalten an: Willys wortreiche Erinnerungen sind zu Ende gekommen und die S können spekulieren, wie das weitere Gespräch verlaufen wird.

Zur Sicherung des Globalverständnisses kann L aussagekräftige Einzeläußerungen von den S erläutern lassen:

◯ *What is meant by the following lines:*
a) *'You didn't crack up again, did you?'* (l. 6) (Howard implies that Willy might have done something strange again like having a break-down, getting upset, etc.)

b) *'we do a road business'* (ll. 23–24) (Howard means that the company earns its money by selling things through its salesmen.)

c) *'he died the death of a salesman'* (l. 60) (Willy means that the man died travelling, but also travelling in style.)

d) *'Pull yourself together.'* (l. 88) (Howard is telling Willy to control his emotions.)

e) *'This is no time for false pride'* (l. 104) (Howard means that Willy has to give up his self-reliance and depend on others.)

→ *WB, ex. 2*

Info

Arthur Miller (born 1915) is one of the USA's most influential playwrights. Born in New York of Jewish parents, he received recognition with his play *All My Sons* (1947), but it was his Pulitzer-Prize-winning play *Death of a Salesman* (1949) that established him as an important playwright. His play *The Crucible* was produced in 1953 as a reaction to the McCarthyite era. Besides other plays, he also wrote the screenplay for *The Misfits* (1961), in which his wife Marilyn Monroe played a leading role.

Death of a Salesman is the story of Willy Loman, a travelling salesman, who is no longer a success at work. After he is fired, he looks back on scenes from his life and decides that he is worth more to his family dead than alive, and kills himself. The play has been performed throughout the world and has been filmed. Miller said once that he wrote the play 'to set forth what happens when a man does not have a grip on the forces of life'.

Lösungs-hinweise

1 **a** Willy accuses Howard of having profited from his work for the company and of being unsupportive now that he is old, while Howard refuses to allow considerations of charity and friendship to get in the way of business success.

b 'I can't take blood from a stone': Howard as a businessman sees it as his task to exploit all the resources he controls to create profit and wealth (blood); Willy, however, is no longer able to yield any revenue because he is old and exhausted (a stone).
'You can't eat the orange and throw the peel away': Willy is trying to make his boss see the whole of him; he feels his life juices have been squeezed out of him and senses that the 'useless' rest of him is expendable as far as the firm is concerned. Willy's image seems rather feeble because that is exactly what most people will do with an orange, but he is trying to say that a human being should not be looked upon as an orange.

c Expressions include:
Howard: 'everybody's gotta pull his own weight' (l 37), 'business is business' (l. 39), 'This is no time for false pride' (l. 103).
Willy: 'I never asked a favour of any man' (l. 25), 'We've got quite a little streak of self-reliance in our family' (l. 48), 'In those days there was personality in it. There was respect, and comradeship, and gratitude in it. Today, it's all cut and dried, [...] They don't know me any more.' (ll. 64ff.), 'I can't throw myself on my sons' (l. 110).
Each man's case:
Howard: He sees Willy as a liability whose further employment, even as a travelling salesman, would jeopardize the company's profitability ('I don't want you to represent us', l. 94). As a young executive, Howard feels he must deal with the world as it is, and not as it was or should be.
Willy: He has lived his life according to the ideals of self-reliance; now that he is old and tired he feels justified in laying claim to humanitarian ideals such as friendship and gratitude.

d Willy asks to speak to Howard and reluctantly admits that he feels too tired to continue working as a travelling salesman. He reminds his young boss of his offer, made at the Christmas party, to find him a job in the central office. Howard remembers but says he has no opening for him. Willy mentions he needs only $65 a week.
When Howard continues to refuse him, Willy talks about old times and how he was asked by Howard's father what he thought about the name Howard for his baby boy. Howard remains unimpressed by such sentimental stories, so Willy backs down and asks for $50.
Again Howard stands firm, and Willy launches into a long speech trying to persuade him to admit considerations of friendship and gratitude into his business ethos. At the end of the speech Willy admits that people nowadays just do not know him any more. Howard seizes on this point to confront Willy with his own failure, so the salesman makes his boss a new offer and tries to sell his work for $40 a week.

Willy becomes desperate and demands that Howard honour the 'promises' which he feels were made to him. Howard is now no longer responding to the content of the old man's ranting, but tells him to pull himself together.

In the final section, Howard fires Willy, who now – too late – offers to go back to his job on the road. He says that he cannot ask his sons for help and finally runs out of arguments and only begs to be allowed to sell merchandise in Boston.

Willy loses the argument because as an aging employee he is in a weaker position. He is no longer able to do his job satisfactorily. Yet he still plays by the rules of the game of business, trying to sell himself to his boss. In a way, this extract is a transaction, and Willy is finally forced by his own arguments to concede that his market value is very low. If you live your life according to the ideals of self-reliance and of profit-making, you will inevitably one day be measured by the same scale yourself, and found wanting. He also loses because his second line of argument stresses the value of friendship and the promises made to him, which for Howard as a business-oriented person do not count.

2 It is definitely sad: We see an old man who has spent his lifetime in the service of a family firm being ruthlessly cast aside. It is tragic since Willy's downfall is also his own fault. He has too much pride to admit his needs to his family. Interestingly, Howard can confront Willy with his own arguments and thereby quite easily defeat him; Willy is brought down by his own stubborn values and lack of flexibility.

3 Bei der Durchführung des Rollenspiels (vgl. auch S. 428) sollten folgende Punkte beachtet werden: Howard sollte seine Frustration über den rechthaberischen alten Mann zum Ausdruck bringen, gleichwohl auch das Bedürfnis zeigen, sich zu rechtfertigen, da Willy ein alter Bekannter des Vaters ist. Dennoch ist Howard eigenen Zwängen unterworfen; er hat eine Fürsorgepflicht nicht nur gegenüber Willy, sondern auch gegenüber der Firma und seiner eigenen Familie. Seine Frau könnte Verständnis für Howards Handlungsweise aufbringen, aber auch Mitleid mit Willy zeigen.

Bei Willy müssen die S entscheiden, wie viel er überhaupt erzählt, ob er z.B. in seinem Stolz versucht, die Entlassung zu kaschieren und dem Gespräch mit Howard einen völlig anderen Verlauf zu geben.

Individual answers.

⬭ *Translate ll. 91–117 into German.*

⬭ *Sum up this scene in about 200 words as part of a German-language guide to modern American drama.*

2 Down and Out – and Up?

„Down and Out – and Up?" greift das in *section* 1 aufgeworfene Thema der sozialen und ökonomischen Verlierer auf und führt es in doppelter Hinsicht weiter: Zum einen wird in Texten A und B Armut in Entwicklungsländern und in industrialisierten Gesellschaften am Beispiel von Indien und Großbritannien kontrastiert; zum anderen werden am Beispiel der britischen Hilfsorganisation Street (UK) (Text C) Mikrokredite als ein Lösungsansatz zur Diskussion gestellt, mit dem die Situation sozial Benachteiligter verbessert werden kann. Im Sinne handlungsorientierten Lernens können die S in einem umfassenden Projekt eine eigene Geschäftsidee entwickeln.

→ WB, ex. 4, 6, 7

SB, S. 95 **A Poverty is Relative** | Mari Marcel Thekaekara

Source:	*The New Internationalist*, March 1999
Topic:	Poverty in Scotland (and India)
Text form:	Essay
Language variety:	BE
Number of words:	300
Level:	Basic/advanced
Skills/activities:	Analysing poverty, comparing one's own views on sth. with those of sb. else

Lern-vokabular

Active vocabulary: 'Poverty Is Relative' (p. 95)

housing estate (l. 4), social change (l. 5), stereotypical image of sth. (l. 6), aid worker (l. 6), by sb.'s standards (l. 10), dispirited (l. 15), depressed (l. 15), alcoholic (l. 15), self-esteem (l. 15), be worse off than sb. (l. 16), fall into the trap of ... (l. 18), material benefits (l. 19), suffer social deprivation (l. 20), be jobless (ll. 20–21)

Didaktisch-methodische Hinweise

Dieser Text dient dazu, einen differenzierten Armutsbegriff zu entwickeln, der nicht nur ökonomische, sondern auch sozialpsychologische Aspekte umfasst. Im Vergleich mit den indischen Adivasi ist die Bevölkerung des Glasgower Easterhouse *housing estate* nach den Beobachtungen der indischen Verfasserin materiell privilegiert, emotional aber benachteiligt. Die S erkennen so die Bedeutung von Hoffnung und Selbstwertgefühl für soziale Randgruppen. Sie erfahren Grenzen einer rein ökonomischen Betrachtungsweise und relativieren ihre Vorstellungen von Privilegierung und Benachteiligung in der Welt und hinterfragen das westliche Überlegenheitsgefühl.

Unterrichts-tipps

Als Vorbereitung bzw. Ersatz für die *pre-reading*-Aufgabe im SB bietet es sich an, die S Ideen zum Thema *poverty in the developing and the industrialized world* sammeln zu lassen (ggf. unterstützt durch Fotos armer Familien in beiden Regionen), die als Mind-Map strukturiert werden können. Alternativ können die S Spontanreaktionen auf die These: „I'd rather be poor in India [than in Great Britain]" (Z. 1) sammeln.

→ *WB, ex. 4, 6, 7*

Info

Adivasi (l. 1): There are about 400 Adivasi communities in India, representing about 7% of the population. They are tribal people, with many of them being hunters and gatherers or rudimentary agriculturists. They are not integrated into the surrounding Hindu or Muslim communities. The term *Adivasi* derives from Sanskrit and means 'original inhabitants', as it is generally believed that the Adivasis were the original inhabitants of India, who lived there before the arrival of the Indo-Europeans, but as India has always been a land of population migration, this might not be the case. The term *Adivasi* only entered into use after the independence of India. During British rule the Adivasis were considered uncivilized people who were encouraged to settle on the land. Since this time they have generally been looked down upon by other Indians.

ACCORD (Action for Community Organisation, Rehabilitation and Development) is an NGO (non-governmental organization) working with tribal people in Gudalur, Tamil Nadu, southern India. Founded in 1986 by Mari Marcel Thekaera and her husband Stan Thekaera, it has been involved with Adivasi land rights issues and runs schools and hospitals as well as subsidizing tea plantations.

Lösungs-hinweise

■■ *Pre-reading*: Das *OALD* definiert *poverty* als „the state of being poor"; *poor* als „having little money; not having enough money for basic needs".

Individual answers.

1 a) Before Thekaekara visits Glasgow, she thinks it is absurd that people with all the facilities available to the inhabitants of a Glasgow housing estate should be considered as living in poverty. In India, such amenities would be considered luxuries. b) Once in Glasgow, she realizes that poverty has more than just a material dimension; the unemployed of Easterhouse are psychologically scarred by their experience, and on the emotional, if not on the material, level, the unemployed in Glasgow are worse off. Both are socially deprived, but in different ways.

2 Individual answers.

○ *The North-South exchange which brought Mari Marcel Thekaekara to Britain was designed to 'reverse the stereotypical image of a Northern aid worker coming to help the Third World' (ll. 6–7). In your opinion, what can the West learn from developing countries?*

○ *PovertyNet (www.worldbank.org/poverty · 1.8.2003) is a World Bank website providing information about poverty, its measurement, its impacts, and initiatives to reduce poverty. In small groups, prepare questions on poverty and poverty reduction, research this website and present your findings to the class.*

○ *Translate ll. 7–17 into German.*

SB, S. 96 **B I Have to Keep the Hot Water for the Kids**   Bob Holman

Source:	*Faith in the Poor* (1998)
Topic:	Personal experience of poverty
Text form:	Diary extract (as part of non-fictional study)
Language variety:	BE
Number of words:	548
Level:	Basic/advanced
Skills/activities:	Analysing a text, supporting a view with evidence from a text, doing research, drawing up a fictional budget

Lern-vokabular

Active vocabulary: 'I Have to Keep the Hot Water for the Kids' (p. 96)

cash (l. 1), keep a diary (l. 4), bus fare (l. 10), spend money (on sth.) (ll. 11–12), be in debt (l. 25), borrow sth. (from sb.) (l. 28), work sth. out (l. 30), lend sb. sth. (l. 31), be on social security (l. 62), calm sb. (l. 64), give sth. up (l. 64), moan (l. 71), be on its last legs (l. 72)
tasks: sense sth., draw up a budget

Didaktisch-methodische Hinweise

Angesichts der gegenwärtig geführten Diskussion um die Zukunft des Sozialstaats können die Tagebucheinträge einer Bewohnerin des Easterhouse *housing estate* die S für die wirtschaftliche und soziale Situation von Sozialhilfeempfängern sensibilisieren. Der Text konkretisiert die in „Poverty is Relative" getroffene Aussage, Armut wiege in Industriestaaten schwerer als in Entwicklungsländern. Der in seiner Ausweglosigkeit bedrückende Text wirft die Frage auf, wie unter den Bedingungen einer globalisierten neoliberalen Marktwirtschaft das Selbstwertgefühl von Randgruppen gesteigert und ihre Zukunftsperspektive verbessert werden kann (vgl. SB, S. 95, Z. 15–23).

Unterrichts-tipps

Da der Text im Wesentlichen aus Einkaufslisten besteht, können die S als Vorbereitung einen typischen Einkaufszettel ihrer Familie zusammenstellen oder reale Einkaufszettel mitbringen, die anonym im Hinblick auf die Frage ausgewertet werden, welche Produkte dominieren und welchen Wert dieser Einkauf (in Euro und Pfund) hat.

Info

Easterhouse estate in Glasgow is Europe's largest council house estate with about 44,000 residents. 77% of the population lives on housing benefit, and unemployment stands at 17% (2002). Infant mortality is twice the national average. Crime, often fuelled by drugs, is an everyday occurrence.

*Lösungs-
hinweise*

1 The expenditure on cigarettes (which Erica comments on and tries to excuse) and on tokens for gas and electricity (obviously the residents are not trusted to pay bills, but have to pay immediately for what they use) take up the largest part of her budget. The family's diet is obviously more filling than it is healthy. The stress is on carbohydrates; there is no fresh fruit or vegetables and no meat or any other protein. Expenditure on transport, hygiene and entertainment seems to be a big problem.

2 Erica as a mother obviously feels upset that she cannot afford to pay for her kids' school trips and even has difficulty feeding them. She resents judgemental comments by others about her need for cigarettes. The family seems to spend a lot of time watching TV, maybe in order to escape from their bleak reality or because other activities are simply unaffordable. Ivor does not bother to get up and do anything at all, which is a clear indication that he is suffering from depression.

3 Die S können auf der Website der Bundesanstalt für Arbeit ein fiktives Arbeitslosengeld ausrechnen (www.arbeitsamt.de/hst/services/lis/alg/selbstberechnung/index. html · 1.8.2003). Die S müssen überlegen, wieviel Geld sie für Miete, Heizung, Lebensmittel usw. veranschlagen müssen.

◯ *Research the benefits available in Britain to unemployed couples with children.*

◯ *Imagine you could interview Charlotte, Deirdre, Gilbert or Mary about their life on the Easterhouse estate and their hopes for the future. Write the interview.*

◯ *Do research on the social and economic situation of the Adivasi in India and compare their lives with what you know about the people on the Easterhouse estate. Present your findings to the class under the title 'Poverty in India and Scotland'.*

SB, S. 97 ## C Starting Your Own Business

Source:	*Street (UK)* website (www.street-uk.com)
Topic:	The experience of two people who want to become self-employed
Text form:	Fictionalized case studies
Language variety:	BE
Number of words:	253
Level:	Basic
Skills/activities:	Working with vocabulary, describing a person's situation, discussing a topic, doing research, writing an e-mail

*Lern-
vokabular*

Active vocabulary: 'Starting Your Own Business' (p. 97)

on your own (l. 1), look after sb. (l. 1), set up a business (l. 4), supply sb./sth. (l. 4), straight away (l. 5), make a living from sth. (ll. 8–9), be in work (l. 11), undertake work for sb. (l. 12), do a good job (l. 14), willing to do sth. (ll. 14–15), hire sb. (l. 15), a waiting list (l. 15), self-employed (l. 16), bank account (l. 16), rented accommodation (l. 17), build up a business (l. 18)

Didaktisch-methodische Hinweise

Nachdem in Texten A und B Arbeitslosigkeit und Armut thematisiert wurden, stellt der Auszug aus der Website der britischen Hilfsorganisation Street (UK) einen Lösungsansatz zur Diskussion, der seit den Siebzigerjahren in verschiedenen Industrie- und Entwicklungsländern erprobt wurde: Mikrokredite als Weg, Eigeninitiative und Eigenverantwortung zu stärken und soziale Randgruppen aus Abhängigkeit und Armut zu befreien. Mikrokredite haben sich in verschiedenen Ländern als geeignet erwiesen, benachteiligten Gruppen (z.B. Frauen in Entwicklungsländern) neue Chancen zu eröffnen; sie können aber nicht alle strukturell bedingten Armutsprobleme lösen. Insbesondere für die Ärmsten der Armen bieten sie keine Lösung; diesen fehlen die Voraussetzungen für den Weg in die ökonomische Selbstständigkeit.

Unterrichts-tipps

Bevor die S den Text lesen, sollten sie in der *pre-reading*-Aufgabe die Frage beantworten, ob sie sich persönlich den Weg in die Selbstständigkeit vorstellen könnten. Als Abschluss kann ggf. in Zusammenarbeit mit den Fächern Politik und Wirtschaftslehre ein Projekt durchgeführt werden, bei dem die S ein virtuelles Unternehmen gründen (vgl. die Zusatzaufgabe unten).

Info

Microcredit system: The micro-finance industry began in 1976 with the establishment of the Grameen Bank in Bangladesh, but has now become a worldwide movement consisting of specialist banks, credit unions, co-operatives, village credit societies, NGOs and charities. The intention of the microcredit system is to offer banking services, especially business credit, to those who do not qualify for normal bank loans. Micro-credits are granted at commercial interest rates, though at much lower rates than those charged by informal money lenders. This allows the lending institution to become self-supporting, not profit-making, while the borrower is able to develop his or her business with loans that are affordable. Typical micro-loans in industrialized countries average between £1,000 and £10,000 and almost invariably they are unsecured, i.e. there is no guarantee that the sum will be paid back. Nevertheless, the worldwide average default rate is less than 2%, better than for most commercial banks.

Lösungs-hinweise

◼◼ *Pre-reading*: Die Ergebnisse können unter geschlechtsspezifischen Gesichtspunkten analysiert werden (z.B. sind Männer eher als Frauen zur Selbstständigkeit bereit?) und sollten nach Möglichkeit mit Statistiken für die Bundesrepublik verglichen werden (vgl. z.B. www.destatis.de/basis/d/erwerb/erwerbtab1.htm · 1.8.2003).

1 a

Sarah	**Leroy**	**both**
start-up with no track record or collateral	a more established entrepreneur	develop a fledgling business unable to secure the credit
a single parent	operate in the grey market	he/she needs to ...
	risk losing your benefits	become self-employed

b Sarah is a single parent who would like to start her own sandwich-making business. As she is trying to develop a fledgling business with no track record or collateral, she is unable to secure the credit she needs.

Leroy is a painter/decorator who operates in the grey market to top up his unemployment benefits. If he becomes self-employed, he risks losing his benefits. Like Sarah, he is unable to secure the credit he needs as he has no bank account.

2 a Possible answers:

Sarah and Leroy need to find someone willing to lend them money. They could:

- apply to banks for a loan;
- take out a personal bank overdraft;

- borrow from a money lender;
- ask friends and family for a loan;
- get a loan from a charity or organization that specializes in credit to small businesses.

b Discussion of their options:
- Banks are unlikely to lend money to Sarah and Leroy (Leroy does not even have a bank account). Sarah and Leroy do not have a fixed income and have no assets to offer the banks as security; in other words, they cannot put up collateral. Sarah, in particular, has little business experience. The size of any loan that Sarah and Leroy may qualify for will be relatively small, the administrative costs of the banks relatively high. (The administrative costs of a £2,000 loan is roughly the same as that of a £20,000 loan; the profit to the bank is only 10%.) Thus banks will have no incentive to lend money to people like Sarah and Leroy.
- Going into overdraft or going into debt on a credit card are not feasible, as the rate of interest paid on such debts is very high.
- Borrowing from a money lender is just as tricky, as they charge very high rates and often use force to get back their money.
- If Sarah and Leroy have friends and family who have money to spare, they might get a loan from them, but if their businesses are successful, they will still need to borrow money from other sources.
- Street-UK suggests the following course of action for Sarah and Leroy:
  Sarah: a four month loan of £500 to develop her business by purchasing more stock and taking on an assistant (cf. www.street-uk.com/sarah.htm · 1.8.03).
  Leroy: a six month loan of £2,000 to enable him to buy a second-hand van, enabling him to develop his business on a full-time basis and build an independent future (cf. www.street-uk.com/leroy.htm · 1.8.03).

3 Possible answers:
a) Street (UK) provides loans for individual lenders but favours the group lending approach: Borrowers join together to form groups of between four and seven members. No collateral is required but borrowers guarantee each other's loans. Further loans are only given if all group members fully repay their loans. Loans are structured to meet the needs of each borrower. The loan is usually very low, and it serves to ensure that the business is merely given a helping start. Borrowers who have successfully met all loan terms qualify for a further loan to gradually build up their businesses.
b) Street (UK) is run by a charitable organization, but its management are people from the world of finance.
c) Microcredit programmes were pioneered in rural Bangladesh. They have inspired similar programmes in developing and industrialized countries and have attracted the attention of institutions like the World Bank. In 1976 Muhammad Yunas, a Bangladeshi economics professor, lent the equivalent of $26 to a group of 42 women, who bought bamboo to make and sell stools. Soon they were able to repay their loans. In 1983 Yunas founded the Grameen Bank, which lends money at a commercial rate and requires its lenders to organize themselves into groups of five. Their members, mostly women, guarantee each other's loans; they discuss their business plans and also address other issues, e.g. health questions. The Grameen Bank reports a repayment rate that is higher than that of commercial banks (cf. www.grameen-info.org · 1.8.03).

4 Individual answers.

5 Opportunities: Microcredits help the poor in developing and industrialized countries to achieve new hope, respect and dignity. They are 'hand-ups' designed to help people help themselves (into work and off benefits) rather than 'handouts' given to those dependent on outside help. Thus microcredits can improve the psychological, social and financial well-being of individuals. At the same time they can strengthen communities by providing opportunities to network with others (e.g. friends, other borrowers, other microenterprises) and by creating new job opportunities.

<u>Limits:</u> Microcredit programs do not help the poorest of the poor, who lack the initiative and skills necessary to start a business. They are no substitute for long-term infrastructure projects and land reform programmes to reduce poverty in developing countries.

⬭ *In groups of five, imagine you are going to start your own business. Decide on:*
- *what product or service you are going to offer (Who is your target group? What do you need to prepare before the launch? How many people will be involved?);*
- *how much capital you will need (How much will you have to spend on things such as a site or office, equipment, transport and communications, initial stock, advertising, labour costs, etc.?);*
- *where you will get the money (Do you and your partners have enough money? Will you need to borrow some, and how much and where from?);*
- *how you will market your product or service (What method is best to achieve publicity? Do you need sales reps?).*

Then design a brochure or video about your business and describe your concepts to the class.

SB, S. 99 ## Context Box

Didaktisch-methodische Hinweise

Der Schwerpunkt der „Context Box" liegt auf Neoliberalismus, ökonomischer Globalisierung und deren Folgen für Industrieländer und Entwicklungsländer. Die S sind gefordert, sich einen Überblick über Entwicklungen in der Weltwirtschaft seit den frühen Neunzigerjahren zu verschaffen. Sie müssen den in der aktuellen Diskussion häufig unscharf verwendeten Begriff der ökonomischen Globalisierung definieren, diesen an Beispielen konkretisieren und sich mit den sozialen Folgen der Globalisierung differenziert auseinander setzen. Unter Berücksichtigung der Erfahrungswelt der S wird der Blick auf kulturelle, politische und ökologische Aspekte der Globalisierung gelenkt und damit bereits die Diskussion über die Rolle des Englischen als internationaler Geschäfts- und Verkehrssprache vorbereitet (vgl. „As Basic as the Screwdriver", SB, S. 101).

Unterrichts-tipps

Bei der Erarbeitung kann von den Fotos auf S. 99 oder 103 ausgegangen werden:

⬭ *What do you think the demonstrators in the photo on p. 99 are protesting about? (Scan the Context Box for information on the WTO.)*

⬭ *Look at the photos of the British phone boxes on p. 103. Why do you think the British government decided to privatize the telecommunications industry? What do the phone boxes tell you about privatization?*

Companies that are privately run are usually more efficient. The modern telephone box might be rather characterless, but it is probably easier to construct and maintain, unlike the traditional telephone box. Thus functionality prevailed over aesthetics.

Lösungs-hinweise

1 Trends in the global economy since the 1990s include: collapse of centrally planned economies, increasing popularity of neoliberal policies such as privatization of state-owned enterprises, cuts in social services and welfare benefits, the liberalization of labour laws, and the acceptance of globalization (e.g. cross-border mergers of companies, transfer of operations to low-wage countries).

Differenzierung **2** Leistungsstärkere S können ihre gesammelten Kollokationen unter den unten angegebenen Überschriften eintragen. Das Sprachmaterial kann als Basis für weitere Wortschatzübungen zu Synonymen (z.B. *cut back / reduce, fire / lay off*) und Antonymen (z.B. *weaken/strengthen, part-time/full-time, hire/fire, foreign/ domestic, developing/ industrialized*) dienen.

adverb	participle/adjective	(compound) noun
centrally	planned	economy
	free	trade/enterprise
increasingly	global	economy
	lower	wage level
	multinational	companies
	economic	power
	foreign	investment
	increasing	unemployment
	developing	world

verb	participle/adjective	(compound) noun
influence		the economy
follow	neo-liberal	policies
weaken		trade unions
privatize	state-owned	enterprises
cut back		social services
change		labour laws
allow		part-time/temporary work
hire/fire		workers
maximize		efficiency/profits
bring		prosperity (to sb./sth.)
move		operations
profit from		globalization
represent		(workers') interests
pull out		capital
reduce	public	spending
lay off		workers

3 **a** Economic globalization is the process that leads to the increasing interdependence and integration of national economies through trade and investment around the world.

Companies such as Daimler Benz and Chrysler merge across countries, acquire stakes in foreign companies (e.g. Daimler Chrysler in Mitsubishi Motors) and transfer part of their production to countries where the wages are lower (e.g. Volkswagen builds Seats in Spain, Skodas in the Czech Republic).

b Benefits: increased prosperity, lower costs, increased competitiveness, emergence of new jobs and capital inflow into developing countries.

Disadvantages: weakening of trade unions operating in multinational companies, no accountability of multinationals, exploitation of cheap labour, inadequate labour standards, increased inequality internationally and within countries, increased dependence of developing countries on foreign capital.

4 Economic aspects: cheaper air travel leading to greater mobility but more rapid spread of diseases (e.g. AIDS, SARS) and air pollution; job opportunities outside Germany; drop in the prices of consumer goods (clothes) bought in shops.

Cultural aspects: global youth culture (e.g. clothes, food, music, sports); domination of American products in the world market; increased contact with people from other cultures through information technology, work experience placements / internships, semesters abroad; increasing use of English words in German; English as a global language; changing holiday traditions (e.g. Halloween, Christmas, Valentine's Day are observed in countries where they were previously not celebrated).

<u>Political aspects:</u> strengthening of Western, especially US influence, on national affairs; strengthening of the economic and political power of corporations; mergers in the media leading to the removal of dissenting voices (e.g. the Australian-born media tycoon Rupert Murdoch used capital from his foreign and satellite TV companies to wage a newspaper war in Britain aimed at destroying rivals to the *Times*).

<u>Environmental aspects:</u> global warming, destruction of the ozone layer, increasing danger of skin cancer, flooding, destruction of natural environment through tourism.

◯ *Identify as many reasons as you can to explain why a corporation would want to locate (or at least establish and maintain) plants in a foreign country.*

◯ *Imagine you are the chairperson of the board of directors of a major corporation. You must decide if it is wise to locate parts of your company in a particular foreign nation. What political/economic conditions would you want to find there so that your company can work successfully? If you decide to locate your new plant in the nation under consideration, what effects might your plant have on it? Assume you have found the ideal country in which to locate your new plant. How will you go about persuading the nation to accept your presence in the country?*

SB, S. 100

Getting Along in English

*Didaktisch-
methodische
Hinweise*

In dieser *section* begegnen die S verschiedenen Situationen, die mit dem Thema Einkaufen zu tun haben (vgl. CD1, *track* 34–36; die Transkripte auf S. 195). Ziel ist es, den S Sprachmaterial zu vermitteln, das insbesondere interkulturell bedeutsame Höflichkeits- und Entschuldigungsfloskeln (z.B. *I wonder if ...*, *I'm afraid*) und andere transaktionsbezogene Redemittel enthält (z.B. *here you go, that's great, there you are*). Diese werden von Deutschen deutlich seltener verwendet als von Muttersprachlern, weshalb Deutsche auf Angelsachsen nicht selten als zu direkt und unfreundlich wirken.

*Lösungs-
hinweise*

1 Die S sollten darauf hingewiesen werden, dass es hier nicht nur um inhaltlich sinnvolle Fragen geht, sondern insbesondere um deren höfliche Formulierung. Folgende Redemittel können hilfreich sein: *I was wondering if ..., Excuse me, but ..., I'm sorry but ..., I'm afraid I ..., Do you happen to ...?.*

Possible questions:
- Excuse me. Have you got any others (in stock)? / You don't happen to have this in a different colour, do you?
- I was wondering if you sell notepaper in this store? / I'm afraid I can't see any wrapping paper here. Do you happen to sell any?
- May I have a look at that watch in that window, please? / Could you please get me one of those earrings in the display case?
- Excuse me, can I try this on, please?
- Excuse me. I'm looking for a bottle of champagne/whisky, but I can't see any anywhere. Do you sell/stock any here?
- I'm sorry but I seem to have run out of cash. Could you tell me if there's a bank or cash dispenser nearby? / Excuse me, I need to get some cash. Could you tell me where I can find a bank or ATM, please?
- Could you help me, please? I was just wondering where can I get hold of a screwdriver.

2 Der Hörtext befindet sich auf CD1, *track* 34; das Transkript auf S. 195.

a Der Anspruch dieser Aufgabe wird dadurch erhöht, dass in dem Dialog Synonyme der im SB angegebenen Begriffe verwendet werden (vgl. „bonus card" / „reward card", „coupon / voucher"). Der Dialog muss deshalb sicher zwei Mal vorgespielt werden.

Bonus card (= reward card), using a coupon (= voucher), options of paying, using a credit card, signing a receipt, wrapping.

b Für diese Aufgabe wird der Dialog ein drittes Mal gespielt werden müssen.

1 I'd like to use this voucher, please.
2 And if you could sign the receipt here.
3 I wonder if you could possibly wrap it as a present?
4 I can only give you a carrier bag.
5 Not to worry.

3 Individual answers.

4 Der Hörtext befindet sich auf CD1, *track* 35 und 36; das Transkript auf S. 195.
Excuse me; let's have a look; righty-ho; here you go; thanks very much; that's great.
I mean; well, I'm sorry but …; I'm afraid; I appreciate that, but …; all I can say is …; I'm very sorry, but there you are; please; excuse me.

In groups of four, imagine the following situation: You take a recently bought pair of swimming goggles back to the shop where you bought them because the strap has started to tear. The assistant, however, believes that the fault is yours (because you pulled the strap too hard). Moreover, the goggles were on sale, so she refuses to take them back. How might the scenario continue? Listen to the recordings again and write down phrases that might help you play your role. Then practise the scene. Take care to be polite but stick to your point of view.

SB, S. 101 # 3 **As Basic as the Screwdriver** Stephen Baker et al.

Text:
Source:	*Business Week*, 13 August, 1999
Topic:	English as the international language of business
Text form:	Feature story
Language variety:	AE
Number of words:	389
Level:	Basic
Skills/activities:	Analysing the global role of English

CD ('Interviews with Braj Kachru and David Crystal'):
Source:	'The Routes of English', *BBC*, 11 October, 2001
Topic:	English in Europe
Text form:	Radio interviews
Language variety:	BE
Length:	3:03 minutes
Level:	Basic/advanced
Skills/activities:	Listening comprehension, analysing metaphors, identifying reasons for the spread of English

Lern-vokabular

Active vocabulary: 'As Basic as the Screwdriver' (p. 101)

win the lottery (l. 1), enroll (BE: enrol) sb. in a school (l. 3), a bright future (l. 4), second language (l. 11), spread beyond sth. (l. 16), link sb./sth. to sb./sth. else (l. 17), move toward(s) political and economic unification (ll. 17–18), a common language (l. 18), crucial (l. 18), labor (BE: labour) market (l. 20), implications (l. 25), engineer (l. 28), blue-collar worker (l. 29), colleague (l. 29), customer (l. 30), factory floor (l. 32)

Didaktisch-methodische Hinweise

Dieser Abschnitt führt das in der „Context Box" eingeführte Thema der Globalisierung unter sprachlichen Aspekten fort. Er unterstreicht die Bedeutung des Englischen als internationaler Geschäfts- und Verkehrssprache für Europa (und die übrige Welt) und thematisiert den Zusammenhang von sprachlicher und politischer bzw. wirtschaftlicher Macht. Während der Text das Englische in einem positiven Licht sieht, sind die Interviews auf der CD eher kritisch (vgl. CD 1, *track* 37, und das Transkript auf S. 196). Hier spricht der in England bekannte Journalist Melvyn Bragg mit Braj Kachru und David Crystal, zwei renommierten Linguisten, die die Entwicklung des Englischen zur *lingua franca* beschreiben und die Machtverhältnisse skizzieren, die zu dieser Entwicklung beigetragen haben.

Den S dürfte bewusst sein, dass Kompetenz im Englischen Vorteile im Berufs- und Alltagsleben bedeutet. Durch die Aufgaben werden sie auch für Probleme sensibilisiert, die sich aus der Verwendung des Englischen als internationaler Verkehrssprache ergeben. Zu ihnen gehören die Gefährdung der kulturellen und sprachlichen Vielfalt und Identität Europas und die Verbindung von Sprache und Macht.

Unter dem Aspekt „Englisch als globale Sprache" ergeben sich von dieser *section* aus Verbindungen zu anderen Texten des SB: „Old Empire", SB, S. 158; „New Empire: The Triumph of English", SB, S. 161; „Imperial Power", SB, S. 171; „A Growing Dislike of the USA", SB, S. 172.

Unterrichts-tipps

Als Einstieg in die Thematik können die folgenden Fragen dienen:

⬭ *How would life be different for you if you could not speak English?*

⬭ *How do you feel about the role of English in the world and in Germany in particular?*

Vor dem Einsatz der Interviews empfiehlt es sich, das Vorwissen der S zur weltweiten Verbreitung des Englischen und zu seinen Varietäten zu erheben:

⬭ *What are the reasons for the spread of English around the world?*

→ WB, ex. 8 ⬭ *There is a journal called* World Englishes. *What do you think is meant by 'Englishes'?*

Info

English in Europe: Generally, English is the first foreign language in education in all EU Member States (except anglophone ones). In secondary education, the language most often taught as a foreign language is English. About 89% of all students in Europe learn English. In Denmark, Germany, Spain, France, Austria, Finland, Sweden and the Netherlands over 90% of all secondary school students learn English. 32% of pupils learn French, 18% German and 8% Spanish. Altogether 47% of all non-native English speakers in the EU say they speak English well.

Lösungs-hinweise

1 The advantages mentioned are:
- English is part of everyday life in European cities, it does not seem foreign (cf. l. 11).
- It has put down deep roots in vital areas of business, finance and technology (cf. l. 15).
- It is helping to connect European people with each other (cf. ll. 16–17, 21–24).
- It is thus a force for European unification (cf. ll. 18–20).

– In the business world it is necessary to speak it as companies enter the global marketplace (cf. l. 27).
– Speakers of English are rewarded by higher incomes (cf. ll. 32–34).

2 Possible answers:
– Other languages will become less important and so people will not bother to learn them, so that really only native speakers will be able to speak them.
– Especially minority languages could lose their status and might be neglected, so there will be fewer media and fewer works of literature or songs in those languages, so that they could die out.
– There might be a greater social gap between educated people who speak English well and less educated ones who can only speak the native language.
– Other European languages will borrow more words and phrases from English.
– There might be a generation gap if older people still feel at home in their native language but younger ones tend to use English more.

3 Possible answers:
The global economy could exist without a global language, but transactions would be harder and slower:
– People would need to translate documents or wait for interpreters to put their speech or publications into a foreign language.
– Personal contact and face-to-face meetings would be more difficult because there would be someone in the middle translating.
– If you do not speak the same language, it is harder to build up the trust you need to do business with each other.
– There would have to be more versions of each product, one for each language area, thereby pushing up prices.

 4 Vgl. CD1, *track* 37, und das Transkript auf S. 196. Da insbesondere Kachrus Aussagen nicht leicht verständlich sind, sollten folgende Wörter semantisiert werden:

trunk: the lower thick part of a tree
whammy (infml): something that has a strong or unpleasant influence
quadruple: consisting of four parts

a Kachru uses the metaphor of the tree. He says that people loved the branches, as they were beautiful and attractive, whereas the trunk was always viewed with suspicion. He suggests that people like the varieties of English, as they are what make the language beautiful, but people are suspicious of where the language comes from, i.e. Britain and America, as it is not always clear what their intentions are.

b Crystal says that English spread due to power, of which he mentions four types:
– political power (which is associated with the British Empire);
– technological power (the Industrial Revolution took place in English-speaking countries, forcing others to learn the language to keep up with developments);
– economic power (the power of the USA has had an important influence on the world);
– cultural power (every significant cultural development in the 20th century either started in an English-speaking country or was facilitated very rapidly by an Englsh-speaking country).

4 Freedom and Opportunity

Section 4 behandelt die Frage, inwieweit der Staat in die Wirtschaft eingreifen sollte. Es werden zwei gegensätzliche Auffassungen dargestellt, die in den letzten Jahrzehnten vielfach diskutiert wurden: der neoliberale Ansatz von Milton und Rose Friedman, die in der Tradition Adam Smiths staatliche Interventionen in der Wirtschaft ablehnen, und der sozialstaatliche Ansatz Huttons, der in der Tradition der europäischen Sozialdemokratie für ein aktives Handeln des Staates plädiert. Die Aufgaben zielen primär auf Verständnissicherung, erst am Schluss sollen die S anhand vorgegebener Aussagen eine begründete Stellungnahme zur Rolle des Staates in der Wirtschaft abgeben. Den Abschluss bildet ein Song des englischen Liedermachers Billy Bragg, der aus der Sicht der Modernisierungsverlierer gegen neoliberale Wirtschaftspolitik protestiert.

Dieser Abschnitt ist wegen seines Abstraktionsniveaus der anspruchsvollste in diesem Kapitel. Er ist im Idealfall in fächerübergreifender Zusammenarbeit mit den Fächern Politik bzw. Wirtschaftslehre zu bearbeiten.

Unterrichts-tipps

Als Einstieg werden die S gebeten, mit Hilfe der Wörter im Kasten die Kernbegriffe *economic freedom* und *economic regulation* zu definieren. Diese Aufgabe ist für leistungsstarke S gedacht, die über gute Politik- bzw. Wirtschaftskenntnisse verfügen. Wird diese Aufgabe ausgelassen, können die S bei der Besprechung der drei Texte auf den Wortschatz im Kasten hingewiesen werden.

SB, S. 102

A Political and Economic Freedom   Milton and Rose Friedman

Source:	*Free to Choose*, 1980
Topic:	The importance of freedom for economic development
Text form:	Extract from a non-fiction book
Language variety:	AE
Number of words:	606
Level:	Advanced
Skills/activities:	Examining American history, comparing two viewpoints, writing a summary

Lern-vokabular

Active vocabulary: 'Political and Economic Freedom' (p. 102)

settlement (l. 1), a magnet for sth. (l. 2), seek adventure (l. 3), flee from sth. (l. 3), make a better life for yourself (ll. 3–4), be attracted by sth. (ll. 8–9), affluence (l. 9), streets paved with gold (l. 10), make the most of sth. (l. 11), encourage sb. to do sth. (l. 13), masterpiece (l. 19), insight (l. 24), the public good (l. 32), proclaim sth. (l. 35), be entitled to do sth. (l. 36), pursue sth. (l. 36), equality of opportunity (ll. 43–44), the free market (l. 48)

Didaktisch-methodische Hinweise

Milton und Rose Friedman präsentieren ein optimistisches Bild der USA als Land, dem es weitgehend gelungen ist, ökonomische und politische Freiheit zu verwirklichen. Als Verfechter einer neoliberalen Wirtschaftsordnung vertreten sie die These, dass ökonomische Freiheit die unabdingbare Voraussetzung für politische Freiheit darstellt. Sie stehen damit exemplarisch für eine Wirtschaftstheorie, die in den letzten Jahrzehnten weltweit an Bedeutung gewonnen hat. Mit ihren Hinweisen auf Adam Smiths *An Inquiry into the Nature and Causes of the Wealth of Nations* und die amerikanische Unabhängigkeitserklärung lenken sie den Blick auf zentrale Dokumente der westlichen Geschichte. An dieser Stelle ist eine Verknüpfung mit dem neunten Kapitel denkbar, insbesondere mit dem Abschnitt „American Dreams" und der „Context Box".

Verständnisschwierigkeiten sind am ehesten bei der komprimierten und lexikalisch anspruchsvollen Darstellung der Wirtschaftstheorie Adam Smiths zu erwarten, die die

meisten S nicht kennen werden. Im Zusammenhang mit den Ausführungen der Friedmans genügt es, wenn die S Smiths Grundposition verstehen: Die Triebkraft der Wirtschaft ist Eigeninteresse; dezentralisierte Märkte lenken diese so, dass das Gemeinwohl
gefördert wird; der Staat hat in wirtschaftlichen Belangen Zurückhaltung zu üben.

Die optimistische Sicht der Friedmans hinsichtlich der Verwirklichung von „equality of
opportunity" und „equality of results" in den USA (Z. 43–44) sollte relativiert werden, z.B.
durch Einbeziehung der Statistiken zur Kinderarmut in den USA und zur Einkommens-
ungleichheit in ausgewählten Ländern (vgl. „Facts and Figures", SB, S. 170). In den USA
unterscheiden sich die Startbedingungen für Kinder aus verschiedenen ethnischen
Gruppen beträchtlich; trotz einiger Verbesserungen seit 1970 leben deutlich mehr
Kinder schwarzer und lateinamerikanischer Herkunft unter der Armutsgrenze als
weiße Kinder. In den sozialstaatlich orientierten europäischen Ländern sind die
Einkommensunterschiede deutlich geringer als in der freien Marktwirtschaft der USA.

Unterrichts-
tipps

❖ Der Einstieg in den Text kann auf zwei Weisen erfolgen: Um die historische Perspektive
der Friedmans zu kontextualisieren, kann vor der Lektüre das Vorwissen der S zur amerikanischen Geschichte reaktiviert werden. Wird eine stärkere Orientierung auf wirtschaftliche Fragen gewünscht, können die S mögliche Gründe für den US-amerikanischen Reichtum zusammentragen. Die S können ggf. arbeitsteilig beide *pre-reading-*
Aufgaben bearbeiten und die Ergebnisse in einem Kugellager (vgl. S. 429) austauschen:

⬭ *What do you know about Jamestown / Plymouth / the War of Independence?*

⬭ *List reasons why you think the USA is the richest and most powerful nation in the*

→ *WB, ex. 7* *world.*

Info

Milton and Rose D. Friedman: Milton Friedman (born 1912) is one of the leading
economists in the United States. The son of Jewish immigrants, he became adviser to
Presidents Richard Nixon and Ronald Reagan. In 1976 he won the Nobel Prize for
Economics. He and his wife Rose D. Friedman, a Polish-born economist, collaborated on
several books, among them the bestselling *Free to Choose* (1980), written to accompany
a TV series on the Public Broadcasting System. They established the Milton and Rose D.
Friedman Foundation (www.friedmanfoundation.org; 01.08.03) to promote competition
and flexibility among schools through educational vouchers, i.e. a system in which
parents are given an amount of money which they can use to send their child to a private
or public school of their choice.

Adam Smith (1723–1790) was a Scottish philosopher and economist who is best known
for his book *The Wealth of Nations* (1776). Raised by his widowed mother in Kirkcaldy,
Smith attended Glasgow University and then Oxford University. He was appointed
Professor of Logic, then Professor of Moral Philosophy at Glasgow University. He also
published *The Theory of Moral Sentiments* (1756), about moral philosophy. The Duke of
Buccleuch engaged him as tutor to his son on the Grand Tour of Europe, where Smith
met other eminent thinkers such as Voltaire, Rousseau, and Franklin. Adam Smith had
an important influence on Western economic thought, particularly at the end of the
20th century when neo-liberalism experienced a rebirth under Prime Minister
Thatcher and President Reagan.

Lösungs-
hinweise

– Jamestown 1607: first permanent English settlement on American soil,
started by the London Company (joint stock company). Investors expected to make
a profit from the trade of the settlers.
– Plymouth 1620: The Pilgrims were a Puritan group who obtained a charter to settle
in Virginia in order to practise their form of religion. They established the first
constitution ('the Mayflower compact') governing civil society in the USA.

- Declaration of Independence 1776: Disagreements over colonial trade, taxation and political representation led to the War of Independence between the colonists and Britain.
- 19th century immigration: Economic and political factors led to increased immigration to the USA from all over Europe as well as Asia.

2 Smith and Jefferson both advocated the freedom of individuals to pursue their own objectives without government interference. Adam Smith was convinced that, in a market economy, self-interest and the common good go hand in hand. In his view, an individual who 'intends only his own gain' (ll. 28–29) is led by 'an invisible hand' (l. 29) to promote the interest of society more effectively than when he intends to trade for the common good (cf. ll. 28–31). According to Jefferson, the pursuit of happiness is an inalienable right. It is one of the principles on which the USA was founded (cf. ll. 36–39).

3 Als Sprachmittlungsaufgabe kann diese Zusammenfassung auf Deutsch erfolgen.

According to the Friedmans, the United States has, since its beginnings, been a magnet for those seeking political freedom and the opportunity to build a better life through hard work, ingenuity and thrift. The success of the United States is based on economic and political freedom as advocated by two documents published in 1776: Adam Smith's *The Wealth of Nations* and the Declaration of Independence. The former argues that economic success derives from pursuing one's own interests, while the latter stated that individuals are entitled to pursue their own interests. The Friedmans see economic freedom as a prerequisite of political freedom. It prevents the concentration of power in the hands of a central authority and thus makes tyranny impossible. (119 words)

⬭ *What stylistic devices do the Friedmans use to make their arguments sound convincing?*
- Words and phrases with positive connotations: 'magnet for' (l. 2), 'promise of freedom and affluence' (ll. 8–9), 'an economic miracle and a political miracle' (ll. 15–16), 'masterpiece' (l. 19).

- Contrast/antithesis: 'misery and tyranny [...] freedom and affluence' (ll. 8–9); 'they did not find streets paved with gold; they did not find an easy life. The did find freedom and an opportunity to make the most of their talents' (ll. 10–12), 'cooperate [...] without coercion' (l. 46).

- Alliteration: 'curious coincidence' (l. 17), 'cooperation and collaboration' (ll. 22–23), 'cooperate [...] coercion' (l. 46), 'slavery [...] settled [...] civil war [...] subsequent' (l. 42).

- Enumeration: 'hard work, ingenuity, thrift, and luck' (l. 12), 'our food, our clothing, our housing' (ll. 23–24).

- Hendiadys [hen'daɪədis] (two nouns joined by a conjunction, used to express a single idea): 'misery and tyranny' (l. 8), 'freedom and affluence' (l. 9), 'hopes and dreams' (l. 13), 'cooperation and collaboration' (ll. 22–23), 'coercion or central direction' (l. 46).

- Repetition: 'they did not find' (l. 10), 'miracle' (ll. 15–16), 'benefit' (ll. 25, 26, 28), 'attempt' (ll. 42–43), 'equality (of opportunity) [...] equality (of results)' (ll. 43–44).

- Parallelism: 'driven by [...] and attracted by [...]' (ll. 8–9).

- Anaphora (here: a triple repetition with a climactic structure): 'No external force, no coercion, no violation of freedom' (ll. 26–27).

- Imagery: metaphors from the world of water ('trickle', 'swell', 'flood', 'stream', cf. ll. 5–9) to suggest the increase in immigration to the United States in the 19th century: images from nature make this increase look natural (and therefore welcome).

B The Fair Society   Will Hutton

Source:	*The World We're In*, 2002
Topic:	The role of government in regulating social affairs
Text form:	Extract from a non-fiction book
Language variety:	BE
Number of words:	103
Level:	Advanced
Skills/activities:	Comparing two texts, giving one's own opinion, discussing a topic

Lern-
vokabular

Active vocabulary: 'The Fair Society' (p. 103)

provide sth. (l. 2), public services (ll. 2–3), regulate sth (l. 3), be conceived as sth. (l. 3), risk (l. 4), allocate sth. (l. 7), market forces (l. 7), enforce sth. (l. 8)
tasks: fulfil a task, issue, impose a tariff, economic growth

Didaktisch-
methodische
Hinweise

Huttons Plädoyer für einen „activist state" (Z. 8) bildet das Gegengewicht zu den Thesen der Friedmans. Sein Bekenntnis zum europäischen Erbe kann die S für Unterschiede zwischen amerikanischer und europäischer Tradition im Spannungsfeld zwischen ökonomischer Freiheit und sozialer Gerechtigkeit sensibilisieren: In den europäischen Sozialstaaten wird im Konfliktfall soziale Gerechtigkeit höher gewertet als individuelle Freiheit. In den USA wird aufgrund anderer historischer Erfahrungen der Eigeninitiative und der individuellen Wahlfreiheit der Vorrang gegeben (vgl. den Buchtitel *Free to Choose*). Eine weitere Rechtfertigung von Steuern, hier aus ökologischen Gründen, findet sich im Text 3C, SB, S. 85.

Unterrichts-
tipps

Huttons Text ist trotz seiner Kürze sowohl lexikalisch wie auch syntaktisch anspruchsvoll. Deshalb sollte einige Zeit auf die Sicherung des Textverständnisses verwendet werden. Nachdem die S den Text mehrfach gelesen und die Wortbedeutungen geklärt haben, kann folgende Aufgabe zur Verständnissicherung bearbeitet werden:

    ⬭ *For each sentence of the text, try to find a couple of words or a phrase which seem central to the meaning of the sentence.*
'fair society' (l. 1), 'larger role for the state' (ll. 1–2), 'conciliating' (l. 2), 'providing public services' (ll. 2–3), 'regulating business and society' (l. 3), 'actor' (l. 4), 'underwrites the
→ *WB, ex. 7*   risks' (l. 5), 'worker rights' (l. 6), 'activist state' (l. 8).

Info

Will Hutton was the editor of the liberal *Observer* newspaper and still writes for it as a columnist. His book *The World We're In* is a critical view of the effects of globalization and a plea for the Europeans to resist US pressure for further economic liberalisation.

Lösungs-
hinweise

1 Possible answers:
– Conciliating partners (e.g. intervening or mediating in industrial unrest, strikes);
– providing public services (e.g. education, health, welfare, roads, police);
– regulating business and society (e.g. monopolies commission, agricultural subsidies, legislation on environmental protection);
– ensuring the fair distribution of risks and rewards (e.g. ensuring that people cannot be cheated in investments, progressive taxation of earnings);
– ensuring everyone has insurance (e.g. unemployment benefit, health insurance);
– supporting worker rights (e.g. adequate payment, against unfair dismissal).

2 Die S können für diese Aufgabe eine Argumentationsübersicht anfertigen. Dabei notieren sie die in beiden Texten vorgebrachten Argumente in strukturierter Form, z.B. in einer Tabelle.

The Friedmans and Hutton basically agree on the aim of promoting equality of opportunity and of results – in Hutton's words, 'a fair society'. They disagree in the means to achieve that end. Hutton envisages a state which intervenes directly and indirectly to guarantee 'fair play'. But the Friedmans believe that an 'invisible hand' (l. 29) will ensure economic success if everybody is allowed to follow his or her own economic interests without hindrance. Indeed, concentration of economic and political power in the hands of politicians is not only likely to wreck the economy, but will endanger liberty itself. Hutton believes that the state needs to harmonize the various interests in society actively and to bear the weaker members of society in mind.

3 Possible answers:
- Governments levy tax and set up welfare systems to ensure that everyone has sufficient food, decent clothing and adequate health care. If there is poverty, one has to ask what social problems this might lead to.
- In state-controlled economies, central planners decide what goods and services are produced, how much is produced, and who produces and consumes these goods and services. Since the collapse of communism in the Soviet Union and Eastern Europe, these centralized economies have been abandoned in favour of market economies. No serious economist today would argue that the state should establish production levels and set prices for goods.
- Governments may be tempted to impose tariffs and import quotas to protect the domestic economy. Economists have long argued that international trade allows all countries to achieve greater prosperity, and most believe that poor countries would be better off opening up their markets to the outside world. However, there is evidence that the free trade policies demanded by international organizations such as the World Bank, the International Monetary Fund and the World Trade Organization have caused serious problems in some developing countries. There seem to be different routes to economic growth and prosperity.
- As small businesses provide employment opportunities, often for disadvantaged groups, governments may hope to promote economic growth by supporting them, e.g. by helping them receive loans or by encouraging them to work together. However, there is controversy among economists as to the roles of public and private support for small businesses.
- Those who enjoy the benefits of selling and consuming a product should pay all the costs they incur, otherwise it falls to the government to pay the costs (and thus the tax-payer in the end).
- Although there is broad agreement among economists that markets are usually a good way to organize economic activity and to determine production levels and prices, even neo-liberal economists accept that there are certain functions that governments have to carry out. These include establishing and protecting the right to private property. Without a system of justice that protects the property rights of owners and enforces contracts in an even-handed manner there would be no incentive for people to set up in business.
- If the market does not produce good results, governments sometimes need to intervene to improve market outcomes in the interest of efficiency and fairness. To prevent monopolies from maximizing profits at the expense of the public, governments take action to limit monopoly power.
- To provide incentives to curb pollution such as exhaust emissions from cars, governments may decide to impose taxes on polluters. In this way they make sure that the costs occurring to society are born by those who cause them.
- Some students will argue that it is unfair to make all taxpayers, including low-income families, pay for what is often enjoyed by a well-to-do cultural elite only.

Others will argue that just as society has accepted responsibility for health, welfare and education, it must support the arts. The arts play a vital role in society providing communities with aesthetic, emotional, intellectual and moral experiences. Companies often consider the cultural life of a city when it comes to making decisions about where to locate their business.

SB, S. 104 **C NPWA**   Billy Bragg and the Blokes

Source:	*England, Half English*, 2002
Topic:	Criticism of the consequences of globalization
Text form:	Song
Language variety:	BE
Length:	5:28 minutes
Level:	Basic/advanced
Skills/activities:	Listening comprehension, giving one's opinion, writing a summary

Didaktisch-methodische Hinweise

In diesem Lied (vgl. CD1, *track* 38, und das Transkript auf S. 197) wird das in *section 1* behandelte Thema des Arbeitsplatzverlustes wieder aufgegriffen. Im Unterschied zu Millers Drama aus den Vierzigerjahren spricht Bragg's Song aus dem Jahr 2002 explizit politische Fragen an. Aus der Sicht eines englischen Arbeitslosen werden die Entscheidungsstrukturen in multinationalen Firmen und internationalen Organisationen wie der Weltbank, dem Internationalen Währungsfond und der Welthandelsorganisation kritisiert. Demokratische Wahlen auf nationaler Ebene werden als unzureichend bezeichnet; von den Entscheidungsträgern in global agierenden Unternehmen und internationalen Organisationen wird Rechenschaft und soziale Verantwortung verlangt. Das Lied wirft Fragen nach dem Verhältnis von ökonomischer und politischer Macht, der Rolle des *shareholder value*, der Verlagerung von Arbeitsplätzen an Standorte mit niedrigerem Lohnniveau und der Bedeutung von Schutzzöllen auf.

Unterrichts-tipps

Da das Lied selbst für Muttersprachler schwer zu verstehen ist, sollten die S durch die erste Aufgabe vorbereitet werden, die sie z.B. in arbeitsteiliger Gruppenarbeit lösen.

Differenzierung

Für leistungsstärkere S dürfte es ausreichen, vor dem ersten Hören die u.a. Wörter zu semantisieren. So können die S den Text global verstehen und die kritische Absicht des Sängers erkennen. Das zweite Hören dient dem Detailverständnis.

company town: (here) town that is based around one industry or firm
accountability: soziale Verantwortung, Rechenschaft(spflicht)
canvass for sb.'s vote: persuade sb. to vote for you
petrol bomb: Molotowcocktail
hold sb. to account: jdn. zur Rechenschaft ziehen
snuff sth. out: etwas auslöschen
ballot box: Wahlurne
cut sb. off: (hier) vom Schuldenerlass / aus der Finanzwelt ausschliessen
wield a sword: ein Schwert schwingen
chairman of the board: Vorstandsvorsitzender

Kopiervorlage

Leistungsschwächeren S kann ein Lückentext vorgelegt werden (vgl. die KV „NPWA", S. 194), in dem sie beim Hören die fehlenden Begriffe ergänzen. Sie bearbeiten die Fragen mit Hilfe des Transkripts.

Info

Billy Bragg and the Blokes: Since his debut album *Life Is a Riot* in 1983, Billy Bragg (born 1957) has recorded dozens of songs and toured the world. The Blokes are his current touring and recording band. Billy Bragg is well-known for his commitment to political and humanitarian issues.

World Bank: Created in 1944, the World Bank was set up to promote development in the world's poorer countries by means of advice and long-term lending. Its loans average $30 billion a year, spread around 100 countries.

International Monetary Fund (IMF): Created by the same conference that founded the World Bank, the IMF is an organization designed originally to supervise the fixed exchange rate between world economies. In the last three decades, it has been more concerned with dealing with the debt incurred by developing countries. It sets the conditions for loans and so often interferes with the way a country is run.

World Trade Organization (WTO): The WTO was set up in 1995 to regulate international trading. It enforces the rules of GATT (General Agreement on Tariffs and Trade), which came into existence in 1947, and punishes the countries that break them.

Lösungs-hinweise

1 Vgl. „Info" oben. Diese Aufgabe eignet sich als Hausaufgabe.

The institutions are criticized because they are seen to interfere in the affairs of sovereign states by demanding that they cut public services and lay off workers, which often results in unemployment. Some people also think that they encourage states to mismanage economic policy and rely on aid to help them out.

CD

2 **a** Vgl. CD1, *track* 38, und das Transkript auf S. 197.

– The speaker is an employee of a company that was taken over and then closed down by a foreign corporation; he became unemployed and lost his job and his house.

– 'No power without accountability!' This is a protest against the power of multi-national corporations to determine the lives of people in foreign lands, and of supra-national organizations even being able to dictate policy without ever being voted into office. Bragg sees this as undemocratic and would like corporations to be made answerable to the people who depend on them.

– The addressee could either be the global corporations who are still able to wield the power so arbitrarily, or the many people who are disenfranchised and who want to show solidarity before their voices are entirely 'snuffed out'.

– The tone is angry and indignant, even aggressive. The repetition of the slogan demanding accountability is reminiscent of a demonstration chant.

b The message is a warning to heed the developments which threaten to undermine the democratic rights of citizens and to stand up to the illegitimate power of multi-nationals. Globalization, according to Bragg, means that traditional economic structures are being destroyed and employees left socially and economically bankrupt. There is little hope that those in positions of power will take note of what consequences their actions have because they are likely to be in distant countries and only interested in shareholder value. National politics are not important because the international economic bodies will only enforce the interests of the powers that are control or influence global trade. People should demand that such power should only go with a sense of responsibility for the people affected.

Watch Your Language

Auf dieser Seite werden zwei sprachliche Problembereiche behandelt, die Verwendung des bestimmten Artikels und Kollokationen.

Insbesondere bei Sachtexten über ein Thema wie Wirtschaft werden viele abstrakte Nomen verwendet, die im Englischen im Allgemeinen nicht mit dem bestimmten Artikel stehen. Werden solche abstrakten Nomen durch einen Relativsatz oder eine *of-phrase* näher bestimmt, muss der bestimmte Artikel verwendet werden. Aufmerksame S werden in den Texten auch Beispielen begegnen, die den Regeln im SB widersprechen (vgl. Lösungsvorschläge). Diese Seite eignet sich daher, mit den S auch die Entstehung

Differenzierung

grammatischer Regeln und ihre gelegentliche Unschärfe zu besprechen. Aufgabe 4 ist v.a. für leistungsstärkere S geeignet.

Kollokationen bereiten den S häufig Schwierigkeiten, da die Kombination von Wörtern keinen wirklich lernbaren Regeln unterliegt und Kollokationen in einsprachigen Wörterbüchern nicht immer einfach auffindbar sind. Ihre Kenntnis von Wortverbindungen

→ *WB, ex. 5*

können die S nur erweitern, indem sie ihren Blick für Beispiele in Texten und Wörterbüchern schärfen und diese lernen.

*Lösungs-
hinweise*

1 Where conditions are right, liberal trade is not only about prosperity and greater freedom of choice but also about fairness. It is about the fairness which ensures that a concern for the welfare of all citizens is set above special interests. The profits of liberalization must be distributed more equally, both within and between countries. This is why politics matter.

2 Wenn die Bedingungen richtig sind, geht es beim Freihandel nicht nur um Wohlstand und größere Wahlfreiheit, sondern auch um Gerechtigkeit. Es geht um die Gerechtigkeit, die sicherstellt, dass die Sorge um das Wohlergehen aller Bürger über die Interessen einzelner gestellt wird. Die Liberalisierungsgewinne / Gewinne aus der Liberalisierung müssen gerechter verteilt werden, sowohl innerhalb als auch zwischen Staaten. Deshalb ist Politik wichtig.

3 Bei der Beantwortung dieser Frage können v.a. zwei Aspekte Schwierigkeiten bereiten. Einige S könnten Einwände gegen die Zuordnung von *politics* zur Kategorie „abstract nouns" äußern, da es sich doch um ein Pluralnomen handele. *Politics* ist allerdings trotz des Plural -*s* ein Singularnomen (vgl. *CEG*, §177d). Ein zweites Problem kann die Wendung *freedom of choice* darstellen, die der Regel „bestimmter Artikel bei abstrakten Nomen mit *of-phrase*" zu widersprechen scheint. Grund hierfür ist, dass *freedom of choice* ähnlich wie z.B. *freedom of speech* bereits ein feststehender Begriff ist und die *of-phrase* nicht als genauere Beschreibung des Nomens zu werten ist.

Plural nouns: 'conditions', 'citizens', 'interests', 'countries'.
Abstract nouns: '(liberal) trade', 'prosperity', '(greater) freedom', 'choice', 'fairness', 'liberalization', 'politics'.
Relative clause: 'the fairness which ensures'.
Of-phrase: 'the welfare of all citizens', 'the profits of liberalization'.
Adjective before such nouns: 'liberal trade', 'greater freedom (of choice)', 'special interests'.

4 No definite article in front of plural nouns: 'Europeans' (l. 1), 'streets' (l. 10), 'friends', 'relatives' (l. 13), 'documents' (l. 17), 'ideas' (ll. 19, 33), 'individuals' (ll. 22, 27), 'results' (l. 44);
No definite article in front of abstract nouns: 'driven by misery and tyranny [...] freedom and affluence' (ll. 8–9), 'hard work, ingenuity, thrift and luck' (l. 12), 'practice' (l. 16), '(modern) economics' (l. 20), 'cooperation' (ll. 25, 27), 'freedom' (l. 27), 'history' (l. 35), 'Life, Liberty [...] Happiness' (ll. 38–39), 'slavery' (l. 42), 'equality' (l. 43), '(economic) freedom [...] (political) freedom' (l. 45), 'coercion or (central) direction' (l. 46), '(political) power' (l. 47), 'concentration of (political) power' (ll. 48–49), '(economic and political) power' (l. 49), 'tyranny' (l. 50).

☞ Vgl. aber 'the society' (ll. 30–31).
Definite article before an *of*-phrase: 'the establishment of the United States' (ll. 5–6), 'the promise of freedom and affluence' (ll. 8–9), 'the freedom of individuals' (ll. 21–22), 'the second set of ideas' (l. 33), 'the pursuit of Happiness' (l. 39).

☞ Streng genommen gehört nur „the freedom of individuals" (ll. 21–22) in diese Kategorie. Bei den anderen Nomen handelt es sich nicht um Abstrakta, da sie nicht ohne den Artikel stehen können; dies sollte allerdings im Unterricht nicht thematisiert werden. Der genannten Regel widersprechen folgende Beispiele: „equality of opportunity [...] equality of results" (l. 43–44) und „concentration of political power" (l. 48–49). Ersteres mag wie im Fall von „freedom of choice" mit einer Lexikalisierung begründet werden, letzteres damit, dass vor dem Nomen der *determiner* „whatever" steht, der den Artikel ersetzt.
Definite article used before a defining relative clause: no examples.
No definite article before an adjective and an abstract noun: 'modern economics' (l. 20), 'economic freedom [...] political freedom' (l. 45), 'central direction' (l. 46), 'political power' (l. 47), 'economic and political power' (l. 49).

5 Individual answers.

6 **a** 'sell sth. with profit' is not a collocation. The proper collocation is 'sell sth. at a profit'.

b Aufgabe 6b sollte arbeitsteilig (unter Verwendung unterschiedlicher Lexika) bearbeitet werden. Die Ergebnisse können der Lerngruppe in übersichtlicher Form (als Liste oder Mind-Map), ggf. mit deutschen Entsprechungen, präsentiert werden. Wenn möglich, sollte den S der Nutzen von Kollokationswörterbüchern wie dem *Student's Dictionary of Collocations* (Cornelsen, Berlin, 1999) vor Augen geführt werden.

Monolingual dictionaries usually list the prepositions commonly used with the headword in brackets and/or in bold type. They often use collocations in the example sentences (where they are not easy to find for students) or enter them under the heading 'idioms', but these are often set expressions that cannot be used that frequently. Sometimes a collocation is given as a separate headword (often there is a cross reference).
Business: business contacts/affairs/interests, a business investment, do business with sb., set up in business as a ..., go into business with sb., business premises, work in the ... business, have/start/run / set up your own business, put sb. / go out of business.
Competition: competition between/with sb. for sth., intense/stiff competition, be in competition with sb./sth.
Supply: water supply, guarantee supplies of sth., be exhausted, run out, supply and demand.
Demand: demand (for sth), meet/satisfy customers' demands, an increased demand for a product, demand exceeds supply.
Industry: heavy/light/local industry, steel/catering/tourist industry, captain of industry, develop an industry.
Money: borrow/lend/save/spend/earn money, get your money back, make/lose money, good money, put money into sth., throw money at sth.
Production: wheat/food/oil/car production, production costs/difficulties, be in production, production starts ..., go out of production, production levels fall, a(n) increase/decline/fall in production, production line.
Wages: wages of £200 a week, a weekly wage of £200, wage reductions/cuts, a wage rise/increase of 3%, wage demands/claims/settlements, pay wages, people on low wages, living wage, minimum wage.

7 Individual answers.

Topic Vocabulary: 'The Economy'

Economic Systems
economy
economist
global economy
world economy
centrally planned economy
market economy
free trade
free/private enterprise

Economic World Order
developed countries
developing countries
'Third World' countries
industrialized countries
economic globalization
economic power
devastate a country's economy

Business
(multinational) company
company
firm
chain store
state-owned/public enterprises
consumer
customer
sales rep(resentative)
set up / start your own business
become self-employed

The World of Work
labour
worker
blue-collar worker
white-collar worker
employee
employer
CEO (= chief executive officer)
chairman/-woman/-person
management
hire sb.
employ sb.
fire sb.
let sb. go
lay off workers
labour laws
part-time/temporary work
full-time work
a nine-to-five job
do/work overtime
a 38-hour week

holiday pay
wage level
inequality
unemployment
tackle unemployment
reduce/increase unemployment
an area of high unemployment
long-term unemployment

Making Money
boom
recession
a slump in profits
fall/increase in share prices
shareholder
stockbroker
investment
invest in sth.
pull out your capital
foreign investor/ investment
open up to foreign investment
merge
make a profit
make money
break even
cut sth. back
cut costs
maximize efficiency
bring prosperity to sb.
competitive
competition
subsidize sth.
subsidy
privatize/nationalize a company

Benefits
health insurance
pension fund/scheme
take out a personal/private pension
a state pension
monthly contribution to a pension
  scheme
be on welfare
welfare/child benefits
unemployment
  benefit(s)/compensation
social services
public services
increase/reduce public spending
increase spending on health
cut back on spending on education

CD **NPWA**

SB, p. 104
(cf. TM, p. 189)   *As you listen to the song, fill in the gaps below.*

1   I grew up in a company town
And I worked real hard 'til that company _____
They gave my job to another man
On half my wages in some _____
5   And when I asked how could this be
Any good for our _____ ?
I was told nobody cares
So long as they _____ when they sell their shares.

Can you hear us? Are you listening?
10   No power without _____ !

I lost my job, my car and my house
When ten thousand miles away some guy _____
He didn't know me, we never spoke,
He didn't ask my _____ or canvass for my vote.
15   I guess it's true, nobody cares
'Til those _____ come spinning through the air.
Gotta find a way to hold them to account
Before they find a way to snuff our _____ out.

Can you hear us? Are you listening?
20   No power without _____ !

The ballot box is no _____ that we achieve democracy;
Our leaders claim their victory when only half the people have spoken.
We have no job security in this global economy,
Our borders closed to refugees but our markets _____

25   The World Bank says to Mexico,
We'll cut you off if you don't keep your _____ low.
But they have no right to wield that sword
'Cos they take their orders from the _____ of the board.

IMF, WTO,
30   I hear these words just every place I go
Who are these people? Who _____ them?
And how do I replace them with some of my friends?

Can you hear us? Are you listening?
No power without _____ !

(© 2002, Billy Bragg. All rights reserved)

▮ CD ▮ Getting Along in English

SB, p. 100
Task 2a

Cashier:	Hello.
	Thank you. Have you got a reward card?
Customer:	No, I haven't. But I'd like to use this voucher, please.
Cashier:	Right, that's fine. That comes to 24.68 then, please. How will you be paying?
Customer:	Credit card, please. Here you go.
Cashier:	Thanks. I'll just swipe your card through the machine. And if you could sign the receipt here – lovely. There's your copy, and your card.
Customer:	Er, I wonder if you could possibly wrap it as a present, please?
Cashier:	Ah, no, sorry, we don't do gift-wrapping. I can only give you a carrier bag, I'm afraid.
Customer:	Not to worry.
Cashier:	All right. There you go. Thank you, dear. Have a nice day.
Customer:	Thanks a lot.

SB, p. 100
Task 4

Dialogue 1

Customer:	Excuse me, but I got this cap as a present for my friend and she doesn't like it.
Shopkeeper:	Let's have a look. Hmm. Got the receipt, have you?
Customer:	Yes, here it is. I bought it yesterday.
Shopkeeper:	Okay, miss. Do you want to take something else or would you prefer a refund?
Customer:	Oh, a cash refund, please.
Shopkeeper:	Righty-ho. I need you to sign on the dotted line for me, please. Here you go – five pounds fifty.
Customer:	Thanks very much. That's great.

Dialogue 2

Customer 1:	Er, hello, we bought this volleyball here this morning, and it's been losing air ever since.
Assistant:	Well, by the looks of it, you've been playing with it.
Customer 1:	Well, yeah, I mean, that's what we bought it for.
Customer 2:	But we only used it on a grass field.
Assistant:	Well, I'm sorry, but it must have hit something sharp then. We can't be held responsible for that, I'm afraid.
Customer 1:	I appreciate that, but you can see that the outside hasn't been damaged at all. The inside must have been faulty when we got it.
Customer 2:	Yeah.
Assistant:	Well, all I can say is that it's the shop's policy not to exchange goods that have been used by the customer. I'm very sorry, but there you are.
Customer 1:	In that case I'd like to talk to the manager about it, please.
Assistant:	All right, sir. I'll see if he's available. Excuse me.

As Basic as the Screwdriver

Interviews with Braj Kachru and David Crystal

Melvyn Bragg: In fact, the worldwide spread of English has this year been the subject of a succession of congresses and conventions from the United States to Sydney. It's the hot story in language study.

Voice: English is the language of international communication ...

Melvyn Bragg: Thirty or more years ago though, very few were talking about it. One who was, was Braj Kachru. He's a Kashmiri by birth but for several decades he's been a guru of the subject at the University of Illinois in the United States. He even founded a journal called *World Englishes*, seen at the time as a controversial title.

Braj Kachu: People see English as a speaking tree and that tree, in mythology, had this trunk ... of the tree created a feeling of awe. People despised the trunk but people loved the branches. The branches used to sing songs: ... the sun and moon and charming and beautiful women, and that's how branches of English are found around the world, but there still is suspicion of the trunk. There is suspicion about what are the motives of Britain, are motives of America, motives of the publishing industry and the media ... those are suspect, so I feel really that there is this sweet and sour feeling.

Melvyn Bragg: David Crystal, is this language take-off entirely to do with power, in a sense the double whammy, if I might use that word, of the British Empire speaking English in the 18th, 19th centuries and then the American Empire speaking American English? Is this the main cause: that language goes where power goes?

David Crystal: It's more than a double whammy, I'd say it was a quadruple whammy, to make it even more a neologism. Yes, power is the key here, but there are many kinds of power: four kinds of power, I think. There's the power that you mentioned that goes with the British Empire – political, military might – and that was the first sort of power that pushed English on its way. But that didn't last forever, I mean, as we now know, secondly, following on from that, in the 18th century, there was the power of technology – scientific power, the industrial revolution-type power. Something like half the people who made that revolution possible worked in the medium of English, either in Britain or America, and people from the continent who wanted to find out about these things had to learn English in order to get somewhere. And then in the 19th century, the third kind of power: economic power – power where money talks, and the money that was talking was the dollar, very largely – and economic power pushed English forward then. And then fourthly, in the 20th century, cultural power, in the sense that every significant cultural development in the 20th century either started in an English-speaking country or was facilitated very rapidly by an English-speaking country – so, four kinds of power.

CD **NPWA**   Billy Bragg and the Blokes

SB, S. 104   I grew up in a company town
And I worked real hard 'til that company closed down.
They gave my job to another man
On half my wages in some foreign land.
And when I asked how could this be
Any good for our economy?
I was told nobody cares
So long as they make money when they sell their shares.

Can you hear us? Are you listening?
No power without accountability!

I lost my job, my car and my house
When ten thousand miles away some guy clicked on a mouse.
He didn't know me, we never spoke,
He didn't ask my opinion or canvass for my vote.
I guess its true, nobody cares
'Til those petrol bombs come spinning through the air.
Gotta find a way to hold them to account
Before they find a way to snuff our voices out.

Can you hear us? Are you listening?
No power without accountability!

The ballot box is no guarantee that we achieve democracy;
Our leaders claim their victory when only half the people have spoken.
We have no job security in this global economy;
Our borders closed to refugees but our markets forced open.

The World Bank says to Mexico,
We'll cut you off if you don't keep your taxes low.
But they have no right to wield that sword
'Cos they take their orders from the chairman of the board.

IMF, WTO,
I hear these words just every place I go
Who are these people? Who elected them?
And how do I replace them with some of my friends?

Can you hear us? Are you listening?
No power without accountability!

„Inform, educate and entertain" – mit diesen Worten beschrieb 1927 Lord Reith, der erste Generaldirektor der BBC, die Funktionen der Medien in der damaligen Zeit. Zweifellos gelten diese Funktionen auch heute noch, selbst wenn Anzahl, Formen und Nutzungsweisen der Medien sich gravierend verändert haben. Beklagt wird häufig, dass besonders bei Jugendlichen die Unterhaltungsfunktion der Medien im Vordergrund steht. Doch auch wenn die Allgegenwart der Medien nach einem überlegten Umgang mit ihnen verlangt, soll in diesem Kapitel trotz aller kritischen Distanz nicht die Freude an der Mediennutzung genommen werden.

Dieses Kapitel thematisiert die wichtigsten Massenmedien:
– *Section 1*, „'Read All about It!'", befasst sich mit Zeitungen, insbesondere mit dem Vergleich der britischen *tabloid press* mit der *quality press*.

– *Section 2*, „The Role of Television", analysiert die wirtschaftliche und soziale Bedeutung des Fernsehens in den USA und Großbritannien.

– *Section 3*, „I Saw It on the Internet ... so it's got to be true", behandelt die Frage nach der Verlässlichkeit des Internets.

– *Section 4*, „You Can Sell Anything", untersucht ein Phänomen, das in allen Medien gleichermaßen prominent ist, die Werbung.

Methodische Schwerpunkte bilden neben analytischen Verfahren schülerorientierte, produktive Vorgehensweisen: Die S erstellen eine Zeitungsseite, führen eine Debatte, stellen Bezüge zu Deutschland her, wenden Qualitätskriterien auf Internetseiten ihrer Wahl an usw.

Didaktisches Inhaltsverzeichnis

SB, p.	Title	TM, p.	Text form	Topic	Skills and activities
106	Lead-in	199	cartoons	news and interactive media	describing and analysing a cartoon; identifying stylistic devices
108	Context Box	201	–	the media	working with vocabulary; writing a short article
109	Germans Destroy Wembley Martin Wallace	202	news story	the demolition of Wembley stadium	analysing the way information; is presented; working with language
110	Work Starts and Stops on Wembley Simon Burnton	204	news story	the demolition of Wembley stadium	comparing newspaper articles; writing a news story
111	The Sheep in Wolf's Clothing James Thurber	206	fable	the responsibility of journalists and readers	analysing a fable
112	Front Pages	208	newspapers	differences in the front pages of newspapers	comparing a tabloid and a broadsheet newspaper; writing headlines
114	A Letter to the Editor	209	letter to the editor	comment on a previous story	analysing a letter to the editor; writing a letter to the editor; creating a newspaper page
115	TV Is Big Business	210	newsmagazine article	TV as a business	analysing connotations; debating
116	Rather than Talking about the Weather	212	essay	the role TV plays in British family life	explaining a text's content in one's own words; devising a questionnaire
117	How to Get on TV Video/DVD	214	TV shows (extracts)	'nasty' host shows and reality shows	analysing TV shows;
118	Nobody Knows You're a Dog	216	cartoon	anonymity on the Internet	describing and analysing a cartoon

118	**The Reliability of Internet Information**	217	non-fictional text	the reliability of information on the Internet	finding out differences between printed and online information; examining the reliability of the Internet
119	**Getting Along in English** CD2, tracks 1–5	218	–	–	making telephone calls
120	**We Are Speaking of Art** Steven Millhauser	219	novel (extract)	the influence of advertising	working with characterization; analysing mode of presentation; converting a text into a film script
122	**AIDA** Kevin Needham	221	non-fictional text	a formula for advertising	examining advertisements; writing an advert
123	**Watch Your Language**	223	–	–	German-English interference

SB, S. 106

Lead-in

Didaktisch-methodische Hinweise

Der Einstieg in das Kapitel erfolgt über Cartoons, in denen verschiedene Probleme heutiger Medien thematisiert werden: der Wahrheitsgehalt von Zeitungs- und Fernsehnachrichten, Konflikte bei der Nutzung neuer Medien, Realitätsverlust durch übermäßige Nutzung von Computerspielen. So werden den S auf humorvolle Weise Problembereiche vor Augen geführt, die später im Kapitel vertieft werden. Gleichzeitig üben sie die Analyse von Cartoons und machen sich ihre eigene Mediennutzung bewusst.

Unterrichts-tipps

Bei der Behandlung des „Lead-in" ist zu beachten, dass den S einige Vokabeln in der Box auf S. 106 unbekannt sein dürften, z.B. „caption", „target", „pun". Diese können entweder vorher gemeinsam besprochen oder von den S selbstständig mit Hilfe des *OALD*, den „Skills Pages" („Working with Cartoons", SB, S. 225) oder des Glossars (besonders „Cartoon", SB, S. 264, und „Wordplay", SB, S. 270) erarbeitet werden.

Lösungs-hinweise

1 **a** The media dealt with are newspapers, television, electronic books and video games.

The first cartoon suggests that people are more interested in gossip and rumour than in serious, real news, and that therefore the former sell better.

The second cartoon implies that TV news is not really based on true facts because those who produce it will do anything to grab the viewers' attention.

The third cartoon seems to be saying that, despite changes as to how sth. is presented, nothing really changes. Here the age-old problem of a person being disturbed when he or she wants to sleep because the other person wants to continue reading remains the same, even with new electronic media.

The fourth cartoon pokes fun at the younger generation, implying that young people cannot differentiate between the real world and the virtual worlds of their computer games. It also appears to be criticizing the violence in such media.

b Die Besprechung der Cartoons kann in kleinen Gruppen erfolgen, wobei es sinnvoll wäre, wenn mindestens jeweils zwei Gruppen sich mit einem Cartoon beschäftigen. Wenn in der Aufgabenstellung von einer Beschreibung „in as much detail as necessary" die Rede ist, bedeutet das nicht, dass die S jedes Detail beschreiben müssen, sondern nur so viel, dass jemand, der den Cartoon nicht gesehen hat, ihn verstehen kann.

Cartoon 1: The cartoon shows a man standing in the street. He is looking at two newspaper vending machines. One vending machine is for 'real news', while the other is for 'stuff we just make up'. While the real news vending machine is still full of newspapers, the vending machine with newspapers containing invented stories is empty, as customers have bought up all the copies. The caption in the box in the top-left-hand corner is 'The write stuff', which is a pun on 'the right stuff'.

The cartoonist is making the point that people are more interested in reading gossip and made-up (but probably interesting) stories than the real news – it also implies that customers know and do not worry that they are reading stories that are lies.

Cartoon 2: A man is standing in a news room, where two workers are sitting typing at their computers. The sign in the man's hand says 'Research shows that ... may cause cancer'. The man has a speech bubble, in which he is asking the news room people to pick a noun to put in the blank space.
The cartoonist has targeted the news media, and implies that they are more interested in scaring people (and thereby attracting viewers) than in reporting real things.

Cartoon 3: The cartoon shows a couple in bed. The woman is reading an e-book, which shines a bright light on her and her husband's faces. The man is annoyed and is telling his wife to turn off her e-book.
The cartoon is humorous because the cartoonist has taken a typical situation in which one partner asks the other to 'close' or 'put down' his or her novel and go to sleep and updated it by having the man say 'turn off' your novel; the implication is that some technological developments do not really change our lives and we find ourselves in the same annoying situations.

Cartoon 4: A father and his son are standing in the countryside. The father is saying to his son that it is good to get away from his computer and see the real world. The son appears hyperactive and excited. The lines around his hands suggest that he is twitching a lot. His speech bubbles say that he is impressed by the graphics of the program and he wants to blow things up.
The cartoonist implies that too many youngsters sit around in front of video games all day and are losing their grasp on reality. He also wants to make a point about violence in video games, as the hyperactive youngster can only think about blowing things up.

⬭ *Cartoon 1: Do you agree that people are more interested in gossip than in serious news?*

⬭ *Cartoon 2: Which TV news do you trust? Do you see differences between privately owned and state-owned TV channels? Explain your answer.*

⬭ *Cartoon 3: Have you ever read a novel or story online, or an e-book? Do you think that this is going to be the future of reading?*

⬭ *Cartoon 4: How much time do you spend playing computer games? What do you get out of them? To what extent do they distract you from other social activities like sports or meeting friends?*

2 **a** Possible answers:
Newspapers, magazines, TV, radio, Internet, mobile phones (BE) = (AE) cell phones.
Although *media* is normally limited to broadcast media (newspapers, magazines, TV, radio), increasingly advertisers and news services broadcast via the Internet and mobile phones, so the boundaries of the media are being extended.

b Vermutlich werden Zeitungen und Zeitschriften an oberster Stelle der informierenden Medien stehen, während als meistgenutzte Medien Fernsehen und Internet genannt werden. Daraus kann man die Schlussfolgerung ziehen, dass die S (wie die meisten Menschen) die Medien v.a. zur Unterhaltung nutzen.

Individual answers.

3 **a** Most people are very visual and so will probably remember a cartoon better than a statement they have heard or read. If the cartoon makes an amusing point, the reader might be inclined to think about the message of the cartoon.

b Hier erkennen die S, dass sich Sprachwitz nur schwer übersetzen lässt, da er häufig auf Homophonen oder Homonymen beruht, die nur in einer Sprache existieren.

Some factors that make translating a cartoon difficult: use of wordplay/puns, use of specialized vocabulary, necessary background knowledge that someone not familiar with the language or country and culture of the original might not have.

SB, S. 108 ## Context Box

Didaktisch-methodische Hinweise Die „Context Box" fordert zur kritischen Betrachtung der Medien auf. Thematisiert werden die Funktion der Medien (Information wie Unterhaltung), die grundsätzliche politische Ausrichtung einer Zeitung oder eines Senders, ethische Standards bei der Informationsverbreitung, die Kontrolle der Medien, Stärken und Schwächen verschiedener Medien.

Unterrichts-tipps Als Einstieg in die Arbeit mit der „Context Box" kann das BBC-Poster analysiert werden:

◯ *In the box at the bottom of the advert there is the following sentence: 'Demand a broader view'. How does this sentence refer to the picture?*
The idea seems to be that very often we need to look at events from different angles in order to be able to consider them objectively. The person in handcuffs in the photo might be considered a hero, terrorist or victim; how he is viewed depends on the individual viewpoint of the observer. There is a saying in English that one man's terrorist is another man's freedom fighter (which is derived from the phrase 'one man's meat is another man's poison'). In order to make an objective judgement we need background information and insights which take the whole situation into account.

◯ *What is the overall message of the advert?*
The implication of the poster is that the world needs the BBC in order to make sense of political events.

◯ *How effective do you think the advert is?*

Aufgrund der neuen Lexik ist die „Context Box" sprachlich anspruchsvoll; die Aufgaben im SB wälzen deshalb v.a. diesen neuen Wortschatz um. Das Textverständnis der S sollte durch Zusatzfragen überprüft werden:

◯ *Why should we be interested in the origin of the information provided by different media?*

◯ *What role do the media play in our everyday lives?*

◯ *How much time per day do we use the media just for fun?*

→ *WB, ex. 2* ◯ *Explain why the topic of censorship is an important one in today's world.*

Lösungs-hinweise **1** **a–c** Vgl. „Topic Vocabulary" (S. 225).

→ *WB, ex. 1* **2** Individual answers.

1 'Read All about It!'

Die Printmedien stehen im Mittelpunkt von *section* 1. Angesichts der heutigen Informationsflut und der immer vielfältigeren Möglichkeiten, Informationen, auch Bilder, zu manipulieren, ist ein kritischer Blick auf die Berichterstattung erforderlich. In dieser *section* werden deshalb besonders die Unterschiede zwischen der britischen *tabloid press* und der *quality press* behandelt. Texte vom selben Tag zum selben Thema aus der *popular* bzw. *quality press* werden einander gegenübergestellt und sowohl inhaltlich als auch sprachlich verglichen. Text D umfasst die Titelseiten zweier Zeitungen desselben Tages aus einer *tabloid* und einem *broadsheet*, deren Vergleich die Gewichtung bestimmter Themen in diesen Zeitungen offen legt. Als literarische Gestaltung des Themas lesen die S die Fabel „The Sheep in Wolf's Clothing". Kreative Textproduktion beschließt die *section*: Die S schreiben einen *letter to the editor* bzw. gestalten eine Zeitungsseite.

Unterrichts-
tipps
Kopiervorlage
Wenn L den Schwerpunkt der Behandlung dieser *section* auf die systematische Gegenüberstellung von *quality* und *popular press* legen möchte, sollten Texte A, B und D nacheinander bearbeitet werden. Zum Abschluss kann die KV „Tabloids and Broadsheets – A Comparison"' verteilt werden (vgl. S. 226): unverändert als zusammenfassende Übersicht oder aber als Arbeitsblatt, auf dem Einzelinformationen oder der gesamte Inhalt der Spalten mit Tipp-Ex unsichtbar gemacht wurden und von den S ergänzt werden.

Differenzierung
Mit leistungstärkeren S kann eine Vertiefung des Themas Berichterstattung und gleichzeitig ein Brückenschlag zum Fernsehen erfolgen, wenn die S Fernsehnachrichten vergleichen. Dafür können von L wie von den S Aufzeichnungen verschiedener Nachrichtensendungen mitgebracht werden, die auch von Weltnachrichtensendern wie CNN oder BBC stammen können. Für eine noch stärker interkulturelle Ausrichtung könnten S ausländischer Herkunft Sender aus ihrer Heimat vorstellen. Die Sendungen sollten auf Video aufgezeichnet werden, damit sie mehrfach gesehen werden können. Bevor der Vergleich durchgeführt wird, sollten mit der Klasse Analysekriterien festgelegt werden. Dazu könnten beispielsweise gehören: Inhalt (z.B. Gegenstand der Nachrichten, Reihenfolge der Präsentation, zur Verfügung stehende Zeit), Moderatoren (z.B. Geschlecht, Alter, Aussehen, Kleidung), Moderation (z.B. Blickkontakt der Moderatoren mit den Zuschauern oder Umgang miteinander), Bild (Ausstattung des Studios; Wirkung von Grafik und Fotos).

→ *WB, ex. 2, 3, 5*

A Germans Destroy Wembley   Martin Wallace

Source:	*The Sun*, 1 October, 2002
Topic:	The demolition of Wembley stadium
Text form:	News story
Language variety:	BE
Number of words:	359
Level:	Basic/advanced
Skills/activities:	Analysing the way information is presented, working with language

Lern-
vokabular
Active vocabulary: 'Germans Destroy Wembley' (p. 109)

demolition (l. 1), get the go-ahead (l. 8), site (l. 21), clear sth. (l. 21), feature sth. (l. 22), stage sth. (l. 24), be financed by sb./sth (l. 27), loan (l. 28), chief executive (l. 29), have the last laugh (l. 31), venue (l. 31)
tasks: consider sth., devote space to sth., merely

Didaktisch-methodische Hinweise	Der Artikel berichtet über den Abriss des traditionsreichen Wembley Stadions im Jahr 2002, bei dem ein deutscher Bulldozer zum Einsatz kam. Der Autor stellt diesen Abriss durch mehr oder weniger subtile Anspielungen als destruktiven Akt der Deutschen gegen die Engländer dar und reiht sich damit in die Tradition der britischen Boulevardpresse ein, die seit Jahrzehnten Deutschland zu einer ihrer Zielscheiben gemacht hat. Vor allem im Bereich des Fußballs werden diese Spannungen immer wieder deutlich. Anhand dieses Textes analysieren die S die manipulative Wirkung von Sprache und vergleichen im Zusammenhang mit „Work Starts and Stops on Wembley" (SB, S. 110) *popular* und *quality press*.
Unterrichts-tipps	Um den Text richtig einordnen zu können, benötigen die S Hintergrundwissen über das Verhältnis zwischen Deutschen und Engländern und über die Bedeutung des Wembley Stadions (vgl. „Info" unten). Fußballinteressierte S können hier Informationen liefern; ggf. sind diese von L zu ergänzen. Hinzuweisen wäre in diesem Zusammenhang z.B. auf das häufig in *tabloids* vorzufindende Bild der Deutschen als Militaristen und Nazis v.a. im Zusammenhang mit Fußballspielen (vgl. z.B. die Kriegsmetaphorik, die einige *tabloids* im Zuge der Fußballweltmeisterschaft 1996 verwendeten: "Achtung! Surrender. For you Fritz ze Euro 96 Championship is over" (*Daily Mirror*), „Let's Blitz Fritz" (*Sun*). Der Text enthält Vokabular aus zwei nützlichen Wortfeldern, die die S arbeitsteilig zusammenstellen können:

<u>Words involved with building:</u> 'demolition' (l. 1), 'rip sth. apart' (l. 2), 'tear into sth.' (l. 3), 'concrete' (l.3), 'flatten sth.' (l. 7), 'a replacement stadium' (ll. 8–9), 'reduce sth. to rubble' (l. 13),' clear a site' (l. 21), 'feature sth.' (l. 22), 'complete sth.' (l. 24), 'design sth.' (l. 26).

<u>Words about football and stadiums:</u> 'home of English soccer' (ll. 3–4), 'a replacement stadium' (ll. 8–9), 'beat sb.' (l. 11), 'an international match' (l. 11), 'a 90,000 seat stadium' (l. 21), 'a sliding roof' (l. 23), 'stage a match' (l. 24), 'a/the cup final' (ll. 24–25), 'a 110,000-seater stadium' (l. 25), 'player' (l. 29), 'fan' (l. 29), 'facilities' (l.30), 'venue' (l. 31), 'triumph' (l. 32), 'the 1966 final' (l. 33).

Info

Wembley Stadium is situated in north-west London. It was built in the 1920s and with its famous twin towers became one of London's landmarks (the twin towers can be seen in the photos on p. 109, as well as in close-up on p. 110). Besides being the home of the annual English cup final, it has also hosted the 1948 Olympic Games and the 1966 World Cup. It was used for the Live Aid concert of 1985, the proceeds of which went to help projects in drought-stricken areas of Africa.

Lösungs-hinweise	**1** **a** Wembley is a legend in England (and in the footballing world) and its demolition gives the *Sun* a chance to talk about football (which is probably interesting for most of its readers) and especially England's football triumph in 1966; it also gives it a chance to indulge in a bit of 'Kraut bashing' ('Kraut' is a derogatory word for a German).

b Da die meisten S Schwierigkeiten mit der Formulierung „other sorts of information" haben werden, sollte zuerst dieser Begriff geklärt werden. Ein Beispiel verdeutlicht, was gemeint ist: Im ersten Satz wird die Tatsache genannt, dass das Stadion mit Hilfe eines deutschen Bulldozers abgerissen wird. Wortwahl („rip apart") und Druck („GERMAN") lassen dies jedoch als aggressiven Akt einer für ihre imperialistischen Neigungen berüchtigten Nation erscheinen. Durch Auswahl und Darstellungsweise der Informationen (Konnotationen) werden negative Emotionen geschürt. Über die Anforderungen der Aufgabe im SB hinaus sollten die S diesen Zusammenhang beschreiben und so Vorarbeit für Aufgabe 3a zum folgenden Text leisten (vgl. SB, s. 110).

– 'rip the stadium apart' (l. 2)
– 'home of English soccer' (ll. 3–4)
– 'The monster excavator carried a St George flag' (l. 5)

- 'flatten the historic arena' (l. 7)
- 'a seven-year saga' (l. 9)
- 'Germany's last demolition job' (ll. 10–11)
- 'reduced to rubble' (l. 13)
- 'She is an old lady.' (l. 17)
- 'The Germans may think they had the last laugh ... England's greatest triumph' (ll. 31–33)

This article illustrates how the mere choice of information can be used to influence readers. The article focuses on the fact that it was a German bulldozer that destroyed Wembley, which is a deliberate attempt to encourage anti-German sentiment.

2
- 'With a German bulldozer ripping the stadium apart' (ll. 1–2)
- 'Germany's last demolition job' (ll. 10–11)
- 'partly financed by the GERMAN bank West LB with a £433 million loan' (ll. 27–28)
- 'The Germans may think they had the last laugh – but ... beating Germany 4–2 ...' (ll. 31–33)

Twice the *Sun* uses capital letters – the only ones in the article – for the word 'German', so clearly this angle is very important for the newspaper. The article, for example, does not use capital letters when it writes 'Aussie' or 'Australia' (l. 25). It seems as if the newspaper is blaming the Germans for demolishing the much loved (if antiquated) Wembley stadium.

'Ripping sth. apart' conjures up a very brutal, aggressive image. Because this aggressive act is being done by the German bulldozer, it immediately becomes associated with Germans, who in Britain are viewed as being aggressive.

In 2000 Germany simply won an international football match against England at Wembley, but 'Germany's last demolition job' again makes this seem a much more aggressive act. The implication is that the Germans were aggressive and destructive, whereas they merely played the better football. The word 'demolition' here also is a pun, as the stadium is being demolished, while a 'demolition job' is an expression used when somebody does something to make another person appear useless (i.e. the Germans beat the English convincingly).

As the Germans are partly financing the replacement stadium, one might also get the impression that the new stadium will be theirs.

The implication of 'the Germans may think they had the last laugh' (by destroying the stadium and winning the last match played there), but the newspaper believes that the World Cup win in 1966 was much more important. The truth is that most Germans are unaware of the fact that it was a German bulldozer that was used for the demolition and the last match was not an important game anyway.

3 Possible answers:
fewer personal anecdotes, more neutral language, less detail about people and unimportant issues, little or no mention of Germany.

SB, S. 110   **B Work Starts and Stops on Wembley**   Simon Burnton

Source:	*The Guardian*, 1 October, 2002
Topic:	The demolition of Wembley stadium
Text form:	Newspaper article
Language variety:	BE
Number of words:	173
Level:	Basic/advanced
Skills/activities:	Comparing newspaper articles, writing a news story

Active vocabulary: 'Work Starts and Stops on Wembley' (p. 110)

site (l. 4), call it a day (ll. 5–6), construction firm (l. 8), in charge of sth. (l. 8), make a speech (l. 9), mark an occasion (l. 9), owe sth. to sb. (l. 10), swing into action (l. 13)
tasks: device, pay attention to sth., make a point, similar

Didaktisch-methodische Hinweise

Dieser Artikel aus dem linksliberalen *broadsheet Guardian* sollte im Zusammenhang mit Text A „Germans Destroy Wembley" (SB, S. 109) behandelt werden, da hier über dasselbe Ereignis berichtet wird. Durch den inhaltlichen wie sprachlichen Vergleich der beiden Artikel erkennen die S die unterschiedliche Berichterstattung in seriöser und Boulevardpresse. Um das Erkannte praktisch umzusetzen, schreiben die S im Anschluss selbst einen Artikel in einem der beiden Formate.

Lösungs-hinweise

1 'At precisely 11.09' (l. 1), 'five years and 287 days' (ll. 1–2), 'Thirteen minutes later workmen ... called it a day' (ll. 4–6), 'John Corocan of Multiplex' (l. 7), 'the 35-ton bulldozer' (l. 15), 'it will take around six months, and some £93 m, to complete the demolition' (ll. 23–25).
Headings: time, money, people.

2 Individual answers.

3 **a** Hierbei kann auf Ergebnisse von Aufgabe 1 zu Text 1A (SB, S. 109) zurückgegriffen werden. In einigen Kursen wird es erforderlich sein, den Begriff *connotation* anhand von Beispielen zu klären. Bei der Suche nach *stylistic devices* stellen die S unter Beweis, inwieweit sie sich mit dem Anhang vertraut gemacht haben. Wichtiger als die eindeutige und lückenlose Identifikation der *stylistic devices* ist die Auswahl derer, die die Leser emotional ansprechen sollen. Ein arbeitsteiliges Verfahren ist möglich, bei dem ein Teil der Klasse sich auf Text A konzentriert, der andere auf Text B.

– 'Rip sth. apart' (Text A, l. 2): connotations of a monster tearing sb. limb from limb: a very aggressive form of demolition;
– 'Goliath [gəˈlaɪəθ] tore into sth.' (Text A, l. 3): reinforces the image of a monster; personification of the bulldozer (called Goliath, after the giant in the Bible): a terrible image of destruction by a real live being;
– 'monster' (Text A, l. 5): a metaphor that underlines the images of destruction and of brutality;
– 'a seven-year saga' (Text A, l. 9): metaphor evoking images of adventures (usually associated with monsters);
– 'Germany's last demolition job' (Text A, ll. 10–11): the connotation of 'demolition' is the total destruction of something, so it is a much more emotional image than winning a football game.
– 'an old lady' (Text A, l. 17): metaphor implying vulnerability and respectability (as opposed to the strong, monstrous, aggressive German bulldozer);
– 'a new Wembley will be born' (Text A, l. 21): personification, which conjures up a strong emotional tie to the stadium;
– 'the last laugh' (Text A, l. 31): has connotations of the Germans indulging in Schadenfreude;
– 'Goliath swung into action' (Text B, l. 13): personification, which evokes an emotional tie to the bulldozer;
– 'punched nervously' (Text B, l. 16): personification, which implies that the excavator respects the old building.
While in Text A the German bulldozer is described as aggressive and destructive, in Text B it appears hesitant and tentative; nevertheless, in both texts the machine is personified. The writer of Text B then puts the (English) human being in charge, and says that 'He bashed ..., ripped off' (Text B, l. 20–22) rather than the machine itself.

b The *Sun* article paints a picture of aggressive destruction, while the *Guardian* writer indicates that it is a great building that is being destroyed. The *Guardian* article uses far fewer emotive images and sticks to describing the events. It lays emphasis on the fact that not much happened; this might be seen as a criticism of the operation as being slow.

The main point that needs to emerge is that the hidden agenda of the *Sun* is to encourage feelings of dislike, even mistrust and fear, of the Germans. It does this by using emotive language and images whereas the *Guardian* sticks mostly to the bare facts.

⬭ *Imagine you are a German journalist reporting for your local TV station. Summarize and comment on British coverage of the demolition of Wembley Stadium.*

4 Diese Aufgabe eignet sich besonders als Hausaufgabe.

Individual answers.

SB, S. 111   **C The Sheep in Wolf's Clothing**   James Thurber

Source:	*Fables of Our Time*, 1940
Topic:	The responsibility of journalists and readers
Text form:	Fable
Language variety:	AE
Number of words:	276
Level:	Basic/advanced
Skills/activities:	Analysing a fable

Lern-vokabular

Active vocabulary: 'The Sheep in Wolf's Clothing' (p. 111)

spy (l. 2), make (some) notes (l. 6), guess sth. (l. 10), slip away (l. 10), suspect sth. (l. 11), publisher (l. 13), message (l. 17), be convinced by sth. (l. 19)

Didaktisch-methodische Hinweise

Während die S bei der Bearbeitung von Text A und B die Problematik von Wahrheit und Manipulation in den Medien nur beschrieben haben, begegnen sie in dieser Fabel Thurbers – dem didaktischen Anspruch dieser Textsorte entsprechend – einer konkreten Handlungsempfehlung: Thurber betont die Verantwortung von Journalisten, wahrheitsgemäß zu berichten, wie auch die Verantwortung der Leserschaft, Skepsis gegenüber den Medien zu wahren. Diese Fabel ist damit ein Beispiel dafür, wie Literatur kritisch auf gesellschaftliche oder politische Realitäten reagiert. Die S sollten auf das Erscheinungsdatum dieser Fabel hingewiesen werden, damit sie sie vor dem Hintergrund des zweiten Weltkrieges betrachten und in ihr die Warnung vor verharmlosenden Bildern erkennen, die Journalisten anfangs von Diktatoren der damaligen Zeit zeichneten.

Die Fragen im SB zielen v. a. auf die Merkmale der Fabel und auf die Charakterisierung von Schaf und Wolf. Inhaltlich sollten diese Fragen keine Probleme bereiten, da die S auf ihr Vorwissen aus dem Deutschunterricht zurückgreifen können.

Unterrichts-tipps

Vor der Analyse erscheint es sinnvoll, das Textverständnis zu überprüfen, indem die S kurz mit eigenen Worten den Inhalt der Fabel wiedergeben. Alternativ kann auch die folgende Frage gestellt werden:

⬭ *Why were the wolves able to kill the sheep so easily?*
The two sheep carried out a very superficial investigation, resulting in false generalizations about the wolves' supposedly peaceful lifestyle. The readers of the reports were no better since they were uncritical about what they read. So when the wolves attacked the sheep one day, they were caught off guard.

Info

James Thurber (1894–1961) was an American cartoonist and writer of humorous prose. As a child, he was partially blinded when his brother accidentally shot an arrow in his eye when they were acting out the story of William Tell. This injury made it impossible for him to play with other children, so he escaped into a fantasy world, which was a source of inspiration for his work. From 1920 onwards he worked as a journalist for several newspapers, among them *The New Yorker*. He is most renowned for his wry humor and his interest in the small events of human life. In Germany, he is best known for his modern fables (*Fables for Our Time*, 1940, and *Further Fables for Our Time*, 1956), while in the English-speaking world his short story 'The Secret Life of Walter Mitty' (1932) is his best-known work. Thurber married twice and had one daughter. In the 1940s his eyesight became worse and by 1950 he was practically blind.

Lösungs-hinweise

1 **a** The two main sheep are ambitious and greedy, as they seem only intent on being the first one to publish their work. They are cunning, as they outwit each other to publish first, and they are stupid, as they make superficial judgements (cf. ll. 4–9, 17–18). The rest of the sheep are depicted as docile and unquestioning.

b Like humans, the wolves know how to enjoy themselves on a public holiday (drinking in pubs and dancing in the streets), but when the holiday is over and things are back to normal, they take on their usual characteristics, i.e. they kill sheep. The wolves are characterized as dangerous and aggressive.

2

– The story is short.
– The animals are depicted as human beings (the sheep have spies, newspapers, publishers, sentinels, etc., the wolves have taverns; both have human personality traits).
– There is a moral tag at the end.

3 **a** The title can be taken at face value as the sheep spies are indeed dressed in wolf's clothing. But the title is also an allusion to (and inversion of) the common phrase 'a wolf in sheep's clothing', which stems from an Aesop fable in which wolves dress up as sheep to disguise their wicked intentions. In Thurber's fable the sheep disguise themselves as wolves to collect secret information about their enemies, and they take on the wolves' competitive, aggressive behaviour. However, they do not use these characteristics to fight their enemy, but to fight each other, which leads to the final catastrophe.

b (i) In the story, the moral could be considered the two sheep's professional credo: It is more important to write anything than to write something that is correct.
(ii) The moral for real life seems to be an ironic one: it pretends to condone a very superficial journalism, where getting the facts right does not matter, just as long as you get something in print. But the consequence is that you get 'eaten up', so that the real moral is, of course, the opposite: do not take things, or portray them, at face value. That may cost you your life.
With this moral, Thurber makes a pun on the verb 'write', since 'right' and 'write' are homophones (words pronounced alike but having different spelling or meaning). This play on words heightens the effect of the moral.

c As news agencies have to sell their news, they are often more interested in getting something published than in checking whether it is correct or not.

D Front Pages

Source:	*Daily Express / The Guardian*, 29 October, 2002
Topic:	Differences in the front pages of newspapers
Text form:	–
Language variety:	BE
Number of words:	–
Level:	Basic/advanced
Skills/activities:	Comparing a tabloid and a broadsheet newspaper, writing headlines

Didaktisch-methodische Hinweise

Broadsheets und *tabloids* unterscheiden sich nicht nur im Hinblick auf die Auswahl und Präsentation von Informationen, wie anhand von Text A und B deutlich wurde, sondern auch in Layout, Format, Themen usw. Die S vergleichen hier jeweils die erste Seite eines *broadsheet (Guardian)* und einer *tabloid (Daily Express)* und vervollständigen damit ihr Wissen über diese beiden Zeitungsarten. Sie lernen die Aufmachung zweier einflussreicher britischer Zeitungen kennen und erweitern so ihr landeskundliches Wissen.

Unterrichts-tipps
Kopiervorlage

Zu Beginn sollten einige Beispielzeitungen mit in die Klasse gebracht werden, so dass die S ihre Untersuchung von *tabloids* und *broadsheets* auf eine umfangreichere Datenbasis stützen können. Zum Schluss kann die KV „Tabloids and Broadsheets – A Comparison" ausgefüllt werden (vgl. S. 226 und die Hinweise auf S. 202).

Wenn eine intensivere Arbeit am Thema gewünscht wird, können den S authentische Zeitungsüberschriften mit dem Auftrag gegeben werden, über den Inhalt der dazugehörigen Artikel zu spekulieren. Leistungsstärkere S könnten einen vollständigen

Differenzierung

Artikel formulieren. Im Anschluss werden Schülerversion und Original verglichen.

Eine wettbewerbsorientierte und deshalb sicher motivierende Aktivität könnte darin bestehen, die Klasse in Gruppen einzuteilen und jeder von ihnen kurze Texte ohne Überschriften und die gleiche Anzahl von Überschriften auszuhändigen, die nicht zu diesen Texten gehören. Die passenden Überschriften sind im Besitz anderer Gruppen. Die Gruppen schauen sich kurz ihre Artikel und Überschriften an. Dann beginnen sie abwechselnd, ihre Texte vorzulesen. Die Gruppe mit der passenden Überschrift muss sich melden, sobald sie der Meinung ist, dass sie den richtigen Artikel erkannt hat. Um die Schüleraktivität dieses Spiels noch zu erhöhen, ist es denkbar, dieses Spiel nicht im Plenum, sondern in Kleingruppen durchzuführen und einzelnen Schüler innerhalb der Kleingruppe Texte und Überschriften zu geben.

Lösungs-hinweise
Kopiervorlage

1 Size of pictures/photographs much bigger in tabloids, banner headlines in tabloids, less text in tabloids, more cover stories in broadsheets, more serious news in broadsheets, sensationalist stories in tabloids (cf. KV 'Tabloids and Broadsheets – A Comparison', p. 226).

2 **a** Wichtig bei dieser Aufgabe ist, dass nicht nur ein grammatisch korrekter Satz entsteht, sondern auch, dass die gegebenen Informationen verständlich sind.

Daily Express:
Stars see Ulrika's sex game on video: Some stars watched Ulrika Johnsson have sex on video.
Divorce letter to William found at butler's home : The letter Princess Diana wrote to her son William about her divorce has been found at the home of her butler.
Revealed: Miracle pill that helps you shed pounds: We reveal a pill that helps you lose weight dramatically.
Guardian:
US weapons secrets exposed: Secrets about US weapons have been revealed to the public.

Chirac cancels summit after row with 'very rude' Blair: President Jacques Chirac has cancelled a summit after having a row in which he said that Tony Blair had behaved in a very rude way.

UK gives 400 tanks to Jordan: The UK has given 400 tanks to Jordan.

Characteristics of headlines:
- The definite article is almost always left out.
- Verbs are often put in the present tense, although the report is about something that happened in the recent past, or just the past participle is used.
- Photos are used to draw attention to people whose names can then be left out (Princess Diana).
- First names or surnames are used instead of complete names (Ulrika instead of Ulrika Johnsson; Blair instead of Tony Blair).
- Some headlines grab the attention of readers through key words ('stars' = celebrities, 'sex game', 'video'; 'exposed' rather than 'revealed', as the former sounds more dramatic).

b Individual answers.

SB, S. 114 **E A Letter to the Editor**

Source:	*The Independent*, 7–8 October 2002
Topic:	Comment on a previous story
Text form:	Photo and caption; letter to the editor
Language variety:	BE
Number of words:	30 (caption); 58 (letter)
Level:	Basic/advanced
Skills/activities:	Analising a letter to the editor, writing a letter to the editor, creating a newspaper page

Lern-
vokabular

Active vocabulary: 'A Letter to the Editor' (p. 114)

inspiration for sth. (ll. 2–3), the high point (ll. 3–4), caption (l. 7), assert sth./that … (l. 8), look to sth. for inspiration (ll. 9–10), check sth. (l. 10)

Didaktisch-
methodische
Hinweise

Die S lernen hier mit dem *letter to the editor* eine in Großbritannien sehr geschätzte und durch ihren intelligenten Witz häufig mit einer besonderen Prägung versehene Textsorte kennen, die eine der wenigen Möglichkeiten darstellt, unmittelbare Reaktionen auf die Presse in der Presse zu veröffentlichen. Methodisch liegt der Schwerpunkt dieses Abschnitts auf produktionsorientierten Verfahren: Die S schreiben selbst einen Leserbrief und bearbeiten ein auf die gesamte *section* bezogenes Projekt. Darin wenden die S ihre Erkenntnisse über die britische Presse an, indem sie in Gruppen Beiträge für eine Zeitungsseite verfassen und sich über Themen, Fotos, und Layout verständigen. Dieses Projekt fördert die Teamfähigkeit der S, da sie unter realitätsnahen Bedingungen (vgl. den Zeitplan) ein Endprodukt herstellen. Ggf. kann mit Hilfe der kreativen Schreibaufgabe aus dem *Youth*-Kapitel eine Vorarbeit zu diesem Projekt geleistet werden (Aufgabe 5, SB, S. 41).

Unterrichts-
tipps

Als Einstieg können die S zu ihren Erfahrungen mit Leserbriefen befragt werden: ob sie schon jemals an eine Zeitung geschrieben haben; wenn ja, warum; ob sie Zuschriften anderer Leser lesen; ob sie den Eindruck haben, dass Zeitungen Leserzuschriften ernst nehmen; warum Zeitungen überhaupt Leserbriefe abdrucken usw. Dann betrachten die S das Bild, lesen die Bildunterschrift und beschreiben, wie *Romeo and Juliet* dem Designer als Inspiration dienen konnte:

What relationship do you see between the clothes the model is wearing and the love story Romeo and Juliet?

Danach lesen sie still den Leserbrief und beschreiben Intention und Ton des Verfassers.

Lösungs-
hinweise

1 Der zweite Teil der Aufgabe eignet sich als Hausaufgabe. Die S sollten sich auf einen englischsprachigen Zeitungsartikel beziehen, um dort erforderliches Sprachmaterial zu finden. Entsprechende Artikel können zur Verfügung gestellt oder von den S im Internet gefunden werden. Dabei sollte L die Artikel kennen, auf die die S reagieren.

When you write an ordinary letter, you always begin 'Dear' and then either a name, or if you do not know the name, 'Sir or Madam'. You never leave the 'Dear' out. You always end a letter with a greeting, which alters according to the degree of formality: 'love from', 'Best wishes from', 'yours sincerely' or 'yours faithfully'. You never end with just your name, unless you want to be deliberately rude.

→ WB, ex. 4 A letter to the editor seems to start with 'Sir' and is finished without a greeting.

2 Hier ist die Organisation der Arbeit besonders wichtig, um zu einem erfolgreichen Resultat zu kommen. Der/die Redakteur/in muss Organisationsgeschick und Überblick besitzen. Sollte es einem Kurs schwer fallen, diese Aufgabe selbstständig zu bewältigen, kann L ihn durch Kontrolle der Ergebnisse einzelner Arbeitsschritte unterstützen. Um zu verhindern, dass die S einfach Artikel aus dem Internet kopieren, sollte die Zeitung das unmittelbare Umfeld der S widerspiegeln, z.B. als *neighbourhood news* oder *school news* enthalten.

SB, S. 115

2 The Role of Television

Das Fernsehen als eines der beliebtesten Massenmedien ist Thema dieser *section*. Zwei nicht-fiktionale Texte behandeln die wirtschaftliche Macht der Fernsehindustrie und die Rolle des Fernsehens in den USA bzw. in Großbritannien. Die S erhalten Einblicke in wesentliche Aspekte der Fernsehkultur dieser beiden Länder und werden dazu angeregt, diese zu ihren eigenen Fernsehgewohnheiten in Bezug zu setzen. In Text C begegnen die S Sendeformaten, die sie aus ihrem eigenen Alltag kennen und die starke emotionale Reaktionen hervorrufen werden: Sie sehen Auszüge aus verschiedenen *quiz shows* und *reality shows*, die zurzeit eine enorme Popularität genießen, und versuchen, dem Erfolgsrezept dieser Sendungen auf die Spur zu kommen. Bei dieser *section* ist eine Verknüpfung mit Materialien aus dem USA-Kapitel möglich (vgl. „The → WB, ex. 6 American Way of Life as Reflected on TV", SB, S. 182).

SB, S. 115

A TV is Big Business

Source:	*The Economist*, 13 April, 2002
Topic:	TV as a business
Text form:	Newsmagazine article
Language variety:	BE
Number of words:	441
Level:	Advanced
Skills/activities:	Analysing connotations, debating

Active vocabulary: 'TV Is Big Business' (p. 115)

beckon (l. 5), tanned (l. 6), home to sth. (l. 7), be set in … (l. 9), export sth. around the globe (l. 11), prime-time television (l. 13), decade (l. 15), be the beneficiary of sth. (l. 19), a turnover of $ … (l. 22), the average (American) (l. 27), the widespread use of sth. (l. 34), personal hygiene (l. 37)

Didaktisch-methodische Hinweise

Dieser Text beschreibt kritisch die Konzentration der Fernsehfilmproduktion in Holly-wood und gibt Informationen zum Fernsehverhalten der Amerikaner. Die kritische Haltung des Autors wird insbesondere durch die Verwendung von Lexik mit starken Konnotationen deutlich, so dass die Arbeit an der Lexik einen Schwerpunkt bei der Behandlung des Textes bildet.

Unterrichts-tipps

Da einige der unbekannten Wörter nicht leicht erschließbar sind, ihre Kenntnis aber zum Verständnis des Textes (und besonders für die Lösung der Aufgabe 2) erforderlich ist, muss viel Zeit für die Semantisierung eingeplant werden. Folgende Möglichkeit bietet sich hierfür an: Der Kurs wird in zwei Gruppen eingeteilt, von denen jede fünf unbekannte Wörter erhält, für die sie die Definition dem *OALD* entnehmen muss: „sear" (l. 1), „tilt" (l.1), „beckon" (l. 5), „bulk" (l. 12), „bonanza" (l. 16) „beneficiary" (l. 19), „sustain sth." (l. 19), „formidable" (l. 23), „array" (l. 23), „captivate sb." (l. 27). Zu jedem ihrer fünf Wörter „erfinden" die S noch eine weitere Definition (sie können auch dem *OALD* Definitionen für andere Wörter entnehmen). Die Gruppen stellen dann der Reihe nach ihre Wörter mit beiden Definitionen vor; die anderen Teams notieren, welche sie für die richtige halten. Gewonnen hat das Team, das die meisten Definitionen richtig zugeordnet hat. Am Ende teilen die einzelnen Gruppen eine Liste ihrer Wörter mit den korrekten Definitionen aus, auf die die S immer wieder zurückgreifen können.

Differenzierung

Insbesondere bei leistungsschwächeren S ist es unerlässlich, das Textverständnis zu sichern. Dies kann z.B. mit den folgenden *true/false*-Aufgabe geschehen. Eine stärkere Schüleraktivierung wird erreicht, wenn die S in Partnerarbeit für jeweils einen Textab-schnitt solche Aussagen selbst formulieren und dem Kurs vorlegen.

⬭ *Read through the following statements, then say whether they are true or false. If they are false, correct them.*

1. *The TV shows mentioned in the text are shot in Chicago, Washington D.C. and New York.* (False: They are all shot in Hollywood, cf. ll. 11–12.)
2. *Friends, ER and The West Wing are shown all over the world.* (True.)
3. *Most of the programmes broadcast in the USA during the evening are filmed outside Hollywood.* (False: Most of the programmes broadcast in the USA during the evening are filmed in Hollywood, cf. ll. 12–14.)
4. *During the last ten years America's TV industry has been incredibly successful and has made an enormous amount of money.* (True.)
5. *Being on television is considered more glamorous than being in movies.* (False: The movie industry is still considered to be more glamorous, cf. ll. 20–21.)
6. *The television industry has a larger turnover than the movie industry.* (True.)
7. *New electronic media like electronic games, computers, etc. have led to people watching less television.* (False: People continue to watch television, cf. ll. 23–27.)
8. *In an average American household the TV is switched on for less than four hours a day.* (False: In an average American household the TV is switched on for more than four hours a day, cf. ll. 27–29.)
9. *Research has shown that Americans are more fond of meeting people than watching TV.* (False: Research has shown that Americans are more fond of watching television than meeting friends, cf. ll. 29–32.)
10. *Americans have given up washing themselves because they enjoy television and the Internet so much.* (False: Americans probably spend less time on personal hygiene due to the amount of time they spend watching television and using the Internet, cf. ll. 36–37.)

Der Text eignet sich, um Vokabeln zum Wortfeld TV-Industrie zusammenzutragen: Wordfield *The Television Industry*: 'a medical drama' (l. 3), 'lot' (l. 3), 'sound stage' (l. 5), 'set' (l. 7),' a drama about sth.' (l. 8), 'interior set' (l. 9), 'TV show' (l. 9), 'set in ...' (l. 9), 'shoot a show' (l. 11), 'studio' (l. 12), 'prime-time television' (l. 13), 'film sth.' (l. 13), 'production company' (l. 14), 'media conglomerate' (l. 15), 'television industry' (l. 15), 'writer' (l. 18), 'producer' (l. 18), 'TV executive' (ll. 18–19), 'actor' (l. 19), 'agent' (l. 19), 'television set' (l. 25), 'media giant' (l. 33).

Lösungs-hinweise

1 Possible answers:

Ll. 1–9: Surprising shooting location for TV shows / The White House ... in Hollywood / Icicles under the California sun.

Ll. 10–23: TV is where the money is / TV earns millions for Hollywood / Not so glamorous, but definitely booming.

Ll. 23–37: The role of TV in the world of electronic media / TV still reigns supreme / Don't wash yourself, watch TV! / The world of electronics wins over the world of humans.

2 Possible answers:
– 'in the grip of' (l. 14): sounds vaguely violent, as if a mafia-like organization is controlling the TV companies;
– 'large media conglomerates' (l. 15): implies impersonal, unscrupulous organizations;
– 'enjoyed a bonanza' (l. 16): positive connotations for those enjoying the bonanza, has the feel of 'the rich getting richer';
– 'an ice-cool attitude' (l. 16), 'an air of entitlement' (l. 17): both imply arrogance;
– 'men in black T-shirts' (l. 17): implies that the people wearing the T-shirts deliberately set themselves aside from the others, as though the T-shirt were a uniform for the successful TV producers, but whereas the black T-shirt is supposed to set them apart, it also makes them look unimaginative as they all wear the same (and rather basic) article of clothing;
– 'picking at salads' (ll. 17–18): recalls the stereotype of the anorexic star;
– 'the smarter Beverley Hills restaurants' (l. 18): the implication is that only the rich are allowed in, though 'smart restaurants' contrasts with the very simple food (salad) that they are picking at;
– 'beneficiaries' (l. 19): implies that these people have reaped benefits without having done anything to earn them;
– 'dwarfs' (l. 21): implies that the position of the TV industry is exceptionally strong.

3 **a** Possible answers:
American culture is popular all around the world; people generally love series set in hospitals (like 'ER') or dealing with successful but neurotic thirtysomethings (like 'Friends'); possibly heavy marketing.

b Bei dieser Aufgabe müssen sich die S vorher mit den Schritten des „debating" (vgl. SB, S. 252) vertraut machen und ihre Debatte gründlich planen.

SB, S. 116 **B Rather than Talking about the Weather**

Source:	*British Cultural Identities*, 1997 (pp. 177–179)
Topic:	The role TV plays in British family life
Text form:	Essay (extract)
Language variety:	BE
Number of words:	334
Level:	Basic
Skills/activities:	Explaining a text's content in one's own words, devising a questionnaire on TV viewing habits

Active vocabulary: 'Rather than Talking about the Weather' (p. 116)

on average (l. 1), accurate (l. 3), a topic of conversation (l. 4), according to sb./sth. (l. 5), leisure time (l. 8), a classic film (l. 15), underestimate sth. (l. 16), attitude (l. 16), social decline (l. 18), the role of sth. (l. 20), deplore sth. (l. 22), current television shows (ll. 22–23), be associated with sb./sth. (l. 25)

*Didaktisch-
methodische
Hinweise*

Dieser Text beleuchtet die Rolle des Fernsehens und seinen Einfluss auf die britische Gesellschaft und ergänzt so Text A. Ein expliziter Bezug zu dessen Thematik wird in Z. 23–27 hergestellt, wo die Vorliebe für amerikanische *TV shows* thematisiert wird. Der Schwerpunkt der Arbeit im Unterricht liegt folglich im Vergleich britischer mit amerikanischen und deutschen Verhältnissen. Insbesondere die Ergebnisse der Befragung, die die S bei Gleichaltrigen durchführen, werden hier von Bedeutung sein.

*Unterrichts-
tipps*

Als Einstieg in die Arbeit am Text bietet sich das Foto an. Die S beschreiben es und die Gefühle, die es bei ihnen auslöst. Aufgrund von Bild und Textüberschrift können die S ihre Erwartungen an den Text formulieren.

*Lösungs-
hinweise*

1 TV gives people something to talk about, and because so much time is spent watching TV, it is fair to say that TV schedules dictate how the British spend their time. Even the holiday period is judged to have been successful or not by the offerings on television, with Christmas, for example, being structured around certain traditional programmes. People's perceptions of what is right or wrong about their country centre around what they think about the quality of TV programming. People in Britain even go so far as to think of the BBC as a family member.

Why do you think that the phrase 'the British way of life' is set in inverted commas? Perhaps because, on the one hand, there is no such thing as the British way of life, just the way some people live, while on the other hand, after reading the text, it seems as if the British way of life is dictated by TV, which is a poor life.

2 This seems to refer to glossy, fast-paced shows with lots of violence and sexy people and to mindless game shows.

Name American TV series that are shown on German TV.

What percentage of feature films shown on German TV is American?

3 Individual answers.

 4 Wenn die S keine Erfahrungen mit dem Erstellen von Fragebögen haben, müssen gemeinsam Grundsätze der Befragungstechnik erarbeitet werden, wie z.B., dass offene Fragen schwierig auszuwerten sind. Wichtig ist der Hinweis, dass die S bereits bei der Erstellung mögliche Antwortvarianten im Kopf haben und sich Gedanken zur Auswertung und Präsentation der Ergebnisse machen sollten. Damit die Arbeit reibungslos läuft, müssen organisatorische Fragen geklärt werden:

Consider the following questions when organizing your work:

– *How are you going to decide which questions to include?*
– *How are you going to phrase the questions so that the results of the questionnaire can be easily analysed?*
– *Who is going to be responsible for photocopying the questionnaire?*
– *How and where are the questionnaires going to be distributed?*
– *How are the questionnaires going to be returned to the group?*
– *Who is going to evaluate the results of the questionnaires?*
– *In what form will the results be presented to the class (e.g. as a poster, as part of a presentation, etc.)?*

Folgende Themen aus Texten A und B könnten im Fragebogen aufgenommen werden:
- average viewing time per day;
- popular ways of spending an evening;
- importance of certain programmes in the daily/weekly routine;
- importance of TV programmes as a topic of conversation;
- the role TV plays during holidays like Christmas or Easter;
- whether people see a relationship between social decline and 'falling standards' on TV.

SB, S. 117

VIDEO

C How to Get on TV

Source:	*Popstars*, 2001, *The Weakest Link*, 2001, *Big Brother 2*, 2001, *Survivor*, 2001
Topic:	'Nasty' host shows and reality shows
Text form:	Reality shows (excerpts)
Language variety:	BE
Length:	ca. 12 mins
Level:	Basic
Skills/activities:	Analysing TV shows

Didaktisch-methodische Hinweise

Als ein vertrautes Fernsehformat werden den S Ausschnitte aus vier in Großbritannien beliebten Fernsehshows gezeigt (vgl. Video/DVD und das Transkript auf S. 227). Einige von ihnen wurden auch im deutschen Fernsehen gesendet. Da diese Shows starke emotionale Reaktionen hervorrufen dürften, sollten sich lebendige Diskussionen ergeben. Die Aufgaben im SB zielen v.a. auf eine Einordnung und Kommentierung dieser Sendeformate, so dass kein detailliertes Hör- oder Sehverstehen erforderlich ist.

Unterrichts-tipps

Zum Einstieg könnten folgende Fragen gestellt werden:

What do you understand by 'reality TV'? Name programmes that you know that you would consider to be 'reality TV shows'.

What do you think of 'reality TV shows'? Do you watch them? Why or why not?

Lösungs-hinweise

VIDEO

1 Vgl. Video/DVD und das Transkript auf S. 227.

Possible answers:
Television is just one of many areas that make up modern life, so it often reflects the mores of the time. If people complain about falling standards being reflected in television, it might be an indication that they themselves have to come to rely on television too much for their entertainment, and so get disappointed when they view shows they dislike. However, it does seem that in many 'reality' shows people without talent or intelligence are being given time on TV, so one could argue that these shows have no real purpose except as mindless entertainment. Perhaps more dangerously, the audience is being asked to make judgements on the personal worth of people.

VIDEO **2** a

<u>Popstars:</u> Most people want to become famous, so by watching normal people on the road to fame, it seems as if one is part of that dream. It is also interesting to see how good people perform and sing, and see if your personal choice makes it through to become a member of the band.

<u>The Weakest Link:</u> The presenter has a strong character, and her nasty remarks and comments entertain the audience. Watching how ordinary people deal with her is also amusing. Especially when showing up representatives of a professional group like teachers the presenter can be certain to have the audience on her side.

<u>Big Brother 2:</u> Here the popularity relies on being able to influence who wins the show, as the audience is able to vote people out. By watching how people behave, move, interact, the audience is indulging in voyeurism and a nicely superficial bit of psychology.

<u>Survivor:</u> This is similar to *Big Brother*, but the fact that the people are living on a tropical island and have interesting tasks to do makes it appealing. Again the tension lies in wondering who will be the winner.

b As with all programmes, the producers want to make money by entertaining audiences.

(i) One could say that they are fair on the participants, as the participants usually know what they are getting themselves into, and they know that embarrassing situations and humiliation might result. In *Big Brother* and *Survivor*, the participants are offered money if they win, but this is not the primary motivation for going on the programme – narcissism and self-promotion are probably the main factors. *The Weakest Link* is more like other quiz shows, except that the presenter has an amusingly harsh tongue and the participants are only briefly on TV, so never become the object of interest that is the case in the other shows. Only one of the programmes (*Popstars*) seems to offer the participants anything lucrative: the possibility of becoming a pop star. It would be interesting to know if the experience leaves deep psychological wounds for those who are humiliated or lose.

(ii) For the audience, one can also say that they are willingly being exploited. They enjoy the fights and problems and traumas, and, in some cases, participate as well by voting people out or in.

3 Possible answers:
In Germany there have been or are equivalents of all these shows, so Germany seems to be following the general trend. There are a lot of chat and talk shows on TV, and American TV series also seem be very popular.

❖ **4** Diese Aufgabe kann in einem Kugellager bearbeitet werden (vgl. S. 429).

Individual answers.

SB, S. 118 **3 I Saw It on the Internet** ... so it's got to be true

Neben dem Fernsehen gehört das Internet zu den von Jugendlichen am häufigsten genutzten Medien. Im Vordergrund stehen dabei zweifellos das Chatten, Einkaufen und die Informationsbeschaffung. Da Jugendliche Internetinformationen oft unkritisch übernehmen, liegt der inhaltliche Schwerpunkt dieser *section* auf den Themen Zuverlässigkeit von Internetinformationen und Überprüfung der Seriosität von Internetanbietern. Dies ist um so wichtiger, als auch an vielen Stellen von *New Context* die Nutzung des Internets angeregt wird und die S dafür in der Lage sein müssen, Internetinformationen zu bewerten.

Unterrichts-
tipps

→ *WB, ex. 7, 10*

Als Einstieg können die S ein Brainstorming durchführen, bei dem sie Assoziationen zum Thema Internet zusammentragen. Das Wort wird an die Tafel bzw. auf Folie geschrieben und durch die von den S erwähnten Stichwörter ergänzt. So werden nicht nur die Nutzungsbreite und unterschiedlichste Meinungen zum Thema offensichtlich, sondern es werden auch nützliche Vokabeln zum Thema festgehalten.

A Nobody Knows You're a Dog

Source:	*The New Yorker*, 7 May, 1993
Topic:	Anonymity on the Internet
Text form:	Cartoon
Language variety:	AE
Number of words:	9
Level:	Basic
Skills/activities:	Describing and analysing a cartoon

Didaktisch-methodische Hinweise

Der Cartoon ermöglicht den Einstieg in die Diskussion über Gefahren oder zumindest negative Auswirkungen, die die Anonymität des Internets haben kann. Die S diskutieren dieses Thema und entwickeln Strategien, wie sie sich selbst vor unseriösen Internetpartnern schützen können.

Auch an anderen Stellen des SB wird das Thema Anonymität im Internet angeschnitten: Im Text „Y2K.CHATRM43" (vgl. SB, S. 47) wird z.B. gezeigt, wie ein junges Mädchen seine Identität im Chatroom verfälscht. Hier ist diese falsche Identität harmlos, aber die S könnten diskutieren, inwieweit solche Anonymität auch gefährlich werden kann.

☞ Bei der Besprechung des Cartoons ist darauf zu achten, dass die S die Doppeldeutigkeit von „be a dog" erkennen: V.a. im amerikanischen *slang* kann es auch auch „be a thing of low quality, a failure" bedeuten.

Lösungs-hinweise

1 The cartoon shows two dogs. One of the dogs is sitting at a desk in front of a computer with one paw on the keyboard, as if he has been typing. He is looking down at the other dog and saying, 'On the Internet, nobody knows you're a dog.'

2 **a** Chatting: The person you are chatting with may not be what he or she claims to be. People sometimes lie about their gender, age and looks. Such people are referred to as 'fakes'. Whereas fakes can be annoying, it is also possible to run into someone truly dangerous, who may lure people into traps or play mind games with them.

Shopping: The company you are buying from may not be a legitimate one, i.e. they are collecting personal information or possibly credit card numbers for the purpose of selling the information to advertisers or even committing credit card fraud. Even non-criminal activities can be annoying: the company may not have things in stock, resulting in long waits for delivery, or it does not have the infrastructure to deliver on its promises or, for example, to handle returns if a customer is dissatisfied. And if it is unclear who is behind an online shop, or if it is in another country, it might be difficult or impossible to enforce legitimate claims against the company in court.

Research: It is often hard to judge whether the information posted on an Internet site is accurate. Some webmasters may deliberately manipulate information in order to fool the gullible or to promote a particular agenda (e.g. hate sites), while others may simply be negligent in their research. Even normally reliable information providers, e.g. university presses, may not have all the same vetting procedures in place for their websites that they have for their print publications.

b Chatting:
– Never give out personal information in chat.
– Ask questions of your chat partner that might cause him/her to reveal him- or herself.
– Have a second email address (i.e. not your main address) with a name that is not connected to you (e.g. xyz123@hotmail.com) if the person wants to continue communicating with you.
– Inform your parents, a teacher or other responsible adult if someone makes you feel uncomfortable.
– Do not arrange to meet anyone personally whom you have met on the Net – if you decide to meet, do so in public place and take someone you trust with you.

<u>Shopping:</u>
- Shop only at well-known, reliable online shops.
- Do not give any more personal information than seems reasonable.
- Only submit personal information, especially sensitive data like credit card information if the page is shown in your browser as being a secure site.
- Read the company's privacy policy to see whether you are comfortable with how they will use your personal information.
- Read the company's terms of business to learn whether you will be able to cancel your order and find out what their return policy is.
- Never do business with a company whose real (as opposed to virtual) address you cannot find on the site.

<u>Research:</u> cf. Text B, below.

SB, S. 118 ## B The Reliability of Internet Information

Source:	McGraw-Hill Higher Educational website
Topic:	The reliability of information on the Internet
Text form:	Non-fictional text
Language variety:	AE
Number of words:	257
Level:	Basic
Skills/activities:	Finding out differences between printed and online information, searching the Internet for unreliable sites

Lern-
vokabular

Active vocabulary: 'The Reliability of Internet Information' (p. 118)

judge sth. (l. 1), the reliability of sth. (l. 1), crucial (l. 1), regulating body (l. 2), a reliable source (l. 5), obtain valuable information (l. 5), questionable (l. 7), tell the difference (l. 8), bias (l. 17), provide information (on sth.) (l. 18), update sth. (l. 20), the purpose of sth. (l. 21), verify information (l. 24)
tasks: imply sth.

Didaktisch-
methodische
Hinweise

Dieser Textauszug verdeutlicht, warum Informationen im Internet nicht unkritisch übernommen werden dürfen. Am Ende steht eine Art Checkliste, mit deren Hilfe die S die Ergebnisse von Internetrecherchen kritisch überprüfen können (vgl. auch „Doing Research on the Internet", SB, S. 231). Somit hat dieser Text eine deutlich anwendungsbezogene Ausrichtung. Es sollte aber erwähnt werden, dass auch Zeitungen oder Bücher nicht über jeden Zweifel erhaben sind. Man denke nur an den Skandal um den *New York Times*-Journalisten Jayson Blair im Jahr 2003, der über Monate hinweg Reportagen fälschte oder erfand. Eine gesunde Skepsis gegenüber Informationen ist immer angebracht – nicht nur, wenn sie im Internet erscheinen.

Lösungs-
hinweise

1 There is no 'regulating body' for the contents of the Internet (cf. l. 2), whereas newspapers such has such a body in the form of its editors. In addition, organizations such as the UK's Press Council watch over journalistic standards.

2 Vgl. auch http://muse.widener.edu/Wolfgram-Memorial-Library/webevaluation/examples.htm · 1.8.2003.

Individual answers.

Getting Along in English

Didaktisch-methodische Hinweise

In dieser *section* liegt der Schwerpunkt auf dem Führen von Telefonaten. Drei Alltagssituationen werden präsentiert (vgl. CD2, *tracks* 1–5, und die Transkripte auf S. 229–232): Die S entnehmen der interaktiven Bandansage einer Fluggesellschaft die gewünschten Informationen zu einem Flug, vereinbaren einen Zahnarzttermin und erfragen die Telefonnummer eines Bekannten. Dabei lernen sie, wie man ein Telefongespräch beginnt, wie man nach bestimmten Informationen fragt und wie man das Gespräch beendet. Sie schulen ihr Hörverstehen und wenden das Gelernte an, indem sie selbst ein Telefongespräch inszenieren.

Unterrichts-tipps

Als Einstieg in das Thema bieten sich folgende Fragen an:

⬭ *Have any of you ever tried to make a phone call when abroad? What were the difficulties you encountered? Were you successful in your attempt to get the information you required? What difficulties might arise when talking on the phone in English?*

Lösungs-hinweise

CD

1 Die Aufnahme befindet sich auf CD2, *track* 1; das Transkript auf S. 229.
Diese Bandansage basiert auf authentischen *recorded messages* von zwei amerikanischen Fluggesellschaften. In den letzten Jahren verwendet man in den USA wie auch in Europa immer häufiger solche *automated messages*, die in der Lage sind, einfache Antworten menschlicher Stimmen zu verstehen.

☞ Bei dieser Übung muss darauf geachtet werden, dass die Pause-Taste an der richtigen Stelle gedrückt und wieder gelöst wird, so dass die S genug Zeit haben zu antworten. Das Transkript gibt die nötigen Hinweise.

CD

2 **a** Der Dialog befindet sich auf CD2, *tracks* 2 und 3; das Transkript auf S. 230.
– Lisa didn't listen properly ('Is that directory enquiries?').
– She was rude right at the start of her conversation ('At last!') and is rude later on ('of course' implies that the operator is at fault).
– She was impolite when saying she could not understand the operator ('I don't understand.' 'Ugh?') and when the dentist's receptionist could not give her the help she wanted.
– She was very abrupt ('I'm not in a phone box. I'm using my handy.').
– She had not thought about what it was she wanted to say beforehand.

b Could you help me, please? / I need to see a dentist/doctor quite urgently. I wonder whether you could tell me where to go to get help / who could help me? / Could you possibly give me the telephone number of a doctor's surgery in …? / Is that the doctor's surgery? / I was wondering whether it's possible for me to make an appointment? I'm over here from Germany for three months and I have a problem with my tooth.

CD

c Der Dialog befindet sich auf CD2, *track* 4; das Transkript auf S. 231.

Individual answers.

3 Starting: Good morning. My name is … I wonder whether you could help me?
Explaining: I come from Germany. I'm here on holiday and I've broken a tooth / twisted my ankle / got a sore throat. It hurts a lot / is swollen, so I was hoping I could see a doctor about it.
Checking: Just one moment. Let me check if I have written down the information correctly. That's 2 Rose Lane at 5.30 this evening?
Ending: Thank you very/so much for your help/patience. I'll see you this evening at 5.30. Goodbye.

CD

4 **a** Der Dialog befindet sich auf CD2, *track* 5; das Transkript auf S. 231.
Bernd does pretty well because he listens carefully and is polite, so people help him and are patient.

I would like to speak to …, please. / I'm not sure. / I think … / and could you please repeat the number? / Thank you very much. / Good morning, my name is …

b directory enquiries; person; hold the line, please; the line is / the telephone is engaged; mobile phone; phone box/public phone.

❖ **5** Um den Anspruch der Aufgabe zu erhöhen, sind folgende Verfahren denkbar:

– Die Telefonpartner stehen Rücken an Rücken, um Hilfe durch Augenkontakt, Mimik oder Gestik auszuschließen.

– Der Kurs wird in eine gerade Anzahl von Gruppen geteilt; jeweils zwei Gruppen erhalten aufeinander abgestimmte Situationen, auf die sie sich entweder als Anrufer oder Angerufener vorbereiten.

Folgende Situationen sind denkbar:
Theatre/film ticket office: information on the current theatre programme for tonight/tomorrow/etc; availability of tickets, length of performance, prices, where and when to collect tickets, how to pay (cash / credit card);
tourist information: you want to book a double room for one night; forms of accommodation, prices, location (e.g. within walking distance of the city centre); when to check in and check out, whether breakfast is included, whether the room has got a TV.

SB, S. 120

4 You Can Sell Anything

Werbung, ein integraler Bestandteil der heutigen Medienwelt, ist das Thema dieser *section*. Anhand eines fiktionalen und zweier nicht-fiktionaler Texte beschäftigen sich die S v.a. mit den Wirkungsweisen von Werbung: Sie lesen einen Romanauszug, einen Sachtext über die bekannte AIDA-Formel und analysieren ein Werbeposter. Die Arbeit an diesen Materialien zielt v.a. auf das Durchschauen von Werbestrategien und somit den kritischen, mündigen Umgang mit Werbung.

→ *WB, ex. 8, 9*

SB, S. 120 **A We Are Speaking of Art**   Steven Millhauser

Source:	*Martin Dressler*, 1996 (from chapter: 'Harwington')
Topic:	The influence of advertising
Text form:	Novel (extract)
Language variety:	AE
Number of words:	738
Level:	Advanced
Skills/activities:	Working with characterization, analysing mode of presentation, converting a text into a film script

Lern-vokabular

Active vocabulary: 'We Are Speaking of Art' (p. 120)

single sth. out (l. 3), admire sth. (l. 5), shape (l. 5), confidence (l. 6), be more likely to do sth. (l. 7), be reputed to be sth. (ll. 19–20), attend university (l. 22), give a lecture on sth. (ll. 24–25), make sth. memorable (l. 28), hold the attention of sb. (l. 40), gather information (l. 41), devise a campaign (l. 51), researcher (l. 55), conduct tests (l. 55), train yourself to do sth. (l. 62), avert your gaze (l. 71)

In diesem Romanauszug bereiten Harwinton, der Leiter einer Werbeagentur, und Dressler, der Manager eines Hotels, eine Werbekampagne für Dresslers neues Hotel vor. Dieser literarische Text gibt den S die Gelegenheit, den Auszug nicht nur im Hinblick auf das Thema Werbung zu untersuchen, sondern auch wichtige literarische Elemente zu analysieren (z.B. Charakterisierung, die Wirksamkeit des *mode of presentation*). Durch seine weitgehend dialogische Struktur eignet sich der Auszug für die Umwandlung in ein Filmskript, wodurch die Erkenntnisse der S über den *mode of presentation* vertieft werden.

*Unterrichts-
tipps*

Durch folgende kreative *pre-reading activity* kann der Text vorentlastet werden: Der Kurs wird in Gruppen aus vier oder fünf S geteilt. Jede Gruppe erhält einen Alltagsgegenstand wie z.B. ein Stück Seife, Kreide oder (in Anlehnung an den Text) einen Stein mit dem Auftrag, innerhalb von 5–7 Minuten einen Werbetext zu erfinden. Nach der Präsentation einiger Texte analysieren die S die eingesetzten Werbestrategien.
Um das Erfassen des Textes zu erleichtern, teilen S den Text nach dem stillen Lesen in Sinneinheiten ein und finden Überschriften. Eine mögliche Einteilung wäre: Z. 1–10: „Selling stones"; Z. 11–36: „Harwinton's appearance and background"; Z. 36–57: „Harwinton's success as an advertiser"; Z. 58–76: „Harwinton's beliefs".

Info

Steven Millhauser (born 1943) is a professor of English at Skidmore College in Saratoga Springs, New York. He has written several novels and collections of short stories and has received several awards for his works, among them the Pulitzer Prize for his novel *Martin Dressler: The Tale of an American Dreamer* (1996), which is about the career of an entrepreneur who, at the turn of the last century, builds fabulous hotels in Manhattan. With his wife and two children, Millhauser lives in Saratoga Springs, New York.

*Lösungs-
hinweise*

– Talking positively about something will make people want to choose it. (ll. 1–7).
– Facts and quality have nothing to do with advertising (ll. 8–10).
– Advertising is an art (ll. 10, 75–76), a science (ll. 33–36).
– The type of product being advertised is not particularly important (ll. 58–60).
– Advertising is about providing things with meaning (ll. 60–63, 65–68).
– Advertising creates desire (ll. 68–69).
– Advertising equates possessing something with happiness (ll. 68–69).
– Advertising is about illusion, not belief (l. 75).

2 Diese Aufgabe setzt die Kenntnis der Termini *implicit/explicit characterization* voraus. Geübte S können die Aufgabe selbstständig, ggf. mit Hilfe des Glossars bearbeiten. Bei weniger erfahrenen S sollten die Termini anhand dieses Textes erarbeitet bzw. wiederholt werden; dazu sammeln die S alle Informationen über Harwinton und erkennen, dass er zum einen durch sein Verhalten, zum anderen durch Dresslers Beschreibung charakterisiert wird. Folgende Fragen können dabei eine Hilfe sein:

⬭ *Find the passages in which we learn something about Harwinton's appearance and character.*

⬭ *How is this information presented to the reader (i.e. does Harwington tell us himself, does someone else talk about him or do we have to form a judgement of his character on the basis of what he says and how he behaves?)?*

The extract uses both direct and indirect characterization.
<u>Direct characterization:</u> Harwinton is described by the narrator from the perspective of Martin Dressler. He provides a physical description (ll. 11–19) as well as information about his background (ll. 19–30). A further description of Harwinton and his manners

and way of talking is also to be found in ll. 70–73; this is partially related directly by the narrator and partly from Dressler's perspective.

Indirect characterization: All instances of direct speech show that Harwinton is educated and eloquent. In several places we can draw the conclusion that he is rather arrogant and revels in his own cleverness (ll. 9–10, 30–31, 60–63, 65–69 [where he also interrupts Dressler], 75–76).

⬭ *What picture of Harwinton emerges from the extract?*
We see that he is ambitious (ll. 53–57) and utterly without scruples (ll. 60–63, 65–69, 75–76). He is obviously also very intense, possibly even unnerving to talk to (ll. 70–73).

3 **a** Diese Aufgabe können erfahrene S allein oder mit Hilfe des Glossars lösen.

The extract makes use of scenic presentation: It allows the reader to experience gradually for him- or herself what Harwinton is like and to draw his or her own conclusions. This is more effective than a quick summary of the conversation.

b Vor Bearbeitung der Aufgabe sollte Einigkeit darüber hergestellt werden, welche Informationen das Drehbuch enthalten sollte, d.h. den Dialog sowie Beschreibungen des *setting* und ungefähre Angaben zu Kameraeinstellungen und -bewegungen. Die S erkennen, dass aufgrund der szenischen Darstellung in dem Ausschnitt wenige Veränderungen nötig sind, um ihn in ein Drehbuch zu verwandeln.

Very few. Obviously stage directions would have to be given, as would instructions for shots and editing cuts. The only problematic passages might be ll. 18–30 and 50–57; here one can decide how much of the information needs to be given. One can either show through the interior decoration of the office, with shots of diplomas and books that Harwinton is a successful and well-educated businessman, or one could include an extra scene in which Dressler asks a friend or colleague whether he knows someone who could advertise his hotel. Alternatively, it could be integrated into the dialogue, as would the studies related in ll. 36–50.

⬭ *Translate ll. 58–76 into German.*

SB, S. 122 **B AIDA**

Source:	The website of Danex Export Marketing Resources
Topic:	How advertising works
Text form:	Essay
Language variety:	BE
Number of words:	228
Level:	Basic/advanced
Skills/activities:	Examining advertisements, writing an advert

Lern-
vokabular

Active vocabulary: 'AIDA' (p. 122)

make sure that (l. 3), catch sb.'s attention (ll. 3, 14), reveal sth. (l. 4), conceal sth. (l. 4), a common interest (ll. 4–5), concern (l. 5), benefit (l. 7), potential (l. 7), enhance sth. (l. 8), irresistible (l. 9), guarantee (ll. 11, 16), overwhelm sb. with sth. (l. 15)
poster: trafficking, assault

Dieser Text behandelt die bekannte AIDA-Formel, auf deren Basis Werbestrategen ihre Kampagnen entwerfen. Die Altersgruppe der S ist für Werbestrategen eine beliebte Zielgruppe. Daher sollte es für die S besonders interessant sein, Werbemechanismen zu untersuchen und ihr eigenes Kaufverhalten kritisch zu überprüfen.

Die Anzeige ist Teil einer Kampagne gegen Rassismus. Die S sollen an dieser Anzeige nicht nur die AIDA-Kriterien überprüfen, sie werden auf einer zweiten Ebene möglicherweise mit eigenen Vorurteilen konfrontiert.

*Unterrichts-
tipps*

Als Einstieg in dieses Thema bringt L eine oder mehrere großformatige Anzeigen aus englischsprachigen Zeitungen oder Zeitschriften mit. Diese können entweder für alle sichtbar an die Tafel geheftet werden, oder die S finden sich in Gruppen zusammen und erhalten je ein Exemplar. Die S betrachten die Anzeigen unter folgender Fragestellung:

⬭ *How does this ad try to make people buy the product?*

Die Ergebnisse werden gesammelt und im Anschluss an die Lektüre mit den im Text beschriebenen Strategien verglichen. Die Anzeigen können auch genutzt werden, um die Ergebnisse von Aufgabe 1 zu illustrieren.

*Lösungs-
hinweise*

1 Attention: Say something in your headline that lots of people are concerned about so they look at the advert;
Interest: Give your customers something that they should think is good for them;
Desire: Offer customers the feeling that they need the product and gifts, etc. to increase their perceived need;
Action: Ask your customers to buy your product or service.

2 **a** Revealing a common interest apparently means that the advertiser should speak directly about something many people are interested in anyway, even before they see your ad. Concealing an interest might mean saying something that hints at something people are interested without actually saying it, which can be very enticing.

b The idea here is that consumers want to know 'what's in it for them'. They will buy a product, which probably is not that much different from a competitor's product, only if they see some sort of added value in the form of improvement of their lifestyle.

3 Diese Aufgabe bezieht sich auf das nebenstehende Poster, das streng genommen nicht der AIDA-Formel entspricht. Seine Effektivität rührt daher, dass es mit den Vorurteilen der Menschen spielt, die spontan das Gesicht des Schwarzen mit den Vergehen auf der rechten Seite in Verbindung bringen werden. Die S erkennen, dass nicht nur die AIDA-Formel erfolgreiche Werbung sichert (vgl. auch SB, S. 44 und 130).

a The ad is trying to 'sell' an attitude change.

b This ad seems to fail the AIDA test.
Attention: There is no headline to grab attention; it relies solely on the photograph of a black man with a scar. However, the face might attract attention.
Interest: There are no enhancements to your life in accepting its message.
Desire: It does not awaken any particular desires in the reader.
Action: It contains no direct call to action.
One could, however, analyse the AIDA formula also in this way:
Attention: The reader could wonder who the black man next to the simple text is.
Interest: Interest could be intellectual, e.g. why am I being informed about this criminal?
Desire: The desire to change your attitude.
Action: The reader could decide to behave differently from now on.

c By and large, it works on the assumption that most readers will assume the man in the photograph is the criminal Michael Conrad because he is black. When their expectations are overturned at the end of the ad, the reader may feel the need to think over his or her racial prejudices, which may be considered an indirect call to action. This shows that AIDA might only be properly used when someone is selling a product.

4 Weitere Anzeigen, auf deren Basis die S Werbestrategien identifizieren können, finden sich im SB auf S. 39, 44, 108, 121, 130, 195; allerdings zielen streng genommen nur die auf S. 39 auf den Verkauf eines Produkts. Wenn L dem oben vorgeschlagenen Einstieg gefolgt ist, haben die S möglicherweise schon zusätzliche Strategien an der Tafel gesammelt.

Individual answers.

5 Individual answers.

SB, S. 123 # Watch Your Language

Didaktisch-methodische Hinweise Schwerpunkte dieser *section* sind typische Interferenzfehler, v.a. falsche Kollokationen und *false friends*. Diese sprachlichen Bereiche bedürfen deshalb der ständigen Übung (vgl. auch SB, S. 105).

Lösungs-hinweise

1 **a**

1 '... <u>spend</u> too much time ...'
2 '... anything on <u>channels one or two</u>. ... watch the private <u>stations</u>'
3 '... <u>on</u> television'
4 'You can <u>have the news sent</u> to your <u>mobile (phone)</u>, which means your <u>information</u> is always <u>up-to-date</u> / you always have <u>up-to-date information</u>'
5 '... these new <u>media</u> ... very early <u>stages</u> of development'
6 '... relatively new <u>technology</u> ...'
7 '... complain <u>to</u> the Ethics Commission ... been <u>treated</u> unfairly ...'
8 '... in a <u>commercial</u> on TV'

b

1 'Take time': 'to need or require a particular amount of time' (*OALD*), clearly not what the student wanted to say. Under 'spend', the second definition is 'to use time for a particular purpose', and one of the examples in fact is 'I spend too much time watching television.'
2 'Programme': defined as 'something that people watch on television or listen to on the radio' (*OALD*), which would not explain to the student why this sentence was wrong. Only the examples make it clear that programme means '*Sendung*'. The first definition of 'channel' is 'a television station'. When speaking with non-Germans, some more clarification might be needed, e.g. 'the two main state-financed stations'. 'Canal': 'a long straight passage dug in the ground' or 'a tube inside the body' (*OALD*), and would be translated with 'Kanal'.
3 'On television' is given as an idiom (*OALD*).
4 'Handy' only exists as an adjective (*OALD*).
'Information' is uncountable ('U' in the dictionary) and so cannot be used in the plural (*OALD*).
'Actual': There is a box under 'actual' in the *OALD* explaining the difference between 'actual', 'current' and 'present'.
5 'Media': this is a plural already (of 'medium') (*OALD*).
'Stadium': 'a large sports ground' (*OALD*).
6 'Technique': 'a particular way of doing sth.' or 'the skill with which sb. is able to do sth. practical' (*OALD*).
7 'Complain (to sb.) (about sth.)' is given in the *OALD*.
'Handle': Of the five definitions in the *OALD*, none means 'treat', etc.
8 'Spot': Of the ten definitions in the *OALD*, none has anything to do with advertisements.

2 Besides the one grammar mistake (4, 'have sent'), the students have made lexical errors: confusing two English words that are used in similar contexts (1), using false friends from German (2,4,5 'stadiums', 6, 7 'handled', 8) or using the wrong prepositions (3). These problems are best avoided by learning words with their correct collocations rather than individually, and by learning an entire word field (e.g. 'media') rather than isolated items. Proper use of a monolingual dictionary would have told the students that their word choices were wrong, but in most cases would not have helped them to find the correct alternative. They would either have had to use a bilingual dictionary, or if that was not possible (e.g. in a test), they would have had to search their memory for the correct expressions, all of which they have learned at one time or another. The best advice one could give these students is to be sceptical every time a word sounds like its German equivalent, and then to check it.

3 **a**

1 self-conscious – *befangen, gehemmt; selbstbewusst* – self-confident
2 sympathetic – *mitfühlend, verständnisvoll; sympathisch* – nice, likeable
3 billion – *Milliarde; Billion* – thousand billion (BE), trillion (AE)
4 meaning – *Bedeutung; Meinung* – opinion
5 critic – *Kritiker/in; Kritik* – review; criticism
6 warehouse – *Lager(haus); Warenhaus* – department store
7 formula – *Formel; Formular* – (blank) form
8 pregnant – *schwanger; prägnant* – succinct, concise

b

1 'Have done sth' is the present perfect of 'to do'; 'have sth. done' is used to indicate that you do not do sth. yourself, but rather you find sb. else to do it.
2 'Let sb. do sth.' means to allow sb. to do sth.; 'leave sb. to do sth.' means to go away so that sb. can get on with whatever they need to do. It could also mean, in another context, to go away from sb. in order to do sth. yourself.
3 'Must not do sth.' means that you are not allowed or should not do sth.; 'need not do sth.' means that you do not have to do sth. if you do not want to.
4 'Stop doing sth.' means that you decide not to continue what you were doing; 'stop to do sth.' means you stop whatever you were doing in order to do sth. else.
5 'Oversee sth.' means to check and control that sth. is done correctly; 'overlook sth.' means to fail to notice sth. or to see sth. wrong and decide to do nothing about it or (of a building) to have a view of sth.
6 'Take a photo of sb.' means that you are using a camera to produce a picture of sb.; 'take a photo from sb.' means that sb. has a photo and you take it physically away.

c

1 'Undertaker' is a person who is responsible for dead people ('Bestatter/in'), while an 'Unternehmer/in' is a 'business person'.
2 To 'overhear sth.' is to hear sth. you were not meant to hear, simply because it is too loud, whereas 'überhören' means that you did not hear sth. that you were supposed to hear. The correct translation of 'overhear' is 'zufällig mitanhören'.
3 'Rest room' is an American expression for 'toilet', while a 'Ruheraum' is a room used to get some rest. The correct translation would have been 'Toilette'.

Topic Vocabulary: 'The Media'

Reporting
the news
reporter
investigative journalism
report
news story
headline
feature story
review
balanced
factual
reliable
judgemental
perceptive
controversial
provocative
predictable
entertaining
harmful
unreliable
sensationalist
biased towards /in favour
    of sth.
downmarket
freedom of the press

Print Journalism
newspapers
broadsheet
quality newspaper
tabloid
gutter press
popular newspaper
daily newspaper
weekly magazine
editor
leading article
editorial
article
commentary
column
cartoon
supplement
gossip column
letter to the editor
publish sth.
television listings

Broadcast Journalism
television
radio
TV station
local radio/TV station
channel
network
public sector
cable television
(compulsory) licence fee
peak-viewing time (BE) =
    (AE) prime time
ratings
viewing figures
a live broadcast
(live) coverage
a news broadcast
the latest news on sth.
broadcast to sb.
transmission via cable
satellite TV
programme
current affairs
programme
quiz show
game show
soap opera
sitcom
series
reality show
documentary (about sth.)
arts programme
popular science
    programme
presenter
anchorman/-woman
newsreader

The Internet
be online
website
search engine
search result
graphics
e-mail
chatroom
virtual

Reacting to the Media
audience
readership
put/turn on/off the
    TV/radio
turn the TV/radio
    up/down
switch sth. on/off
watch TV
watch sth.
see/watch a TV
    programme
watch a lot of television
listen to the radio /
    a programme
hear sth. on the radio
listen to sth.
rely on sth.
question the source of
    information
exercise caution in
    approaching the media
blame the media for sth.
be suspicious of sth.
be up to date

Selling Products
advertisement
classified ads
commercial
commercial break

© 2003 Cornelsen Verlag, Berlin • Alle Rechte vorbehalten • New Context

SB, pp. 109–113
(cf. TM, pp. 202, 208)

Read All About It

Tabloids and Broadsheets – A Comparison

	Tabloids / Yellow Press / Gutter Press	Serious/Quality Press / Broadsheets
Size, layout	small in size big headlines eye-catching layout lots of colour about 25% of the total area of the paper taken up by pictures most pictures from private lives of celebrities, often half-naked women	large in size smaller headlines black and white mostly about 10% of the total area of the paper taken up by pictures most pictures show celebrities at premieres or doing charity work
Readership	working class, people who are not intellectual	educated people who are interested in politics, etc.
Content	shocking and sensational stories lurid details of crime and scandals more focus on person-alities when dealing with political stories foreign affairs, politics only dealt with in a very biased and personal manner	objective, factual news coverage politics, economics, foreign affairs
Length of articles	relatively short articles usually one main story on front page	longer articles featuring political stories with focus on the actual issue
Language	more subjective language use of emotive language opinions are presented like facts	more objective language more complex sentences
Examples	*Daily Express* *The Daily Mail* *The Daily Mirror* *The Daily Star* *The Sun*	*The Daily Telegraph* *The Guardian* *The Financial Times* *The Independent* *The Times*

VIDEO **How to Get on TV**

SB, p. 117 ### Popstars

Voice-over:	From a series of open auditions, *Popstars* will bring together five undiscovered talents to create a new and exciting band. And from first auditions through to the release of their single, the cameras will follow them, every step of the way.

Clips of various unsuccessful candidates singing, and comments by the main auditioner:

Auditioner:	Sheridan ... he can't sing, can he?

A candidate tries to sing 'La Vida Loca'.

Auditioner:	Good, thank you. It's difficult at this time of the morning to get excited about that, isn't it?

Various candidates try to sing 'La Vida Loca'.

Auditioner:	Next! *(Coaching a candidate)* 'The smile on your face lets me know that you love me ...' *(Candidate tries to sing, badly.)*
Auditioner:	It's a bit like going pearl diving. You can open up a lot of oysters and find nothing in there. And then you find one and you go 'yes, thank you'. And it is well worth it.

The Weakest Link

Anne Robinson:	But at least actors don't pretend to be intelligent, unlike teachers – those important people in charge of our children's education. Here's some of those so-called experts. This is going to really reassure parents.
Anne Robinson:	Catherine, how many corners does a cube have?
Catherine:	Four?
Anne Robinson:	Eight. Wayne, in drawing, what pencil has the softer lead: a 2H or a 2B?
Wayne:	2H.
Anne Robinson:	No, a 2B. What T is the Irish word for the Prime Minister of the Republic of Ireland?
Wayne:	Tinwault.
Anne Robinson:	No, the Taoiseach. Steve.
Steve:	Still here, Miss.
Anne Robinson:	What's your job?
Steve:	I'm a head teacher.
Anne Robinson:	Of what sort of school?
Steve:	Primary school.
Anne Robinson:	Right. And how do you think the kids will react to the fact that you haven't a clue what the Irish prime minister is called?
Steve:	They won't notice.
Anne Robinson:	David, in maths, what is the cube of 3?
David:	1?
Anne Robinson:	27. David.
Steve:	Yes, Ma'am.
Anne Robinson:	Did you ever become a head teacher?
David:	No, Ma'am, I was once a temporary acting deputy.
Anne Robinson:	And then what happened?
David:	I went back to the classroom.
Anne Robinson:	Did they not want you to carry on?

David:	It was something to do with my administration.
Anne Robinson:	You mean, your lack of administration?
David:	Uh ... I stand corrected.
Anne Robinson:	In geography, Lower Saxony is a state in which European country?
Andy:	France.
Anne Robinson:	No, Germany.
	Andy, the trainee Geography teacher who doesn't know the difference between France and Germany. You've got a lot to learn. You are the weakest link. Goodbye.

Big Brother 2

Penny:	Hello, Bubble.
Narrator:	The star of the first two weeks was Penny, one of the more eccentric housemates.
Fellow housemate:	Where's your bra?
Brian:	I think you should show us all your breasts. They're nice, aren't they, girls?
Penny:	You won't survive a night out with me, mate. I'm joking. [...] Look me in the eye and tell me you're not going to shag me. [...] I'm not in the kitchen. In the kitchen, out the kitchen, in the kitchen, out the kitchen, in the kitchen, out, in, in, in, get that chicken out, wash it , scrub it, rub its insides out, black pepper it, put a bit of garlic under its skin, put a bit of oil on it, whack it in the oven, out the kitchen.
Brian:	How long for?
Penny:	Five seconds. [...]
Fellow housemate:	Oh, God Almighty, you child!
Narrator:	Within three days, Penny hit the tabloids with a full frontal flash when she accidentally let her towel drop and the scene slipped past the live TV censors.
	In week two, Penny and Helen were the first housemates to face a public vote.
Presenter:	The first person to leave the Big Brother house will be ... Penny.

Survivor

Presenter:	So, the big question: which of the two groups of strangers has bonded sufficiently as a tribe to win the first challenge? This challenge is all about fire. Here's what you have to do: There are two rafts, about a hundred and fifty foot out to sea. You have to bring those rafts back, lighting every torch along the way. If you fail to light even one torch, you will be disqualified. When you get back, you also have to light your side of the Malaysian fire spirit. Survivors: Ready? Go!!!
Presenter:	Welcome, Nick, to Tribal Council. Can you take your torches? You take your torches and gather round the fire. Dip them into the flame, light the torches and replace them on the stands, and take your seats at the Tribal Council. We begin with this ritual because, as I told you yesterday, fire represents your life on this island. Now, the bad news is that for one of you, your flame will be extinguished tonight. Could you start the voting please?
Tribe Member 1:	This is nothing personal. I'm just really, really sorry to do this to you.

Nick:	... gone for Jackie. It's not really anything you have or you haven't done. It's just that we have to look at protecting the tribe to make sure we're the strongest we possibly can be for the next events. Sorry, Jackie.
Tribe Member 2:	Nick – he doesn't say 'please', he doesn't say 'thank you'.
Presenter:	I'll count the votes: Jackie, Jackie, Nick, Nick, Nick, Jackie. That's three votes for Nick and three votes for Jackie. Nick, Nick. Nick, could you fetch your torch and bring it to the stand, please? As I said yesterday, Nick, fire represents your life on this island. I'm afraid your life on this island has come to an end. Could you extinguish your flame, please? The tribe has spoken, Nick, you must leave.

Nick leaves.

Tribe Member 3:	I'd like to vote Nick off because the other members of the team and I can't let our fires burn while he's on the island because he's such a control freak.
Nick:	I may have pushed people too hard at several stages, but for me it was to get life as comfortable as possible as soon as possible.

CD **Getting Along in English**

SB, p. 119
Task 1a

Thank you for calling American United Airlines, the only airline with more room throughout coach for more coach passengers. Lower fares may be available at our website at americanunited.com. This call may be recorded for quality assurance. Choose automated service. To check flight arrival, departure and gate information, to reconfirm an existing reservation, to request a prereserved seat, or to hear a list of security and check-in procedures, press 1.
For fares, schedules and general travel information, press 2.
For assistance with American United Airlines vacation, press 3.
To repeat this menu, press the star key.
    (Pause. Die richtige Antwort ist „1".)

For flight information, press 1.
To reconfirm an existing reservation and request a prereserved seat, press 2.
For a list of security and check-in procedures, press 3.
    (Pause. Die richtige Antwort ist „1".)

Welcome to the flight information system for American United Airlines. To get you up to date on departure and arrival information, I am going to ask you a few questions. By the way, if you have already used this sytem, you can say the answer before I finish the question. I don't mind interruption.
First, what's the flight number? Tell me just the flight number or say 'I don't know'.
    (Pause. Hier werden die S „I don't know" sagen müssen.)

Ok, let's find out which flight you want. What's the departure city?
    (Pause. Die richtige Antwort ist „Chicago".)

Next, tell me the arrival city.
    (Pause. Die richtige Antwort ist „Orlando".)

Thanks. Now is that for departure or arrival information?
    (Pause. Die richtige Antwort ist „arrival information".)

And finally, around what time does that flight arrive?
    (Pause. Die richtige Antwort ist „10.30".)

Is that in the morning or evening?
(Pause. Die richtige Antwort ist „in the morning".)

Let me make sure I got that right. From Chicago O'Hare to Orlando, Florida, arriving at about 10:30 am. Did I get that right?
(Pause. Die richtige Antwort ist „yes".)

One moment. Flight 2031 is scheduled to arrive Orlando, Florida, at 10:30 a.m., Gate 15, baggage claim area 5.
Remember gate assignment can change, so please be sure to check those monitors at the airport. That's it! You can hang up now.

SB, p. 119
Task 2a,b

Dialogue 1

Operator:	Directory enquiries; which town, please?
Lisa:	Is that directory enquiries?
Operator:	Yes, it is.
Lisa:	At last! The number was engaged for a long time.
Operator:	Which town, please?
Lisa:	I don't understand.
Operator:	Do you want a number in the town you're calling from?
Lisa:	Ugh?
Operator:	Are you phoning from a phone box? Because if you are, it says in the phone box where you are.
Lisa:	I'm not in a phone box. I'm using my handy.
Operator:	I beg your pardon?
Lisa:	I mean my ... mobile phone.
Operator:	Perhaps you could just tell me the number you want.
Lisa:	I need the number of a dentist.
Operator:	In which town?
Lisa:	Here, in Cornwall, of course.
Operator:	Cornwall is not a town, Madam. I need to know in which town you want to see a dentist.
Lisa:	Oh, in Camborne.
Operator:	Hold the line please ...
Computer voice:	The number you require is 01209 ...

Dialogue 2

Receptionist:	Good morning, Trelliske Dental Surgery: how may I help you?
Lisa:	I need to see a dentist very quickly.
Receptionist:	Are you a patient of ours?
Lisa:	I come from Germany. I have lost a filling and my tooth hurts a lot.
Rec:	I'm afraid if you're not registered with us, the dentist won't be able to give you an appointment. But you could come late this afternoon and wait till the end of surgery.
Lisa:	But I'm in pain!
Receptionist:	If you'd like to give me your name and number, we could phone you if we have a cancellation during the day.
Lisa:	A what?
Receptionist:	If someone can't use their appointment. Could you give me your name, please?
Lisa:	In Germany if you have an emergency, the dentist will always see you.
Rec:	The dentist will see you, Miss, but later today. If the pain is too bad, you could always go to the A and E department.

Lisa:	What's 'A and E'?
Rec:	Accident and Emergency.
Lisa:	Where?
Receptionist:	At Truro Hospital.
Lisa:	That's too far! I'll try another dentist.
Receptionist:	Well, really!

SB, p. 119
Task 2c

Receptionist:	Camborne Dental Centre, good morning.
Lisa:	Good morning. I wonder, can you help me, please?
Receptionist:	Well, I'll try. Are you a patient of ours, dear?
Lisa:	No, I'm afraid I'm not. I'm on holiday here and I've lost a filling and now I have terrible toothache.
Receptionist:	Oh, dear. Well, first of all, give me your name.
Lisa:	It's Lisa, Lisa Bauer.
Receptionist:	How do you spell the family name?
Lisa:	B-A-U-E-R, Bauer.
Receptionist:	And where do you come from, Miss Bauer?
Lisa:	I'm from Germany.
Receptionist:	EU, that's fine.
Lisa:	Excuse me, I didn't understand what you just said.
Receptionist:	Well, we can only take you as a private patient – you have to pay us. But Germany is part of the European Union, and that means your health insurance may pay you back.
Lisa:	Oh, I see. Yes.
Receptionist:	Well, let me have a look ...
Lisa:	I would be very grateful if you could help me, the pain really is awful.
Receptionist:	Well now, you may have to wait a bit, but if you come towards the end of morning surgery – say around half past twelve – I think Mr Penhaligon will be able to see you and at least give you something for the pain. All right?
Lisa:	Thank you so much.
Receptionist:	Now, do you know how to get here?
Lisa:	No, I'm sorry, I don't.
Receptionist:	Well, it's quite easy, really. Do you know the church at the end of Fore Street?
Lisa:	Yes, I do.
Receptionist:	Well, you turn left, just before that, into Victoria Street and we're the third house on the right.
Lisa:	The third house on the right ... in Victoria Street?
Receptionist:	That's it. Well, we'll see you at about half past twelve then, Miss Bauer.
Lisa:	Half past twelve, yes. And thank you again. Goodbye.
Receptionist:	Goodbye.

SB, p. 119
Task 4a

Computer voice:	Directory Assistance. State clearly the name of the party.
Bernd:	Directory assistance? Oh, er ...
Computer voice:	Directory Assistance. State clearly the name of the party.
Bernd:	Kretschko and Kremer Instruments.
Computer voice: (Fade out and in.)	Please hold ... The number you require is 1-800 ...
1st Receptionist:	Kretschko and Kremer Instruments. Good morning. Nancy Holbrook speaking, how may I help you?
Bernd:	I would like to speak to Mr Reinecke, please.
1st Receptionist:	Which division does he work for, sir?

Bernd:	Oh! I'm not sure. I think maybe he works in engineering.
1st Receptionist:	Would you hold please, sir? Ah, Mr Reinecke: he works in the Technical Division. You'll have to call our New Jersey offices, sir. The number is 201 355 4646.
Bernd:	Technical Division ... and could you please repeat the number?
1st Receptionist:	That's 201 355 4646, sir.
Bernd:	201 355 4646?
1st Receptionist:	That's correct, sir.
Bernd:	Thank you very much.
1st Receptionist:	You're welcome, sir. Have a nice day.
(Fade out and in.)	
2nd Receptionist:	Good morning, Kretschko and Kremer Technical Division, Lily Winters speaking. How may I help you?
Bernd:	Good morning. My name is Bernd Schmees. I would like to talk to Mr Reinecke, please.
2nd Receptionist:	Mr Shmays? Please hold while I try to connect you. Mr Shmays, I'm sorry, but Mr Reinecke's line is busy. Can his secretary help you?
Bernd:	Well, maybe ...
2nd Receptionist:	Are you calling from a cell phone, Sir? You could give me the number and I could get his office to call you.
Bernd:	No, I don't have a cell phone. I'm calling from a phone booth.
2nd Receptionist:	Oh, dear. Well, I'll try his secretary. Please hold.
Secretary:	Good morning. Mr Reinecke's office, Monica Franks speaking. How may I help you?
Bernd:	Good morning. My name is Bernd Schmees. I'm over from Germany and I'm trying to contact Mr Reinecke.
Secretary:	Bernd Schmees?
Reinecke:	Bernd?!
Bernd:	Martin?!
Reinecke:	Na, das find ich toll: Du bist hier in New York? Dann müssen wir uns treffen ...

Ziel dieses Kapitels ist es, die S für Formen und Funktionen von Kunst zu sensibilisieren und diese von ihnen diskutieren zu lassen. Die S begegnen dabei unterschiedlichen Bereichen der Kunst; der Schwerpunkt liegt auf der Literatur (Lyrik, Drama und Kurzgeschichte):

- *Section 1*, „Transforming Misery into Words", zeigt anhand zweier Texte von Hemingway, wie dieser ein reales Ereignis in eine Kurzgeschichte umwandelt.

- *Section 2*, „Poetry: Soothing the Soul", diskutiert die Funktion von Lyrik.

- *Section 3*, „Theatre: A Battle on Stage", enthält Auszüge aus Shakespeare-Dramen.

- *Section 4*, „Music: Offering Hope", widmet sich dem befreienden Aspekt von Musik.

- *Section 5*, „Architecture: Rising from the Ashes", zeigt anhand der Beispiele Coventry und Dresden, wie Architektur der Vergangenheitsbewältigung dienen kann.

Die S lernen in diesem Kapitel, Kunstwerke zu beschreiben, sich ihrer unterschiedlichen Wirkungsweisen bewusst zu werden und sich – sprachlich oder auch nicht-sprachlich – mit ihnen auseinander zu setzen. Neben der Förderung der Sprachkompetenz dient dies der Enkulturation der S, d.h., sie lernen Kunst als einen zentralen Teil der Kultur kennen und erkennen ihre gesellschaftliche Bedeutung. Die S reflektieren über die Rolle der Kunst in ihrem eigenen Leben, indem sie ihre persönliche Sicht einbringen oder selbst kreativ tätig werden. Seiner Thematik entsprechend, eignet sich dieses Kapitel besonders für fächerverbindenden Unterricht.

Um das Thema Kunst an Beispielen zu konkretisieren, wurde mit „Konflikt und Krieg" ein alle Teilkapitel verbindendes Thema gewählt, das in der Kunst, vor allem in der englischsprachigen Welt, besonders häufig gestaltet worden ist. Gleichzeitig ist es von herausragender Bedeutung für den pädagogischen Bereich, man denke nur an die zentrale Aufgabe des Fremdsprachenunterrichts, die S zu Frieden und Toleranz zwischen Menschen und Kulturen zu erziehen.

Da es sich um ein sprachlich wie inhaltlich anspruchsvolles Kapitel handelt, empfiehlt

→ *WB, ex. 8, 9, 10* sich der Einsatz am Ende der Oberstufe.

Didaktisches Inhaltsverzeichnis

SB, p.	Title	TM, p.	Text form	Topic	Skills and activities
124	Lead-in	235	painting	children at the end of a war	describing and analysing a painting; writing an interior monologue; presenting a favourite work of art;
			novel (extract)	artists dealing with catastrophes	analysing a text; comparing a text with a painting
126	Context Box	237		the arts and their role in society	working with words; writing a brochure
127	The Flight of Refugees (April 3, 1938) Ernest Hemingway	238	news report	refugees fleeing the fighting in the Spanish Civil War	reading comprehension
128	Old Man at the Bridge Ernest Hemingway	240	short story	the effect of war on an ordinary old man	comparing two texts; describing a character; writing a short story; identifying the differences between fiction and non-fiction
130	The Ultimate Pain Relief	243	advert	poetry's soothing effect	analysing an advert/a photo; analysing the effectiveness of an advert; presenting a favourite poem

131	**In Flanders Fields** John McCrae	244	poem	death in war and the call to continue the struggle	analysing a poem;
131	**Grass** Carl Sandburg	244	poem	the way grass covers over battlefields	analysing a poem; comparing the message and effectiveness of two poems; giving a personal opinion; presenting a poem with a similar topic
132	**A Shakespearian Performance** Video/DVD	250	feature film (extract)	a play performed in Shakespeare's time	examining the problems involved in performing plays; analysing how a film deals with a theatrical performance
132	*Henry V*: **Prologue** William Shakespeare	251	drama (extract)	the demands made upon an audience	examining the problems of putting on a play; comparing Shakespeare's theatre with modern-day theatres
	Video/DVD		feature film (extract)	the demands made upon an audience	viewing comprehension
133	**Battle of Agincourt** William Shakespeare	253	drama (extract)	the lead-up to and aftermath of the Battle of Agincourt	rewriting a text in modern English; speculating about the reasons for the outcome of the battle; writing and performing a play
134	**Two Performances of** *Henry V* Video/DVD	255	films (extract)	the lead-up to and aftermath of the Battle of Agincourt	commenting on a performance; writing a review; analysing film techniques
135	**Extracts from the** *Resurrection Symphony* Gustav Mahler CD2, track 6	257	symphony (extract)	the power of music	listening to music; expressing one's feelings and reactions
135	**An Infinitely Hopeful Message** Martin Goldsmith	259	fictionalized biography (extract)	the effects of stirring music	examining the effect of music; comparing reactions to music; writing a letter; presenting a favourite piece of music
137	**Coventry: Destruction and Reconciliation** Video/DVD	261	photos	the role of architecture in dealing with the past	analysing architecture
			documentary film	the destruction and rebuilding of a cathedral	
138	**Dresden: Obliteration and Rebirth**	263	photos	the role of architecture in dealing with the past	doing a role play; analysing architecture
140	**Getting Along in English** CD2, tracks 7–9	264	–	talking about the arts	
141	**Watch Your Language**	267	tenses		

Lead-In

Extract from *A History of the World in 10 1/2 Chapters*	
Source:	*A History of the World in 10 1/2 Chapters*, 1989
Topic:	catastrophes and art
Text form:	Novel (extract)
Language variety:	BE
Number of words:	114
Level:	Basic/advanced
Skills/activities:	analysing a text, comparing a text with a painting

Didaktisch-methodische Hinweise

Das „Lead-In" stellt eine Hinführung sowohl zu der übergreifenden Thematik „war/conflict" dar als auch zu den Wirkungsweisen von Kunst. Über das Gemälde „Liberation" von Ben Shahn werden die S mit dem Thema des Kapitels vertraut gemacht, bevor ein Abschnitt aus *A History of the World in 10 1/2 Chapters* von Julian Barnes die Verbindung zwischen Katastrophen wie dem Krieg und verschiedenen Kunstformen herstellt.

Bei der Beschäftigung mit dem Bild stehen eine detaillierte Bildanalyse und das Verfassen eines inneren Monologs am Anfang. Transferaufgaben lassen die S sich über die Funktionen von Kunst und über ihren persönlichen Bezug zur Kunst bewusst werden. Nach der Besprechung des Textes sollen die S die Aussage Barnes' überprüfen, indem sie konkrete Beispiele suchen und den Text auf das Bild beziehen.

Unterrichts-tipps

Als Ausgangspunkt für die Arbeit mit dem „Lead-in" könnte der Titel des Kapitels „Turning Conflict into Art" dienen. Die S stellen Vermutungen an, was sich hinter diesem Titel verbergen könnte, und formulieren ihre Erwartungen an das Kapitel. Dabei kann L um Präzisierung bitten, sollte aber davon absehen, die Beiträge der S zu kommentieren. Folgende Fragen können hilfreich sein:

⬭ – *What do you think the phrase 'Turning Conflict into Art' could mean?*
– *How would you interpret 'conflict' here?*
– *How can conflicts be turned into art?*
– *What forms can 'art' take, and how does the conflict reveal itself in art?*

⬭ *'Turning Conflict into Art' is the title of the next chapter we are going to work with: what do you think the chapter might deal with?*

Info

Ben Shahn (1898–1969) was born in Kaunas, Lithuania (then part of Russia), to an Orthodox Jewish family. His family immigrated to the USA in 1906, where they settled in Brooklyn. In the 1930s he became known as a socially and politically involved artist, painting in the style of Social Realism, whose main intention was to criticize social injustice. In response to the horrors of World War II, however, he moved from Social Realism to a more subjective way of painting, transforming his own experiences and the historical events of the time into universal commentaries on social injustice. In 'Liberation' (1945) Shahn used tempera on cardboard mounted on composition cardboard.

Julian Barnes (born 1946) is one of Britain's leading contemporary novelists. His works include *Flaubert's Parrot* (1984), *A History of the World in 10 1/2 Chapters* (1989) and *England, England* (1999; cf. SB, p. 156). He has also published a collection of short stories and various essays. He also writes a regular weekly column in the *Guardian*.

A History of the World in 10 1/2 Chapters views history as a series of catastrophes. This extract is taken from a chapter in which Barnes describes how the artist Théodore Géricault turned the catastrophe of a shopwreck into art: the result was the masterpiece 'The Raft of the Medusa'.

Lösungs-
hinweise

'Liberation'

1 Individual answers.

2 Zur Vorbereitung, ggf. als Hausaufgabe, können die S „Working with Pictures" (vgl. SB, S. 223) durcharbeiten.

a In the foreground, slightly left of centre, there is a reddish-brown pole, probably a telegraph pole, and on the ground behind it there is a pile of rubble. On the delicate wires which hang from the pole three children are swinging round in circles. Their leg movements and their hair, which is flying out behind them, and the way one of them is flying almost horizontally, indicate that they are spinning round quite fast. One child, whose face is concealed, is dressed in black; she is only holding on with one arm, as if she is about to fall off. The face of the child in the centre is completely visible; her eyes are lowered, and her facial expression seems to communicate fear instead of pleasure. This impression is emphasized by the fact that her face is a colourless greyish-white. The wire that the third child is holding is longer and she is spinning further out. In the background there are the ruins of a house, which consists of four storeys, and is leaning towards the left, as if it is about to collapse. The sky is visible through the holes which used to be the windows. The front wall of the house is missing, and the scraps of wallpaper still hanging on the walls show that the house was once lived in. As the house is white it does not stand out very clearly against the grey-blue and white sky. The colours the artist has used are pale: the children's faces, the ground and the heap of rubble, and the outside wall of the house all seem to be the same colour. The colours of the children's clothes are dark and stick out against the background. The only brightly coloured areas are the patches of wallpaper in the ruins.

◆◆ **b** Wegen der Schwierigkeit der Aufgabe sollten die S sie zunächst in Partnerarbeit diskutieren.

On the one hand, the atmosphere created by the painting is cheerful: we see children playing. The brightly coloured patches of wallpaper and the blue bits of sky underline this impression. On the other hand, the painting also implies sadness and a kind of hopelessness: everything is in ruins, the bright patches of wallpaper in the ruins show that the people who lived there have lost their homes and perhaps even their lives. The face of the child facing the viewer also shows anxiety and fear instead of happiness. The feeling of danger is created by the child in the black dress, as she seems to be falling off the 'roundabout'; this seems to imply the presence of death.

3 Diese Aufgabe kann zu Hause oder in einer Stillarbeitsphase im Unterricht vorbereitet werden.

Individual answers.

4 The painting was completed in 1945 and the title has two meanings: liberation from the 'enemy' – in this case facism – but also liberation from war in general and the establishment of freedom and happiness. Shahn communicates this idea by showing children who are free to play again; they play regardless of the fact that everything around them is destroyed. However, Shahn also conveys the horrors of war in general: the children, who are innocent victims, have been robbed of their childhood and cannot feel real happiness. None of the children is laughing or showing joy. They seem isolated from each other, with their eyes avoiding each other. Some of them may even be so sick due to the hardships of war that they may not survive.

 5 **a** Für diese anspruchsvolle Aufgabe sollten die S drei Minuten Zeit bekommen, um ggf. gemeinsam mit einem Partner Stichwörter zu notieren, die anschließend im Plenum in Form eines Mind-Maps gesammelt werden:

functions of art: to entertain, to express yourself, to illustrate something, to make somebody aware

b Es bietet sich an, die S von den einzelnen Zweigen des Mind-Maps ausgehen und sie begründen zu lassen, welche Funktionen 'Liberation' erfüllt oder nicht.

6 Die Beispiele, die die S mitbringen, können in der Klasse ausgestellt und bei einem Rundgang kurz erläutert werden. Für Musikstücke sollte ein CD-Player vorhanden sein.

Lösungs-hinweise

Auszug aus *A History of the World in 10 1/2 Chapters*

1 **a**

Catastrophes	Art
Explosion in a nuclear plant	plays
Assassination of a president	books and films
A series of murders	poetry

b Art helps to understand, to imagine, to explain, to justify and to forgive.

2 Mögliche Beispiele, die den S bekannt sein könnten:

<u>Plays:</u> Arthur Miller's *The Crucible.*
<u>Novels:</u> Kurt Vonnegut's *Slaughterhouse-Five*; Robert Westall's *Gulf*, Graham Greene's *The Quiet American*, Joan Lingard's *Twelfth Day of July*, Robert C. O'Brien's *Z for Zachariah*, Julian Barnes's *A History of the World in 10 1/2 Chapters.*
<u>Films:</u> *Titanic, Schindler's List, Seeking Private Ryan, Pearl Harbour, JFK, Apocalypse Now, Born on the 4th of July.*
<u>Other forms:</u> 'Guernica' by Pablo Picasso (painting); *Miss Saigon* (musical).

3 'Liberation' helps us to understand and to imagine the horrors of war, particularly for children, and it helps to explain how people felt after the war. Barnes speaks of an 'automatic' process of responding to catastrophe in a negative tone, but with 'good' art the response goes deeper. Perhaps the students might feel that Shahn, does attempt to 'understand' the catastrophe and reflects this in a quiet way to the viewer (which contrasts with Barnes's sarcastic expressions 'send in the novelists', 'tramp', etc.).

SB, S. 126
Context Box

Didaktisch-methodische Hinweise

Die „Context Box" verzichtet auf eine abstrakte Definition des Begriffs *art* und geht stattdessen von der Gegenüberstellung von *art* und *(fine) arts* aus. Verschiedene Kategorien und Medien der Kunst werden aufgelistet. Auch der Stellenwert von Kunst und Fragen des Kunstmarkts in der industriellen Gesellschaft werden thematisiert. Das Foto zeigt Louise Bourgeois' „Spider" in der Tate Modern in London.
Bevor die S Aufgabe 1 beantworten, sollten sie auf die Hinweise zu Mind-Maps in den „Skills Pages" verwiesen werden.

Lösungs-hinweise

1 Diese Aufgabe kann sinnvoll in arbeitsteiliger Gruppenarbeit gelöst werden, bei der die Aufgaben 1 a, b und c auf Gruppen von jeweils vier bis fünf S verteilt werden.

❖ **a – c** Individual answers.

2 Mass production and technology means that more people than ever before have access to art. Art attracts people for various reasons: it can attract people by means of the medium chosen, because of the function it fulfils (which can be entertaining, provocative or simply decorative or aesthetic), because it is controversial, because it attracts people's attention and makes them think about the subject and the art form, or because it is an investment. Wealthy people often buy works of art not only because they appreciate them but also because they are a means of guaranteeing their wealth and are often regarded as status symbols. Patrons of the fine arts often donate their collections to museums and art galleries, and large firms and businesses have realized that it is important to show an interest in arts by sponsoring artists.

3 Individual answers.

SB, S. 127

1 Prose: Transforming Misery into Words

In diesem Abschnitt begegnen die S der Verarbeitung einer Katastrophe in einem literarischen Prosatext: Ernest Hemingway gestaltet das Flüchtlingselend während des spanischen Bürgerkrieges. Als Kriegsberichterstatter erlebte Hemingway den Bürgerkrieg in Spanien unmittelbar; als Schriftsteller glaubte er daran, dass man eine Sache nur dann überzeugend wiedergeben könne, wenn man sie direkt miterlebt oder zumindest genau beobachtet habe. So lesen die S im Text A ein Ausschnitt aus einer Depesche, die Hemingway im April 1938 schrieb, im Text B erfahren sie, wie Hemingway das Erlebte literarisch verarbeitet. Die S sollen die Darstellung der Realität in einem fiktionalen und einem nicht-fiktionalen Text vergleichen und entscheiden, welche Darstellungsweise die Schreckens des Krieges am drastischten vermittelt.

→ *WB, ex. 1*

SB, S. 127 ## A The Flight of Refugees (April 3, 1938) Ernest Hemingway

Source:	*By-Line: Ernest Hemingway*, 1998
Topic:	Refugees fleeing the fighting in the Spanish Civil War
Text form:	News Report
Language variety:	AE
Number of words:	289
Level:	Basic/advanced
Skills/activities:	Reading comprehension

Lern-vokabular

Active vocabulary: 'The Flight of Refugees (April, 3, 1938)' (p. 127)

refugee (l. 1), sob (l. 2), sewing machine (l. 4), mattress (l. 5), look back over your shoulder (ll. 11–12), civilian population (l. 18), troops (l. 18), cheerful (l. 19), ridiculous (l. 20)

Didaktisch-methodische Hinweise

In diesem Text schildert Hemingway seine Beobachtung, die er als Kriegsbericht-erstatter während des spanischen Bürgerkrieges am 3. April 1938 machte: Auf der Flucht vor den Faschisten Francos bewegen sich die Flüchtlinge voran, allmählich kommen die Truppen der Republikaner dazu, die Stimmung ist entspannt; von Panik ist nichts zu spüren. Die S erleben hier, wie Hemingway das Geschehen nicht kommentiert, sondern nur die Szene präzise beschreibt, wenn auch gelegentlich mit literarischen Stilmitteln. Es bleibt den Lesern überlassen, sich eine eigene Meinung zu bilden.

Unterrichts-tipps

Der Einstieg erfolgt, indem die S von der Gegenwart ausgehend ihre Erfahrungen mit Kriegsberichterstattung beschreiben. L leitet zur Kriegsberichterstattung über, wie sie vor 70 Jahren ausgesehen haben könnte. Anschließend kann L Hemingway und seine Tätigkeit als Kriegsberichterstatter vorstellen:

⬭ *When there is a war or an armed conflict anywhere in the world, how do we learn about it nowadays?*
Immediate information via TV or radio; often 24-hour coverage; reports by embedded journalists.

⬭ *Think back 50, 60, 70 years ago: where did people get their information from?*
Perhaps from the radio, but more often through newspapers. They relied on correspondents for information.

⬭ *Look at the photo on p. 127. Imagine you were the photographer. What were you thinking when you took this photo?*

Differenzierung Nach einer Still-Lesephase kann L in leistungsschwächeren Gruppen das Verständnis mit den folgenden Fragen überprüfen und so den Vergleich mit Text 1B erleichtern:

⬭ *Answer the following questions on the text to show you have understood the text.*

1 *How many individuals does Hemingway mention, and what are they doing?* (An old woman who is crying while driving a cart, cf. ll. 1–3;, eight children who are walking behind a cart, cf. l. 3; one little boy who is pushing on a wheel, cf. ll. 3–4; a woman who is riding a mule and holding her new-born baby, cf. ll. 8–9; a man who is leading the mule on which the mother is sitting, cf. ll. 11–12).

2 *Name some of the things the refugees brought with them.* (Bedding, sewing machines, cooking utensils, goats and sheep, cf. ll. 4–7).

3 *What was the general mood of the people?* (There was no panic and many people seemed cheerful, cf. ll. 7, 18–21).

4 *What was the weather like?* (It was a beautiful day, cf. l. 20).

Als Überleitung auf den zweiten Text kann die folgende Frage dienen:

⬭ *Later, Hemingway wrote about refugees in the Spanish Civil War in a short story. What changes might he have had to make to turn it into a short story? Think of how he might have dealt with the point of view (cf. Glossary, p. 258), incidents, dialogue, background information, etc.*

Info

Ernest Hemingway (1899–1961) was born in Oak Park, Illinois. He became a reporter for the *Kansas City Star*, but left the job after only a few months to become an ambulance driver in Italy during World War I. He then settled in Paris, but spent long periods of time in Florida, Spain and North Africa. During the Spanish Civil War (cf. below) he went to Spain as a correspondent, and during World War II he was a correspondent for the US First Army. After World War II he moved first to Havana, Cuba, and then to Ketchum, Idaho, where he was killed by a self-inflicted gunshot. Hemingway started as a short-story writer, but wrote many novels, including *A Farewell to Arms* (1929) and *For Whom the Bell Tolls* (1940), which deals with the Spanish Civil War. In 1952 Hemingway published *The Old Man and the Sea*, a novella about an elderly Cuban fisherman, for which he won the Pulitzer Prize for fiction. In 1954 Hemingway was awarded the Nobel Prize in Literature. Hemingway's writings and personal life had a strong influence on other American writers. He described his writing as being like an iceberg, which reveals only 1/8 of itself while 7/8 remains under the surface. He felt by omitting certain things from a story (e.g. the characters' emotions, the surroundings and the outcome) he could actually strengthen it.

Info

The Spanish Civil War: In February 1936, the leftist government of the Spanish republic exiled the army chief-of-staff Francisco Franco to the Canary Islands. In July 1937 he launched a revolt against the republic. In October 1937 he was made commander-in-chief and head of state of the new Nationalist (=fascist) regime. During the war that followed, Franco's forces advanced slowly but steadily to complete victory in April, 1939. Franco governed Spain from 1939 until his death in 1975.

SB, S. 128   **B Old Man at the Bridge**   Ernest Hemingway

Source:	*The First Forty-Nine Stories*, 1938
Topic:	The effect of war on an ordinary old man
Text form:	Short story
Language variety:	AE
Number of words:	289
Level:	Basic/advanced
Skills/activities:	Comparing two texts, describing a character, writing a short story, identifying the difference between fiction and non-fiction

Lern-
vokabular

Active vocabulary: 'Old Man at the Bridge' (p. 128)

truck (l. 2), stagger (l. 3), bank (l. 4), peasant (l. 6), take care of sb./sth. (l. 15), shepherd (l. 19), look out for oneself (l. 34), blankly (l. 45), urge (l. 60), sway (l. 61), advance toward(s) sth. (l. 66), overcast (l. 66), good luck (l. 68)

Didaktisch-
methodische
Hinweise

Diese Kurzgeschichte ist charakteristisch sowohl für den Stil Hemingways, der die amerikanische Literatur in der zweiten Hälfte des 20. Jahrhunderts entscheidend geprägt hat, als auch für die Themen, mit denen er sich vorwiegend beschäftigt hat: soziale, wirtschaftliche und politische Ungerechtigkeit und die universelle Gefährdung der Freiheit. Hemingways Schilderung wirkt distanziert, da er versucht, durch eine einfache Sprache eine Szene genau einzufangen. Er beschreibt weder die Emotionen noch die Gedanken seiner Figuren und verzichtet weitgehend darauf, als Erzähler die Ereignisse zu kommentieren (vgl. allerdings die letzte Zeile). Auf diese Weise wird der Leser zum Augenzeugen, der unmittelbar das Geschehen miterlebt. Er muss mitdenken, um die Äußerungen und Aktionen der Figuren zu verstehen.

Die Aufgaben zielen v.a. auf den Vergleich zwischen Depesche und *short story* und schließlich auf einer abstrakteren Ebene zwischen fiktionalen und nicht-fiktionalen Texten. Eine kreative Schreibaufgabe gibt den S die Gelegenheit, ihr theoretisches Wissen umzusetzen.

Unterrichts-
tipps

Bevor die S den Text still lesen, sollten sie ihre Erwartungen an die Kurzgeschichte formulieren. L erläutert, dass die *short story* auf der Depesche basiert, die sie zuvor gelesen haben, und fragt die S, welche inhaltlichen Schwerpunkte Hemingway gewählt und wie er das Geschehen dargestellt haben könnte.

Differenzierung

Für leistungsschwächere Gruppen kann L nach der Lektüre das Textverständnis durch folgende *true or false*-Sätze überprüfen. Die S belegen ihre Antworten am Text:

⬭ *Old Man at the Bridge – True or false?*

1 *The soldiers are helping the peasants to push their carts.* (True; cf. ll. 4–5).
2 *It is the narrator's job to help the people.* (False: He must find out how far the enemy has advanced; cf. ll. 8–9).
3 *The old man is on the road with his family.* (False: He is alone; cf. ll. 32–33).

4 *The old man is a farmer.* (False: He was taking care of a few animals; cf. ll. 28–29).

5 *He is fleeing because he supports the Republicans.* (False: He has no politics and he is fleeing because the artillery is approaching; cf. ll. 31, 37).

6 *He set the pigeons free before he left.* (True; cf. ll. 56–57).

7 *After a while he gets up and moves on.* (False: He gets up only to sit down again; cf. ll. 61–62).

8 *It is a beautiful day.* (False: It is grey and overcast; cf. ll. 66).

9 *Enemy planes were flying in their direction.* (False: They were not flying because of the low clouds; cf. ll. 66–67).

Lösungs-hinweise

1

	The Flight of Refugees	Old Man at the Bridge
Characters	an old woman, children, a man, a woman and a baby, the reporter refugees: mostly cheerful and carrying many belongings	one old man and the narrator the old man: tired and without belongings.
Setting	on a road	on a road by a pontoon bridge over the Ebro, going towards Tortosa and Barcelona
Story/plot	beautiful weather no story, only description	a dull and cloudy day the story of the old man unfolds – reader understands his misery open ending
Role of the 'I' figure	describes what he sees only asks the man a question about the baby an outsider.	involved in the war talks to the old man and tries to help him

2 Diese Aufgabe kann in Partnerarbeit bearbeitet werden.

The old man:
– has no family (ll. 31–33);
– is not interested in politics (l. 37);
– seems polite (l. 61);
– was looking after his animals in the village he comes from (l. 15);
– is worried about the animals and wants to talk about them (ll. 28–59);
– is too tired to move on and has nowhere to go anyway (ll. 7, 43–44, 61–62);
– has lost everything due to the war (ll. 22, 67–68);
– is an innocent victim.

3 Bei dieser Aufgabe können die S durchaus unterschiedlicher Meinung sein.

Effectiveness

The Flight of Refugees	Old Man at the Bridge
Shows the situation of the refugees in general.	
The fate of different people is shown. Report shows human misery on a wider scale.	The old man symbolizes the injustice of war. Story shows how war affects individuals and destroys their existence.
Reader catches glimpses of people's lives.	Reader becomes emotionally involved.

→ *WB, ex. 2* **4** Bevor die S diese Aufgabe bearbeiten, sollten sie die Merkmale von Hemingways Stil herausarbeiten (vgl. „Info" oben). Dabei bietet es sich an, sie zuvor die Einträge „Narrator and Point of View", „Style", „Tone" und „Register" im Glossar (SB, S. 258 und 265ff.) nachlesen zu lassen:

⬭ *Find and list characteristic elements of Hemingway's short story. Consider the role of the narrator, his sentence structure, his use of description, his use of nouns, adjectives and adverbs, his use of connectors as well as his style and tone.*
- Simple sentences (few subordinate clauses);
- simple language: only a few adjectives, no connectors (e.g. 'and then', after that, etc.);
- narrator makes no comments, the reader must draw his own conclusions;
- neutral style and objective tone.

⬭ *In your group divide the short story into the following parts: ll. 1–11, ll. 12–26, ll. 27–44, and ll. 45–68. Alone (or in pairs if there are more than four people in your group) translate one of the parts into German so that your group translates the entire short story.*

5 Possible answers:

Non-fiction	Fiction
relates to particular events	tries to show the universal truth behind events
description of setting less important	setting important for the story
few personal details	fewer characters, but more personal details, so the reader becomes emotionally involved, must interpret
reader less emotionally involved	
less direct speech	direct speech used to characterize the figures;
reporter often remains objective as an outsider his job is to report	narrator sometimes plays a part in the narrative

⬭ *Look at the photos of the refugees in the photo on p. 129, and compare them with the refugees described in the dispatch and the short story. What differences do you notice, and what do they have in common with the refugees you have read about in this section?*

SB, S. 130 # 2   Poetry: Soothing the Soul?

Die Funktionen von Literatur als einem zentralen Bereich von Kunst lassen sich wahrscheinlich am Beispiel von Gedichten mit den S leichter erörtern als mit narrativen Texten (vgl. *section* 1), weil Lyrik von den meisten selbstverständlicher als „Kunst" identifiziert wird.
Die Thematik wird auf doppelt überraschende Weise eingeführt. Die S werden nicht, wie sie vielleicht erwarten, mit Gedichten, sondern mit einer Anzeige für Lyrik konfrontiert. Die zweite Provokation liegt in der Therapieankündigung „to calm, comfort and soothe the soul": Die „Einnahme" von Gedichten als einem schmerzstillenden Medikament wird damit als etwas der (seelischen) Gesundheit Dienliches empfohlen. Wenn die S nicht schon andere Funktionen von lyrischen Texten kennen, so wird ihnen spätestens durch die zwei sich anschließenden Gedichte, durch die die Verbindung mit dem Rahmenthema hergestellt wird, die beunruhigende, aufrüttelnde Wirkung von Lyrik bewusst. Diese Gedichte nehmen – auf den ersten Blick nicht leicht erkennbar – eine völlig unterschiedliche Haltung zu Krieg, Kampf und Tod ein und tragen gerade durch diesen Kontrast und den Bezug zu den „soothing elements" dazu bei, die S für das Lesen von Gedichten zu sensibilisieren.
Die Erschließung der formalen Elemente sowohl der Anzeige als auch der Gedichte sollte nicht Selbstzweck sein, sondern mit Blick auf die inhaltliche Aussage und die Wirkung auf die S geschehen.

SB, S. 130 **A The Ultimate Pain Relief**

Source:	*Times Literary Supplement*, 10 April, 2002.
Topic:	Poetry's soothing effect
Text form:	Advert
Language variety:	BE
Number of words:	20
Level:	Basic/advanced
Skills/activities:	Analysing an advert/ a photo, analysing the effectiveness of an advert, presenting a favourite poem

Lern-vokabular

Active vocabulary: 'The Ultimate Pain Relief' (p. 130)

ultimate, pain relief, calm sb./sth., soothe sb./sth., comfort sb./sth., soul
tasks: evaluate sth., effectiveness

Didaktisch-methodische Hinweise

Die Aufgaben zu dieser Anzeige zielen v.a. auf die Analyse von Form und Inhalt. Dabei sollten die S sich nicht auf die Herausarbeitung der lustigen Gleichsetzung von „pain relief" und „poem" beschränken, sondern die ernstzunehmende Aussage der Anzeige genauer unter die Lupe nehmen. Deren Gültigkeit für sie selbst überprüfen die S, indem sie nach tröstenden Gedichten oder Liedtexten suchen.

Unterrichts-tipps

Die S werden mit der Anzeige konfrontiert und bearbeiten die Aufgaben 1–3 ggf. in Partnerarbeit, wobei sie die Definition von „advertisement" im Glossar (vgl. SB, S. 264) und ggf. die Informationen über „AIDA" (vgl. SB, S. 122) zu Hilfe nehmen. Als Alternative zu diesem Einstieg könnte auch das Wortfeld „pain/medicine" erstellt werden (vor allem, wenn zuvor schon „Getting Along in English" aus Kapitel 3 behandelt wurde, vgl. SB, S. 65).

Nach Bearbeitung der Gedichte auf S. 131 kann auf die Anzeige zurückgegriffen werden, indem die S sich eine neue Beschriftung für die Flasche ausdenken, in die die Aussage eines der Gedichte einfließt.

Info

In 1995 the BBC conducted a survey to find the nation's favourite poem. 12,000 votes were cast and the results were printed in the BBC publication *The Nation's Favourite Poems*. (The 'winner' was 'If' by Rudyard Kipling; cf. www.everypoet.com/archive/poetry/Rudyard_Kipling/kipling_if.htm · 1.8.2003). Anthologies such as *101 Poems To Keep You Sane* or *101 Poems To Get You Through the Day (and Night)* are extremely popular, and this is the context in which this 'advertisement' could be read.

Lösungs-hinweise

Picture: A bottle of pain-killers
Copy: Text promises the same soothing effect as painkillers.
AIDA (cf. SB, p. 122):
A   Attention is attracted by the unusual association of painkillers and poetry.
I   Interest is aroused by thinking how poetry could have the same effect as painkillers; links are formed through the reader's personal experience.
D   The viewer wants this calming, comforting and soothing effect (but without the possibly unpleasant side-effects of medicine).
A   The viewer will, hopefully, go out and start reading poetry.

2   Andere Anzeigen mit ähnlicher, nicht-kommerzieller Ausrichtung finden sich auf S. 44 und 122 des SB.

Traditional advertisements usually want to sell a product so that a company can make money. Here, however, nothing specific is being sold and no one is really trying to make money.

However, many advertisements (e.g. anti-racism, environmental awareness, anti-alcohol and driving) try to educate the viewer and want to sell a message rather than a product. This advertisement falls into this category. It is trying to educate the viewer about the value of poetical words and is encouraging the viewer to read more poetry.

3 It is effective because in today's world everyone wants pain relief. People want to be calmed, soothed or comforted at some time or other. However, it could be that people are just amused by this original form of getting people to read poetry. The advert might be seen as implying that poetry is a product like everything else, which might annoy some people.

4 Individual answers.

SB, S. 131 **B In Flanders Fields**   John McCrae

C Grass   Carl Sandburg

In Flanders Fields:	
Source:	*Punch*, 1915
Topic:	Death in war and the call to continue the struggle
Text form:	Poem
Language variety:	Can E
Number of words:	97
Level:	Basic/advanced
Grass:	
Source:	*Cornhuskers*, 1918
Topic:	The way grass covers over battlefields
Text form:	Poem
Language variety:	AE
Number of words:	67
Level:	Basic/advanced
Skills/activities:	Analysing poems, comparing the message and effectiveness of two poems, giving a personal opinion, presenting a poem with a similar topic

Lern-vokabular

Active vocabulary: 'In Flanders Fields' and 'Grass' (p. 131)

In Flanders Fields: cross (l. 2), row (l. 2), dawn (l. 7), sunset (l. 7), quarrel (l. 10), foe (l. 10), hold sth. high (l. 12), grow (l. 14)
Grass: pile sth. (ll. 1, 4, 5), cover sth. (l. 3), conductor (l. 7)
tasks: stand for sth., represent sth., convey a message

Didaktisch-methodische Hinweise

Die Auswahl der beiden Gedichte wurde durch ihre Gemeinsamkeiten und Gegensätze bestimmt:

– Beide thematisieren den Krieg und das Sterben im Krieg.

– Beide haben eine ungewöhnliche Perspektive: Bei McCrae sprechen die gefallenen Soldaten, bei Sandburg das Gras, das die Gräber überwuchert.

– Das Leben und die Natur werden in „Flanders Fields" mit dem Tod kontrastiert; in „Grass" wird die Natur nur sichtbar als das alles bedeckende Gras.

– „In Flanders Fields" gibt dem Sterben einen Sinn, der allerdings erst dann realisiert wird, wenn die Leser des Gedichts den Kampf gegen den Feind aufnehmen. Es fordert damit zur Fortsetzung des Kämpfens auf, ist ein Kriegsgedicht. In „Grass" hingegen wird durch die Fragen von Lebenden der Nachwelt die Sinnlosigkeit des Kriegs verdeutlicht: Touristen besuchen die Schlachtfelder, wissen aber nichts über die Schlachten und die Gefallenen. Das Gedicht verdeutlicht damit die Sinnlosigkeit des Kriegs und ist ein Friedensgedicht.

In dem Erkennen dieser Gemeinsamkeiten und Gegensätze, die für die S nicht leicht zu durchschauen sind, liegt eine der zentralen Zielsetzungen der *section 2*. Das Erfassen der Struktur und der verwendeten künstlerischen Mittel sowie der Vergleich der Wirkungsweisen bilden den zweiten Schwerpunkt.

'In Flanders Fields'

„In Flander Fields" ist das einzige Gedicht von John McCrae, das die Zeit überdauert hat. Dafür wird es von vielen als das berühmteste Kriegsgedicht des ersten Weltkrieges angesehen, und seine Bilder sind zu Bestandteilen des kollektiven Kriegsgedächtnisses geworden: Jedes Jahr werden in Großbritannien anlässlich des *Remembrance Day* kleine (künstliche) Mohnblumen verkauft, die sich die Menschen ins Knopfloch stecken. Ein amerikanischer Soldatenfriedhof in Flandern wurde nach dem Gedicht benannt, und eine Statue am Fuße eines kanadischen Kriegerdenkmals in Nordfrankreich zitiert das Bild des sterbenden Soldaten, der die Fackel weiterreicht.
Das Gedicht ist nicht unumstritten, da der Aufruf, die Fackel aufzunehmen und den Kampf weiterzuführen, als nicht mehr zeitgemäßer, blinder Patriotismus ausgelegt werden könnte – McCrae war in der Tat kein Pazifist.
Die S sollen dieses berühmte Gedicht und seine Topoi kennen lernen (die Gegenüberstellung von Schlachtfeld und Natur in der ersten Strophe, in der zweiten die Analogie „soldier – lover" und in der letzten Strophe die Bedeutung des Symbols „torch") und nach dem Vergleich mit dem Gedicht von Sandburg ihre eigene Meinung bilden. Da das Gedicht einfach und klar strukturiert ist, eignet es sich gut für eine formale Gedichtinterpretation.

Unterrichts-tipps

Das Gedicht sollte zunächst für sich präsentiert werden. Die S lesen die erste Strophe (die ggf. als Kopie verteilt wird) und spekulieren über die Aussage des Gedichts. Um ein besseres Gefühl für das Versmaß und den Rhythmuswechsel (z.B. durch die Enjambements) zu bekommen, sollte das Gedicht laut vorgelesen werden, zumal der Wortschatz keine Ausspracheschwierigkeiten birgt. Es bietet sich an, das Gedicht in Partnerarbeit gegenseitig vortragen zu lassen, entweder als Ganzes oder abwechselnd Strophe für Strophe. Auf diese Weise kommen alle zum Vorlesen, und Korrekturen sind möglich, ohne dass die ganze Klasse zuhört.

'Grass'

Sandburg schrieb in *free verse* und setzte die Techniken der *imagists* ein, d.h., er verwendete klare, präzise Bilder und knappe Sprache als Mittel des poetischen Ausdrucks. Statt durch Formelemente wie Versmaß und Reimschema erhält „Grass" seine Struktur durch die knappe Syntax, durch Parallelismen und Wiederholungen. Der Sprecher des Gedichts ist das Gras, und es scheint mit jedem zu sprechen, der es hören will. Sandburg war Realist, und in diesem Gedicht führt uns das Gras die Unfähigkeit des Menschen vor Augen, aus der Geschichte zu lernen. Tausende Menschen sterben in Schlachten, Schlachten, die allenfalls als berühmte Namen und Daten im Gedächtnis bleiben, denn das Gras hat die Spuren des Krieges verwischt: Man hat Gras darüber wachsen lassen. Die Aussage Sandburgs ist ambivalent: Die Zeit und die Natur heilen Wunden, aber diese heilende Kraft birgt die Gefahr des Vergessens, was dazu führen könnte, dass das Gras wieder Spuren verwischen muss.

„Grass" ist nicht so leicht zugänglich wie „In Flanders Fields", daher sollte der Einstieg erleichtert werden, z.B. indem die S ihre Assoziationen zu *grass* sammeln. Die Wendung *let the grass grow over sth.* sollte unbedingt genannt werden, ggf. unter Verweis auf die deutsche Wendung:

⬭ *Close your eyes for a moment and think of grass. What kind of grass do you see? Where is it? How do you feel when you see it?*

⬭ *Do you know any expressions/idioms which use the word 'grass'?*
'As green as grass', 'the grass is always greener on the other side of the fence', 'let the grass grow over sth.'

→ *WB, ex. 3* Der Text wird wie das erste Gedicht durch stilles Lesen und anschließendes Vortragen präsentiert.

Info

'In Flanders Fields'
John McCrae [mə'kreɪ] (1872 – 1918) was born in Guelph, Ontario, Canada. He became a doctor, but then served in the Boer War in South Africa from 1900 until 1901. In World War I he served in the medical corps in a hospital in France. His poem 'In Flanders Fields' was inspired by the death of a close friend. It was published in *Punch* in 1915 and became immediately popular. It was often used to inspire young men to enlist in the army. McCrae died of pneumonia on the western front.

Flanders (l. 1) is the north-western part of Belgium. Traditionally Flanders includes the flat coastal areas around Bruges and Ghent but is now used for the Flemish-speaking region of Belgium. It was the main area in which the Western Front in World War I was fought.

Poppies (l. 1) flower when all other plants around them are dead. Their seeds can lie on the ground for years and years, but only when the ground has been dug up will the seeds sprout. As the soil on the First World War battlefields was dug up as never before, thousands and thousands of poppies flowered. On Remembrance Day (11 November), when the dead of both world wars are honoured, people in Britain still buy small, artificial poppies. The money goes to charities which support the war-wounded. The poppy is also regarded as a symbol of sleep: opium is derived from poppies and is used to make morphine, one of the strongest painkillers.

'Grass'
Carl Sandburg (1878–1967) was an American poet born of Swedish parents in Galesburg, Illinois. He first gained recognition with the poem 'Chicago', which was published in 1914, and his published anthology *Chicago Poems* (1916) brought him popular success.

Austerlitz (l. 1) (near Slavkov in the present-day Czech Republic) was one of the greatest military battles won by Napoleon. It took place on 2 December, 1805, between a French army of about 68,000 and an Austrian–Russian army of nearly 90,000. The French lost 9,000 men; the Austrians and Russians about 25,000.

Waterloo (l. 1) was the final battle fought between the French army under Napoleon, and the British, Dutch and Prussian allies near Waterloo, in what is now Belgium. It took place on 18 June, 1815. Napoleon was defeated and the battle is considered as a turning point in modern history. It was one of the bloodiest in modern history: French casualties totalled about 40,000, British and Dutch about 15,000, and Prussian about 7,000.

Gettysburg (l. 4) was a battle fought during the American Civil War from 1–3 July, 1863, and is often considered to be the turning-point in the war. The Federal army of the North lost 3,000 men, the Confederates 3, 500. President Lincoln made his famous address, the Gettysburg Address, on the battlefield.

Info

Ypres (l. 5) ['iprə; in British soldier's slang often called 'waɪpəz] is the name given to three battles of World War I fought around the town of Ypres, Belgium. Throughout the war Ypres was under constant attack as it blocked a German approach to the English Channel. During the battles, fought between 1914 and 1917, over 500,000 casualties were recorded.

Verdun (l. 5) was one of the major battles of World War I, fought between German and French forces from February to December 1916. The losses on both sides were high: the French suffered 350,000 casualties and the Germans 330,000. The battle itself was totally indecisive, as neither side won a strategic advantage.

Lösungs-hinweise

1 The speaker in 'In Flanders Fields' is the voice of the dead soldiers. In 'Grass' it is the grass.

Differenzierung
❖

2 Diese Aufgabe sollte schriftlich nach der Anleitung in „Reading Poetry" (vgl. SB, S. 241) bearbeitet werden. In leistungsschwächeren Lerngruppen kann eine Besprechung des Gedichts im Unterricht als Vorbereitung dienen. Die anschließende Auswertung der schriftlichen Interpretation kann mittels *peer group monitoring* erfolgen: In Vierergruppen lesen sich die S ihre Interpretationen vor, die anderen hören aufmerksam zu, loben oder machen Verbesserungsvorschläge. Die S können dann zu Hause ihre Interpretationen überarbeiten.

The poem 'In Flanders Fields' by John McCrae was written in 1915. In it he expresses his despair in the face of the loss of life on the battlefields of Flanders during World War I, and expresses the hope that the battle will not have been in vain, but that others will continue the fight. In the first stanza the speaker (the voice of the dead soldiers) introduces the reader to the scene and contrasts nature with the ongoing battle. The reader can picture the crosses, which mark the graves, and the red poppies, and can hear birds sing despite the noise of the guns. In the second stanza the speaker arouses pity by referring to the dead as human beings who once enjoyed the beauty of nature and who now lie in their graves instead of their beds. He speaks collectively for all those who have died, and in the last stanza he addresses the reader directly, saying that he must carry on the battle, otherwise the soldiers will have died in vain. This implies that the soldiers were fighting for a just cause, that they sacrificed their lives and that this sacrifice must go on until victory has been achieved.

The poem is composed of three stanzas. The first stanza has five lines, which follow the rhyme scheme a a b b a, the second consists of four lines, which follow the scheme a a b c, and the final stanza has six lines, with the rhyme scheme a a b b a c. This creates an impression of regularity and repetition (this can be seen as a reflection of the orderly rows of graves). In the first stanza ll. 3–4 and 4–5 run on into each other (enjambement), which underlines the flow of the poem, making it similar to normal speech. The same applies to ll. 6–7, ll. 8–9, ll. 11–12 and ll. 14–15. The speaker occasionally speaks in a military tone (the lark sings 'bravely', l. 4, 'foe', l. 10) and sometimes his use of the language is old-fashioned (l. 5: 'scarce heard amid', l. 5, word order in l. 11, 'ye', l. 13), so the atmosphere created is very solemn.

The most significant image is that of the torch in the third stanza. The torch symbolizes the soldiers' fight against the enemy and is passed on from the dead to the living so that they can continue the fight. The speaker underlines the urgency of his message in the last two lines by means of the metaphor of 'sleep', which stands for death, and by the figurative use of 'poppies', which also symbolize sleep (as poppies are used to produce opium). If the battle is not continued the dead soldiers will not be able to rest in peace.

❖❖ **3** Die Bearbeitung dieser Aufgabe findet am sinnvollsten zunächst in einem Partnergespräch statt, damit die S vor allem Teil b diskutieren können.

a The names stand for battles in which hundreds of thousands of soldiers lost their lives. They could be seen as standing for war in general.

b Grass: This could have two meanings, a literal and a figurative one.
Literal: Nature and life, in contrast to the piles of bodies which stand for death and decay. The grass grows over everything, has healing powers, like time.
Figurative: The scenes of battles are covered by grass, and this makes people forget, so the grass could stand for forgetfulness.

Passengers: This refers to people on a literal or figurative journey.
Literal: The people are just visiting the area. They are possibly tourists.
Figurative: People in general on their journey through time, who forget about the terrible things which happened in the past, which is one reason why wars continue to take place.

Conductor: This belongs to the image of the passengers. On a journey it is the conductor's job to inform the passengers of where they are or help them if they do not know where they are. The passengers rely on the conductor for information.

4 Damit die S ein Gerüst für den Textvergleich haben, wird ihnen das leere Schema präsentiert (s.u.). In Partnerarbeit wird es dann von den S vervollständigt. Bei der Beurteilung der Effektivität können die S zu unterschiedlichen Einschätzungen kommen.

Possible answers:

	In Flanders Fields	Grass
Form and structure	clearly structured regular rhyme scheme run-on lines create fluidity rhythm	free verse parallelisms, repetition (names of the battles, 'pile', 'let me work', 'I am the grass') and short sentences give the poem its structure
Speaker / point of view	dead soldiers	the grass
Language	frequent allusions to nature military tone old-fashioned language	poet speaks in images; simple language
Attitude to war	poet does not condemn war the fight for a just cause must go on dying makes sense, i.e. in favour of certain wars	horrors of war summed up in the single image of piling the bodies high; people do not learn from history: the battles continue the dead are anonymous and soon forgotten dying senseless, i.e. against wars.
Effectiveness	addresses the emotions arouses feelings of pity, sadness and despair; inspires young soldiers/ people to fight ambivalence of the message perhaps more effective as it is better known (because it made the bereaved feel better?)	addresses the intellect via the images makes the reader think depressing

❖ **5** Damit bei der Beantwortung der Aufgaben 5 und 6 alle S zu Wort kommen, empfiehlt sich folgende Variante des Kugellagers (vgl. hierzu auch S. 429): Zuerst machen sich alle stichwortartig Notizen zu den beiden Aufgaben. Die S setzen sich in zwei gegenüberliegende Reihen, damit jeder einen Gesprächspartner hat. Zuerst wird Aufgabe 5 im Zweiergespräch bearbeitet. Danach bewegt sich jeder einen Stuhl nach rechts weiter. Im Gespräch mit dem neuen Partner wird die Aufgabe 6 bearbeitet.

<u>'In Flanders Fields'</u>: It is calming, as there seems to be an acceptance of death in the middle of carnage, yet it is disturbing, as the speaker wishes the carnage to carry on in order to make the dead rest at ease.

<u>'Grass'</u>: The idea of grass is usually consoling, as it is pleasant to lie on or touch, but here it encourages people to forget. Moreover, the grass is seen as an active ingredient of the battlefield ('let me work', l. 2).

6 Vgl. Aufgabe 5.

Individual answers.

7 Die gesammelten Gedichte können dem Plenum vorgetragen und evtl. anhand des oben angewandten Schemas analysiert werden. Eine Alternative wäre es, die Klasse eine kleine Anthologie zusammenstellen zu lassen, die auch mit Illustrationen (z.B. mit Kunstpostkarten, eigenen Bildern) versehen wird.

SB, S.132 # 3 Theatre: A Battle on a Stage

Diese *section* hat drei thematische Schwerpunkte:

- die *performing arts* und ihre Funktionen im Rahmen des Kapitels;
- die Themen Krieg und Konflikt auf der Bühne und im Film;
- Shakespeare-Texte als Kulminationspunkt und als Schnittstelle der ersten beiden Schwerpunkte.

In der Palette der Künste, die in diesem Kapitel thematisiert werden, kommt der darstellenden Kunst (Theater, Film) ein hoher Stellenwert zu. Zum einen gehört der Film zu den bei den S beliebtesten Kunstformen. Auch wirkt das Rahmenthema dieses Kapitels durch die Gestaltung der Schrecken des Krieges im Film vielleicht eindringlicher als bei den meisten anderen Kunstformen. Schließlich ist die Umsetzung eines Textes von einem Medium (geschriebenes Wort) in ein anderes (Aufführung oder Film) besonders reizvoll. Wichtig ist aber hierbei, die S selbst schauspielerisch tätig werden zu lassen. Dabei geht es weniger darum, vor Publikum zu spielen, als um die Erfahrung des gemeinsamen Spielens. Einen interessanten Teilaspekt stellt dabei die Frage dar, wie es möglich ist, eine Schlacht mit Tausenden von Soldaten auf die Bühne zu bringen. Am Anfang der *section* steht ein Ausschnitt aus dem populären Film *Shakespeare in Love*, der die Probleme der Shakespeare-Bühne beschreibt und zugleich eine Überleitung zu den Auszügen aus Shakespeares *Henry V* (vgl. auch die Informationen zu Shakespeare und Musik und seinen *pastoral comedies* auf S. 143). Nachdem die S sich Gedanken über die Inszenierung der Auszüge gemacht haben, vergleichen sie zwei Verfilmungen. Aus Gründen der Motivation sollten möglichst die Interesse weckenden Elemente der Verfilmungen in den Vordergrund gerückt werden und nicht so sehr die Schwierigkeiten wie die Sprache Shakespeares.

→ *WB, ex. 4*

A A Shakespearian Performance

`VIDEO`

Source:	*Shakespeare in Love*, 1998
Topic:	A play performed in Shakespeare's time
Text form:	Feature film (extract)
Language variety:	BE
Length:	13:40 minutes
Level:	Advanced
Skills/activities:	Examining the problems involved in performing plays, analysing how a film deals with a theatrical performance

Didaktisch-methodische Hinweise

In diesem Filmausschnitt (vgl. Video/DVD und das Transkript auf S. 269–271) sehen die S einige Szenen aus *Romeo and Juliet*, aufgeführt auf einer Shakespeare-Bühne. Sie sollen erkennen, unter welchen Bedingungen zur Shakespeare-Zeit Aufführungen stattfanden (z.B. keine Kulissen, Requisiten oder künstliche Beleuchtung), um vor diesem Hintergrund die folgenden Ausschnitte aus *Henry V* besser verstehen zu können. Als moderner und schülernaher Film bildet *Shakespeare in Love* sicher einen motivierenden Einstieg in das Thema Shakespeare.

Unterrichtstipps

Nachdem die Arbeitsaufträge 1 und 2 vorgestellt wurden, kann der Ausschnitt den S ohne große Vorbereitung präsentiert werden. Sie sollten aber darauf aufmerksam gemacht werden, dass sie sich eher aufs Sehen als aufs Hören konzentrieren sollten. Sie notieren ihre Antworten und vergleichen sie in Partnerarbeit. Wegen der Länge der Sequenz mag es sinnvoll sein, die Aufgaben arbeitsteilig von zwei S bearbeiten zu lassen. Das Sammeln der Ergebnisse erfolgt im Unterrichtsgespräch.

Info

Shakespeare in Love (director: John Madden; filmscript: Tom Stoppard): Set in 1593, the film introduces Shakespeare as a young playwright who is suffering from writer's block. His theatre manager is in debt to the local moneylender and the future of their theatre looks bleak. A wealthy merchant's daughter, Viola De Lesseps, decides to disguise herself as a boy (women were not allowed to perform on the stage at that time) and audition for the play which Shakespeare is working on (called *Romeo and Ethel, the Priate's Daughter*). She is given the role of Romeo, but Shakespeare soon discovers her disguise. He and Viola fall in love, and as a result the play is transformed into *Romeo and Juliet*. Viola has been promised in marriage to Lord Wessex. The marriage takes place on the same day as the first performance of *Romeo and Juliet*. After the wedding ceremony, Viola rushes off to the theatre. The play is a great success, but Viola and Shakespeare are forced to part.

Lösungshinweise

`VIDEO`

1 Vgl. Video/DVD und das Transkript auf S. 269–271.

Circumstances:
– A performance was a social occasion, which all kinds of people attended, and the less educated people in the audience were entertained by humorous scenes (comic relief), sword fights, etc.
– Plays were considered politically and morally sensitive (cf. Puritan preacher).

Technical limitations:
– There was no curtain to signal the beginning of the performance, so there was often a fanfare.
– There was no scenery to show where the action was set, so a chorus told the audience of the setting.
– The audience listened carefully to what was going on, as the acoustics were not good.

- There was no artificial lighting, so the performance took place during the day.
- The stage was very small, so there were never too many people on the stage at once.
(– Actors wore their own clothes; this is not evident in the film.)

The actors:
- No females were allowed to act, so younger females were acted by young boys whose voices had not yet broken, and older women were acted by men.

`VIDEO` **2**

- The action on and behind the stage are presented simultaneously, so that they flow into each other (e.g. when they kiss each other).
- Use of cuts to move the action quickly on, so that even those who do not know the play can follow the basic plot.
- Only the best known scenes and the climax of *Romeo and Juliet* are shown.

SB, S. 132 **B** *Henry V:* **Prologue**   William Shakespeare

Text:	
Source:	*Henry V*, ca. 1599.
Topic:	The demands made upon an audience
Text form:	Drama (extract)
Language variety:	BE
Number of words:	126
Level:	Basic/advanced
Skills/activities:	Examining the problems of putting on a play, comparing Shakespeare's theatre with modern-day theatres

`VIDEO`

Video:	
Source	*Henry V*, 1944.
Topic:	The demands made upon an audience
Text form:	Feature film (extract)
Language variety:	BE
Length:	6:10 minutes
Level:	Basic/advanced
Skills/activities:	Viewing comprehension

Lern-vokabular

Active vocabulary: 'Henry V: Prologue' (p. 132)

cram sth. (with) in sth. else (l. 2), confined (l. 8), imperfections (l. 11), imaginary (l. 13), accomplishment (l. 18)
tasks: be faced with sth.

Didaktisch-methodische Hinweise

In diesem Abschnitt – einem Teil des Prologs – fasst der Chor die Situation zusammen: Die Soldaten zweier Königreiche (England und Frankreich) stehen sich beiderseits des engen Ärmelkanals gegenüber und werden in Agincourt aufeinandertreffen. All das soll auf der kleinen Bühne des Theaters dargestellt werden. Ferner müssen die Geschehnisse mehrerer Jahre in die kurze Zeit der Aufführung gepresst werden. Dies alles bedeutet, dass hohe Anforderungen an die Vorstellungskraft der Zuschauer gestellt werden.
Die Bearbeitung dieses Abschnitts verfolgt drei Ziele:
- Die S sollen ihr Vorwissen aus „A Shakespearian Performance" anwenden.
- Die S sollen Unterschiede und Ähnlichkeiten des hier dargestellten Shakespeare-Theaters und die Möglichkeiten des heutigen Theaters herausarbeiten.
- Die S sollen erkennen, mit welchen Mitteln das Theater die Realität einfangen kann.

Unterrichts-tipps

Der Text sollte zunächst von L laut vorgelesen werden, während die S mitlesen. Leistungsschwächere Gruppen können die Übersetzung hinzuziehen (vgl. die KV 'The Battle of Agincourt: German Translation' online). Danach kann der Auszug aus einer älteren Verfilmung von *Henry V* von Sir Laurence Olivier gezeigt werden (vgl. das Video/die DVD und das Transkript auf S. 271–272), in der der Schauspieler Leslie Banks zu sehen ist (Zeilen 5 sowie 12–13 fehlen dabei). Obwohl diese Inszenierung den S nicht so nahe sein wird wie der Auszug aus *Shakespeare in Love*, bietet sie eine gute Ergänzung und erleichtert das Textverständnis. Anschließend bearbeiten die S die Aufgaben in Partnerarbeit. Zum Schluss können die S den Text unter Beachtung von Intonation und Emphase und eventuell mit Einsatz von entsprechender Gestik vortragen.

Info

Sir Laurence Olivier (1907–1989) is often considered one of the finest English stage actors. He began his acting career in the 1920s, and was co-director of the Old Vic Shakespeare company from 1944 to 1949. The film version of Shakespeare's *Henry V* not only starred Olivier but was also produced and directed by him. Olivier also starred in film versions of Shakespeare's *Hamlet* (1948), *Richard III* (1956) and *Othello* (1965). Other films include *Rebecca* (1940), *The Entertainer* (1960) and *Sleuth* (1972).

Henry V (ca. 1599): This is one of Shakespeare's history plays and concludes the sequence of *Richard II* and *Henry IV*. It is one of his most overtly patriotic plays, celebrating the exploits of the warrior king over the French. Henry V quells a rebellion at home before defeating the French at the Battle of Agincourt. Afterwards he woos the French princess and the play ends with their marriage plans.

This wooden O (l. 3): This refers to the inner courtyard of contemporary theatres such as the Globe, which was round and encircled by wooden balconies. (Cf. illustration on p. 132 for the exterior view.)

Agincourt (l. 4) (now Azincourt): The Battle of Agincourt was fought in France on 25 October, 1415, as part of the Hundred Years' War, between an English army under King Henry V of England and a French army. Henry, who claimed the French throne, invaded France. Weakened by disease and hunger, Henry's army of 6000 men was on its way to Calais, where Henry planned to sail back to England. In the course of the march to Calais the English force, for the most part lightly equipped archers, was met by the French army of about 25,000 men, who were heavily armoured knights on horseback and footsoldiers. It rained heavily before the battle, which left the French troops at a disadvantage because of their heavy armour. The knights on horseback soon became stuck in the mud, which made them easy targets for the English archers. Whereas the French army suffered losses of over 5000, the English losses numbered about 200.

Lösungs-hinweise

1 The audience had to use their imagination in order to:
- picture in their minds the vast landscape of France (cf. l. 2);
- picture huge armies and two kingdoms (cf. ll. 8–13);
- convert the normal clothes of the actors into those of a king's (cf. l. 16);
- understand what might have happened between scenes (cf. ll. 17–19);
- be able to picture the horses in battle (cf. ll. 14–15);
- be able to understand that the period of time portrayed in the play was not identical with the length of the play (cf. ll. 17–19);
- accept the limitations of the theatre (cf. ll. 1–3).

2 Other elements: swords being rattled offstage, fanfares (cf. 'A Shakespearian Performance'), banners, fireworks, small cannons.

Similarities	Differences
Even a larger stage cannot hold an army. The audience must still listen carefully.	Lighting, sounds and special effects (e.g. a revolving stage, the use of videos to convey the background, etc.) can help to create the illusion. Female roles are acted by females.

SB, S. 133

C Battle of Agincourt   William Shakespeare

Source:	*Henry V*, ca. 1599.
Topic:	The lead-up to and aftermath of the Battle of Agincourt
Text form:	Drama (extract)
Language variety:	BE
Number of words:	396
Level:	Advanced
Skills/activities:	Rewriting a text in modern English, speculating, writing and performing a play

Lern-vokabular

Active vocabulary: 'Battle of Agincourt' (p. 133)

fresh (l. 6), (the) odds (l. 7), warrior (l. 12), honour (l. 22), garments (l. 26), sin (l. 28), noble (l. 35), dispose of sth. (ll. 43–44)
tasks: outcome, rehearse sth.

Didaktisch-methodische Hinweise

Die zwei Szenen aus Akt IV wurden vorrangig wegen ihrer Funktion ausgewählt. Sie verdeutlichen, wie Shakespeare das Problem löst, eine Schlacht auf der Bühne darzustellen, und wie er unterschiedliche Haltungen zu Krieg und Sterben gestaltet.

In Szene iii befürchtet Westmorland eine Niederlage und wünscht Verstärkung; Salisbury sieht es als seine Pflicht an, in die Schlacht zu gehen und sich seinem Schicksal zu fügen. Henry wendet die zahlenmäßige Unterlegenheit seiner Männer ins Positive: Einerseits bedeute sie, dass weniger Engländer auf dem Schlachtfeld sterben müssen, andererseits sei der Anteil des Einzelnen an der Ehre um so größer, wenn England siegen sollte.

In Szene vii grenzen sich Engländer und Franzosen, repräsentiert durch Montjoy und Henry, deutlich voneinander ab, und ihr unterschiedliches Auftreten verdeutlicht jeweils das Auftreten des anderen: Als Montjoy vor den König tritt, zeigt er auch in der Niederlage die Arroganz, mit der Shakespeare alle Figuren auf der französischen Seite ausgestattet hat. Er bittet darum, die Toten zählen und die Edelmänner von den einfachen Soldaten trennen zu dürfen, die nicht der Ehre, sondern des Geldes wegen gekämpft haben. Henrys Bescheidenheit wirkt vor diesem Hintergrund um so eindringlicher. Als er vom Ausgang der Schlacht erfährt, sieht er darin die Gnade Gottes. Diese Haltung steht in deutlichem Kontrast zu seinem Auftreten in Szene iii und lässt ihn als *round character* erscheinen.

Unterrichts-tipps

Durch die *pre-reading activity*, die in Kleingruppen bearbeitet werden sollte, wird eine Erwartungshaltung aufgebaut. Die S lesen dann Szene iii und lösen Aufgaben 1 und 2, um das Textverständnis zu sichern und die unterschiedlichen Haltungen der Figuren herauszuarbeiten. Nachdem die S Szene vii still gelesen haben, bearbeiten sie Auf-

Differenzierung

gaben 3–5. Leistungsschwächere S können auch die deutschen Übersetzungen heranziehen (vgl. die KV „Battle of Agincourt: German Translation" online).

Info

King Henry: Henry V came to the throne in 1415 and set out to conquer France and claim the French throne. He defeated the French in the Battle of Agincourt (cf. p. 252). In the next two years, Henry captured much of northern France. The French king Charles VI agreed that Henry would marry his daughter Catherine, and on Charles's death would become King of France. Henry's death in 1422 meant he never became King of France, and his son, Henry VI, lost all of his French possessions.

Gloucester ['glɔstə], *Bedford:* King Henry's brothers.

Westmorland: King Henry's cousin.

Men in England that do no work today (ll. 16–17): The Feast Day of Crispin and Crispianus (cf. l. 54) was a holiday for shoemakers.

Crispin Crispianus (l. 53): Crispin and Crispian were two brothers who were martyred for preaching Christianity during the time of the Roman Empire.

Lösungs-hinweise

● *Pre-reading:* Individual answers.

1 **a** The soldiers are outnumbered and weak, as they have been campaigning in France, whereas the French soldiers, on their own ground, are still fresh.

b <u>Salisbury</u>: He bravely resigns himself to his fate, feeling that God will be on his side (he takes it for granted that they will all meet again in heaven).
<u>Westmorland</u>: He is anxious and frightened by the numbers of French soldiers; he wishes they had more men.
<u>Henry</u>: He thinks of his soldiers and wishes to avoid unnecessary sacrifices; on the other hand, he thinks of the greater share in the honour and glory fewer men would have.

2 If we survive, then being so few in number, we shall have a greater share of the honour. Please don't wish for more soldiers. God knows, I'm not interested in wealth, and I don't care how many people I have to support, and I don't mind other people wearing my clothes. Material things like that don't interest me. But if it is a sin to want too much honour, then I sin more than anyone else.

3 The English soldiers are victorious, and the battlefield is covered with the dead bodies of French noblemen and ordinary soldiers.

4 At the end of the battle Henry seems subdued and displays more modesty than in scene iii:
– When he learns of the victory his only reaction seems to be one of relief: his short speeches seem plain and simple when compared with what Montjoy says.
– He thanks God for the victory, not himself (cf. l. 50).
– His one thought is to commemorate the day by naming the battle after the place it was fought at (cf. l. 53).
– He thinks of the Saints' day it was fought on (a reflection of his piety) (cf. l. 54).
There is a contrast between these reactions and his attitude before the battle:
– He dismisses the fear of death (cf. ll. 20–21).
– He is energetic when it comes to the subject of honour, emphasizing what he says with expletives such as 'God', 'By Jove' (cf. ll. 21–29).
– He tries to motivate the others (cf. ll. 20–29).

5 Für die Beantwortung dieser Aufgabe kann die Zusatzaufgabe unten hilfreich sein.

Possible answers:
– The English soldiers fought very bravely, perhaps because the King makes no difference between noblemen and 'ordinary' soldiers, unlike the French.

– The French were too confident of themselves and their victory, while the English had to make their inferior numbers work more effectively.

⬭ *Look carefully at the illustration on p. 133. Describe it and say what hints it gives about the battle and the reasons for the English victory.*

It shows the Battle of Agincourt. On the right is the English army, on the left are the French forces (this can be seen from the flags: the *fleur-de-lis*, the lily, is the symbol of the French monarchy, the lion of the English monarchy; the English flag also has the *fleur-de-lis*, as the English claimed the French throne up until the 17th century). To the right of the centre one can see Henry V (his armour has the same decoration as the English flag and he is wearing a crown). The French knights, like the English knights, are wearing heavy armour, but in the foreground one can see the English long-bow archers, who were the main reason for the English victory (cf. also the two soldiers below the main picture). The arrows devastated the French knights. The French were also fighting on muddy terrain while the English were on higher dry terrain (cf. the ground below the French knights and that below the English archers). Many French knights literally drowned in the mud, when their horses were killed by the archers.

❖ **6** Die „Aufführung" dieser Szenen sollte vor dem Plenum erfolgen. Zunächst bereiten die S jedoch in kleinen Gruppen eine der beiden Szenen vor. Nachdem von dem Kurs (der in die Rolle einer Schauspielertruppe schlüpfen soll) beschlossen wird, welche der Gruppen die jeweilige Szene vorspielen wird, überlegt die Klasse gemeinsam, wie die eigentliche Schlacht dargestellt werden soll. Dabei greifen sie unter Beachtung der Begrenzungen des Theaters auf ihre Überlegungen in der *pre-reading activity* zurück.

SB, S. 134 **D Two Performances of *Henry V***

VIDEO

BBC TV version:
Source:	Henry V, 1979.
Topic:	The lead-up to and aftermath of the Battle of Agincourt
Text form:	Film (extract)
Language variety:	BE
Length:	4:35 minutes
Level:	Advanced

VIDEO

Film version:
Source:	Henry V, 1989.
Topic:	The lead-up to and aftermath of the Battle of Agincourt
Text form:	Film (extract)
Language variety:	BE
Length:	5:58 minutes
Level:	Advanced
Skills/activities:	Commenting on a performance, writing a review, analysing film techniques

Didaktisch-methodische Hinweise Damit die S einen Eindruck davon bekommen, wie professionelle Schauspieler diese Szenen dargestellt haben, werden ihnen zwei unterschiedliche Fassungen von *Henry V* gezeigt (vgl. Video/DVD). Eine wurde in der 70er Jahren von der BBC mit David Gwillim als Henry V produziert, die andere ist die Kinofassung von und mit Kenneth Branagh. Da Branagh sich bei dem Text sehr viele Freiheiten genommen hat (vgl. auch den Hinweis in Aufgabe 6b, „the script is unimportant"), wird in beiden Fassungen die
→ *WB, ex. 5* gesamte Rede Henrys V wiedergegeben (vgl. das Transkript auf S. 272–274).

Info

David Gwillim (born 1947) has appeared mostly in TV series or films, with Henry V being his only important leading role.

Kenneth Branagh (born 1960) is the best-known Shakespeare interpreter of the late 20th century. He has been responsible for bringing many of Shakespeare's works to the screen. However, his film *Mary Shelley's Frankenstein* (1994), showed that he was principally an interpreter of Shakespeare rather than a good director. Born in Belfast to a working-class family, he was later accepted at the Royal Academy of Dramatic Arts (RADA) in London, where he established himself as a Shakespearian actor. *Henry V* (1989) was the first film he directed, and was followed by *Dead Again* (1991) and *Peter's Friends* (1992). He has also appeared in many films, including *Harry Potter and the Chamber of Secrets* (2002).

Lösungs-hinweise

VIDEO

1 Vgl. Video/DVD und das Transkript auf S. 272–274.

Possible answer:
Branagh's Henry V is more inspirational and seems to motivate his men, while David Gwillim is quiet and almost timid in his portrayal.

2 Points that might be mentioned:
– The acting, particularly that of the actor playing Henry V (Film: Branagh delivers his speech in scene iii in a way that motivates and rouses the soldiers, changing tone from loud to soft to loud; TV film: Gwillim delivers his speech as a good humoured attempt to overcome the worries of the nobles (no common soldiers hear his speech), but he does bring some emotion in towards the end of the speech)
– The stage or setting (Film: outdoors with trees and ground, muddy; TV film: indoors, landscape very flat and clean).
– Music and incidental noise (Film: stirring music and background noise, e.g. birds, thunder; TV film: no music or battle noise, so the words stand out by themselves).
– Text (Film: cuts out parts that might not interest the audience; TV film: keeps the entire text).
– Props (Film: costumes, wagons, blood and mud on Henry's face; TV film: just armour and a tent, no feeling that a battle has taken place).

VIDEO

3 Film: The camera work is quite complex and there is a lot of movement, which keeps the interest of a modern audience. The two groups of nobles are not together. Gloucester arrives, then speaks, then the camera tracks the movement of Westmorland as he moves down to Exeter and Salisbury. When Henry starts his speech, he summons the nobles and soldiers, the camera tracks the nobles walking towards Henry. Henry is shown in long shot surrounded by his men, then in close-up. The camera cuts occasionally to the attentive faces of the soldiers. In scene vii, Montjoy and Henry are filmed together in the shot, emphasizing the nearness of rivals achieved during a bloody battle. When it is clear that the battle has been won, Henry breaks free and is filmed in a medium shot with only the (defeated) French herald behind him.

TV film: The camera work is relatively static and concentrates on group ensembles. When Henry appears in scene iii there is a low-angle shot of him and his entourage to make his appearance look impressive (but the shot is too short to be really effective). During his speech in scene iii there are medium shots showing him interacting with the other nobles, but at the end he is filmed in close-up (which means the actor has to have more control of his facial expression). In scene vii there are medium shots of the two main actors, and they are not shot together in the same cut, which emphasizes the distance between a king and a herald.

4 Music: Offering Hope

Section 4 bietet den S die Gelegenheit, die Wirkung von klassischer Musik auf Menschen in einer Situation nachzuempfinden, die von Angst und Verzweiflung gekennzeichnet ist. Dies geschieht exemplarisch anhand eines Auszugs aus einer Biographie, in dem eine Aufführung von Mahlers „Auferstehungssinfonie" durch das Orchester des Jüdischen Kulturbundes in Berlin im Frühjahr 1941 geschildert wird. Davor machen die S Bekanntschaft mit Auszügen aus der Sinfonie, deren Leitmotiv die Auseinandersetzung mit dem Tod (der „menschlichen Katastrophe" schlechthin) ist.

Diese Inhalte stellen eine große Herausforderung für die S dar, die noch keine Begegnung mit dem Tod oder extremen Notsituationen gehabt haben und sich dieser Thematik nun in einer fremden Sprache stellen müssen. Auch ist davon auszugehen, dass die Beschäftigung mit klassischer Musik nicht für alle S selbstverständlich ist. Hier werden die Grenzen des Fremdsprachenunterrichts überschritten, wobei es natürlich weniger um die musiktheoretische Auseinandersetzung mit Mahlers Werk geht als um das ganzheitliche Einfühlen in eine für viele fremdartige Form von Musik, um das Erfassen ihrer Funktionen gerade in Zeiten äußerster Be-drohung und um die Verbalisierung von Eindrücken. Dass Musik beruhigen und Trost spenden kann, werden die meisten S bereits selbst erfahren haben, und deshalb sollen sie die Möglichkeit erhalten, diese Erfahrungen – auch anhand eines eigenen Beispiels – zu versprachlichen. Schließlich besitzt *Section 4* eine spürbare ethische Komponente: Sie soll die S anregen, sich mit dem Schicksal von Unterdrückten und Verfolgten (auch aus der jüngeren deutschen Geschichte) zu beschäftigen und Empathie für sie zu entwickeln.

A Extracts from the *Resurrection Symphony* Gustav Mahler

`CD`

Source:	*Symphony No. 2 (Resurrection Symphony)*.
	Extract 1: 1st movement (ca. 12:30–16:00)
	Extract 2: 2nd movement (ca. 7.30–10:40)
	3rd movement (0:00–1:15)
	Extract 3: 5th movement (ca. final 6 minutes)
Topic:	The power of music
Text form:	Symphony
Length:	13:55 minutes
Skills/activities:	Listening to music, expressing one's feelings and reactions

Didaktisch-methodische Hinweise

Um den S die Gelegenheit zu geben, die Emotionen nachzuvollziehen, die Mahlers Auferstehungssymphonie bei der Aufführung des Jüdischen Kulturbundes in „An Infinitely Hopeful Message" auslöst, hören sie einige Auszüge aus der Symphonie (vgl. CD2, *track* 6; Die Aufnahme stammt vom City of Birmingham Symphony Orchestra unter der Leitung von Simon Rattle aus dem Jahr 1987; die Sängerinnen sind Arleen Auger und Janet Baker).

Unterrichts-tipps

Die Symphonie sollte möglichst zu Beginn einer Doppelstunde präsentiert werden, damit genügend Zeit vorhanden ist, um die Musik zwei Mal zu hören, die Fragen zu beantworten und den folgenden Text zu lesen. (Die Erstbegegnung mit dem Text sollte idealerweise nicht erst am nächsten Tag erfolgen, damit den S die Eindrücke besser präsent sind, die die Symphonie auf sie gemacht hat.) Vor dem ersten Hören sollten die S nur den Auftrag bekommen, sich der Emotionen bewusst zu werden, die die Musik in ihnen auslöst. Erst vor dem zweiten Hören sollte Aufgabe 1 gelesen werden, da sie genaueres, analytisches Hören verlangt. Soll der fächerverbindende Aspekt ausgeweitet werden, können Referate über Mahler und seine Symphonie gehört werden.

Info

Gustav Mahler (1860–1911) was an Austrian composer and conductor, whose music was a major influence on such 20th-century composers as Arnold Schoenberg and Alban Berg. He was the conductor of several central European opera houses, and in 1897 he renounced his Jewish faith in order to become artistic director of the Imperial Opera in Vienna. Besides his nine symphonies, he also composed the symphonic song cycle *Das Lied von der Erde* (1908) and the song cycle *Kindertotenlieder* (1902).

Resurrection Symphony [rezəˈrekʃn]: The Symphony No. 2 in C minor by Gustav Mahler, known as the *Resurrection Symphony*, was written between 1888 and 1894. It was written for an orchestra consisting of wind instruments (e.g. flutes, piccolos, oboes and clarinets), brass instuments (e.g trumpets, trombones), percussion (e.g. drums, cymbals), two harps, an organ and strings. The fourth movement requires an alto soloist, and the last movement a soprano soloist and a choir. The work in its finished form has five movements:

1. *Allegro maestoso*, in which Mahler presents a funeral scene ('Totenfeier') and asks questions such as 'Is there life after death?';
2. *Andante moderato*, in which Mahler used traditional Austrian folk music in the form of a 'Ländler' and which is a remembrance of happy times;
3. *In ruhig fließender Bewegung* (With quietly flowing movement), in which Mahler depicts a complete loss of faith, and belief in life as meaningless;
4. *Urlicht* (Primeval Light), a song praising the rebirth of faith ('I am from God, and will return to God');
5. *Im Tempo des Scherzos* (In the tempo of a scherzo). After a return of the doubts of the third movement and the questions of the first, Mahler ends his symphony with a realization of God's love, and recognition of everlasting life. The text in the extract is the following:

> Hör auf zu beben!
> Bereite Dich zu leben!
> O Schmerz! Du Alldurchdringer!
> Dir bin ich entrungen!
> O Tod! Du Allbezwinger!
> Nun bist Du bezwungen!
> Mit Flügeln, die ich mir errungen,
> in heißem Liebesstreben,
> werd ich entschweben
> zum Licht, zu dem kein Aug gedrungen!
> Sterben werd ich, um zu leben!
> Alles Liebe, auferstehn wirst du
> Mein Herz, in einem Nu!
> Was du geschlagen
> Zu Gott wird es dich tragen.

A performance of the whole symphony lasts approximately 85 minutes.

Lösungs-hinweise

CD

1 Die Symphonie befindet sich auf CD2, *track* 6. Bevor die S die Ausschnitte hören, sollten der Hörauftrag besprochen und unbekannte Vokabeln geklärt werden. Nach dem Hören tauschen die S in einem Partnergespräch ihre Eindrücke aus.

 2 In einem Unterrichtsgespräch können S über die Intentionen Mahlers spekulieren; L kann abschließend Informationen dazu geben. Das Gespräch sollte jedoch nicht zu ausführlich sein, damit die Musik noch präsent ist, wenn die S den Text lesen.

Mahler shows that beyond suffering and death there is the hope of resurrection.

B An Infinitely Hopeful Message   Martin Goldsmith

Source:	*The Inextinguishable Symphony*, 2000
Topic:	The effects of stirring music
Text form:	Fictionalized biography
Language variety:	AE
Number of words:	510
Level:	Advanced
Skills/activities:	Examining the effect of music, comparing reactions to music, writing a letter, presenting a favourite piece of music

Lern-vokabular

Active vocabulary: 'An Infinitely Hopeful Message' (p. 135)

audience (l. 4), applaud (l. 5), take possession of sth. (l. 9), be conscious of sth. (l. 10), acknowledge (l. 12), be aware of sth. (l. 12), cough (l. 14), sneeze (l. 14), humiliation (l. 17), in vain (l. 22), radiant (l. 32), stunned (l. 35), reign (l. 41), peak (l. 42), endeavour (l. 44)

Didaktisch-methodische Hinweise

In diesem Abschnitt erleben die S, wie die Musik, die sie soeben gehört haben, auf das jüdische Publikum im Berlin des Jahres 1941 wirkte. Die S vergleichen diese Wirkung mit ihren eigenen Eindrücken. In einem kreativen Schreibauftrag verarbeiten sie das Gelesene. Sie reflektieren ihre eigenen Reaktionen, indem sie andere Musikstücke beschreiben, die für sie persönlich von Bedeutung sind, und ihre Wirkung zu ergründen versuchen.

 Vor der Lektüre des Texts sollte der Begriff „inextinguishable" geklärt werden.

Info

Martin Goldsmith (born 1956) is the son of Rosemarie and Günther Goldschmidt, two German Jews who met in Germany and emigrated to the USA in 1941, shortly after the concert described in the text. Most of the members of Günther Goldschmidt's family were killed in the Holocaust. Martin Goldsmith is a music critic, and for years presented the popular radio programme *Performance Today* on National Public Radio, which brought classical music closer to a wider audience. His book *The Inextinguishable Symphony* takes its name from the symphony of the same name by Carl Nielsen, which the *Kulturbund* was preparing to perform when it was dissolved.

The Jüdische Kulturbund was founded in Berlin in 1933, as Jews were starting to be excluded from their professions. As it was forbidden for Jewish artists to perform in public, the *Kulturbund* provided them with opportunity to work. It opened with a performance of Lessing's *Nathan the Wise*. Performances, concerts, lectures and exhibitions were financed by membership fees, and by 1934, the Kulturbund had 20,000 members. In 1941, the *Kulturbund* was closed down and many of its members were killed. The *Kulturbund* gave the Nazis the chance to deny Jews were facing discrimination, and for this reason its members were also criticized by other Jews.

Rudolf Schwarz (1905–1994) (l. 3) was a pianist and conductor. He was born and studied in Austria before working in Düsseldorf and Karlsruhe. From 1936 until 1941 he was the musical director of the *Jüdische Kulturbund* in Berlin. Deported to Auschwitz in 1943, he survived the death marches and was interned in Sachsenhausen and then Bergen-Belsen. After the war he moved first to Sweden and then to Britain, where he was the director of various symphony orchestras, including the City of Birmingham Symphony Orchestra and the BBC Symphony Orchestra.

1 **a** L könnte den S das folgende Schema geben, das sie in Still- oder Partnerarbeit ausfüllen, bevor die Ergebnisse gesammelt werden. Als Vorbereitung auf Aufgabe 2 könnte auch eine Spalte „My own experience of the music" hinzugefügt werden:

Why the performance is special for

Rosemarie and Günther	Musicians and audience in general
Rosemarie felt someone besides the conductor was leading the orchestra; feeling of awe, like that experienced when in the presence of a natural phenomenon.	The music took possession of them; not aware of time passing; united by the spirit of the music; realize others have been in similar, desperate situations; given hope by the message of the symphony; audience were stunned at first, then showed their emotions.

b Bei der Bearbeitung dieser Aufgabe sollen die S versuchen zu abstrahieren.

Possible answers:
– The experience of music unites the audience and the orchestra.
– Music helps people to forget the outside world.
– Music can mirror personal experience and show listeners they are not alone.
– Music can console and give hope.
– Experiencing a concert can be a pleasure shared with others.
– It can be an unforgettable experience.

2 Diese Aufgabe sollte mit Hilfe der bei Aufgabe 1 erstellten Tabelle einzeln bearbeitet und in Partnerarbeit und/oder im Unterrichtsgespräch verglichen werden.

Individual answers.

3 Bei dieser Schreibaufgabe sollen S nicht nur den Text umwälzen, sondern spekulieren, was aus Rosemarie und Günther in den USA geworden ist. Deshalb könnte es hilfreich sein, sie zunächst in Partnerarbeit die Geschichte weiterspinnen und stichwortartig notieren zu lassen. Alternativ können Sie eine *writing conference* durchführen (vgl. S. 429). Die S sollten beachten, dass die beiden an eine Respektsperson schreiben, auch wenn es sich um einen persönlichen Brief handelt.

Individual answers.

4 Bei der Präsentation der Musikstücke oder bei der schriftlichen Ausarbeitung müssen sich die S darüber im Klaren sein, dass sie nicht einfach irgendein „Lieblingsstück" beschreiben, sondern die Wirkung differenziert begründen sollen.

Individual answers.

⌒ *Translate ll. 8–23 into German.*

5 Architecture: Rising from the Ashes

Nachdem die S die Verarbeitung von Konflikten in verschiedenen Kunstformen untersucht haben, steht dieser letzte Abschnitt im Zeichen der Versöhnung. Den S soll bewusst werden, welche Rolle die Architektur bei der Überwindung einer konfliktreichen Vergangenheit spielt, denn sie prägt die Umgebung, in der wir leben, und beeinflusst Vergessen und Erinnern.

Versöhnung wird anhand der Städte Coventry und Dresden exemplarisch demonstriert, symbolisiert durch den Wiederaufbau der Kathedrale von Coventry und der Frauenkirche in Dresden. Neben der für sie charakteristischen Architektur bietet die Kathedrale von Coventry Skulpturen, mit deren symbolischem Gehalt die S sich auseinandersetzen sollen.

Unterrichts-tipps

Im Gegensatz zu den anderen Abschnitten dieses Kapitels treten hier Texte bewusst in den Hintergrund. Anstatt die Bauwerke durch den Filter von Texten kennen zu lernen, sollen sich die S mit Bildmaterial beschäftigen und ihre Reaktionen in Rollenspielen und Diskussionen umsetzen. In einer projektorientierten Aufgabe können die S über die einzigartige europäische Städtepartnerschaft zwischen Coventry und Dresden recherchieren. Als Transfer stellen sie Beispiele für Architektur oder Skulpturen vor, die ihnen persönlich etwas bedeuten.

Als Einstieg in diesen Abschnitt sollen die S in Partner- oder Kleingruppenarbeit die Frage nach dem Wiederaufbau zerstörter Bauwerke diskutieren und stichwortartig die wichtigsten Gedanken notieren, die für oder gegen die drei im SB genannten Optionen sprechen. Sie dienen als Anhaltspunkte und Wegweiser durch diesen Abschnitt.

→ *WB, ex. 6*   Anschließend lesen die S die kurze Einführung.

A Coventry: Destruction and Reconciliation

VIDEO

Video	
Source	*Coventry: Rising from the Ashes*, 1994
Topic:	The building of the new Coventry Cathedral
Text form:	Documentary
Length:	11:19 minutes
Level:	Basic/advanced
Skills/activities:	Analysing architecture

Didaktisch-methodische Hinweise

Sofort nach ihrer Zerstörung im November 1940 wurde der Wiederaufbau der Kathedrale Coventrys beschlossen, und zu Weihnachten 1940 rief der Dompropst zu Vergebung und Versöhnung auf. Seit dieser Zeit setzt sich die Gemeinde von Coventry weltweit für Frieden und Versöhnung zwischen Konfliktparteien ein. Durch Betrachtung von Fotos der Kirche und zweier bedeutender Skulpturen, die dort zu finden sind, sollen die S diese Friedensbotschaft nachvollziehen und im Anschluss noch einmal das grundsätzliche Für und Wider eines Wiederaufbaus abwägen. Als Materialbasis dienen die Fotos; der Ausschnitt auf dem Video / der DVD (vgl. das Transkript auf S. 275–277) kann v.a. für leistungsstärkere S ergänzend eingesetzt werden.

Unterrichts-tipps

Der kurze Einführungstext bietet Hintergrundinformationen zu dem Filmausschnitt, den die S un-mittelbar im Anschluss an die Lektüre sehen sollten. Aufgaben 1–2 sollten in Kleingruppen bearbeitet werden, damit alle S die Möglichkeit haben, sich an dem Gespräch zu beteiligen.

Der folgende Wortschatz kann für die Bearbeitung des Themas von Nutzen sein:
architect, medieval, modern, integrate sth. into sth. else, rubble, altar, beams, skeleton of a building, arched window, tower, spire, stone, brick, chapel, sculpture, sculptor, two figures, cast-iron, bronze, embrace, majestic, triumphant, folds of the tunic, spear, wings, horns, in chains.

Info

Coventry is a city in the English Midlands. Today, it is an industrial centre known for the production of motor cars and aircraft engines. During the first half of the 20th century it gained importance as an armaments centre, which made it a target during the Second World War. The air raid on Coventry in November, 1940, destroyed the medieval cathedral, much of the old city centre and killed 568 of its citizens. At Christmas 1940, Provost Howard called on Britain and the British Commonwealth to forgive and to rebuild links with Germany once the war was over. At the time, this was considered a controversial viewpoint.

Coventry Cathedral: The original cathedral, destroyed during the air raid on Coventry, dates back to the middle ages. The day after the air raid in November 1940 it was decided that a new cathedral should be built. It was designed by the British architect Sir Basil Spence and was consecrated in 1962. Cf. also www.know-britain.com/churches/coventry_cathedral_1.html · 1.8.2003.

Saint Michael, the Archangel: Saint Michael's Feast Day is celebrated on 29 September. Venerated by the Jews as the highest angel, St Michael has also been revered by Christians. A well-known passage in the Revelations (12:7–9) about the 'war in heaven' led to St Michael being honoured as 'captain of the heavenly host', protector of Christians in general and soldiers in particular. The cathedral of Coventry is dedicated to St Michael.

Josefina de Vasconcellos (born 1904) comes from a wealthy Brazilian family, but has lived all her life in England. In 1921 she was awarded a scholarship to the Royal Academy in London. Her religion has always influenced her art and her naturalistic style. The statue 'Reconciliation', which was donated to Coventry Cathedral in 1995 by Sir Richard Branson, can also be seen at the Berlin Wall and in Hiroshima.

Sir Jacob Epstein (1880–1959) was a British sculptor of portraits and monumental figures. He was born in New York City of Russian-Polish descent. He studied at the Art Students League in New York and at the École des Beaux-Arts in Paris with Auguste Rodin. After 1905 Epstein lived in England, and became a British citizen in 1910.

Lösungs-hinweise

1 a
- He wanted the ruins to be a reminder of the destruction caused by war.
- He wanted to make sure that people never forget what happened.
- He wanted to emphasize the fact that there has always been a cathedral in Coventry.
- He wanted the cathedral to be a monument to the people of Coventry who lost their lives in the Second World War.
- He wanted to contrast old and new.

b
- Visitors will be reminded of the past; perhaps it will come alive for them and they will think about the destruction caused during the war.
- They will be impressed by the new, modern building, which perhaps gives hope that life continues after destruction.
- The contrast between old and new will make them think more about the building they are visiting.
- It will underline the message of forgiveness and reconciliation.

2 'St Michael Subduing the Devil':
- The figure of St Michael stands with his wings spread out wide, with open arms and legs wide apart, which demonstrates strength and power: this could be the strength and power of goodness.

- His pose also demonstrates peace: he is holding his spear upright and not pointing it at the enemy, and his open arms signify an attitude of peace and not of aggression.
- The devil is lying at St Michael's feet, his arms are tied behind him, his feet are tied together, too: he is the prisoner who has been overcome by the Angel, so good has overcome evil.
- Altogether, this shows that good overcomes evil, and that goodness should always be prepared to meet the enemy with open arms and not with hostility.

'Reconciliation':
- The two figures represent opposites: man and woman, whose bodies are facing each other from opposite directions.
- They are kneeling, and whereas their knees are some distance apart, their upper bodies are leaning towards each other, and their arms are round each other, so that their bodies seem to form a bridge.
- Their heads are bowed, and their faces are hidden, which shows extreme sadness.
- They do not seem to be enemies: there is no good or bad.
- They are united in their sorrow.
- These seem to symbolize the idea that people should overcome their differences and realize what they share – sorrow and loss.

⬭ *What did you note down about rebuilding towns, buildings or monuments as a symbol of reconciliation and forgiveness (cf. note on p. 137)? Has what you have learned about and seen from Coventry Cathedral made you reconsider any of your ideas? Explain your answer.*

❖ ⬭ *In groups of four, imagine you are visiting Coventry Cathedral, and you are interviewed by a reporter from a local radio station, who is doing a feature on why young people visit Coventry Cathedral. He wants to know whether young people understand the cathedral's message and whether it is relevant for them. Based on tasks 1a and b and 2, prepare the interviewer's questions and your answers. You can then either act out the interview or record it and present it to the class as a radio feature.*

SB, S. 138   **B Dresden: Obliteration and Rebirth**

Topic:	The role of architecture in dealing with the past
Text form:	Photos
Level:	Basic
Skills/activities:	Analysing architecture

Didaktisch-methodische Hinweise

Nach ihrer Zerstörung 1945 blieb die Frauenkirche im Zentrum Dresdens Ruine. Erst nach der Wiedervereinigung wurde entschieden, sie originalgetreu und unter Verwendung der erhaltenen Steine bis zum 800-jährigen Stadtjubiläum Dresdens 2006 wieder aufzubauen. Somit lernen die S eine Form des Wiederaufbaus kennen, die der Coventrys entgegensteht. Die Gedanken der S zum Einstiegsimpuls auf S. 137 werden hier erneut reflektiert, wenn die S in einem Rollenspiel das Für und Wider eines originalgetreuen Wiederaufbaus diskutieren. Recherchen zur Städtepartnerschaft Coventry–Dresden ermöglichen es, das Thema Vergebung und Versöhnung weiter zu verfolgen.

Unterrichts-tipps

Folgender Wortschatz könnte bei der Bearbeitung nützlich sein:
dome (wobei auf den Unterschied zum deutschen *Dom = cathedral* hingewiesen werden sollte), *wipe out, air raid, reunification, orb and cross* (= *Turmkreuz*), *craftsman, restore, symbolize, landmark, intention, observer.*

Info

Dresden is the capital of Saxony. The city developed as an important cultural centre in the 17th century, but suffered severe damage during the Seven Years' War (1756–1763). It was rebuilt in the baroque and rococo styles, the beauty of which gave it the name 'the Florence on the Elbe'. Dresden developed into an important industrial centre in the late 19th century. On the night of 13 February, 1945, hundreds of Allied bombers released a firestorm of bombs on Dresden, killing over 13,000 people and destroying 80 percent of the city. In the 1950s young people from Coventry travelled to Dresden to help rebuild the Deaconess Hospital, which had been destroyed by British bombers, and a group of Germans went to Coventry to build the vestry of the Cathedral – the process of reconciliation had begun. Coventry and Dresden were twinned in 1956.

Frauenkirche: Designed by Georg Bähr, it was completed in 1743. With its concave sandstone dome it resembled a huge bell. The *Frauenkirche* miraculously survived the massive bomb attacks of February, 1945, but as the interior had been destroyed by fire, the sandstone pillars could not withstand the weight of the dome, and the building collapsed on 15 February, 1945. Its ruins stood as a reminder of the horrors of war. After the reunification of Germany an initiative was started to raise funds for the restoration of the church. Although initially many citizens of Dresden were against the project, worldwide offers of support from private sponsors led to the restoration, which has been financed exclusively by donations. Much of the old material has been used in rebuilding the church.

Lösungs-hinweise

1 **a** Die offen gestellte Aufgabe im Rollenspiel dient weniger einem Transfer als der Konfrontation mit der Idee des Wiederaufbaus. Dabei beziehen sich die S auf die Auseinandersetzung mit den Bildern der Kathedrale von Coventry und auf die Auflage, die Kirche originalgetreu und unter Verwendung des ursprünglichen Materials wieder aufzubauen. Das Rollenspiel soll ihnen helfen, sich eine eigene Meinung zum Wieder-aufbau der Kirche zu bilden.

Individual answers.

b Individual answers.

2 Individual answers.

3 Diese Transferaufgabe ergibt sich vor allem aus der Betrachtung der Kathedrale von Coventry und der Skulpturen.

Individual answers.

◯ *Has what you have learned about and seen from the* Frauenkirche *in Dresden made you reconsider any of your ideas about rebuilding monuments which have been destroyed in war? Would you still stand by what you noted down? Explain your answer.*

SB, S. 140 ## Getting Along in English

Didaktisch-methodische Hinweise

Drei unterschiedliche Situationen, in denen Menschen im alltäglichen Leben mit Kunst in Kontakt kommen, bilden die Grundlage für diesen Abschnitt (vgl. die Dialoge auf CD2, *track* 7 und 8; die Transkripte auf S. 277–278). Die S erfahren, wie man sich nach dem kulturellen Angebot einer Stadt erkundigt, wie man ein Gespräch über einen Film führt und wie man mangelnde Kenntnisse im Bereich der Malerei überspielt. So weit wie möglich wird *everyday English* benutzt. Die ersten zwei Dialoge stehen im Zusammenhang miteinander, während der letzte Dialog eine neue Situation darstellt.

Info

Lady Godiva's Church [gə'daɪvə] (task 1a, dialogue): In 1043 a Benedictine monastery was established in Coventry by the Earl of Mercia and his wife, Lady Godiva. In a dispute over taxes which the earl demanded from Coventry, he promised to ease the taxes if she rode naked through the marketplace. Lady Godiva took up the challenge and rode naked through the town (possibly covered only by her long hair). In the 17th century, a detail was added that Lady Godiva had ordered the people of the town to stay indoors during her ride, but that a boy named Tom dared to look at her. This is the origin of the term 'peeping tom'. Whether any part of the story is true is uncertain.

*Lösungs-
hinweise*

CD

1 **a** Der Dialog befindet sich auf CD2, *track 7*; das Transkript auf S. 277.
Neben den Ortsnamen und der Fülle von Angeboten, die aufgelistet werden, könnten Michaels Begeisterung für Automobile und der leicht gereizte Unterton seiner Freundin Sandra die S irritieren, so dass es sich zunächst empfiehlt, den Text ein Mal ohne Vorbereitung von der CD zu präsentieren. „Vintage cars" sollte semantisiert und darauf hingewiesen werden, dass der Begriff *Oldtimer* im Englischen nicht in diesem Kontext verwendet wird. Danach lesen die S die Einführung und den Hörauftrag und hören den Text ein zweites Mal. Beim Sammeln der Ergebnisse sollten folgende Begriffe erklärt bzw. ergänzt werden: *crafts, craftspeople, pottery, carving, antiques, collectables.*

- Michael is interested in vintage cars.
- Sandra definitely does not share his interests, and is annoyed because his old car has broken down.
- Coventry was destroyed during the war, and was rebuilt in the 1950s and 60s, it is an ugly mixture of old and new; it has a cathedral, a transport museum and Lady Godiva's church.
- Ansley has an Antiques centre with crafts, made by local craftspeople, such as pottery and carvings; it also offers antiques.
- (i) free of charge (ii) calendar of events (iii) we're sold out.

b Bevor die S diese Aufgabe bearbeiten, kann der Text zur Vorbereitung ein drittes Mal vorgespielt werden, um den S die Gelegenheit zu geben, auch die sprachlichen Mittel, die für einen solchen Dialog notwendig sind, zu notieren, z.B.
'How can I help you?', 'one of the finest examples of', 'a map of the city centre', 'have a quick look at sth.', 'it's definitely worth visiting', 'available'.

CD **2** **a** Der Dialog befindet sich auf CD2, *track 8*; das Transkript auf S. 278.
In einem Unterrichtsgespräch können Wendungen, die für die Bewertung eines Films nützlich sein können, gesammelt und an der Tafel geordnet werden. Um uniforme Begriffe wie *nice* zu ersetzen, muß L genügend Hilfen geben, damit möglichst differenzierte Wendungen gesammelt werden, z.B.:

Like	Dislike
The casting was good.	The casting was bad.
The acting was excellent.	The acting was poor/unconvincing/wooden.
The story(line) was exciting/interesting/intriguing.	The story was unlikely/boring/dull/confusing.
The screenplay was successful / well thought-out.	The screenplay was not well written / amateurish.
The photography was brilliant / breath-taking.	The photography was not very imaginative.

The music was beautiful/stirring/moving.	The music did not fit the story / was too overpowering.
The special effects were spectacular. You could really identify with the characters.	The special effects were unspectacular. The characters were shallow.
The film was highly enjoyable.	The film was awful.
I would recommend everyone to see it.	I wouldn't wish it on my worst.

b <u>Michael</u>: a great film; plenty of action; a thrilling ending; the acting was superb; Jennifer Lopez is a great actress; special effects were great.

<u>Sandra</u>: I didn't find the ending that convincing; her make-up still perfect after all the bombing; at least the characters in Titanic were more interesting; they were all wooden; that ghastly film.

c Individual answers.

CD **3** Der Dialog befindet sich auf CD2, *track* 9; das Transkript auf S. 278.
Vor dem Hören lesen die S die Anleitung und Aufgabe 3a. Es sollte der Hinweis erfolgen, dass Anitas Verhalten nicht ganz ernst zu nehmen ist. Hierbei könnte die Wendung *tongue in cheek* eingeführt werden.

a It's very harmonious; well-structured; the use of colour is autumnal; extremely original; the way he covers the canvas; a very interesting composition.

b
– It's harmonious and well-structured;
– it's extremely original, a very interesting composition;
– the way he covers the canvas.

c Possible answers:
– I wouldn't say I was an expert, but ...
– That reminds me of Picasso/Renoir/Mondrian/etc.
– I think I've seen something similar in London/Paris/etc.
– The use of colour is impressive/original/spectacular/calming/soothing.
– Your paintings are very interesting. What did you have in mind when you were painting them?
– I can't say I quite understand what the artist is trying to express.

⃝ In folgendem Spiel, das auch das Improvisationstalent der S und ihr sprachliches Können trainiert (Fähigkeiten, die sie im fremdsprachigen Ausland jeden Tag einsetzen müssen), wenden die S das soeben Gelernte an. Das Spiel greift auch auf das „Lead-in" und die Seite „Working with Pictures" (SB, S. 223) zurück.
L bringt Kalenderblätter, Poster usw. mit moderner Kunst mit. Die Klasse bildet Gruppen, und jede Gruppe erhält ein Bild und folgenden Auftrag:

Imagine you are a guide in a museum of modern art. Present your picture to a group of tourists. Describe what it represents, interpret it for the tourists, and comment on it. The tourists do not know anything about modern art, so you must give them the impression that they are learning something new.

Nach einer kurzen Vorbereitung wählt jede Gruppe einen Experten, der der Klasse das Bild eindrucksvoll erläutert und es mit seinem ganzen Sachverstand kommentiert.

Watch Your Language

Auf dieser Seite wird vor allem die Verwendung der Präsens-Zeitgruppe thematisiert – ein Bereich der englischen Grammatik, der besonders beim Verfassen von Inhaltsangaben und von Buch- und Filmbesprechungen wichtig ist und den S oft Probleme bereitet. Während in Erzählungen bzw. narrativen Texten zumeist das *past tense* (vgl. *CEG* §86b, 89c) verwendet wird, benutzt man bei der zusammenfassenden Wiedergabe das *present tense* (*CEG* §75c). Nur wenn auf etwas zurückgeblickt wird, was vor der Erzählgegenwart geschehen ist, wird – entsprechend den üblichen Regeln der Zeitenverwendung – entweder das *past tense* oder das *present perfect* gebraucht.

Im einführenden Text werden zunächst häufige Fehler lokalisiert. Dabei werden auch einige lexikalische bzw. stilistische Fehler einbezogen, damit sich die S nicht einseitig auf die *tense*-Problematik konzentrieren können. Anschließend wenden die S ihre Kenntnisse an, indem sie bei der Wiedergabe vergangener Ereignisse eine Form der *past tense*-Gruppe verwenden (Aufgabe 2a), in einer Inhaltsangabe aber eine Form der *present tense*-Gruppe (Aufgabe 2b). Zum Schluss verfassen die S unter Verwendung der *present tense*-Gruppe eine kurze Inhaltsangabe.

*Unterrichts-
tipps*

S mit einem ausgeprägten expliziten Grammatikwissen können die Aufgaben in der vorgesehenen Reihenfolge bearbeiten. Da der Einführungstext keine Formen der *past-tense*-Gruppe enthält, müssen sie beim Ausfüllen der Zeile „Telling a Story" in der Tabelle auf ihr Vorwissen zurückgreifen. Bei einem stärker induktiv ausgerichteten Vorgehen korrigieren die S zunächst den Text und bearbeiten – nach mündlicher Sicherung der Regeln für die Verwendung der *present*- bzw. *past tense*-Gruppe – Aufgabe 2, bevor sie abschließend die Tabelle ausfüllen.

*Lösungs-
hinweise*

1 a

	Referring to what happens ('Erzählgegenwart')	Referring to what happened in the past (Handlung vor der 'Erzählgegenwart')	Referring to what will happen in the future (Handlung nach der 'Erzählgegenwart')
Telling a story	Simple Past or Past Progressive	Past Perfect or Past Perfect Progressive	*would* + infinitive
Writing a review, book report, etc.	Simple Present or Present Progressive	Simple Past, Past Progressive or Present Perfect	*will*-future

b who; cannot / are unable to; is; by the name of / named / called; turns up; suspects; is; represents; i.e. / that is; begins; plant; reach; takes; the latter / Fowler; decides; betrays.

2 a Hier muss deutlich darauf hingewiesen werden, dass es sich hierbei um eine auf Tatsachen beruhende Biographie, d.h. eine „wahre" Geschichte handelt.

1 met; would change
2 fled; returned; could not; had begun / were beginning
3 made; would remain / remained

b
1 meets; will change
2 flees; returns; cannot; have begun / are beginning
3 make; will remain / remains

3 Individual answers.

Topic Vocabulary: 'The Arts'

Art
work of art
creator
creative
aesthetic

Displaying Art
art gallery
museum
display sth.
be on display
exhibition
exhibit sth.
an exhibit

The Creative Process
skill
produce a work of art
imagination
an artist's medium

Visual Arts
painting
drawing
portrait
still life
oil paints
watercolour
tempera
collage
graphics
video installation
paint sth.
visual
graphic
decorative
(make a) sculpture
statue
made of sth.
bronze
cast-iron
wood
painter
craftsman/-woman

Architecture
architect
interior designer
cathedral
dome
arched window
spire
tower

Literature
literary
poetic
write sth.
author/writer
poet
playwright

Performing Arts
acting
act (in a play/film)
actor/actress
perform a play
production (of a play)
direct a play
curtain
scenery
lighting
props
costumes
revolving stage
music
compose a piece of
  music
give a concert
composer
musician
orchestra
musical
concert hall
venue

Reacting to Art
audience
visit / go to an ex-
  hibition /a concert
observe sth.
experience sth.
have access to art
controversial
innovative
luxury
investment
appreciate sth.
soothing
console sb.
disturb sb.
provocative
inspirational
make you ask questions
give hope
mirror personal
  experience
help sb. forget the outside
  world
entertain sb.

Patronage
support an artist /
  art with public/
  private funds
rely on public grants /
  private sponsorship
corporate sponsorship
private donation
tax-deductible
donate sth. to a museum
subsidy

VIDEO A Shakespearian Performance

SB, p. 132   *The passages in blue typeface are from* Romeo and Juliet.

Fennyman:	Is this alright?
Preacher:	Licentiousness is made a show! Vice is made a show! Vanity and pride likewise made a show. This is the very business of show!
Wabash:	T-t-t-two; t-t-two households ...
Shakespeare:	We're lost
Henslowe:	No, it will turn out well.
Shakespeare:	How will it?
Henslowe:	I don't know. It's a mystery.
Chorus:	Two households, both alike in dignity,
	In fair Verona (where we lay our scene),
	From ancient grudge break to new mutiny,
	Where civil blood makes civil hands unclean.
	From forth the fatal loins of these two foes
	A pair of star-cross'd lovers take their life;
	Whose misadventur'd piteous overthrows
	Doth with their death bury their parents' strife. [...]
	The which if you with patient ears attend,
	What here shall miss, our toil shall strive to mend.
Shakespeare:	Wonderful.
Wabash:	Was it ... good?
Sampson:	Gregory, on my word, we'll not carry coals.
Gregory:	No, for then we should be colliers.
Sampson:	I mean, and we be in choler, we'll draw.
Sam:	Master Shakespeare.
Shakespeare:	Luck be with you, Sam. Sam!
Sam:	It's not my fault, Master Shakespeare. I could do it yesterday.
Shakespeare:	Do me a speech. Do me a line.
Sam:	'Parting is such sweet sorrow.'
Henslowe:	Another little problem.
Shakespeare:	What do we do now?
Henslowe:	The show must, you know, ...
Shakespeare:	Go on!
Henslowe:	Juliet does not come on for 20 pages. It will be alright.
Shakespeare:	How will it?
Henslowe:	I don't know. It's a mystery.
Sampson:	Let them begin.
Gregory:	I will frown as I pass by, and let them take it as they list.
Sampson:	Nay, as they dare. I will bite my thumb at them, which is disgrace to them if they bear it.
Abram:	Do you bite your thumb at us, sir?
Sampson:	I do bite my thumb, sir.
Abram:	Do you bite your thumb at us, sir?
Henslowe:	Excuse me. Can we talk? We have no Juliet.
Burbage:	No Juliet?
Viola:	No Juliet?
Henslowe:	It'll be alright, Madam.
Juliet:	What happened to Sam?
Henslowe:	Who are you?
Viola:	Thomas Kent.
Henslowe:	Do you know it?
Viola:	Every word.

Romeo:	I'll go along no such sight to be shown,
	But to rejoice in splendour of mine own.
Lady Capulet:	Nurse, where's my daughter? Call her forth to me.
Nurse:	Now by my maidenhead at twelve years old,
	I bade her come. What, lamb! What, ladybird!
	God forbid, where's this girl?
	What, lamb! What, ladybird! What, Juliet?
Juliet:	How now, who calls?
Burbage:	We'll all be put in the clink.
Henslowe:	See you in jail.
Nurse:	Your mother ... your mother.
Juliet:	Madam, I am here, what is your will?
Lady Capulet:	This is the matter. Nurse, give leave a while,
	We must talk in secret. Nurse, come back again,
	I have remember'd me, thou'st hear our counsel.
	Thou knowest my daughter's of a pretty age.
Nurse:	Faith, I know her age unto an hour.
Lady Capulet:	She's not fourteen.
Nurse:	I'll lay fourteen of my teeth –
	And yet to my teen be it spoken, I have but four–
Lady Capulet:	Tell me, daughter Juliet,
	How stands your dispositions to be married?
Juliet:	It is an honour that I dream not of.
Romeo:	Hold, Tybalt! Good, Mercutio!
Mercutio:	I'm sped.
Romeo:	Courage, man, the hurt cannot be much.
Mercutio:	Ask for me tomorrow and you shall find me a grave man.
Fennyman:	'Such mortal drugs I have, but Mantua's law
	Is death to any he that utters them.'
	Then him, then me.
Benvolio:	Romeo, away, be gone!
	The citizens are up, and Tybalt slain.
	Stand not amaz'd, the prince will doom thee death
	If thou art taken. Hence be gone, away!
Romeo:	O, I am fortune's fool.
Benvolio:	Why dost thou stay?
Officer:	Which way ran he that kill'd Tybalt?
	That murderer, which way ran he?
Benvolio:	There lies Tybalt.
Officer:	Up, sir, go with me;
	I charge thee in the prince's name obey.
Prince:	Where are the vile beginners of this fray?
Shakespeare:	'O, I am fortune's fool!' You are married? 'If you be married, my grave is like to be my wedding bed.'
Juliet:	Art thou gone so, love, lord, ay husband, friend?
	I must hear from thee every day in the hour,
	For in a minute there are many days.
	O, by this count I shall be much in years
	Ere I again behold my Romeo!
Romeo:	Farewell!
Juliet:	O think'st thou we shall ever meet again?
	Methinks I see thee now, thou art so low,
	As one dead in the bottom of a tomb.
	Either my eyesight fails, or thou look'st pale.
Romeo:	And trust me, love, in my eye so do you:
	Dry sorrow drinks our blood. Adieu, adieu!

Friar Lawrence:	Take thou this vial, being then in bed,
	And this distilling liquor drink thou off,
	No warmth, no breath shall testify thou livest;
	And in this borrow'd likeness of shrunk death
	Thou shalt continue two and forty hours,
	And then awake as from a pleasant sleep.
Romeo:	What ho, apothecary!
	Come hither, man. I see that thou art poor.
	Hold, there is forty ducats; let me have
	A dram of poison ...
Apothecary:	Such mortal drugs I have, but Mantua's law
	Is death to any he that utters them.
Romeo:	Art thou so ...
Apothecary:	My poverty, but not my will, consents.
Romeo:	I pay thy poverty and not thy will.
Romeo:	Eyes, look your last!
	Arms, take your last embrace! and lips, O you
	The doors of breath, seal with a righteous kiss
	A dateless bargain to engrossing Death!
	Come bitter conduct, come, unsavoury guide!
	Thou desperate pilot, now at once run on
	The dashing rocks thy seasick weary bark!
	Here's to my love! O true apothecary!
	Thy drugs are quick. Thus with a kiss I die.
Juliet:	Where is my lord?
	I do remember well where I should be;
	And there I am. Where is my Romeo?
Nurse:	Dead.
Juliet:	What's this? A cup clos'd in my true love's hand?
	Poison I see hath been his timeless end.
	O happy dagger,
	This is thy sheath; there rest, and let me die.
Chorus:	A glooming peace this morning with it brings,
	The sun for sorrow will not show his head.
	Go hence to have more talk of these sad things;
	Some shall be pardon'd and some punished:
	For never was a story of more woe
	Than this of Juliet and her Romeo.

VIDEO ## *Henry V:* Prologue

SB, p. 132	*Chorus:*	O for a Muse of fire that would ascend
		The brightest heaven of invention,
		A kingdom for a stage, princes to act
		And monarchs to behold the swelling scene.
		Then should the warlike Harry, like himself,
		Assume the port of Mars, and at his heels
		(Leash'd in, like hounds) would famine, sword and fire
		Crouch for employment. But pardon, gentles all,
		The flat unraised spirits that have dar'd
		On this unworthy scaffold, to bring forth
		So great an object. Can this cockpit hold
		The vasty fields of France? Or may we cram

Within this wooden O the very casques
That did affright the air at Agincourt?
On your imaginary forces work.
Suppose within the girdle of these walls
Are now confin'd two mighty monarchies,
Whose high upreared and abutting fronts
The perilous narrow ocean parts asunder:
Piece out our imperfections with your thoughts;
Think when we talk of horses that you see them
Printing their proud hoofs i' th' receiving earth;
For 'tis your thoughts that now must deck our kings,
Carry them here and there, jumping o'er times,
Turning th' accomplishment of many years
Into an hour-glass. For the which supply
Admit me Chorus to this history,
Who, Prologue-like, your humble patience pray,
Gently to hear, kindly to judge, our play.

VIDEO Two Performances of *Henry V*

SB, p. 134 The BBC TV film version starring David Gwillim uses the text shown below. The film version starring Kenneth Branagh does not use the full text; omissions are shown in square brackets [ ]. There are also occasional variations in words and pronunciations between the two versions.

Act IV, Scene iii

Gloucester:	Where is the king?
Bedford:	The king himself is rode to view their battle.
Westmorland:	Of fighting men they have full threescore thousand.
Exeter:	There's five to one; besides, they all are fresh.
Salisbury:	[God's arm strike with us!] 'tis a fearful odds.
	[God be wi' you, princes all; I'll to my charge:
	If we no more meet till we meet in heaven,
	Then, joyfully, my noble Lord of Bedford,
	My dear Lord Gloucester, and my good Lord Exeter,
	And my kind kinsman, warriors all, adieu!
Bedford:	Farewell, good Salisbury; and good luck go with thee!
Exeter:	Farewell, kind lord; fight valiantly to-day.
	And yet I do thee wrong to mind thee of it,
	For thou art fram'd of the firm truth of valour.
Bedford:	He is full of valour as of kindness;
	Princely in both.]
Westmorland:	O that we now had here
	But one ten thousand of those men in England
	That do no work today.
King Henry V:	What's he that wishes so?
	My cousin Westmorland? No, my fair cousin.
	If we are mark'd to die, we are enough
	To do our country loss; and if to live,
	The fewer men, the greater share of honour.
	God's will, I pray thee, wish not one man more.
	[By Jove, I am not covetous for gold,
	Nor care I who doth feed upon my cost;

It yearns me not if men my garments wear.
Such outward things dwell not in my desires:
But if it be a sin to covet honour,
I am the most offending soul alive.
No, faith, my coz, wish not a man from England.
God's peace! I would not lose so great an honour
As one man more, methinks, would share from me,
For the best hope I have. O, do not wish one more!]
Rather proclaim it, Westmorland, through my host,
That he which hath no stomach to this fight
Let him depart. His passport shall be made
And crowns for convoy put into his purse.
We would not die in that man's company
That fears his fellowship to die with us.
This day is called the Feast of Crispian.
He that outlives this day, and comes safe home,
Will stand a-tiptoe when the day is nam'd,
And rouse him at the name of Crispian.
He that shall see this day and live old age,
Will yearly on the vigil feast his neighbours,
And say 'Tomorrow is Saint Crispian'.
Then will he strip his sleeve and show his scars.
And say 'These wounds I had on Crispin's day.'
Old men forget, yet all shall be forgot,
But he'll remember, with advantages,
What feats he did that day. Then shall our names,
Familiar in his mouth as household words,
Harry the king, Bedford and Exeter,
Warwick and Talbot, Salisbury and Gloucester,
Be in their flowing cups freshly remember'd.
This story shall the good man teach his son,
And Crispin Crispian shall ne'er go by
From this day to the ending of the world
But we in it shall be remember'd.
We few, we happy few, we band of brothers –
For he today that sheds his blood with me
Shall be my brother; be he ne'er so vile,
This day shall gentle his condition –
And gentlemen in England, now a-bed,
Shall think themselves accurs'd they were not here,
And hold their manhoods cheap whiles any speaks
That fought with us upon Saint Crispin's day.

Act IV, Scene vii

King Henry V: How now! what means this, herald?
Com'st thou again for ransom?

Montjoy: No, great king:
I come to thee for charitable licence,
That we may wander o'er this bloody field
To book our dead, and then to bury them,
To sort our nobles from our common men,
For many of our princes – woe the while –
Lie drown'd and soak'd in mercenary blood,
[So do our vulgar drench their peasant limbs
In blood of princes, and their wounded steeds

Fret fetlock deep in gore and with wild rage
Yerk out their armed heels at their dead masters,
Killing them twice.] O, give us leave, great king,
To view the field in safety and dispose
Of their dead bodies!

King Henry V: I tell thee truly, herald,
I know not if the day be ours or no,
[For yet a-many of your horsemen peer
And gallop o'er the field.]

Montjoy: The day is yours.
King Henry V: Praised be God, and not our strength, for it.
What is this castle call'd that stands hard by?

Montjoy: They call it Agincourt.
King Henry V: Then call we this the field of Agincourt,
Fought on the day of Crispin Crispianus.

Coventry: Destruction and Reconciliation

SB, p. 137

Presenter:	The centre of the city itself was left in ruins. Where once had stood proud factories, shops, offices and houses, now, in a matter of hours, was rendered a mass of rubble.
Newsreader:	The martyred city of Coventry. Amid the wholesale wreckage of a noble city, crushed by the force of hundreds of tons of bombs, the steeple of her one-time beautiful fourteenth-century cathedral looks down on a scene of indescribable desolation.
Presenter:	But the most dreadful news was that St. Michael's Cathedral was now no more than a standing shell.
	The pinnacle of the city's many achievements, however, would be the building of the new cathederal, a symbol of resurrection and reconciliation. Plans for a new cathedral had been discussed back in 1941. Now, ten years later, the project was to begin. A competition was held to select a design and 219 entries were received from all over the Commonwealth. The winning design was Sir Basil Spence's. The design was the subject of some controversy. Comments in the vein of 'a wicked waste of money' summed up the feelings of those opposed to the new construction. Fortunately, the council and reconstruction committee held firm and Sir Basil Spence made a forthright defence of his plans for the new cathedral.
Basil Spence:	Of course, you're bound to start an argument if you build a cathedral now. Because people love the old buildings. So do I, I love the old cathedrals, but remember this: when these old cathedrals that everybody admires were first built, they were modern, they were new. This is the tradition and this is exactly what I am trying to do at Coventry.
Presenter:	Laurence Lee had begun to design the nave windows back in 1952.
Lawrence Lee:	The architect gave us only one condition: that there should be a colour symbolism representing man's life from birth to death, getting richer as it gets towards old age, and finally one light window representing the resurrection. We decided that we would adopt the usual Christian symbolism but that it would be impossible to use bible stories and lives of saints, but rather we should do the thing in a more abstract form.
Presenter:	The entire west wall of the cathedral would consist of 90 panels of glass engraved with figures of saints and martyrs. After working on his sketches for more than five years, John Hutton then laboured for a further two years to recreate the effect on glass.
John Hutton:	This is not coloured glass, it's ordinary British plate glass on which I engrave these figures. Glass engraving has been done for upwards of a thousand years, but in a rather different way. Normally, the glass is laid on the revolving grindstone, but I use a small grindstone on a hand drill and draw on the glass as an artist would. I had to do a lot of experimenting to get the kind of effects that I'm going to need for this job – the degree of brilliance and at the same time the boldness that we needed for the figures at the top of the screen.
Presenter:	By the spring of 1959 the wall of the cathedral was almost complete. A forest of scaffolding was then erected to assemble the roof. Across the channel in France, work had begun on a tapestry of Christ in Glory, designed by Graham Sutherland. This would be the largest tapestry in the world, and the skillful mixing of colours would be the key to matching the artist's original intention.

Weaving the giant tapestry would be the sole occupation of twelve weavers for the next three years. The skills of generations of weavers brought to bear on a tapestry the size of a tennis court made in one piece. This magnificent work would cover the entire east wall of the cathedral.

John Piper was the designer of the baptistry window.

John Piper: When I was first asked to design this window, the shape and size of it, the actual form, had already been decided upon. What it seemed to me to need most of all, was simplifying, unifying in some way, and it's this that I've attempted to do. To me, the colour and form of the whole thing symbolizes the spirit of God descending.

Presenter: By 1960 the roof was finished. In June, a sculpture of St. Michael and the devil by Sir Jacob Epstein was unveiled by his widow.

Mrs. Epstein: Ladies and gentlemen, it is a great pleasure that I now unveil this statue by Jacob Epstein of St Michael overcoming the devil.

Presenter: This was to be one of the last great works by Epstein before he died.

News reporter: The chapel of unity is an independent building linked with the cathedral by a cloister. The building is in the shape of a ten-pointed star, and ten tapered concrete buttresses support the concrete roof. On the north-east side, the walls of the ruins were strengthened, and over them a great arch and porch erected, the architectural link between old and new. The second external chapel, the circular chapel of Christ the servant. This charming architectural feature rounds off the massive end of the cathedral nave.

Presenter: In 1962, the cathedral was almost complete. The problem with mounting the 80-foot spire was overcome by fitting it using a helicopter. This task was actually achieved within 11 minutes. The finishing touch was Geoffrey Clark's flying cross, which was delicately lowered into position.

Presenter: Essentially, Sir Basil Spence's design is a triumph of the spirit and imagination which provides a unique home for the word and spirit of Christ for future generations. The old cathedral tower and the ruins are preserved to symbolize sacrifice, while the new building comfirms the promise of resurrection. The new cathedral was completed in only seven years. Queen Elizabeth and Princess Margaret attended the service of consecration on the 25th May, 1962.

Connie Downes: Just after the cathedral was consecrated, they came to see a new building. They wanted to see a twentieth-century cathedral, and of course a lot of them were quite shocked. The first thing that people notice when they come into the cathedral is the last major work of Jacob Epstein: St. Michael and the devil. And that to me is a very powerful sculpture. We also have in the ruins another of his sculptures, rather a large one, called Ecce Homo.

Presenter: Inside the cathedral the eye is drawn to the magnificent vaulted ceiling and the tapered columns converging on the dominant great tapestry. Either side of Christ are the living creatures mentioned in Revelations, which symbolize the four apostles: St Matthew is depicted as a man, St Luke as a calf, while St John is an eagle and St Mark represented as a lion. Between the feet of Christ is man. The simple beauty of the holy table contrasts beauti-fully with the magnificent cross of silver overlaid with gold. The ages of man: youth, passion, liberal life, old age, wisdom and the gift of the afterlife are represented by the ten great windows. The canopies of the cannon stalls, set beneath the windows, form an avenue of thorns. Gethsemane chapel is used for private prayer. The crown of thorns designed by Sir Basil Spence was a gift of the royal engineers constructed in their own workshops. Here is found the mosaic mural of the angel holding the cup of bitterness designed by Steven Sykes. The chapel of unity provides a stage for religious drama and is devoted to all denominations. From Swe-den comes a mosaic of marble laid as a floor. Elizabeth Shrink's design of a bronze eagle commands a position above the lectern in the nave. The baptistry window is glorious colours ablaze, and the font formed from a boulder brought from Bethlehem in the Holy Land.

Connie Downes: They were impressed, some of them, by the tapestry and by the baptistry window and by the great west window. Others thought it looked like a theatre or a battleship, so you got all sorts of reactions. Now, I think people come just to see it because it's known world-wide.

Getting Along in English

SB, p. 140
Task 1a

Tourist Information: Hello, how can I help you?

Michael: Well, we're waiting for our car to be repaired – we can't pick it up till tomorrow morning, so we'd like to know how we can spend a day in Coventry.

Sandra: Is there anything to see here? It all looks very modern and ugly.

Tourist Information: Well, here's a map of the city centre. As you probably know, Coventry was destroyed during the war, and was rebuilt in the 1950s and 60s. At the time it was considered very up-to-date, but tastes change. However, Coventry Cathedral remains one of the finest examples of post-war modern buildings.

Michael: Aha. Well, we could go and have a quick look at it. Where is it?

Tourist Information: Right here on the map. It's built next to the ruins of the old cathedral as a reminder of the horrors of war. Although theoretically entrance is free of charge, they do request a £3 donation.

Michael: Gosh, that's a bit steep. Are there any museums here?

Tourist Information: Well. I might be touching a sore point considering your car's broken down, but the Coventry Transport Museum has a wonderful collection of vintage and modern vehicles including the ThrustSSC, which broke the world land speed record in 1997.

Michael: That sounds great. I'm a real car enthusiast. More vintage than modern cars, really, which is why I have a Morris.

Sandra: Don't talk to me about your Morris. I think the weather is too nice to be hanging around in museums all day, and I think I have seen enough of cars for today!

Tourist Information: Well, there are the remains of Lady Godiva's church, but you could also go on a coach trip to the Granary Antiques Centre near Ansley.

Sandra: Ah, that sounds better.

Tourist Information: Oh, it's definitely worth visiting. Within the courtyard, there's a selection of crafts available – pottery, carvings, you know – produced by the working craftspeople, together with a range of antiques and collectables.

Sandra: Great. Let's go there! And what shall we do this evening, Michael?

Michael: Do you have a calendar of events?

Tourist Information: Certainly ...

Michael: Hey there's a performance of *Henry V* at the Warwick Arts Centre. Can we buy tickets here?

Tourist Information: I'm sorry, but we're sold out.

Sandra: Well, why don't we just go to a nice pub? So where shall we go now? The Cathedral or the Granary Antiques Centre?

Michael: Well, I would really like to see the Transport Museum, and afterwards we could go to the ...

SB, p. 140
Task 2a

Michael: Well, that was a great film. What a good idea to spend the evening at the cinema!

Sandra: Hmm, I think I would rather have gone to the pub and had a drink.

Michael: What? Didn't you like it? It was great. The photography was excellent and the screenplay was brilliant – there was plenty of action and it had a thrilling ending.

Sandra: I think I really wanted to see something more relaxing than a war film. I don't know why you chose that film. And I didn't find the ending that convincing. It was obvious it was going to end like that. You could see the twist coming a mile away. It was all too obvious.

Michael: Well, perhaps, but the acting was superb. Come on, you have to admit that Jennifer Lopez is a great actress.

Sandra: Yes, I suppose if you could accept her playing the part of an American general, you could believe anything. I didn't find her at all convincing.

Michael: Well, at least the special effects were great.

Sandra: Which special effects? You mean the close-ups on her face as she lay in bed with her make-up still perfect after the bombing?

Michael: Don't be so tetchy. No, I mean the scene where the battleships were sinking. Didn't you find that impressive and moving?

Sandra: Well, give me a sinking *Titanic* any day. At least the characters in *Titanic* were more interesting. You can at least identify with them, whereas here they were all wooden. At least the ending of *Titanic* was moving.

Michael: I didn't realise you were such a romantic. Well, at least this film had a happy ending. When we went to see *Titanic*, I seem to remember you found it all a little too moving. Well, let's go and have a drink before closing time.

Sandra: As I had to sit through that ghastly film, I think the drinks should be on you.

SB, p. 140
Task 3

Anita: Hallo, I'm Anita Woodward from the newspaper *The Kentish Express*. I'm here to ...

Mark: Hallo, I'm Mark Cook from the municipal council. Can I show you around? Erm ... now, the artists exhibiting here are all amateurs, but I think you'll be impressed with the quality of the work. This watercolour, for instance: 'October in Canterbury' ...

Anita: Yes ... it's very ... harmonious, and ... well-structured. And the use of colour is, well, ... autumnal ...

Mark: Erm ... Ah, and what about this one by John, we call him our local Picasso, ...

Anita: Ah. Erm ... extremely ... original, especially the way he covers the canvas ... A very interesting composition indeed.

Mark: Oh, absolutely. Ah, here he is. John, this is Anita, the local rag's new art critic. She certainly knows what she's talking about ...

Die britische Gesellschaft ist von einer Vielzahl von Aspekten geprägt: dem Abschied vom *Empire*, als dessen Vermächtnisse die multikulturelle Gesellschaft und die englische Sprache gelten können, die Monarchie, *devolution*, das Nord-Süd-Gefälle, ein Hang zur Nostalgie. Dieses Kapitel soll den S zu einem differenzierten und zeitgemäßen Verständnis des *United Kingdom* und seiner Einwohner verhelfen.

– In *section 1*, „What It Means to Be British", erfahren die S anhand zweier Reden, welche Werte Großbritannien bestimmen.
– In *section 2*, „The Great Immigrant Experiment", wird den S auf der Basis eines Romanauszugs vor Augen geführt, wie unterschiedlich Einwanderer der ersten und der zweiten Generation ihre ethnische Identität im neuen Land bestimmen.
– In *section 3*, „On Tour in the UK", lernen die S die touristischen Angebote nicht nur Englands, sondern auch der anderen Teile des Vereinigten Königreichs kennen.
– *Section 4*, „The Parts of the Whole", behandelt die *devolution*, mit der Macht an die kleinen Länder des Königreichs zurückgegeben wurde.
– In *section 5*, „This England", stellt England als einen Teil des *United Kingdom* in den Mittelpunkt und betont die Vielschichtigkeit dieser Region.
– *Section 6*, „Pride in Our Past, Confidence in Our Future", behandelt das Thema *Empire* mit seinen Auswirkungen auf die Gegenwart und seiner kontroversen Bewertung.

Neben Sachtexten regen Reden, literarische Texte, ein Gemälde, viele Fotos und ein Sketch die S dazu an, eine eigene, fundierte Sicht auf das Vereinigte Königreich zu entwickeln.

Da es schwer möglich ist, für das Thema *United Kingdom* eine umfassende und repräsentative Wortschatzliste zu erstellen, entfällt für dieses Kapitel die KV „Topic → WB, ex. 9 Vocabulary".

Didaktisches Inhaltsverzeichnis

SB, p.	Title	TM, p.	Text form	Topic	Skills and activities
142	Lead-in	278	photos quotes	images and ideas of Britain	discussing; making a collage
144	Chicken Tikka Massala Robin Cook	282	speech	Britain as a traditionally multicultural country	summarizing a text; writing an editorial; making a timeline
145	Golden Jubilee Speech to Parliament Queen Elizabeth II CD2, track 10	285	speech	the changes that have taken place in GB over 50 years	listening comprehension; comparing texts
146	The Great Immigrant Experiment Zadie Smith	287	novel (extract)	the experience of immigrants	reading comprehension; examining narrative techniques; doing a role play
148	On Tour in the UK	289	–	planning a trip to GB	doing research on the Internet; giving a talk
149	Getting Along in English CD2, track 11	290	–	reserving accommodation	planning a telephone call; writing an email;
150	Devolution in the UK	291	official report	devolution in the UK	information gap activity; comparing results; doing research
151	A New Flag for a Changing Country	293	flags quotes	redesigning the Union Jack	describing pictures; intelligent guessing
152	Down in the North	295	newsmagazine report	social differences in multicultural England	reading comprehension; writing a comment

SB, S. 142 Lead-in

Lern-vokabular

Active vocabulary: Quotes in the 'Lead-in' (p. 142)

innovation, patriotic, epitomize sth., eccentricity, moan about sth.

Didaktisch-methodische Hinweise

Im „Lead-in" wird ein Kaleidoskop von Eindrücken aus Großbritannien präsentiert: Fotos und Zitate zum Thema *Britain and Britishness* entwerfen ein vielschichtiges Bild, das Altes und Neues, Kontroverses und Populäres, Touristisches und Politisches verbindet (zu den Motiven der Fotos vgl. den Lösungshinweis zu Aufgabe 1). Bei den Zitaten wurde auf eine möglichst breite Streuung der Interviewpartner Wert gelegt: Ihre Namen, ihre Sprache oder Angaben zu ihrem Wohnort weisen auf unterschiedliche regionale oder ethnische Hintergründe und verschiedene Bildungsniveaus hin. Ihre Assoziationen zu Großbritannien sind vielfältig und reichen vom Geistreichen zum Trivialen.

Ausgangspunkt für die Arbeit mit dem „Lead-in" sind die Eindrücke der S von Großbritannien, die sie, angeregt durch Fotos und Originalzitate, ergänzen und zu einer allgemeinen Vorstellung von *Britishness* zusammenfügen. Dabei sollten sie erkennen, dass jeder Versuch einer Definition zugleich eine Reduktion ist, die vom Erfahrungshorizont der Person bestimmt wird, die sie formuliert. Am Ende lenken die S ihren Blick auf ihr eigenes Land und erstellen eine Collage zu Deutschland.

Lösungs-hinweise
❖

1 Diese Aufgabe kann zunächst bei geschlossenem Buch durchgeführt werden, um die S nicht durch die Fotos zu beeinflussen. Für die Ideensammlung ist das Kugellagerverfahren möglich (vgl. S. 429). In Kleingruppen notieren die S dann ihre Ideen und strukturieren sie. Eine Gruppe schreibt ihre Ergebnisse an die Tafel (in Form eines Mind-Map oder als Tabelle); die anderen ergänzen.

The photos show (in a clockwise direction starting at bottom left on p. 142):

- Indian women wearing saris outside Buckingham Palace; this illustrates two aspects of modern Britain: the multicultural nature of the country and the traditional institutions, as represented by the monarchy.

- Queen Elizabeth II is not only head of state of the United Kingdom, but also of many other countries, including Canada, and is Head of the Commonwealth. Here she is visiting Canada and talking to some native Canadians. This is an example of the British legacy of Empire and colonialism.

- A pod of the London Eye is directly in front of the Clock Tower of the Houses of Parliament. The Houses of Parliament are often considered to be the mother of Parliaments. The London Eye was erected to commemorate the Millennium. It is a big wheel which is 135 m high and takes about 20 minutes to go round. The picture stands for modern and traditional England side by side.

- A boy group (here, 'Westlife'): Britain's creativity is often expressed in its pop music, which has had global success ever since the Beatles in the 1960s.

- Fox-hunting divides the nation. These young people are not only protesting against cruelty to animals; they also see fox-hunting as a symbol of the decadence of the upper class. It shows also the ambivalent attitude of British people to animals, being both animal lovers and great hunters.

- A young man is doing a street performance in a kilt (in the streets of Edinburgh). Britain has a lively arts scene, and the Edinburgh festival with its many street performers is one of the world's most important arts festivals.

- The Edinburgh tattoo: Each year, the army puts on a spectacle for visitors. This is a symbol of the role the military plays in public life, and the tattoo reveals the prestige and excellence of the British armed forces.

- A Welsh rugby supporter: People in the UK are proud of their national teams and heritages. Sport plays an important role in the British psyche.

2 **a** Possible answers:
'innovation', 'nostalgia trip', 'nation', 'patriotic pride', 'the monarchy', 'fish and chips', 'pint', 'be epitomized by sth.', 'tradition of sth.', 'eccentricity', 'reverberations', 'bundle of countries', 'moan about sth.', 'appreciate sth.', 'proud', 'royal family', 'melting pot'.

b Individual answers.

Differenzierung   **3**   Um das entstandene Bild von *Britishness*, das auch die Ergebnisse aus Aufgabe 1 umfassen soll, zu strukturieren und zu kommentieren, können v.a. für leistungsschwächere S die unten aufgelisteten Zusatzfragen hilfreich sein. Anschließend fügen die S in Gruppen ihre Eindrücke zu einem Gesamtbild zusammen und präsentieren sie, z.B. in Form eines Wandplakats, eines Interviews (z.B. mit einer der zitierten Personen) oder eines Zeitungsartikels.

⬭ *Are there any elements or aspects which appear repeatedly in the pictures or quotes?*

⬭ *Which aspects refer to life in Britain and which to the people of Britain?*

⬭ *Could you imagine any of the quotes coming from Germans talking about their country?*

❖   **4**   Diese Aufgabe sollte zu Hause vorbereitet werden. In der Folgestunde stellen die S in Kleingruppen Ausstellungen von etwa fünf Bildern (oder Bildbeschreibungen) zusammen Der Kurs geht von Ausstellung zu Ausstellung und lässt sich von der

→ *WB, ex. 1*   jeweiligen verantwortlichen Gruppe das Produkt erläutern.

1 What It Means to Be British

In diesem Abschnitt setzen sich die S mit zwei Versuchen auseinander, die Briten als Nation zu erfassen und zu beschreiben. Während Robin Cook Großbritannien als multikulturelle Gesellschaft beschreibt, betont Queen Elizabeth II die menschlichen Werte, die traditionell mit Großbritannien verbunden werden, wie z.B. Pragmatismus und Offenheit. Die hier anklingende Frage nach nationaler Identität kann mit Materialien aus Kapitel 10 vertieft werden (vgl. z.B. „Context Box", SB, S. 189; „My Region, Myself", SB, S. 192).

SB, S. 144 ## A Chicken Tikka Massala Robin Cook

Source:	*Guardian*, 19.04.2001
Topic:	Britain as a traditionally multicultural country
Text form:	Speech
Language variety:	BE
Number of words:	625
Level:	Basic/advanced
Skills/activities:	Summarizing a text, writing an editorial, making a timeline

Lern-vokabular

Active vocabulary: 'Chicken Tikka Massala' (p. 144)

the ethnic composition (ll. 1–2), indigenous to (a place) (l. 4), be driven out by sb. (l. 11), ransom (l. 16), without parallel (l. 21), be home to sth. (l. 22), asset (l. 26), contribute to sth. (l. 26), social cohesion (l. 31), illegal migrant (l. 32), cultural diversity (l. 36), staff (l. 39), recruit sb. (l. 39), broaden sb.'s horizons (l. 42), open to new influences (l. 44), come to terms with sth. (l. 51)

Didaktisch-methodische Hinweise

Cook charakterisiert in seiner Rede die Briten als seit Jahrhunderten multikulturelles Volk. Er betont, dass die Völkervielfalt für die Zukunft Großbritanniens ein bedeutendes Kapital darstellt. Als Symbol für die gelungene Integration ethnischer Gruppen erhebt Cook *Chicken Tikka Massala* zum neuen Nationalgericht: das indische Gericht *chicken tikka*, dem die *massala*-Soße hinzugefügt wurde, um das britische Bedürfnis nach Soße zu befriedigen. Damit verdrängt Cook die üblicherweise mit Großbritannien assoziierten Speisen *fish and chips* und *roast beef and Yorkshire pudding*. *Chicken tikka massala* ist nicht nur ein Beispiel für die Flexibilität der Briten, sondern auch für die Bereitschaft, ausländische Einflüsse anzunehmen.

Unterrichts-tipps

Als Einstimmung können die S ihr Wissen oder Halbwissen, Vorurteile oder Erfahrungen zum Thema britisches Essen äußern:

⬭ *What do you know about British food?*

Anschließend wird den S eine Abbildung von *Chicken Tikka Massala* gezeigt:

⬭ *Does this look like typical English food? What do you think the ingredients could be? Where do you think it might come from?*

Nach der Lektüre kann anhand folgender Aussagen das Verständnis gesichert werden:
1 *Cook maintains there is no such thing as the British race.* (True: cf. l. 2.)
2 *London was first established as the capital by the Angles and Saxons.* (False: It was established by the Romans, cf. l. 10.)
3 *Over 30 different languages are spoken in London.* (False: Over 300 languages are spoken, cf. l. 23.)
4 *In all countries, strict but just immigration laws should exist.* (True: cf. ll. 29–30.)

5 *London is a favourite location for multinational companies because everyone in London speaks English.* (False: It is chosen because the people of London speak so many different languages, l. 39.)

→ WB, ex. 2, 4 6 *Older Britons adapt to new influences more slowly.* (True: ll. 43–44.)

Info

Robin Cook (born 1946) is a member of the Labour Party. Born and educated in Scotland, he entered Parliament in 1974. He was Foreign Secretary (1997–2001) and Leader of the House of Commons (2001–2003), but resigned as a result of Tony Blair's stance on the war in Iraq.

Norman Bishops (l. 12): Although most bishoprics were founded during the Anglo-Saxon time, the invasion of the Normans in 1066 resulted in the rebuilding of most of the cathedrals in England. The cathedrals of Durham, Norwich, Peterborough, St Albans and Winchester are among the finest examples of Norman (also called Romanesque) architecture in England.

A Dutch Prince (l. 13): A reference to William of Orange. After the death of Charles II in 1685, Charles's Catholic brother, James II, became king, much to the dismay of the Protestant Establishment. In 1688 they asked William of Orange, who was married to James's daughter, Mary, to invade Britain and remove James. William did so and was crowned William III and in 1690 James and his forces were defeated at the Battle of the Boyne. This established the Protestant supremacy in Britain.

Richard the Lionheart (l. 14): Richard I, called the Lionheart, was born and raised in France, much of which at the time belonged to the English monarch. In 1189 he became king and in 1190 he joined the Third Crusade. On his journey home, in 1192, he was captured by Duke Leopold of Austria and imprisoned. He was sold to the Holy Roman Emperor, Henry VI, who demanded a huge ransom for him. The English were taxed to pay for Richard's release. As the richest community in England, the Jews paid a large portion.

London as 'home to over 30 ethnic communities' (l. 22): The 2001 census revealed that London has the highest proportion of people from minority ethnic groups. Whereas ethnic minorities comprise 9% of the population of England and Wales, in London it is 29%.

Lösungs-hinweise
◆◆

1 Diese Aufgabe kann am effektivsten in Partnerarbeit gelöst werden. Je zwei Paare vergleichen ihre Ergebnisse untereinander und verständigen sich über die Kriterien, die ihren Gliederungen zu Grunde liegen. Die Einteilungen können unterschiedlich sein.

Possible answers:
Ll. 1–9: Introduction – a mixed race
Ll. 10–17: examples from the past
Ll. 18–26: positive effects of pluralism
Ll. 27–35: controlled immigration
Ll. 36–51: a multi-cultural lifestyle
Ll. 52–53: conclusion – future prospects

◆◆ 〇 Partner A: Paraphrase the following expressions for your partner; they must guess which expression you are referring to: 'naval supremacy' (l. 7), 'pluralism of ancestry' (l. 9), 'without parallel' (l. 21), 'multi-ethnic environment' (l. 44–45). Now listen to your partner's explanation and try and locate the original expressions in the text.

Partner B: Listen to your partner's explanations and try and locate the original expressions in the text. Now paraphrase the following expressions for your partner; he/she must guess which expressions you are referring to: 'imperial expansion' (l. 8), 'hub of the globe' (l. 22), 'trafficking in human beings' (l. 30–31), 'cultural horizons' (l. 42).

Differenzierung **2** Leistungsschwache S sollten zuerst Stichwörter sammeln und dann die Definition formulieren:

'The changing ethnic composition' (ll. 1–2); 'a gathering of countless different races' (l. 3); 'not indigenous to these islands' (l. 4).
According to Cook, the British are not a race, but a people of many different ethnic origins, which are continually changing. Most of them are not natives of the British Isles.

Differenzierung **3** Vgl. den Tipp bei Aufgabe 2.

'London is a perfect hub of the globe' (l. 22); 'an immense asset [...] to the cultural and economic vitality of our nation' (ll. 25–26); 'preferred location for multinational companies' (l. 37); 'young Britons [...] are more open to new influences' (ll. 43–44); 'Chicken Tikka Massala [...] a true British national dish [...] an Indian dish [...] the desire of British people to have their meat served in gravy' (ll. 48–50).
Multi-ethnicity has made London into a multi-cultural centre, and many international firms have set up their headquarters in Britain, which will benefit the country's economy and culture. Young people in Britain are particularly open to the changes brought by different ethnic groups, and this has changed their lifestyle. The dish Chicken Tikka, which was originally an Indian dish, was adapted by adding the Massala sauce to accommodate British taste.

4 Diese Aufgabe eignet sich als Hausaufgabe Die S sollten daran erinnert werden, dass Aufgaben 1–3 diesen Essay vorbereitet haben.

Possible answer:
In Robin Cook's speech yesterday he emphasized the mixed origins of most Britons and made it clear that this pluralism should be regarded as an asset, and that legitimate immigration is necessary to the British economy. Cook went on to point out how not just the economy but other areas of life in Britain as well had benefitted from cultural diversity. As an example of the willingness of the British to accept and adapt to various ethnic influences he named Chicken Tikka Massala as the new British national dish.
In our opinion ...

⬭ *Write a letter to the editor of your local newspaper, reacting – in German – to Cook's speech.*

❖
❖❖ **5** Diese Aufgabe könnte als *on-going task* gestellt werden, den die S auch zu Hause, in Partner- oder Kleingruppenarbeit durchführen können und bis zum Ende der Arbeit am Kapitel „The UK" abgeschlossen haben sollten. Bei den Ergebnissen ist auf eine anschauliche Darstellung zu achten. Als fachübergreifende Alternative könnte ein Zeitstrahl zu den wichtigsten Ereignissen der britischen Geschichte angefertigt werden.

2000 years ago: Celts in Britain (from central Europe) – 43 AD: Roman invasion – 5th century: Angles, Saxons (from Germany, Denmark, the Netherlands) – 9th century: the Vikings (from Scandinavia) – 1066: Norman invasion (from France) – 11th century: Jews arrive from France – 17th century: slaves from Africa – end of WWII: Poles, Italians, West Indians – 1950s/60s: immigrants esp. from the Commonwealth ...

⬭ *Translate ll. 10–21 into German.*

B Golden Jubilee Speech to Parliament   Queen Elizabeth II

Source:	Website of the BBC, 30.4.2003
Topic:	The changes that have taken place in GB over 50 years
Text form:	Speech
Language variety:	BE
Length:	6:35 minutes
Level:	Advanced
Skills/activities:	Listening comprehension, comparing texts

Didaktisch-methodische Hinweise

Königin Elizabeth II beschreibt in dieser Rede (vgl. CD2, *track* 10, und das Transkript auf S. 311–312) den Wandel als Konstante der heutigen Zeit und betont, wie gut die Briten aufgrund ihrer Eigenschaften in der Lage seien, sich diesem Wandel zu stellen. Großbritannien blicke auf eine lange, stolze Geschichte zurück, die den Briten überdauernde Werte vermittelt habe: Pragmatismus, Offenheit, Kreativität, Fairness und Toleranz, insbesondere aber die Bereitschaft, ehrenamtlich tätig zu werden. Die Königin setzt damit trotz partieller Übereinstimmung mit Cook (Großbritannien als multikulturelle Gesellschaft) andere Akzente als der frühere Außenminister. Der Vergleich der beiden Reden zeigt die Schwierigkeit, nationale Identität zu beschreiben. Der Text wird als Hörverstehenstext angeboten; entsprechend dienen die Aufgaben v.a. der Verständnisüberprüfung und dem Vergleich mit der Rede Cooks.

Unterrichts-tipps

Vor dem ersten Hören müssen die S den Hörauftrag zum globalen Erfassen des Texts in Aufgabe 1 gelesen haben. Nachdem sie den Text gehört haben, vergleichen und ergänzen sie in Dreiergruppen ihre Notizen. Vor dem zweiten Hören lesen die S Aufgabe 2 und arbeiten dann arbeitsteilig: Jeder im Dreierteam konzentriert sich auf ein bestimmtes Thema, anschließend tauschen die S ihre Ergebnisse aus. Da der Text nun nicht mehr gehört wird, sind die S dafür verantwortlich, dass ihre Teamkameraden umfassend informiert werden, damit alle (evtl. als Hausaufgabe) Aufgabe 3 lösen können.

Info

Golden Jubilee: The Queen celebrated the 50th anniversary of her accession to the throne in 2002.

The emergence of the Commonwealth: The Commonwealth emerged in the early part of the 20th century, as the 'white' colonies (e.g. Australia and Canada) became more independent from Britain. After World War II, however, it became increasingly difficult for Britain to sustain and control her Empire. Many colonies started to demand independence, which most of them achieved in the 1950s and 60s. Most members of the former Empire chose to remain within the Commonwealth.

Tradition of service: The countless charities in Britain depend to a large extent on voluntary helpers. Devoting free time to voluntary work is common in Britain.

Armed forces: In Britain, the reigning monarch is also Head of the Armed Forces.

Whitehall: The government offices are located in Whitehall.

The Queen's Golden Jubilee Award: This new award was created for voluntary groups in recognition of their outstanding work in the community.

Lösungs-hinweise

1 Der Hörtext befindet sich auf CD2, *track* 10; das Transkript auf S. 311–312.

a She describes it as time of change.

b The British are pragmatic, open-minded, fair, tolerant, inventive and creative.

c The aspect of service is highlighted.

d She thanks the people for their service, and expresses her wish to continue to serve the people of Britain.

CD

2 Changing Times: The Commonwealth has developed; the European Union has expanded; the Cold War has ended; and now there is the danger of international terrorism; devolution; changing society; developments in technology and communications.

National Identity: The British people have a long and proud history, with the monarchy and Parliament being at the heart of British life; a moderate, pragmatic people, more comfortable with practice than theory; Britain is a seafaring nation; the British are outward-looking and open-minded, making it easy for them to cope with development, especially because of their language; the British also have a tradition of fairness and tolerance, which has helped them achieve a multicultural society

The Tradition of Service: The Queen refers to those who serve the community voluntarily; she also mentions the Armed Forces who serve the country and protect the people; she talks about those who give service in the public sector, either in government, or in hospitals, schools, the police or emergency services; voluntary service is particularly important: she has started the Golden Jubilee Award Scheme; as Queen, she herself serves the nation.

3 Im Folgenden finden sich nur Abstraktionen der Antworten, die bereits bei Aufgabe 2 aufgeführt wurden. Die S sollten aber eine vollständige Tabelle erstellen, die aus Beispielen und Abstraktionen besteht.

	Robin Cook	Queen Elizabeth II
History	history of Britain as a history of multi-ethnicity	history of Britain as a sea-faring nation, history of Britain during her reign
Identity	British identity: cultural diversity, tolerance and openness	aspects which define British identity: its history, institutions, tolerance, multi-culturalism and the tradition of service
Change	changes in culture, economy and in lifestyle due to cultural diversity	changes in politics, society, technology, within Britain, international changes

Differenzierung Leistungsstärkeren S wird die Rede als Kopie ausgehändigt, und anhand der folgenden Fragen vergleichen sie detailliert die beiden Reden:

Who do the speakers address and how do they convince their audiences?
Describe the language they use: is it elevated or ordinary, do they use stylistic devices, etc.?
Which speech do you think is more effective, and why?

	Robin Cook	Queen Elizabeth II
Audience	general public (white British to show them their multicultural past; ethnic minorities to make them feel part of the nation); gives a lot of examples from history to underline what he says about the British; examples: emphasizes London as a multi-cultural centre; uses Chicken Tikka Massala as a symbol of British identity	Parliament, but also the British people; always speaks of 'we': everyone who hears the speech feels they are being addressed; nothing negative is mentioned (except terrorism); emotional ending (she will continue to serve the people)

Language	plain, ordinary language and no complicated sentence structures, but some superlatives ('countless', 'sheer', 'without parallel', 'no more evil business', 'true', 'perfect')	elevated language (e.g. 'change has become a constant'); uses metaphors, many of which are nautical ('chart its course', 'beacons')
Effectiveness	Individual answers	Individual answers

⬭ *Choose one of the people who are quoted in the Lead-in (cf. pp. 142–143). Imagine they listened to either one of the speeches. The next day they are interviewed in the street. The interviewer asks: 'What was your reaction to Robin Cook's / the Queen's speech yesterday?' Answer the question for them. (You can act out the interview in class and get your classmates to guess who you are.)*

SB, S. 146 # 2 The Great Immigrant Experiment Zadie Smith

Source:	*White Teeth*, 2000
Topic:	The experience of immigrants
Text form:	Novel (extract)
Language variety:	BE
Number of words:	754
Level:	Advanced
Skills/activities:	Reading comprehension, examining narrative techniques, doing a role play

Lern-vokabular

Active vocabulary: 'The Great Immigrant Experiment' (p. 146)

mass exodus (l. 6), cramped (l. 6), mistake sb. for sb. else (ll. 8–9), comfort (l. 12), admit sth. (l. 13), infection (l. 18), puddle (l. 20), bring sb. back home (ll. 27–28), weep (l. 28), preach (l. 32), disappointment (l. 33), merge with sth. (l. 41), occur to sb. (l. 42), sneak into sth. (l. 47), leave it at that (l. 49)

tasks: concern, increase sth., anxiety, contradict sb., convince sb., concerning

Didaktisch-methodische Hinweise

Der Auszug aus *White Teeth*, dem Erstlingswerk von Zadie Smith (vgl. auch S. 381 und das SB, S. 196), ist die literarische Gestaltung des multikulturellen Gedankens. Der Ausschnitt zeigt die Ängste zweier Immigrantinnen, Clara und Alsana, im Hinblick auf ihre Kinder, Irie und Millat, die in einer „weißen", englischen Umgebung aufwachsen. Claras Familie stammt aus Jamaika, ihr Mann Archie ist Engländer; Alsana und ihr Mann Samad stammen aus Bangladesch. Ihre Kinder haben ganz selbstverständlichen Kontakt mit weißen Jugendlichen; Irie ist beinahe magisch angezogen von dem englischen Leben der Chalfens, was bei beiden Müttern Ängste vor der Anglisierung ihrer Kinder auslöst. Darüber hinaus beschreibt der Auszug die Situation zweier Heranwachsender, für die der Ablösungsprozess vom Elternhaus begonnen hat und für die ihre ethnische Herkunft eine untergeordnete Rolle spielt.

Unterrichts-tipps

Der Einstieg kann über das Bild erfolgen:

⬭ *Choose one of the people in the photo and invent their biography. The following questions might help: Who is he/she? Where does he/she come from? How did he/she come to be in the photo? Is he/she happy with his or her life? Why or why not?*

Differenzierung

Der Text ist aufgrund der komplexen Personenkonstellation nicht einfach zu verstehen; die S sollten den Text daher in einer Stillarbeitsphase, ggf. auch als Hausaufgabe lesen und das Diagramm in der Randspalte zu Hilfe nehmen. In leistungsschwächeren Gruppen sind eine Unterbrechung nach Z. 26 und die Beantwortung von Aufgaben 1 und 2 möglich.

Info

Zadie Smith (born 1975) was born to a Jamaican mother and British father, and grew up in Willesden, north London. She studied English Literature at Cambridge University. She has written two novels. *White Teeth* (2000) was well-received by the public and by many critics. It was adapted as a four-part television drama on Channel 4. *The Autograph Man* (2002) was nominated for the 2002 Booker Prize.

White Teeth is a meandering story of two London families, the Joneses and the Iqbals. The two men meet in the army during the Second World War and remain friends. Archie Jones marries Clara, a Jamaican, with whom he has one daughter, Irie. Samad Iqbal marries the boisterous Alsana, and has two twins, Magid and Millat. Samad wants both boys to be brought up as good Muslims, but can only afford to send Magid back to Bangladesh to receive a proper Muslim upbringing. Millat becomes a juvenile delinquent before embracing fundamental Islam. Meanwhile Irie has a crush on Millat, and following an incident when they are busted for drugs, Irie and Millat are forced to go to study sessions with the Chalfen family, a liberal Jewish family. Marcus Chalfen is a geneticist developing a new form of mice called FutureMice. When Magid returns from Bangladesh, he reveals he has become an agnostic and starts to work with Marcus Chalfen. At the launch of FutureMice all the protagonists come together, and Archie and Samad are forced to confront a figure from their past.

Willesden (l. 8) belongs to the London borough of Brent, in north-west London. Among the ethnic groups which form the non-white population of Brent are Indians, black Caribbeans, black Africans. There are some but not many Bangladeshis. Besides being the centre of London's main Catholic shrine, Willesden also houses the world's largest Hindu temple outside India.

Bengali (l. 21) is the term used to describe people from Bangladesh or West Bengal.

BB, aa (ll. 21–24): capital letters are used in genetics to classify dominant genes, while small letters are used for weak genes. This is slightly different from their use in the text.

Lösungs-hinweise

1 They show how diverse the population of London has become. The names in ll. 3–5 do not seem to belong together. Either couples from different ethnic groups give their children names that reflect their background, or some parents find names that come from different ethnic backgrounds exotic or more conformist (cf. ll. 9–10).

⬭ *Look at the names and try and guess where they come from:*

First names:	Isaac (l. 3)	(Jewish, also American Protestant)
	Danny (l. 3)	(Irish, also British)
	Quang (l. 4)	(Vietnamese)
	Irie (l. 4)	(Jamaican)
	Sita (l. 8)	(Indian)
	Sharon (l. 8)	(British)
Last names:	Leung (l. 3)	(Chinese)
	Rahmann (l. 4)	(Jewish, German, also Arabic)
	O'Rourke (l. 4)	(Irish)
	Jones (l. 5)	(Welsh)

2 What the young white men are angry about: immigrants come to the country and claim the same rights as the white people (cf. l. 13); the immigrants feel as though they belong; mixed marriages reduce the number of white people (cf. l. 18). Not only do immigrants become English, but the English adopt immigrant characteristics (l. 14).
What immigrants worry about: Their children might marry people from other ethnic groups and lose their race, skin colour and traditions (l. 19); in a few generations it will no longer be possible to recognize people's origins (l. 25), and immigrants feel distant from their offspring.

3 **a** Alsana is worried that her son will marry a white girl, whose child then marries a white person resulting in grand-children with whom Alsana feels no affinity. Millat's behaviour increases these concerns as he is always bringing home white girlfriends to spend the night.

b Irie is aware of her mother's concerns about her being assimilated into white English society, which she herself desires, so she visits the Chalfens regularly but lies to her mother about it. She herself feels that the Chalfens are the essence of Englishness and so wants to become a part of them, hence the need to lie to her black mother.

4 Contradicting each other: 'on a direct collision course' (l. 6);
hide: 'secrete' (l. 6);
not worth mentioning: 'small fry/peanuts' (l. 18);
not speaking although one really wants to: 'biting of tongues' (l. 30);
mix or unite with sb.: 'mate/merge with sb.' (l. 41);
in a way: 'after a fashion' (l. 42).

5 Diese Aufgabe kann als Hausaufgabe oder in einer Stillarbeitsphase bearbeitet werden. Die S sollten ggf. auf die Einträge im Glossar (S. 258) und die Seite „Reading Narrative Prose" (S. 238) verwiesen werden.

Narrative technique: third-person narrator with a limited point of view, as he only presents the reader with what Alsana, Clara and Irie think. The reader does not know what is going on in Samad's or Millat's minds.
Effect: the reader can understand Alsana's, Clara's and Irie's attitudes, and therefore sympathize with these characters. The reader must work out for him- or herself why Samad 'attacks' the coriander (cf. l. 29), why Millat keeps bringing white girls home despite the inevitable arguments.

6 Die S sollten genügend Zeit bekommen, das Rollenspiel vorzubereiten (ca. 30 Minuten). Sie sollen die Haltung der jeweiligen Figuren festlegen und mögliche Argumente sammeln. Dies sollte nur stichwortartig geschehen, damit das Rollenspiel natürlich wirkt und Raum für Improvisation bleibt.

a–c Individual answers.

◯ *Choose one of the following and give a five-minute presentation to the class:*
- *Jamaica's history and people;*
- *Bangladesh's history and people;*
- *The history of the Jewish community in Britain;*
- *The history of immigration to Britain from former colonies.*

SB, S. 148 # 3 On Tour in the UK

Didaktisch-methodische Hinweise In diesem Abschnitt machen sich die S mit verschiedenen Regionen des Vereinigten Königreichs vertraut, indem sie im Rahmen eines Projekts eine fiktive Reise planen und die anderen S als Mitreisende zu gewinnen versuchen. Dazu müssen sie überlegen, was für andere S von besonderem Interesse sein könnte. Sie üben verschiedene Fertigkeiten, z.B. Internetrecherche, Planung einer Reise und Gestaltung eines ansprechenden Posters. Das SB gibt genaue Anleitungen, die die S als Checkliste verwenden können. Dabei ist besonders der Hinweis zu betonen, dass die S exakt recherchieren und eine realistische Tour planen sollen. Sie arbeiten während der Unterrichtszeit oder zu Hause, je nach Ausstattung der Schule bzw. der Haushalte.

Unterrichts-tipps S, die mit dem *UK* wenig vertraut sind, könnten anhand einer physischen Karte oder der Fotos im SB in das Thema eingeführt werden. Von der physischen Karte her erschließen sie Freizeitmöglichkeiten und Aktivitäten. Die Fotos im SB helfen, sich eine genauere Vorstellung zu machen; sie zeigen folgende Motive (von links unten im Uhrzeigersinn): Reiterinnen in Cornwall (im Hintergrund St Michael's Mount); Läden in The Shambles, einer alten Gasse in York; Micklegate Bar, York (eines der alten Stadttore Yorks); einen viktorianischen Pub (The Crown Bar), Belfast; Portobello Road Market, London; Brighton Pier, Sussex.

SB, S. 149

Getting Along in English

Didaktisch-methodische Hinweise

Es empfiehlt sich, diese *section* im Zusammenhang mit *section 3* zu besprechen, da die S hier die sprachlichen Mittel erwerben, mit denen sie eine Unterkunft finden und buchen können. Die Seite lässt sich in einer Unterrichtsstunde bewältigen, wobei Aufgabe 4 am sinnvollsten als Hausaufgabe zu bearbeiten ist. Der Dialog zu Aufgabe 3 befindet sich auf CD2, *track* 11, das Transkript auf S. 312.

Lösungs-hinweise

1 Die S bilden Dreiergruppen; jeder S liest eine Anzeige. Anschließend tauschen sich die drei S über die Angebote aus und diskutieren deren Vor- und Nachteile:

❖

	Antrim Bay YHA	Ramsey Hotel	Aberdeen University accommodation
Type of place	youth hostel	hotel	students' accommodation
Facilities and services offered	simple accommodation; no private showers or toilets; no food offered	private showers and toilets; TV and telephone; (breakfast)	self-catering, but breakfast offered
Comments	cheap; good for meeting other young people; maybe not so comfortable	central London; comfortable	interesting; probably more comfortable than the youth hostel but not as comfortable as the hotel; says nothing about double or single rooms, private showers and toilets

2 Other useful words might be: 'price', 'how to get there', 'noise', 'methods of payment'.

CD **3** **a** Der Dialog befindet sich auf CD2, *track* 11, das Transkript auf S. 312.
Die Aufnahme mit der Anfrage Marcs wird einmal ohne Hörauftrag vorgespielt. Danach lesen S die Aufgabe, hören sich den Text ein zweites Mal an, und versuchen, Marcs Liste aufzustellen. Nach dem zweiten Hören vergleichen die S ihre Listen in Partnerarbeit und ergänzen sie. Ein dritter Durchgang dient dazu, ihre Ergebnisse zu überprüfen.

☞ Die S sollten auf die Verwechslungsgefahr der umgangssprachlichen Zeitangabe *half eleven* mit dem deutschen *halb elf* hingewiesen: *half eleven* steht für *half past eleven*.

Marc's list:
Booking for 3 people from Friday, 15 July – Monday, 18 July
Price / How much?
Time of arrival / When should we be there by?
German Youth Hostel Cards acceptable?
Bedsheets provided?
How to get there.

b Useful words: 'self-catering'; 'minimum stay'; 'single', 'double', 'triple room', 'private shower and toilet', 'bed and breakfast', 'make a booking/reservation', 'hold a booking', 'make a deposit', 'provide bedsheets', 'be located near / on the road to / off the road to (a place)'.

4 Example of an e-mail from Marc:

Hello,

I'm enquiring about the student self-catering accommodation. Do you have a double room for three nights from Friday, 15th August to Monday, 18th July? Your advert says you offer bed and breakfast – what kind of breakfast would that be? As we are keen on sports, we were wondering whether it would be possible to use the university's sports facilities during our stay? As we will be travelling by train we need to know whether the accommodation is located near the station, how easy it is to get into the town centre and back and whether we have to be in by a certain time in the evening.

I look forward to hearing from you soon.

Yours sincerely

Marc Stein

SB, S. 150 # 4 The Parts of the Whole

Im Mittelpunkt dieser *section* stehen verschiedene Entwicklungen, die die Einheit des Vereinigten Königreichs auf den Prüfstand stellen. Aspekte wie Dezentralisierung, der Übergang von einer industriellen zu einer Dienstleistungsgesellschaft – mit zum Teil schwer wiegenden Konsequenzen für den Norden Englands mit seinen Bergwerken und Schwerindustrien –, die Verschärfung der *north-south-divide* und der Wandel von einer Klassengesellschaft zu einer multikulturellen Gesellschaft rufen diejenigen auf den Plan, die den Begriff *United Kingdom* mitsamt seinen Symbolen gerne ersetzt sehen würden.

SB, S. 150 ## A Devolution in the UK

Source:	The website of the Foreign and Commonwealth Office
Topic:	Devolution in the UK
Text form:	Official report
Language variety:	BE
Number of words:	102
Level:	Basic/advanced
Skills/activities:	Information gap activity, comparing results, doing research

Lern-vokabular

Active vocabulary: 'Devolution in the UK' (p. 150)

provide for sth. (l. 1), be located in (a place) (l. 2), take over certain functions (ll. 2–3), local government (ll. 5–6), retain responsibility for sth. (l. 7), foreign policy (l. 8)

Didaktisch-methodische Hinweise

Dieser Abschnitt behandelt eine grundlegende Änderung, die sich seit den 1990er Jahren im politischen System des Vereinigten Königreichs vollzogen hat: die Dezentralisierung. Die bisher subsumierten anderen „Teile des Ganzen", Wales, Nordirland und Schottland, wehrten sich im 20. Jahrhundert zunehmend gegen die Bevormundung durch Westminster, besannen sich auf ihre Traditionen und eigenen Sprachen und strebten ihre Autonomie an. Wie diese Autonomie aussieht, erarbeiten die S, indem sie in einer *information gap activity* die bereitgestellten Informationen zusammentragen

Kopiervorlage und die Situation mit der in Deutschland vergleichen. Ergänzend kann die KV „The United Kingdom at a Glance" (vgl. S. 310) eingesetzt werden.

Unterrichts-tipps

Der Einstieg kann über ein Gespräch über die Regionen des *United Kingdom* erfolgen, in dem die Unterscheidung zwischen *United Kingdom*, *Great Britain* und *England* verdeutlicht wird: Das *United Kingdom of Great Britain and Northern Ireland* besteht aus *Great Britain* (England mit Wales als eine administrative Region und Schottland) und *Northern Ireland*. Eine Abgrenzung von *The British Isles* (England, Irland, Schottland und Wales) ist sinnvoll. Bevor die S die Aufgaben bearbeiten, sollte sie daran erinnert werden, dass die Regionen bis 1997 weitgehend von Westminster regiert wurden.

→ *WB, ex. 5*

Info

Wales: In 1282 Edward I of England presented his first-born son to the people of Wales as their prince – a symbolic act which, on the one hand, was meant to demonstrate that Wales had its own ruler, but, on the other hand, subordinated the Welsh to English rule.

Northern Ireland: Ireland was invaded by England in 1169. Despite the Reformation, the people of Ireland remained largely Catholic. Following revolts in the northern province of Ulster, northern Ireland was colonized in the 17th century by Protestant settlers from Scotland and England. In 1690 William of Orange defeated the Catholic James II of England and VII of Scotland at the Battle of Boyne, which was fought in Ireland, thus ensuring Protestant supremacy in Ireland until the southern counties were given dominion status in 1922. Northern Ireland remained part of the United Kingdom with its own parliament that represented the interests of the Protestant majority. The parliament was dissolved in 1972 as a result of the civil strife in the province – it was clear that it was not interested in taking on the concerns of the large Catholic minority. With the Good Friday Agreement in 1998, Northern Ireland was given its own assembly, which was set up in 1999. Following intelligence gathering for the IRA by Sinn Fein members of the Assembly, the Secretary of State for Northern Ireland suspended and then dissolved the Northern Ireland Assembly in 2002.

Scotland: Following long wars, Scotland managed to have its independence recognized by England in 1314. Following the death of Elizabeth I in 1603, James VI of Scotland became King James I of England, thereby uniting the two crowns. Separate parliaments for the two kingdoms continued until the Act of Union in 1707. Scotland retained its laws, system of justice and Church, while its parliament was united with the English parliament at Westminster. Many areas of Scotland had not been pleased to see the Stuarts replaced with the Hanoverians in 1714, and two revolts took place against the new royal house. Called the Jacobites, they aimed to restore the Catholic Stuarts to the throne, but were finally defeated at the Battle of Culloden in 1746. After this the Hanoverians brutally crushed Scottish opposition, especially in the Highlands. In 1929 the Scottish National Party was formed, whose aim was independence from the United Kingdom.

Devolution: In 1979 a first referendum was held to see whether there was support for devolution in Wales and Scotland. In both countries the referendum was not accepted as not enough voters turned out to vote, but in the 1997 referenda, both Scotland and Wales voted for devolution. In 1998 Northern Ireland voted in favour as part of the peace process.

Lösungshinweise

1 Hier kann das „Active vocabulary" (vgl. S. 291) einbezogen werden.

2 a–b

Country	Wales	Northern Ireland	Scotland
Population	2.94 million	1.7 million	5.1 million
Year of referendum	1997	1998	1997
Turnout	50%	81%	60%
Name of Parliament	National Assembly of Wales	Northern Ireland Assembly	The Scottish Parliament
Seat	Cardiff	Belfast	Edinburgh
Powers	Welsh language; water; arts and heritage; industry; education and training; economic development; social services; agriculture and fisheries; environment; housing; health; highways; local government; town and country planning; tourism	Legislative & executive powers in areas like agriculture, arts, education, and economic policy	Wide range of powers in areas like health, education, social services, environment, law-making, economic development, income tax

3 Die S sollten zunächst in Partnerarbeit Unterschiede suchen und begründen.

Possible suggestions:
Turnout for the referendum was much higher in Northern Ireland than in Wales and Scotland. Perhaps this is because the people of Wales and Scotland were not too unhappy about their situation, while the people of Northern Ireland saw the referendum as a chance to support the peace process. It seems that the Welsh Assembly has the most far-reaching power in areas ranging from arts and heritage to town and country planning. The Scottish Parliament seems to have more legislative power and it can levy taxes; this may be due to the large population, and the fact that it was already independent in many areas (e.g. law, education, etc.)

4 Diese Aufgabe kann zur Schulung von *presentation skills* dienen, bei der die S einzeln oder in Gruppen ihre Fähigkeit zur Recherche, zur Materialauswahl (die wiederum Lesefertigkeiten wie *skimming* und *scanning* beeinhaltet), zur Aufbereitung und Präsentation demonstrieren können. Die S sollten von verschiedenen Visualisierungstechniken Gebrauch machen und den im SB angegebenen Wortschatz nutzen. Für Informationen vgl. www.wales.gov.uk · 1.8.2003, www.scotland.gov.uk · 1.8.2003 und www.northernireland.gov.uk · 1.8.2003.

SB, S. 151 **B A New Flag for a Changing Country?**

Source:	*Guardian*, 2002
Topic:	Redesigning the Union Jack
Text form:	Flags and quotes
Language variety:	BE
Number of words:	264
Level:	Basic/advanced
Skills/activities:	Describing pictures, intelligent guessing

Lern-vokabular **Active vocabulary: 'A New Flag for a Changing Country?' (p. 151)**

represent sth. (l. 1), out of control (ll. 1–2), reference to sth. (l. 7), a reminder of sth. (l. 8), a symbol of unity (l. 11), acknowledge sth. (l. 21)
tasks: match sth. to sth. else, to what extent

Im Jahr 2002 wurden Leser der Tageszeitung *Guardian* aufgerufen, eine Flagge zu entwerfen, die das neue Verständnis des *United Kingdom* veranschaulichen sollte. Natürlich wird keine der Fahnen den *Union Jack* ersetzen, aber Flaggen wie die zu ihnen gehörenden Zitate spiegeln wider, wie Briten heute ihre Identität definieren, und bieten somit eine Ergänzung zu „Lead-In" und *sections* 1 und 2. In sprachlicher Hinsicht dient diese *section* der Schulung des Beschreibens.

Unterrichts-
tipps

Als Einstimmung können folgende Fragen dienen (vgl. ggf. SB, S. 165):

⬭ *What do flags represent? When and where do you see them? What do you think people feel when they see their national flag?*

⬭ *Which flag am I describing – It has a circle of 12 yellow or gold stars on a dark blue · background?*
The flag of the European Union.

Anschließend beschreiben die S Flaggen, die ihre Mitschüler erraten sollen. Haben die S dabei den *Union Jack* nicht gewählt, sollte L ihn beschreiben.

Info

The Union Jack: The three crosses represented in the flag of the United Kingdom (called the 'Union Jack') are named after the patron saint of the three kingdoms: St George, (patron saint of England), St Andrew (patron saint of Scotland) and St Patrick (patron saint of Ireland). Wales is a principality within England and has therefore historically been considered part of England. When King James VI of Scotland became king of England (as King James I) it was decided that the union of the two kingdoms under one monarch should be represented symbolically by a new flag. Originally it consisted of the red cross of England superimposed on the white cross of Scotland on the blue background of the Scottish flag. However, the flag was usually restricted to use at sea until the two kingdoms were formally united in 1707. It was most probably from its use at sea that the flag got the name 'Union Jack' (a jack is the name given to a flag on a ship). The flag continued to be used in this form until 1801, when Great Britain and Ireland were formally united; the cross of St Patrick was included. The flag as we now know it was created. When the southern part of Ireland gained its independence in 1921 and became the Irish Free State no alteration was made to the Union Jack, as the northern part of Ireland remained part of the United Kingdom. The name 'Union Jack' became official when it was approved by Parliament in 1908.

Lösungs-
hinweise

1 The Union Jack comprises two red crosses, one straight and one diagonal within white crosses. The background is dark blue.
Flag No. 1: In the bottom left-hand corner there is a lion roaring. There are wavy lines which could be red flames or blue waves, and on the right-hand side there a four stars, which are green, red, blue and white.
Flag No. 2 looks like the Union Jack, but the colours have been changed: the background is red. The red crosses have been replaced with green crosses, and the white crosses with yellow crosses.
Flag No. 3: On the left-hand side the flag still looks like the Union Jack, but on the right-hand side the colours have been changed to brown, black, purple, green, yellow, pink. The middle stripe has been divided up into various colours: there is a blue flag with a miniature Union Jack in the top left-hand corner, and a green bit on the right; the stripe then is divided between red and yellow.
Flag No. 4 has a swirl of different colours – red, white, blue, yellow, green, black and mauve – which move inwards in a clockwise direction.

a Vgl. „Info" oben.

b Individual answers.

2 Für diese Aufgabe empfiehlt sich Partnerarbeit.
1C; 2D; 3B; 4A

❖ ⬭ *In groups of four to five, decide which of the designs you prefer (one group, however, must represent the Union Jack). Prepare a one-minute speech in which each of you speaks in favour of your flag. After all five flags have been presented, the class takes a vote on which flag should be the flag of the United Kingdom.*

⬭ *Translate ll. 11–14 into German.*

SB, S. 152 ## C Down in the North

Source:	*Economist*, 15.12.2001
Topic:	Social differences in multicultural England
Text form:	Newsmagazine report
Language variety:	BE
Number of words:	554
Level:	Advanced
Skills/activities:	Reading comprehension, writing a comment

Lern-vokabular

Active vocabulary: 'Down in the North' (p. 152)

the health service (l. 3), low-skilled workers (l. 4), prosperous (l. 6), prosperity (l. 6), community (l. 7), be integrated (ll. 8–9), economic prospects (l. 15), unemployment rate (l. 24), breeding ground for sth. (l. 27), racial tension (l. 27), the wealth gap (ll. 30–31), social housing (l. 43), be in short supply (l. 43), a high-growth area (l. 44)
tasks: division, distribution

Didaktisch-methodische Hinweise

Der Text dient dazu, das Großbritannienbild der S zu differenzieren. Er befasst sich mit den sozialen und wirtschaftlichen Unterschieden in der britischen Gesellschaft, insbesondere der Situation von Zuwanderern und der wirtschaftliche Lage im Norden und Süden des Landes. Während v.a. Einwanderer aus der Karibik nicht selten einen englischen Ehepartner haben, gehen Einwanderer aus Pakistan und Bangladesch viel seltener eine Mischehe ein. Arbeitslosigkeit unter Weißen wie Einwanderern trifft vor allem den armen Norden Englands, der durch den Wandel von einer industriellen zu einer Dienstleistungsgesellschaft wirtschaftlich geschwächt ist.

Unterrichts-tipps

Zur Einstimmung auf den Text wählen die Schüler eines der Fotos und spekulieren über die Lebenssituation der abgebildeten Personen:

⬭ *Write a short text on the photo you have chosen, describing what it shows (e.g. the kind of people, surroundings, etc.). Then imagine what kind of life the people in the photo, or in these surroundings, live, what hopes and fears they might have.*

Da der Text lang ist und viele statistische Angaben enthält, kann eine Zäsur nach Z. 26 angebracht sein. Zur Sicherung des Verständnisses können folgende Aussagen bearbeitet werden:

1 *West Indians came to Britain to work in public services.* (True, cf. ll. 2–3.)
2 *African Asians were forced to leave Africa because they were disliked for being too rich.* (True, cf. ll. 4–6.)
3 *Intermarriage with whites is high among Pakistanis and Bangladeshis.* (False: It is low, cf. ll. 13–14.)
4 *Pakistanis and Bangladeshis have the highest employment rate.* (False: They have the highest unemployment rate, cf. ll. 15–17.)
5 *Poverty and racial tension are closely connected.* (True, cf. ll. 20–27.)

6 *Many poor people rely on social housing.* (True, cf. l. 43)

7 *There is plenty of social housing in the south of England.* (False: Social housing is scarce, cf. ll. 40, 43–44)

Kopiervorlage
→ *WB, ex. 3, 4*

Ergänzend kann die KV „The United Kingdom at a Glance" (vgl. S. 310) eingesetzt werden.

Lösungs-
hinweise

████ *Pre-reading:* Hierbei geht es um Spontanreaktionen ohne Begründungen oder Erklärungen.

❖ **1** Wegen des hohen Anspruchs des Texts stellt die Bearbeitung dieser Aufgabe in arbeitsteiliger Gruppenarbeit eine Entlastung dar. Die Gruppen notieren ihre Ergebnisse und präsentieren sie. Überlappungen sind möglich.

a Tendencies among Britain's ethnic groups are not uniform:
– In many areas of London intermarriage leads to racial integration.
– Ethnicity is not a distinction either: Pakistanis and Bangladeshis are less qualified than any other ethnic group and their rate of unemployment is highest, but in poor white areas unemployment is just as high; in some areas unemployment among the whites is even higher than among Asians.
– Unemployment is highest among low-skilled workers, regardless of whether they are white or non-white.

b
– Among whites, those who live in poorer areas, especially the North, are less well off.
– Many East-African Asians have become prosperous in Britain.
– Unemployment among Asians is sometimes, but not always, lower than among whites, but Pakistanis and Bangladeshis are less qualified and less employed than any other ethnic group.
– Poor people who rely on social housing have less chance of improving their situation.

c
– There is a wealth gap, or prosperity gulf, between the north and the rich south-east.
– This is larger than in any other European country.
– In recent years this wealth gap has grown by 30%.
– High house prices in the south-east make it difficult for people from the north to move, as there is less social housing in the south-east.
– Even if they have their own property in the north, the money they get from selling it will not buy much in the south.

2 Als Hilfestellung kann zuerst nach Synonymen für die beiden Schlüsselbegriffe gefragt werden, die an der Tafel notiert werden, z.B.:

<u>have sth. in common with sb.:</u> share sth. with sb., be connected with / linked to sb. by sth., have the same interests, etc. as sb.;

<u>be divided from sb.:</u> differ from sb.; be distinct/separated / cut off from sb.

The fact that Pakistanis and Bangladeshis are often low-skilled means that their unemployment is high, but this applies to white people, too, especially if they live in the poorer north. This is what connects both groups. On the other hand, Pakistanis and Bangladeshis have a different skin colour, a different cultural background and different traditions from the whites. This is what separates them from whites.

3 Bevor diese Aufgabe besprochen wird, sollten Wendungen gesammelt werden, mit denen eine Meinung, Zustimmung oder Dissens ausgedrückt werden können, z.B.:
– my original reaction was ..., but now I've changed my mind / and I still think this is the case;
– the text shows / points out / illustrates / has convinced me that ...;

– I agree; I feel the same; in my opinion; if you ask me, ...;
– I disagree; I don't think so; I wouldn't say that ...;

Die S suchen im Text nach Stellen, die die vier Aussagen beweisen oder widerlegen. Folgende Kettenübung integriert möglichst viele S in die Besprechung:

○ *Say what your original reaction to the statement was and whether you have changed your mind or not. Use one example from the text to underline what you think, then ask your neighbour whether he or she agrees. Your neighbour continues in the same way.*

Possible answers:

1 There are marked differences between the different ethnic minorities (ll. 6–7, 10–14, 15–16).

2 Blacks seem to be more integrated, because of the high rate of intermarriage with whites (ll. 10–12).

3 In some areas unemployment rates are higher for whites than for ethnic minorities (ll. 20–26).

4 Economic inequalities are not declining in England, but growing (ll. 39–42, 46–48).

SB, S. 154

5 This England

Wie in *section* 4 aufgezeigt wurde, ist das Vereinigte Königreich kein einheitliches Gebilde, sondern setzt sich aus vier Regionen mit eigener Identität zusammen: Wales und Schottland definieren sich über ein ausgeprägtes Nationalbewusstsein, das seinen Ausdruck in einer eigenen Kultur und einer eigenen Sprache findet. Die Protestanten in Nordirland definieren sich, bedingt durch den Nordirlandkonflikt, über die Loyalität zu Großbritannien. Wie aber definiert sich England? Dieser Abschnitt versucht, Aspekte dessen einzufangen, was England bedeutet und anziehend macht. Ein Shakespeare-Text zeigt England als von Gott gesegnete, uneinnehmbare Inselwelt, ein Bild von Constable stellt England als Idylle dar. Ein Auszug aus einem Interview mit dem Schriftsteller Julian Barnes geht der Spannung zwischen Selbst- und Fremdbild Englands als Land der Exzentriker nach; er leitet über zu einer Parodie auf englische Eigenarten durch Monty Python.

SB, S. 154

A **This Sceptred Isle** William Shakespeare

Source:	*Richard II*, ca. 1595
Topic:	The beauty and uniqueness of England
Text form:	Drama (extract)
Language variety:	BE
Number of words:	83
Level:	Advanced
Skills/activities:	Working with metaphors

Lern-
vokabular

Active vocabulary: 'This Sceptred Isle' (p. 154)

throne (l. 1), fortress (l. 4), infection (l. 5),
tasks: create an impression, be referred to as sth., select sth.

Didaktisch-
methodische
Hinweise

Um drei zentrale Metaphern („royal throne of kings", „seat of Mars, „demi-paradise") entwirft Shakespeare in dieser berühmten Textstelle aus seinem *Richard II* das Bild eines erhabenen, mächtigen und idyllischen England. Dieser Auszug soll im Unterricht in erster Linie im Hinblick auf seine Metaphorik untersucht werden.

☞ Sollten die S Schwierigkeiten mit der Syntax des Auszugs haben (es handelt sich um eine hymnische Aneinanderreihung von Nomen mit Attributen und einen Relativsatz) kann ein Verweis auf den Eintrag „enumeration" im Glossar (SB, S. 267) hilfreich sein.

Unterrichts-tipps

Als Einstieg können die Fotos auf S. 154 betrachtet werden:

▢ *What impression do you get from the picture in the centre? How would you describe the countryside?*

▢ *Look at the other two pictures: what might the fortress and the cliff have in common?*

☞ Der Text wird von L vorgetragen (wobei die Betonung des Wortes „blesséd" in Z. 11 zu beachten ist), die S lesen mit und halten in Stichwörtern ihre Eindrücke fest. In Partnerarbeit teilen sie sich gegenseitig mit, wie der Text auf sie gewirkt hat, bevor sie, ebenfalls in Partnerarbeit, die Aufgaben 2 und 3 bearbeiten.

Info

Richard II was a controversial play, because it deals with the true story of the murder of a king. Richard II is deposed by Henry Bolingbroke, whose lands have been confiscated by Richard. This serves as a pretext for him to invade and depose the unpopular king. Richard is then murdered by a supporter of Henry Bolingbroke, who repudiates the murder but is crowned Henry IV. The speech in the SB is made by John of Gaunt on his deathbed, and is a criticism of Richard II – he is eulogizing the ideal England, which under Richard II has become corrupted.

Lösungs-hinweise

1 Individual answers.

2

Royal throne of kings	Seat of Mars	Demi-paradise
sceptred isle (l. 1) earth of majesty (l. 1)	fortress built by Nature (l. 4) against [...] the hand of war (l. 5) a wall or a moat defensive to a house (l. 9)	this other Eden (l. 3) this happy breed of men (l. 6) this little world (l. 6) this precious stone set in a silver sea (l. 7) the envy of less happier lands (l. 10) this blessed plot (l. 11)

❖ **3** Vor der Besprechung im Plenum können die S sich in Kleingruppen austauschen und ihre Ergebnisse ggf. korrigieren und ergänzen.

'This royal throne of kings', 'this sceptred isle', 'this earth of majesty': these metaphors refer to objects that denote that someone is king or queen; they imply that England is the embodiment of royalty, which is anointed by God.
'This seat of Mars': this implies that England is a warrior-nation.
'This other Eden, demi-paradise': England is compared with the garden of Eden, or paradise. These metaphors are biblical and imply that God has blessed the country.
'This fortress built by Nature for herself against infection and the hand of war': This metaphor refers to the fact that England is an island, like a fortress, and is therefore protected from attack.
'This happy breed of men, this little world': England is a contented world of its own, independent from other countries.
'This precious stone set in the silver sea': Here the island is compared to a precious stone (e.g. diamond) in the centre of a ring, with the sea around it as the silver band. It refers

to the wealth and beauty of England (a wealth that is derived from the land and the sea). 'Which serves it in the office of a wall or as a moat defensive to a house against the envy of less happier lands': These similes refer to the sea which surrounds the island like a moat does a castle and guarantees its protection, and again refers to the luck and contentedness of the English compared to other nations.

'This blessed plot, this earth, this realm, this England': Here again, biblical language is used, implying that God protects the country.

SB, S. 155 **B Chocolate Box Englishness**

Topic:	The English landscape
Text form:	Painting
Language variety:	BE
Level:	Basic/advanced
Skills/activities:	Reacting to a painting

Didaktisch-methodische Hinweise

Dieser Abschnitt stellt ein nostalgisches Englandbild vor und präsentiert den S die Idylle, die viele Menschen mit England assoziieren und die jährlich von Touristen gesucht wird. Constable ist neben Turner (vgl. SB, S. 76) einer der bekanntesten englischen Maler; seine Landschaftsbilder gelten als Inbegriff des Englischen. Als Vorbereitung auf die Begegnung mit dem kurzen Text soll zunächst ein emotionaler Bezug zu dem Bild hergestellt werden. Eine detaillierte Bildbeschreibung ist entbehrlich, da sie bei der Erfassung der Atmosphäre des Bildes störend wirken kann. Bei der Besprechung können folgende Wörter nützlich sein: *depict sth., portray sth., rural scene, (water)mill, country cottage, stream, cart, wagon* (die S sollten darauf hingewiesen werden, dass *wain* heute ungebräuchlich ist), *shady, tranquil, rustic*. Ein Transfer auf andere Regionen Großbritanniens oder Deutschland rundet diese Einheit ab.

Info

John Constable (1776–1837) was born in East Bergholt, south Suffolk, and became a master of landscape painting in the romantic style. His works greatly influenced the French painters of the impressionist movement. After studying at the Royal Academy he exhibited his first landscape paintings in 1802 and then continued to paint English rural life. His paintings, composed entirely outdoors, were an innovation in English art. Constable achieved natural, luminous lighting effects through the use of broken bits of colour, applied with a palette knife. He was fascinated by reflections in water and the effect of light on clouds. Although he lived in London, he painted his native country around the Stour River in Suffolk, as well as Salisbury and Dorset. For many years Constable received little recognition or support in England. In France, however, he was much admired. He became a member of the Royal Academy in 1829.

'The Hay Wain' (1821, National Gallery, London) portrays a cottage (which is seen from Flatford Mill) on the River Stour. Constable depicted details from the rural life which was so familiar to him and which he loved: two horses drawing a hay wagon, a dog watching from the river bank, a figure who seems to be mooring a boat, a mill. Constable always observed the weather conditions very closely, and the painting portrays a typically English summer, in which spells of cloudy weather and sunshine follow each other in quick succession. The 'Hay Wain' depicts a natural universe in which the harmony between man, beast and countryside is still intact.

Lösungs-hinweise

1 Individual answers.

2 Individual answers.

3 Folgende Erläuterung zum kulturellen Hintergrund wird hilfreich sein:
'A box of chocolates is always a welcome gift in Britain. Whereas in Germany the lid of a box of chocolates usually displays what is inside, British chocolate boxes are often decorated with romantic scenes or old paintings.'

a Boxes of chocolates are often decorated with scenes taken from the past, which are always pretty and picturesque. There is obviously a strong connection between the senses, as the delicious taste of the chocolates is enhanced by the aesthetic pleasure of the box's picture. People obviously have an image of England that is pleasurable and perhaps somewhat kitchy.

b
– They are looking for something which is missing in their everyday lives, which are often full of problems and worries.
– Maybe they are searching for the quiet, peaceful and harmonious life which Constable's painting depicts.
– Visiting an idyllic and tranquil place like Flatford Mill helps them to forget and makes them feel good.
– Everyone is familiar with the painting, so when they visit the place they already feel that they know it.
– Having visited Flatford Mill, when they see the painting they can say 'I have been there'. There is a sort of 'holiness' in being exactly on the same spot where something famous happened.
– Visiting famous sights is part of cultural tourism, and one can then say to what extent the sight, view or landscape has changed since the painting was composed.

4 Individual answers.

SB, S. 156 ## C Those Wild and Crazy English

Text:	
Source:	*Observer*, 30.8.2003
Topic:	The English, as they see themselves and as others see them
Text form:	Interview
Language variety:	BE
Number of words:	180
Level:	Basic/advanced
Skills/activities:	Summarizing

VIDEO

Video:	
Source:	*Monty Python's Flying Circus*, 11.2.1972
Topic:	A strange argument
Text form:	Comedy series
Language variety:	BE
Length:	4:24 minutes
Level:	Basic/advanced
Skills/activities:	Viewing comprehension, writing a text

Lern-vokabular

Active vocabulary: 'Those Wild and Crazy English' (p. 156)

(the) essence of sth. (l. 4), boil sth. down to sth. else (l. 4), in terms of sth. (l. 8), a tendency to sth. (l. 10), suicide (l. 10), eccentric (l. 13)
tasks: according to sb., depend on sth., an example of sth., indifference

Der Textauszug in diesem Abschnitt befasst sich mit Selbst- und Fremdbild der Eng-länder. Während das Selbstbild von Begriffen wie Demokratie und Zivilisation geprägt ist, betrachten andere Nationen die Engländer häufig als exzentrisch. Als Beispiel wird die Gruppe Monty Python genannt, deren Sketche z.B. von Franzosen als typisch englisch, von Engländern allerdings als *Ironisierung* des typisch Englischen verstanden werden. Der Sketch „The Argument Clinic" soll diese Idee veranschaulichen (vgl. das Video / die DVD und das Transkript auf S. 313–315).

*Unterrichts-
tipps*

Der Einstieg kann über die Themen *theme parks* (ausgehend vom Bild im SB) oder britischer Humor erfolgen. Entscheidet man sich für die erste Option, soll das Gespräch auf die Einsicht zielen, dass durch die Auswahl von Bauwerken oder Symbolen eines Landes in einem solchen *theme park* ein verzerrtes Bild entsteht, das wiederum von Betrachtern als repräsentativ verstanden werden kann. Dies ist der Hauptgedanke des Texts von Barnes:

◯ *Have you ever been to Legoland Deutschland (situated near Günzburg, Bavaria)? What impression did it give of Germany and other countries?*

◯ *Imagine it was your job to create a theme park called Mini-Germany. What would you put in it? How would you attract visitors (especially from other countries) and what would you offer them? Write a two-minute speech to convince sponsors that they should finance your project, and give your speech to the class, who represent the sponsors.
After you have listened to all the speeches, discuss what impressions visitors would go home with after they have visited the park.*

Ein alternativer Einstieg könnte darin bestehen, die S nach Beispielen für britischen Humor zu fragen (z.B. Monty Python oder Rowan Atkinson als Mr. Bean). Sie sollten beschreiben, was sie als charakteristisch für britischen Humor empfinden und welchen Eindruck von den Engländern er vermittelt.

Info

Julian Barnes: cf. p.235.
In *England, England* the country is re-constructed as a massive theme park on the Isle of Wight. The park contains everything considered English and is aimed at attracting wealthy tourists so that they do not have to see the 'real' England. In the course of time the replica becomes the real thing, and England, England begins to replace Old England, which eventually becomes a backwater.

'Brown Heritage signposts' (l. 2; cf. the photo on p. 156): The organization English Heritage ensures the upkeep and care of the historic environment of England.

Windsor Castle (l. 3) is one of the Queen's official residences and is the largest inhabited castle in the world. A castle has existed on the site for 900 years.

Legoland (Windsor) (l. 3) is located on the road to Ascot, near Windsor Castle. 150 acres of park offer 50 different rides, attractions and shows. It was opened in May 1998. It is one of four legolands worldwide.

Royal Ascot (l. 3) is perhaps the most famous race course in the world. The best known race meeting (Royal Ascot) takes place every year in June, and the Queen herself usually attends every day.

Mme de Stael (1766–1817) (l. 10) was a French writer and intellectual, famed for her international salon and her letters.

Lewis Carroll (1832–1898; real name Charles Dodgson) (l. 13) was an English author, mathematician and logician, and is best known for his fantasy *Alice's Adventures in Wonderland* (1866).

*Lösungs-
hinweise* **1** The English see themselves as quiet, civilized, peace-loving; others see them as wild and crazy, as eccentrics.

VIDEO **2** Vgl. das Video / die DVD und das Transkript auf S. 313–315.

a Room 12: abuse room, where the man is insulted;
room 12 A: argument room where he starts arguing; his time runs out, and the other man stops; he pays for some more time, but the man starts an argument claiming he is not having an argument;
next room: complaints room, but the other man here just complains about things himself;
last room: being-hit-on-the-head room, where everyone is hit on the head.

b Individual answers.

3 Individual answers.

SB, S. 157 ## Context Box

*Didaktisch-
methodische
Hinweise*

Die „Context Box" bietet einen Überblick über die Entwicklungen, die Großbritannien seit dem Beginn des 20. Jahrhunderts geprägt haben: die Entwicklung vom Empire zum Commonwealth, die wirtschaftlichen Krisen der 70er Jahre und das Verhältnis Großbritanniens zu den USA einerseits und zu Europa andererseits. Parlamentarische Reformen innerhalb des Landes könnten die Entwicklung der Zukunft prägen.
Die Aufgaben verlangen eine inhaltliche Zusammenfassung, vertiefte Wortschatz-

→ *WB, ex. 3, 4* arbeit und den Transfer auf Deutschland.

*Unterrichts-
tipps* Der Text hat eine hohe Informationsdichte. Aus diesem Grund wird ein arbeitsteiliges Verfahren vorgeschlagen (vgl. Aufgabe 1).

Info

Jeremy Paxman is a TV news presenter and journalist. In his book *The English – a Portrait of a People* (2001), he examines English identity.

*Lösungs-
hinweise* **1** Der erste Absatz sollte gemeinsam gelesen werden, so dass die S die vier Einflüsse benennen können. Dann wird jedem S durch Abzählen eine Zahl von 1–4 zugeordnet, und jeder S ist für das Thema „seiner Zahl" zuständig. Mittels *skimming* identifizieren die S relevante Passagen und notieren alles, was zu ihrem Thema gehört. Anschließend werden alle Informationen an der Tafel gesammelt.

End of Empire	Pressures for Britain to integrate in Europe	Uncontrollability of international business	Divisions within UK
end of global power formation of the Commonwealth immigration multi-cultural society	special relationship with the USA lack of faith in the EU not part of monetary union	trust in free market forces modernization cuts in social benefits privatization	decentralization self-government for Northern Ireland, Scotland and Wales democratic reforms

2 Diese Aufgabe sollte – neben der vertieften Wortschatzarbeit – den Umgang mit dem einsprachigen Wörterbuch trainieren. Wenn alle S ein Wörterbuch haben, wird sie am sinnvollsten zu Hause erledigt. Anderenfalls empfiehlt sich Freiarbeit.

a–c Individual answers.

3 Die folgenden Einträge der „Skills Pages" könnten hilfreich sein: „Doing Research" (S. 230), „Doing Research on the Internet" (S. 231), „Skimming" (S. 236), „Scanning" (S. 236), „Note Making" (S. 243), „Giving a Talk or Presentation" (S. 254).

SB, S. 158 # 6 Pride in Our Past, Confidence in Our Future

Da das heutige Großbritannien nur vor dem Hintergrund seiner Geschichte wirklich zu begreifen ist, erfolgt in diesem Abschnitt anhand von Auszügen aus Niall Fergusons Buch *Empire: How Britain Made the Modern World* und einer kritischen Rezension ein Exkurs in die Geschichte des *British Empire*. Ziel ist es, den S ein differenziertes Bild des *Empire* und seiner Vermächtnisse zu vermitteln.

→ WB, ex. 6

SB, S. 158 **A Old Empire**   Niall Ferguson

Source:	*Empire – How Britain Made the Modern World*
Topic:	The British Empire and its legacy
Text form:	Non-fiction
Language variety:	BE
Number of words:	557
Level:	Advanced
Skills/activities:	Speculating, analysing metaphors, discussing

Lern-vokabular

Active vocabulary: 'Old Empire' (p. 158)

(i) dominate (l. 3), bar none (l. 4), off the coast of (a place) (l. 4), seek to do sth. (l. 6), address a question (l. 7), on balance (l. 9)

(ii) awe sb. (l. 3), the transient nature of sth. (l. 5), solitary (l. 5), astounding (l. 7), the better part of sth. (l. 7), stretch from (one place) to (another place) (l. 13), how on earth ...? (l. 16)

(iii) supremacy (l. 2), the burden of sth. (l. 5), debtor (l. 5), expansion (l. 7), dwindle (l. 10)

Didaktisch-methodische Hinweise

In seiner Abhandlung über das *British Empire*, aus der einige Auszüge präsentiert werden, geht Ferguson der Frage nach, wie das *Empire* nicht nur das heutige Vereinigte Königreich, sondern die ganze Welt geprägt hat. Demokratische Strukturen und die englische Sprache sind für ihn zwei Aspekte, die die Welt dem *Empire* zu verdanken hat. In dieser *section* treten geschichtliche Daten in den Hintergrund. Dies bedeutet nicht, dass sie vernachlässigt werden können, sondern dass S ihre Kenntnisse aus dem Geschichtsunterricht aktivieren sollen.

Info

Niall Ferguson (born 1964) is a history professor, who has taught at Cambridge and Oxford Universities and who now teaches at New York University. He has published works on 19th and 20th century European political and financial history. His books include a history of the Rothschilds bank, *The World's Banker* (1998), a history of the First World War, *The Pity of War* (1998). His book *Empire: How Britain Made the Modern World* (2003) was a follow-up to a television history of the British Empire.

Info

India: The British competed with the Portuguese and the French for trade with India for about a century, before the British finally defeated the French in 1757 during the Seven Years War, thereby putting Bengal in the hands of the East India Company. In 1784 all land under the control of the East India Company was given to the British government. During the 19th century most of India came under British control. Although Britain never ruled all parts of India directly, it sought to dominate the Indian states so that they remained allied with Britain, which was responsible for all foreign policy of the subcontinent. India gained independence from Britain in 1947.

SB, S. 158

(i) Introducing the Empire

Dieser kurzer Auszug ist die Einleitung in Fergusons Buch und formuliert dessen zwei Kernfragen: Wie konnte ein so kleines Land wie England ein so großes Reich regieren und wie ist das *Empire* abschließend zu bewerten? Die S können hier im Sinne der Wissenschaftspropädeutik erkennen, dass zu Beginn einer wissenschaftlichen Abhandlung Fragen zu stellen sind, die im Lauf der Untersuchung beantwortet werden. An diesem Muster können sie sich für ihre Facharbeiten orientieren.

Lösungs-hinweise

1 The two questions that are posed are:
– How could a small nation like Britain build up and support such a vast Empire?
– Was the British Empire a good or a bad thing?

2 Bei dieser Frage müssen die Schüler ihr Vorwissen reaktivieren. Sie kann in einem Unterrichtsgespräch beantwortet werden. In leistungsstarken Klassen eignet sich diese Frage für eine *fishbowl discussion* (vgl. 428).

Good	Bad
The Empire brought the following to many parts of the world: – modern technology (e.g. railways); – democracy; – education; – medical care; – fair system of justice. It provided the mother country with raw materials and markets, which helped industry. It gave people from Britain the chance to start a new life in one of the colonies.	The Empire: – brought slavery; – robbed the colonies of raw materials; – stole the land from native people; – robbed the people of their independence, made them dependent on the colonizers; – encouraged racism; – led to many present-day problems (e.g. an inferiority complex).

Translate the excerpt into German.

SB, S. 159

(ii) The Raj

Dieser Abschnitt beschreibt ein Denkmal, das der Königin Victoria in Kalkutta gesetzt wurde, und erläutert seine Funktion als Symbol britischer Macht über Indien.

Unterrichts-tipps

Als Einstimmung können die S das Foto im SB, S. 158 betrachten:

Why do you think buildings like this were necessary for the Empire? What impression do you think it made on the Indian people who saw it? What impression could the building have on people today?

Differenzierung

In lernschwächeren Gruppen können zusätzlich die folgenden Wörter semantisiert werden: „gaze wearily" (Z. 4), „miasmic" (Z. 7), „astounding" (Z. 7).

1

Intended effects of the monument	Actual effects of the monument
monument to the British Empire;	appears to be out of place;
to impress people with its splendour;	implies that the Empire is a thing of the past,
an answer to the Taj Mahal.	that the Empire is no longer relevant.

2 The metaphor uses the elements island and sea: an island stands alone, surrounded by sea. The white marble monument is compared to an island which stands out in a sea of dark-skinned Bengalis in the overpopulated city of Calcutta. British rule in India was characterized by the fact that only 900 British civil servants and 70,000 British soldiers were capable of controlling over 250 million people. This is symbolized by the solitary building surrounded by thousands of Indians.

SB, S. 160

(iii) The End of Empire

In diesem Ausschnitt wird eine Bilanz gezogen und nach den Spuren des *Empire* in der heutigen Welt und insbesondere in Indien gefragt. Neben Aspekten wie parlamentarischer Demokratie, der Organisation von Armee, Beamtenapparat und Presselandschaft nennt Ferguson auch die englische Sprache (vgl. Text C).

Unterrichts-
tipps

Mit der folgenden *pre-reading activity* kann eine Brücke zwischen Gegenwart und Vergangenheit geschlagen werden:

▢ *When you look at the world today, what would you say is the legacy of the British Empire? How do you think the Empire has affected the world we live in?*
Elements of the British way of life in some of the former colonies (e.g. Canada, Australia, New Zealand), the English language, problems of racism and underdevelopment due to concentration on one resource or industry, Britain's lack of interest in Europe.

Lösungs-
hinweise

1 It resulted in Britain's commercial, financial and industrial supremacy, it allowed for Britons to go abroad and seek their fortune outside in foreign lands.

2 The English language has resulted in all the world's regions being able to communicate with others and therefore being able to trade with each other and pick up new developments rapidly.

SB, S. 160

B A Book Review: 'Sweet Taste of Empire'   Michael Brunton

Source:	*Time*, 20.1.2003
Topic:	A review of Ferguson's book
Text form:	Review
Language variety:	AE
Number of words:	248
Level:	Advanced
Skills/activities:	Scanning, doing research

Lern-
vokabular

Active vocabulary: 'A Book Review: Sweet Taste of Empire' (p. 160)

a span of x years (l. 2), lay claim to sth. (l. 2), surface (l. 3), contemporary (l. 4), be good at doing sth. (l. 7), be hooked on sth. (l. 9), evolve sth. (l. 10), navy (l. 10), dub sth. sth. else (l. 11), frown on sth. (l. 14), doubt sth. (l. 19)

Didaktisch-methodische Hinweise

Diese Rezension stellt Fergusons positive Bewertung des *Empire* in Frage und fordert die S damit zu einer eigenen Stellungnahme auf. Der Autor kritisiert v.a., dass Ferguson die zweifelhaften Aspekte des *Empire* wie Sklaverei und Massaker nicht wirklich in seine Bilanz einbezieht, sondern sie als notwendige Übel auf dem Weg der Welt in die Moderne darstellt.

Unterrichts-tipps

Vor der Behandlung des Texts sollte an die Erwartungen erinnert werden, die die S vor der Lektüre des ersten Auszugs formuliert haben:

⬭ *Did the extracts you read from Niall Ferguson's book live up to your expectations? Would you read the book now? Why / Why not?*

Zur Inhaltssicherung und Wortschatzarbeit eignet sich die folgende Aufgabe, bei der die S ggf. durch *intelligent guessing* und Beachtung des Kontexts die Antworten finden.

⬭ *Find words or expressions from the text which have the same meaning:*
surprise greatly ('astound', l. 4); *very positive compliments* ('glowing praise', l. 4); *pirates* ('buccaneers', l. 8); *addicted to sth.* ('hooked on sth.', l. 9); *develop sth. with time* ('evolve sth.', l. 10); *give sth. a particular name* ('dub sth.', l. 11); *disapprove of sth.* ('frown on sth.', l. 14); *perfect* ('without blemish', l. 17).

Info

Elizabethan buccaneers (l. 8): Sir Francis Drake and Sir Walter Raleigh are two of the most famous sailors of the Elizabethan era. Due to their practices of attacking and robbing other ships (especially Spanish ships) they should, however, be considered pirates.

East India Company (ll. 10–11): the aim of the trading companies was to monopolize trade. The English East India Company was founded in 1613 to win a share in the lucrative spice trade. For more info cf. 'India' on p. 304.

The Battle of Omdurman (l. 14): An Anglo-Egyptian force of nearly 30,000 soldiers marched on the town of Omdurman in Sudan, which was the capital of the Mahdists. The Mahdists were the followers of al-Mahdi, the creator of a vast islamic state in present-day Sudan. The reserves were attacked from behind by 20,000 Mahdists. It was the use of modern machine guns such as the Maxim that resulted in the British victory. At the end of the battle, 10,000 Mahdists were dead and 16,000 were wounded, while only 43 British soldiers had been killed. It marked the end of opposition to British rule in Sudan.

Lösungs-hinweise

1
– Ferguson is too positive (cf. l. 5).
– He does not pay sufficient attention to the negative side of Empire (cf. ll. 16, 19).

2 Examples for Ferguson's positive attitude: text (i), l. 9; text (iii), ll. 13–16.

3 <u>Language:</u> it gave the people access to a widely used language, hence to knowledge, information and progress; groups of people who spoke different dialects (e.g. in Africa or in India) could communicate with each other in English.
<u>Liberty:</u> many groups in the colonies depended on local leaders, whom they had to obey, so the idea of liberty showed them the way to democracy.

⬭ *Explain the metaphor Brunton uses in ll. 13 and 16. How does it fit in with Ferguson's texts (especially excerpt i)?*
Brunton uses a metaphor from the world of economics ('a balance sheet'). In the world of commerce a balance sheet is composed of a credit and a debit column, the former showing how much one has earned, the latter how much one has spent. Brunton says that Ferguson has written a balance sheet to decide whether the Empire was a good or

a bad thing and claims that the 'debit column' (i.e. a listing of the negative aspects) has been underused. He claims that Ferguson is guilty of 'creative accounting', a popular term used to describe incorrect figures in a balance sheet, and which is often used by company accountants to indicate that their firm has done better than it actually has done. It fits in with what Ferguson has written because in the first excerpt he says that one of the aims of his books is to decide whether the Empire was a good or a bad thing and says that people consider it 'on balance' to have been a bad thing. So Ferguson is also weighing things up to work out whether a negative or plus comes out at the end.

4 Bevor die S diese Aufgabe beantworten, sollten ihnen *credit/debit column* als Elemente einer Bilanz bekannt sein. Bei der Präsentation der Ergebnisse sollten sie Visualisierungstechniken anwenden. Ggf. können einige der „Skills Pages" durchgearbeitet werden: „Doing Research" (SB, S. 230), „Doing Research on the Internet" (SB, S. 231), „Skimming" (SB, S. 236), „Scanning" (SB, S. 236), „Note Making" (SB, S. 243), „Giving a Talk or Presentation" (SB, S. 254). Für Hintergrundinformationen können die S auf die Webseite www.britishempire.co.uk · 1.8.2003 hingewiesen werden.

SB, S. 161 **C New Empire: The Triumph of English**

Source:	*Economist*, 19.12.2001
Topic:	English as a world language
Text form:	News article
Language variety:	BE
Number of words:	428
Level:	Advanced
Skills/activities:	Making a timeline

Lern-vokabular **Active vocabulary: 'The Triumph of English' (p. 161)**

in some sense (l. 3), be exposed to sth. (l. 3), predict sth. (l. 4), be proficient in sth. (l. 4), official document (l. 7), global language (l. 12–13), supremacy (l. 17), decline (l. 19), farther afield (l. 32), negotiate sth. (l. 33)
tasks: based on sth., for what purpose, be exposed to sth., exposure, responsible for sth.

Didaktisch-methodische Hinweise Anknüpfend an Fergusons Aussage, die Verbreitung der englischen Sprache gehöre zu den größten Verdiensten des *Empire*, verdeutlicht dieser Text die Omnipräsenz des Englischen und seine Wandlungsfähigkeit. Er blickt zurück auf die *linguae francae* der Antike und identifiziert die USA als heutigen Motor der Verbreitung des Englischen.

Unterrichts-tipps Der Einstieg kann über Schätzfragen erfolgen. Die S notieren zunächst ihre Schätzungen, dann werden „Gebote" gesammelt und die richtigen Antworten gegeben:

◯ *How many native speakers of English are there in the world today?* (ca. 380 m)

◯ *How many countries have English as an official language?* (44)

◯ *How many Indian newspapers are published in English?* (3,000)

◯ *What percentage of world mail is written in English?* (70%)

◯ *Which is higher: a) the number of people who live in the United States or b) the number of people in China who are learning English?* (b)

→ *WB, ex. 8*

Lösungs-
hinweise

1 Die folgenden Daten sollten in dem Zeitstrahl dargestellt sein:

14th century: English is spoken by the 'low people' of England.
19th century: English spreads across the Empire.
20th century: English becomes the language of diplomats.
21st century: English is spoken by half the world.

2 The main areas of exposure are: science and technology, international trade, the internet and computing, consumer electronics, travel, sport, fashion, food.

3 The message of the poem is that Latin and Greek were lasting languages in the sense that they did not change or develop, which is why they can still be understood today. English, however, is flexible; it changes and develops continually, which is why it is hard to understand the English that was spoken centuries ago. It is like writing in the sand on a beach: when the water flows over it, it is washed away and disappears.

4 a) The Empire:
- by founding colonies in countries which were not populated or which only had a very small native population (e.g. the USA, Canada, Australia, New Zealand);
- by colonizing countries in which English had not been spoken before, e.g. India or other parts of Asia or Africa.

b) The Commonwealth, which grew out of the former colonies: its member countries trade and negotiate not only with Britain but also with each other, so English is the language they use; this ensures that English continues to be learned.

c) The USA:
- before World War II: music;
- after World War II: NATO; developments in science and technology; spread of American culture throughout the world; America's growing role as world police; the media and communication.

❖ **5** Hier kann ein *pyramiding* (vgl. S. 428) eingesetzt werden. Dabei beschäftigt sich eine Hälfte der S mit den verbindenden, die andere mit trennenden Aspekten.

Possible answers:
<u>Things that bind Britain to Europe:</u> the EU, commerce, history, religion and culture, holidays, modern transport (Chunnel, cheap air travel).

<u>Things that keep it apart:</u> geography, the Commonwealth, history, the English-speaking world.

SB, S. 163 # Watch Your Language

Didaktisch-
methodische
Hinweise
Diese Seite setzt folgende Schwerpunkte: die Differenzierung zwischen Adverb und Adjektiv; die Steigerung der Adverbien; die Verwendung eines Adverbs, um ein Adjektiv näher zu beschreiben; die Verwendung des Adjektivs nach Verben wie *look, feel, smell.* In diesen grammatischen Bereichen machen deutsche Lerner häufig Interferenzfehler, da die Unterscheidung Adjektiv/Adverb im Deutschen nicht existiert.

Lösungs-
hinweise
1 a a <u>beautifully</u> built cottage ... a <u>highly paid / well-paid</u> job ... the house was <u>well-equipped</u> ... they felt very <u>proud;</u>
express myself more <u>easily</u> ... talk more <u>slowly;</u>
spoke to me <u>jokingly / in a humorous way</u> ... to be taken <u>totally</u> seriously ... They often appeared <u>serious;</u>
my host family <u>usually went</u> to the pub ... <u>eternally</u> grateful

b <u>beautifully built:</u> *CEG* §203 (Index under 'adverb: use');
<u>highly paid / well-paid:</u> *CEG* §203 (Index under 'adverb: use');
<u>well-equipped:</u> *CEG* §203 (Index under 'adverb: use');
<u>felt proud:</u> *CEG* §209a (Index under 'adverb: after verbs');
<u>easily:</u> *CEG* §203 (Index under 'adverb: use');
<u>slowly:</u> *CEG* §203 (Index under 'adverb: use');
<u>jokingly / in a humorous way:</u> This is really a lexical problem; *funny*: 'amusing', 'strange';
funnily / in a funny way: 'in a strange way';
<u>totally seriously:</u> *CEG* §203 (Index under 'adverb: use');
<u>serious:</u> *CEG* §196b (Index under '*appear*: + adjective), *CEG* §209a (Index under 'adverb: after verbs');
<u>usually went:</u> *CEG* §214, 215 (Index under 'adverb: position');
<u>eternally grateful:</u> *CEG* §203 (Index under 'adverb: use').

c Mistakes such as 'beautiful built', 'a high paid job': since there are no adverbs in German, students tend to use adjectives in English where an adverb would be required. 'Take sth. serious': here students tend to translate the German phrase 'etwas ernst nehmen' literally, forgetting to use the adverb instead of the adjective.
'Went usually to the pub': in German, adverbs can be placed between verb and object, but not in English.

→ *WB, ex. 7* **2 a** Individual answers.

b extremely difficult, highly amusing, surprisingly easy, well-dressed, strictly regulated, truly amazing, naturally shy, etc.

c The classroom looks untidy. I feel very tired at the moment. That perfume smells terrible. The teacher sounds annoyed. The coffee I drank at break tasted horrible. Everyone seems very lazy.

d Individual answers.

The United Kingdom at a Glance

Government

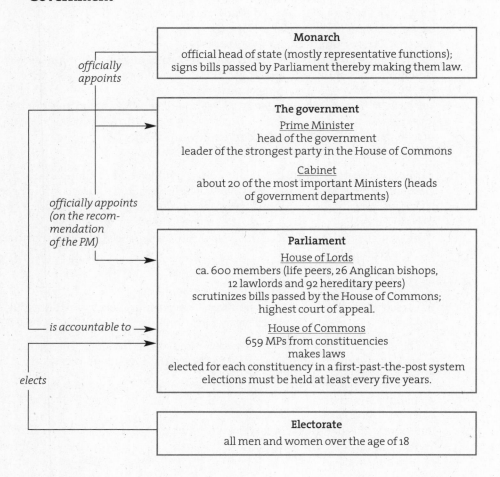

Monarch
official head of state (mostly representative functions);
signs bills passed by Parliament thereby making them law.

officially appoints

The government
<u>Prime Minister</u>
head of the government
leader of the strongest party in the House of Commons

<u>Cabinet</u>
about 20 of the most important Ministers (heads
of government departments)

officially appoints (on the recommendation of the PM)

Parliament
<u>House of Lords</u>
ca. 600 members (life peers, 26 Anglican bishops,
12 lawlords and 92 hereditary peers)
scrutinizes bills passed by the House of Commons;
highest court of appeal.

<u>House of Commons</u>
659 MPs from constituencies
makes laws
elected for each constituency in a first-past-the-post system
elections must be held at least every five years.

is accountable to

elects

Electorate
all men and women over the age of 18

Population

Total Population (2001):   58,789,000
England: 49,139,000
Scotland: 5,062,000
Wales: 2,903,000
Northern Ireland: 1,685,000

Ethnicity (England and Wales, 2001)
White: 91.3%
Indian: 2.0%
Pakistani: 1.4%
Mixed Ethnicity: 1.3%
Black Caribbean: 1.1%

45% of all ethnic minorities live in London,
where they form 28.8% of the population.

Religion (United Kingdom, 2001)
Christian: 71.6%
Muslim: 2.7%
Hindu: 1.0%
Sikh: 0.6%
Jews: 0.5%
Other: 0.6%
No religion/
none given: 23.2%

Some Figures for the UK
Unemployment rate (2003):   5%
Inflation rate (2003):   3.1%
GDP (2002): $25,300
Life expectancy: 78 years

CD Golden Jubilee Speech to Parliament

SB, p. 145 If a Jubilee becomes a moment to define an age, then for me we must speak of change – 1
its breadth and accelerating pace over these years. Since 1952 I have witnessed the
transformation of the international landscape through which this country must chart
its course: the emergence of the Commonwealth, the growth of the European Union,
the end of the Cold War and now the dark threat of international terrorism. This has 5
been matched by no less rapid developments at home: in the devolved shape of our
nation, in the structure of society, in technology and communications, in our work and
in the way we live. Change has become a constant; managing it has become an
expanding discipline. The way we embrace it defines our future.

It seems to me that this country has advantages to exploit in this exciting challenge. We 10
in these islands have the benefit of a long and proud history. This not only gives us a
trusted framework of stability and continuity to ease the process of change, but it also
tells us what is of lasting value. Only the passage of time can filter out the ephemeral
from the enduring. And what endure are the characteristics that mark our identity as a
nation and the timeless values that guide us. These values find expression in our 15
national institutions – including the monarchy and Parliament – institutions which in
turn must continue to evolve if they are to provide effective beacons of trust and unity
to succeeding generations.

I believe that many of the traditional values etched across our history equip us well for
this age of change. We are a moderate, pragmatic people, more comfortable with 20
practice than theory. With an off-shore, seafaring tradition we are outward-looking
and open-minded, well suited by temperament – and language – to our shrinking
world. We are inventive and creative – think of the record of British inventions over the
past 50 years or our present thriving arts scene. We also take pride in our tradition of
fairness and tolerance; the consolidation of our richly multicultural and multi-faith 25
society, a major development since 1952, is being achieved remarkably peacefully and
with much goodwill.

But there is another tradition in this country which gives me confidence for the future.
That is the tradition of service. The willingness to honour one another and seek the
common good transcends social change. Over these 50 years on visits up and down this 30
country I have seen at first hand and met so many people who are dedicating
themselves quietly and selflessly to the service of others.

I would particularly pay tribute to the young men and women of our armed forces who
give such professional service to this country often in the most demanding and
dangerous circumstances. They have my respect and admiration. I also wish to express 35
my gratitude for the work of those in the public service more widely – here in
Westminster or the corridors of Whitehall and town halls, as well as in our hospitals
and schools, in the police and emergency services. But I would especially like to thank
those very many people who give their time voluntarily to help others. I am pleased
that the Jubilee is to be marked by the introduction of The Queen's Golden Jubilee 40
Award, a new annual award for voluntary service by groups in the community. I hope
this will give added recognition to those whose generosity of time and energy in the
service of others is such a remarkable tradition in our society.

These enduring British traditions and values – moderation, openness, tolerance,
service – have stood the test of time, and I am convinced they will stand us in good stead 45
in the future. I hope that the Golden Jubilee will be an opportunity to recognize these
values and to celebrate all we as a nation have achieved since 1952. For my part, as I
travel the length and breadth of these islands over the coming weeks, I would like to
thank people everywhere for the loyalty, support and inspiration you have given me
over these 50 unforgettable years. I would like to express my pride in our past and my 50
confidence in our future. I would like above all to declare my resolve to continue, with
the support of my family, to serve the people of this great nation of ours to the best of
my ability through the changing times ahead.

Getting Along in English

SB, S. 149	*Warden:*	Antrim Bay Youth Hostel, Warden speaking.
Task 3	*Marc:*	Good morning, this is Marc Stein. I'm calling from Germany and I'd like to make a reservation at your youth hostel, please.
	Warden:	Fine, go ahead.
	Marc:	Sorry?
	Warden:	When would you like to stay, Marc?
	Marc:	Well, I'm with three friends, and we'd like to stay from Friday, 15th July, to the Monday, that's the 18th.
	Warden:	You're leaving on the 18th.
	Marc:	Yes, that's right.
	Warden:	And that's four males?
	Marc:	Er, no, it's two girls and two boys actually.
	Warden:	Yes, I can do that.
	Marc:	Oh great. And how much will it cost us?
	Warden:	You under 18 or over?
	Marc:	I'm 19. Oh, you mean our group. Erm, all over except one.
	Warden:	Well, it's £11.50 for the older ones and £9 for your friend. Do you want me to make a booking?
	Marc:	Well, yes please. Erm, what time do we need to arrive, because we might be late.
	Warden:	Well, the hostel closes at half eleven.
	Marc:	Oh, we'll be in by then.
	Warden:	But we only hold the booking until six. So if you want it guaranteed, I'm afraid I'll be needing a deposit of one night's stay, let's see 34.50 plus 9, that's £43.50.
	Marc:	Right. How can I pay?
	Warden:	Have you got a credit card? Or you can send a postal order?
	Marc:	I'll send a postal order. I'll put it in the post tomorrow. Another thing, do you accept German Youth Hostel cards?
	Warden:	No problem, sir. Now, I need your full name, it was Marc ...
	Marc:	Stein: S - T - E - I - N. And Marc with a C.
	Warden:	I've got you down.
	Marc:	Thanks a lot. Oh, one last thing: do you provide bed sheets and blankets?
	Warden:	You must be new to hostelling. I'm afraid you have to bring your own sheets or sleeping bag or you can borrow a linen sleeping bag from us, that's £3. Blankets are provided free of charge. Breakfast is an extra too, but you can see all about that when you get here, okay?
	Marc:	Yes – er, oh, it says there's a bus that goes past the Youth Hostel – does that still run?
	Warden:	We're located 200 yards off the coast road. You catch the 172 from Ballycastle, about every two hours.
	Marc:	Every two hours. Thanks very much for your help.
	Warden:	Right you are. Bye now.

Those Wild and Crazy English

SB, S. 156
Task 2

The Argument Clinic

Receptionist:	Yes, sir?
Man:	I'd like to have an argument, please.
Receptionist:	Certainly, sir. Have you been here before?
Man:	No, this is my first time.
Receptionist:	I see. Do you want to have the full argument, or were you thinking of taking a course?
Man:	Well, what would be the cost?
Receptionist:	Well, yes. It's one pound for a five-minute argument, but only eight pounds for a course of ten.
Man:	Well, I think it's probably best if I perhaps start with the one and then see how it goes from there, OK?
Receptionist:	Fine. I'll see who's free at the moment. Mr DuBakey's free, but he's a little bit conciliatory. Yes. Try Mr Barnard. Room 12.
Man:	Thank you.
Abuser:	What do you want?
Man:	Well, I was told outside ...
Abuser:	Don't give me that, you snotty-faced heap of parrot droppings!
Man:	What?
Abuser:	Shut your festering gob, you tit! Your type makes me puke, you vacuous, toffee-nosed, malodorous, pervert!!!
Man:	Look, I came in here for an argument.
Abuser:	Oh, oh, I'm sorry. This is abuse.
Man:	Oh, I see, well, that explains it.
Abuser:	Ah no, you want 12A, next door.
Man:	I see. Sorry.
Abuser:	Not at all. No, that's alright. Stupid git!!
Arguer:	Come in.
Man:	Is this the right room for an argument?
Arguer:	I've told you once.
Man:	No, you haven't.
Arguer:	Yes, I have.
Man:	When?
Arguer:	Just now.
Man:	No, you didn't.
Arguer:	Yes, I did.
Man:	Didn't
Arguer:	I did!
Man:	Didn't!
Arguer:	I'm telling you I did!
Man:	You did not!!
Arguer:	Oh, I'm sorry. Is this a five-minute argument or the full half hour?
Man:	Oh, just the five minute one.
Arguer:	Fine. Thank you. Anyway, I did.
Man:	You most certainly did not.
Arguer:	Now, let's get one thing quite clear; I most definitely told you.
Man:	You did not.
Arguer:	Yes, I did.
Man:	You did not.
Arguer:	Yes, I did.
Man:	Didn't.

Arguer:	Yes I did.
Man:	Didn't.
Arguer:	Yes, I did.
Man:	Look, this isn't an argument.
Arguer:	Yes, it is.
Man:	No, it isn't. It's just contradiction.
Arguer:	No it isn't.
Man:	Yes, it is!
Arguer:	It is not.
Man:	It is. You just contradicted me.
Arguer:	No, I didn't.
Man:	Oh you did!!
Arguer:	No, no, no.
Man:	You did just then.
Arguer:	No, no, nonsense!
Man:	Oh, look, this is futile!
Arguer:	No it isn't.
Man:	I came here for a good argument.
Arguer:	No, you didn't; no, you came here for an argument.
Man:	Well, an argument's not the same as contradiction.
Arguer:	It can be.
Man:	No it can't. An argument is a connected series of statements to establish a proposition.
Arguer:	No, it isn't.
Man:	Yes, it is! It isn't just contradiction.
Arguer:	Look, if I argue with you, I must take up a contrary position.
Man:	But it isn't just saying 'No it isn't.'
Arguer:	Yes, it is!
Man:	No, it isn't!
Man:	Argument is an intellectual process. Contradiction is just the automatic gainsaying of anything the other person makes.
Arguer:	No, it isn't.
Man:	Yes, it is.
Arguer:	Not at all.
Man:	Now look.
Arguer:	Thank you. Morning.
Man:	What?
Arguer:	That's it. Good morning.
Man:	I was just getting interested.
Arguer:	Sorry, the five minutes is up.
Man:	That was never five minutes just now!
Arguer:	I'm afraid it was.
Man:	No, it wasn't.
Arguer:	Sorry, I'm not allowed to argue anymore.
Man:	What?!
Arguer:	If you want me to go on arguing, you'll have to pay for another five minutes.
Man:	But that was never five minutes, just now. Oh come on! This is ridiculous.
Arguer:	I'm very sorry, but I told I'm not allowed to argue unless you've paid!
Man:	Oh, alright. There you are.
Arguer:	Thank you.
Man:	Well?
Arguer:	Well what?
Man:	That was never five minutes, just now.
Arguer:	I told you, I'm not allowed to argue unless you've paid.

Man:	I just paid!
Arguer:	No you didn't.
Man:	I did! I did! I did! Look, I don't want to argue about that.
Arguer:	Well, I'm very sorry but you didn't pay.
Man:	Aha. Well, if I didn't pay, why are you arguing? Got you!
Arguer:	No you haven't.
Man:	Yes I have. If you're arguing, I must have paid.
Arguer:	Not necessarily. I could be arguing in my spare time.
Man:	I've had enough of this.
Arguer:	No, you haven't.
Man:	Oh, shut up.
Man:	I want to complain.
Complainer:	You want to complain! Look at these shoes. I've only had them three weeks and the heels are worn right through.
Man:	No, I want to complain about ...
Complainer:	If you complain nothing happens, you might as well not bother, and my back hurts ...
Man:	Hello, I want to ... Ooooh!
Hitter:	No, no, no. Hold your head like this, and then go 'waaah'. Try it again.
Man:	Ohhhh!!
Hitter:	Better, better, but ... waah, waah! Hold your hands here.
Man:	No.
Hitter:	Now.
Man:	Waaaaah!!!
Hitter:	Good! That's it. Good!
Man:	Stop hitting me!!
Hitter:	What?
Man:	Stop hitting me!!
Hitter:	Stop hitting you?
Man:	Yes!
Hitter:	What did you come in here for?
Man:	I came here to complain.
Hitter:	Oh no, that's next door. It's being-hit-on-the-head lessons in here.
Man:	What a stupid concept.

Das neunte Kapitel befasst sich unter verschiedenen Aspekten mit amerikanischen Selbst- und Fremdbildern und zielt auf ein differenziertes Urteil über die amerikanische Gesellschaft in ihrer Vielfalt und Widersprüchlichkeit. Der Kapiteltitel zitiert die ersten drei Wörter der amerikanischen Verfassung und kann als Hinweis auf amerikanisches Demokratieverständnis und Sendungsbewusstsein verstanden werden.

- *Section 1*, „American Dreams", stellt durch eine Auswahl patriotischer und amerikakritischer Lieder und Gedichte gegensätzliche Sichtweisen der USA vor.
- *Section 2*, „God Bless America", vertieft diese Sichtweisen anhand der Antrittsrede von Präsident George W. Bush (2001)und einiger Statistiken zu den USA.
- *Section 3*, „America in the Eyes of the World", zeigt aktuelle ambivalente Reaktionen auf den weltweiten amerikanischen Führungsanspruch.
- *Section 4*, „An American Quilt", verdeutlicht die inneren Spannungen einer Einwanderergesellschaft.
- *Section 5*, „The American Way of Life", skizziert verschiedene Elemente des amerikanischen Alltagslebens wie Baseball, Auto und Fernsehen.

Da es schwer möglich ist, für das Thema USA eine repräsentative Wortschatzliste zu erstellen, entfällt die KV „Topic Vocabulary" für dieses Kapitel.

Didaktisches Inhaltsverzeichnis

SB, p.	Title	TM, p	Text form	Topic	Skills and activities
164	Lead-in	317	photos	views of the USA	identifying symbols; making a collage; summarizing different views
			novel (extract)	views of the Statue of Liberty and the US flag	
166	America the Beautiful Katherine Lee Bates	321	poem	America as the land blessed by God	comparing various texts
166	The New Colossus Emma Lazarus	322	poem	America as the land that welcomes the poor and the oppressed	comparing various texts
167	Dirty Blvd. Lou Reed	324	song lyrics	America as the land that treats its poor badly	comparing various texts
167	American Dream Bad Religion	325	song lyrics	criticism of the American Dream	comparing various texts
168	Context Box	327	–	the development of the American self-image	writing a fact sheet; analysing a painting; finding synonyms; writing an A–Z
169	Inaugural Speech George W. Bush Video/DVD	328	speech	presidential inaugural speech	identifying themes; analysing stylistic devices; giving a personal reaction; doing research
170	Facts and Figures	331	figures	income inequality; children living in poverty; prisoners in the USA	working with figures
171	America Triumphant	334	editorial	the world a year after 11 September, 2001	
171	Imperial Power George Monbiot	335	newspaper column	the need for Europe to prevent US imperial power	
172	A Growing Dislike of the USA	335	online news report	global reactions to the USA	examining the global role of the USA; writing a letter

173	**Bound by a Common Thread** Jesse Jackson	336	speech	the USA as a quilt	analysing the use of language; designing a quilt
174	**Lifeblood of the Nation** T. Coraghessan Boyle	339	novel (extract)	the rights and wrongs of immigration to the USA	examining two sides of an argument; writing a summary; identifying the mode of presentation; converting a novel into a filmscript
175	**Assimilation, American-style** Robert J. Samuelson	341	newsmagazine column	the assimilation of immigrants in the USA	working with definitions; comparing different views; writing a text
177	**Getting Along in English** CD2, track 13	343	–	–	working out strategies to avoid rudeness
178	**The Magic of Baseball** Doris Kearns Godwin	344	essay	sport as an activity that binds generations	analysing metaphors; working with idioms
180	**A Sedentary Nation** Bill Bryson	347	essay	the love of cars and its effect on American behaviour	analysing the use of humour; working with vocabulary; examining American and European views
182	**Car Culture and the Shopping Mall** CD2, track 14	349	radio documentary	the role of the car and the shopping mall	examining the popularity of malls
182	**The American Way Way of Life as Reflected on TV** Video/DVD	350	TV series (extract)	American family life and American values	analysing the Americanness of TV programmes
183	**Watch Your Language**	351	–	–	participles, relative clauses and sentence variety

SB, S. 164

Lead-in

Didaktisch-methodische Hinweise

Das „Lead-in" eröffnet durch die Bilder und den Textauszug aus Paul Austers *Leviathan* einen differenzierten Zugang zu den USA als umstrittener ökonomischer, politischer, kultureller und militärischer Supermacht und ihren weltanschaulichen Grundlagen.

Fotos

Dieses Kaleidoskop beinhaltet positiv wie negativ konnotierte Aspekte der USA:

– Die Lincoln-Statue im Washingtoner Lincoln Monument erinnert an eine Zentralfigur des amerikanischen Selbstbewusstseins: „Honest Abe", den aufrechten Kämpfer gegen Sklaverei und für Demokratie, der in seiner „Gettysburg Address" die berühmte Formel „government of the people, by the people and for the people" prägte.
– Das Bild der Feuerwehrleute in den Ruinen des World Trade Center markiert den amerikanischen Selbstbehauptungswillen angesichts des 11. September 2001.
– Der Flugzeugträger und die Kampfflugzeuge stehen für die militärische Hegemonie der USA.
– Das Wortspiel der Demonstranten „God (b)less America" greift die traditionelle Schluss- und Segensformel amerikanischer Politiker auf (vgl. SB, S. 167) und stellt das religiöse Selbstverständnis einer puritanisch geprägten Nation in Frage.
– Der Hamburger und das Museum „The World of Coca Cola" in Las Vegas stehen für den weltweiten Einfluss amerikanischer Popkultur.
– Der amerikanische Dollar repräsentiert die amerikanische Finanzmacht.

– Die amerikanischen Fahnen stehen als Integration stiftendes nationales Symbol für den Patriotismus einer Einwanderernation.Bei der Arbeit mit den Fotos aktivieren die S ihr Vorwissen, machen sich Aspekte des Amerikabildes bewusst, stellen Überlegungen über ihr eigenes Amerikabild an und recherchieren arbeitsteilig zu ausgewählten Aspekten.

SB, S. 165

Auszug aus *Leviathan*

Source:	*Leviathan*, 1992
Topic:	American ideals as reflected in the Statue of Liberty and the American flag
Text form:	Novel (extract)
Language variety:	AE
Number of words:	241
Level:	Basic/advanced
Skills/activities:	Summarizing different views

Lern-vokabular

Active vocabulary: 'Leviathan' (p. 165)

replica (l. 1), town hall (l. 3), divide people (l. 4), bring people together (l. 4), be proud of sth. (l. 5), feel ashamed of sth. (l. 6), regard sth. as sth. else (l. 7), be immune from sth. (l. 8), transcend sth. (l. 9), emblem (l. 10), represent sth. (l. 11), live up to your ideals (l. 15), give comfort to sb. (l. 16)

Didaktisch-methodische Hinweise

Der Auszug aus Paul Austers *Leviathan* [lə'vaɪəθən] kontrastiert unterschiedliche Einstellungen zur amerikanischen Fahne und zur Statue of Liberty, nennt grundlegende amerikanische Werte (*democracy, freedom, equality under the law*) und spricht die Kluft zwischen amerikanischen Idealen und amerikanischer Wirklichkeit an. Der kurze Romanauszug bietet damit einen Anknüpfungspunkt für die oft sehr ambivalenten Einstellungen der S gegenüber den USA. Die Bedeutung der Statue of Liberty für das amerikanische Selbstverständnis kann in *section* 1 anhand des Auszugs aus Emma Lazarus' „The New Colossus" (vgl. SB, S. 166) erarbeitet werden; Austers idealisierte Sicht der Freiheitsstatue wird relativiert durch Lou Reeds „Dirty Blvd." (vgl. SB, S. 167).

Unterrichts-tipps

Als Ausgangspunkt für die Erarbeitung der Auftaktseiten können die Abbildungen dienen. Die S identifizieren und beschreiben die Bildinhalte, wobei sie sich ggf. arbeitsteilig jeweils mit einem Bild genauer beschäftigen sollten. Als Überleitung zum Text können die S gebeten werden, andere amerikanische Symbole zu nennen, zu denen auch die Freiheitsstatue gehören wird.

→ *WB, ex. 1*

Info

The American flag: First used in 1777 during the Revolutionary War against Britain, the US flag has always been treated with reverence in the USA. Many Americans see the flag not just as a symbol of national unity, but as something sacred that represents what is best in the nation. Any disrespect to the flag is therefore considered a sacrilege. Other Americans feel the flag is a mere symbol and should not be treated in a way that contradicts the basic ideals of the USA; for them being able to desecrate the flag reveals the value attached to free speech in the USA. The Supreme Court has always struck down laws that have prosecuted people for desecrating the flag, as it argues this falls under the First Amendment as free speech.

Info

The dollar bill: The federal government first started to print its own paper money in 1861. The current $1 bill dates from 1957. It contains the mottos 'In God we trust', 'E pluribus unum' (Out of many one), 'Annuit Coeptis' (It, i.e. the eye of Providence, has favoured our undertakings), 'Novus ordo seclorum' (A new order of the ages), and the year 1776 at the base of the pyramid. For background information on the symbolism of the Great Seal of the USA cf. www.greatseal.com · 1.8.2003.

Paul Auster (born 1947) studied at Columbia University. He gained success with his *New York Trilogy* (1985–1986), which he followed up with novels such as *Moon Palace* (1989) and *Music of Chance* (1991). *Leviathan* (1992) deals with the activities of Ben Sachs, who blows up replicas of the Statue of Liberty as a sign that America should mend its ways.

Lösungs-hinweise

1 **a** The Lincoln Memorial is a symbol of the unity of the USA (the Civil War divided the country) and of the emancipation of black Americans.
Flags as symbols of national unity; unifying symbols are especially important in immigrant societies. Raising the American flag in the ruins of the World Trade Center was a symbolic act expressing American pride and determination after 11 September, 2001.
The demonstrators' wordplay 'God (b)less America' is a reaction to American exceptionalism, i.e. the belief that America, as God's own country, has to fulfil a mission: to bring prosperity and democracy to the world.
The dollar note (informally known as the 'greenback') is a symbol of American economic power, as was the World Trade Center, the attacks on which revealed global (especially from the Muslim world) hostility to American power.
The hamburger and the Coca Cola museum symbolize the global influence of American popular culture.
The American aircraft carrier and the fighter squadron flying overhead stand for American military power.

b The firefighters see the flag as a symbol of American pride at a difficult time, whereas the demonstrators seem to reject the flag by writing anti-US statements on it.

2 **a–c** Individual answers.

⬭ *If you have a partner school in the USA, exchange a 'culture discovery list/box' with your partner class. To do this, you have to select objects you consider typically German. As many of the objects will be unknown in the other country (an American is unlikely to know, for example, what a Currywurst is), both schools can decide whether it might help to add information about what the object is or to allow the partner school to do research on it. You can also add explanatory notes about why the objects play an important role in your country. When you receive the American 'culture discovery list/box', speculate about the choices of your partner class, especially about their cultural significance before studying the explanatory notes.*

3 **a** According to Auster, Americans are united in their respect for the Statue of Liberty as a symbol of basic American values (democracy, freedom, equality under the law). Americans are divided, however, in their attitudes to the American flag. Some are proud of it, while others are ashamed of it; some regard it as a sacred object while others want to desecrate it.

b 'divide people' (l. 4), 'bring people together' (l. 4), 'cause controversy' (l. 5), 'be proud of sth.' (l. 5), 'be ashamed of sth.' (l. 6), 'regard sth. as a holy object' (l. 7), 'spit on sth.' (l. 7), 'burn sth.' (l. 8), 'drag sth. through the mud' (l. 8), 'transcend politics and ideology' (l. 9), 'stand as an emblem of sth.' (l. 10), 'represent sth.' (l. 11).

4 Individual answers.

○ *Do Germans have a different attitude to their flag from Americans?*

○ *What role do historical buildings such as the Brandenburg Gate and the Reichstag have as symbols of German identity? Are they more important than flags?*

○ *To what extent does the European flag serve as a symbol of European unity?*

4 Individual answers.

○ *Having looked at the photos in the Lead-in, do research on the following, taking into consideration their role in the American psyche. Present your results to the class:*

– *'Honest Abe', the Civil War and the Gettysburg address;*

– *9/11 (the terrorist attacks on the World Trade Center and the Pentagon);*

– *the significance of the American flag in the USA (consider terms such as 'The Star-Spangled Banner', 'Old Glory', 'the Stars and Stripes', 'Flag Day', 'the Pledge of Allegiance', 'flag burning and desecration');*

– *the dollar bill and its symbolism;*

– *McDonald's and Coca Cola as multinational companies.*

SB, S. 166 # 1   American Dreams

In diesem Abschnitt werden anhand von Auszügen aus patriotischen wie auch amerikakritischen Liedern und Gedichten unterschiedliche Reaktionen auf die USA vorgestellt: auf der einen Seite die idealisierte Sicht der Vereinigten Staaten als gesegnetes Land („America the Beautiful") und Heimstatt der Entrechteten („The New Colossus"), auf der anderen Seite Desillusion und aggressive Kritik an Ausbeutung („Dirty Blvd.") und Heuchelei („American Dream") in der amerikanischen Gesellschaft.

Die gegensätzlichen Amerikabilder greifen die im „Lead-in" (SB, S. 164) angesprochenen Ambivalenzerfahrungen der S auf. Sie illustrieren – aus amerikanischer Sicht – die von Paul Auster (vgl. den Auszug aus *Leviathan*, SB, S. 165) beklagte Kluft zwischen amerikanischem Ideal und amerikanischer Wirklichkeit und relativieren damit den bei den S möglicherweise vorhandenen Eindruck eines übergreifenden unkritischen amerikanischen Patriotismus. Dabei sollte aber betont werden, dass patriotische Stimmen in der Mehrzahl sind (und möglicherweise nach dem 11. September 2001 noch zugenommen haben). Die Gedichte aus den Achtzigerjahren können nicht als repräsentativ für das Verhältnis heutiger US-Amerikaner gegenüber den Idealen ihres Landes gelten.

Diese Auswahl bietet verschiedene Verknüpfungsmöglichkeiten mit anderen Abschnitten des USA-Kapitels:
– Das Lied „America the Beautiful" war Teil des Rahmenprogramms bei Präsident Bushs Amtseinführung am 20. Januar 2001 (vgl. „Inaugural Speech", SB, S. 169);

– „Dirty Blvd." relativiert Austers Aussagen zur Akzeptanz der *Statue of Liberty* in den USA und kann zur Frage der Integration von Wirtschaftsflüchtlingen und Einwanderern in den USA überleiten (vgl. *section* 4, SB, S. 173);

– „America the Beautiful", „Dirty Blvd." und „American Dream" enthalten alle den für das amerikanische Selbstverständnis zentralen Begriff „dream", der in der „Context Box" untersucht wird.

Differenzierung

→ WB, ex. 5

Leistungsstärkere S können die vier kurzen Texte nacheinander still lesen und dann die Aufgaben beantworten. Für leistungsschwächere Kurse empfiehlt sich eine sukzessive Behandlung.

A America the Beautiful   Katherine Lee Bates

Source:	'America the Beautiful', 1893
Topic:	America as the land blessed by God
Text form:	Poem
Language variety:	AE
Number of words:	37 (all 4 verses: 141)
Level:	Basic/advanced

*Didaktisch-
methodische
Hinweise*

Den Ausgangspunkt dieser *section* bildet Katherine Lee Bates' „America the Beautiful",
das häufig als Ersatz für die schwer zu singende amerikanische Nationalhymne vorgeschlagen worden ist. Der Ton ist hymnisch, das Lied besingt den Reichtum, die Erhaben-
heit der amerikanischen Natur und den Idealismus und den Patriotismus der amerikanischen Siedler. Die wiederholten Segensformeln („God shed ..., God mend ... May
God ..."), die Erwähnung der *pilgrims* und die Anspielungen auf die biblische
Verheißung des neuen Jerusalem, in dem Gott alle Tränen abwischt („undimmed by
human tears"), verweisen auf das religiöse Fundament der USA. Der Patriotismus des
Liedes wird relativiert durch die Einsicht in die Unvollkommenheit der amerikanischen
Gesellschaft („God mend thine every flaw" und „May God thy gold refine") und bietet
somit auch Identifikationsmöglichkeiten für Menschen, die amerikanischer Politik
und Lebensweise kritisch gegenüberstehen.

Im SB ist nur die erste Strophe abgedruckt; die S müssen zunächst den gesamten Text
auf ihrer Basis rekonstruieren, bevor sie weiterarbeiten (vgl. die KV „America the
Beautiful" auf S. 353, s.u.). Die Rekonstruktion der Strophen dürfte ohne größere
Probleme möglich sein, wenn die S sich an dem Reimschema a b a b in der ersten
Strophenhälfte und dem Strophenaufbau (z.B. Einleitung mit dem Ausruf „O",
Anrufung Amerikas und abschließender Segenswunsch) orientieren. Zu beachten ist
allerdings, dass es sich bei „skies/majesties" in der ersten Strophe lediglich um einen
Augenreim handelt.

Lexikalische und syntaktische Schwierigkeiten bei der Rezeption des Lieds können die
Ellipse („beautiful for", Z. 1), die archaisierende Sprache („thee", „thy", Z. 6,7), die Stellung
des direkten Objekts vor dem Verb („Who more than self their country loved", „May God
thy gold refine") und der Gebrauch des „subjunctive" bereiten („God shed", Z. 6). Hier
sind je nach Leistungsstand der Lerngruppe sprachliche Hilfen erforderlich.

Inhaltlich bietet der Text Ansatzpunkte für Schülerrecherchen zu den Themen „The
Pilgrims and the Puritan heritage" und dem *War of Independence*. Der religiöse Hintergrund des Liedes kann vertiefend in Zusammenarbeit mit dem Religionsunterricht
bzw. Ethik oder Werte und Normen geklärt werden.

*Unterrichts-
tipps
Kopiervorlage*

Der Einstieg sollte über die im SB abgedruckte Strophe erfolgen. Die S bearbeiten die KV
„America the Beautiful" (vgl. S. 353) und erhalten Einsicht in Strukturmerkmale des
Lieds, indem sie die von ihnen gewählte Reihenfolge der Zeilen begründen. Erst danach
sollte die Musik (vgl. CD2, *track* 12) gespielt werden.
Strophen 2–4 lauten im Original:

2. O beautiful for pilgrim feet
Whose stern, impassioned stress
A thoroughfare for freedom beat
Across the wilderness!
America! America!
God mend thine every flaw,
Confirm thy soul in self-control,
Thy liberty in law!

3. O beautiful for heroes proved
In liberating strife.
Who more than self the country
loved
And mercy more than life!
America! America!
May God thy gold refine
Till all success be nobleness
And every gain divine!

4. O beautiful for patriot dream
That sees beyond the years
Thine alabaster cities gleam
Undimmed by human tears!
America! America!
God shed his grace on thee
And crown thy good with brotherhood
From sea to shining sea!

Die Aufgabe auf der KV könnte folgendermaßen gelöst werden:
Geographical features: prairies ('amber waves of grain'), Rockies/Appalachians/etc. ('purple mountains'), two coasts ('from sea to shining sea').
Historical events: Civil War (insistence on 'brotherhood'), Pilgrims ('pilgrim feet'), Constitution ('liberty in law'), Revolutionary War ('liberating strife').
Values: goodness ('good'), brotherhood, self-improvement ('mend thine every flaw', 'sees beyond the years thine alabaster cities gleam undimmed by human tears'), self-control, liberty, heroism ('heroes'), patriotism ('more than self the country loved', 'patriot dream'), mercy, nobleness.

⬭ *Find photos and pictures that could be used to illustrate and comment on 'America the Beautiful'. Explain your choice.*

Info

Katharine Lee Bates (1850–1929) wrote 'America the Beautiful' in 1893 on a visit to Pike's Peak, Colorado (cf. photo on p. 166). She revised the lyrics in 1904, and again in 1911. For most of her adult life, Bates was a professor of English at Wellesley College. She wrote children's books and published several collections of poetry. However, her lasting fame comes from her authorship of 'America the Beautiful'. With its lyrics and its stirring tune ('Materna', composed by Samuel A. Ward in 1882), 'America the Beautiful' appeals to Americans of all political persuasions as an expression of what is good about the USA.

SB, S. 166 **B The New Colossus**   Emma Lazarus

Source:	'The New Colossus', 1883
Topic:	America as the land that welcomes the poor and the oppressed
Text form:	Poem
Language variety:	AE
Number of words:	67
Level:	Basic/advanced

Lern-vokabular

Active vocabulary: 'The New Colossus' (p. 166)

mighty (l. 2), imprisoned (l. 3), beacon (l. 4)

Didaktisch-methodische Hinweise

Im SB sind aus Platzgründen nur 10 der 14 Zeilen von Emma Lazarus' Sonett abgedruckt. Der Auszug enthält viele Licht-Metaphern („torch", l. 2, „flame", l. 2, „lightning", l. 3, „beacon", l. 4, „lamp", l. 10) und endet mit dem Willkommensgruß an die Heimatlosen und Entrechteten aller Länder („Give me your tired, your poor", l. 6).

Kopiervorlage

Die KV „The New Colossus" (vgl. S. 354) enthält den vollständigen Text mit Fragen zu einer vertiefenden Gedichtanalyse. Literarisch interessierten Lerngruppen bietet sich die Gelegenheit, die im Glossar enthaltene Sonettdefinition zu erweitern (vgl. SB, S. 256). Das 14-zeilige Gedicht besteht aus einer *octave* und einem *sestet* und ist somit als

Italian oder *Petrarchan* *sonnet* zu klassifizieren (vgl. die Lösung zu Aufgabe 5 der KV). Wenn die S Shakespeare-Sonette kennen (z.B. „Sonnet 130", SB, S. 43), können die formalen Unterschiede festgestellt werden.

Eine Lösung zur KV „The New Colossus" könnte folgendermaßen aussehen:

1 The old world has history and rich cultural heritage, but its people are downtrodden and oppressed, so that those who are not part of the rich establishment feel they do not belong (cf. 'homeless', l. 13)

2 a) It is the Colossus of Rhodes.
   b) The Colossus of Rhodes seems to serve as a symbol of power and strength and conquest ('conquering limbs', l. 2). It is arrogant and bold ('brazen', l. 1). By contrast, the Statue of Liberty is the 'Mother of Exiles' (l. 6), who welcomes those who have been cast out and are poor and miserable.

3 The poet uses the symbolism of light in ll. 3–7 ('sunset', 'torch', flame', 'lightning', beacon', 'glows') and l. 14 ('lamp') to show that America is a beacon or light to the world, offering refuge and hope. People always move towards light, so this is a very comforting image. In l. 14 she uses the symbol 'the golden door', the door being a traditional symbol for entering a new life or starting again, the adjective 'golden' implying a better (and wealthier) future for the exiles.

4 She uses alliteration and personification ('world-wide welcome').

5 The poem is divided into two parts: an octave rhyming a b b a a b b a and a sestet ryhming c d c d c d. The octave deals with the contrast between the two statues, the sestet are the words of the Statue of Liberty. In Shakespeare's sonnets there are three quatrains rhyming a b a b c d c d e f e f which develop the theme and then a couplet which concludes the sonnet.

Unterrichts-tipps   Bevor die S den Text lesen, können sie ihr Wissen oder ihre Assoziationen zum Titel und zum Koloss von Rhodos (vgl. „Info", S. 324) sammeln. Für eine kurze Inhaltssicherung unmittelbar nach der Lektüre eignen sich die folgenden Fragen:

⬭ *What is the new colossus?*
The Statue of Liberty.

⬭ *What does she stand for?*
She stands for the welcome that is given to exiles, the poor, the tired and the oppressed.

⬭ *Where did the 'tired', 'poor', 'masses' 'refuse', 'homeless' come from, and why? Does that still apply today?*
At the time immigrants came principally from Europe, where there was much oppression (especially for Jews in Eastern Europe) and poverty (especially in the Mediterranean countries). As most present-day immigrants come from developing countries such as Mexico, one can say that it still applies today.

Info

Emma Lazarus (1849–1887) wrote 'The New Colossus' in 1883 for the pedestal of the Statue of Liberty. The statue was a gift from France as a sign of the friendship between the two nations. The French had aided the Americans in their struggle for independence from Britain, and the Statue of Liberty was intended to celebrate the centenary of American independence. The Americans were responsible for the pedestal, while the French constructed the statue. It was only in 1886 that the statue was finally dedicated. Lazarus's sonnet was only noticed after her death, when it was found in a portfolio of poems written to raise money for the pedestal. Its last five lines were inscribed on a plaque and set on the pedestal in 1903. While the Statue of Liberty was primarily intended to be a symbol of enlightenment for the countries of Europe still battling tyranny and oppression, Lazarus's sonnet resulted in the statue becoming the symbol of American freedom and unrestricted immigration to the USA.

Info

The Colossus of Rhodes was a 30 m high bronze statue of the sun god Helios that stood by the harbour of the Greek island of Rhodes and was one of the Seven Wonders of the World. It was built by Chares of Lindos between ca. 292 and 280 BC. The statue, which commemorated the ending of a long siege, was toppled by an earthquake in about 225 BC. The fallen Colossus was left in place until 653 AD, when the Arabs raided Rhodes and had the bronze sold for scrap.

SB, S. 167 · **C Dirty Blvd.** Lou Reed

Source:	*New York*, 1989
Topic:	America as a country that treats its poor badly
Text form:	Song lyrics
Language variety:	AE
Number of words:	107
Level:	Basic/advanced

Lern-vokabular

Active vocabulary: 'Dirty Blvd.' (p. 167)

landlord (l. 2), dream of being sth. (l. 3), bigotry (l. 6), get it over with (l. 8), dump sb./sth. (l. 8), end up (l. 9)

Didaktisch-methodische Hinweise

Dieser Text bezieht sich explizit auf Lazarus' Gedicht und reflektiert dessen Aussage kritisch. Der pessimistische Ton ist in vielerlei Hinsicht typisch für die Enttäuschung vieler US-Amerikaner in den Siebziger- und Achtzigerjahren, die angesichts von Vietnamkrieg, Watergate-Affäre und der immer größer werdenden Kluft zwischen Reich und Arm feststellten, dass ihr Land nicht länger als *beacon* für die Welt diente. Dabei sollte betont werden, dass Reed nicht die Ideale selbst in Frage stellt, sondern ihre Umsetzung. Der komplette Text von „Dirty Blvd." befindet sich unter www.lyricsfreak.com/l/lou-reed/85219.html · 1.8.2003.

Unterrichts-tipps

Den S könnte folgende Frage zum Textverständnis gestellt werden:

⬭ *What does the 'dirty boulevard' stand for?*
It stands for all the poverty and broken dreams of the USA. Here it is where the poor and oppressed end up, homeless and trodden on.

Info

Lou Reed (born 1942) is a musician whose career has taken different turns. Although Reed achieved his greatest success as a solo artist, his most enduring accomplishments were as the singer-songwriter of *Velvet Underground* in the 1960s, despite the fact that they were largely unappreciated at the time. In 1970 Reed started his solo career. Among his best early albums are *Berlin* (1973), *Sally Can't Dance* (1974) and *Transformer* (1979). *New York* (1989) was both a commercial and critical success for Reed. His album *Ecstasy* (2000) was also well received. Reed is one of the few stars from the 1960s who has managed to create work that is meaningful, contemporary and well-received.

D American Dream Bad Religion

Source:	*How Could Hell Be Any Worse?*, 1982
Topic:	Criticism of the American Dream
Text form:	Song lyrics
Language variety:	AE
Number of words:	66
Level:	Basic/advanced
Skills/activities:	Comparing various texts

Lern-
vokabular

Active vocabulary: 'American Dream' (p. 167)

tasks: attitude towards, in the light of, view of, take sth. into consideration

Didaktisch-
methodische
Hinweise

Der Song bildet mit seiner emotionalen Ablehnung des amerikanischen Lebensstils eine scharfe Antithese zu der Amerika verherrlichenden Sicht in „America the Beautiful". Literarisch ist er wenig anspruchsvoll. Er lebt von den Wiederholungen und den Aufzählungen dessen, was der Sänger hasst. Der vollständige Text befindet sich unter www.lyricsdepot. com/bad-religion/american-dream.html · 1.8.2003.

Info

Bad Religion is one of the most successful southern Californian hardcore punk bands that emerged in the 1980s. They retained their underground credibility while producing a series of records that always managed to reflect different trends; they added psychedelia, heavy metal as well as melody to their records. Their first record was *How Could Hell Be Any Worse?* (1982). Still teenagers at the time, it was only with *Into the Unknown* (1983) that they gained some attention on the US punk scene. Other albums include *Against the Grain* (1990), *Stranger Than Fiction* (1994) and *New America* (2000).

Lösungs-
hinweise

1 For Bates the American dream is the promise of a New Jerusalem 'from sea to shining sea' (l. 8). With God's help America is destined to fulfil the dream of abundant nature, natural beauty, freedom and brotherhood. Similarly, Lazarus's poem 'New Colossus' paints a positive picture of the USA as being a land of freedom, tolerance and hope as well as being a haven for the poor and homeless. By contrast, 'Dirty Blvd.' depicts the USA as a land in which the rich oppress the poor and where there is no hope for those living in poverty; it criticizes exploitation and insensitivity. The 'American Dream' is partly a teenage reaction against civil society as represented by middle-class America. It does also criticize the way that American society considers people who are old and not productive as useless.

2

a Lazarus sees the USA as generously welcoming the poor and needy from all over the world. The Statue of Liberty is personified as a mother, but is also symbolized as a 'beacon' to the world, offering light, shelter and prosperity to the poor. Reed's song aims to expose the hypocrisy of a nation that sees itself as a haven for the poor and the homeless from all over the world but treats its homeless with callous indifference. There is no hope of upward social mobility or success through education and hard work on dirty boulevard; the only dream left is the hope of escaping poverty and exploitation through drug-dealing.

b According to Auster, the Statue of Liberty transcends politics and ideology. In his view, it is universally accepted by Americans. Reed's song shows that this is not quite the case. His wordplay (cf. Glossary, p. 270) 'Statue of Liberty/Bigotry' is an attack on one of the central symbols of America, which is motivated by the pain that some Americans feel at 'America's failure to live up to [its] ideals' (Auster).

3 Bad Religion rejects everything the American Dream stands for: the belief in the American family, upward social mobility through education, rules and good behaviour. In particular, the group criticizes middle-class hypocrisy (cf. l. 2) and the neglect of the old (cf. l. 4). Bad Religion sees the American dream as a threat rather than a promise, swallowing those who who try to achieve it (cf. ll. 3, 6).

4 Der vollständige Text von „Dirty Blvd." befindet sich unter www.lyricsfreak. com/l/lou-reed/85219.html · 1.8.2003, der von „American Dream" unter www. lyricsdepot.com/bad-religion/american-dream.html · 1.8.2003. Weitere geeignete Lieder sind:„God Bless America" (Irving Berlin), „This Land is Your Land" (Woody Guthrie), „God Bless the USA" (Lee Greenwood), „My country, 'tis of thee" (Samuel F. Smith), „America" (Simon and Garfunkel), „Born in the USA" (Bruce Springsteen).

	America the Beautiful	Dirty Blvd.	American Dream
Content	highlights the spaciousness, fertility and grandeur of America from the Atlantic Ocean to the fertile plains of the Midwest and the Pacific Ocean (1st stanza); praises the Puritan heritage, the idealism of the settlers in the War of Independence and their commitment to freedom	criticizes broken promises of the American Dream, exposes the hollowness and hypocrisy of the Statue of Liberty ('Statue of Bigotry'); attacks inner-city life/ child abuse, drug dealing, insensitivity to the plight of the homeless / slum lords exploiting immigrants ('Pedro') / inequality of American society / prostitution; dreams seen as escapist, no hope of improving inner-city conditions	rejects middle-class lifestyle/hypocrisy, nuclear family ('family', 'one boy one girl'), school, rules ('speed limits') norms ('golden rule') religion ('your god'), neglect of the old ('old thus useless'), status symbols ('Chevrolet, with white walls on the side')
Tone	solemn, like a hymn	angry, critical, bitter, sarcastic (Statue of Bigotry), hopeless (desperate)	aggressive, bitter, scornful, critical
Language/ style	formal, archaic	colloquial (club 'em, 'cause), slang (piss), explicit/offensive language (TV whores calling out the cops for a suck)	colloquial, frequent repetitions of 'I hate' (anaphora), 'American Dream' and 'people who aren't what they seem'
Music	majestic, solemn, stirring	bright pop chords	heavy and loud, angry

⬭ *Imagine you are an immigrant arriving from Europe to the USA in 1900. Write down your feelings as you sail into New York Harbour and see the Statue of Liberty.*

⬭ *Imagine you are an American citizen, and a foreigner refers to the Statue of Liberty as the Statue of Bigotry. What might you say to persuade him or her that this view of America is wrong?*

Context Box

Didaktisch-
methodische
Hinweise

Die „Context Box" verfolgt das in *section 1* aufgeworfene Thema amerikanischer Träume und Alpträume weiter. Vor dem Hintergrund der Besiedlungsgeschichte der USA zeigt sie das Bedeutungsspektrum des Begriffs des *American Dream* im Wandel der Zeiten und liefert so einen Schlüssel zum Verständnis der amerikanischen Gesellschaft. Die im Begriff des *American Dream* enthaltenen Wertvorstellungen werden in den folgenden Abschnitten zur amerikanischen Innenpolitik (*section 2*) und Außenpolitik (*section 3*), zur amerikanischen Einwanderungsgesellschaft (*section 4*) und zum amerikanischen Lebensstil (*section 5*) konkretisiert. Vertiefend kann das Plädoyer der Friedmans für politische und wirtschaftliche Freiheit („Political and Economic Freedom", S. 102) im Kapitel „A Global Marketplace" herangezogen werden.

→ WB, ex. 1, 3

Lösungs-
hinweise

1 In schwächeren Lerngruppen kann zunächst die (zeitliche) Struktur des Texts herausgearbeitet werden. Leistungstärkere S können aufgefordert werden, die Informationen aus anderen Quellen zu ergänzen.

- 16th century: English adventurers and colonists hoping for wealth and glory.
- 17th century: Pilgrims desiring the establishment of a New Jerusalem.
- 18th century: Religious minorities seeking freedom from oppression; people seeking freedom to farm and to escape European feudal society.
- 19th century: The USA expands westwards and offers unlimited possibilities to new immigrants; people are able to realize their full potential regardless of their socio-economic and ethnic background.
- 20th century: There was no more open space to be conquered. The American dream had to be redefined and new frontiers in the sense of challenges (e.g. space, overcoming inequality, fighting for a better society) were sought.

2 John Gast depicts the settling of the North American continent in the 19th century. Two elements of the picture illustrate the belief that Americans were a chosen people: the figure in the middle of the picture and the light. The painting is dominated by an angelic figure dressed in a flowing white gown. Floating above the prairie, she seems to be leading the way (three trains are moving behind her towards the West), casting light on all below her. She can be seen as representing destiny, the driving force behind the westward movement. She is carrying a schoolbook, which represents education, and a telegraph wire, which represents communication. The right side is much lighter than the left: the sun is shining, the light is warm and bright, while on the left-hand side there are dark clouds and the colours are darker and more threatening. White settlers are moving across the prairie and driving Native Americans (together with the native animals they hunted) from their ancestral lands into the dark area. The city on the extreme right represents civilization. The light–dark contrast in the picture represents the belief that the settlers are bringing enlightenment and civilization to a dark and hostile land. In conquering the North American continent, they are fulfilling a divine mission, which was called Manifest Destiny.

3 Die Aufgabe kann durch die folgenden Wörter ergänzt werden, deren Synonyme die S suchen sollen: *attract*: 'lure' (1st paragraph); *achieve*: 'realize' (1st paragraph); *answer*: 'response' (2nd paragraph); *endless*: 'unlimited' (3rd paragraph); *mentality*: 'attitude' (4th paragraph); *large number*: 'host' (4th paragraph). Als Hilfestellung kann der Absatz genannt werden, in dem das gesuchte Wort enthalten ist.

dubious of: 'sceptical of' (2nd paragraph)
act of depending on oneself: 'self-reliance' (2nd paragraph)
typical of: 'characteristic of' (4th paragraph)

4 Für das A–Z kommen aus dem USA-Kapitel u.a. folgende weitere Stichwörter in Betracht: *flag, Statue of Liberty* („Lead-in"), *Pilgrims (section 1), inauguration, 9/11*

(11 September, 2001), unilateral power (section 2), quilt, melting pot, rainbow, pizza (section 3), Tortilla Curtain, immigration, assimilation, Protestant work ethic (section 4), popular culture, baseball, cars, shopping mall, TV shows (section 5). Stichwörter aus anderen Kapitel sind u.a.: family, Thanksgiving („Chapter 1"), television, advertising („Chapter 6"), personal statement („Chapter 11").

American Dream: the dream of a land of plenty and a land in which people are able to realize their full potential, regardless of their socio-economic and ethnic background.
Frontier: the moving borderline between civilization and wilderness. The frontier was closed when the settlers reached the Pacific coast in the second half of the 19th century.
Manifest Destiny: the 19th belief that the USA was chosen by God to settle most of North America.
Puritans: Protestant group of Christians in England in the 16th and 17th centuries who wanted to worship God in a simple way. They led strict lives and wanted to make America the New Jerusalem.

SB, S. 169

2 God Bless America

Section 3 behandelt die politische Vision, die George W. Bush bei seiner Amtseinführung als neu gewählter Präsident der USA 2001 entwarf. Durch die Auszüge aus der *inauguration address* lernen die S ein zentrales, Integration stiftendes Ritual der amerikanischen Gesellschaft kennen. Sie setzen sich mit amerikanischer politischer Rhetorik auseinander, fragen nach politischen Absichten, analysieren den Einsatz rhetorischer Mittel und überprüfen politische Aussagen anhand statistischer Angaben.

SB, S. 169

A Inaugural Speech   George W. Bush

VIDEO

Source:	*George W. Bush: Election & Inauguration*, 2001
Topic:	Presidential inaugural speech
Text form:	Speech
Language variety:	AE
Length:	11:06 minutes
Level:	Basic/advanced
Skills/activities:	Identifying themes, analysing stylistic devices, giving a personal reaction, doing research

Didaktisch-methodische Hinweise

Die Antrittsreden der amerikanischen Präsidenten vermeiden traditionell tagespolitische Probleme und konzentrieren sich auf mehrheitsfähige Grundsätze und Perspektiven. Sie dienen dem Ziel, die nach dem Präsidentschaftswahlkampf gespaltene Nation zu einen und auf die Politik der neuen Regierung einzustimmen. Sie sind daher in besonderer Weise geeignet, die S für amerikanische Themen und Motive zu sensibilisieren und ihre Kritikfähigkeit gegenüber politischer Rhetorik zu schärfen.
Mit ihrem Rückgriff auf amerikanische Geschichte und Wertvorstellungen, ihrem patriotischen Pathos und ihren religiösen Bezügen ist Bushs Antrittsrede vom 10. Januar 2001 ein typisches Beispiel einer *inaugural speech*. Angesichts der kontroversen Außenpolitik Bushs seit dem Angriff auf das World Trade Center am 11. September 2001 und der im Zusammenhang mit dem zweiten Irakkrieg (2003) belasteten deutsch-amerikanischen Beziehungen ist davon auszugehen, dass viele S der Rede emotional und sehr kritisch begegnen werden. Anliegen dieses Kapitels ist es aber nicht, die Diskussion über Bush und seine Amtsführung zu vertiefen. Der Schwerpunkt sollte vielmehr auf den exemplarischen Merkmalen einer Antrittsrede liegen, die diese *inaugural speech* mit vielen anderen gemein hat, und die auf spezifische ameri-

kanische Werte und Traditionen verweist. Entsprechend fragt die *pre-reading*-Aufgabe nach den Erwartungen an die Antrittsrede eines beliebigen neu gewählten Presidenten, nicht nach den Erwartungen an George W. Bush.

Für politisch interessierte S bietet der Projektvorschlag, Bushs Innen- und Außenpolitik mit den in seiner Antrittsrede geäußerten Absichtserklärungen zu vergleichen (Aufgabe 4), eine anspruchsvolle Herausforderung. Die Ergebnisse der Schülerrecherchen können zu Diskussionen über die Kluft zwischen Ideal und Wirklichkeit führen. Als

Kopiervorlage grundlegende Information über Bevölkerung und Wahlrecht kann die KV „The United States at a Glance" (vgl. S. 357) verwendet werden.

Bushs Bekenntnis zur Bereicherung Amerikas durch Einwanderung bietet eine Überleitungsmöglichkeit zu „An American Quilt" (SB, S. 173). Sein Hinweis auf den „simple dream of dignity" kann anhand der „Context Box" (SB, S. 166) vertieft werden.

Unterrichts- Der Redeauszug befindet sich auf dem Video / der DVD; das Transkript wird als Kopier-
tipps vorlage (KV „George W. Bush: Inaugural Speech", S. 355–356) angeboten, da die S es für
Kopiervorlage die Bearbeitung von Aufgabe 2 benötigen. Die ungekürzte Fassung der Rede ist unter www.cnn.com/ ALLPOLITICS/inauguration/2001/transcripts/template.html · 1.8.2003 zu finden.

Aus Gründen der Zeitökonomie werden die Auszüge aus der Rede (ca. 11 Minuten) nur ein Mal vorgespielt werden können, so dass die S darauf hingewiesen werden sollten, sich während des Sehens Notizen zu machen. Ggf. können die S sich mit einem Partner oder in Kleingruppen austauschen und ihre Notizen vervollständigen. Bei leistungsschwächeren S kann nach der ersten Präsentation mit dem Transkript weitergearbeitet werden.

Info

George W[alker] Bush (born 1946) was born in Connecticut but grew up in Texas. He attended Yale University and then served as an F-102 fighter pilot in the Texas Air National Guard. He later attended the Harvard Business School and began a career in the oil and gas industries. After working on his father's (George Bush, Sr) successful 1988 presidential campaign, he too entered politics and was elected Governor of Texas in 1994; in 2000 he was elected 43rd President of the USA after a bitterly disputed election; in Florida George W. Bush and his Democratic rival (Al Gore) were only a few hundred votes apart. There were allegations that some ballots might not have been counted properly, and many felt that the ballot paper had misled them to vote for the wrong candidate. After weeks of recounting and legal action by both sides, the Supreme Court finally decided in George W. Bush's favour. His presidency was overshadowed by the terrorist attacks of 11 September, 2001, and the collapse of energy giants (e.g. Enron) due to false accounting. The Bush administration also removed two foreign governments by force: the Taliban in Afghanistan (in 2002) and Saddam Hussein in Iraq (in 2003).

Lösungs-
hinweise
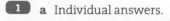

1 **a** Individual answers.

b According to Bush, America at its best is marked by civility (a commitment of each citizen to work for a fair and free society), courage (the willingness to confront domestic and foreign policy issues), compassion (concern, of the government and the nation as a whole, for the poor and disadvantaged) and character (personal responsibility, sacrifice and commitment to the community) (cf. KV, p. 355, ll. 37–78).

2 Vgl. die KV „George W. Bush: Inaugural Speech" auf S. 355–356.

a The ongoing American story (cf. transcript, ll. 8–15), pursuit of American ideals (ll. 16–28), the responsibility of everyone to build America (ll. 12–15, 31–36, 67–79), America at its best (ll. 37–79).

b Contrast (antithesis): 'slave-holding society ... servant to freedom' (cf. transcript, l. 10), 'to protect but not possess, to defend but not to conquer' (l. 11); 'flawed and fallible people ... grand and enduring ideals' (ll. 12–13); 'everyone belongs, that everyone deserves a chance, that no insignificant person was ever born' (ll. 14–15); 'inspire ... condemn' (l. 43); 'confronting problems ... passing them on' (ll. 44–45); 'reclaim America's schools ... claim young lives' (ll. 46–47); 'not acts of God ... failures of love' (l. 61); 'not strangers ... citizens, not problems ... priorities' (ll. 63–64); 'all of us ... when any ...' (ll. 64–65); 'sacrifice ... deeper fulfillment' (l. 77).

Alliteration: 'story ... slave-holding society ... servant' (l. 10); 'flawed and fallible' (l. 12); 'prosper ... promise' (l. 23); 'continent ... country' (l. 27); 'been ... blood ... birth ... bound ... beyond ... backgrounds' (ll. 32–33); 'courage, compassion and character' (l. 38); 'fair ... forgiveness' (l. 40); 'power ... prevent' (l. 48); 'persistent poverty ... promise' (l. 59); 'proliferation of prisons' (l. 61); 'strangers ... citizens' (ll. 63–64); 'problems ... priorities' (l. 64); 'church ... charity' (l. 69); 'pain ... poverty' (l. 72); 'community ... commitment' (ll. 78–79).

Assonance: 'abandonment ... abuse ... acts' (ll. 60–61).

Metaphor: American history as: 'the American story' (ll. 8–12); a journey: 'halted ... delayed ... follow no other course ... a long way yet to travel' (ll. 17–22);
American ideals as: 'rock in a raging sea' (ll. 19–20), 'seed upon the wind, taking root' (l. 19).

Repetition: 'story' (ll. 8, 9, 10, 12).

Anaphora: 'every child must ... every citizen must ... every immigrant' (ll. 34–35); 'We will ...' (ll. 47–49, 52, 56–58).

Use of the first person plural: ('we', 'our'), e.g. ll. 8, 17, 21, etc.
The stylistic devices serve to make the speech more memorable, stirring and to reinforce the message.

3 **a** Individual answers.

⌒ *Read the following reaction to Bush' speech: 'It wasn't a stirring speech, it wasn't a speech full of applause lines but it was a carefully crafted speech, [...] a well delivered speech with some language that [...] we can spend some time talking about' (Judy Woodruffe, CNN, 20.01.2001). Do you agree with this verdict? Explain your answer.*

b Pride in national history; belief in America's mission; emphasis on individual freedom, justice and opportunity; community service; strong belief in religion (cf. biblical allusions) and a higher power guiding America.

4 Issues that might be researched include: civil liberties (e.g. US Patriot Act) (ll. 66–67), education (ll. 24, 46, 67), poverty and Social Security (ll. 47, 58–61), health care (ll. 47, 65), tax cuts (l. 48), national security (l. 50), the non-proliferation of biological, chemical and nuclear weapons (ll. 50–51), the prison system (l. 62), individual responsibility, volunteerism and charitable organizations (ll. 68–71, 76–79).

⌒ *Bush has been described as a compassionate conservative who shapes policy based on the principles of limited government, personal responsibility, strong families and local control. How are these principles reflected in Bush's inaugural address?*
Limited government: ll. 66–68; personal responsibility: ll. 76–79, 80–82 (note the importance attached to religious communities, ll. 68–71), strong families: ll. 78, 80.

⌒ *Translate ll. 8–22 into German.*

⌒ *Imagine you are a German journalist covering President Bush's inauguration for a German newspaper or radio/TV station. Briefly summarize in German what Bush said in his inaugural address.*

SB, S. 170 **B Facts and Figures**

Source:	Working Paper N° 252, *Luxembourg Income Study*, 2000; *Statistical Abstract of the United States*, 2001
Topic:	Income inequality, children living in poverty, prisoners in the USA
Text form:	Figures
Language variety:	AE
Level:	Basic/advanced
Skills/activities:	Working with figures

Didaktisch-methodische Hinweise

Die vereinfacht dargebotenen Statistiken zu Einkommensunterschieden, Kinderarmut und Zahl der Gefängnisinsassen in den USA nehmen die in Bushs „Inaugural Speech" angesprochenen Themen der sozialen Ungleichheit und Kriminalität auf. Die S können anhand der Statistiken exemplarisch lernen, ihre Urteile über Anspruch und Wirklichkeit der USA empirisch abzusichern. Dabei ist vor allem auf eine differenzierte Auswertung der Daten zur Kinderarmut zu achten. Die Statistik zu Einkommensunterschieden in ausgewählten Ländern ermöglicht internationale Vergleiche und illustriert die Unterschiede zwischen dem sozialstaatlichen Modell Westeuropas (vgl. „The Fair Society", SB, S. 103), und der neoliberalen Gesellschaftsordnung der USA (vgl. „Political and Economic Freedom", SB, S. 102). Die Statistiken zur Armut in verschiedenen ethnischen Gruppen bietet Querverbindungen zu den Abschnitten „An American Quilt" (SB, S. 173) und „Down and Out – and Up?" (SB, S. 95).

Eine vertiefte sozio-ökonomische Analyse der USA bedarf zusätzlicher Daten; sie erfolgt im Idealfall in Zusammenarbeit mit dem Politik- bzw. Wirtschaftsunterricht bzw. Gemeinschaftskunde.

Unterrichtstipps

Zum Auftakt können die S unter Rückgriff auf Kernaussagen aus Bushs Antrittsrede aufgefordert werden, Hypothesen zu den USA zu bilden:

⬭ *Bush promises to build a single nation of justice and opportunity. How successful do you think has the United States been in this attempt in comparison with other nations? Rank the following countries from most to least egalitarian: Australia, Canada, Germany, Luxembourg, the Netherlands, Sweden, the United Kingdom, the United States.*

⬭ *Bush says that persistent poverty is unworthy of the American promise. As far as you know, is child poverty in the USA increasing or decreasing? Which ethnic group has seen the greatest reduction in child poverty between between 1970 and 1999: whites, blacks, Asians and Pacific Islanders, or Hispanics?*

⬭ *Bush deplores the proliferation of prisons. As far as you know: Has the prison population in the USA more than doubled, tripled, quadrupled, or quintupled from 1980 to 1998?*

Info

The Gini index (also known as Gini ratio or Gini coefficient) is a measure commonly used by economists for making international comparisons of income inequality. A Gini index of 0.000 represents perfect equality; a Gini index of 1.000 implies perfect inequality. In practice, the Gini usually falls between 0.200 (egalitarian societies) and 0.450 (unequal societies).

Poverty level: A household with an income below a fixed level (poverty threshold) is poor. To find the annual poverty threshhold cf. www.census.gov/hhes/poverty/threshld.html · 1.8.2003. The guidelines were set in the early 1960s and have simply been adjusted for inflation ever since – it is a notion of poverty that takes no note of changing consumption patterns or rising GDP (gross domestic product).

Info

Prison system: America's incarceration rate was roughly constant from 1925 to 1973, with an average of 110 people behind bars for every 100,000 residents. By 2000, however, the rate of incarceration in state and federal prisons had more than quadrupled, to 478. American convicts are more likely to go to prison and to draw longer sentences than European criminals for similar offences. America is particularly tough when dealing with drug offences. Figures suggest that some 13m Americans – 7% of the adult population and nearly 12% of men – have been found guilty of a serious crime; with black men, the figure is even higher: roughly one in five black men has been incarcerated at some point in his life, and one in three has been convicted of a felony. The USA also has a higher crime rate than most West European countries. America's homicide rate is about six times higher than most developed countries, largely due to the easy access to guns.

*Lösungs-
hinweise*

1 a

General: Income discrepancies are considerably higher in the USA than in other Western countries. Countries which have followed neo-liberal policies in recent years (like the USA and the United Kingdom) are more unequal than countries that have a strong welfare state model (e.g. Sweden).

Childhood poverty: Between 1970 and 1990 childhood poverty increased significantly. Childhood poverty declined somewhat between 1990 and 1999 but remained higher than in 1970 for all races except blacks. In 1999, black children were still the poorest ethnic group with almost a third living below the poverty level, despite some improvements in the 1990s: in 1999, the percentage of black children below the poverty level was almost 10 percentage points lower than in 1970. The data also shows that large numbers of Hispanic children live in poverty. Between 1990 and 1999, the poverty level of Hispanic children declined less than that of blacks. In 1999, the Hispanic poverty level was almost as high as that of black children (29.9 percent compared with 32.7 percent). Interestingly, there has also been a rise in poverty levels amongst white children since 1970 (though it did decrease between 1990 and 1999).

Prisons: The number of prisoners in the USA more than quadrupled in less than 20 years. This may be either due to a significant increase in crime, or due to a stronger reaction of the government to crime.

b The data support what Bush says. There is a large income gap in the USA: 'While many of our citizens prosper, others doubt the promise, even the justice of our own country' (ll. 23–24). The increase in the number of prisoners is a cause for concern: 'The proliferation of prisons ... is no substitute for hope and order in our souls' (ll. 62–63). The high level of child poverty, especially among minorities, runs counter to the American promise 'that everyone belongs, that everyone deserves a chance, that no insignificant person was ever born' (ll. 14–15) and 'The ambitions of some Americans are limited by failing schools and hidden prejudice and the circumstances of their birth' (ll. 24–25).

2 Individual answers.

3 The top photo suggests there is overcrowding in some American jails. Three men are in one cell. This is reflected in the figures 'State and federal prisoners in the USA' in 'Facts and Figures' and in Bush's reference to 'the proliferation of prisons' (l. 62).
The middle photo reveals that there is real hardship in some areas, but that individuals are responsible for supporting themselves. This is reflected in the figures under 'Income Inequality' and in Bush's comment that 'America ... is a place where personal responsibility is valued and expected' (l. 75). It does reveal, however, that determination to work alone does not guarantee personal success.

The bottom photo reveals again the hardship of many homeless or jobless people in the USA, as they have to go to soup kitchens to get food. It also reflects Bush's view that 'church and charity, synagogue and mosque lend our communities their humanity, and they will have an honored place in our plans and in our laws' (ll. 69–71).

⬭ *Discuss the immediate and lasting effects of childhood poverty.*
Negative effects include increased stress on families, poor diets, hunger, housing problems, homelessness, restricted access to health services, more difficulty in school, greater possibility of becoming a teenage parent, with the consequence that one remains trapped in poverty (cf. www.childstats.gov/ac2000/econtxt.asp • 1.8.2003).

SB, S. 171 # 3 America in the Eyes of the World

Section 3 thematisiert die Rolle der Vereinigten Staaten als globale politische, militärische, wirtschaftliche und kulturelle Führungsmacht und ergänzt die innenpolitisch orientierte *section 2* um die außenpolitische Perspektive. Sie zielt auf eine Schülerrecherche zu einem aktuellen außenpolitischen Thema eigener Wahl und auf eine Stellungnahme zum deutsch-amerikanischen Verhältnis in Form eines Briefes an einen amerikanischen Freund. Zur Vorbereitung auf diese Aufgaben dienen Bildmaterialien, konträre Stellungnahmen zur weltpolitischen Rolle der USA sowie ein Bericht über eine internationale Umfrage zum Amerikabild in verschiedenen Kulturen.

Unterrichts-
tipps
Der Einstieg in *section 3* kann über die Bildmaterialien erfolgen. Die S analysieren in Gruppen eine der Illustrationen, bevor sie in der Klasse besprochen werden:

⬭ *Choose one of the illustrations on pp. 171–172. Describe it and explain what it shows.*
P. 171 (top): The photo shows the second plane crashing into one of the towers of the World Trade Center on 11 September, 2001, while the other tower –already hit – burns. The World Trade Center represented the strength of the USA's financial and economic system. The attack revealed the hatred some Muslims feel towards the USA and the terrorism that holds the world in grip. Following the attack the USA commenced its 'war on terror' (Text C, l. 29).

P. 171 (bottom): The photo shows an American soldier patrolling in Afghanistan following the defeat of the Taliban government. We can only see the soldier's machine gun and the uniform with the American flag on it. Two dirty-looking children are sitting on the ground. The girl's expression is one of fear or uncertainty, while the boy seems more relaxed and interested in the soldier. One can say the soldier represents American military might (which is even able to invade a landlocked country far from the USA successfully), or American hegemony or American determination to fight its enemies. The different expressions on the faces of the two children might be seen as standing for the ambivalence many feel towards the USA.

P. 172 (top): The cartoon shows the world wearing an American gallon hat (which is the symbol of cowboys, and is worn today especially by people from Texas, where President Bush comes from). The implication is that the world is becoming more American; the world is like a head on which the American hat is sitting. It might also imply that this is how the Americans would like to see the world.

P. 172 (bottom): The photo shows a McDonald's restaurant in an Arab country. McDonald's is written in Arabic. Two veiled women are walking by. It represents the worldwide strength of American products and firms, and reveals the attraction for the American way of life even in countries where there is resentment of the USA.

⬭ *Which of the four illustrations do you find most interesting?*

Bei der Bearbeitung der Texte übernehmen je zwei Schülergruppen die Lehrerrolle (*learning by teaching*) und beschreiben der jeweils anderen Gruppe in eigenen Worten den Inhalt der Texte A bzw. B; Text C wird gemeinsam erarbeitet. Der Vergleich wird mit Hilfe von Aufgabe 1 vorgenommen. In schwächeren Lerngruppen mag es sinnvoll sein, die Texte zunächst einzeln zu besprechen.

→ *WB, ex. 2, 3, 5*

SB, S. 171

A America Triumphant

Source:	*Economist*, 2002
Topic:	The world a year after 11 September, 2001
Text form:	Newsmagazine editorial
Language variety:	BE
Number of words:	163
Level:	Basic/advanced

*Lern-
vokabular*

Active vocabulary: 'America Triumphant' (p. 171)

set off (l. 1), hijack (a plane) (l. 2), civilians (l. 3), nightmare (l. 6), vulnerable (l. 9), cowardly (l. 9), show resolve (ll. 9–10), liberate sb. from sth. (l. 10), base (l. 11), forces (l. 11), war-torn country (l. 11), alliance (l. 13), back sb. (l. 13), respectively (l. 14)

*Didaktisch-
methodische
Hinweise*

Dieser Textauszug aus dem neoliberalen *Economist* stammt aus der Zeit nach dem US-Einsatz in Afghanistan. Er erinnert an den 11. September und an die Verunsicherung, die dieses Datum in der Welt hervorrief, und stellt vor diesem Hintergrund die neu gewonnene Sicherheit der USA dar, die sich als Befreier Afghanistans von vielen Nationen unterstützt sahen.

*Unterrichts-
tipps*

Als Leitfrage für die Textauswertung bietet sich die folgende Frage an:

⬭ *How does the author view the USA and its role in the world?*

⬭ *Translate the text into German.*

Info

11 September, 2001 is the day on which four planes were hijacked by the Muslim terrorist group al-Qaeda. Two of the planes were crashed into the twin towers of the World Trade Center in New York, causing them to collapse. The third plane crashed into the Pentagon, while the fourth crashed in a field after the passengers fought with the hijackers. Altogether about 3000 people died.

The Taliban (l. 10) are an Islamist group that emerged from the Afghani religious schools in Pakistan in 1994 (their name means 'students'). They captured the Afghan capital, Kabul, in 1996 and established an Islamic state based on an ultra-conservative interpretation of Islamic law. They banned music, games and all forms of visual representations of humans. Beards and traditional non-Western dress were mandatory for men, while women had to wear burqas (a piece of clothing which covers the whole body and has a mesh over the face). Girls were forbidden to go to school. Women were not allowed to work outside the home except in the health sector, and they could not go out unless accompanied by a male relative. Despite pressure from the USA and other countries, the Taliban regime continued to harbour Osama bin Laden, the leader of the al-Qaeda movement that carried out the attacks of 11 September, 2001; the Taliban was ousted from power by an American-led coalition in 2002.

SB, S. 171 **B Imperial Power**   George Monbiot

Source:	*Guardian*, 2002
Topic:	The need for Europe to prevent US imperial power
Text form:	Newspaper column
Language variety:	BE
Words:	110
Level:	Basic/advanced

Lern-
vokabular

Active vocabulary: 'Imperial Power' (p. 171)

imperial power (l. 1), empire (l. 2), meet with resistance (l. 2), resist sb./sth. (l. 3), by military/economic means (l. 3), response to sth. (l. 4), a policy of sth. (l. 5), non-cooperation (l. 5), act unilaterally (l. 6), resume sth. (l. 8)

Didaktisch-
methodische
Hinweise

Auch dieser Text steht im Zusammenhang mit dem Einsatz der USA in Afghanistan. Anders als „America Triumphant" warnt dieser Kommentar aus dem linksliberalen *Guardian* vor US-Imperialismus und einem amerikanischen Alleingang.

Unterrichts-
tipps

Als Leitfrage für die Textauswertung bieten sich die folgenden Arbeitsaufträge an:

  ◯ *How does the author view the USA and its role in the world?*

  ◯ *Give examples of how Europe might be able to impede the USA's attempts to act unilaterally.*

Possible answers:
More integration within Europe so that its becomes a power to be taken seriously, more use of the the veto of the UK and France in the Security Council of the UN.

SB, S. 172 **C A Growing Dislike of the USA**

Source:	*BBC website*, 2002
Topic:	Global reactions to the USA
Text form:	Online news report
Language variety:	BE
Number of words:	303
Level:	Basic/advanced
Skills/activities:	examining the global role of the USA, writing a letter

Lern-
vokabular

Active vocabulary: 'A Growing Dislike of the USA' (p. 172)

increasing (l. 1), trend (l. 2), discontent (l. 6), traditional ally (l. 6), embrace sth. (l. 8), spread of sth. (l. 11), beneficial (l. 11), paint sb./sth. in a bad light (l. 14), news agency (ll. 14–15), growing (l. 23), a dislike of sth. (l. 23), hold a (favourable) view of sb./sth. (ll. 23–24), enjoy support (l. 29), be critical about sth. (ll. 30–31), business practices (l. 31)

Didaktisch-
methodische
Hinweise

Dieser Text wurde geschrieben, als die USA den Krieg gegen den Irak 2003 vorbereiteten. Er diskutiert die Ergebnisse einer Studie, die ein großes Misstrauen vieler Länder gegenüber den USA zeigte, gleichzeitig aber auch die ungebrochene Popularität des amerikanischen Lebensstils in vielen dieser Länder offenbarte; eine Haltung, die vermutlich auch bei den meisten S sichtbar wird.

Identify *which areas of the world: a) largely hold a favourable view of the USA; b) have seen a growing criticism of US policy; c) seem to dislike the USA most of all.*
a) Russia and non-Muslim areas of Africa and Asia; b) Canada, Germany and France; c) the Muslim world.

Info

The Pew Research Center is an independent opinion research group that studies attitudes toward the press, politics and public policy issues (including America's place in the world). It is best known for regular national surveys that measure public attentiveness to major news stories, and for polling that charts trends in values and fundamental political and social attitudes.

Lösungshinweise

1 As the only remaining superpower, the USA evokes ambivalent reactions among most non-Americans. On the one hand, most people in most countries like American culture, science and technology (Text C, ll. 10–12); on the other hand, there is widespread criticism of the economic, military and political role of the USA, in particular among Muslim nations (Text C, ll. 27–28). Interestingly, criticism seems to be coming from traditional allies, while developing countries and Russia have a more favourable view (Text C, ll. 23–24, 25–26,29, 30–31). While some praise the USA for its resolve and its leadership in liberating Afghanistan from the Taliban after 11 September, 2001 (Text A), others like George Monbiot see the USA as an imperial power pursuing its own interests unilaterally and urge a policy of non-cooperation (Text B).

2 Individual answers.

3 Individual answers.

4 Individual answers.

Translate ll. 22–31 into German.

SB, S. 173

4 An American Quilt

Die Metapher des *quilt* (vgl. das Bild, SB, S. 173) in der Überschrift dieser *section* lenkt die Aufmerksamkeit auf amerikanische *folk art* und das Ideal einer multikulturellen Gesellschaft, in der das Ganze mehr ist als die Summe seiner Teile. Der Vision einer gerechten, Minderheiten integrierenden Gesellschaft steht die Realität ökonomischer und kultureller Spannungen einer Einwanderernation gegenüber. Der Abschnitt kann ergänzt werden durch die Kurzgeschichte „Origami" (SB, S. 186) über die Identitätsprobleme einer jungen Amerikanerin japanisch-europäischer Abstammung.

SB, S. 173

A Bound by a Common Thread   Jesse Jackson

Source:	*PBS website*, 1988
Topic:	The USA as a quilt
Text form:	speech
Language variety:	AE
Number of words:	339
Level:	Basic/advanced
Skills/activities:	analysing use of language, designing a quilt

Active vocabulary: 'Bound by a Common Thread' (p. 173)

afford sth. (l. 3) complain (l. 3), freeze (l. 3), wool (l. 4), silk (l. 4), sew sth. together (l. 6), fight for/against sth. (ll. 16, 17), a cure for sth. (l. 17), right/left wing (l. 19), hawk (l. 19), dove (l. 19) *tasks*: briefly, convince sb., a wide range of sth., concept

Didaktisch-methodische Hinweise

Jesse Jacksons liberale Utopie eines amerikanischen *quilt* bildet den Einstieg in die Diskussion über die Herausforderungen einer multiethnischen Gesellschaft. Der Demokrat Jackson betont die Bedeutung, die Minderheiten und ihre Anliegen für die Gesellschaft haben, und setzt damit andere Akzente als der Republikaner Bush in seiner Vision Amerikas (vgl. SB, S. 167). Jacksons Rede ist ein herausragendes Beispiel amerikanischer Rhetorik; daher lohnt sich eine eingehende Analyse.

Unterrichts-tipps

Jacksons Metapher des *quilt* kann die S zu eigenen Gestaltungsversuchen ihres Ameri-kabildes inspirieren, ggf. in Zusammenarbeit mit dem Kunstunterricht. Der Einstieg kann über eine kurzen Schülerpräsentation zu *quilts* und *quiltmaking* erfolgen. Dabei sollten verschiedene Abbildungen von *quilts* vorgestellt werden, um die Fantasie der S für die kreative Projektarbeit (Aufgabe 5) anzuregen.

Info

Jesse Jackson (born 1941) was born out of wedlock to a teenage mother and grew up in Greenville, South Carolina. In 1959 Jackson got a football scholarship to the University of Illinois, but he left after a year due to racism at the university and enrolled in the North Carolina Agricultural and Technical State University. In 1963 Jackson became a student activist leader. He led marchers into restaurants and public buildings that did not let blacks in and was sent to jail. Later he moved to Chicago to study to become a Baptist minister. He then joined with the leader of the Civil Rights Movement, Martin Luther King, Jr.. In the 1980s he twice attempted to become the Democratic presidential candidate. At the Democratic Convention in 1988 he came second to George Dukakis, who was defeated in the presidential election by the Republican George Bush, Sr.

Lösungs-hinweise

1 Die S sollten bei dieser Aufgabe die betreffenden Personengruppen und ihre jeweiligen Forderungen auflisten.

Farmers:	fair prices;
workers:	fair wages;
women (and mothers):	improved educational and medical services (Head Start, day care, prenatal care), respect and pay equality for women (rather than jail care and welfare);
students:	scholarships;
blacks and Hispanics:	civil rights;
gays and lesbians:	acceptance of their sexual orientation (no discrimination); cure for AIDS;
conservatives:	right-wing agenda;
progressives:	left-wing agenda;
hawks:	military intervention;
doves:	peace initiatives.

2 Jackson envisages an inclusive society that integrates but transcends minority interests: 'a great quilt of unity and common ground' (ll. 22–23).

3 Jackson aims to unify the Democratic party and reach out to a wide range of voters.
– He directly addresses ('you') special interest groups (farmers, students, women), disadvantaged minorities (blacks and Hispanics, gays and lesbians) and voters of different political persuasions (conservatives and progressives, hawks and doves).

- His speech is rich in associations (but vague on detail) that strike a chord with Americans: He talks about his personal experience and childhood; he implicitly appeals to the American Dream (he was poor, now he is successful), the American sense of family, and the American sense of self-reliance (his grandmother exemplifies family solidarity and the American can-do mentality).
- Jackson's appeal to ordinary people is reflected in his language. He uses short, simple sentences and vocabulary that is easy to understand and at times emotive ('my grandmama', l. 21).
- His speech is unified by the extended metaphor of the quilt, the repetition of key elements ('you are right but your patch is not big enough') and the frequent use of parallelism ('you seek / fight for')
- He makes use of various stylistic devices:
  <u>Alliteration:</u> 'pieces ... patches' (l. 4); 'sturdy ... strong' (l. 6); 'Pool the patches and the pieces' (ll. 21–22); 'health care and housing ... hope' (ll. 23–24);
  <u>Contrast:</u> 'could not afford a blanket; she didn't complain and we did not freeze' (ll. 2–3); 'pieces of old cloth ... barely good enough to wipe off your shoes with ... a quilt, a thing of beauty and power and culture' (ll. 4–7); 'Head Start and day care and prenatal care on the front side of life, rather than jail care and welfare on the back side of life' (ll. 12–13); 'Conservatives and progressives', 'right wing, left wing, hawk, dove' (ll. 18–19)
  <u>Assonance:</u> 'day care and prenatal care ... jail care' – 'welfare' (ll. 12–13);
  <u>Enumeration:</u> 'one thread, one color, one cloth' (l. 1); 'patches, wool, silk, garbadine, crockersack' (l. 4); 'a thing of beauty and power and culture' (l. 7); 'Head Start and day care and prenatal care' (l. 12), 'health care and housing and jobs and education' (ll. 23–24).

4 The traditional metaphor of the USA as a melting pot refers to the mixing of people of different backgrounds and emphasizes the fact that cultural groups change when they are in contact with others. When different metallic elements are melted, alloys are formed which have different properties from the original elements. Similarly, different ethnic and cultural groups in the USA have been blended together into a new common American culture through education, intermarriage, etc. New immigrants were traditionally encouraged to become Americans, to embrace basic American values, adopt English as the language of communication, observe national holidays and customs, etc. (cf. 'Assimilation, American-style', p. 176, ll. 19–23).

In recent years, the metaphor of the melting pot has come under criticism as implying rigid cultural conformity. By contrast, the metaphors of the quilt, salad bowl, rainbow and pizza have been used to describe the fact that US society is composed of many different groups, all of which have contributed to the formation of that society and many of which have retained their heritage and identity. While the quilt, salad bowl, rainbow and pizza metaphors emphasize cultural diversity and variety in unity, they suggest that cultural groups remain unchanged and thus they do not do justice to the dynamic character of cultural interaction and social change.

5 Individual answers.

⬭ *Compare Jackson's and Bush's visions of America.*
Both paint a positive picture of the USA, both share a belief in the importance of family bonds, but they emphasize different aspects (which are not mutually exclusive):
- Bush, cf. answer to task 1b (p. 329);
- Jackson: unity in variety (inclusive, multicultural society); accepts gays.

⬭ *Do research on one of the following:*
- *the Democratic and Republican parties;*
- *the social situation of blacks and Hispanics.*

B Lifeblood of the Nation   T. Coraghessan Boyle

Source:	*The Tortilla Curtain*, 1995
Topic:	The rights and wrongs of immigration to the USA
Text form:	Novel (extract)
Language variety:	AE
Number of words:	527
Level:	Basic/advanced
Skills/activities:	Examining two sides of an argument, writing a summary, identifying the mode of presentation, converting a novel into a film script

Lern-vokabular

Active vocabulary: 'Lifeblood of the Nation' (p. 174)

accept immigrants (l. 1), legal immigrants (l. 3), people with skills (l. 3), have sth. to offer (l. 6), at a fraction of the cost (l. 8), be in a hurry (l. 10), in the heat of the moment (l. 11), times have changed (l. 23), in terms of sth. (l. 24), social services (l. 25), contribute sth. (l. 30), tax revenues (l. 30), use up sth. (l. 30), welfare (l. 31), schooling (l. 31), crime (l. 32), deserve a chance in life (l. 37), assimilate (l. 38)
tasks: deal with an issue, argue one's case, evaluate sth., convert sth. into sth. else

Didaktisch-methodische Hinweise

Der Auszug aus T. Coraghessan Boyles *Tortilla Curtain* präsentiert in Form eines Dialogs zwischen zwei Bekannten konträre Ansichten zur illegalen Einwanderung nach Kalifornien. Unter literarischen Gesichtspunkten steht bei der Bearbeitung das für die Lesersteuerung wichtige Element der *mode of presentation* im Vordergrund. Diese Untersuchung kann erweitert werden durch eine Analyse der Erzählperspektive (vgl. „Narrator and Point of View", SB, S. 258). Leser tendieren dazu, Sympathie für die Figur zu entwickeln, deren Gedanken sie kennen lernen – im vorliegenden Fall ist dies Delaney (vgl. Z. 36–40), selbst wenn er vom Gespräch überfordert zu sein scheint.

 Die S werden sicher Schwierigkeiten haben, im letzten Satz „besides which" (vgl. Z. 38–39) syntaktisch richtig einzuordnen. Sie können auf Paraphrasen wie *apart from this* oder *moreover* verwiesen werden.

Info

T. Coraghessan Boyle (born 1948) grew up in New York State. He studied English and History at the State University of New York. After a period of drug addiction he studied creative writing at the University of Iowa. Boyle then joined the English Department at the University of Southern California, and lives now near Santa Barbara in California. His stories are filled with quirky, memorable characters, colourful descriptive prose, and have been widely praised for their inventiveness and vision. He has a keen sense of satire and cynical sense of humour. Amongst his novels are *World's End* (1987), *The Road to Wellville* (1993), *The Tortilla Curtain* (1995), and *Drop City* (2003).
Tortilla Curtain is Boyle's most popular work to date. Set in Southern California, in and around the American-Mexican border area where white middle-class Americans co-exist alongside impoverished, homeless Mexican illegal immigrants, the novel explores the lives of two families, the Mossbachers, a rich white American family, and the Pincons, a family of illegal Mexicans, who come into contact following an accident.

'*We'd stolen California from them in the first place*' (l. 39): Reference to the Mexican-American War (1846–1848), in which Mexico lost Texas and California to the USA.

Lösungs-hinweise

1 The excerpt deals with American reactions to immigration to California, in particular the illegal immigration of unskilled Mexicans.

2 The Tortilla Curtain is the name given to the Mexican–US border (*tortilla* is a traditional Mexican dish).

3 **a**

Jack: The USA accepts more immigrants than all the other countries of the world combined (cf. ll. 1–2); half of them settle in California (cf. ll. 2–3); they arrive illegally, are unskilled in a society that has no need for unskilled labour (cf. ll. 5–8); the saturation point has been reached (l. 16); the Jardines are not immigrants, as they have been in the USA since the Revolutionary War (cf. ll. 16–17); the economic and social costs of immigrants (e.g. welfare, emergency care, schooling, crime, uninsured motorists, etc.) outweigh the economic benefits (cf. ll. 28–35).

Delaney: Immigrants are the lifeblood of this country (cf. l. 14); the USA is a nation of immigrants (cf. ll. 14–15); every American is a descendant of immigrants (cf. l. 18) irrespective of when they arrived; everyone deserves a chance in life (cf. ll. 37–38); Mexicans will assimilate just like earlier generations of immigrants (cf. l. 37); Mexicans have a right to be in California as the USA annexed ('stolen', l. 39) California from Mexico.

b Jack moves from the general to the particular. He argues that immigration to the USA and to California needs to be restricted. He begins by referring to the large number of legal immigrants and then moves on to the problem he is most worried about: illegal immigration from Mexico (cf. l. 4). Using strong emotive language, he asserts that unskilled economic migrants from Mexico 'are killing us' (l. 4). He supports this view by pointing out that the only asset illegal immigrants have, their physical strength, is no longer needed in modern society. He sums up his case by claiming that a point of saturation has been reached (cf. l. 16). He brushes aside Delaney's counter-argument about the USA as a nation of immigrants and goes on discuss the economic implications of illegal immigration (cf. ll. 22–35). Asking Delaney a series of personal rhetorical questions (cf. ll. 32–35), he aims to show that the costs of immigration outweigh the benefits.

c In this passage from T. Coraghessan Boyle's *The Tortilla Curtain*, Delaney Mossbacher and Jack Jardine discuss immigration to the USA. Jack is concerned about the large numbers of unskilled labourers crossing illegally from Mexico into California. In his view, physical strength, the only asset illegal immigrants have, is no longer needed in a modern technology-based society; a saturation point has been reached. Upset, Delaney answers that the USA has always been a nation of immigrants. Jack brushes this argument aside and asks Delaney if he is willing to pay the extra costs caused by immigrants. Delaney is lost for words but thinks that everyone deserves a chance, that Mexicans will assimilate just like immigrants have always done and that Americans have a moral obligation to accept Mexicans as California was originally Mexican. (132 words)

4 Individual answers.

❖ ◯ Die folgende Aufgabe kann in einem Kugellager (vgl. S. 429) besprochen werden: *Would you say that the argument between Jack and Delaney is relevant for the European Union too?*

◯ *Debate the motion: 'Immigration to the USA has to be severely restricted'.*

5 In a panoramic presentation the reader would be given a summary of the arguments. Here the mode of presentation is mostly scenic as it is dialogue. This allows the reader to experience the words of the characters (and so find out more about them). Other details like Delaney putting down the milk (cf. l. 10) and the woman getting the olives (cf. ll. 21–33) add to the authenticity. The reader feels part of the scene.

6 As most of the passage is dialogue, it would be relatively easy to convert the extract into a film script. Delaney's thoughts at the end could be given as a dialogue or monologue in a scene in which Delaney talks about his discussion with Jack. The way the woman picks up the olives and perhaps the inability of Delaney to express his thoughts could be used to relieve tension.

◯ *Translate ll. 28–40 into German.*

SB, S. 175 **C Assimilation, American-style**   Robert J. Samuelson

Source:	*Newsweek*, 9 April, 2001
Topic:	The assimilation of immigrants in the USA
Text form:	Newsmagazine column
Language variety:	AE
Number of words:	472
Level:	Advanced
Skills/activities:	Working with definitions, comparing different views, writing a text

Lern-vokabular

Active vocabulary: 'Assimilation, American-style' (p. 175)

census (l. 1), consciousness (l. 1), have a huge impact (l. 5), assimilate sb. (l. 7), change for the worse (l. 11), multiculturalism (l. 15), diversity (l. 16), dated (l. 16), retain (your) ethnic traditions (l. 18), take pride in your (American) identity (ll. 20–21), self-reliant (l. 22), hardworking (l. 22), morally upright (ll. 22–23), third-generation (Latinos) (l. 30), mirror sth. (l. 30), backlash (l. 36), recession (l. 36), benefit from sth. (l. 37), economic boom (l. 40) *tasks*: cultural diversity, enrich sth., endanger sth.

Didaktisch-methodische Hinweise

Samuelsons Kolumne führt die in „Lifeblood of the Nation" (SB, S. 174) aufgeworfene Frage nach Assimilationsbereitschaft und -kapazität in den USA weiter. Angesichts der Belastungen des sozialen Systems vertritt der Autor trotz grundsätzlicher Bejahung der Ein- bzw. Zuwanderung eine restriktive Position. Sein Text kann Anstöße für Recherchen zur Situation von Immigranten in den USA und für Vergleiche mit der Situation in Deutschland geben. Die von Samuelson genannten wirtschaftlichen Motive des „anti-immigrant backlash" sind nach den Angriffen des 11. September 2001 um sicherheitspolitische Gesichtspunkte zu ergänzen. Insbesondere muslimische Einwanderer erfuhren den Stimmungsumschwung gegen Einwanderer, etwa in Form verschärfter Melderechte, Befragungen durch das FBI, Überfälle auf Familien und Religionsstätten oder Benachteiligungen bei der Arbeitssuche.

Unterrichts-tipps

Nachdem die S den Text gelesen haben, kann eine Verständniskontrolle im *Cloze*-Verfahren durchgeführt werden, bei dem in einem oder mehreren Absätzen des Textes jedes fünfte Wort getilgt wird und von den S ersetzt werden muss.

Wegen seines Abstraktionsniveaus ist Samuelsons Kolumne anspruchsvoll. Im Unterrichtsgespräch sollten Konzepte wie „rigid cultural conformity" (Z. 17), „retain ethnic traditions and affections" (Z. 18) oder „anti-immigrant backlash" (Z. 36) an Beispielen konkretisiert werden. Dabei können Erfahrungen oder Wissen über US-amerikanische Familien und Schulen einbezogen werden (z.B. der *Pledge of Allegiance*, amerikanische Flaggen in Klassenzimmern usw.).

Info

Robert J. Samuelson (born 1945) is an American journalist who has written a weekly column on political, economic and social issues for *The Washington Post* since 1977. He has won numerous journalism awards.

Census: There is a census in the USA every ten years. Samuelson is referring to the 2000 census.

Lösungs-hinweise

1 **a** Some people criticize the concept of assimilation as imposing rigid cultural conformity on minority groups (cf. ll. 13–14, 17). For others like Samuelson, it is a positive term, which implies:
– joining the economic mainstream (l. 8);
– adopting English as the national language (ll. 19–20);
– taking pride in America and its democratic principles (ll. 20–21);
– embracing the Protestant work ethic (ll. 22–23).
While assimilation requires immigrants to think of themselves primarily as Americans (l. 9), it does not require them to give up their 'ethnic traditions and affections' (l. 18).

b <u>Immigration</u>: immigrant families / children / Hispanic men (ll. 19, 33, 34), third-generation Latinos (l. 30), anti-immigrant backlash (l. 36), newcomers (l. 39), skilled/unskilled immigrants (l. 41);

<u>assimilation</u>: a spontaneous process driven by the economy, popular culture and the belief in individual opportunity (ll. 24–25);

<u>assimilate</u>: join the economic mainstream (l. 8), adopt English (l. 19), take pride in one's American identity (ll. 20–21).

2 Samuelson sees immigration as potentially beneficial to the USA (l. 37). In this respect he is like Delaney. But like Jack, he emphasizes the difficulties involved in assimilating a growing number of immigrants, e.g. for institutions like schools and hospitals. He warns of an anti-immigration backlash in times of recession and favours limiting immigration, in particular immigration of unskilled workers (ll. 1–5, 31–41).
Samuelson's language reflects the middle position between Delaney and Jack. Whereas Jack is quite explicit in stating his anti-immigration sentiment (e.g. ll. 28–35), Samuelson is much more cautious, pointing out that Americans 'may need a little less' immigration and that they 'need time to adjust' (ll. 37–38). Delaney refers to immigration as the 'lifeblood' of the nation (l. 14) and sees a moral responsibility of Americans to accept Mexican immigrants (l. 39). Samuelson is less enthusiastic: he wants to 'benefit' from immigration and to improve 'the odds for assimilation' (l. 41).

3 Students may refer to new cultural perspectives, the greater culinary variety, the dynamism of upwardly mobile immigrants and the economic advantages associated with immigration. Immigrants may occupy economic niches, create employment and open up new business opportunities in their countries of origin. Societies with an ageing population may benefit from the influx of immigrant families with a large number of children, provided these can be integrated into the education system and the job market.

4 Individual answers.

SB, S. 177

Getting Along in English

Didaktisch-
methodische
Hinweise

Diese *section* widmet sich charakteristischen Schwierigkeiten in der Kommunikation zwischen Deutschen und Amerikanern. Für amerikanisches Verständnis äußern Deutsche zu häufig und zu direkt Kritik und verstärken so das Vorurteil gegenüber den „unhöflichen" Deutschen. Für deutsches Empfinden dagegen sind Amerikaner oft „oberflächlich"; sie verstellen sich und sagen nicht offen, was sie denken. Ähnliche Kommunikationsprobleme gibt es mit Angehörigen anderer angelsächsischer Kulturen. Diese Seite dient deshalb dazu, die S für die Problematik zu sensibilisieren und ihnen Strategien höflicher, indirekter Kritik zu vermitteln (vgl. auch SB, S. 34). Dazu untersuchen sie ein Gespräch zwischen einer Amerikanerin und einer deutschen Touristin (vgl. CD2, *track* 13 und das Transkript auf S. 358), lernen Redemittel kennen und schreiben schließlich selbst einen Dialog.

→ WB, ex. 4

Lösungs-
hinweise

CD

1 Der Dialog befindet sich auf CD2, *track* 13; das Transkript auf S. 358.

- An American woman is talking to a young German woman.
- The American woman initiates the conversation and tries to establish contact with the German through some shared experience or interest ('Is that German ... my son is stationed in Germany'). She is friendly and encouraging ('How nice. How do you like it here?'). The German is not very forthcoming in her responses. Her answers are short; she does not volunteer any additional information. The conversation turns sour when she starts to criticize Americans for their superficiality. She does not pick up on the warning signals in the conversation – the change in the woman's tone of voice, followed by 'I beg your pardon' (an extremely strong signal). The conversation can no longer be saved. The American woman gets her own back in the end, implying that the Americans who invited the German did not know her ('No, I don't suppose she did'), otherwise they would not have invited such an unfriendly and rude person, but the German probably does not notice this criticism.

2 1d, 2c, 3a, 4e, 5b.

Listen to the dialogues from the 'Getting Along in English' page of Chapter One (cf. SB, p. 34; CD1, tracks 3–9). Note down all the times when the German is impolite and all the times when he or she is polite.

3 All of these strategies are non-confrontational 'I-messages', i.e. messages that are phrased as personal observations, concerns, etc. They do not pass judgement on what is perceived as different or irritating, but explicitly or implicitly ask for a comment or clarification. Some Germans may feel strategy 5 to be dishonest. For English-speaking people, however, it is a perfectly acceptable way of avoiding direct criticism.

4 Zusätzliches Sprachmaterial finden die S im SB, S. 34, Aufgaben 2a–b.

a) is based on an American saying but would be socially unacceptable in the situation on the bus as it implies a refusal to enter into conversation.
b) takes account of the human interest in cultural variety and is relatively safe, especially if the observations are phrased as 'I-messages'. In a conversation with a stranger, however, it might be more appropriate to start with a positive remark.
c) is the reaction expected by Americans and would be the safest way to open a conversation.
d) risks alienating Americans and should be used with caution and only if one knows the other well. In the case of the low temperatures in air-conditioned buildings, for example, it is advisable not to phrase one's 'honest' opinion as an attack on wasteful Americans, but as an I-message saying that, as a German, one is not used to air-conditioning, that one feels easily cold, or that, as a citizen of a densely populated country, one is concerned about the environmental impact of rising energy consumption.

5 The American Way of Life

Section 5 eröffnet den Zugang zu interkulturell bedeutsamen Facetten des amerikanischen Alltagslebens. „The Magic of Baseball" (SB, S. 178) macht die Faszination des amerikanischen Nationalsports verständlich. In „Why No One Walks" (SB, S. 180) beschreibt Bill Bryson die Vorliebe der Amerikaner für das Auto mit ironischer Distanz. Der Ausschnitt aus der BBC-Dokumentarsendung „The American Century" (SB, S. 182) setzt sich mit dem globalen Siegeszug des Autos und der *shopping mall* als Beispiel amerikanischer Kultur auseinander. „The American Way of Life as Reflected on TV" (SB, S. 182) behandelt die Rolle amerikanischer Fernsehserien als Vermittler amerikanischer Kultur.

Weiteres Material zu Aspekten amerikanischen Alltagslebens findet sich an anderen Stellen des SB: vgl. Rockwells „Freedom from Want" (S. 21) und „Giving Thanks" (SB, S. 31) zu *Thanksgiving*; „TV Is Big Business" (SB, S. 115) zur Rolle des Fernsehens.

A The Magic of Baseball   Doris Kearns Goodwin

SB, S. 178

Source:	*Boston Globe*, 6 October, 1986
Topic:	Sport as an activity that binds generations
Text form:	Essay
Language variety:	AE
Number of words:	809
Level:	Advanced
Skills/activities:	Analysing metaphors, working with idioms

Lern-vokabular

Active vocabulary: 'The Magic of Baseball' (p. 178)

memories of sb./sth. (l. 3), recall sth. (l. 7), relive sth. (l. 11), permit sb. to do sth. (l. 14), recapture sth. (l. 14), settle into sth. (l. 29), curse sb./sth. (l. 32), cheer sb./sth. (l. 33), break sb.'s heart (l. 34), tease sb. about sth. (l. 37), obsession (l. 37), committed to sth. (l. 39), create a bond between sb. (l. 40), in deep conversation (l. 41), share sth. with sb. (l. 45), in the presence of sb. (l. 53), a bond between sb. (l. 56), link sb./sth. to (l. 57)

Didaktisch-methodische Hinweise

Goodwins autobiographischer Text „The Magic of Baseball" steht für amerikanische Sportbegeisterung und bietet Vergleichsmöglichkeiten zur Rolle des Sports in den USA und Deutschland. In sprachlicher Hinsicht kann anhand des Texts untersucht werden, wie Sportbegeisterung ihren Niederschlag in der Sprache findet.

Unterrichts-tipps

Eine Annäherung an den Text kann über das Foto auf S. 178 erfolgen:

⬭ *What might make the boy in the photo remember his visit to the baseball stadium when he is older?*
He is with his father, he has been given a baseball glove (and possibly ball) and baseball cap (which might be presents from his father for his first trip); the noise and the large stadium will probably remain engrained in his memory.

Um das Textverständnis zu überprüfen und kleinschrittige Fragen zu vermeiden, können den S nach dem Stilllesen des Texts Stichwörter vorgelegt werden, die sie inhaltlich ausfüllen müssen, z.B. „childhood memories", „the role of the scorebook", „a miserable summer", „women friends", „a parent myself", „a bond between generations".

→ WB, ex. 6
Differenzierung

Für leistungsstarke S eignet sich die folgende Aufgabe:

⬭ *What do you understand by the following phrases? Rewrite them to show you understand what they mean:*
– *'my personal renderings of all those games' (ll. 18–19)* (everything I wrote down about those games);

- *'the cozy ballfield scaled to human dimensions' (ll. 30–31)* (the intimate ballfield which is small enough so that human beings do not feel overwhelmed by it);
- *'directing my old intensities towards my new team' (l. 35)* (feeling all my forgotten passions awaken and using them to support my new team);
- *'defied the ravages of modern life' (l. 48)* (managed to avoid being destroyed by new technology or commercialism).

Info

Doris Kearns Goodwin (born 1943) is a historian and television presenter. She was Professor of Government at Harvard before serving in 1969 as assistant to President Johnson in his last year in the White House. Her memoir *Wait Till Next Year. Summer Afternoons with My Father and Baseball* (1997) deals with her childhood and her love for the Brooklyn Dodgers. Goodwin served as a consultant for the PBS documentary *The History of Baseball* (1994). As a commentator on baseball, she became the first woman to enter the Red Sox locker room.

Baseball is the second most popular spectator team sport in the USA after American football. The game takes a long time to play and for this reason lends itself well as an outing with family or friends. For information on the rules of baseball, cf. www.learnetix.de/home/de/htdocs/Englisch/Moonpalace/Pdf/Chapter1/BaseballRules. pdf · 1.8.2003.

'the Dodgers taken away' (ll. 22–23): The Dodgers were based in Brooklyn until the 1950s. The club's president, Walter O'Malley, wanted to build a more modern stadium for his team, but New York officials refused to give O'Malley the land he wanted, so in 1958 the Dodgers moved to Los Angeles, which also ensured that baseball no longer remained the preserve of the East Coast and Mid-West.

Lösungs-hinweise

1 Goodwin's journey through time comprises her life from childhood (cf. l. 2) to parenthood (cf. l. 45). As a young child, she was introduced to the game of baseball by her father, who gave her his time and attention, shared his baseball memories with her and treated her as someone he needed and took seriously. After her father's death, when she was at college, Goodwin lost interest in the game of baseball for a while, as baseball seemed linked to her childhood. But as a young professor at Boston, her childhood interest in baseball was rekindled. As a mother, she now plays the role for her three sons that her father played for her in her childhood: her journey has come full circle.

2

Metaphor	Associations
'mystic texture of childhood' (ll. 1–2)	'Texture' implies fabric, so it is associated with feelings and the sense of touch; different strands are woven in a piece of fabric which makes childhood seem to have a host of different feelings.
'instant/ invisible bond' (ll. 40, 56)	Bonds fasten and hold things together, so 'bond' is associated with closeness, feelings of love and friendship.
'I have circled back to my childhood' (l. 43)	To go in a circle implies that you are back where you started, so the connection between childhood and parenthood is emphasized, as is the idea of life as something complete.
'anchor of loyalty' (l. 57)	An anchor is something that gives you a feeling of safety and stability.

3 Goodwin likes the coziness and human scale of the baseball stadium, the excitement and passion of the spectators, the ups and downs of the players and teams (cf. ll. 30–35), the instant bond felt among baseball enthusiasts (cf. ll. 40–41).

Baseball represents for her 'the mystic texture of childhood' (ll. 1–2). It is a sensual experience bringing back 'the sounds and smells' of childhood summers (l. 2).

On another level, 'this most timeless of all sports' (ll. 58–59) is a way to overcome the passing of time. Baseball 'has defied the ravages of modern life' (l. 48); its basic rules and its pace have remained unchanged for a century (ll. 48–50). It is an 'anchor' of stability and loyalty in the flux of time (cf. l. 57).

Most importantly, it is also the link between the generations (cf. ll. 47–59). It evokes nostalgic memories of a much-loved father. It links the young and the old, the dead and the living: three generations (cf. l. 57) or even four, if one includes Goodwin's grandfather (cf. l. 7).

 4 Zur Erschließung der amerikanischen Sportmetaphern wird ein einsprachiges Wörterbuch benötigt.

Expression	Meaning	Sport
play hardball	be determined to get what you want and behave accordingly	baseball
quarterback (v)	direct or organize sth.	American football
touch base (with sb.)	make contact with sb. you live or work with while you are away	baseball
ballpark	number, amount, figure that is approximately right	baseball
way off base	completely wrong about sth.	baseball
in a league of your own	much better than others	baseball
out of your league	too expensive for you	baseball
not in sb.'s league	much better than sb.	baseball
throw sb a curve	surprise sb. by asking a difficult question	baseball
the ball is in your court	it is your responsibility to take action next	tennis
not to get to first base	fail to make a successful start in a project, relationship, etc; fail to get to through the first stage	baseball
in a different league	(usually) much better than others	baseball

Other idioms from the world of sport:
not by a long shot, another ball game, below/above par, bull's eye, get the ball rolling, give something your best shot, jump the gun, level playing field, off to a running start, par for the course, sticky wicket, three strikes and you're out.

⬭ *Choose one of the following:*
- *Research the rules of one American team sport (e.g. baseball, American football);*
- *Research the role of sports in American high schools and colleges (e.g. the significance of the homecoming).*

⬭ *Translate ll. 4–15 into German.*

⬭ *Explain in German to a German friend the attraction baseball has for many Americans. Refer to Goodwin's article.*

SB, S. 180 **B A Sedentary Nation**   Bill Bryson

Source:	*Daily Mail*, 18 May, 1997
Topic:	The love of cars and its effect on American behaviour
Text form:	Essay
Language variety:	AE
Words:	961
Level:	Basic/advanced
Skills/activities:	Analysing the use of humour, working with vocabulary, examining American and European views

Lern-
vokabular

Active vocabulary: 'A Sedentary Nation' (p. 180)

sedentary (title, l. 11), have sb. round for dinner (l. 2), blank look (l. 5), make a study of sth. (l. 9), barely (l. 12), be no stranger to sth. (l. 12), within walking distance of sth. (l. 16), insist (l. 30), leave the scene of an accident (l. 34), occur to sb. (l. 36), ludicrous (l. 37), leave the motor/engine running (ll. 40, 43), an acquaintance of (mine/ours) (l. 46), adjust sth. (l. 52), urban planners (l. 65), suburban malls (l. 68), thrive (l. 72)

Didaktisch-
methodische
Hinweise

Mit dem Blick des Satirikers auf sich und seine Umwelt beschreibt Bryson für das britische Massenblatt *Daily Mail* die Erfahrungen eines Amerikaners, der sich aufgrund eines mehrjährigen Europaaufenthalts fremd im eigenen Land fühlt. Mit ironischem Ton stellt er die Gewohnheit der meisten Amerikaner, selbst kürzeste Strecken mit dem Auto zurückzulegen. Dabei bedient er die amerikakritischen Tendenzen seiner britischen Leserschaft. Die Frage nach den geographischen und historischen Gründen für die unterschiedlichen Verhaltensmuster in den USA und Europa wird nicht gestellt; das amerikanische Verhalten erscheint als seltsam und unverständlich. Bei aller Freude an Brysons satirischen Beobachtungen und Formulierungen muss seine Kolumne deshalb auch gegen den Strich gelesen werden. Ihre textsortenbedingten Grenzen sind den S zu verdeutlichen. Die S müssen erkennen, dass die ökologisch bedenkliche Autoliebe der meisten Amerikaner v. a. durch die geographischen Gegebenheiten der USA entstanden ist – Fragen der Stadt- und Verkehrsentwicklung stellen sich in einem großräumigen, dünn besiedelten Land wie den USA anders als in dem kleinräumigeren, dicht besiedelten Europa. So sollten die S zumindest das Entstehen dieses Verhaltens differenziert beurteilen, wenn auch die Kritik an heutigen Auswüchsen, wie sie Bryson schildert, durchaus berechtigt ist.

Unterrichts-
tipps

Der Einstieg kann über Assoziationen zur Überschrift über Einstellungen zur amerikanischen Autoliebe oder die Fotos einer fußgängerfreundlichen idyllischen Kleinstadt (SB, S. 180) und einer autogerechten, gesichtslosen Vorstadt (SB, S. 181) erfolgen.

Differenzierung

Leistungsschwächeren S könnte die folgende Aufgabe das Verständnis erleichtern:

⬭ *What examples does the writer give of people not walking in the USA?*
Using the car to go next door (cf. ll. 1–2), not walking into the nearby town (cf. ll. 19–21); not walking from shop to shop (cf. ll. 37–43); driving to a nearby gym to walk on a treadmill (cf. ll. 46–50), refusing to go shopping in a town where one could not park outside the shops (cf. ll. 66–68)

→ *WB, ex. 7, 8, 9*

Info

Bill Bryson (born 1951) was born and grew up in Iowa. He moved to England as a young man, where he became a journalist and travel writer. He is far better known in Britain than in the USA. His books include *The Lost Continent* (1989), which is about the USA, *Neither Here nor There* (1991), which is about Europe, and *Notes from a Small Island* (1995), which is about Britain. In 1996 he moved to New Hampshire with his English wife and children.

1 The writer enjoys walking. When he and his family moved to the USA, they chose a place 'within walking distance of shops' (l. 16) and he refuses lifts from well-meaning neighbours so he can walk to town (cf. ll. 22–32). He favours pedestrianizing town centres (cf. ll. 61–72). It makes him angry if people waste petrol when they leave their engines running (cf. ll. 39–43).

His neighbours use the car wherever they go, even for very short distances (ll. 1–2). To make up for their sedentary lifestyle, they exercise. They jog, play squash or go to the gym for personalized workout programmes (cf. ll. 44–54). Walking is part of their exercise programme and no longer serves the purpose of getting from A to B. Americans have made themselves psychologically so dependant on cars for movement that they feel that Bryson is strange because he walks.

2 Die Herausarbeitung der humoristischen Mittel kann für viele S schwierig sein. In diesem Fall sollten sie, z.B. anhand der Karikatur auf S. 107 unten, an das Mittel der Übertreibung in Cartoons erinnert und aufgefordert werden, Beispiele für Übertreibungen in Brysons Kolumne zu finden.

<u>Humour directed at himself:</u> He describes himself as 'no stranger to sloth' (l. 12). He makes himself appear to be a TV junkie by comparing the movement involved in finding the remote control to the distance covered by the average American. He says if he is 'feeling particularly debonair, I stop at Rosey Jekes Café for a cappuccino' (ll. 23–24), which makes something trivial appear more glamorous. He talks about having something 'rash and lively' done to his hair, showing he is not at all cool or stylish. 'All this is a big part of my life' (l. 26): Bryson describes everyday routines like going to the post office or the barber's as if they were important events. By poking fun at himself, he tries to make the reader more sympathetic to his message; Bryson is not an arrogant person but an amusing normal person, whose message comes across more effectively.

<u>Exaggeration:</u> 'Nobody walks anywhere in the USA nowadays' (l. 8); 'they would … reluctantly, even guiltily as if leaving the scene of an accident' (l. 34), which is an amusing comparison considering they are indeed leaving somebody by the road; 'it would never occur to them to unfurl their legs and see what they can do' (ll. 35–36), making legs seem like unusual untried out appendages; 'as if I were tragically simple-minded' (l. 51); 'Americans not only don't walk anywhere, they won't walk anywhere' (ll. 61–62).

<u>Irony:</u> 'I'll tell you this, but you have to promise that it will get no further' (l. 1): Bryson pretends that he is telling a secret but is actually writing in a mass-circulation daily; 'curious and eccentric behaviour' (l. 27): by European standards, there is nothing curious or eccentric about Bryson's behaviour, rather it is American behaviour that appears curious and eccentric; 'It had not occurred to me how thoughtlessly deficient nature was in this regard' (ll. 53–54): Bryson personifies nature and implies that American think that nature is at fault and needs improvement. What he really means is that Americans lead very artificial lives.

3 **a** Die Erläuterungen können weiter differenziert werden, wenn – arbeitsteilig – mehrere einsprachige Lexika, insbesondere Synonymwörterbücher, ausgewertet werden. Zur Ergebnissicherung bietet es sich an, die Verben in Sinngruppen (z.B. 'walk slowly', 'walk quickly') zusammenfassen zu lassen.

'move' (l. 2): (here) change the place where you live
'drive' (l. 3): operate a car so that it goes in a particular direction
'get to' (ll. 4–5): arrive at a place
'walk' (l. 8): move or go somewhere on foot, but without running
'stroll' (l. 19): walk somewhere in a slow relaxed way
'pop (out/in)' (ll. 39, 43): (BrE, infml) go out of / into a place quickly or for a short time
'dash (inside)' (l. 39): go (inside a place) very quickly
'come out' (l. 41): leave a place

'get in' (l. 41): go into sth. (especially a vehicle)
'pace off' (l. 42): measure sth. by walking across it with regular steps
'jog' (l. 44): run slowly and steadily for a long time, especially for exercise

b Tiptoe, creep, edge, limp, shuffle, trudge, step, tread, wander, roam, prowl, hike, trek, wade, paddle, totter, stagger, stride, swagger, strut, parade, march, hurry, run, trot, bound, rush, race, sprint, tear, charge.

4 Some of the differences between public perception of transportation in Europe and in the USA can be attributed to the differences in population density. It is probably useful to examine different modes of transportation:

Urban public transport: To be economically viable, public transport requires a certain number of passengers. Apart from in very large cities such as New York and Chicago, which came largely of age in the 19th century, public transportation is less viable in the USA than in Europe. In the densely populated countries of Western Europe ecological awareness is likely to be higher than in more sparsely populated countries with plenty of open space (urban areas and roads take up only about 3 percent of the land area of the USA). Other cities like Los Angeles only expanded significantly in the middle of the 20th century, by which time the car had become the preferred means of transport.

Railways/Buses: Buses are cheaper than trains and planes and are often used by poorer people in the USA for long-distance travel. Railways were an important factor in connecting the vast spaces of the USA before the 1960s, but now it is easier to fly. This has led to little investment in train travel except on important routes along the East Coast (e.g. New York–Washington, D.C.), so travelling by train in the USA is much slower than in most European countries. European countries are small enough to support extensive rail networks. As European cities are compact, travelling by train allows you to get into the centre of a city (which is often the commercial hub) quicker than by car.

Car: As the middle-class American families live in suburbs where there is no public transport, cars are essential. For women, who had been home-bound up to the 1950s, the car meant more independence and the ability to look for work. Car ownership contributed to urban sprawl, making it easier to live in suburbia. Suburbia, in turn, made car ownership a virtual necessity, requiring families to own more than one car.

Planes: Americans and Europeans use planes for middle- and long-distance flights. The USA is much larger than continental Europe and one must consider the fact that a flight is quick and often not too expensive. Here there is no difference in perceptions between Americans and Europeans.

SB, S. 182   **C Car Culture and the Shopping Mall**

Source:	*BBC World Service*, 2003
Topic:	The role of the car and the shopping mall
Text form:	Radio documentary
Language variety:	BE
Length:	6:02
Level:	Advanced
Skills/activities:	Examining the popularity of malls

*Didaktisch-
methodische
Hinweise*

Dieser Hörtext knüpft inhaltlich an „A Sedentary Nation" an und vertieft die dort gewonnenen Erkenntnisse, indem er die Beliebtheit von *shopping malls* beschreibt. Einkaufszentren außerhalb der Stadt bieten Einkaufs- und Unterhaltungs-möglichkeiten unter einem Dach, sind aber meist nur mit dem Auto zu erreichen. Wie der Hörtext zeigt, ist dieser Trend nicht spezifisch amerikanisch, sondern international. Bei diesem Text (vgl. CD2, *track* 14 und das Transkript auf S. 358–360) begegnen die S einer Vielfalt verschiedener englischer Akzente: Es gibt Sprecher aus England, den USA, aus Südafrika und Singapur.

Bevor die S den Text hören, sollten die folgenden Begriffe und Wörter semantisiert werden:

Jack in the Box: a hamburger restaurant chain
Eisenhower era: the mid- and late 1950s when Dwight Eisenhower (1953–1961) was president of the USA – it was a boom time in the USA.
outskirts: the parts of a town that are furthest from the centre
window-shopping: looking in shop windows without buying anything

mischief: bad behaviour
gated community: a small community of houses surrounded by a fence or wall to keep out intruders or criminals
subliminal message: a message that is so soft that you are not aware that is affecting your mind
ingenious: very clever

Lösungs-hinweise

1 The global popularity of malls is due to several factors, which may differ from place to place. Firstly, there is the fact that so many shops and restaurants can be found under one roof; this makes shopping (and eating and drinking easy); secondly, they are easy to reach by car (or by public transport in Singapore); they are air-conditioned; they are safe; finally and probably most important of all, they are economic to run.

2 The mall is laid out so that you cannot just go straight up but when you reach one floor, you have to walk round (and therefore see lots of shops) in order to get the next escalator up. All the restaurants are located on the top floor, so that customers actually do go up to the top floor, as at some point everyone needs to eat or drink something.

3 Individual answers.

SB, S. 182

D The American Way of Life as Reflected on TV

Source:	*The Sopranos*, 1999
Topic:	American family life and American values
Text form:	TV series
Language variety:	AE
Length:	8:23 minutes
Level:	Basic/advanced
Skills/activities:	Analysing the Americanness of TV programmes

Didaktisch-methodische Hinweise

Zum Abschluss dieses Kapitels begegnen die S amerikanischer Popkultur, wie sie in Fernsehserien aus den USA dargestellt wird. Preisgekrönt in den USA und beliebt in der gesamten angelsächsischen Welt, handelt *The Sopranos* von einem Mafiaboss aus New Jersey, der unter psychologischem Stress und den üblichen Familienproblemen leidet. Anhand des Ausschnitts (vgl. das Video / die DVD und das Transkript auf S. 360–362) und aufgrund ihres Vorwissens zu deutschen und US-amerikanischen Fernsehserien sollen die S charakteristische Themen US-amerikanischer Fernsehserien identifi-zieren: die Suche nach dem persönlichen Glück (z.B. *Sex and the City, Ally McBeal*), Familienleben (z.B. *Dawson's Creek, Married with Children* [deutsch „Eine schrecklich nette Familie"], *The Cosby Show, The Simpsons*), alternative Formen des Zusammen-lebens (z.B. *Friends, Buffy the Vampireslayer, Friends*), der Umgang mit dem Über-natürlichen (z.B. *X Files*). Gelegentlich (z.B. *Married with Children, Roseanne*) stellen die Serien das Leben jenseits des *American Dream* von Wohlstand und Statussymbolen dar.

Da die Figuren in *The Sopranos* mit dem für S schwer verständlichen New-Jersey-Akzent sprechen, sollten vorab mögliche Verständnisschwierigkeiten minimiert und folgende Wörter semantisiert werden:

physician: general doctor
black out: faint, lose consciousness
from the ground floor: (here) from the beginning
mating season: Paarungszeit
yard (AE): garden
poo (sl): shit
do it: have sex
gross: disgusting
sfogliatelle (Italian): type of biscuits eaten for breakfast
Aspen: famous US ski resort

Skeet Ulrich: US actor
Gordon Willis, Jeez Luiz: expressions of surprise
putty: Kitt
jimmy a window: open a window with a tool
sneak out – snuck out – snuck out (infml): leave the house secretly
cunniving: deception
grounded: forbidden to leave home
boot: Italy (which has the shape of a boot)
Sally Jessy Raphael: talk show host
va fan culo (Italian): fuck you

Sollten die S nach der ersten Präsentation Schwierigkeiten haben, Aufgabe 1 zu beantworten, kann ihnen vor dem zweiten Sehen das Transkript ausgehändigt werden.

Info

The Sopranos was first broadcast in 1999 and was immediately well-received. It chronicles a suburban American family, who are part of the New Jersey Mafia. Tony Soprano finds himself in a deep depression seeking psychotherapy due to the pressure of heading two families – his murderous mob clan and his own family. The tension between Tony Soprano (played by James Gandolfini) and his psychiatrist Jennifer Melfi (played by Lorraine Bracco) adds an extra touch to the comic drama of the series.

---

1 Vgl. das Video / die DVD und das Transkript auf S. 360–362.

Possible answers:

The American Dream (wealth, large suburban house with swimming pool), work, immigration (both Soprano and Melfi are aware of their immigrant Italian past), beauty (cf. daughter's obsession with keeping skinny, compared to the overweight son), family (father and children relationship), value of education (school grades), pursuit of happiness (psychotherapy, love of nature in the form of ducks), guns (cf. Carmel's gun when she thinks someone is breaking in – a necessary precaution for a mafia boss, but a possible scenario in many American households), movies (cf. Soprano's reference to Gary Cooper, Carmel watching movies with the priest), sense of community (e.g. what it is to be an American, 'A lot of Americans feel that way').

2 Individual answers.

3 **a–b** Individual answers.

Watch Your Language

Anhand von Texten zum Thema USA werden den S typische Fehler beim Verknüpfen von Sätzen vor Augen geführt. Insbesondere die Unterscheidung von notwendigen und nicht-notwendigen Relativsätzen und daraus folgende Konsequenzen für die Kommasetzung sowie Partizipialkonstruktionen erweisen sich als schwierig. In Aufgabe 2 müssen die S einen überwiegend parataktischen Text durch Satzgefüge, Partizipialkonstruktionen und Konnektoren stilistisch verbessern.

→ WB, ex. 7

 a–b

'people who': *CEG* §260 (Use of relative pronoun: Index under 'relative pronouns', 'who: relative pronoun'); *CEG* §259b, 304e (Use of comma: Index under 'defining relative clauses', 'comma');
'which': *CEG* §266 (Index under 'relative clause: *which* relating to a clause');
'America has always been a land of liberty and opportunity for millions of immigrants fleeing from' ...: *CEG* §162 (Index under: 'participle: subject in participle constructions');
'native countries': German-English dictionary under 'Geburtsland';
'a country that': *CEG* §259b, 304e (Use of comma: Index under 'defining relative clauses', 'comma');
'those who': *CEG* §259b, 304e (Use of comma: Index under 'defining relative clauses', 'comma');
'The inauguration of the president, who is elected in November, does not ...': *CEG* §162 (Index under: participle: subject in participle constructions');
'what': *what* is used as a nominal relative pronoun, which means that it does not (as other relative pronouns do) refer to a noun coming before it, but that it functions as noun + relative pronoun together, meaning 'the thing which'.

c The student needs to revise relative pronouns, punctuation in defining and non-defining relative clauses, and participle constructions (avoiding misrelated or dangling participles).

2 In the old days, when quilts were made as warm bedcovers, the tasks of caring for their homes and family filled up so many hours that most women had little leisure time in which to express their creativity. Many of them channeled their inventive talent and imagination into quiltmaking. Hundreds of hours were spent composing quilts from bits of fabric accumulated and kept in scrap bags. One piece might be from a favourite dress, while another came from a child's bonnet – all of them reminders of the past when these were worn. A twentieth-century writer on quilts quotes her great-grandmother as saying, 'My whole life is in that quilt. It scares me sometimes when I look at it. All my joys and all my sorrows are stitched into those little pieces.'

SB, p. 166
(cf. TM, p. 321)

America the Beautiful   Katherine Lee Bates

Below is the first stanza of 'America the Beautiful'. On the right are jumbled up couplets from the poem's succeeding stanzas. Cut them out and try to reconstruct the stanzas 2–4 by putting the couplets into the right order. It will help you if you look at the form of stanza 1 and follow the rhyme scheme.

O beautiful for spacious skies,
For amber waves of grain,
For purple mountain majesties
Above the fruited plain!
America! America!
God shed His grace on thee,
And crown thy good with brotherhood
From sea to shining sea!

O beautiful for pilgrim feet
Whose stern impassion'd stress

Thine alabaster cities gleam
Undimmed by human tears!

America! America!
God shed his grace on thee

America! America!
May God thy gold refine,

Who more than self their country loved,
And mercy more than life!

Till all success be nobleness,
And ev'ry gain divine!

O beautiful for patriot dream
That sees beyond the years

America! America!
God mend thine ev'ry flaw,

Confirm thy soul in self-control,
Thy liberty in law!

O beautiful for heroes prov'd
In liberating strife,

A thoroughfare of freedom beat
Across the wilderness!

And crown thy good with brotherhood
From sea to shining sea!

stern: streng · *thine* (old use): your · *gleam:* shine softly · *undimmed by human tears:* allusion to the vision of the New Jerusalem in Revelations 21:4 ('God [...] will wipe every tear from their eyes') · *mend sth.:* repair sth. · *flaw:* defect, imperfection · *strife:* fight · *thoroughfare:* public road

What geographical features, historical events and values does 'America the Beautiful' celebrate?

SB, p. 166
(cf. TM, p. 322)

The New Colossus   Emma Lazarus

Here are the complete lyrics to the poem. Read them and answer the questions below.

1   **N**ot like the brazen giant of Greek fame
With conquering limbs astride from land to land;
Here at our sea-washed, sunset gates shall stand
A mighty woman with a torch, whose flame
5   Is the imprisoned lightning, and her name
Mother of Exiles. From her beacon-hand
Glows world-wide welcome; her mild eyes command
The air-bridged harbor that twin cities frame,
'Keep, ancient lands, your storied pomp!' cries she
10   With silent lips. 'Give me your tired, your poor,
Your huddled masses yearning to breathe free,
The wretched refuse of your teeming shore,
Send these, the homeless, tempest-tost to me,
I lift my lamp beside the golden door!'

1 *brazen:* made of bronze; shameless and bold   **2** *limb:* (here) leg
2 *astride:* apart   **3** *sunset:* (here) western   **6** *beacon-hand:* (here) hand
holding a beacon (= Leuchtfeuer) **8** *twin cities:* New York and Brooklyn
(which until 1895 were two separate cities)   **9** *storied:* recorded in
history; well-known   **11** *huddle:* be crowded close together **12** *refuse*
['refjuːz]: waste material   **12** *teeming* (adj): full, crowded   **13** *tost* (old-
fashioned) = *tossed:* thrown about

1   Compare Emma Lazarus's vision of the old and the new world.

2 a   What was the 'brazen giant of Greek fame' that the poet refers to?

   b   How is the Statue of Liberty different from that statue?

3   Identify and analyse the symbolism in the poem.

4   What stylistic device does the poet use in l. 7?

5   Analyse the structure and rhyme scheme of the poem.
A poem with this formal arrangement is called a sonnet. How does it
differ from other sonnets (cf. SB, p. 256)?

SB, p. 169
(cf. TM, p. 328)

George W. Bush: Inaugural Speech

1 Thank you all. Chief Justice Rehnquist, President Carter, President Bush, President Clinton, distinguished guests and my fellow citizens. The peaceful transfer of authority is rare in history, yet common in our country. With a simple oath we affirm old traditions and make new beginnings. As I begin, I thank President Clinton for his service
5 to our nation, and I thank Vice-President Gore for a contest conducted with spirit and ended with grace. I am honored and humbled to stand here where so many of America's leaders have come before me and so many will follow.

We have a place, all of us, in a long story – a story we continue, but whose end we will not see. It is the story of a new world that became a friend and liberator of the old, the
10 story of a slave-holding society that became a servant of freedom, the story of a power that went into the world to protect but not possess, to defend but not to conquer.

It is the American story – a story of flawed and fallible people, united across the generations by grand and enduring ideals. The grandest of these ideals is an unfolding American promise that everyone belongs, that everyone deserves a chance, that no
15 insignificant person was ever born.

Americans are called to enact this promise in our lives and in our laws. And though our nation has sometimes halted, and sometimes delayed, we must follow no other course. Through much of the last century, America's faith in freedom and democracy was a rock in a raging sea. Now it is a seed upon the wind, taking root in many nations. Our demo-
20 cratic faith is more than the creed of our country, it is the inborn hope of our humanity, an ideal we carry but do not own, a trust we bear and pass along. And even after nearly 225 years, we have a long way yet to travel.

While many of our citizens prosper, others doubt the promise, even the justice, of our own country. The ambitions of some Americans are limited by failing schools and
25 hidden prejudice and the circumstances of their birth. And sometimes our differences run so deep, it seems we share a continent, but not a country. We do not accept this, and we will not allow it. Our unity, our union, is the serious work of leaders and citizens in every generation. And this is my solemn pledge: I will work to build a single nation of justice and opportunity.

30 I know this is in our reach because we are guided by a power larger than ourselves who creates us equal in His image. And we are confident in principles that unite and lead us onward. America has never been united by blood or birth or soil. We are bound by ideals that move us beyond our backgrounds, lift us above our interests and teach us what it means to be citizens. Every child must be taught these principles. Every citizen must
35 uphold them. And every immigrant, by embracing these ideals, makes our country more, not less, American.

Today, we affirm a new commitment to live out our nation's promise through civility, courage, compassion and character. America, at its best, matches a commitment to principle with a concern for civility. A civil society demands from each of us good will
40 and respect, fair dealing and forgiveness. [...]

America, at its best, is also courageous. Our national courage has been clear in times of depression and war, when defeating common dangers defined our common good. Now we must choose if the example of our fathers and mothers will inspire us or condemn us. We must show courage in a time of blessing by confronting problems instead of
45 passing them on to future generations.

Together, we will reclaim America's schools, before ignorance and apathy claim more young lives. We will reform Social Security and Medicare, sparing our children from struggles we have the power to prevent. And we will reduce taxes, to recover the momentum of our economy and reward the effort and enterprise of working Americans.

50 We will build our defenses beyond challenge, lest weakness invite challenge. We will confront weapons of mass destruction, so that a new century is spared new horrors. The enemies of liberty and our country should make no mistake: America remains engaged in the world by history and by choice, shaping a balance of power that favors freedom. We will defend our allies and our interests. We will show purpose without arrogance.

55 We will meet aggression and bad faith with resolve and strength. And to all nations, we will speak for the values that gave our nation birth.

America, at its best, is compassionate. In the quiet of American conscience, we know that deep, persistent poverty is unworthy of our nation's promise. And whatever our views of its cause, we can agree that children at risk are not at fault. Abandonment and

60 abuse are not acts of God, they are failures of love.

And the proliferation of prisons, however necessary, is no substitute for hope and order in our souls. Where there is suffering, there is duty. Americans in need are not strangers, they are citizens, not problems but priorities. And all of us are diminished when any are hopeless.

65 Government has great responsibilities for public safety and public health, for civil rights and common schools. Yet compassion is the work of a nation, not just a government. And some needs and hurts are so deep they will only respond to a mentor's touch or a pastor's prayer. Church and charity, synagogue and mosque lend our communities their humanity, and they will have an honored place in our plans and

70 in our laws.

Many in our country do not know the pain of poverty, but we can listen to those who do. And I can pledge our nation to a goal: When we see that wounded traveler on the road to Jericho, we will not pass to the other side.

America, at its best, is a place where personal responsibility is valued and expected.

75 Encouraging responsibility is not a search for scapegoats, it is a call to conscience. And though it requires sacrifice, it brings a deeper fulfillment. We find the fullness of life not only in options, but in commitments. And we find that children and community are the commitments that set us free.

Our public interest depends on private character, on civic duty and family bonds and

80 basic fairness, on uncounted, unhonored acts of decency which give direction to our freedom. Sometimes in life we are called to do great things. But as a saint of our times has said, every day we are called to do small things with great love. The most important tasks of a democracy are done by everyone. [...]

God bless you all, and God bless America.

12 *fallible:* able and likely to make mistakes 20 *creed:* system of religious beliefs 28 *solemn:* serious 28 *pledge:* promise 37 *civility:* politeness, consideration 38 *compassion:* pity for the suffering of another person 47 *Social Security:* (in the USA) government programme providing unemployment benefits and old-age insurance 47 *Medicare:* (in the USA) system of medical care for old people provided by the government 50 *lest* (fml): damit nicht 60 *act of God:* an event caused by natural forces beyond human control, such as a storm, a flood or an earthquake 61 *proliferation:* rapid increase in numbers 72–73 *wounded traveler [...] Jericho:* allusion to the Biblical parable of the Good Samaritan (Luke 10:25–37) 75 *scapegoat:* Sündenbock 81 *a saint of our times:* Mother Teresa of Calcutta

The USA at a Glance

Government

System of Checks and Balances

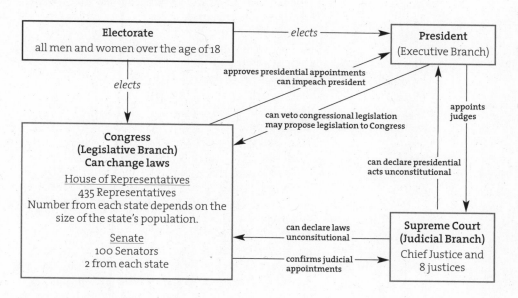

Population

Total Population (2000): 281,422,000

Race/Ethnicity	
White:	69.1%
Black:	12.1%
Hispanic:	12.5%
Mixed Race:	1.9%
Asian:	3.6%
Native American:	0.8%

(Depending on their origins,
Hispanics may consider themselves white,
black or Native American.)

Religion

Protestant:	52%
Catholic:	25%
Mormon:	2%
Jews:	1.3%
Muslim:	0.5%
Buddism:	0.5%

Some Figures for the USA

Area:	9,372,600 km²
Unemployment rate (2002):	5.8%
Inflation rate (2002):	1.6%
GDP per capita (2002):	$37,600
Life expectancy:	77 years

CD · **Getting Along in English**

SB, p. 177

Woman:	Excuse me. I couldn't help but notice that you're reading something in a foreign language. Is that German?
Maren:	Yes.
Woman:	That's interesting. My son is stationed in Germany. Wiesbaden, I think. He's in the army.
Maren:	Oh really?
Woman:	So, are you just visiting the US, or are you living here?
Maren:	I'm just a tourist.
Woman:	How nice. And do you like it here?
Maren:	Well, not all that much, actually.
Woman:	Oh my! Why ever not?
Maren:	Well, the people ...
Woman:	What about the people?
Maren:	I find Americans terribly superficial.
Woman:	I beg your pardon?
Maren:	You know – the way everybody wishes you a nice day. 'Have a nice day', all the time. Nobody really means it. And they always smile and pretend to like you.
Woman:	Maybe they're just trying to be nice and friendly. I like it when people smile and are cheerful.
Maren:	But why? I don't know these people. And I've already received two invitations to people's houses, from people I just met.
Woman:	That's our way of being friendly. Did you take these people up on their invitations?
Maren:	No. They didn't mean it anyway. I mean, they hardly knew me.
Woman:	No, I don't suppose they did. Now, if you'll excuse me, I think I see an empty seat over there by the window.

CD · **Car Culture and the Shopping Mall**

SB, S. 182

1st Speaker:	It's crucial to keep in mind that the car culture and fast-food culture came from the same place and the same time. We're really talking about post-war southern California. Los Angeles was the first major city that was built around the automobile and developed to serve the needs of the automobile, and the fast-food restaurant kind of built upon that, where you drove up, got out, ordered your food or – as Jack in the Box introduced – you just drove through. So these restaurants, their design and their sensibility really comes from this Eisenhower era, car culture, belief in technology and progress, and whenever you go to a MacDonalds, anywhere in the world, you're walking into a little bit of southern California in the 1950s.
2nd Speaker:	That was the model then, but in the 1950s they created a new kind of shopping center, the first one was in Minneapolis in about 1955, called mall. First they were being built in areas on the outskirts of traditional cities but then they were being built in areas which had no city centres at all, so they de facto became the town centers of these communities and this took over the country. This became the most popular form of retail activity.
3rd Speaker:	At some point in the 20th century, shopping became, you know, one of the most significant cultural activities. The temple of

suburban culture is, of course, the shopping mall and that's where worshippers of the American Dream do their religious observations.

Presenter: And the sacred rights of mall shopping are now performed in every continent. Here's Siva Choi in Asia.

Siva Choi: Shopping malls are a huge thing in Singapore and there's a reason for that. If you are living as, well say, I think nearly 80% of the population is living, in high-rise apartments, it's a great thing to be able to get out of the apartment, take a bus or the train down into the city and then walk through these huge air-conditioned shopping malls where you don't have to buy anything, you can just walk up there and do some window-shopping. You can meet up with friends, hang around the burger joints, have a nice day and go home. So a huge meeting-point culture has evolved around the malls. The one distinctive thing, I think, which must be said about shopping malls in Singapore is that they're extremely safe places; a lot of the kids gather there but there is relatively very little mischief. You don't get kids going around spraying graffiti on walls, getting into fights – it happens, but not very often. And so a lot of people will go to malls because they know they're not threatened by the presence of juveniles, for example.

Presenter: Down in South Africa, Greg Kusier has also seen a world made safe for shopping.

Greg Kusier: Along with the urban decay of city centres in South Africa, alongside that has been the rise of American-style shopping malls. It's really fed into South Africa's emerging siege mentality, you know, people go straight from their little gated community homes: you can get into your air-conditioned car, drive from your gated community, go as quickly as you can along the highway and hope you don't get hijacked, straight into the shopping mall, into the air-conditioned parking lot and do your shopping without actually having to get outside at any point. And I think it's a very unfortunate thing because when I grew up you could still go to the city centre, you still went to the city centre to do your shopping. And I still do, to a large extent. Especially in summer in Durban, you know, I mean, or even in winter in Durban, it's a pleasure being outside in this country, and to go into these shopping centres with this awful recycled air conditioning, these teenage mall rats hanging around the escalators, and there's that funny white noise in the background in shopping malls, I'm sure it's full of subliminal messages, telling us to buy things.

2nd Speaker: These places have been shown to be the most economical for certain kinds of development, and so people in other countries, when they copy them, they're not copying them to give any homage to America, they're copying them because this is the way they themselves in their countries are going to make the most money. So, in effect, this becomes a kind of standard practice. You know, it's just that we were there first, we figured this stuff out first, and so it becomes a kind of American model. And the layout of these places is incredibly ingenious; if you ever go in them, you'll know this, for example the way they cunningly split the up-escalators so that you in fact have to keep circulating around the mall to keep going up and up and up. They don't let you just kind of step on and step off again, they want you to make a circuit each time. The way that, for example, they put the food court, as they call it – the place with all the restaurants, they gather them all together, they don't let them sort of be interspersed with the other stores, unlike a real city, where restaurants are just usually in between stores. They gather them all and they put them in on the top floor and this has several advantages: first of all, the top floor space is the least attractive to retailers – it's the one they want the least 'cause the fewest people reach it, so they get to lease that out to another use; and the other thing is it then actually brings people up there because, at some point or another, everyone gets hungry or thirsty and needs to get something to eat, so they're kind of lured up to the least attractive part of the mall, the part they might least naturally go to.

Presenter: And that's why I'm travelling up on the escalator at the shopping mall: more fries. 'It's all functional', says the sociologist Professor George Ritzer.

George Ritzer: You know, much of what a shopping mall, a supermarket, a department store, a theme park, and many of these other kinds of settings are about is that they are essentially people-moving machines, and indeed a fast-food restaurant is that, that's the point of a drive-through window – you want to move people through as quickly as possible, or making uncomfortable seats, so people move through as quickly as possible.

VIDEO The American Way of Life As Reflected on TV

SB, S. 182 Extract from *The Sopranos*.

Dr Melfi: Mr Soprano?
Tony Soprano: Er, yeh.
Dr Melfi: Have a seat.
Tony Soprano: Hm.
Dr Melfi: My understanding from Dr. Cusamano, your family physician, is that you collapsed. Possibly panic attack? You were unable to breathe?
Tony Soprano: They said it was a panic attack. Of course, all the blood work and the neurological work came back negative. And they sent me here.
Dr Melfi: You don't agree that you had a panic attack?
How are you feeling now?
Tony Soprano: Good. Fine. Back at work.
Dr Melfi: What line of work are you in?
Tony Soprano: Waste management consultant. Look it's impossible for me to talk to a psychiatrist.
Dr Melfi: Any thoughts at all on why you blacked out?
Tony Soprano: I don't know. Stress maybe.
Dr Melfi: About what?
Tony Soprano: I don't know. The morning of the day I got sick I'd been thinking, it's good to be in something from the ground floor. I came too late for that. I know. But lately I'm getting the feeling that I came in at the end. The best is over.
Dr Melfi: Many Americans, I think, feel that way.
Tony Soprano: I think about my father. He never reached the heights like me. But in a lot of ways he had it better. He had his people. They had their standards. They had pride. Today what have we got?
Dr Melfi: Did you have these feelings of loss more acutely in the hours before you collapsed?

Tony Soprano:	I don't know. A couple of months before there was these two wild ducks landed in my pool. It was amazing. They're from Canada or some place and it was mating season. They had some ducklings. My daughter's friend was here to drive my daughter Meadow to school.
Hunter:	Meadow, your father with those ducks!
Meadow:	I know, the whole yard smells like duck poo. It's like embarrassing.
Carmela Soprano:	Girls, you've got to have more than just cranberry juice for breakfast, alright? You need brain food for school. Happy birthday, handsome. Thirteen!
Meadow:	Yeh, he doesn't act it.
Anthony Junior:	Shut up.
Hunter:	A male and female duck just made a home in your pool and did it.
Meadow:	Iiiiow!
Hunter:	Disgusting!
Meadow:	Get out of here. You're so gross.
Carmela Soprano:	Girls, you want some of last night's *sfogliatelle*?
Meadow:	Get out of here with that fat.
Carmela Soprano:	One bite.
Hunter:	How do you stay so skinny, Mrs Soprano?
Carmela Soprano:	Him with those ducks!
Tony Soprano:	Listen, if you don't like that ramp, I'll build you another one. Maybe it's the wood. Hey, hey, kids. Come here! Come here, they're trying to fly. Come here, the babies, they're trying to fly. Look, they're trying to fly.
Meadow:	*National Geographic*, Dad.
Anthony Junior:	You showed us yesterday.
Tony Soprano:	It's great. Now my wife feels this friend is a bad influence.
Hunter:	It's so cool you're going to be able to come to Aspen with my family at Christmas. Last year at Aspen I saw Skeet Ulrich as close as from where you're sitting.
Meadow:	Oh my God!
Carmela Soprano:	Miss Meadow, we made a deal. You keep your school grades up and you keep your curfew between now and Christmas. Then you get to go.
Meadow:	I know that.
Tony Soprano:	Morning, ladies.
Hunter:	Hey, Mr Soprano.
Meadow:	We're late, dad.
Tony Soprano:	Hey, happy birthday.
Anthony Junior:	Thanks, dad.
Carmela Soprano:	You're going to be home tonight for Anthony Junior's birthday party, right? Birdman! Hello!
Tony Soprano:	Yeh, yeh. I'll get home early from work.
Carmela Soprano:	I'm not talking about work.
Tony Soprano:	This isn't going to work. I can't talk about my personal life.
Dr Melfi:	Finish telling me about the day you collapsed.
Tony Soprano:	My wife and my daughter were not getting along.
Priest:	Darn. These laser discs are incredible.
Carmela Soprano:	Tony watches *Godfather 2* all the time. He says the camera work looks just as good as in the movie theater.
Priest:	Gordon Willis. Tony prefers 2 not 1?
Carmela Soprano:	Yeh. He likes the part when Vito goes back to Sicily. With 3 he was like, 'What happened?'
Priest:	Where does Tony rank *Goodfellas*? ... What, do you have raccoons?
Carmela Soprano:	Someone's jimmying a window.

Priest:	What? Yeh, but you have all these security lights. Who would try and ...? uh? Oh no. Jeez Luiz!
Carmela Soprano:	Hold it! Meadow!
Meadow:	I noticed the glass rattles every time I go to the laundry room. Do we have any, what do you call, putty?
Carmela Soprano:	Don't give me that. You snuck out!
Anthony Junior:	What's going on?
Meadow:	You locked my bedroom window on purpose, so I'd get caught.
Anthony Junior:	Hey!
Carmela Soprano:	Normal people thought you were upstairs doing your homework. You have become a master of lying and cunniving.
Meadow:	Yeah, I know I'm grounded but Patrick's swim meet is tomorrow and he needed me.
Carmela Soprano:	Grounded for this? Oh, no, you're not grounded. You're not going to Aspen with Hunter Scangarelo. That's where you're not going.
Anthony Junior:	Yes!
Tony Soprano:	But this shit I'm telling you. It'll all blow over.
Dr Melfi:	Didn't you admit to Dr. Cusamano that you were feeling depressed?
Tony Soprano:	Melfi! What part of the boot are you from, huh?
Dr Melfi:	Dr. Melfi. My father's people were from Caserta.
Tony Soprano:	Avellino. My mother would have loved it if you and I got together.
Dr Melfi:	Anxiety attacks are legitimate psychiatric emergencies. Suppose you were driving and you passed out?
Tony Soprano:	Let me tell you something. Nowadays everybody's got to go to shrinks and counsellors and go on *Sally Jessy Raphael* and talk about their problems. Whatever happened to Gary Cooper? The strong, silent type. That was an American! He wasn't in touch with his feelings. He just did what he had to do. See what they didn't know is, once they got Gary Cooper in touch with his feelings, that they wouldn't be able to shut him up and then it's dysfunction this and dysfunction that and dysfunction *va fan culo*!
Dr Melfi:	You have strong feelings about this.
Tony Soprano:	Let me tell you something. I had a semester and a half at college, so I understand Freud. I understand therapy as a concept. But in my world, it does not go down. Could I be happier? Yeah. Yeah. Who couldn't?
Dr Melfi:	Do you feel depressed? Do you feel depressed?
Tony Soprano:	Since the ducks left. I guess.
Dr Melfi:	The ducks that preceded your losing consciousness. Let's talk about them.

Das Ende der Schulzeit ist für die Jugendlichen eine Phase, in der die Frage nach ihrer persönlichen Identität einen großen Raum einnimmt, wenn sie Überlegungen zu Berufs- oder Studienwahl oder allgemeiner Lebensplanung anstellen. Die S erfahren in diesem Kapitel, welche Faktoren die Identität eines Menschen bestimmen können:

– In *section* 1, „Origami", lernen sie die Problematik der Identitätsbestimmung in einem Immigrationskontext kennen.

– In *section* 2, „I'm Not Lying Any More", erleben sie anhand eines Drehbuchs und eines Filmausschnitts, wie zwei Jugendliche ihre ethnische Identität bestimmen, indem sie zwischen ihrer Herkunftskultur und der Kultur vermitteln, in der sie leben.

– In *section* 3, „My Region, Myself", erkennen die S am Beispiel englischer Dialekte, dass auch Sprache über ein identitätsstiftendes Potential verfügt.

– In *section* 4, „Believing in Me: Goals and Ambitions", werden die S ermuntert, ihre Stärken und Schwächen zu erkennen und selbst-bewusst ihren eigenen Weg zu gehen, in beruflicher wie privater Hinsicht.

Die besondere Relevanz dieses Kapitels für Jugendliche in einer Lebenssituation, in der sie Weichen für ihr weiteres Leben stellen, zusammen mit dem hohen Abstraktionsvermögen, das von ihnen verlangt wird, lassen dieses Kapitel insbesondere für das Ende der Oberstufe angemessen erscheinen.

→ *WB, ex. 9*

Didaktisches Inhaltsverzeichnis

SB, p.	Title	TM, p.	Text form	Topic	Skills and activities
184	**Lead-in**	364	personal statements	aspects of identity	allocating statements to pictures; collecting words to do with identity; writing a portrait of a person
186	**Origami** Susan K. Ito	366	short story	determing one's ethnic and cultural identity	writing a description of a character; analysing the structure of a short story; identifying imagery; working with language
189	**Context Box**	369	–	aspects of a person's identity	making a diagram or mind map; listing self-doubts
190	**Beckham Is the Best**	370	screenplay (extract)	the problems involved when sexual and ethnic identity collide	converting a screenplay into a film
191	**We Have Some-Thing to Tell You** Video/DVD	372	film (extract)	telling one's parents the truth about one's needs	viewing comprehension; analysing a character's development; writing a screenplay
192	**Four English Accents** CD2, tracks 15–18	373	read text	various English accents	comparing different accents
192	**A Question of Accent** Rose George	374	newspaper article	people's reactions to different accents	discussing attitudes to accents
193	**Why Can't the English?** Alan Jay Lerner	376	song	criticism of different English accents	listening comprehension; comparing attitudes
194	**Getting Along in English**	378	–	being interviewed	analysing interviews; creating a personal interview code

195	**Aim Higher**	379	advert	higher education as a means of getting a good job	analysing an advert; creating an advert
196	**I Have an Ambition** Simon Hattenstone	381	newspaper article	one person's path to success	analysing the meaning of ambition; writing a short text
197	**Find Your Hidden Strengths** Marty Nemko	382	magazine article	finding out what one's personal strengths are	skimming; summarizing; discussing one's strengths and future plans
198	**The Road Not Taken** Robert Frost	383	poem	personal fulfilment by taking an unusual path	interpreting a poem; working with imagery
198	**Ships?** Maya Angelou	383	poem	life's enriching experiences	interpreting a poem; working with imagery
199	**Watch Your Language**	385	–	tenses	–

SB, S. 184

Lead-in

Lern-vokabular

Active vocabulary: 'Lead-in: Statements' (p. 184)

a) assume sth.   b) withdrawn, outgoing, overcome sth.   c) have a fit, bring sb. home with you, dating   e) show an interest in sth.   g) faith   k) self-confident, assertive   m) easy-going, get upset, go with the flow   n) earn money, fulfilment   o) lack of sth., socialist

Didaktisch-methodische Hinweise

Dieser Abschnitt vermittelt einen Überblick über verschiedene Aspekte persönlicher Identität: soziale und ethnische Herkunft, Erziehung, religiöse und politische Ausrichtungen, sexuelle Präferenzen, Mentalität und Temperament usw. Die S sollen in die Lage versetzt werden, diese Aspekte zu differenzieren und ansatzweise zu systematisieren.

Um dieses komplexe Thema zu konkretisieren, sollen die S die abgedruckten Zitate den Personen auf den Fotos zuordnen und somit deren – fiktive – Identität erschaffen. Dabei müssen sie darauf achten, dass in sich stimmige Personenporträts entstehen und nicht derselben Person widersprüchliche Zitate zugeordnet werden. Die S runden diese „Identität" ab, indem sie aus Sicht einer dieser Personen einen Text zum Thema „Who am I?" schreiben. Es ist dabei wichtig, den S deutlich zu machen, dass es nicht um eine „korrekte" Zuordnung von Zitaten zu den Personen geht, die ja nicht möglich ist, da es sich um fiktive Persönlichkeiten handelt. Vielmehr soll ein Bewusstsein für die verschiedenen Aspekte geweckt werden, die die Identität eines Menschen ausmachen. In Aufgabe 2a werden die S aufgefordert, ihre Zuordnungen zu hinterfragen, um stereotype Vorstellungen aufzudecken.

Unterrichts-tipps

Um die Identitäten der Personen detaillierter herauszuarbeiten und themenrelevantes Vokabular aus den Zitaten zu erfassen und mit bekanntem Wortschatz zu verbinden, können die S tabellarisch die im SB gegebenen Informationen und deren mögliche Implikationen auflisten (s.u.). Auf diese Weise kann auch das Personenporträt in Aufgabe 3 vorbereitet werden.

Person	Information given	Implied personality traits
A	from working-class background to university	good at school, intelligent, ambitious, self-confident

→ WB, ex. 1

1 Individual answers.

2 **a** Bei der Diskussion der Zuordnungen werden sicher einige S von selbst darauf hinweisen, dass diese auf der Basis stereotyper Vorstellungen erfolgt sind; ggf. sollten die Begriffe *stereotype* und *stereotypical* eingeführt werden.

Individual answers.

b Possible answers:

background	attitudes	personality	others
be working-class	fanatic	withdrawn	date people from different
be middle-class	go with the flow	insecure	races/cultures
be upper-class	content	outgoing	marry outside one's religion
	be (overly) ambitious	easy-going	have friends from different
	want a good education	religious	races / one's own ethnic
	be liberal	quiet	group
	be happy with oneself	a dreamer	not sure what to do with
	look for a nine-to-five job	be straight/gay	one's life
	want respect/ tolerance	homophobic	want to earn good money
	be kind to everybody	self-confident	
	want to have children	assertive	
	establish one's career first	to get upset easily	
	not interested in politics		
	want to find fulfilment		
	at work		

3 Bevor die S diese Aufgabe bearbeiten, sollten sie sich möglichst detaillierte Notizen zu einer fiktiven Biographie machen. Folgende Aspekte könnten dabei berücksichtigt werden:

– name, age
– situation at home (parents, siblings, finances, housing)
– ethnic and social background
– (family) values, conflicts
– education
– sexual orientation
– housing situation now
– hobbies and leisure-time activities
– personality traits
– plans for the future, worries and interests

⬭ Die folgende Aufgabe dient der Selbstreflexion und Wortschatzerweiterung:

Find the opposites of the following adjectives and write them on the right. Then try to assess yourself, e.g. if you think you are very generous, circle '3' on the left side, if you think you are a little mean, circle '1' on the right side.

generous	*3*	*2*	*1*	*0*	*1*	*2*	*3*	mean
hard-working	*3*	*2*	*1*	*0*	*1*	*2*	*3*	...

Folgende Adjektive eignen sich für diese Aufgabe: *careful, optimistic, light-hearted, quick-tempered, extroverted, relaxed, polite, talkative, courageous* usw. Leistungsstärkere S können selbstständig Adjektivpaare suchen und den Fragebogen von einem Partner ausfüllen lassen.

1 Origami Susan K. Ito

Source:	*Two Worlds Walking*, 1994
Topic:	Determining one's ethnic and cultural identity
Text form:	Short story
Language variety:	AE
Number of words:	1448
Level:	Advanced
Skills/activities:	Writing a description of a character, analysing the structure of a short story, identifying imagery, working with language

Lern-vokabular

Active vocabulary: 'Origami' (p. 186)

follow directions (l. 9), be lost (l. 11), confusion (l. 15), persevere (l. 18), give up (l. 19), impostor (l. 23), fuss over sb. (l. 30), minimum wage (l. 34), smell of sth. (l. 40), party (of people) (l. 43), greet sb. (l. 45), hand sb. sth. (l. 47), moist (l. 55), blush (l. 65), tainted (l. 68), scoff (l. 71), not have a clue (l. 73), freckles (l. 87), feel guilty (l. 92), awkward (l. 105)
tasks: refer to sth., attitude, achieve sth., self-confidence

Didaktisch-methodische Hinweise

Anhand dieser Kurzgeschichte können die S Empathie für die Identitätskonflikte einer jungen Frau entwickeln: In den USA als Tochter eines europäischen Vaters und vermutlich einer japanischen Mutter geboren und von japanischstämmigen Adoptiveltern großgezogen, bemüht sie sich vergebens, ihre Zugehörigkeit zur japanischen Kultur unter Beweis zu stellen, indem sie einen Kranich in der traditionellen japanischen Origami-Technik faltet. Sie lehnt ihre europäischen Wurzeln ab, die sich vor allem in ihrem Aussehen bemerkbar machen. Während ihr japanisches Umfeld sie als vollwertiges Mitglied zu akzeptieren scheint, wird sie von einem offensichtlich angelsächsischen Gast in dem japanischen Restaurant, in dem sie arbeitet, als nicht authentisch beschimpft. Am Ende jedoch erlebt sie am Beispiel der alten Japanerin, dass das Fehlen einer mit der japanischen Kultur verbundenen Fähigkeit wie dem Origami nicht notwendigerweise die Zugehörigkeit zu dieser Kultur in Frage stellt. In diesem Spannungsfeld zwischen Eigen- und widersprüchlichen Fremdwahrnehmungen steht die Suche der jungen Frau nach ihrer ethnischen Identität. Ähnliche Fragen werden auch in „The Great Immigrant Experiment" (SB, S. 146) behandelt.

Der Text wurde als Einstiegstext ausgewählt, da er als *coming-of-age story* (vgl. SB, S. 255) zeigt, wie eine junge Frau lernt, ihre ethnische Identität zu definieren. Der Text wirft die Frage nach Kriterien individueller Identitätsfindung auf, die oft von Vorurteilen und Intoleranz beeinflusst werden.

Unterrichts-tipps

Als Alternative zum *pre-reading* im SB können die S ihr Wissen über Origami zusammentragen, ggf. selbst einen Origami-Kranich basteln und über den Inhalt der Kurzgeschichte spekulieren:

⬭ *The story we are going to read is called 'Origami'. What do you know about origami? What could it have to do with the topic personal identity?*

Mit der folgenden Aufgabe kann eine Verständnissicherung durchgeführt werden:

⬭ *Decide whether the following statements are true or false. If they are false, correct them.*

1 *The story takes place in a Japanese restaurant.* (False. It takes place in a cafeteria; cf. l. 4). The speaker only remembers an incident that took place in a Japanese restaurant.)

2 *The protagonist is an American woman who was born in Japan.* (False. She seems to have been born in America (to a European father, cf. l. 81, and a Japanese mother, cf. l. 70) and was adopted by parents of Japanese ancestry, cf. ll. 84–85.)

3 *Doing origami is difficult for the protagonist.* (True.)
4 *The American customer is annoyed because the protagonist cannot speak Japanese.* (False. He is annoyed because she is not totally Japanese, cf. ll. 71–72.)
5 *Kimi is a Japanese waitress in the restaurant.* (False. To Westerners, she looks Japanese, but she is actually from Korea, cf. ll. 73–74.)
6 *The American customer decides to go to McDonald's instead.* (False. He says that he wants to be served in a Japanese restaurant by Japanese staff only. If he wanted waitresses of mixed ancestry, he could have gone to McDonald's, cf. ll. 75–77.)
7 *The protagonist dislikes all the physical parts of her that come from her European genes.* (True.)
8 *The old Japanese woman sitting next to the protagonist produces very delicate Origami cranes.* (False. Her fingers are not skilful enough to fold one, so her crane is terrible, cf. ll. 108–109.)

→ *WB, ex. 2*

Info

Susan K. Ito was born in New Rochelle, New York, of mixed European and Japanese ancestry. She was adopted and was raised in New Jersey.

Lösungs-hinweise

 Pre-reading: Possible answers:
When you are asked to take part in a ceremony you are not familiar with; when you are expected to do something your culture forbids you to do (e.g. eat pork), etc.

1 a
Background: she has been around Japanese-speaking people (parents), but does not really understand the language (ll. 2–3); she worked as a waitress in a Japanese restaurant when she was young (ll. 25–26); her father was not Japanese, but European (ll. 81–88); she was adopted by a Japanese-American couple (l. 85), who laid emphasis on her Japanese heritage.

Appearance: she has a mixture of European and Japanese looks (ll. 81–88), which makes it difficult for people to know where she comes from (ll. 89–90).

Identity: she is confused about her identity. She wants to be more Japanese, but her European looks belie this, so she is unhappy about herself. She thinks the Japanese art of paper-folding should come naturally to her, but she falls short of her own expectations.
Her mixed heritage makes her feel as though she does not really belong anywhere, which leads to a certain lack of self-confidence. She continually strives to be part of the Japanese community, but never feels totally at home, even though the Japanese community seems to accept her (cf. the old lady at the end of the story).

b She uses words like 'inauthentic ... version of the real thing' (l. 24), 'watered-down' (l. 24), 'half-authentic, tainted blood' (l. 68). The implication is that she is not pure, but that she is only partially real.

c While working as a waitress, she had to dress up in traditional Japanese costume, but she still did not pass for a Japanese girl. All the same, she feels comfortable in a Japanese setting and wants to master the Japanese skill of origami. At the end she accepts the fact that external things like being good at paper-folding do not determine one's identity – this is the lesson the old woman teaches her. One might say that the human factor has overcome the ethnic factor. However, it remains doubtful whether she has accepted that she is neither Japanese nor European but a mixture of different traditions.

2 The man is poorly and cheaply dressed ('beige polyester jacket', l. 51) and he seems dirty ('ring of perspiration soaked into his shirt', l. 60). He is rude, as he seems to take pleasure in insulting the protagonst and is very aggressive. He is also revealed as being ignorant when he thinks Kimi must be Japanese (cf. ll. 73–74). We get all this information through description, not through the judgement of the narrator (i.e. through indirect characterization, cf. „Glossary", SB, p. 260).

3 The story has a frame situation (the situation with the women making paper cranes) and a flashback scene (the narrator's experience at the Japanese restaurant). This is quite an effective way of telling the story because it gives the reader the background to understand the extent of the identity crisis the narrator is currently going through while attempting to do something which involves the traditions of (half) her heritage. One might say that she learned little from the incident in the restaurant, as she still feels that mastering a skill will be proof that she is Japanense.

4 a From least self-confident to aggressive: 'falter' (l. 58), 'murmur' (l. 62), 'whisper' (l. 70), 'mutter' (l. 109), 'demand' (l. 64), 'scoff' (l. 71).

b On a stylistic level, the passages read better, as they avoid repetition. Moreover, the different expressions help the reader to imagine the described scenes better. The description of how someone speaks in a given situation is also part of indirect characterization: the fact that the man at the restaurant demands to know something (rather than just asking) and scoffs at the protagonist show him to be arrogant and aggressive, while the narrator is shown to be lacking in self-confidence.

5
a) 'follow all the directions' (l. 9)
b) 'persevere' (l. 18)
c) 'not have a clue' (l. 73)
d) 'blame sb. for sth.' (l. 88)
e) 'it's not for lack of experience' (l. 107)

Why is the short story called 'Origami'?
Origami is a skill which is particularly mastered by the Japanese. As the main character needs to feel more in touch with her Japanese identity, she wants to learn this skill. She feels that by mastering it, she will prove to herself and others that she is indeed Japanese. However, she learns that being able or not able to do origami has little to do with ethnic identity, because the old Japanese woman is also useless at origami. Origami is merely a paper-folding technique that some people can master and others cannot, regardless of ethnicity. Hence, origami can be considered a symbol of the narrator's more mature attitude towards ethnicity.

Translate ll. 48–77 into German.

In groups of three create a freeze frame for one scene in the story.

If the protagonist had one wish, what would she ask for? Explain your answer.

What do you think the oba-san and the protagonist will talk about in the kitchen? Write their dialogue.
Hier können verschiedene Elemente aus der Kurzgeschichte herausgearbeitet werden, z.B. kann die *oba-san* nach der Herkunft des Mädchens fragen, sie kann über ihre Probleme mit Origami sprechen, sie kann auch über ihre Erfahrung im „Tule Lake internment camp" (Z. 7) erzählen, da sie alt genug ist, um dort interniert gewesen zu sein.

In the short story the protagonist has difficulties dealing with her mixed ethnic background. What advantages might there be in having two different ethnic backgrounds?

Context Box

Die „Context Box" bietet eine Übersicht über die Aspekte, die die Identität eines Menschen bestimmen, und über Identitätskrisen und ihre Folgen. Sie kann damit als Hilfestellung bei einem einführenden Gespräch über die zu erwartenden Inhalte dieser Unterrichtseinheit dienen, aber auch als eine Zusammenfassung, bei der die S noch einmal über die Aspekte der bearbeiteten Texte reflektieren.

Zur Veranschaulichung und Vertiefung können Texte aus anderen Kapitel herangezogen werden: zum Thema nationale Identität SB, S. 142, 144, 145; zum Thema ethnische Identität SB, S. 146.

→ WB, ex. 3

1 a

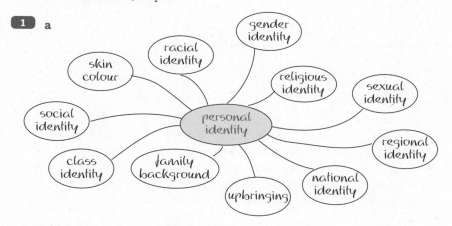

b Things affected by one's personal identity: values, attitudes, doubts, success, faith, beliefs, moral code, sex life, self-perception, happiness.

2 Possible answers:
Feelings of inferiority concerning appearance, intelligence, class, education; feelings of being torn between contradictory norms concerning dress, role models, sexuality; rootlessness due to a life in two or more different places or communities.

2 I'm Not Lying Anymore Paul Berges et al.

Diese *section*, der ein Ausschnitt aus dem Drehbuch und aus dem Film *Bend it Like Beckham* zugrunde liegen, führt die Thematik der Identitätsfindung in einem Immigrationskontext fort. Sie zeigt zwei Jugendliche, die auf unterschiedliche Weise im Konflikt zwischen den Normen ihrer Familien und denen der sie umgebenden Kultur stehen: Tony ist homosexuell, Jess spielt Fußball und ist in einen Weißen verliebt – drei Dinge, die in der britischen Kultur, in der die beiden leben, relativ unproblematisch sind, für ihre nach traditionell indischen Prinzipien lebenden Familien jedoch unvorstellbar. Die S erleben hier also zwei Jugendliche, deren ethnische Identität durch die Verankerung in zwei Kulturen konfliktbehaftet ist.

Im Gegensatz zur Protagonistin von „Origami" ist Jess eine selbstbewusste junge Frau, die weiß, wer sie ist und was sie will. Während sie im ersten Auszug noch versucht, nach den Regeln beider Kulturen zu leben, indem sie ihre Eltern täuschen und ihnen eine standesgemäße Verbindung mit Tony vorspielen will, strebt sie im zweiten Auszug nach einer Vermittlung zwischen beiden Kulturen: Sie lässt Tony nicht bei ihren Eltern um ihre Hand anhalten, sondern erzählt ihnen offen von ihrer Fußballleidenschaft, ihrem Erfolg und ihrem Wunsch, professionelle Fußballerin zu werden.

A Beckham Is the Best

Source:	*Bend It Like Beckham. The Screenplay*, 2002
Topic:	The problems involved when sexual and ethnic identity collide
Text form:	Screenplay
Language variety:	BE
Number of words:	348
Level:	Basic/advanced
Skills/activities:	Converting a screenplay into a film

Lern-
vokabular

Active vocabulary: 'Beckham Is the Best' (p. 190)

don't mind sb. (l. 3), fancy sb. (l. 8), nod (one's head) (ll. 17, 31), fall for sb. (l. 22), the penny drops (l. 29), shrug one's shoulders (l. 35), marry sb. (l. 37), punch sb. (l. 38)
tasks: reveal sth., issue, leave sth. unsaid, indication, according to sb./sth.

Didaktisch-
methodische
Hinweise

Anhand des Auszugs aus dem Drehbuch von *Bend It Like Beckham* sollen die S sich zunächst mit den Aspekten sexuelle, ethnische und soziale Identität auseinander setzen. Darüber hinaus dient der Auszug der Medienerziehung. Die S stellen Überlegungen zur Umsetzung des Dialogs im Film an und vergleichen diese schließlich mit dem wirklichen Film (vgl. das Video / die DVD und das Transkript auf S. 388).

Unterrichts-
tipps

Die S lesen den Dialog zunächst still für sich, ggf. auch als Hausaufgabe. Nachdem sie Aufgabe 2a bearbeitet haben, lesen sie den Text in Kleingruppen mit verteilten Rollen, wobei ein S die Rolle des Regisseurs übernimmt und die S den Text gemäß seiner Interpretation lesen und ggf. vorspielen lässt. Es ist auch denkbar, anhand einzelner zentraler Zeilen verschiedene Lesarten auszuprobieren und zu bewerten (z.B. Z. 8, 26, 40, 42).

Info

Bend It Like Beckham: The film is set in Hounslow, west London. Jess (played by Parminder Nagra) and her best friend Jules (played by Keira Knightley) play football for a girls' team. However, Jess has to keep this secret from her traditional Sikh family. When the team travels to Hamburg for a match, the coach shows an interest in Jess, much to Jules's annoyance. The day a talent scout for an American football team is due to watch the girls play also happens to be the day that Jess's sister is due to marry. Seeing the misery of his daughter, Jess's father gives her permission to play and she is good enough to impress the scout and get a scholarship to an American university, where she can also play football. Whereas Jess finds happiness in realizing her dream, Tony (played by Ameet Chana) does not reveal his homosexuality to his family.

David Beckham (born 1975) was born in Leytonstone, near London. He signed for Manchester United as a trainee in 1991. In 1995, he made his league debut for Manchester United. He made his name for his excellence at free kicks and penalties. In 1996 he first played for England. He was sent off for a foul in the World Cup in 1998 against Argentina, which made him unpopular. He became the captain of the England team, and in 2002 he redeemed his earlier foul by scoring the winning penalty against Argentina in the World Cup. In 1999 he married Victoria Adams (better known as 'Posh', a member of the former pop group Spice Girls). Besides his kicking skills, he is well-known for his continually changing haircuts. In 2003 he transferred to Real Madrid.

1 **a** The scene deals primarily with sexual and ethnic identity, but also with social identity.

<u>Sexual identity:</u> Jess is waking up to the fact that she feels sexual attraction to her coach; this worries her, as she feels she should not feel attracted to him (it is harming her relationship with her best friend, Jules, and it is considered unusual for an Indian to go out with a white man); Tony, on the other hand, feels attracted to men; in this scene he tells Jess about his homosexuality, but urges her to keep it secret.

<u>Ethnic identity:</u> Jess feels she needs an Indian boyfriend (this will appear more normal to those around her; Jules, for example, will not feel threatened if she believes that Jess is looking for love within her own community); Tony is gay, but to Indians, homosexuality is not seen as something that is a part of their community ('But you're Indian?', l. 32), so he has to keep it secret.

<u>Social identity:</u> Here the friends one chooses play an important role. Jess and Tony are friends and become open and honest with each other. Jess also sees her friendship with Jules as being important. She feels her attraction to her coach is a betrayal of her friendship with Jules, which she highly values, hence her willingness to sacrifice her feelings and go out with Tony (who she likes, but is probably not attracted to). Tony reveals his friendship by refusing Jess's clumsy attempt to make him her boyfriend, and gives her good advice. Jess is also loyal to Tony by keeping his secret.

b In both the areas of sexual and ethnic identity the families presume that the two teenagers will settle down with partners of the opposite sex from their own community. In <u>Jess</u>'s case this is not so evident in the excerpt (it seems her friendship with Jules is the main reason she thinks she needs an Indian boyfriend). With <u>Tony</u>, Jess's sister presumes that Tony must fancy Jess (she presumes that if two Indian teenagers are friends, there must be sexual attraction). The question 'what're your mum and dad going to say?' (l. 34) refers to the expectations that his family will have that he marries an Indian girl.

c Jess mentions the fact that she needs an Indian boyfriend (l. 14). Having an Indian boyfriend will make her life easier, as her parents know what to expect from someone from their own community. An English boyfriend would create problems. Neither Tony nor Jess talk explicitly about Tony's homosexuality: Tony talks about 'really' liking Beckham, and Jess leaves her sentence 'You mean…' (l. 30) uncompleted. This is certainly due to the fact that homosexuality is a taboo in their Indian culture.

2 **a** Possible answers:

<u>Jess</u> is emotionally confused in ll. 2–15, so she should act in a way that is perhaps overenthusiastic. She is embarassed in ll. 16–21, as she is confessing intimate details, so her voice might be lower. In ll. 22–27 she relaxes somewhat when they talk about Beckham, as the topic is her favourite (football). She is surprised when she learns of Tony's secret in ll. 28–34 (perhaps she raises her voice when she says: 'But you're Indian?', l. 32), and relaxes somewhat for the rest of the scene, as her problems seem minor compared to Tony's – his confession leads to a general release of tension for her. <u>Tony</u> is perplexed and embarrassed by Jess's behaviour (ll. 5–15), as her sexual interest is probably threatening for him; he is sympathetic towards Jess, as he listens to her problems. He is probably a little nervous about Jess's reaction to his confession (l. 40), so he might speak in a low nervous voice. He might react quickly and nervously in l. 40, but is relaxed for the rest of the scene. For him telling someone he is gay is a big step, and his feelings will be more confused than Jess's during this scene, whose feelings are much more on display. The director will probably tell Tony to play down the emotions, while Jess might be told to show her feelings more directly.

VIDEO **b** Individual answers.

→ WB, ex. 4 **c** Parts of the dialogue were deleted. In some ways this makes the message of the scene clearer. When the characters are discussing their problems, they are shown in close-up, over the shoulder of the character who is listening. This makes the confessions more intimate. They are shown in medium shots when the tension is partially relieved – this is signalled by Tony laughing when he says 'wow ... and that's why you need an Indian boyfriend?' and 'What's your mum going to say?' After Tony says he does not want to marry Jess, he moves out of the scene. This enables Jess to approach him. In a long shot we see Tony isolated (perhaps his white shirt was also deliberately chosen to make him stick out). Jess then comes up to him and in a medium shot reassures him she has no problem with him being gay.

◯ *How do you think Jess and Tony will deal with their respective situations? Speculate as to what might happen in the film and how the story ends.*

SB, S. 190

VIDEO

B We Have Something to Tell You

Source:	*Bend It Like Beckham*, 2002
Topic:	Telling one's parents the truth about one's needs
Text form:	Film
Language variety:	BE
Length:	3:34 minutes
Level:	Basic/advanced
Skills/activities:	Viewing comprehension, analysing a character's development, writing a screenplay

Didaktisch-methodische Hinweise

Nachdem die S im Drehbuchauszug die beiden Figuren Tony und Jess und ihre Probleme kennen gelernt haben, sehen sie hier, wie Jess ihren Konflikt löst: Sie versucht eine Vermittlung zwischen den beiden Kulturen, in denen sie lebt, indem sie ihren Eltern offen ihre Wünsche und Zukunftspläne offenbart. Ihr Charakter hat sich gegenüber dem ersten Auszug gewandelt, in dem sie versuchte, eine Anpassung an die indischen Normen vorzutäuschen. Tony vollzieht einen gegenläufigen Wandel: Während er im ersten Auszug nicht bereit ist, Jess' Heuchelei zu unterstützen, tut er es nun, da er keinen anderen Ausweg sieht. Die Aufgaben zielen v.a. auf die Nachzeichnung dieser Entwicklungen.

Unterrichts-tipps

Da den S Personen und Konflikt bereits bekannt sind, sollten sie den Auszug auf dem Video / der DVD (vgl. auch das Transkript auf S. 388) verstehen können, ohne vorher eine schriftliche Version gelesen zu haben. Eine produktionsorientierte Aufgabe fordert sie auf, den umgekehrten Weg wie bei Text A zu gehen und zu Ausschnitten aus der Filmszene ein Drehbuch zu verfassen. Dabei vertiefen sie ihre *viewing skills* insbesondere im Hinblick auf Kameraeinstellungen.

Bevor die S den Ausschnitt sehen, sollten folgende Wörter semantisiert werden:

solicitor: Rechtsanwalt/Rechtsanwältin
final: Endspiel
sneak off: leave a place secretly
Guru Nanak (1469–1539): founder of the Sikh religion
leave it: stop it
vow: swear

Lösungs-hinweise

VIDEO

1 **a** Tony makes the announcement so that Jess can go to the university of her choice with a good conscience. On the one hand, he pretends to be her boyfriend, which he did not want to do in the first extract; on the other hand, it is consistent with his character, as he is Jess's friend and will help her when necessary. In the first extract, Jess wanted him as a boyfriend without knowing he was gay, which he rejected; now that they are open with each other, he is prepared to help her. In the first scene, the reason for becoming her boyfriend was trivial, while in the second it is important, as it touches on her ethnic identity.

b Possible answers:

Brave: She stands up for herself and tells her family what she really wants in life.

Stupid: She might lose her family by telling them about her plans, which are connected with playing football. Everyone tells lies to get by.

c She is still nervous and uncertain, but obviously she has learned that football makes her happy and she is talented at it, and therefore she wants to pursue her dream without lying to her family. One can say that she has matured and is more self-confident.

VIDEO **2** Individual answers.

SB, S. 192 # 3 My Region, Myself

Diese *section* thematisiert die identitätsstiftende Funkton von Dialekten und Soziolekten. Für Jugendliche, die ihr Leben ausschließlich in ihrer Heimatregion verbracht haben, mag es eine neue Erkenntnis sein, dass Identität auch durch Sprache konstituiert wird. Andere S, die erlebt haben, wie über ihren Akzent gelacht wurde oder wie ein gemeinsamer Dialekt eine Verbindung zwischen Menschen herstellte, sollten für das Thema dieser *section* sensibilisiert sein. Die S erfahren anhand von zwei Textbeispielen (einem journalistischen Text und einem Lied aus einem Musical), mit welcher Leidenschaft Akzente (und damit auch die sie sprechenden Menschen) abgelehnt und für minderwertig erklärt werden können – ein Phänomen, das in England ungleich stärker vertreten ist als in Deutschland, aber dort ebenso vorzufinden ist. Sie erkennen auch, dass in Großbritannien das Sprechen mit regionalem Akzent traditionell etwas über die Klassenzugehörigkeit aussagte, auch wenn heute im Zuge von Globalisierung und Migration die Haltung zu regionalen Akzenten deutlich entspannter geworden ist. Die meisten S werden britische und amerikanische Sprecher voneinander unterscheiden können. In Text A begegnen sie jedoch vier englischen Akzenten, die sie sicher nicht differenzieren können, und lernen einige phonetische Unterschiede zwischen ihnen kennen. Anschließend werden sie mit verschiedenen Einstellungen zu Akzenten konfrontiert.

Als Hintergrund oder zur Vertiefung kann die BBC-Dokumentarsendung *Routes of English* verwendet werden; vgl. www.bbc.co.uk/radio4/routesofenglish · 1.8.2003.

SB, S. 192 ## A Four English Accents

CD

Topic:	Various English accents
Text form:	Read text
Language variety:	BE
Length:	1:20 minutes
Level:	Basic/advanced
Skills/activities:	Comparing different accents

Didaktisch-methodische Hinweise Den S wird hier ein kurzer Text vorgespielt, der in vier englischen Varietäten vorgetragen wird (vgl. CD2, *tracks* 15–18, und die Transkripte auf S. 192): *Received Pronunciation*, *Estuary* (vgl. „Info"), Midlands und Yorkshire. Neben der als Standard betrachteten *Received Pronunciation* begegnen die S damit auch Varietäten aus dem Norden, dem Süden und der Mitte Englands. Der Text enthält Wörter wie „raspberry", „car" und „bus", an deren Aussprache im Text B festgemacht wird, ob eine Person zur eigenen oder einer fremden Gruppe gehört.

Die Aufgaben zielen v.a. auf eine Sensibilisierung für das Phänomen Akzent und mit ihm verbundene affektive Reaktionen. Da die S sicher keine ausgeprägten Einstellungen gegenüber englischen Akzenten haben, beschreiben sie ihre persönliche Reaktion auf deutsche Akzente und klassifizieren die englischen Akzente auf der CD im Hinblick auf ihre Verständlichkeit.

Unterrichts-tipps Als Einstieg in die Thematik könnte die folgende Frage dienen:

⬭ *Explain how it is possible to define where a person comes from.*
Looks, dress, language.

Nachdem die S die Akzente auf der CD gehört haben, sollten sie versuchen, einige Unterschiede zwischen ihnen zu beschreiben. Ggf. können sie gebeten werden, auf die Aussprache der folgenden Wörter zu achten: „aunt", „day", „raspberries", „car", „hat", „handbag". Die *RP*-Aussprache (Sprecher 1) wird den S bekannt sein. Folgende Beispiele für abweichende Aussprachen in den anderen Akzenten könnten sie nennen (die Transkriptionen stellen Annäherungen an die Laute dar): Der *Estuary*-Sprecher (2) spricht kein anlautendes *h* und kein auslautendes *t* und *k*; „side" klingt bei ihm wie [soɪd]. Die Sprecherin aus den Midlands (3) spricht „day" als [daɪ], „other" als [ʊðə]; ihre Intonation ist steigend wie bei einer Frage. Der Sprecher aus Yorkshire (4) spricht lange Vokale kürzer als im *RP*, z.B. „aunt" als [ʌnt], „raspberries" als ['ræzbəriz], „car" als [kɑ].

Differenzierung Leistungsstarke und linguistisch interessierte S können mit Hilfe des OALD die folgende Aufgabe bearbeiten:

⬭ *What is the difference between a dialect and an accent?*
A dialect is a form of a language that is spoken by a particular group of people, especially living in one area. It has different pronunciation, words and grammar from other forms of the language.
An accent is the way of pronouncing a language or dialect.
For example, a Scot may speak standard English with a Scottish accent. One might have difficulty understanding it due to lack of experience with the accent. However, in Scotland there are also dialects, which are variations of English. They differ from standard English in lexis and grammar, not just in pronunciation (e.g. 'I amn't' for 'I am not', 'bairn' for 'child), but are still recognizable as English, even if one understands very little.

Info

Estuary English: The predominant English accent in London and in the southeast of England, which is gradually replacing Received Pronunciation as the standard accent.

Lösungs-hinweise **1** Individual answers.

2 Vgl. CD2, *tracks* 15–18 und die Transkripte auf S. 389.

Individual answers.

SB, S. 192 **B A Question of Accent**   Rose George

Source:	*Independent Magazine*, 6.4.2002
Topic:	People's reactions to different accents
Text form:	Newspaper article
Language variety:	BE
Number of words:	424
Level:	Advanced
Skills/activities:	Discussing attitudes to accents

Lern- *vokabular*	**Active vocabulary: 'A Question of Accent' (p. 192)** posh (l. 4), snobby (l. 4), admittedly (l. 5), cruelty (l. 7), be doomed (l. 11), unrelenting (l. 11), grief (l. 11), pariah (l. 25), giggle (l. 32), feel humiliated (l. 33), distingush between sth. (l. 39), womb (l. 41), be obsessed by sth. (l. 42) *tasks:* refer to sth., be associated with sth.

<table>
<tr>
<td>Didaktisch-
methodische
Hinweise</td>
<td>Dieser Text beschreibt an mehreren Beispielen, wie das Sprechen mit Akzent zur emotionalen und sozialen Ausgrenzung von Menschen durch ihre Umwelt führen kann, deren Auswirkungen traumatische Folgen für die Betroffenen haben können: Englische Erwachsene erinnern sich an die Reaktionen ihrer Mitschüler, als sie als Jugendliche in Südengland mit einem nördlichen Akzent sprachen bzw. im Norden mit einem südlichen Akzent. Dabei unterstreicht die Tatsache, dass derselbe Akzent in einem Kontext zu Akzeptanz, in einem anderen jedoch zu Ausgrenzung führt, die Bedeutung von Sprache als Identifikationsmittel. Die S sollten diese Bewertung von Personen durch ihren regionalen Akzent kritisch hinterfragen.</td>
</tr>
<tr>
<td>Unterrichts-
tipps</td>
<td>Da dieser Text viel nicht aus dem Kontext erschließbares Vokabular enthält, empfiehlt sich dessen Einführung und Semantisierung vor der Textpräsentation. Die folgenden Aufgaben dienen der Verständnissicherung:</td>
</tr>
</table>

⬭ *Who said the following things? The formulations may have been changed slightly.)*

1 *'I came from a common background but went to a posh school.'* (Mother: ll. 22–23)
2 *'When I was a child I spoke with a Hertfordshire accent in Yorkshire.'* (Writer: l. 5)
3 *'I remember panicking because I could not remember how I was supposed to pronounce the word "aunt".'* (Tom: l. 13)
4 *'Don't ever read in my class again until you learn to speak correctly.'* (Miss Crout: ll. 29–31)
5 *'England is the country which is most obsessed by accent in the world.'* (Writer: ll. 29–30)

⬭ *Explain in one sentence what you learned about the following characters:*
a) the writer, b) Claire Lemon, c) Tom, d) the writer's mother, e) Sally Parker, f) Miss Crout.

a) The writer was bullied as a child for her accent and still remembers it today (cf. ll. 1–7).
b) Claire Lemon was a playmate of the writer's who treated her cruelly due to her accent (cf. ll. 1–4).
c) Tom is a friend of the writer's and suffered at school because he once pronounced a word with a southern accent (cf. ll. 10–20).
d) The writer's mother was humiliated by her teacher for not reading in an educated accent (cf. ll. 21–33).
e) Sally Parker was a classmate of Tom's and was the first to tease him because he pronounced a word differently (cf. ll. 17–20).
f) Miss Crout was the teacher who would not tolerate her students speaking 'incorrectly' (cf. ll. 25–33).

⬭ *Choose the statement that best sums up what the text is about and then discuss your choice with a partner:*
1 *It is about childhood bullying.*
2 *It is about how people fail to communicate when others do not understand their accent.*
3 *It is about how people must learn to change their accent to fit in with the people around them.*
4 *It is about how the different accents in England should be celebrated.*
5 *It is about the trauma that some English people experience when they speak with a different accent from the one used around them.*
6 *It is an attempt to show why the English are more obsessed by accents than other nations.*

The most accurate statement is 5.

Info

Hertfordshire accent (l. 5): This has now virtually died out, having been replaced by Estuary English and Received Pronunciation.

Lösungs-hinweise

1 Being tied to a radiator (cf. l. 3); being shouted at or teased (cf. ll. 4, 10–20), being humiliated by teachers (cf. ll. 28–33).

2 Southern accents are associated with being posh (cf. l. 34).

⬭ *Why might this be so?*
London is situated in the south, and has for over 1000 years been the centre of government, the monarchy and commerce in England. It is the richest part of the United Kingdom and dominates the cultural and political life of the country.

3
– In England accents play an important role as to whether an individual will be accepted or not: The wrong accent can lead to you being ridiculed and being made to feel like an outsider.
– You can tell not only where someone comes from by his or her accent, but you can also tell what class someone belongs to, since speaking 'posh' is apparently connected with having a southern accent.

SB, S. 193 **C Why Can't the English?**   Alan Jay Lerner

CD

Source:	*My Fair Lady*, 1964
Topic:	Criticism of different English dialects
Text form:	Song
Language variety:	BE
Length:	2:36 minutes
Level:	Basic/advanced
Skills/activities:	Listening comprehension, comparing attitudes

Didaktisch-methodische Hinweise

Dieser Auszug aus dem Musical *My Fair Lady* (vgl. CD2, *track* 19, und das Transkript auf S. 389) ist ein populäres Beispiel für die Auseinandersetzung mit der „verbal class distinction", hier besungen von Henry Higgins, einem englischen Professor für Phonetik. In seinem Lied beklagt Higgins die schlechte Qualität verschiedener Varietäten des Englischen, die die Menschen, die sie verwenden, in einer sozial untergeordneten Position verharren lässt. Er ignoriert damit die Identifikationsfunktion von Akzenten, wie sie in „A Question of Accent" impliziert ist, und betrachtet sie nur unter sozialen Gesichtspunkten.
Die Aufgaben dienen der Schulung des Hörverstehens und der differenzierten Würdigung von Akzenten. Dabei sollten Higgins' Arroganz gegenüber allen nicht-standardsprachlichen englischen Varietäten und die identitätsstiftende Funktion von Dialekten aufgezeigt werden.

Unterrichts-tipps

Die S könnten sich als vorbereitende Hausaufgabe über den Inhalt des Musicals oder des Dramas informieren. Alternativ kann L eine kurze Einführung in die Situation geben. Anschließend hören die S das Lied und machen sich Notizen für Aufgabe 1a. Für Aufgabe 1b muss das Lied sicher noch einmal vorgespielt und ggf. auch das Transkript ausgeteilt werden.

Wichtig für das Textverständnis ist die vorherige Einführung und Semantisierung des neuen Vokabulars:

◯ *Match the following words and their definitions. You may want to use the OALD.*

1	'gutter'	A	say sth.
2	'condemn sb.'	B	have a conversation
3	'utter sth.'	C	large farm building
4	'tongue'	D	punish sb. / doom sb.
5	'converse'	E	have no respect for sb./sth.
6	'barn'	F	a channel at the edge of the road where water collects and is carried away
7	'wretched'	G	to think about sth./sb. in a particular way
8	'despise sb./sth.'	H	(here, old-fashioned) language
9	'regard sth./sb. as'	I	extremely bad

Die Lösungen sind: 1F, 2D, 3A, 4H, 5B, 6 C, 7I, 8E, 9G.

Die S sollten darauf hingewiesen werden, dass es *hanged* und *Arabic* heißen sollte und nicht, wie Higgins sagt, „hung" und „Arabian". „Garn" ist ein Ausdruck des Nicht-Glaubens, des Widerspruchs.

Literarisch interessierte S können das Drama *Pygmalion* von George Bernard Shaw lesen, auf dem das Musical basiert.

Info

Alan Jay Lerner (1918–1986) was one of Broadway's great lyric writers. Among the many musicals he wrote are *Brigadoon* (1947), *Paint Your Wagon* (1951), *My Fair Lady* (1956) and *Camelot* (1960). He usually worked in collaboration with Frederick Loewe, who wrote the music to his lyrics.

My Fair Lady is a musical based on the stage play *Pygmalion* (1913) by George Bernard Shaw. Henry Higgins is a professor of languages and a rather snobbish and arrogant man. A friend, Colonel Pickering, makes a bet with him that he cannot take a 'commoner' and turn her into someone who would not be completely out of place in the social circles of upper-class English society. The dirty Cockney flower girl, Eliza Doolittle, who Higgins discovers in front of Covent Garden, becomes the girl he transforms. He succeeds, but his arrogance takes no account of her role in the matter and she leaves him. It is only then that Higgins realizes that he is in love with her. The musical opened in New York in 1956 and in London in 1958. In 1964 the film version was made, starring Rex Harrison and Audrey Hepburn, whose singing was dubbed by Marni Nixon. The film won eight Academy Awards.

Lösungs-
hinweise

CD

1 Vgl. CD2, *track* 19, und das Transkript auf S. 389.

a He dislikes the way the following people speak: people down in Soho Square (i.e. Londoners), Yorkshiremen, Cornishmen, the Scottish (here called 'the Scotch'), the Irish and the Americans.

b He means that working-class people and people from other English-speaking countries will never be able to do much with their lives as long as they refuse to speak Standard English. Eliza Dolittle is described as a 'prisoner of the gutters, condemned by every syllable she ever utters'. Higgins tells Pickering that if Pickering spoke as she did, he 'might be selling flowers, too', despite his education and competence. He says it is speech and not appearance that result in people being forced to live in bad circumstances: 'It's "Aoooow" and "Garn" that keep her [Eliza] in her place. Not her wretched clothes and dirty face.' If people speak bad English, it implies that they have not received a good education, hence the question to the man 'did you go to school?' This is taken up in the refrain of the song: 'Why can't the English teach their children how to speak?'

CD **2** The two texts reflect the same idea: that accents make English people hate each other: 'An Englishman's way of speaking absolutely classifies him; the moment he talks he makes some other Englishman despise him. One common language I'm afraid we'll never get.' Rose's catalogue of traumas (cf. 'A Question of Accent', answer to task 1) shows the same attitude. Higgins represents a person who is not dissimilar to Miss Crout ('A Question of Accent', ll. 25–33), as he believes that people should speak 'correctly'.

SB, S. 194

Getting Along in English

Didaktisch-methodische Hinweise

Diese Seite widmet sich den kommunikativen Fehlern, die S in Situationen machen können, in denen sie über sich selbst oder andere Themen Auskunft geben müssen. Dabei handelt es sich um Fehler, die sie in der Mutter- wie in der Fremdsprache gleichermaßen machen können: die falsche Einschätzung der Formalität einer Situation und entsprechend die Wahl des falschen Registers, zu kurze bzw. zu ausführliche Antworten, Antworten auf Fragen, die nicht gestellt wurden usw. In der Fremdsprache kann für die S erschwerend hinzukommen, dass sie nicht über die sprachlichen Mittel verfügen, um situationsadäquat zu antworten. Dieser Abschnitt soll die S für die Problematik sensibilisieren. Die S schätzen die Formalität verschiedener Dialoge ein und identifizieren die Fehler von Dialogpartnern (vgl. die Dialoge auf CD2, *tracks* 20–25, und die Transkripte auf S. 390–393). Anschließend werden ihnen Redemittel zu verschiedenen Sprachabsichten wie Begrüßung, Verabschiedung, Entschuldigung an die Hand gegeben, mit denen sie formelle wie informelle Situationen meistern können.

Lösungs-hinweise

1 **a** Possible answers:
At a dinner party, when you are being asked questions about yourself by people who have just met you; at immigration when you enter an English-speaking country; when applying for a grant to go to college in the USA.

b Individual answers.

CD **2** Vgl. die Dialoge auf CD2, *tracks* 20–23, und die Transkripte auf S. 390–392.

a Dialogue 1: interview for the job of babysitter;
dialogue 2: interview by a police officer at the scene of an accident;
dialogue 3: interview by a fellow student for a school magazine;
dialogue 4: questions being asked by a neighbour on the doorstep.

b
Dialogue 2: formal, as the police need to know the exact details of the accident to write a report;
dialogue 1: quite formal, as the teenager has to impress the mother and show she is reliable;
dialogue 4: informal, as they are two strangers talking casually;
dialogue 3: very informal, as it is two teenagers just talking.

c Formal:
Dialogue 1: 'Good afternoon', 'I've come to see … about …', 'do come in / sit down', 'thank you', 'well, now, tell me a bit about yourself', 'we'd want you to …', 'splendid';
dialogue 2: 'sir', 'officer', 'can you tell me exactly …', 'thank you very much', 'that'll be all for now', 'we may need to get in touch with you again', 'I'd be pleased to help', 'you've already been most helpful';
dialogue 4: 'I am sorry', 'I beg your pardon', 'I am ever so sorry', 'pleased to meet you, I'm sure'.

Informal:
Dialogue 1: 'I think I'd manage OK';
dialogue 2: 'And your name is?';
dialogue 3: 'This won't take long', 'that's OK', 'go on', 'wow', 'what about ...?', 'that sounds posh', 'oh bother', 'can I get back to you?', 'no problem', 'thanks', 'see you';
dialogue 4: 'Oh my goodness', 'who are you?', 'I only popped over ...', 'that's OK', 'just till ...', 'been to the pub yet?', 'Thanks'.

CD **3** Vgl. die Dialoge auf CD2, *tracks* 24–25, und die Transkripte auf S. 392–393.

Dialogue 1: The shopper greets the interviewer formally and he introduces himself very formally. He offers opinions that were not asked for; he ignores the contents of a question; he rounds off the interview in a very formal manner although the setting and the relationship with the interviewer should be informal.

Dialogue 2: An interview for a place on a course is a formal occasion. Pat's greeting is too informal, as she introduces herself with a 'hi' and just her first name, although the interviewer has greeted her with 'good morning' and asked her for her name (one can presume he expects her full name). Her first answer is too blunt and short and comes over both as arrogant and unjustified; twice she uses 'What?' to get a question repeated and therefore appears rude – if she is is uncertain, she should say something like 'I'm sorry, but ...'; she uses words like 'mum' and 'cool' and she ends the interview on a far too informal note: 'Fingers crossed then, eh? Bye.'

→ WB, ex. 7

4 Individual answers.

5 Individual answers.

SB, S. 195 # 4 Believing in Me: Goals and Ambitions

Zur Identität eines Menschen gehören Aspekte wie Persönlichkeit, Selbstwahrnehmung, Stärken und Schwächen sowie Strategien, mit ihnen umzugehen. In *section 4* stehen das Erkennen eigener Stärken und die bewusste Entscheidung für einen Lebensweg im Vordergrund. Somit ist dieser Abschnitt weniger theoretisch und stärker auf konkrete Fragen der Identitätsfindung ausgerichtet, die sich den S in der Zeit vor dem Schulabschluss stellen werden.

Text A, eine Anzeige für *higher education*, macht deutlich, dass jemand, der nicht die Qualitäten für ein Leben als Star mitbringt, in anderen Bereichen brillieren kann. In Text B lesen die S die Überlegungen der Schriftstellerin Zadie Smith zum Thema Berühmtheit. In Text C werden die S angeregt, über ihre verborgenen Talente nachzudenken und daraus berufliche Perspektiven zu entwickeln. Abschließend lesen sie zwei Gedichte aus verschiedenen Zeiten, die sich mit der Entwicklung eines individuellen Lebenswegs befassen.

SB, S. 195 ## A Aim Higher

Source:	*Sugar*, February 2002
Topic:	Higher education as a means to get a good job
Text form:	Advert
Language variety:	BE
Level:	Basic/advanced
Skills/activities:	Analysing an advert, creating an advert

Active vocabulary: 'Aim Higher' (p. 195)

so what if ..., photographer, editor, be brilliant at sth., loads of sth., have a say in sth.,
higher education

Didaktisch-
methodische
Hinweise

Mit den hier abgedruckten Anzeigenseiten warb das britische *Department of Edu-*
cation and Skills im Rahmen der Kampagne *Aim Higher* in Jugendzeitschriften für die
Hochschulbildung. Es macht anhand zweier fingierter Cover der Frauenzeitschrift
Vogue darauf aufmerksam, dass nicht alle Menschen Berühmtheit erlangen können
wie Naomi Campbell, dass aber viele Menschen auf ihre Weise berufliche Verwirk-
lichung finden und Aufgaben erfüllen können, die es den Menschen des öffentlichen
Lebens erst ermöglicht, im Rampenlicht zu stehen. Wie in *section* 4C steht auch hier der
Aspekt der Selbstfindung zur beruflichen Selbstverwirklichung im Vordergrund. Die
Aufgaben zielen auf die Analyse der Anzeige und auf die Erstellung einer ähnlichen
Anzeige für männliche Adressaten.

Unterrichts-
tipps

Den S könnte zunächst als stummer Impuls die Anzeige mit Naomi Campbell auf Folie
präsentiert werden. Sie können ggf. durch die folgenden Fragen und Impulse auf die
zweite Seite der Anzeigen vorbereitet werden:

⬭ *Have a look at this cover. Does anything strike you?*
No date given, just one article referred to, normally there would be a little more
information about the article.

⬭ *Actually, this is not a real cover of* Vogue, *but the first part of an advert (issued by*
the British Department for Education and Skills) which appeared in teen magazines.
What would you guess was the point of the advert?

Lösungs-
hinweise

1 **a** The advert shows two similar pictures. The top picture appeared before the
lower larger one. The first picture shows the model Naomi Campbell looking
glamorous. The photo (with its typeface and use of colour) is made to look like the front
cover of the magazine *Vogue*, but it is not (the 'O' is missing). It simply asks the question:
'So what if you're not the next Naomi Campbell?' The second picture is similar and
shows a smiling black girl, who is dressed in a school uniform; she is not as glamorous
as Naomi Campbell, but has a big smile and emanates self-con-fidence. Using the same
typeface and magazine elements, the advert says that one can become a photographer,
fashion designer or magazine editor. The small print below shows that the advert is
aimed to encourage youngsters to apply for higher education.

b The government (here the Department of Education and Skills) issued the ad. It
wants young people to have realistic goals. Having a higher education is a more likely
path to success than being a model.

c The message is that everybody can achieve a position in life or on the job market that
meets his or her talents and interests. The advert implies that a schoolgirl in a uniform
has the opportunity to move in the glamorous world of fashion – though not necessarily as a top model.

d Individual answers.

B I have an Ambition ...   Simon Hattenstone

Source:	*Guardian*, 11.12.2000
Topic:	One person's path to success
Text form:	Newspaper article
Language variety:	BE
Number of words:	471
Level:	Basic/advanced
Skills/activities:	Analysing the meaning of ambition, writing a short text

Lern-
vokabular

Active vocabulary: 'I Have an Ambition ...' (p. 196)

extraordinary (l. 1), be affected by sth. (l. 4), fame (l. 5), have the fortune/misfortune to be sth.(l.7), swotty (l. 15), true to oneself (l. 17), be fooling yourself (l. 21), make the grade (ll. 21–22), decade (l. 23), academic (l. 24), map out your future (l. 25), read up about sth. (ll. 25–26), ambition (l. 31), strive for sth. (l. 35)
tasks: celebrity, distinction, goal, achieve sth.

Didaktisch-
methodische
Hinweise

In diesem Text berichtet der Journalist Simon Hattenstone über den Weg der jungen britischen Schriftstellerin Zadie Smith, deren Erstlingsroman *White Teeth* eine Medien-sensation war (vgl. auch „The Great Immigrant Experiment", SB, S. 146, und weitere Informationen zu Roman und Autorin auf S. 88). Er beleuchtet dabei die Zielstrebigkeit und das Engagement der Autorin, die nicht nur einfach berühmt sein, sondern als Schriftstellerin besondere Qualitäten entwickeln möchte, worin sie sich ihrer Meinung nach von vielen anderen jungen Autoren unterscheidet. Der Text bietet eine Vorlage für die S, sich mit eigenen Ambitionen und Lebenszielen auseinander zu setzen und sie zu formulieren.

Unterrichts-
tipps

Die im SB abgedruckte *pre-reading*-Aufgabe eignet sich als Einstieg in den Text und als Vorbereitung für Aufgabe 3.

Lösungs-
hinweise

■■■ *Pre-reading*: Da diese Aufgabe als Arbeitsgrundlage für Aufgabe 3 dient, sollte sichergestellt werden, dass die S den gesammelten Wortschatz notieren. Ggf. sollte L die Liste ergänzen:

plan to do sth, intend to do sth., do sth with the intention of ..., to have no/an idea of what to do, choose to do sth., choose between two things, make a choice, consider doing sth., take sth. into consideration, be determined to do sth., decide to do sth., decide on sth., reach a decision, change one's mind about sth., make up one's mind, postpone a decision, enrol on a course at university/college.

1 As a child, she wrote poems and stories; later she wrote pastiches of Agatha Christie novels. She worked hard at school. She changed her name slighty to make it seem more exotic. As a teenager she read up about the writing methods of her favourite authors. One can say that she knew that she loved writing and that she practised and worked hard to achieve her goal of becoming a good writer.

2 Smith's ambition is to write a great novel, while other people seem to want to be famous for having done nothing. Her ambition is literary, not fame in itself.

3 Individual answers.

SB, S. 197

C Find Your Hidden Strengths   Marty Nemko

Source:	*Cosmo Girl*, February 2002
Topic:	Finding out what one's personal strengths are
Text form:	Magazine article
Language variety:	AE
Number of words:	220
Level:	Basic/advanced
Skills/activities:	Skimming, summarizing, discussing one's strengths and future plans

Lern-
vokabular

Active vocabulary: 'Find Your Hidden Strengths' (p. 197)

dream job (l. 1), obvious (l. 2), talent (l. 2), hidden strengths (l. 3), be great at sth. (l. 9), point sb. toward(s) sth. (l. 10), have a knack for sth. (l. 14), fix sth. (l. 15), endure sth. (l. 19), device (l. 25), struggle with sth. (l. 26)

Didaktisch-
methodische
Hinweise

Dieser Text schließt inhaltlich an Texte 4A und B an. Die S werden ermutigt, über ihre Fähigkeiten und Ziele nachzudenken, was ihnen bei der Berufswahl behilflich sein kann. Dabei lenkt der Text die Aufmerksamkeit der S von der Schule auf außerschulische Aktivitäten. Da der Text aus einer US-amerikanischen Jugendzeitschrift stammt und recht jugendnah geschrieben ist, sollten die S motiviert sein, mit ihm zu arbeiten.

Unterrichts-
tipps
→ WB, ex. 5

Es empfiehlt sich, den Text im Zusammenhang mit Text B zu behandeln. Er ist in Verbindung mit Aufgabe 1a als Hausaufgabe geeignet, so dass Aufgabe 1b im Unterricht bearbeitet werden könnte.

Lösungs-
hinweise

▬▬ *Pre-reading:* The feature is about trying to find your hidden strengths, as this will help you decide on what sort of career you should follow. The writer, a career counsellor, poses four questions, which ask you to consider what you are good at, what you have endured in your life, what tools you like to work with and what subject particularly interests you. On the basis of your answers it might become clear what sort of work would suit you best.

 1 a–b Aufgabe b kann zu Spannungen in der Lerngruppe führen, wenn Partner zusammenarbeiten müssen, die einander nicht ihre persönlichen Lebenspläne offenbaren möchten. Daher sollte den S die Partnerwahl freigestellt werden.

Individual answers.

⬭

a *As a class collect the different fields students from your class might like to work in, e.g. music, medicine, the law, TV, etc.*
b *Divide into pairs, with each pair choosing a different field. With your partner, research some of the jobs you can think of that might be associated with that field and find out as much as you can about each.*
c *Together prepare a five-minute presentation. Try to offer a variety of jobs suitable for different abilities and personalities. If you want to offer information sheets – with qualifications necessary for each job, for example – then prepare these too.*
d *Do a presentation for the class.*

⬭ *In German, write a similar article for a German teenage magazine or school newspaper.*

D The Road Not Taken   Robert Frost

E Ships?   Maya Angelou

CD

The Road Not Taken
Source:	*Atlantic Monthly*, 1916
Topic:	Personal fulfilment by taking an unusual path
Text form:	Poem
Language variety:	AE
Number of words:	134
Level:	Basic/advanced

CD

Ships?
Source:	*Atlantic Monthly*, 1916
Topic:	Life's enriching experiences
Text form:	Poem
Language variety:	AE
Number of words:	66
Level:	Basic/advanced
Skills/activities:	Interpreting poetry, working with imagery

*Lern-
vokabular*

Active vocabulary: 'The Road Not Taken', 'Ships?' (p. 198)

'The Road Not Taken'
diverge (l. 1), undergrowth (l. 5), sigh (l. 16), make all the difference (l. 20)
'Ships?'
sail (a ship) (l. 1), float (l. 4), breath (l. 13), failure (l. 16), (not) be ashamed to do sth. (l. 17)
tasks: experience, message, outlook on sth., appropriate, content

*Didaktisch-
methodische
Hinweise*

Die beiden Gedichte „The Road Not Taken" und „Ships?" gestalten auf unterschiedliche Weise das Thema Lebensentscheidungen – Entscheidungen, die oft getroffen werden müssen, ohne ihre Konsequenzen vollständig abzuschätzen zu können. Während Frost die Entscheidungsfindung selbst thematisiert, beschreibt Angelou eine Art, mit Fehlentscheidungen umzugehen. Auch die S stehen in dieser Phase ihres Lebens vor wichtigen Entscheidungen, die große Auswirkungen auf ihr weiteres persönliches und berufliches Leben haben, und können sich hier anhand zweier literarischer Vorlagen mit eigenen Entscheidungen auseinander setzen: Frost zeigt ihnen die Notwendigkeit von Entscheidungen als existenzielle Grundsituation des Menschen, Angelou vermittelt eine lebensbejahende Perspektive, die auch Fehlentscheidungen einschließt.

Frost beschreibt in seinem sehr regelmäßig aufgebauten Gedicht (vgl. Reimschema, Strophenzahl, inhaltliche Struktur) anhand des Symbols des sich gabelnden Waldwegs den Prozess einer Entscheidungsfindung: Da beide Wege sich nur in dem Maß unterscheiden, in dem sie benutzt wurden, entscheidet das lyrische Ich sich für denjenigen, der weniger benutzt erscheint und gibt damit seinem Leben eine Richtung, von der es nicht weiß, ob sie besser oder schlechter ist, als es die andere gewesen wäre. Die ruhige Stimmung des Gedichts legt jedoch den Schluss nahe, dass der Sprecher mit der Entscheidung nicht unzufrieden ist. Sein Seufzen (vgl. Z. 16) weist auf das Bedauern hin, nicht zu wissen, welchen Weg sein Leben bei der anderen Entscheidung genommen hätte.

Angelous Gedicht ist nicht ganz so regelmäßig gebaut wie Frosts (vgl. aber Struktur und Reimschema der Strophen 1–3) und wirkt durch die ungleiche und insgesamt geringe Verslänge dynamischer und weniger reflektierend. Dies spiegelt den Inhalt des Gedichts wider: Das lyrische Ich nimmt die Dinge des Lebens, wie sie kommen, ohne lange zu reflektieren. Entsprechend grübelt es auch über falsche Entscheidungen nicht nach, sondern akzeptiert sie als Bestandteile seines Lebens, nicht als Dinge, die hätten anders gelöst oder vermieden werden können.

Unterrichts-
tipps
Differenzierung

Die Aufgaben im SB sind so angelegt, dass beide Gedichte zusammen gelesen und verglichen werden. Da insbesondere Frosts Gedicht von der Lexik her nicht leicht zu verstehen ist, sollten in leistungsschwächeren Kursen beide Gedichte nacheinander gelesen und kurz besprochen werden, bevor die Aufgaben im SB beantwortet werden. Leistungsstärkere S können die Gedichte zu Hause vorbereiten und im Unterricht beide Gedichte von CD hören (vgl. CD2, *tracks* 26 und 27), bevor sie die Aufgaben lösen.

Die S sollten auf den *if*-Satz in Z. 4 von Angelous Gedicht hingewiesen werden, der nicht der im Unterricht behandelten Zeitenfolge von konditionalen Satzgefügen entspricht (*will* in der *if-clause*). Hierbei handelt es sich um eine nicht-standardsprachliche Form.

→ WB, ex. 6

Info

Robert Frost (1874–1963) was born in California, where he lived until he was 11, when his father died. His family then moved to Massachusetts. In 1912 he moved to England, following a depression brought on by his mother's death. It was there that he started to write and have his poems published. Encouraged by his success, he moved back with his wife and children to New England, the region of the USA with which he is most associated. From the publication of his first book of poems in the USA until his death he was probably the nation's best-known and best-loved poet. President John F. Kennedy invited him to read a poem at his inauguration in 1961. He wrote many of the poems from the perspective of a wise country person living close to nature and approaching life in a spirit of compassionate realism. 'The Road Not Taken' is probably his most famous poem; other well-known poems include 'Mending Wall' and 'Stopping by Woods on a Snowy Evening'.

'The Road Not Taken' is written from the perspective of a man looking back at a point in his life when he was faced by two roads in a wood. One road has been well trodden, while the other is less trodden. Although the situation has been interpreted on a metaphorical level, it is actually based on the real experience of walking with his English friend Edward Thomas in the countryside. Thomas always hesitated before choosing which path to take and wondered whether indeed the other path might not have been more interesting.

Maya Angelou (born 1928) was born in St Louis, Missouri. Besides her many poems, she has written several novels including *I Know Why the Caged Bird Sings* (1970). She has also acted on stage and in films, including the TV series *Roots* (1977). She was asked by President Bill Clinton to read her poem 'On the Pulse of Morning' at his inauguration in 1993.

Lösungs-
hinweise

1 They are a symbol of choice, of different options, etc.

2 **a** In the last stanza, there are only four lines instead of five. The second and third lines are longer than in the other stanzas. The rhyme scheme is different: a b b a instead of a b c c b (the first stanza is a b c c d). The first line of the last stanza has two syllables, while all the rest have one syllable. Moreover, it deals with a negative quality, 'failure', which she then refuses to accept; in the other stanzas she deals with 'ships', 'men' and 'life', all of which make a positive impression.
Angelou sets up a rhythmic pattern, which soothes the reader. The change in rhythm emphasizes the last stanza.

b The speaker will try anything, but with determination: the one thing she is not prepared to do is to fail. Even failures are to be overcome or rather, they are not to be called and considered failures.

3 The speaker in 'The Road Not Taken' seems to relish the prospect of having choice, as one can consider one's options, look back on what might have been with a sigh and still be content that one took the path one did.

The <u>speaker in 'Ships?'</u> seems to enjoy everything that life can offer and believes that failure does not really exist (one can tell it, but never spell it).

4 Individual answers.

5 All the texts in this section have something to do with people making choices that affect their future.

SB, S. 199
Watch Your Language

Didaktisch-methodische Hinweise
Im Mittelpunkt dieses Abschnitts steht die Wiederholung der Zeiten mit den Schwerpunkten *present perfect, simple past* und *future time*. Ausgehend von der Bearbeitung des Fehlertexts finden die S mit Hilfe einer Grammatik und eines einsprachigen Wörterbuchs die richtigen Lösungen. Der Abschnitt mündet in die produktive Verwendung der Zeiten und die Erläuterung ihrer Verwendung durch die S.

Lösungs-hinweise

1 a

1 The school <u>has had</u> a course in cross-cultural studies <u>for</u> three months.
2 '<u>I'll</u> help you,' is what Sharon always says when she sees someone with a problem.
3 Matthew <u>has been working / has worked</u> in the job he dreamed of since 2001.
4 Tom <u>hasn't been</u> ('isn't' also possible) the same since his mother <u>died</u> last year.
5 Sharon <u>was taking</u> a shower when her girlfriend rang, so she <u>couldn't</u> come to the phone.
6 They'<u>re meeting</u> after work tonight to talk about their problems.
7 Ginny <u>has seemed</u> somewhat depressed lately.
8 An important decision <u>was reached</u> at the conference yesterday.

b

1 <u>has had / for</u>: *CEG* §84 (Index under 'present perfect: with *since/for*, '*since*: + present perfect'); *OALD*: explanation under '*since*: HELP';
2 <u>I'll help you</u>: *CEG* §73, §96b (Index under 'future time: ways of expressing future time');
3 <u>has been working</u>: *CEG* §84 (Index under 'present perfect: with *since/for*', '*since*: + present perfect');
4 <u>hasn't been</u>: *CEG* §84 (Index under 'present perfect: with *since/for*, '*since*: + present perfect');
  <u>died</u>: *CEG* §86a (Index under 'simple past');
5 <u>was taking</u>: *CEG* §89b (Index under 'past progressive'), §90 (Index under 'past progressive: and simple past');
  <u>could not</u>: *CEG* §26, 36–37 (Index under 'can: substitute forms', 'could/couldn't');
6 <u>are meeting</u>: *CEG* §73, §99 (Index under 'future time: ways of expressing future time', 'present progressive: expressing future time');
7 <u>has seemed</u>: *CEG* §80b; *OALD* under 'lately: examples';
8 <u>was reached</u>: *CEG* §86a (Index under 'simple past'); *CEG* §108 (Index under 'passive').

2 The class mainly needs to study and practise tenses, including the substitute forms of the modal auxiliaries. The use of 'since' and 'for' and the effects the two have on the tense in English also need looking at.

3 a

1 The family has/have lived in Britain longer than I can remember. They'll never leave.
2 We first met back in 1999, and since then we've only seen each other twice.
3 They knew they had to come to a decision before last night's press conference.

b Information about future time can be found in *CEG* §73, 95–106.
1 present progressive (*CEG* §99)
2 *going to*-future (*CEG* §98a)
3 simple present (*CEG* §100)
4 *will*-future (*CEG* §96b)
5 *will*-future (*CEG* §96a)

c
1 The camera will cost more tomorrow. – OK, I'll take it.
2 The project group is meeting this evening to prepare the presentation.
3 Daniel has known that he's gay since he was a child / since his childhood. He will tell
his parents sometime. He thinks they'll have problems with it (better: accepting it).

→ *WB, ex. 8*

Topic Vocabulary: 'Personal Identity'

Aspects of Identity
appearance
background
born into (a rich family)
born of/to (poor parents / a German family)
region
national identity
social class
upper/middle/working class
racial/ethnic identity
ethnicity
mixed ethnic background
of mixed ancestry
religious identity
upbringing
education
hereditary
acquired

Strengths
realize your full potential
have a positive outlook on life
find fulfilment in sth.
ambition
ambitious
aim high
achiever
seek self-fulfilment/happiness
be good/talented at sth.
work hard for sth.
focus on sth.
strong point
self-confidence/self-respect
overcome a problem
mature
self-assured
feel accepted

Personality
have/show personality traits
self-confidence
self-confident
assertive
aggressive
self-awareness
shape an individual's personality
attitudes
beliefs
(stick to your) principles
morals
interests
be interested in sth.
share values
role model
find yourself
deny your origins

Weaknesses
self-doubt(s)
lack of self-confidence/self-respect
shortcomings
self-consciousness
go/pass through an identity crisis
have an inferiority/superiority complex
failure
fail in sth.
be nervous/uncertain/confused about sth.
feel rootless
feel threatened by sth.
feel like an outsider
be a snob

Goals/Ambitions
have realistic goals
achieve your goals
find a dream job
pursue a dream
consider your options

Sexuality
gender identity
sexual identity
sexual orientation
heterosexual
homosexual
bisexual
enter into / end a relationship

VIDEO **Beckham Is the Best**

SB, p. 190

Jess:	Do you fancy me, Tony?
Tony:	I like you, yeah.
Jess:	Well, good. Maybe we can go out then, yeah?
Tony:	Jess, what's going on?
Jess:	I just think I need an Indian boyfriend.
Tony:	What is going on, Jess? You're acting all weird.
Jess:	Sorry. You know my coach, yeah?
Tony:	Yeah!
Jess:	I nearly kissed him in Germany.
Tony:	Wow. And that's why you need an Indian boyfriend?
Jess:	Well, Jules likes him too and now she hates me.
Tony:	Look Jess, you can't plan who you fall for, it just happens. I mean, look at Posh and Becks.
Jess:	Beckham is the best.
Tony:	Yeah, I really like Beckham too.
Jess:	Of course you do. No one can cross a ball or bend it like Bendham.
Tony:	No, Jess. I really like Beckham.
Jess:	What, you mean … But you're Indian!
Tony:	I haven't told anyone.
Jess:	God, what's your mum going to say? My sister thinks you're mad about me.
Tony:	I am. I just don't want to marry you.
Jess:	I wonder what all those tossers would say if they knew?
Tony:	Jess, you're not going to tell anyone.
Jess:	Of course not. It's okay, Tony. I mean it's okay with me.
Tony:	Yeah, well you fancing your gora coach is okay with me. Besides, he's quite fit.

VIDEO **We Have Something to Tell You**

SB, p. 191

Jess:	How am I going to tell them, Tony? I have to now or I'll end up a solicitor bored out of my mind.
Tony:	Come with me.
	Mum, Uncle Biji, Auntie Biji, we've got something we want to tell you.
Aunt Biji:	Why is he holding her hand?
Tony:	You know how we have been good friends for a long time now. We'd like to ask for your blessings. We'd like to get engaged. But look, there's one condition. I want Jesminder to go to college first anywhere that she wants.
Dad:	Of course, Putar!
Jess:	Mum, dad, Tony's lying. We're not getting married. Tony only said that to help me but I'm not lying any more. I played in the final today and we won.
Mum:	How? When?
Jess:	I wasn't going to but Dad let me. And it was brilliant. I played the best ever and I was happy because I wasn't sneaking off and lying to you. I didn't ask to be good at football. Guru Nanak must have blessed me. Anyway there was a scout from America there today and he's offered me a place at a top university with a free scholarship and a chance to play football professionally. And I really want

	to go and if I can't tell you what I want now, then I'll never be happy, whatever I do.
Mum:	You let her leave her sister's wedding to go to football match?
Dad:	Maybe you could handle her long face. I could not. I didn't have the heart to stop her.
Mum:	And that's why she's ready to go all the way to America now?
Tony:	It's alright, mum. Just leave it.
Dad:	When those bloody English cricket players threw me out of their club like a dog, I never complained. On the contrary, I vowed that I will never play again. Who suffered? Me. But I don't want Jessie to suffer. I don't want her to make the same mistakes that her father made of accepting life, accepting situations. I want her to fight. And I want her to win, because I've seen her playing. She's brilliant. I don't think anybody has the right of stopping her. Two daughters made happy in one day. What else can a father ask for?
Mum:	At least I've taught her full Indian dinner. The rest is up to God.

`CD` Four English Accents

SB, p. 192   My aunt had an accident the other day. She had picked some raspberries from her garden and wanted to take them to her friend who lives on the other side of town. She got in the car, but it wouldn't start – it's very old. So she took the raspberries, put on her hat, grabbed her handbag and went to catch the bus. But just as she turned the corner into the high street, a great big dog came running round the corner and crashed into her. She fell over and the raspberries went all over the pavement.

`CD` Why Can't the English?

SB, p. 193		
	Henry Higgins:	Look at her, a prisoner of the gutters, Condemned by every syllable she utters. By right she should be taken out and hung, For the cold-blooded murder of the English tongue.
	Eliza Doolittle:	Aaooooww!
	Henry Higgins:	Aaooooww! Heaven's! What a sound! This is what the British population Calls an elementary education.
	Colonel Pickering:	Come, sir, I think you picked a poor example.
	Henry Higgins:	Did I? Hear them down in Soho Square, Dropping 'h's everywhere. Speaking English anyway they like. You sir, did you go to school?
	Man:	Wadaya tike me for, a fool?
	Henry Higgins:	No one taught him 'take' instead of 'tike'! Hear a Yorkshireman, or worse, Hear a Cornishman converse, I'd rather hear a choir singing flat. Chickens cackling in a barn – just like this one!
	Eliza Doolittle:	Garn!
	Henry Higgins:	'Garn' – I ask you, sir, what sort of word is that? It's 'Aoooow' and 'Garn' that keep her in her place. Not her wretched clothes and dirty face.

Why can't the English teach their children how to speak?
This verbal class distinction by now should be antique.
If you spoke as she does, sir, instead of the way you do,
Why, you might be selling flowers, too.

Colonel Pickering: I beg you pardon.
An Englishman's way of speaking absolutely classifies him,
The moment he talks he makes some other
Englishman despise him.
One common language I'm afraid we'll never get.
Oh, why can't the English learn to set
A good example to people whose
English is painful to your ears?
The Scotch and the Irish leave you close to tears.
There even are places where English completely disappears.
Well, in America, they haven't used it for years!
Why can't the English teach their children how to speak?
Norwegians learn Norwegian; the Greeks are taught their Greek.
In France every Frenchman knows his language from A to Zed
The French don't care what they do, actually,
As long as they pronounce it properly.
Arabians learn Arabian with the speed of summer lightning.
And Hebrews learn it backwards,
which is absolutely frightening.
But use proper English you're regarded as a freak.
Why can't the English,
Why can't the English learn to speak?

CD   **Getting Along in English**

SB, p. 194   **Dialogue 1**
Task 2

Mrs Smith:	Yes? Can I help you?
Helen:	Oh, good afternoon. I'm Helen Minter. I've come to see Mrs Smith about the babysitting job.
Mrs Smith:	Ah, you're Helen Minter! Good afternoon, Helen. I'm Mrs Smith. Do come in.
Mrs Smith:	Do sit down, Helen.
Helen:	Thank you.
Mrs Smith:	Well, now, tell me a bit about yourself, Helen. First of all, how old are you?
Helen:	I'm fourteen, well, nearly fifteen. I'll be fifteen in two weeks' time.
Mrs Smith:	And have you done babysitting before?
Helen:	At home, yes. I have two younger brothers. One's seven years old and the little one's just three.
Mrs Smith:	And you look after them sometimes, do you?
Helen:	Yes, I do. It's really quite fun – I play all sorts of games with them. And I think I'm quite good at getting them to do what I want: I almost always get them to bed on time.
Mrs Smith:	That's good, because our last babysitter was hopeless at that. Well, we'd want you to come once a week. Could you manage that?
Helen:	Yes, that would be fine. Erm … how many children do you have?

Mrs Smith:	Three. They're five years old, three and one. Do you think you can handle that?
Helen:	Er ... well, it's a challenge! Yes, I think I'd manage OK.
Mrs Smith:	Splendid! Well, we'd pay you five pounds an hour. Could you start this Saturday?
Helen:	Does that mean I've got the job?
Mrs Smith:	Yes!
Helen:	That's marvellous. Thank you very much, Mrs Smith. I really will look after the children well, I promise. When would you like me to come on Saturday?

Dialogue 2

Police Constable:	Now, sir, did you see the accident?
Mark:	Yes, officer, I did. I was standing right here.
PC:	And your name is?
Mark:	Whittaker, Mark Whittaker.
PC:	How do you spell that, sir?
Mark:	W - H - I - T - T - A - K - E - R.
PC:	Whittaker. And your address, sir?
Mark:	15 Jubilee Road, Kew.
PC:	And your phone number, sir?
Mark:	That's 020 8992 1155.
PC:	Right. Now ... Mr Whittaker, can you tell me exactly what you saw?
Mark:	Yes, well, I was standing here, on the corner, waiting for my friend, when the red van came round the corner. Next I saw a football roll into the road. Then the little boy ran into the road after the ball.
PC:	Which little boy, sir?
Mark:	That one there: the blonde, curly-haired one with the glasses and the blue T shirt.
PC:	Right. And what happened next?
Mark:	Well, the red van jammed on its brakes and the silver car drove straight into the back of it. There was an enormous crash and we all ran over to help.
PC:	Thank you very much, sir. That'll be all for now. We may need to get in touch with you again.
Mark:	Of course, officer, I'd be pleased to help, if I'm needed.
PC:	Thank you, sir. You've already been most helpful. Goodbye.
Mark:	Goodbye, officer.

Dialogue 3

Jane:	This won't take long, Max. We've only got half a page in the magazine!
Max:	That's OK, Jane. It's *pause* ... er, I mean break, anyway.
Jane:	OK now, first of all where do you come from?
Max:	I come from Germany.
Jane :	I know that, Max! I meant where in Germany.
Max:	Oh! Weimar, I come from Weimar.
Jane:	And is there anything special about Weimar?
Max:	Oh, yes, lots!
Jane:	Go on.
Max:	Well, Weimar is very famous because it is the place where Goethe and Schiller wrote many of their most famous works.
Jane:	Goethe and Schiller?

Max:	Yes. Goethe is for Germany what Shakespeare is for England, I think. You know, every school child knows his name. But he didn't just write plays and poems, he also wrote novels and scientific works and he drew and he was a politician ...
Jane:	Wow! And he did all this in Weimar. When was that?
Max:	The late 18th and early 19th century, I think.
Jane:	Ah ... but what about Weimar today?
Max:	Well, Weimar was part of the GDR until 1990, but since the re-unification of Germany, it's become a real tourist attraction – sightseers come by the busload. Weimar was even one of the European 'Cities of Culture'.
Jane:	That sounds posh! How do you find life in Weimar compared with life in Bristol?
Max:	It's very different. Firstly there are all the differences between Germany and England: Life here in Bristol is more easy-going. And there's more of a racial mix – in Weimar you see mainly white faces, here you see lots of black faces, too. Then, of course, here you have the lovely countryside – which we have too, but you also have the sea, the port – it's all very lively ...
Jane:	Oh, bother, we'll have to stop. If I need any help when I write my notes up, can I get back to you, Max?
Max:	Of course, no problem.
Jane:	Thanks. See you.
Max:	See you.

Dialogue 4

Tom:	Coming, coming!
Mary:	Oh, my goodness! Who are you?
Tom:	I beg your pardon?
Mary:	Oh, I am sorry, it's just I wasn't expecting a stranger. I'm Mary ... from next door ... and I only popped over to borrow a cup of sugar from Susan ... I'm ever so sorry.
Tom:	That's OK, Mary. I'm Tom, Susan's nephew.
Mary:	Oh! You're Tom! Well, pleased to meet you, I'm sure. How long are you here for, Tom?
Tom :	Just till Friday. I thought it'd be nice to get out of the city and visit my aunt.
Mary:	Oh, that's not long. What a pity! And do you like our little village?
Tom:	Oh, yes, it's very pretty.
Mary:	Been to the pub yet?
Tom:	No, not yet.
Mary:	Oh, goodness, I've only just noticed. Did I get you out of the bath?
Tom:	Well, yes, but that's OK.
Mary:	Oh, I am sorry. Well, I mustn't keep you on the doorstep any longer. Could I just borrow that sugar? Do you know where the sugar is?
Tom:	Yes, I do. Hold on just a minute. Here you are.
Mary:	Thanks. Bye.
Tom:	Bye.

Dialogue 1

Interviewer:	Excuse me, could I just ask you a few questions? We're doing research on shoppers and public transport.
Shopper:	Good afternoon. Let me introduce myself: My name is Jonathan Puttick – you can call me Johnny, though, and of course I'd really like to help you with your survey: I think it's a fantastically interesting subject. In fact I once read a book all about ...
Interviewer:	Yes, thank you. First question: how did you travel into the shopping centre this afternoon?
Shopper:	As I was saying, this book put forward the theory that if you had more car parks then more shoppers would come, but that if you ...
Interviewer:	It sounds very interesting, but I need to fill this form in: would you mind telling me how you travelled this afternoon?
Shopper:	I came by car, of course.
Interviewer:	And do you ever use public transport?
Shopper:	No! Never!
Interviewer:	Ah. Well, that's it then. Thank you.
Shopper:	Well, goodbye and thank you so much. It's been delightful talking to you.

Dialogue 2

Interviewer:	Next candidate, please. Good morning, and you are ...?
Pat:	Hi, I'm Pat.
Interviewer:	Pat. Pat who?
Pat:	Pat Furse.
Interviewer:	Ah, Patricia Furse. Well now, Miss Furse, as you know, there are only a limited number of places on this fashion course. So, why do you think you deserve a place on it?
Pat:	'Cos I'm good?
Interviewer:	Would you like to expand on that a bit?
Pat:	What?!
Interviewer:	Would you like to explain why you think you're good?
Pat:	Well, I got good marks in my exams ... Two As and two Bs ... and I – well, I just love designing and making clothes. I make all my clothes and my mum's and my friends' – I even designed a really cool waistcoat for my boyfriend. I'm really interested in the textiles, too: I did a tie-dye course when I was on holiday last year ...
Interviewer:	If we offer you a place, how would you see your future at the end of the course?
Pat:	What?
Interviewer:	What job would you like to do?
Pat:	Well, if I could, I'd love to design clothes – I think that's really exciting, but otherwise I'd try to get into textile design.
Interviewer:	Thank you, Miss Furse. You'll hear from us by the end of the month.
Pat:	Thanks. Fingers crossed, then, eh? Bye.

Dieses Kapitel versteht sich als Ausstieg aus der Arbeit mit dem Buch und aus dem Schulleben. Es befasst sich mit Abschied und Neubeginn – einem Thema, das die S unmittelbar betrifft, da sie in Kürze die Schule verlassen und einen Neubeginn machen werden. Dabei stellt sich ihnen die Frage, wie sie den nächsten Lebensabschnitt gestalten: ob sie z.B. reisen, studieren, eine Berufsausbildung beginnen, Bundeswehr oder Zivildienst absolvieren, eine Familie gründen wollen.

Die Texte dieses Kapitels spiegeln diese Umbruchssituation wider. Es finden sich fiktionale wie nicht-fiktionale Texte, in denen Jugendliche in unterschiedlichen zeitlichen Kontexten und unterschiedlichen Situationen gezeigt werden, die ihr Elternhaus oder ihre Heimat verlassen und Pläne für ihr weiteres Leben schmieden.

– In *section* 1, „Leaving Home", begegnen die S einem jungen Mann, einer Ausreißerin, einer Schulabgängerin und einem Flüchtling, die über das Verlassen ihres Zuhauses reflektieren.

– In *section* 2, „Choices", stehen praktische Fragen zu Berufswahl und Studienbeginn (in den USA) im Vordergrund.

→ *WB, ex. 4*

– In *section* 3, „Eveline", vollziehen die S anhand der bekannten Kurzgeschichte von James Joyce eine Entscheidungsfindung zwischen Aufbruch und Bleiben nach.

Didaktisches Inhaltsverzeichnis

SB, p.	Title	TM, p.	Text form	Topic	Skills and activities
200	Lead-in	395	photo	a girl moving out	analysing a photo; writing an interior monologue; doing a hot seating activity; working with words
	A Fantasy Journey CD2, track 28				making a fantasy journey; talking about one's plans
202	**The Road to London** Laurie Lee	397	novel (extract)	a young man leaving home to seek his fortune	describing a character's motives; analysing a relationship; analysing imagery; writing an account of one's feelings when leaving home
204	**Running Away** Melvin Burgess	400	novel (extract)	advice on running away from home	analysing the narrator's attitude
205	**Free!** Lauren Krugel	401	article from a website	reflections about how to live one's life	discussing the writer's view; analysing stylistic devices
207	**So I Have a New Name – Refugee** Ruvimbo Bungwe CD2, track 28	403	poem	a refugee's loss of identity	listing associations; interpreting a poem; comparing people in various texts
208	**Context Box**	404	–	reasons for and conditions of moving out	working with words; discussing a statement
209	**Career Plan**	405	extract from an advice column	developing a career plan	commenting on and developing a career plan; writing a CV & covering letter
211	**Doomsday**	406	feature story	waiting for exam results	listing options after school; comparing school systems and presenting the results
212	**Applying to a US University**	408	information for university applicants	applying to a US university	writing a 'personal statement'; collecting collocations; explaining a table; debating
214	**Victoria, not Vicky** Andrea Levy	409	novel (extract)	meeting other students on the first day at college	describing a person's character; telling the story from another perspective

215	**Off to College** Video/DVD	411	TV documentary	students moving into halls of residence	viewing skills; writing a diary entry
216	**Getting Along in English** CD2, tracks 30–32	412	–	finding a place to stay	understanding small ads; writing a small ad; acting out a dialogue
217	**Eveline** James Joyce	413	short story	deciding whether to leave home or stay	tracing a character's life story; describing a character; considering pros and cons; identifying external and internal action; analysing imagery; writing a letter
221	**Watch Your Language**	221	–	future time	–

Lead-in

SB, S. 200

Didaktisch-methodische Hinweise

Im Zentrum des „Lead-in" steht das Foto eines Mädchens, das mit einer kleinen Katze und einem Schlafsack unter dem Arm an einer befahrenen Straße steht. Die abgebildete Situation ist mehrdeutig; die Aufgaben zielen darauf, dass die S sich in das Mädchen hineinversetzen und die Situation beschreiben, in der es sich befindet. Anschließend sollen sich die S in einer Fantasiereise mit ihrer eigenen Aufbruchssituation auseinander setzen und gedanklich verschiedene Lebensentwürfe durchspielen.

Unterrichts-tipps

Der Einstieg ist über den Hörtext (vgl. CD2, *track* 28 und das Transkript auf S. 423), das Foto, Aufgabe 4 oder ein Brainstorming der S über ihre Zukunft nach dem Schulabschluss möglich. Dabei können die S ihre Überlegungen in Anlehnung an die Kategorien der Aufgabe 3 strukturieren. Wird das Bild als Einstieg gewählt, sollte den S zunächst Zeit gegeben werden, das Foto auf sich wirken zu lassen und sich frei dazu zu äußern, bevor Aufgabe 1 ihre Gedanken steuert.

Lösungs-hinweise

→ *WB, ex. 1*

1 **a** Individual answers.

b The photo is a black and white photo of a girl. She has a rolled up sleeping bag over her shoulder and a kitten in her hand. The photo is quite grainy. In the background there is a street with parked cars; there are some cars driving towards the girl; as they have their headlights on, one can presume it is dusk or night. The expression on the girl's face, and the way that she is looking not into the lens but past it, seem to indicate that she is lost in thought.
The fact that she is holding a vulnerable little kitten in her hand and that she is the only human being in the photo, emphasizes her loneliness and vulnerability. The light falls most strongly on the sleeping bag, which makes the viewer suppose that she is on the move and is possibly homeless. She looks thoughtful, as if things are not working for her or as if she is not sure what her next steps will be.

c Individual answers.

2 Für weitere Informationen zu *hot seating activities* vgl. S. 429. Die Fragen können als Hausaufgabe vorbereitet werden.

Individual answers.

3 Bei der Zuordnung der Begriffe sind Überschneidungen möglich.

Possible answers:

<u>Qualifications</u>: foreign languages, A-levels, exam, pass a test, get good marks/grades, subjects, gain experience, do an internship, acquire 'soft skills';

<u>Education after school</u>: go to university, get a university degree, attend lectures, go to college, do vocational training;

<u>Careers</u>: law, medicine, engineering, IT, office worker, self-employed, entrepreneur, parenting, teaching;

<u>Special interests</u>: hobbies, people, languages, natural sciences, teaching;

<u>A place to live</u>: house, garden, pets, family, apartment, balcony, tropical island, sea, sun, one's own home;

<u>Hopes</u>: salary, fulfilment, nice colleagues, responsibility, freedom, lack of pressure, power, family, partner, friends;

<u>Fears</u>: unemployment, pressure, working overtime, social exclusion, loneliness, being stuck in a job, divorce, illness.

4 Possible answers:
A young person might leave home because he/she:
– wants to study in another town/country;
– does not get on well with his/her parents;
– wants to live in a flatshare with people of his/her own age;
– wants privacy;
– wants to live in a place where there is a better chance of finding work;
– wants to move to a country that is safer;
– wants to move to a place that promises to be more interesting;
– wants to broaden his/her horizons;
– wants to move to a country/region with higher wages.

CD **5** **a–c** Der Hörtext befindet sich auf CD2, *track* 28; das Transkript auf S. 423.

Individual answers.

SB, S. 202 # 1 Leaving Home

Die Texte dieser *section* eint die Thematik des Fortgehens von Zuhause; jedoch werden jeweils unterschiedliche Aspekte in den Vordergrund gerückt. Die S begegnen einem jungen Mann, der in den Dreißigerjahren sein Elternhaus auf dem Land in Richtung London verlässt. Sie lesen die Ratschläge einer Jugendlichen von heute über das Weglaufen von zu Hause und vollziehen die Gedanken einer Schulabgängerin über Freiheit und Lebenspläne nach. Einen Kontrapunkt setzt der letzte Text, in dem ein Flüchtling klagt, einen Teil seiner Identität verloren zu haben. Durch ihn werden die S aufgefordert, innezuhalten und sich auf eine viel existenziellere Form des *moving out* einzulassen, als ihnen unmittelbar bevorsteht.

Unterrichts-tipps

→ *WB, ex. 2*

Da jeder Text einen anderen Aspekt der Thematik berührt, bietet sich arbeitsteilige Partner- oder Gruppenarbeit an, bei der die S einzelne Texte lesen, die dazugehörigen inhalts- und formbezogenen Aufgaben bearbeiten und die Ergebnisse der Lerngruppe präsentieren. Die Transferaufgaben sollten gemeinsam diskutiert werden.

A The Road to London   Laurie Lee

Source:	*As I Walked Out One Midsummer Morning*, 1969
Topic:	A young man leaving home to seek his fortune
Text form:	Novel (extract)
Language variety:	BE
Number of words:	759
Level:	Basic/advanced
Skills/activities:	Describing a character's motives, analysing a mother–son relationship, analysing imagery, writing an account of one's feelings when leaving home

Lern-vokabular

Active vocabulary: 'The Road to London' (p. 202)

discover sth. (l. 3), farewell (l. 4), blessing (l. 4), make up your mind (l. 10), belongings (l. 12), appeal (l. 13), persuasion (l. 13), settle down (l. 25), unease (l. 26), inevitable (l. 26), vigour (l. 36), reluctance (l. 37), indifference (l. 39), solitary (l. 41), be on your own (ll. 45–46)
tasks: relationship, mood, be intended to, comparable, account

Didaktisch-methodische Hinweise

Der Ich-Erzähler dieses Romanauszugs, ein 19-jähriger Mann aus England in den Dreißigerjahren, verlässt sein Zuhause, um die Welt zu entdecken. Sein Traum ist es, in die Hauptstadt London zu gelangen und das Meer zu sehen. Dafür nimmt er den Umweg über Southampton auf sich. Mit diesen für die S sicherlich fremden Wünschen und der Art und Weise, sie zu erreichen (zu Fuß, mit etwas zu essen, einer Violine und einem kleinen Zelt ausgestattet), bietet dieser Romanauszug die Gelegenheit, über Motive des Fortgehens und seine materiellen Voraussetzungen zu diskutieren.

Auch wenn die Situation des jungen Mannes sich von der der S unterscheidet, gibt es Berührungspunkte: den Wunsch, Neues zu entdecken; die Sorgen der Eltern; den Widerspruch gegen oder die Anpassung an das traditionelle Lebensmodell der Zeit; die materielle Situation. Durch diese Berührungspunkte dient der Text auch als Vorbereitung auf die kreative Schreibaufgabe, in der die S ihren eigenen Prozess des *moving out* darstellen. Die Schwerpunkte der Textaufgaben liegen auf der Analyse der Beziehung von Mutter und Sohn und der Bildlichkeit.

Unterrichts-tipps

Der Einstieg erfolgt über die *pre-reading*-Aufgabe. Bevor die S den Text lesen, bilden sie Hypothesen über den Aufbruch eines Jugendlichen aus dem ländlichen England der Dreißigerjahre: seine Motivation, Ziele, die Reaktionen seiner Umwelt, Transportmittel usw. Um deutlich zu machen, wie viel Zeit sich der Ich-Erzähler nimmt und welchen Umweg er einschlägt (Z. 30–34), kann eine Englandkarte eingesetzt werden.

Nach Bearbeitung der zweiten Frage können die S aufgefordert werden, die Aufbruchssituation aus Sicht der Mutter zu betrachten und ihre Gedanken in einem inneren Monolog zu formulieren.

Info

Laurie Lee (1914–1997) was born to a large family and lived in a small overcrowded cottage in Gloucestershire. His father lived in London and worked there as a civil servant, and never returned home. Lee left school at 15. When he was 19, he left for London, where he worked for a year as a builder's labourer. He then spent four years travelling in Spain at the time of the Civil War and around the eastern Mediterranean. Before devoting himself entirely to writing in 1951, Lee studied art, but worked as a journalist and as a scriptwriter. His first collection of poems, *The Sun My Monument*, was published in 1944. He is best known for his autobiographical trilogy (cf. the note in the SB, p. 202), which depicts Lee's boyhood in Gloucestershire, his journey to London to seek his fortune, and his experiences in the Spanish Civil War.

Info

As I Walked Out One Midsummer Morning (1969) narrates Lee's first trip to Spain in 1936. He leaves his childhood village and ends up in Spain. He walks across the country and finally returns to England when Franco's troops win the Civil War.

Lösungs-hinweise

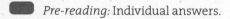 *Pre-reading:* Individual answers.

1 Lee set out on the road to London because:
– three sisters and a brother had already left home;
– he is 19 and confident about the future;
– he felt claustrophobic in the valley he had always lived in;
– local girls wanted him to marry and settle down;
– he was attracted to the sea, and above all, to London.

2 The relationship between Lee and his mother is obviously a warm one. She appears to be an old-fashioned caring but not questioning mother from another age. She never tries to prevent her son from leaving as she knows this is the way of the world: 'not questioning why I went' (ll. 4–5). He describes her realistically ('stooping', l. 1, 'old and bent', l. 3, 'gnarled hand', l. 4) – and he shows she does care: 'raised in farewell and blessing' (l. 4). Her physical appearance reveals a hard life in the country raising seven children (ll. 1, 3–4). She feels sympathy and understanding for her son wanting to leave home (ll. 10–13), but also feels the need to 'mother' him one last time in her own way (l. 10). She is concerned for Lee's welfare, hence her 'long and searching look' (ll. 13–14) to see if he is really ready to leave.

⬭ *What does this relationship reveal about parent–child relationships in the 1930s as compared to today? (To answer this question, imagine you were leaving your home at the age of 19 with no plans and no money. How might your parents react?)*
When a son from poor parents reached a certain age it was accepted that he would leave home and start his own life (girls left home when they got married). A mother cared for her children as long as necessary but it was accepted that after a certain age, an individual must make his or her own way in life (cf. l. 9). Lee writes that he 'closed that part of my life for ever' (l. 7), indicating he never returned to see his family again.

 3 Diese Aufgabe ist besonders für leistungsstarke S geeignet. Zu Beginn sollte der Begriff „emotive words and phrases" geklärt werden: Hier wird darunter Sprachmaterial verstanden, das Auskunft über die Gefühlslage des Erzählers gibt. Als Hilfestellung können die S zunächst die Passagen nennen, in denen ein bestimmtes Gefühl dominiert, und dann die Bilder und sprachlichen Mittel zusammentragen, mit denen dieses Gefühl ausgedrückt wird.

His mother – wistfulness:
– 'I ... saw the gold light die behind her' (ll. 5–6): a wistful image making one think both of religious paintings (Mary, mother of Jesus, with golden halo and beams of sunlight) and of the dying sun and therefore of old age as being the last phase before death. It reflects the strong feelings the son has for his mother.

The weather – optimism:
– 'It was bright Sunday morning' (l. 8), 'early sunshine' (ll. 14–15): The use of 'bright' and 'sunshine' lifts the mood after the parting and reveals Lee's optimism about his future.

His country background – a place to flee from:
– 'and walked away from the sleeping village' (l. 20): 'sleeping' (personification) implies an untroubled, but also slightly boring cosiness from which he is awakening.
– 'propelled' (l. 22) evokes energetic movement, but also the implication that Lee has been thrown out of his old life by these forces.

- 'small tight valley closing in around one, stifling the breath with its mossy mouth' (ll. 23–24): here the entire valley is personified and reveals the sense of claustrophobia which is one of the reasons why he is happy to be leaving; the vivid metaphor of the 'mossy mouth' shows that even the beauty of the country can also make one feel suffocated, and that breathing is connected with freedom and moving away.
- 'the cottage walls narrowing like the arms of an iron maiden' (ll. 24–25): a simile for the physically almost painful lack of hope in the small village; there is also a pun on 'maiden' as he then goes on to refer to the girls (maidens) wanting him to stay and settle down with one of them.

The journey – optimism and strength:
- 'And now I was on my journey in a pair of thick boots and with a hazel stick in my hand' (ll. 29–30): a jaunty optimism returns, enhancecd by the image of him striding along with the hazel stick.

The landscape – weariness and uncertainty:
- 'as I tramped through the dust '... weighed me down'(ll. 36–37): 'tramped' implies tiredness and lack of joy while 'dust' implies that the clear views of the early morning sunshine are gone, and with them maybe the clarity of purpose, too, while 'weigh' implies heaviness.
- 'elder-blossom and dog roses hung in the hedges' (ll. 37–38): 'hung' also implies weariness, an unusual way of describing blossom and roses bursting with life.
- 'blank as unwritten paper' (l. 38): the image is one of uncertainty, just as the flowers are young, so too is he.
- 'sulky summer sucked me towards it' (l. 40): this phrase contains an alliteration (the repetition of 's') and an assonance (the repetition of the ʌ sound), the latter producing a negative effect, reinforced by the word 'sucked' implying as with 'propelled' (l. 22) that he is not in charge of his destiny.

Thoughts of home – longing for its familiarity and noisiness:
- 'solitary morning' (l. 41), 'I was affronted by freedom' and 'the day's silence' (l. 44) reveal his loneliness, which makes him think of home.
- 'I was taunted by echoes of home' (ll. 44–47): the sounds and sights of home reinforce the element of loneliness and leads to self-doubts.
- 'the honeyed squalor of home' (ll. 51–52) is an image of sweetness and pleasantness on the one hand and untidiness, dirt, mess on the other, which together suggests 'home' in a very real and therefore very emotional way.

4 London represents all that is the contrary of his small village. It represents life, opportunity, new experiences and new people as compared to the stifling expectations of village life: a small cottage, limited horizons ('tight valley', l. 23), marriage. Today, people have similar attitudes to big cities, but they might take negative aspects, such as dirt, crime, isolation, lack of human values, etc. into account.

⬯ *'I had all the summer and all time to spend' (ll. 33–34). Compare this attitude to that of young people today.*
Similarities: Many young people today take some time or even a year off before going to college or starting their vocational training.

Differences: Many feel they do not have time to lose as employers are looking for people who have demonstrated purposefulness/single-mindedness.

5 Hier können verschiedene Textarten vorgeschlagen werden, z.B. Tagebucheintrag, innerer Monolog, Telefongespräch, E-mail, Brief, Postkarte, Gespräch usw.

⬯ *Translate ll. 1–15 into German.*

⬯ *Write a speech to be given at the presentation of the* Abitur *certificates in which you compare the situation of young people leaving home in the 1930s and today.*

B Running Away Melvin Burgess

Source:	*Junk*, 1996
Topic:	Advice on running away from home
Text form:	Novel (extract)
Language variety:	BE
Number of words:	298
Level:	Basic/advanced
Skills/activities:	Commenting on something

Lern-vokabular

Active vocabulary: 'Running Away' (p. 204)

run away from home (l. 2), malcontent (l. 3), underwear (l. 5), waterproof (l. 5), sleeping bag (l. 6), wits (l. 8), abduct sb. (l. 10), pervert (l. 11), binliner (l. 12), rubbish tip (l. 12), get fed up with sb. (l. 13), leave of your own accord (l. 14), leave home (l. 17), no hard feelings (l. 20), unbearable (l. 22), beware (l. 23), undermine sth. (l. 24), credibility (l. 24), book sth. (l. 25)

Didaktisch-methodische Hinweise

In diesem Text steht mit dem Weglaufen von zu Hause ein weiterer Aspekt des *moving out* im Vordergrund. Die Jugendliche Gemma gibt Nachahmern eine Reihe von Ratschlägen, wie das Weglaufen organisiert werden sollte, die kühle Berechnung und genaue Planung ihres Vorhabens verraten. Gemmas Anleitung ist als Provokation und als Ausdruck von Vertrauensverlust und Enttäuschung zu verstehen. In sprachlicher Hinsicht eignet sich der Text für Übungen zum Register (vgl. das Glossar, SB, S. 265).

Unterrichts-tipps

Die im SB abgedruckte *pre-reading*-Frage eignet sich zur Bearbeitung als Hausaufgabe, bevor die S den Text lesen. Aufgabe 1 ist wegen ihrer Offenheit und Komplexität anspruchsvoll. Zur Vorbereitung könnten – v.a. bei leistungsschwächeren S – Aufgaben 1 und 2 umgestellt und zusätzlich nach den Motiven für Gemmas Verhalten gefragt werden (vgl. die Zusatzaufgabe). Nach der Textbearbeitung kann ein *hot seating* durchgeführt werden (vgl. S. 429), bei dem nicht nur Gemma, sondern auch ihre Eltern zu Wort kommen.

Info

Melvin Burgess (born 1954) was brought up in southern England. He was not good at school, but managed to get a training programme as a journalist for a local newspaper. He then decided to become a full-time writer. With his novel *The Cry of the Wolf* (1989) he finally achieved recognition. *Junk* (1996) is probably his best-known novel, but he also wrote the novelisation of the feature film *Billy Elliot* (2001). He lives in Manchester. *Junk* is set in Bristol. The main characters, Tar and Gemma, decide to run away from home and move to Bristol, where they meet up with some squatters. In the squat they experiment with drugs and become addicted to heroin.

Lösungs-hinweise

■■■ *Pre-reading:* Individual answers.

1 Individual answers.

2 Yes: Points 3 and 4 indicate that, though she sounds quite tough, she does not want her parents to worry too much.

No: If she was worried about them a) she would not go and b) she would not steal their money. She would confront them with her problems.

◯ *From what you can gather from the text, what things have led to Gemma's resentment of her parents?*

Gemma seems to be very angry with her parents because they treat her like a little child rather than seeing her as an adolescent who is moving towards adulthood. Phrases like 'my little girl' (l.10), 'little Lucinda' (l.13) and 'little you' (l.15) indicate that the parents still view her as a little child in need of care and protection from the evil world; the fact that the parents presume some pervert is harming their child also shows that they only see their child as being defenceless. So she turns sarcastic when she uses this language against her parents by calling them 'Mumsy and Dadsy' (l.13).

⬭ *Identify elements of informal English in Gemma's handbook.*
'stuff' (l. 5), ' 'em' (l. 8), 'Mumsy' (l. 13), 'Dadsy' (l. 13), 'copper' (l. 14) 'on your tail' (ll. 13–14), 'piccy' (l. 17), 'local rag' (l. 17), elliptical sentences (cf. ll. 5–8, 17).

⬭ *Imagine that Gemma's parents come across Gemma's 'handbook'. On a website designed to reach out to runaway children, they decide to write a letter to Gemma in response to the fact that she has run away and to what she wrote in her 'handbook'. Write their letter.*

SB, S. 205 **C Free!**   Lauren Krugel

Source:	*Website of Young People's Press*, 2001
Topic:	Reflections about how to live one's life
Text form:	Essay
Language variety:	CanE
Number of words:	782
Level:	Basic/advanced
Skills/activities:	Discussing the writer's view, analysing stylistic devices

Lern-vokabular

Active vocabulary: 'Free!' (p. 205)

good riddance (l. 3), have time on your hands (l. 5), convertible (l. 7), all day long (l. 8), rape sb. (l. 14), murder sb. (l. 14), resent sth. (l. 16), waste sth. (l. 21), plan for sth. (l. 22), retirement (l. 22), prepare for sth. (l. 26), retire (l. 28), refuse to do sth. (l. 29), look back on sth. (l. 29), responsibility (l. 33), drudgery (l. 33), tedium (l. 33), pretentious (l. 35), catch sb.'s drift (l. 38), ultimately (l. 38), raise a family (l. 44), have a point (l. 48), die of sth. (l. 48)

Didaktisch-methodische Hinweise

Die S lesen hier die Gedanken einer literarisch und philosophisch interessierten Schülerin, deren Situation am ehesten mit der vergleichbar ist, in der sich die S in Kürze befinden werden: Nach erfolgreichem Schulabschluss wägt sie ihre weiteren Optionen ab. Dabei spielt der Wunsch nach Freiheit eine zentrale Rolle: Ähnlich wie der Ich-Erzähler in Text A (SB, S. 202) will sie aus ihrer bisherigen Welt ausbrechen. Das Sicherheitsdenken ihrer Eltern lehnt sie ab; sie räumt aber selbstkritisch ein, dass ihr Bemühen um gute Philosophienoten darauf abzielt, sich eine gute Ausgangsbasis für Universität und Berufsleben zu verschaffen. Bei ihrem Freiheitsstreben ist sie von dem französischen Existenzialismus (Jean Paul Sartre) und der Jugendrevolte der Fünfziger- (Kerouac) und Sechzigerjahre (Simon and Garfunkel) beeinflusst. Sie sieht sich in der Tradition der amerikanischen *hobos*. Abschließend plädiert sie für einen Ausgleich von Zukunftsplanung und erfüllter, selbstbestimmter Gegenwart, die Ziellosigkeit, Zufälligkeit, Kreativität und Freiheit einschließt.

Unterrichts-tipps

Die S werden sich mit der Grundaussage der Verfasserin weitgehend identifizieren. Hilfestellungen dürften bei der Erschließung der literarischen und philosophischen Anspielungen erforderlich sein (vgl. „Info"). Die Aufgaben zielen auf das Verständnis und eine kritische Auseinandersetzung mit Laurens Auffassung. Dabei ist zu erwarten, dass die S über ihre eigenen Erfahrungen bei der Realisierung ihrer Pläne berichten.

Der Text kann als Hör- oder Lesetext präsentiert werden. Mit Hilfe der folgenden Aufgabe kann (z.B. beim zweiten Hören) eine Verständnissicherung erfolgen:

⬭ *Choose the correct alternatives:*

1   *Lauren will be graduating from college / high school soon.* (high school)

2   *She is sure/ isn't sure about what to do with the seven months she has ahead of her.* (isn't sure)

3   *The idea of travelling in an old convertible / coach across America appeals to her.* (in an old convertible)

4   *She is especially interested in seeing oceans / jungles / her relatives / other countries / Jack Kerouac.* (oceans, jungles and other countries)

5   *Her mother warned her that she might get lost in the jungles / get raped / have a car accident / be murdered.* (she might get raped and be murdered)

6   *Lauren regrets having missed the sixties / the seventies / the eighties.* (the sixties)

7   *She doesn't want to waste her youth on planning for retirement / buying an expensive apartment / raising a family.* (on planning for retirement)

8   *She agrees / doesn't agree with Jean Paul Sartre's view that we are all condemned to be free.* (agrees)

9   *She realises that it is necessary to plan her life carefully / to lead a life that has no meaning / to plan for only what makes her happy.* (plan for only what makes her happy)

Kopiervorlage   Um die Aufmerksamkeit der S auf die vielen umgangssprachlichen Wörter des Texts zu lenken, eignet sich die KV „Informal English", z.B. als Hausaufgabe (vgl. S. 420). Die Lösungen zur KV sind: 1I, 2G, 3K, 4C, 5J, 6B, 7A, 8H, 9D, 10L, 11F, 12E.

Info

Jack Kerouac (1922–1969) (l. 7) has often been called a chronicler of the so-called 'beat generation' of the 1950s, a social and literary movement mostly characterized by criticism of the so-called establishment, by a rejection of social and artistic convention. His most influential work is *On the Road* (1957), a semi-autobiographical novel in which the main character hitchhikes across the USA and enjoys casual friendships, love affairs and new sensations.

'Look for America' (ll. 12–13): reference to the 1968 song 'America' by Simon and Garfunkel, in which the singer describes his feelings when travelling through the USA, in search of 'America' (cf. www.lyricsdepot.com/simon-garfunkel/america.html · 1.8.2003)

'Hobo-itis' (l. 18): A hobo is a person who travels the country in order to find short-time work, especially on farms. Hoboism came into being in the USA after the Civil War and boomed again during the Great Depression. While people used to be driven into hoboism out of economic necessity, today they tend to be attracted by the freedom and adventure attached to this way of living.

Chrissy Hynde (born 1951) (l. 19) is a songwriter, guitarist, and the lead singer of the band 'The Pretenders'.

Jean-Paul Sartre (1905–1980) (l. 32) was a French philosopher and writer and a leading exponent of 20th-century existentialism. In his writings, he denies the existence of God and conceives of man as a being living in a meaningless universe. Man is totally responsible for all his deeds, and is burdened with a terrifying freedom to choose.

1

- The risk of rape and murder;
- the world is not the same as it used to be;
- freedom brings responsibility, as you need to earn money;
- living recklessly might mean you have no money for college, and so no future;
- you could end up dead if you don't take care of yourself.

2 Individual answers.

3

- L. 3: <u>enumeration</u>. The effect on the reader is to build up the feeling of the initial thought – that of leaving – by the repetition of 'goodbye' in several languages. Cleverly, she adds 'good riddance' at the end, which is an unpleasant way of saying goodbye. She implies that she now wants her freedom.
- Ll. 10–11 and 25–29: <u>parallelism</u> ('I want[ed] to see/buy ...'). In the first case she lists all the possibilities, which creates the effect of endlessness (and reveals her enthusiasm), while juxtaposing opposites (e.g. 'oceans' and 'deserts'). Lauren allows the reader to feel that nothing has been left out. In the second case the parallelism lies in the repetition of 'You go to ... to ...' (<u>anaphora</u>) in a slow rhythm creating the impression of endless drudgery involved in the process of living, so much so that she forgets what the final point is: 'what will we be preparing for again?'.

SB, S. 207 **D So I Have a New Name – Refugee** Ruvimbo Bungwe

`CD`

Source:	*Credit to the Nation*, 2002
Topic:	A refugee's loss of identity
Text form:	Poem
Language variety:	BE
Number of words:	80
Level:	Basic/advanced
Skills/activities:	Listing associations, interpreting a poem, comparing people in various texts

Lern-
vokabular

Active vocabulary: 'So I Have a New Name – Refugee' (p. 207)

personality (l. 3), refugee (l. 4), share sth. (l. 5), comfort (l. 8), restore sth. (l. 9), offer sth. (l. 11), borrow sth. (l. 12), seek sth. (l. 13)
tasks: association, preference, contrast sth. with sth. else

Didaktisch-
methodische
Hinweise

Im Vordergrund dieses Gedichts steht eine völlig andere Form des *moving out* als in den übrigen Texten dieses Kapitels: Es beschreibt die Gefühle eines Flüchtlings, der sich durch wirtschaftliche, soziale oder andere Gründe gezwungen sah, sein Land zu verlassen. In dem neuen Land angekommen, beklagt er den Identitätsverlust, der mit seinem Status als Flüchtling einhergeht, und wünscht sich, als Freund aufgenommen zu werden. Durch dieses Gedicht sollen die S für die schwierige Lage von Flüchtlingen sensibilisiert werden und erkennen, dass *moving out* auch ein *moving in* bedeutet, das nicht nur positive Erlebnisse beinhaltet. Die Identitätsproblematik erlaubt Verbindungen zu Kapitel 10, v.a. *section* 1 und 2 (SB, S. 186 bzw. 190). Für weitere Informationen zum Refugee Council vgl. www.refugeecouncil.org.uk · 1.8.2003.

Unterrichts-
tipps

Es empfiehlt sich, das Gedicht am Ende dieser *section* zu besprechen, um den Kontrast zur Situation der S stärker hervortreten zu lassen. Als Einstimmung können die S *acrostics* zu den Begriffen *refugee* und *friend* anfertigen, ggf. als Hausaufgabe. Danach wird das Gedicht von CD2 (*track* 29) präsentiert.

1 The name the speaker has been given is 'refugee', the name he wants is 'friend'.
<u>Associations for 'refugee'</u>: person who has fled, who has nothing, who is afraid/
traumatised/hunted, who you feel sorry for, who you do not trust (bogus asylum
seekers), who has no real home, who does not belong.
<u>Associations for 'friend'</u>: a person you like / you spend time with / you have chosen to
be close to, a person who can help you / you can rely on / you can confide in, a person
you have fun with / you value, a person who you feel is your equal.
The speaker does not like the word 'refugee' because:
– it takes no account of the fates of individuals (ll. 1–3);
– it implies taking (shelter, help, etc.) and not giving (ll. 11–12);
– it takes away a person's self-esteem (l. 8).
He would prefer 'friend' because:
– it implies giving and taking, not just being dependent (ll. 11–12);
– it implies equality and sharing (ll. 9–10).

2 **a** The speaker means refugees are not alike, neither in their personality nor in
their history nor in their aspirations nor even in their reasons for being a refugee, but
that refugees are always looked upon from one viewpoint, that of being a person living
in a new country as a result of persecution.

b Individual answers.

3 The speaker may have left home due to war or political oppression.
In <u>text A</u>, Lee chose to leave home because he was beginning to feel closed in and
wanted new experiences.
In <u>text B</u>, Gemma implies that she chose to leave home because she was finding it
difficult to cope with her parents, and there was maybe an element of being hemmed
in and not being taken seriously.
In <u>text C</u>, Lauren plans to leave home in order to experience adventure, travel, freedom
in whatever way she chooses, regardless of what her parents and others think, so that
when she is older she can look back on her life and think it was worthwhile.

⬭ *Translate the poem into German.*

⬭ *Write a diary entry for one day in the life of a teenage refugee living in Germany. It
may be helpful to remember what you have heard or read about refugees in the media.*

Context Box

Die „Context Box" fokussiert auf die Aspekte der Thematik, die der Lebenssituation der
S recht nah sind: Die verschiedenen Optionen der Lebensplanung nach dem Schulabschluss werden aufgeführt (Studien- und Berufswahl, Wohnungssuche, Verhältnis zu
den Eltern), aber auch die Problematik der *runaways* wird angesprochen.
Die „Context Box" kann im Zusammenhang mit dem „Lead-in" zur Einführung in das
Kapitel genutzt werden oder am Ende als inhaltliche Zusammenfassung dienen. Sie
kann ebenso nach einer bestimmten *section*, vorzugsweise *section 1*, als Reflexion über
die dort behandelten Inhalte und Ausblicke auf weitere Aspekte fungieren.

Nachdem die Aufgaben im SB bearbeitet worden sind, erhalten die S den Auftrag, fünf
der hervorgehobenen Wörter auf einen Zettel zu schreiben. Diese Zettel werden in
Kleingruppen ausgetauscht und die S halten eine kurze, zusammenhängende Rede mit
den Begriffen, die auf ihrem neuen Zettel stehen.

1 **a–b** Possible answers:
be dependent on, stay at home;
grow increasingly independent, have a bit of freedom and privacy, desire for inde-

pendence, support oneself;
run away from home, stay away, move out of our childhood home, set out on our own,
get away from their parents, start out in life;
rush into marriage;
rite of passage;
student housing, move in with sb. in a flat-share arragement, 'place of one's own', rents;
attend college or university;
suffer from 'empty nest syndrome'.

2 Individual answers.

⬭ a) Explain what role parents play in the upbringing of a child.
b) Consider what effect their children leaving may have on them.

⬭ Do you intend to continue living at home once you leave school, or will you move out? Explain your choice.

⬭ Find useful websites, magazines, leaflets and brochures providing school leavers with information about cheap accommodation, study facilities at a particular place of your choice. Speak about your plans or design an information board with your group.

→ WB, ex. 7

SB, S. 209 **2 Choices**

Viele S setzen ihre Ausbildung nach der Schule, dem Wehr- bzw. dem Zivildienst an einer Hochschule fort. Ist die Phase der Orientierung und Entscheidung für ihren persönlichen Bildungs- und Berufsweg abgeschlossen, stehen die S vor neuen Herausforderungen: Bewerbungen für Universität oder Beruf, die im Zuge globaler Arbeitsmärkte auch außerhalb Deutschlands angesiedelt sein können, und schließlich die Eingewöhnung am Studienort oder Ausbildungsplatz.
Das Anliegen dieser *section* ist es, die S über das Bewerbungsverfahren an einer US-amerikanischen Universität zu informieren, das sich grundlegend von dem in Deutschland üblichen unterscheidet, und ihnen praktische Hilfestellungen bei der Einschätzung ihrer Fähigkeiten und der Formulierung von Bewerbungsunterlagen in englischer Sprache zu geben. Dem Thema entsprechend, stehen nicht-fiktionale Texte im Vordergrund, doch durch einen Romanauszug und einen Ausschnitt aus einem Dokumentarfilm ist mediale Vielfalt gewährleistet. Der abschließende fiktionale Text wirft einen Blick auf die zwischenmenschliche Seite des Neubeginns. Er zeigt das Unbehagen einer jungen Studentin aus einer bildungsfernen Schicht am ersten Tag an der Universität.

SB, S. 209 **A Career Plan**

Source:	Website of 'Mapping Your Future'
Topic:	Developing a career plan
Text form:	Advice column
Language variety:	AE
Number of words:	457
Level:	Basic/advanced
Skills/activities:	Commenting on and developing a career plan, writing a CV and a covering letter

Lern-
vokabular

Active vocabulary: 'Career Plan' (p. 209)

available (l. 2), make a decision (l. 2), determine sth. (l. 7), evaluate (l. 10), challenging (l. 11), be employed (l. 14), activities (l. 17), volunteer (l. 19), intern (l. 26), internship (l. 26), gain experience (l. 27), network (l. 28), assess sth. (l. 29), work experience (l. 33), focus on sth. (l. 34)

Didaktisch-
methodische
Hinweise

Dieser Text gibt den S Anregungen, wie sie ihren Berufsfindungsprozess strukturieren und bewusst gestalten können. Sie gehen die Denkanstöße des Texts Schritt für Schritt durch und werden so auf Kriterien hingewiesen, die ihre individuelle Entscheidung für eine berufliche Laufbahn bestimmen können. Im Anschluss simulieren sie eine Bewerbungssituation, indem sie ein Unternehmen aussuchen, bei dem sie sich für ein Praktikum bewerben könnten, und einen Lebenslauf und ein Bewerbungsschreiben in englischer Sprache verfassen.

Lösungs-
hinweise

1 A career plan is a statement of your career goals and an outline of the steps needed to attain that goal. Developing a career plan can help you to understand what skills and experiences you can offer a potential employer.

2 It seems to be useful for German teenagers too:
– It suggests that young people define their interests and skills, to see if there are common themes which might help them choose their profession.
– It suggests they do research about what options they have.
– It advises them to find out more about the career they are considering to see if it is really what they want to do.
– It advises them to find out what skills, training and qualifications are necessary to follow a particular career.
– It urges them to network, i.e. talk to people already involved in that profession.
– It suggests that practical work experience in the form of internships will give them more experience.
– It mentions work experience and volunteer work, all of which are quite common in Germany, too.

3 **a** The imperative: The text is meant to give advice, so it tells you what to do in order to achieve a given goal.

b Questions make the reader think about particular points (and make the advice sound friendlier than would be the case if only the imperative was used).

→ *WB, ex. 5*   **4** Individual answers.

→ *WB, ex. 5*   **5** **a** Individual answers.

b Als Anregung können fertige Anschreiben verwendet werden (vgl. z.B. SB, S. 250 und die „Study Pages" B14 und B15 im *OALD)*. Im Internet finden sich ebenfalls viele hilfreiche Seiten, z.B. http://career.berkeley.edu/Guide/Resume.stm · 1.8.2003.

SB, S. 211   **B Doomsday**

Source:	*Independent*, 14.8.2002
Topic:	Waiting for exam results
Text form:	Newspaper feature
Language variety:	BE
Number of words:	262
Level:	Basic/advanced
Skills/activities:	Listing options after school, comparing school systems and presenting the results

Active vocabulary: 'Doomsday' (p. 211)

apply for sth. (l. 6), course (l. 6), reconsider sth. (l. 7), reapply (l. 7), refer to sth. as sth. (l. 8), doomsday (l. 8), scared (l. 9), revise (l. 10), social life (l. 10), expectations (l. 14), a degree in (a subject) (l. 16), retake (an exam) (l. 17), dread (doing) sth. (l. 17), tension (l. 18), take a gap year (l. 19)

tasks: in particular, consider sth., rigorous

In diesem Zeitungsartikel kommt eine junge Britin zu Wort, die voller Anspannung und Ungewissheit auf den „doomsday" wartet, den Tag, an dem britische S die Ergebnisse ihrer *A-level*-Prüfungen erhalten. Auch wenn die beschriebene Gefühlslage wohl kaum interkulturelle Differenzen aufweist, werden Unterschiede zwischen britischem und deutschem Schulsystem deutlich (z.B. die Prüfungsfächer, der „doomsday" usw.). Neben der Auseinandersetzung mit den Plänen der Verfasserin zielt die Behandlung des Texts daher auf den Vergleich des deutschen mit dem britischen und dem amerikanischen Schulsystem.

Es kann davon ausgegangen werden, dass viele S bereits an den Tag der Zeugnis-ausgabe gedacht haben. Daher empfiehlt es sich, Assoziationen zu diesem Tag zu sammeln, anhand derer der Begriff „doomsday" eingeführt werden kann.

1 15 August is the day when the A-level results come out, which then decide the future of all British sixth-formers. For this reason the sixth-formers are full of apprehension. Emma Prest is particularly apprehensive because she knows she did not prepare very well for her exams, having left everything to the last minute.

2 Emma could go to university, do a gap year before going to university, work for a charity, retake her exams or get a job. Her current plans are to get a job to earn some money for travelling and for university, then to travel to the Americas. After that she intends to study, but she does not know what she will study and does not think it is that important what she studies, as she intends to work for a charity after graduating.

⬭ *Which prefix is used to indicate that something is done again? There are three examples in the text of verbs with this prefix. Find them. Then use your dictionary to find three more examples. Use them in sentences to show you have understood their meanings.* Reconsider (l. 7), reapply (l. 7), retake (l. 17).

❖ **3** **a–b** Diese Aufgabe kann sinnvoll arbeitsteilig in einem Gruppenmixverfahren bearbeitet werden. Die Klasse wird in zwei Gruppen geteilt, die über das englische bzw. US-amerikanische Schulsystem recherchieren und somit zu „Experten" des jeweiligen Systems werden. (Das schottische und das nordirische Bildungssystem bleiben hier der Einfachheit halber ausgeklammert, da sie sich aus historischen Gründen vom englischen unterscheiden.) In einer zweiten Phase setzen sich die S in Zweiergruppen zusammen, die aus je einem Experten für jedes Bildungssystem bestehen, und stellen

den anderen jeweils ihr System vor. Die KV „The English and Welsh Education System" und „The US Education System" (vgl. S. 421 bzw. S. 422) können anschließend zur Sicherung dienen. Werden einzelne Informationen mit Tipp-Ex überdeckt, können die KVs auch zur Überprüfung der Kenntnisse genutzt werden.

4 Possible answers:
The A-Level system usually requires more intense study of a limited area. This is due to the fact that only three subjects are studied. Moreover, students are required to sit different papers in one particular subject (cf. '14 exams', l. 9).
In Germany, each *Land* has its own regulations, but it could be said that the *Abitur* requires more knowledge over a wider field, since German students have to study a larger number of subjects and cannot opt out of the main subjects such as German, English and Maths. In the *Abitur*, they have to sit exams in four or five subjects.

C Applying to a US University

Source:	Website of UC Berkeley Office of Undergraduate Admissions, August 2002
Topic:	Information on applying to a US university
Text form:	Information brochure
Language variety:	BE
Number of words:	444
Level:	Basic/advanced
Skills/activities:	Writing a personal statement, working with collocations, extracting information from a chart, debating

Lern-vokabular

Active vocabulary: 'Applying to a US University' (p. 212)

vital (l. 2), apply to (a university) (l. 3), evaluate sth. (l. 4), academic record (l. 5), accomplishment(s) (l. 7), activity (l. 7), gain insight into sth. (l. 7), evident (l. 10), a frame of reference (l. 14), initiative (l. 16), motivation (l. 16), leadership (l. 16), persistence (l. 17), overcome sth. (l. 18), challenge (l. 18), internship (l. 21), establish a goal (l. 24), effective (l. 30), allow time for sth. (l. 33), contribute to sth. (l. 35)

Didaktisch-methodische Hinweise

Immer mehr S wählen eine Universität im Ausland für ihr künftiges Studium. Daher ist die Kenntnis der Aufnahmebedingungen und der Auswahlverfahren dieser Universitäten für sie von besonderer Relevanz. Hier lernen sie mit dem „personal statement" ein Schriftstück kennen, das viele US-amerikanische Universitäten zur Bewerberauswahl verwenden, das aber dem deutschen, bisher v.a. an Noten und Wartezeiten orientierten System widerspricht. Die S erfahren, was sich die renommierte „University of California at Berkeley" von diesen Bewerbungsschreiben verspricht und welche Erwartungen ein Bewerber erfüllen muss. Neben der pragmatischen Zielsetzung, die S zu befähigen, selbst ein solches „personal statement" zu verfassen, wird mit diesem Text auch die Absicht verfolgt, den S einen Einblick in das US-amerikanische Bildungswesen zu geben.

Unterrichts-tipps

Als Einstieg eignet sich eine kurze Verständigung über das Bewerbungsverfahren für eine deutsche Universität, um den Kontrast zum Verfahren Berkeleys deutlicher hervortreten zu lassen:

Direct registration for degree courses with no restriction of admissions; application to the university if the university restricts the number of students; application to the ZVS if there is a nationwide restriction of admissions; ZVS: a central organization which admits and places applicants in universities; criteria: *numerus clausus* (i.e. a grade point average in your school-leaving exam beyond which you are not admitted to a specific course) and waiting period; 20% of university places: allotted after interviews.

Info

Personal statement: Applicants to Berkeley are required to write 1000 words in answer to three questions. Two of the answers must be of approximately 200 words each, while the third must be of at least 600 words. The student can decide which of the three questions he or she wishes to write most about.

The first question is headed 'Academic Preparation': 'How have you taken advantage of the educational opportunities you have had to prepare for college?'

The second question is headed 'Potential to Contribute': 'Tell us about a talent, experience, contribution or personal quality you will bring to the University of California.'

The third is headed 'Open-ended': 'Is there anything you would like us to know about you or your academic record that you have not had the opportunity to describe elsewhere in this application?'

Lösungs-hinweise **1** Students who have the following qualities: creativity, intellectual curiosity and achievement, exceptional personal or academic recognition, unusual talent or ability, initiative, motivation, leadership, persistence, service to others, special potential, substantial experience with other cultures, the ability to overcome or manage significant challenges (cf. ll. 15–18.). The university is interested in these things because applicants often have very similar academic records (cf. ll. 4–5), and to decide between candidates it is useful to know what other qualities a student has.

2 **a–b** Individual answers.

3 **a** apply to a campus (l. 2), discover/evaluate distinctions (ll. 4–5), review sb.'s personal statement / academic record / accomplishments / activities (ll. 6–7), gain insight into sth. (l. 7), afford sb. an opportunity (ll. 8–9), provide sb. with information (l. 9), consider achievement (l. 12), have an opportunity (l. 13), respond to an opportunity (l. 13), seek certain characteristics (ll. 14–15), overcome/manage a challenge (l. 18), address a prompt (l. 19), focus on an aspect of sth. (l. 20), an experience changes an attitude / crystallizes a conviction (l. 23), establish a goal (l. 24), a quality emerges (ll. 24–25), give sb. a sense of sth. (ll. 26–27), make a choice (l. 28), allow time for sth. (l. 33), evaluate sb.'s ability (l. 34).

b Individual answers.

4 The difference in housing, food and utilities indicates that a residence hall is much more expensive than renting a flat – this is due also to the fact that the residence hall calculates that all meals will be eaten on campus; living at home is obviously the cheapest option. Personal expenses are estimated to be highest for people living off campus and away from home because they spend more for certain living needs like furniture and cooking utensils, as well as for activities and entertainment that people living on campus may not have to pay for. For transportation the situation is reversed. People living on campus rarely need to use a car or public transport because they are already at the university. Students who live off campus but not at home will try to find a flat near the university, so their expenses for transport may be lower than those living at home.

5 Individual work.

SB, S. 214 **D Victoria, not Vicky** Andrea Levy

Source:	*Never Far from Nowhere*, 1996
Topic:	Meeting other students on the first day at college
Text form:	Novel (extract)
Language variety:	BE
Number of words:	569
Level:	Basic/advanced
Skills/activities:	Describing a person's character, telling the story from another perspective

Lern-vokabular **Active vocabulary: 'Victoria, not Vicky' (p. 214)**

make an entrance (ll. 3–4), smile at sb. (l. 11), introduce yourself (l. 12), turn to sb. (l. 12), titter (ll. 13–14), inhale deeply (l. 38), wash your hair (l. 42), look a fright (l. 42), tell sb. the truth (l. 42), stink of sth. (l. 43), move away from sb./sth. (l. 44), delicate (l. 50)

Didaktisch-
methodische
Hinweise

Mit seiner Thematik stellt dieser fiktionale Text ein Gegengewicht zu den pragmatisch ausgerichteten anderen Texten dieser *section* dar, da er die emotionale Seite eines Neuanfangs in den Blick rückt. Vivien, die Hauptfigur dieses Romanauszugs, fühlt sich aus mehreren Gründen unbehaglich in ihrem neuen Kurs am College: Sie kommt zu spät und wird von allen anderen Studierenden im Raum angestarrt. Die Begegnung mit der jovialen, selbstbewussten Victoria schüchtert sie ein; sie fühlt sich ungepflegt und schämt sich ihrer ärmlichen Herkunft.

Unterrichts-
tipps

Der Einstieg könnte über eine Sammlung der stärksten Angstfaktoren an einem ersten Tag an der Hochschule oder dem Ausbildungsplatz sein, die die S in Gruppen erarbeiten und im Plenum vorstellen. Anschließend wird der Text still gelesen. Um die Spannung zwischen Victoria und der Ich-Erzählerin erlebbar zu machen, bietet sich ein Vortrag des Dialogs mit verteilten Rollen an.

Info

Andrea Levy (born 1956) was born in London to Jamaican parents. She has written three novels: *Every Light in the House Burnin'* (1994), *Never Far from Nowhere* (1996) and *Fruit of the Lemon* (1999). In each of these novels she explores the problems faced by black British-born children of Jamaican immigrants.

Never Far from Nowhere is set on a council estate that forms the backdrop to the lives of two very different sisters, Olive and Vivien, whose parents are from Jamaica. The novel is about the tension between local identity and ethnicity, as the two sisters move in different directions. Olive considers herself to be authentically 'black' and longs to 'return' to Jamaica, while Vivien, who has a lighter complexion than Olive, 'passes' as white.

Lösungs-
hinweise

1
- She arrives late, the introductory session has already started.
- Her hair is untidy.
- She is 'puffing, sweating and cursing' (l. 4).
- She has a Torremolinos sticker (a working-class holiday destination) on her bag.
- She is not wearing deodorant and has BO, due to the hot and difficult walk from the station.
- She feels intimidated by immaculate, self-assured Vivian.
- She feels ashamed of her poor background.

2 Victoria is characterized both indirectly and directly.

The <u>indirect characterization</u> is in her own words, which make her sound very self-assured, indeed almost conceited. She wants to be addressed by her full name (cf. ll. 36–37); this makes her appear snobbish; she then talks about the fact that she was a debutante, which is a way of showing that she comes from a wealthy family; this makes her sound rather arrogant. She then talks about her appearance in a way that seems to be fishing for compliments (cf. ll. 41–42).

The <u>direct characterization</u> comes from Vivien's comments about her. There is a fair amount of physical description (cf. ll. 27–31, 48–51). Vivien lets the reader know that she does not particularly like Victoria: 'her face was so pretty it was boring' (ll. 27–28), 'lifeless hair' (l. 31), 'they all looked the same to me' (l. 31), but also by the description in ll. 48–51, which leads her to deny her origins, i.e. she recognizes that Victoria is not like her.

The effect of Vivien's description is to make the reader dislike her. Victoria's own words further add to the negative impression, as she comes across as too self-confident and arrogant.

3 Stretching the 'BO' test out over several paragraphs has two effects: Firstly, it adds humour to the passage, as Vivien is trying to find out whether she smells or not, while having a conversation with a girl who seems immaculate. It also adds tension, as the reader wants to know whether indeed she does smell or not. The irony is that she discloses the fact that she 'stinks of BO' (l. 43) at exactly the point when Victoria is saying that she herself probably 'looks an absolute fright' (l. 42).

4 Die S können hierfür auch andere Darstellungsformen als eine Erzählung wählen (z.B. Victorias innerer Monolog, eine E-mail, ein Gespräch mit ihrer Freundin, ein Telefongespräch, bei dem nur Victorias Gesprächsanteile hörbar sind, usw.)

Individual answers.

SB, S. 215 **E Off to College**

VIDEO

Source:	*College Girls*, 2002
Topic:	Students moving into halls of residence
Text form:	TV documentary
Language variety:	BE
Length:	9 min
Level:	Basic/advanced
Skills/activities:	Viewing skills, writing a diary entry

Didaktisch-methodische Hinweise

Dieser Ausschnitt aus einem Fernsehdokumentarfilm zeigt junge Frauen an ihrem ersten Tag an der Oxford University (vgl. Video/DVD und das Transkript auf S. 423). Sie schreiben sich ein, beziehen ihre Zimmer und verabschieden sich von ihren Eltern. Wie in Text D stehen auch hier die Emotionen der Studentinnen am Beginn eines neuen Lebensabschnitts im Vordergrund; hier jedoch sind sie nicht fiktional. Der Schwerpunkt der Behandlung liegt auf *viewing skills* und auf kreativem Schreiben.

Unterrichts-tipps

Bevor die S den Auszug sehen, sollten sie Aufgaben 1 und 2 lesen, um sich Notizen machen zu können. Für Aufgabe 3 werden sie den Auszug noch weitere zwei Mal sehen müssen.

Lösungs-hinweise

1

- Picturesque Oxford at the start of the new academic year (autumn);
- the entrance to St Hilda's College as new students arrive;
- students who are already at the college helping new students register and showing them their rooms;
- new students in their rooms, reacting to their rooms, expressing hopes and worries;
- new students saying goodbye to their parents.

VIDEO **2** Laura has always been influenced by her father. She admires him a lot and has always thought that whatever he says and does is right. She thinks it is time she gained a little distance from him and made up her own mind about some issues. She needs to prove that she can be independent.

VIDEO **3**

- In the opening scenes the use of filters and of shooting against the sunlight produces very romantic images so that at the start of the film it is the myth and dreamy beauty of Oxford that is emphasized. The fact that the film is made from a moving bus (and then the camera always moves past objects, e.g. on the river) gives a general impression of the city.
- When the film cuts to the students arriving the camera is handheld. This has the effect of (i) suddenly bringing us back to the real world of human beings and

(ii) putting us in the same position as the newcomers. The camera makes the viewer feel as if he or she is there too.
- In the rooms (and in the first shots of Laura and Natasha arriving at St Hilda's) the director uses 'point of view' shots, i.e. shots taken so that we are seeing the room or the view from the position of the student who is looking at it. The camera is directly behind the girls. Again this device helps us identify with the student.
- The use of the 'flashback' with Laura's father gives context and some depth to at least one of the characters.

3 Individual answers.

SB, S. 216 ## Getting Along in English

Didaktisch-methodische Hinweise
Auf dieser Seite bekommen die S sprachliche Hilfestellungen für die Suche nach einer geeigneten Unterkunft bei einem längeren Auslandsaufenthalt, z.B. während eines Studiums, eines Praktikums oder eines *gap year*.
Die S entschlüsseln zunächst eine Wohnungsanzeige mit ihren typischen Abkürzungen und ordnen dann drei weitere Anzeigen möglichen Mietern mit ihren besonderen Bedürfnissen zu. In drei Dialogen zwischen Wohnungsinteressenten und Vermietern (vgl. CD2, *tracks* 30–32 und das Transkript auf S. 426) üben die S zielgerichtetes Hörverstehen und sammeln Anregungen für Dialoge, die sie selbst führen sollen.

Lösungs-hinweise
1
'dble': double – means not too tiny;
'gdn': garden – means ground floor or basement (giving on to a small garden);
'mod cons': modern conveniences – can mean many things, e.g. washing machine, dishwater, etc.;
'suit': suitable for – means that what follows are qualities that the applicant should have;
'n/s': non-smoking;
'BR': British Rail – means a railway station is nearby to get one quickly into central London;
'months dep': a month's deposit – means one month's rent is required in advance as a deposit;
'ref req': reference required – means a written reference from your employer, your previous landlord/-lady or someone with a good job in the community (e.g. lawyer, doctor) is required;
'prof': professional – means that the landlord/-lady only accepts somebody with a job requiring a high level of education;
'pcm': per calender month.

2

a) The male nurse should try for the room in Hackney because the two people living in the flat also have unusual work patterns, so the nurse's shifts should not be a problem: also it's the cheapest and nurses do not earn a lot of money. Additionally there's no mention of wanting a non-smoker.

b) The female secretary should try for the room in Camden; the wording of the ad indicates that the people living there are fun-loving and there are good tube and bus connections, which means she can get to see her friends easily.

c) The teacher should try for the Clapham room because if she wants to get out of town at the weekends it is an advantage to be near a railway station. Being an animal lover means that she will probably like having a spaniel in the flat. As she is a teacher, she counts as a 'professional female'.

- Very close: here it means 'right on top of'.
- Charming: here it means run-down, old-fashioned or down at heel.
- Semi-furnished: (literally 'half-furnished') here it means almost no furniture at all, just the minimum (a bed and a small table).

CD 4 ◆◆ **a–d** Bei Aufgabe b sollten die S aufgefordert werden, auf Wortmaterial zu hören, das sie in ihren Dialogen verwenden können. Sie sollten es notieren und in Partnerarbeit austauschen.

→ *WB, ex. 6*   Individual answers.

SB, S. 217 # 3 Eveline   James Joyce

Source:	*Dubliners*, 1914
Topic:	The difficulty of deciding whether to leave home or stay
Text form:	Short story
Language variety:	IrE
Length:	1825
Level:	Basic/advanced
Skills/activities:	Tracing a character's life story, describing a character, considering pros and cons, identifying internal and external action, analysing imagery, writing a letter

Lern-vokabular

Active vocabulary: 'Eveline' (p. 217)

odour (l. 2), where on earth (l. 21), familiar (l. 22), casual (l. 28), consent to do sth. (l. 30), run away with sb. (l. 34), elated (l. 72), forbid sb. to do sth. (l. 83), quarrel with sb. (l. 85), lap (l. 87), indistinct (l. 88), remind sb. of sth. (l. 98), catch a glimpse of sth. (l. 117), distress (l. 123), grip sth. (l. 128), railing (l. 128), clutch sth. (l. 130), frenzy (l. 130), anguish (l. 131), farewell (l. 135), recognition (l. 135)
tasks: trace sth., justify sth., play a major role, achieve an effect

Didaktisch-methodische Hinweise

Mit dieser berühmten Kurzgeschichte werden die S in eine historisch wie geographisch fremde Welt versetzt. Sie erleben den Entscheidungsprozess einer jungen Irin zu Beginn des letzten Jahrhunderts mit, die sich zwischen zwei Möglichkeiten entscheiden muss: dem Verbleiben in ihrem bisherigen Zuhause, das ein Leben in einfachen Verhältnissen, mit harter Arbeit und schwierigen Beziehungen zu ihrem Vater und ihrer Vorgesetzten bedeutet, und dem Fortgehen mit ihrem Freund, das ein Leben als verheiratete, respektierte Frau in einer ganz anderen Welt, in Buenos Aires, verspricht. Joyces Hauptfigur entscheidet sich gegen das *moving out*: Sie bleibt in ihrem vertrauten Leben, das sie schließlich nicht mehr „wholly undesirable" findet (Z. 63).

Die S erhalten, bedingt durch Joyces Erzähltechnik, einen intensiven Einblick in das Innenleben der Figur Eveline. Es wird fast keine externe Handlung geschildert: Alle Dialoge, Rückblicke, Geschehnisse finden – scheinbar spontan und assoziativ – in Evelines Gedanken statt (vgl. auch die Lösung zu Aufgabe 5). Auf diese Weise können die S den Prozess, der zu Evelines Entscheidung führt, genau nachvollziehen.

Der Aufgabenapparat enthält Aufgaben zur detaillierten Informationsentnahme und -darstellung sowie zur Textanalyse mit dem Schwerpunkt Erzähltechnik. Die S sollen sich abschließend mit der Entscheidung Evelines auseinander setzen und darüber spekulieren, wie ihr weiteres Leben verlaufen könnte.

Unterrichts-tipps

Der Text ist sprachlich recht einfach; lediglich die komplexe Zeitstruktur mit ihren Rückblenden in verschiedene Ebenen der Vergangenheit jedoch könnte den S Schwierigkeiten bereiten. Aus diesem Grund sollte der Text als Hausaufgabe gelesen werden. Im Unterricht können die S ein Flussdiagramm anlegen, in dem sie stichwortartig Evelines Gedankengänge notieren. Auf diese Weise wird nicht nur das Verständnis gesichert, sondern auch ein Einblick in die Erzähltechnik des *interior monologue* (vgl. SB, S. 259) gegeben. Das Flussdiagramm kann an der Tafel begonnen werden:

→ *WB, ex. 3, 8, 10* „Eveline's childhood: playing with other children – her parents – change – …".

Info

James Joyce (1882–1941) was born in Dublin to an impoverished middle-class family. He was educated at Jesuit schools before attending University College, Dublin. He subsequently travelled throughout Europe, rarely returning to Ireland. While living in Trieste, he wrote *Dubliners* (1914) and most of *A Portrait of the Artist as a Young Man* (1916). During World War I he moved to Zurich, where he wrote most of *Ulysses* (1922), which was banned in the USA and Britain for many years. The book is based on the classic work of Homer, but recalls the events of one day, as Leopold Bloom's life in Dublin is narrated. Joyce lived in Paris between the two world wars, and there he finished *Finnegan's Wake* (1939). On the fall of France in 1940, he returned to Zurich, where he died. Joyce's novels are characterized by major technical innovations, especially his extensive use of interior monologue and complex networks of symbols drawn from mythology, history, and literature; he created a unique language of invented words, puns, and allusions, which often makes his works difficult to read.

Lösungs-hinweise

- As a child she used to play with friends and her brothers and sisters in a field near the house (cf. ll. 6–15).
- Since then her brothers and sisters have all moved away or, in the case of Ernest, died (cf. ll. 48–50).
- Her mother is also dead. Since then she seems to have looked after two young children and her father (cf. ll. 15, 61–62)
- Fear of her father has given her health problems ('palpitations', l. 45)
- She found a job in the Stores, which she does not like (cf. ll. 33–40).
- She met Frank, a sailor, and they started seeing each other (cf. ll. 66–82).
- Frank and her father quarreled so they started to see each other secretly (cf. ll. 85–86).
- Frank suggested they move to Buenos Aires, a proposal she accepted (cf. ll. 30, 65–66).

2 **a** Facts: he has a home in Buenos Aires, is fond of music, likes to sing, started life as a deck boy on a ship, has since been on many ships and to many countries, somehow came into money.

Impression: The reader has very little information to form an opinion about Frank, but there is some lingering doubt about his background; he seems to be a shady character. He could act as the saviour in Eveline's small world.

b
- There is almost no indication in the short story that she loves Frank, the exception being that she felt 'pleasantly confused' (l. 75) when he sang the song about the lass and the sailor.
- She seems more interested in being treated with respect (ll. 42–43).
- She finds him 'kind, manly, open-hearted' (ll. 64–65), not exactly words used for passion.
- She seems to find him attractive (ll. 69–70), and she enjoys the attention he gives her.
- At first she found it exciting to be with a man (ll. 75–76) – not necessarily with Frank – and only later did she begin to 'like' him (l. 76).

- She seems to think of Frank as someone who can save her from her dreary life (ll. 110–113), but he would only 'perhaps' give her love (l. 111).
- The final indication that she did not love Frank is the final scene: Frank, she felt, would 'drown her' (l. 128); she chose not to go with him, and her eyes showed 'no sign of love' (l. 135).

3 **a** Reasons to stay at home:
- She has her memories there.
- She is surrounded by familiar objects.
- She has shelter and food there.
- Her life at home is not 'wholly undesirable' (l. 63).
- She knows her father will miss her, and he is getting old and can be nice at times.
- She promised her mother 'to keep the home together as long as she could' (l. 99).

b Reasons to leave home:
- She has to work very hard at home.
- She dislikes her job, where she is not treated with respect.
- She believes she will be treated with respect in her new home.
- Her father is prone to violence and has threatened her, and there was no one there to protect her from him.
- Her father is difficult, especially about money.
- Her father tried to drive away the man she was dating.
- She has a right to be happy, to have a life.
The ranking will be subjective.

Look again at ll. 6–113. Identify which lines deal with Eveline's past, which with the present, and which with the future. What does this say about her and the likelihood that she will leave home?
Past references: ll. 6–19, 23–29, 36–39, 43, 45–47, 67–86, 90–94, 98–109

Present: ll. 20–22, 31–33, 43–44, 47–62, 64–65, 87–90, 95–98, 110

Future: ll. 22–23, 30, 33–36, 40–43, 64–66, 90, 110–113
There is a clear predominance of past and present references, showing that Eveline is preoccupied with the past and with her life as it is. She is not thinking of a life with Frank, and when she does it is in very abstract terms. From this we might conclude that she is inclined to stay at home, although she may not be aware of that herself.

4 She opts for a continuation of the same dreary life she has been leading so far. She will probably stay at home and do what she feels is 'her duty' (l. 120). There is a possibility that her life will be a bit different because of her experience with Frank. He has made her feel special and offered her opportunities she had never dreamed of before. She knows she is desirable, which could increase her self-confidence and make her more assertive in dealing with her father and her boss, Miss Gavan. On the other hand, having once given up a chance to experience freedom she may lead a life of quiet desperation like her mother.

5 **a** Most of the story takes place in Eveline's mind. The only exceptions are:
- the opening, where she is sitting in the window (ll. 1–6: '... way home');

- interruptions of her train of thought where the reader is reminded that she is physically present, e.g. 'she looked around the room' (l. 20), 'she stood up' (l. 110);

- the scene at the quay (ll. 114–135). Even here where there is external action and where Frank for the first time is physically present (unlike her father, who is never present), there are examples of internal action (ll. 119–120, 121–123, 128, 130).

The rest of the scenes are Eveline's reminiscences and hopes. Under the deceptive appearance of memory by association, she recalls her life in a very orderly fashion although with many side glances as she meditates selectively on things she sees before her:

- She remembers the field in which she and others once played until a man from Belfast bought it and built houses on it (cf. ll. 6–8).
- The word 'home' (l. 19) brings her back to her present, and she looks around her room; she notices the picture of a priest, a school-friend of her father's. The priest is a half-forgotten subject of a yellowing photograph. Next to his picture are the promises made to Blessed Mary Margaret Alacoque (cf. ll. 20–29).
- Eveline then considers her job as a department store clerk under her abusive superior. She hates being treated as an inferior in the store and this allows her to consider her future as a respected wife (unlike her dead mother). She considers her miserable life with her violent father (cf. ll. 33–40).
- She reminisces about Frank's courtship and his conflict with her father (cf. ll. 66–86).
- She recalls her father before her mother's death (cf. ll. 90–94).
- The sound of a street organ reminds her of the night that her mother died. Her mother seems to have slowly lost her mind (cf. ll. 97–109).
- Eveline then experiences panic at what she sees as her fate if she remains in Ireland. Frank will be her rescue (cf. ll. 110–113).

b By telling the story of Eveline's life through her thoughts, Joyce has allowed us to look inside her character and gain an intimate knowledge of her. We feel we know her much better than we could if we had only observed her outward behaviour or had the occasional glimpse of her thoughts. It takes us longer to read Eveline's thoughts than it takes her to have them, so we experience her entire thought process and feel the agony of her decision. This, in turn, has the effect of leaving us as much in the dark about what Eveline will decide as the character herself, and makes us want to read to the end.

◯ *How does the author give structure to the short story despite his use of interior monologue?*
By starting with and returning to the narrative present (cf. task 5a), with Eveline in the window, Joyce gives his story unity of time and place. This helps to structure it, reminding the reader that everything else is background. Her thoughts do not jump around as much as they might in real life, and Joyce is careful to provide some time references when telling the story of Eveline's life.

 6 Die S sollten ggf. darauf hingewiesen werden, dass *imagery* im Sinn nichtwörtlicher Bedeutung verwendet wird und in vielfältiger Form erscheinen kann (vgl. das Glossar, SB, S. 268). Da es vielen S schwer fällt, bildhafte Sprache zu identifizieren, können als Hilfestellung einige Bilder genannt werden, die die S deuten sollen. Eine eindeutige Zuordnung der Bilder in die beiden Kategorien ist oft nicht möglich.

Images of being closed in:
- dusty heavy curtains (cf. ll. 2–3, 96): keep out the freedom of the outside world;
- 'dust' (l. 21): makes Eveline's world seem darker and gloomier;
- yellow photo of priest (cf. l. 24): shows, on the one hand, how Eveline's world is decaying, and, on the other hand, it shows how closed her world is: although she has seen the photo every day for her entire life, she has yet to find out who exactly it depicts;
- 'broken harmonium' (l. 25): symbolizes the run-down and dysfunctional ('harmonium' ~ harmony) world in which Eveline lives;
- 'mist' (l. 121): when Eveline is at the quay, away from home, she is still surrounded by a mist which prevents her seeing into the distance, where 'freedom' awaits her;
- 'barrier' (l. 133): Frank rushes 'beyond the barrier' and is now free; Eveline stays behind, with the barrier, like prison bars, between her and 'freedom' (cf. 'iron railing', l. 128).

<u>Images of being free:</u>
- Frank (the name means 'free' in Middle English) is the person who is supposed to save her from the narrow confines of her world, but he comes across as a shady character;
- 'the window' (ll. 1, 95): opens out in the world, but here only serves to emphasize the closed in feeling of Evelin's house and the life there (so it can also be seen as an image of confinement);
- 'cinder path' (l. 6): leads away from the house where Eveline is trapped, but at the same time it is a dark path which no longer leads to open fields;
- 'bright brick houses with shining roofs' (l. 9): the outside world is brighter than Eveline's world, this again serves to emphasize her imprisonment;
- 'England' (l. 18), 'Melbourne' (l. 29): two far-away places that symbolize escape from Eveline's little world, but they are places others have escaped to, thus emphasizing how entrapped Eveline is;
- 'down somewhere in the country' (l. 50): the outside world is a place where her brother can go but from which Eveline is excluded;
- 'night-boat' (l. 65): although this is Eveline's escape route to another life, her boat is to leave at night, meaning she will not be able to see the freedom that awaits her;
- 'Buenos Ayres' (l. 66) (the name means 'good airs') and can be seen as a contrast to Eveline's dusty little house;
- *The Bohemian Girl* (l. 72): bohemianism means freedom, so the opera she sees with Frank seems to be an image of freedom;
- 'street organ' (l. 97): the music should be a pleasant air, but it only makes her relive the memories of her mother's death in the house where Eveline is trapped.

By making extensive use of images of freedom and limitation, Joyce has the reader feel the conflict Eveline finds herself in. The experience is sensory. The reader smells the dusty and stifling atmosphere of Eveline's home. Through the wide open doors of the shed one catches a glimpse of the freedom awaiting Eveline, and feels the cold iron railings that mark the end of her attempt to break out of the world confining her.

7 Bei der Beantwortung der Frage ist zu beachten, dass der Text keinen ausdrücklichen Hinweis darauf gibt, dass Frank tatsächlich nach Buenos Aires fährt. Es wäre auch möglich, dass er in Dublin bleibt.

a–b Individual answers.

SB, S. 221 # Watch Your Language

Lösungs-
hinweise

 a

1 I want / hope / would like to ...
2 I expect to do / I am going to do ...
3 ... so I should / hope to / expect to get ...
4 By then I will have completed ...
5 I am taking / am planning to take / am going to take a gap year ...
6 If you hire me ...
7 Since I will be finishing / will finish school ...
8 I intend to / am going to do ...

b All entries (except for 'should' in 3 and the *if*-clause in 6) can be found in the *CEG* index under 'future time: ways of expressing future time'.

1 Cf. *CEG* §106
2 Cf. *CEG* §106, §98a
3 Cf. *CEG* §47a, b (Index under 'possibility' or under 'probability', §106
4 Cf. *CEG* §104
5 Cf. *CEG* §99, §106, §98a
6 Cf. *CEG* §252 (Index under 'conditional sentences')
7 Cf. *CEG* §106c, §102a, §99, §96
8 Cf. *CEG* §106b, §106a, §98a

2 The students need to revise 'ways of expressing future time' (*CEG* §95–106) and, to a lesser extent, modals and *if*-clauses. These are grammar topics best done using a standard learner's grammar.

→ *WB, ex. 9* **3** **a** The *will*-future is used to make predictions or assumptions about the future and to express spontaneous decisions such as offers or promises (cf. *CEG* §95–96).
The *going to*-future is used to talk about intentions and plans as well as things that are more or less sure to happen based on signs of them happening (cf. *CEG* §97–98).
The future perfect is used for actions or events that will be complete at a point of time in the future (cf. *CEG*, §103–105).
'Shall' is sometimes used in formal British English instead of 'will' in the first person, whereas 'should' is used to express obligation, to give advice or talk about something that will probably happen (cf. *CEG* §95, 35).
'Be about to' is used to talk about something that will happen in the very near future (cf. *CEG* §106c).
'Expect/hope to' are used to say what the speaker feels or thinks about the future (cf. *CEG* §122).

b In a little more than a year's time, I will finish / will be finishing / expect to finish school. But I'm going to look for something to do with my life before that. I should have good grades in my *Abitur*, so I shouldn't have problems getting a place at university. The questions is: What am I going to do until then? I'm going to / I want to start talking to people who have done volunteer work in developing countries soon – maybe that would be a good idea.

c
1 Hopefully / I hope the position will still be open in six months.
2 By then I will have finished/completed all the necessary courses successfully / passed all the necessary course exams / got all the necessary qualifications.
3 With my yodelling diploma / certificate and two year's experience / two years of yodelling experience I'll be able to apply/look for a job anywhere. I'll probably go to America with it.
4 They'll welcome/greet me there with open arms. I've read that they will need at least 10,000 yodellers in the States by 2015.

Topic Vocabulary: 'Moving Out'

The World of Education
leave school
finish school
A-levels (BE)
GCSEs (BE)
high-school diploma (AE)
graduate from school (AE)
high school graduation (AE)
school-leaver (BE)
high-school graduate (AE)
revise (BE)/study/prepare for an exam
sit (BE)/take an exam
pass an exam
fail an exam
retake an exam
get good/bad grades
attend / go to college/university
receive/get a scholarship/bursary
do a degree (in a subject) (BE)
major in (a subject) (AE)
study (a subject)
get a student grant
pay back a student grant
apply for a student grant
take out a loan
(cheap/affordable) student
　accommodation/housing
live on campus
have time on your hands
see the world
take a year off
take a gap year

The World of Work
decide on a career
gain/get work experience
look for a temporary/full-time job
support yourself
internship
intern
work as an intern (for a company)

Moving towards Independence
start out in life
leave home
move to a big city
share a flat
run away
live on the streets
move out
move in with sb.
grow/become independent from sb.
get along on your own
have some freedom

SB, S. 205
(cf. TM, p. 402)

Free!

Informal English

The text contains many examples of informal English. Match the following words and phrases with their definitions. Then put a German translation into the space below the phrase.

1 have time on your hands (l. 5)

_____

2 find yourself (l. 6)

_____

3 a beat-up convertible (l. 7)

_____

4 stuff your face (l. 8)

_____

5 flat-out (l. 13)

_____

6 itchy (l. 20)

_____

7 hit the highway (l. 20)

_____

8 bite your thumb at sb. (l. 21)

_____

9 buddy (l. 35)

_____

10 catch sb.'s drift (l. 38)

_____

11 pee sth. away (ll. 41–42)

_____

12 money doesn't grow on trees
    (ll. 44–45)

_____

A start travelling

B restless, wanting
   to move

C eat a lot

D friend

E money needs to
   be earned

F spend sth. in a frivo-
   lous way

G discover more about
   who you are

H indicate to sb. that you
   dislike them

I have nothing much to do

J completely, in a direct way

K an old and damaged car
   with an open top

L understand what sb. is
   trying to say

SB, p. 211
(cf. TM, p. 407)

Doomsday

The English and Welsh Education System

Age	Institution					Certificates/Degrees
26 25 24	University (postgraduate studies)					Doctor of Philosophy (PhD)
23 22	University (postgraduate studies)					Master of Arts (MA) Master of Science (MSc)
21	University		Polytechnic			Bachelor of Arts (BA) Bachelor of Science (BSc)
20 19	(undergraduate studies)					
18 17	Public/ Private School	Grammar School	Secondary Modern School	Compre- hensive School	Sixth-form College	A-levels (3 subjects); also AS-levels
16 15 14 13						General National Vocatio- nal Qualification (GNVQ)
12 11 10 9 8	Prep School		Primary School			GCSE (General Certificate of Secondary Education, 9 subjects)
7 6 5	Private Infant School					
4 3		Nursery School				
	Private school system (7% of all pupils)	**State school system**				

Compulsory education (vertical label spanning ages 5–18)

SB, p. 211
(cf. TM, p. 407)

Doomsday

The US Education System

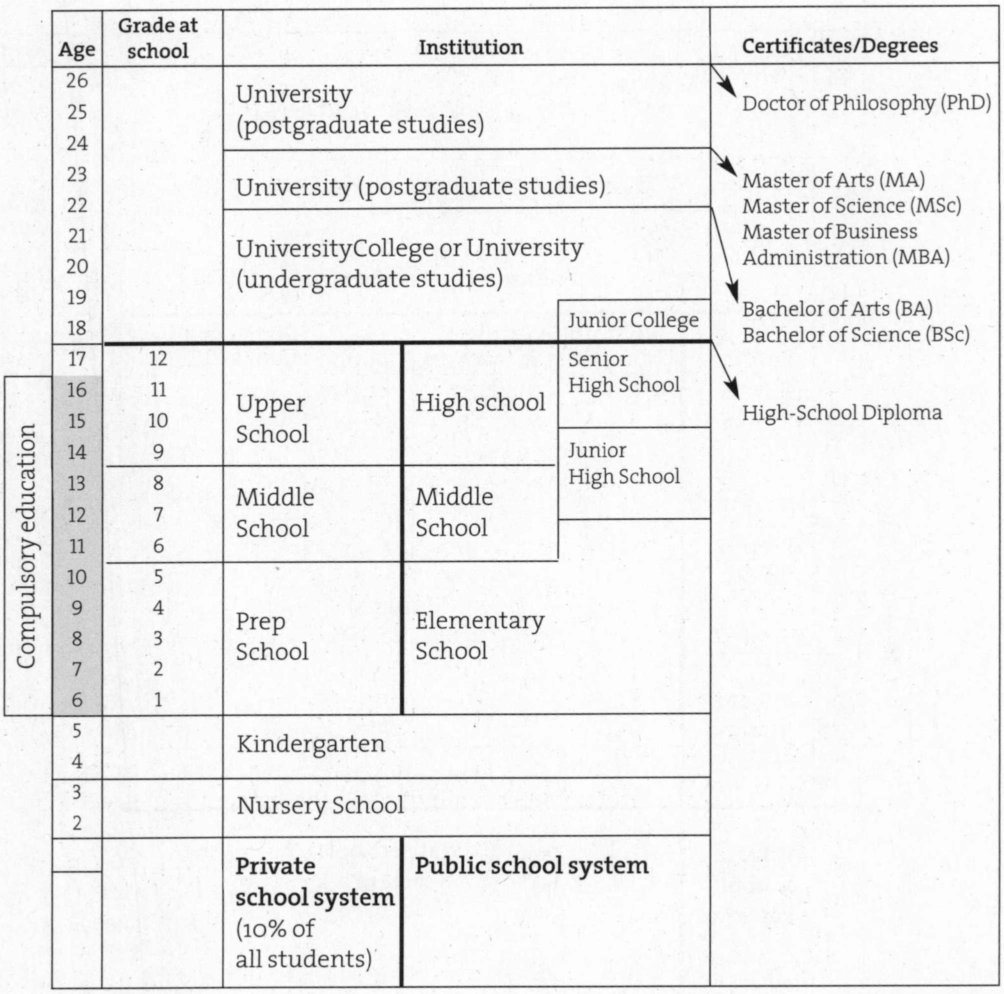

Age	Grade at school	Institution				Certificates/Degrees
26 25 24		University (postgraduate studies)				Doctor of Philosophy (PhD)
23 22		University (postgraduate studies)				Master of Arts (MA) Master of Science (MSc) Master of Business Administration (MBA)
21 20 19 18		UniversityCollege or University (undergraduate studies)			Junior College	Bachelor of Arts (BA) Bachelor of Science (BSc)
17 16 15 14	12 11 10 9	Upper School	High school	Senior High School		High-School Diploma
				Junior High School		
13 12 11	8 7 6	Middle School	Middle School			
10 9 8 7 6	5 4 3 2 1	Prep School	Elementary School			
5 4		Kindergarten				
3 2		Nursery School				
		Private school system (10% of all students)	**Public school system**			

Compulsory education (vertical label at left of table)

TRANSKRIPTE

CD ## A Fantasy Journey

SB, p. 201   *Kids:*   *Ciao! Tschüss! Wiedersehen!*
     Task 5   *Voice:*   *Abitur* is over. The party is over. School is behind you forever. Close your eyes ... relax. It's time for bed ... time for sleep ...

It's time to put school right behind you, to go to sleep and to wake up to a new life. What might that new life be? Where might it be? Relax ... come with me in your dreams ...

Listen ... beyond the music ... what do you hear? Seagulls? Yes, seagulls ... circling up in the blue, blue sky and calling to one another ... and the sea itself ... you can hear the waves lapping at the shore ... coming in, going out ... coming in, going out ... you can smell the sea, feel the warmth of the sun on your body ... and the gentle breeze ... you hear it rustle in the palm trees ... you run the sand through your fingers ... you feel free ... aimless ... relaxed ... no pressure, no purpose, no goal ... just the sun and the sea ...

Do you dream of going to a tropical island? A year away from it all? A life away from it all?

Or does your journey take you straight to university? Listen ...

The buzz of the lecture hall.... It's crowded, there's someone sitting on either side of you, your shoulders are touching ... it's hot ... you hear papers rustle ... pens scratch ... people coughing ... the lecture is interesting ... you look round, most of the students are listening, concentrating ... it feels good to be with all these people ... to share this new knowledge ... to share thoughts about life, the world, the future ...

Someone drops a book ... that dream is over. Is it yours? Will you go to college or university?

Or is home life what you think of most? Your own home ... a partner ... children ... it's evening ... you can hear the meat sizzling in the frying pan ... the smell of good home cooking ... the sound of the potatoes boiling ... and the baby gurgling in its high chair ... home is warm and light and cosy ... the baby smiles at you ... it's the most important thing in your life now ... you must look after it and protect it ... it bangs a spoon on the table in front of it ... you laugh ... it laughs ... in your own home you feel safe, contented ... is that your dream?

Or is your dream a different one altogether? ... Go there ... now ... listen to the sounds ... smell the smells ... feel the place ... see the people ... let yourself go there ... go ...

And now the journey is coming to an end. Come back now ... slowly ... gently ... back to the classroom ... back to the present.

VIDEO ## Off to College

SB, p. 215   *Guide:*   Where is the university? People often ask us, 'Where is the university?' Well, there's no campus as such. If you're successful, you'll be given a tutor of the subject you want to study and you'll meet your tutor on a one-to-one or two-to-one basis each week to be given reading, to hand in your essay ...

            Presenter: It is autumn in Oxford. They call it Michaelmas. Once on this river a don at the university began telling the story of *Alice in Wonderland*. And in Oxford there is still something of wonderland.

Guide:	Where is the university? Then the University Church. Very much the centre of things at one time. And the History of Science Museum here ...
Presenter:	In Oxford, the university is everywhere.
Guide:	There are 39 colleges all over the city. Each college is completely individual. You live in your college. You eat in your college. And over there on the left with shutters, is St. Hilda's College. That's the last all-women college, the last single-sex college.
Laura:	Hi, do you know where I'm supposed to ... go ...?
Nicole:	Are you a fresher?
Laura:	I am.
Nicole:	Do you want to sign up and get all the paper work and stuff?
Laura:	Okay, alright.
Nicole:	Okay. What's your name?
Laura:	Laura Pascal.
Nicole:	Hi, I'm Nicole. Do you know what building you're living in?
Laura:	Er, Garden 302.
Nicole:	Garden 302.
Gillian:	Excuse me. Hi! Are you Afshan? ... I'm Gutienne. I'm the welfare officer. Vice-President. If you'd like to take the car round here and then I'll give you your keys and everything.
Afshan:	Do I need my, erm, like ...?
Gillian:	You don't need anything. No. You don't need anything at the moment. No.
Natasha:	Is this where I come to get my key?
Girl:	Yeh.
Natasha:	Yeh.
Cheryl:	Hi. Are you a fresher?
Natasha:	Yeh.
Cheryl:	What's your name?
Natasha:	Uh, Natasha Rodrington.
Cheryl:	Right. Let's get your key.
Natasha:	I'm really scared.
Cheryl:	Have you just come, yeh?
Natasha:	Yeh.
Cheryl:	Yeh. Where do you live?
Natasha:	Crystal Palace. In London.
Cheryl:	Oh, so it's not that far.
Natasha:	No.
Nicole:	Just follow! Ok, right. You know where everything is. That's South.
Laura:	Uhuh.
Nicole:	Bad food and general administrative stuff.
Gillian:	How long did it take you to drive down?
Afshan:	Uh, ages!
Gillian:	Yeh?
Afshan:	I thought we were lost.
Gillian:	No! You've got a mild Welsh accent.
Afshan:	Have I?
Gillian:	South Wales. Yes.
Cheryl:	There's a bath in there.
Natasha:	Alright.
Gillian:	Okay, this is your welcoming letter and your fresher's pack and just tells you what's going on.

Nicole:	Are you kind of excited? Nervous?
Laura:	Er, oh, yeh! I've got butterflies in my stomach all of a sudden.
Natasha:	Feels like a dodgy hotel.
Nicole:	Right, here we are.
Laura:	Aha. Great. OK, which key is it?
Natasha:	Oh!
Cheryl:	This is your room.
Natasha:	Hello, room!
Laura:	Wahey! Well, it's er ... lots of character.
Gillian:	Okay? So this is your room. It's quite spacious.
Afshan:	Yeh.
Gillian:	And then there's quite a lot of storage space here. And up there as well.
Afshan:	Alright.
Gillian:	You can leave stuff over there, over the vacation if you want.
Afshan:	Oh, I can, can I?
Gillian:	Well you can. You have to lock it yourself.
Afshan:	Okay.
Gillian:	Okay? Right I have to go now.
Afshan:	Alright then.
Gillian:	Bye.
Afshan:	Bye.
Interviewer:	Well, this is it. What do you think?
Afshan:	What do I think? Well, it's not as nice as the room I had like when I came up for my interview but I've got a nice view. Yeh. It's okay. It's nice. Just got to make it home.
Laura:	Yeh, it's alright. It's alright. I'm not sure about this third floor business, but, um, yeh. It's, it's bigger and nicer than I thought. I'm going to have to get something on these walls. It looks really bare, doesn't it? Look at the bed!
Natasha:	It's alright actually. It's not as big as the one I stayed in before but it'll do. It's mine. My little retreat from now on, I say. Mmm.
Afshan:	Mum, I'm really going to miss you.
Afshan's mother:	Oh, don't start again, Afshan. Afshan, don't be like that. Okay? It's alright. Really ...
Laura's mother:	Give us a ring when you've got something to tell. You know, you don't have to ring before you want to. Just ring when either you've just got something to interesting or you feel lonely or you've forgotten something vital and want us to send it. And remember we'd, we'd like to come and see you sometime this term if you feel like it. As I said, I don't want to cramp your style. So give us a hug and ring us soon. It's going to be great. It really is. Oh, come on. So. Don't be daft. Come on, you're going to be fine.
Afshan's mother:	Okay. Okay. Okay, don't cry.
Natasha's mother:	And it's the weather, isn't it? ... So.
Natasha:	You take care, alright?
Natasha's mother:	Yes, I will. Don't worry. It won't be the first time I've gone wrong.
Natasha:	In life generally, yeh! Okay.
Natasha's mother:	Right, okay. Come on!
Natasha:	Oops. What're you doing? Okay. Bye.

Natasha's mother:	Bye, sweetheart.
Natasha:	Bye.
Voices:	*Socialist Worker, Socialist Worker ....*
Laura:	For as long as I remember, I remember watching my Dad argue with people. I totally swallow everything my father says still. Because, you know, he talks in such a way that you think, 'Oh, it must be true. Because he says it like that, it must be true.' I think, I mean, it will be good for me to get away from my father for a while. I want to get down there and prove something to myself and to my parents and to everybody that I can do this. And I can. If I try.

⬛ CD   Getting Along in English

SB, p. 216   ### Dialogue 1

Landlady:	268 5544
Man:	Er, hello. I'm phoning about the room.
Landlady:	Hold on a sec! Hey, someone turn the music down! OK. So you think you might like the room?
Man:	Well, first I'd like a few more details.
Landlady:	Well, there are three of us here, two girls and a bloke – so another bloke would be good.
Man:	What was that?
Landlady:	That? A bus hooting – sometimes people stop even though there's a red line along this bit of the high road.
Man:	No, before that.
Landlady:	Oh, the tube? You only really hear that if you have the windows out the back open.
Man:	Is the room to let at the back or the front?
Landlady:	It's at the front – so there's no problem really, is there?
Man:	Mmm. You say in the ad 'very close to shops and pubs' ...
Landlady:	Yeah, that's really good. There's the 24-hour supermarket next door and we're right over one of the best pubs – 'the Dog and Whistle' – do you know it?
Man:	As a matter of fact I do ...
Landlady:	It's really good, isn't it? Well now, tell me about you.
Man:	I don't think that'll be necessary. I really need a room where I can sleep at night! Thank you!
Landlady:	Oh!

Dialogue 2

Landlady:	Hello?
Young woman:	Is that 020 8954 231?
Landlady:	Yes.
Young woman:	I'm phoning about the room to let.
Landlady:	Yes?
Young woman:	Er, could you maybe tell me a little more about it? Erm, how big is it?
Landlady:	Big. It's got a double bed, a table and two chairs and an armchair. OK?
Young woman:	Er, that sounds great. Er ... it says in the ad 'Victorian' ...
Landlady:	Yeah – it's old.
Young woman:	Er, does everything work? I mean the kitchen and the bathroom and that?

Landlady:	Most of the time. We have an old gas cooker – but we don't, by the way, have a washing machine. That's not a problem, though, as there's a launderette round the corner. There's a gas fire in each room that runs off a slot meter – you know, you have to put 50p in. Oh, and the loo is in the bathroom. You know: it's very charming – it's got lots of character.
Young woman:	You mean ... it's a bit down at heel?
Landlady:	We were going to have a decorating weekend soon: you know, we all get some paint and brushes and brighten the place up a bit – it's really not bad. Why don't you come round and look at it? You're from Scotland, aren't you?
Young woman:	Yes, I am. I've just come down to London.
Landlady:	My Dad came from Scotland. Aberdeen.
Young woman:	I'm from Aberdeen!
Landlady:	Well, come over for a cup of tea and see if you like the room! 3.30?
Young woman:	OK, I will. Thank you. Can you give me the address? ...

Dialogue 3

Landlord:	8775 4987.
Woman:	Hello. I'm phoning about the room you advertised in today's Evening Standard.
Landlord:	Oh, right. Well, what do you want to know?
Woman:	You say the flat's near a railway station?
Landlord:	Yes, it's near Clapham Junction mainline station.
Woman:	How near?
Landlord:	Five minute's walk?
Woman:	That's great. Err, it says in the ad 'semi-furnished'.
Landlord:	Ah, yes.
Woman:	So, is there a bed?
Landlord:	Yes, of course.
Woman:	And a table?
Landlord:	A small one.
Woman:	One you can work at?
Landlord:	Erm, not really.
Woman:	Eat at?
Landlord:	Well, actually, it's a bedside table.
Woman:	Chairs?
Landlord:	Err, to be honest, that's it: a bed and a bedside table.
Woman:	I see. And who are the other two people?
Landlord:	I'm one of them – the flat actually belongs to me. And the other tenant is a lady who works in television. What about you?
Woman:	I'm a teacher.
Landlord:	And you did see about the non-smoking and the dog?
Woman:	Yes, I did. I've never smoked and I love animals. Could I maybe come and look at the room?
Landlord:	Sure.

Pyramiding

This is particularly useful for deciding on how to structure a discussion or arguments.
- The teacher gives a topic.
- Each student is required to write down quickly four to five terms that he or she associates with the topic.
- In partner work, the students agree on four of the terms from their lists, which are then ranked according to the importance which the pair believes the terms have for the topic.
- Each pair finds another pair, and together they look at the eight terms which have been gathered, agree on four of them and rank them as above.
- This activity can be done until the whole class has come together or just until groups of eight or 16 have come together.
- Then they present their lists, starting with the term which they think is most important, and give reasons why they think it is, e.g. 'We think that x is the most important for the following reasons', 'we think x is less important because ...'.

Fish Bowl

This is useful for giving feedback on discussion techniques.
- The teacher gives a topic.
- A group of four to five discusses either the pros or cons of the topic.
- One representative from each of the groups takes a chair and places it with those of the other representatives in a circle. There is also one chair for a moderator.
- One more chair is put into the circle and is left empty.
- The rest of the class sits around this group.
- The moderator gets the discussion going by asking one of the people in the circle their opinion on the topic. He or she also ensures that each person in the circle is allowed to speak, and that no one dominates the discussion.
- The rest of the class can contribute by sitting on the empty chair. Once they have said what they want to, they leave the chair, so that someone else can contribute.
- Once the discussion is over, the representatives say how they felt being in the circle.
- The rest of the class then comments on the discussion. The observers can comment, for example, on the following:
  Was there anything missing?
  How did the representatives argue?
  Did they look each other in the face when addressing each other?
  Did they speak clearly?
  Did they listen and allow others to make their point?
  Did they respond to the arguments that were put forward by others?
  Did they deviate from the topic?

Role Play

A role play involves a group of students acting out a scene or situation.
- The group decides who is going to play which role.
- The students write role cards for each of the characters. This should involve a few details about the age and appearance of the character, as well as some information about his or her personality.
- The group considers what the situation is that it is going to act out. On the role cards the students write down how the character will act and why he or she will act in this way. This serves to help the role players when it comes to the role play itself.
- The group rehearses the situation before presenting it to the class, but does not write down lines or a script for the role play.

Hot Seating

This is particularly useful for working out the motivation of characters in literary texts.
- A student has to prepare him- or herself to take on one of the characters in a story that has been read.
- He or she should make a few notes about how he or she felt at particular times of the story and be prepared to explain why he or she acted in a certain way. The student might also consider events outside the story, e.g. what happened afterwards. It often helps if a group of four to five students discuss these points together. Then they can elect one of their group members to sit on the hot chair. The student should not have any notes at his or her disposal.
- The student sits in the hot chair in the middle of the class, while the other students ask him or her questions about the particular character, addressing him or her as the character of the story. The other students should have written down questions they would like to ask.
- During the questioning a moderator can select people to ask the questions.

Double Circle *(Kugellager)*

This is a useful way of developing one's discussion skills.
- The teacher gives a topic.
- The class is divided into two groups, with one group forming an outer circle and the other an inner circle. The two groups should be facing each other.
- The students in the inner circle start the discussion on the topic with the student facing them.
- They discuss the topic for about three minutes.
- The students in the outer circle then move one place to the right.
- The discussion starts again and continues ideally until the two original partners are facing each other to talk one last time about the topic, but can be interrupted by the teacher beforehand.
- The teacher can then open a new discussion by asking the following questions: 'What was the most important aspect you discussed?', 'Which aspects kept cropping up?', etc.

Writing Conference *(Schreibgespräch)*

This can be used to get ideas and arguments for topics or for creative writing.
- The teacher gives the title of a topic.
- The students work in groups of four to five. Within a certain time limit, each student writes down on a piece of paper a few lines reacting to the topic.
- The papers are then given to a student sitting next to them. The students comment on what has been written (again within the time limit).
- This continues until everyone in the group has reacted to every original statement and the comments on them and the papers have been returned to the original students.
- This activity should be done in silence.

Freeze Frames *(Standbild)*

These are useful for understanding situations and the reasons for particular behaviour in fictional texts.
- Groups choose a situation from the text, which they must present to the class. The group presents it as though it is a freeze frame from a video.
- The group has to present the situation so that the rest of the class can guess what situation is being shown.
- Either the class or the group describes the characters and their emotions during the situation.

ACTIVE VOCABULARY

Introduction

Land/scape
p. 8

dread sth. (l. 8), spend time together (l. 9), have an opinion on sth. (l. 13), have different opinions (l. 17), expect more of sb. (ll. 39–40), keep on doing sth. (l. 34), actually (l. 42), polite (l. 77), be busy doing sth. (l. 92), for that matter (l. 94), embarrassing (l. 112), make an effort to do sth. (l. 126), control yourself (l. 126), lose your temper (l. 127), challenge (l. 131), right on cue (l. 158), defiant (l. 167), possession (l. 168), avoid sth. (l. 185), lose courage (l. 224), live up to sth. (l. 243), fit in (l. 248)

Young, Talented
and Rebellious
p. 18

excel in sth. (l. 1), refuse to do sth. (ll. 3, 12), stick to sth. (l. 4), grasp the opportunities before you (ll. 5–6), regret sth. (l. 7), get a degree (l. 10), A-level results (l. 10), turn your back on sth. (l. 18), go along with sth. (ll. 20–21), end up (l. 21), give sth. up (l. 26), leave sth. too late (l. 27), cope with sth. (l. 32), take advantage of sth. (l. 44)

Chapter I: All in the Family

The Trouble
with Mother
p. 22

Partner A, p. 22: be pretty strict (l. 1), be unbearable (l. 4), have some privacy (l. 5), I can't help feeling jealous (l. 20), worry (l. 25), not mind sth. (l. 25), reassure sb. (l. 27)
Partner B, p. 25: call sb. sth. (l. 4), accuse sb. of doing sth. (l. 6), argue back (l. 7), embarrassing (l. 9), concerned (l. 12), watch sb.'s every move (ll. 12–13), quiz sb. about sth. (l. 16), be embarrassed by sb./sth. (l. 18), get on well with sb. (l. 32), constant questions/accusations (ll. 33–34), take sth. the wrong way (l. 36)
tasks: appropriate, comfortable

Households and
Families:
1990 and 2000
p. 28

grow by sth. (l. 1), increase (l. 2), the vast majority of sth. (l. 7), be related to sb. (l. 8), the average (family) size (ll. 16–17), decrease (l. 17), over (a period of time) (l. 17), decline (l. 18), respectively (l. 18), downward trend (l. 18)

Giving Thanks
p. 31

save sb. from sth. (l. 2), turn into sth. (l. 4), set a goal for sb./sth. (l. 9), beg sb. to do sth. (l. 12), plead with sb. to do sth. (ll. 12–13), suggest sth. (l. 20), be impressed (by sth.) (l. 23), mean sth. to sb. (l. 24), obligation (ll. 24–25), have nothing in common (l. 26), do a better job (l. 66), grade (l. 72), bury sth. (l. 88)

Chapter II: Youth Culture

This
Thing Called
'Youth Culture'
p. 38

emergence (l. 1), phenomenon (l. 2), leisure time (l. 2), rite of passage (l. 5), provoke a response (ll. 10–11), contradictory (l. 10), a defining moment (l. 15), inspire sth. (l. 15), impact (l. 18), lead the way (l. 22), slow down (l. 27), distinct (l. 28), contemporary (l. 30), dull (l. 30)
tasks: contain sth., make a point, relate to sth.

I'm Britain's
Top Teen DJ
p. 40

honest, keen, be over the moon, get used to sth., have a laugh (1st column); dedicated to sth., have a chat, down to earth, wish sb. luck (2nd column); in the meantime, ambition (3rd column)

Diet-crazy
Girls ...
and Boys
p. 42

diet (ll. 3, 27), self-esteem (l. 2), concern about sth. (l. 2), survey (l. 4), lose weight (l. 6), appearance (l. 8), skip sth. (l. 10), desire (l. 13), anxiety (l. 14), shape (l. 18), be aware of sth. (l. 19), make sb. comfortable with sth. (ll. 20–21), health campaigner (l. 22), encourage sb. to do sth. (l. 23), be sceptical about sb./sth. (l. 23), exercise (l. 27), question sth. (l. 28)

ACTIVE VOCABULARY

Chapter III: Science and Technology

Chapter IV: Our Fragile Planet

If the Earth   diameter, marvel at sth., layer, creature, surface, sacred, heal sb./sth., gain knowledge
p. 74

The Lake   *tasks:* convey sth., achieve sth., artificial
at Petworth
p. 76

The Lake Isle   hive (l. 3), veil (l. 6), glow (l. 7), shore (l. 10), pavement (l. 11)
of Innisfree   *tasks:* support sth., quote, feature sth., reflect sth.
p. 77

Nice Places   sit next to sb. (l. 1), chop sth. down (l. 9)
p. 78   *tasks:* based on sth., examine sth., background, advantage

What Happened   branch (l. 3), glisten (l. 3), livestock (l. 4), barn (l. 4), ditch (l. 7), huddle (l. 12),
during   expect sb. to do sth. (l. 19), pounce on sb./sth. (l. 19), yell (l. 19), barbed-wire fence (ll. 20–21),
the Ice Storm   seed (l. 21), yolk (l. 22), layer (l. 27), shell (l. 30), soak through sth. (l. 32)
p. 80   *tasks:* cover sth., reveal sth., behave

Too Much   become apathetic (l. 8), perform sth. (l. 9), deal with sth. (l. 9), car-pooling (l. 10),
Trouble?   recycling (l. 10), be passionate about sth. (l. 10), environmental awareness (l. 13),
p. 83   deplorable (l. 24), passion (l. 26), convenience (l. 28), abandon sth. (l. 32),
   craving for sth. (l. 37), evident (l. 37), dependence on sth. (ll. 37–38), replace sth. (l. 39),
   consumerism (l. 41), resources (l. 45)
   tasks: loss, take up an interest, consist of sth.

What Is 'Eden'   symbol of (l. 1), mankind (l. 1), rejection (l. 2), conservation policy (l. 2),
about?   keep sb. out of sth. (l. 4), live in harmony with nature (l. 6), destruction (l. 6),
p. 84   a beneficial effect (l. 7), challenges lie ahead (l. 7), meet a challenge (l. 8)

Economists   enthusiastic (l. 1), well-educated (ll. 2–3), well-off (l. 3), sentimental (l. 4),
Are Also   favo(u)r sth. (l. 10), incentive (l. 18), a tax on sth. (l. 18), tend to do sth. (l. 24),
Environmentalists   discourage sb. from doing sth. (l. 28), revenue from sth. (l. 29), income tax (l. 31),
p. 85   reduction in sth. (l. 33), aside from sth. (ll. 35–36), the general consensus (l. 39),
   on balance (l. 39), so what? (l. 41), leisure time (l. 44), agree on sth. (l. 46), cuddly (l. 47)
   tasks: affect sth., convice sb. of sth.

Chapter V: A Global Marketplace

Business $65 a week (l. 19), frankly (l. 21), ask a favour of sb. (l. 25), appreciate sth. (l. 30),
Is Business   desperately (l. 38), admit sth. (l. 39), streak (l. 48), self-reliance (l. 48),
p. 92   make a living (l. 55), career (l. 56), funeral (l. 62), comradeship (l. 65), gratitude (l. 65),
   pull yourself together (l. 88), fire sb. (l. 96), give sb. a hand (l. 102), false pride (l. 104),
   cripple (l. 110), stop by (l. 115)

Poverty Is   housing estate (l. 4), social change (l. 5), stereotypical image of sth. (l. 6), aid worker (l. 6),
Relative   by sb.'s standards (l. 10), dispirited (l. 15), depressed (l. 15), alcoholic (l. 15), self-esteem (l. 15),
p. 95   be worse off than sb. (l. 16), fall into the trap of ... (l. 18), material benefits (l. 19),
   suffer social deprivation (l. 20), be jobless (ll. 20–21)

© 2003 Cornelsen Verlag, Berlin • Alle Rechte vorbehalten • New Context

ACTIVE VOCABULARY

'I Have to Keep
the Hot Water
for the Kids'
p. 96

cash (l. 1), keep a diary (l. 4), bus fare (l. 10), spend money (on sth.) (ll. 11–12), be in debt (l. 25), borrow sth. (from sb.) (l. 28), work sth. out (l. 30), lend sb. sth. (l. 31), be on social security (l. 62), calm sb. (l. 64), give sth. up (l. 64), moan (l. 71), be on its last legs (l. 72)
tasks: sense sth., draw up a budget

Starting Your Own
Business
p. 97

on your own (l. 1), look after sb. (l. 1), set up a business (l. 4), supply sb./sth. (l. 4), straight away (l. 5), make a living from sth. (ll. 8–9), be in work (l. 11), undertake work for sb. (l. 12), do a good job (l. 14), willing to do sth. (ll. 14–15), hire sb. (l. 15), a waiting list (l. 15), self-employed (l. 16), bank account (l. 16), rented accommodation (l. 17), build up a business (l. 18)

As Basic as the
Screwdriver
p. 101

win the lottery (l. 1), enroll (BE: enrol) sb. in a school (l. 3), a bright future (l. 4), second language (l. 11), spread beyond sth. (l. 16), link sb./sth. to sb./sth. else (l. 17), move toward(s) political and economic unification (ll. 17–18), a common language (l. 18), crucial (l. 18), labor (BE: labour) market (l. 20), implications (l. 25), engineer (l. 28), blue-collar worker (l. 29), colleague (l. 29), customer (l. 30), factory floor (l. 32)

Political and
Economic
Freedom
p. 102

settlement (!l. 1), a magnet for sth. (l. 2), seek adventure (l. 3), flee from sth. (l. 3), make a better life for yourself (ll. 3–4), be attracted by sth. (ll. 8–9), affluence (l. 9), streets paved with gold (l. 10), make the most of sth. (l. 11), encourage sb. to do sth. (l. 13), masterpiece (l. 19), insight (l. 24), the public good (l. 32), proclaim sth. (l. 35), be entitled to do sth. (l. 36), pursue sth. (l. 36), equality of opportunity (ll. 43–44), the free market (l. 48)

The Fair Society
p. 103

provide sth. (l. 2), public services (ll. 2–3), regulate sth (l. 3), be conceived as sth. (l. 3), risk (l. 4), allocate sth. (l. 7), market forces (l. 7), enforce sth. (l. 8)
tasks: fulfil a task, issue, impose a tariff, economic growth

Chapter VI: Inform, Educate and Entertain

Germans
Destroy Wembley
p. 109

demolition (l. 1), get the go-ahead (l. 8), site (l. 21), clear sth. (l. 21), feature sth. (l. 22), stage sth. (l. 24), be financed by sb./sth (l. 27), loan (l. 28), chief executive (l. 29), have the last laugh (l. 31), venue (l. 31)
tasks: consider sth., devote space to sth., merely

Work Starts
and Stops on
Wembley
p. 110

site (l. 4), call it a day (ll. 5–6), construction firm (l. 8), in charge of sth. (l. 8), make a speech (l. 9), mark an occasion (l. 9), owe sth. to sb. (l. 10), swing into action (l. 13)
tasks: device, pay attention to sth., make a point, similar

The Sheep in
Wolf's Clothing
p. 111

spy (l. 2), make (some) notes (l. 6), guess sth. (l. 10), slip away (l. 10), suspect sth. (l. 11), publisher (l. 13), message (l. 17), be convinced by sth. (l. 19)

A Letter
to the Editor
p. 114

inspiration for sth. (ll. 2–3), the high point (ll. 3–4), caption (l. 7), assert sth./that … (l. 8), look to sth. for inspiration (ll. 9–10), check sth. (l. 10)

TV Is
Big Business
p. 115

beckon (l. 5), tanned (l. 6), home to sth. (l. 7), be set in … (l. 9), export sth. around the globe (l. 11), prime-time television (l. 13), decade (l. 15), be the beneficiary of sth. (l. 19), a turnover of $ … (l. 22), the average (American) (l. 27), the widespread use of sth. (l. 34), personal hygiene (l. 37)

Rather than Talking about the Weather p. 116	on average (l. 1), accurate (l. 3), a topic of conversation (l. 4), according to sb./sth. (l. 5), leisure time (l. 8), a classic film (l. 15), underestimate sth. (l. 16), attitude (l. 16), social decline (l. 18), the role of sth. (l. 20), deplore sth. (l. 22), current television shows (ll. 22–23), be associated with sb./sth. (l. 25)
The Reliability of Internet Information p. 118	judge sth. (l. 1), the reliability of sth. (l. 1), crucial (l. 1), regulating body (l. 2), a reliable source (l. 5), obtain valuable information (l. 5), questionable (l. 7), tell the difference (l. 8), bias (l. 17), provide information (on sth.) (l. 18), update sth. (l. 20), the purpose of sth. (l. 21), verify information (l. 24) *tasks:* imply sth.
We Are Speaking of Art p. 120	single sth. out (l. 3), admire sth. (l. 5), shape (l. 5), confidence (l. 6), be more likely to do sth. (l. 7), be reputed to be sth. (ll. 19–20), attend university (l. 22), give a lecture on sth. (ll. 24–25), make sth. memorable (l. 28), hold the attention of sb. (l. 40), gather information (l. 41), devise a campaign (l. 51), researcher (l. 55), conduct tests (l. 55), train yourself to do sth. (l. 62), avert your gaze (l. 71)
AIDA p. 122	make sure that (l. 3), catch sb.'s attention (ll. 3, 14), reveal sth. (l. 4), conceal sth. (l. 4), a common interest (ll. 4–5), concern (l. 5), benefit (l. 7), potential (l. 7), enhance sth. (l. 8), irresistible (l. 9), guarantee (ll. 11, 16), overwhelm sb. with sth. (l. 15) *poster:* trafficking, assault

Chapter VII: Turning Conflict into Art

The Flight of Refugees (April 3, 1938) p. 127	refugee (l. 1), sob (l. 2), sewing machine (l. 4), mattress (l. 5), look back over your shoulder (ll. 11–12), civilian population (l. 18), troops (l. 18), cheerful (l. 19), ridiculous (l. 20)
Old Man at the Bridge p. 128	truck (l. 2), stagger (l. 3), bank (l. 4), peasant (l. 6), take care of sb./sth. (l. 15), shepherd (l. 19), look out for oneself (l. 34), blankly (l. 45), urge (l. 60), sway (l. 61), advance toward(s) sth. (l. 66), overcast (l. 66), good luck (l. 68)
The Ultimate Pain Relief p. 130	ultimate, pain relief, calm sb./sth., soothe sb./sth., comfort sb./sth., soul *tasks:* evaluate sth., effectiveness
'In Flanders Fields' and 'Grass' p. 131	*In Flanders Fields:* cross (l. 2), row (l. 2), dawn (l. 7), sunset (l. 7), quarrel (l. 10), foe (l. 10), hold sth. high (l. 12), grow (l. 14) *Grass:* pile sth. (ll. 1, 4, 5), cover sth. (l. 3), conductor (l. 7) *tasks:* stand for sth., represent sth., convey a message
Henry V: Prologue p. 132	cram sth. (with) in sth. else (l. 2), confined (l. 8), imperfections (l. 11), imaginary (l. 13), accomplishment (l. 18) *tasks:* be faced with sth.
Battle of Agincourt p. 133	fresh (l. 6), (the) odds (l. 7), warrior (l. 12), honour (l. 22), garments (l. 26), sin (l. 28), noble (l. 35), dispose of sth. (ll. 43–44) *tasks:* outcome, rehearse sth.
An Infinitely Hopeful Message p. 135	audience (l. 4), applaud (l. 5), take possession of sth. (l. 9), be conscious of sth. (l. 10), acknowledge (l. 12), be aware of sth. (l. 12), cough (l. 14), sneeze (l. 14), humiliation (l. 17), in vain (l. 22), radiant (l. 32), stunned (l. 35), reign (l. 41), peak (l. 42), endeavour (l. 44)

Chapter VIII: The UK – Redefining a Nation?

Quotes in the 'Lead-in' p. 142	innovation, patriotic, epitomize sth., eccentricity, moan about sth.
Chicken Tikka Massala p. 144	the ethnic composition (ll. 1–2), indigenous to (a place) (l. 4), be driven out by sb. (l. 11), ransom (l. 16), without parallel (l. 21), be home to sth. (l. 22), asset (l. 26), contribute to sth. (l. 26), social cohesion (l. 31), illegal migrant (l. 32), cultural diversity (l. 36), staff (l. 39), recruit sb. (l. 39), broaden sb.'s horizons (l. 42), open to new influences (l. 44), come to terms with sth. (l. 51)
The Great Immigrant Experiment p. 146	mass exodus (l. 6), cramped (l. 6), mistake sb. for sb. else (ll. 8–9), comfort (l. 12), admit sth. (l. 13), infection (l. 18), puddle (l. 20), bring sb. back home (ll. 27–28), weep (l. 28), preach (l. 32), disappointment (l. 33), merge with sth. (l. 41), occur to sb. (l. 42), sneak into sth. (l. 47), leave it at that (l. 49) *tasks:* concern, increase sth., anxiety, contradict sb., convince sb., concerning
Devolution in the UK p. 150	provide for sth. (l. 1), be located in (a place) (l. 2), take over certain functions (ll. 2–3), local government (ll. 5–6), retain responsibility for sth. (l. 7), foreign policy (l. 8)
A New Flag for a Changing Country? p. 151	represent sth. (l. 1), out of control (ll. 1–2), reference to sth. (l. 7), a reminder of sth. (l. 8), a symbol of unity (l. 11), acknowledge sth. (l. 21) *tasks:* match sth. to sth. else, to what extent
Down in the North p. 152	the health service (l. 3), low-skilled workers (l. 4), prosperous (l. 6), prosperity (l. 6), community (l. 7), be integrated (ll. 8–9), economic prospects (l. 15), unemployment rate (l. 24), breeding ground for sth. (l. 27), racial tension (l. 27), the wealth gap (ll. 30–31), social housing (l. 43), be in short supply (l. 43), a high-growth area (l. 44) *tasks:* division, distribution
This Sceptred Isle p. 154	throne (l. 1), fortress (l. 4), infection (l. 5), *tasks:* create an impression, be referred to as sth., select sth.
Those Wild and Crazy English p. 156	(the) essence of sth. (l. 4), boil sth. down to sth. else (l. 4), in terms of sth. (l. 8), a tendency to sth. (l. 10), suicide (l. 10), eccentric (l. 13) *tasks:* according to sb., depend on sth., an example of sth., indifference
Old Empire p. 158	(i) dominate (l. 3), bar none (l. 4), off the coast of (a place) (l. 4), seek to do sth. (l. 6), address a question (l. 7), on balance (l. 9) (ii) awe sb. (l. 3), the transient nature of sth. (l. 5), solitary (l. 5), astounding (l. 7), the better part of sth. (l. 7), stretch from (one place) to (another place) (l. 13), how on earth ...? (l. 16) (iii) supremacy (l. 2), the burden of sth. (l. 5), debtor (l. 5), expansion (l. 7), dwindle (l. 10)
A Book Review: 'Sweet Taste of Empire' p. 160	a span of x years (l. 2), lay claim to sth. (l. 2), surface (l. 3), contemporary (l. 4), be good at doing sth. (l. 7), be hooked on sth. (l. 9), evolve sth. (l. 10), navy (l. 10), dub sth. sth. else (l. 11), frown on sth. (l. 14), doubt sth. (l. 19)
New Empire: The Triumph of English p. 161	in some sense (l. 3), be exposed to sth. (l. 3), predict sth. (l. 4), be proficient in sth. (l. 4), official document (l. 7), global language (l. 12–13), supremacy (l. 17), decline (l. 19), farther afield (l. 32), negotiate sth. (l. 33) *tasks:* based on sth., for what purpose, be exposed to sth., exposure, responsible for sth.

Chapter IX: We the People

Extract from *'Leviathan'* *p. 164*	replica (l. 1), town hall (l. 3), divide people (l. 4), bring people together (l. 4), be proud of sth. (l. 5), feel ashamed of sth. (l. 6), regard sth. as sth. else (l. 7), be immune from sth. (l. 8), transcend sth. (l. 9), emblem (l. 10), represent sth. (l. 11), live up to your ideals (l. 15), give comfort to sb. (l. 16)
The New Colossus *p. 166*	mighty (l. 2), imprisoned (l. 3), beacon (l. 4)
Dirty Blvd. *p. 167*	landlord (l. 2), dream of being sth. (l. 3), bigotry (l. 6), get it over with (l. 8), dump sb./sth. (l. 8), end up (l. 9)
American Dream *p. 167*	*tasks*: attitude towards, in the light of, view of, take sth. into consideration
America *Triumphant* *p. 171*	set off (l. 1), hijack (a plane) (l. 2), civilians (l. 3), nightmare (l. 6), vulnerable (l. 9), cowardly (l. 9), show resolve (ll. 9–10), liberate sb. from sth. (l. 10), base (l. 11), forces (l. 11), war-torn country (l. 11), alliance (l. 13), back sb. (l. 13), respectively (l. 14)
Imperial Power *p. 171*	imperial power (l. 1), empire (l. 2), meet with resistance (l. 2), resist sb./sth. (l. 3), by military/economic means (l. 3), response to sth. (l. 4), a policy of sth. (l. 5), non-cooperation (l. 5), act unilaterally (l. 6), resume sth. (l. 8)
A Growing *Dislike* *of the USA* *p. 172*	increasing (l. 1), trend (l. 2), discontent (l. 6), traditional ally (l. 6), embrace sth. (l. 8), spread of sth. (l. 11), beneficial (l. 11), paint sb./sth. in a bad light (l. 14), news agency (ll. 14–15), growing (l. 23), a dislike of sth. (l. 23), hold a (favourable) view of sb./sth. (ll. 23–24), enjoy support (l. 29), be critical about sth. (ll. 30–31), business practices (l. 31)
Bound by a *Common Thread* *p. 173*	afford sth. (l. 3) complain (l. 3), freeze (l. 3), wool (l. 4), silk (l. 4), sew sth. together (l. 6), fight for/against sth. (ll. 16, 17), a cure for sth. (l. 17), right/left wing (l. 19), hawk (l. 19), dove (l. 19) *tasks*: briefly, convince sb., a wide range of sth., concept
Lifeblood of *the Nation* *p. 174*	accept immigrants (l. 1), legal immigrants (l. 3), people with skills (l. 3), have sth. to offer (l. 6), at a fraction of the cost (l. 8), be in a hurry (l. 10), in the heat of the moment (l. 11), times have changed (l. 23), in terms of sth. (l. 24), social services (l. 25), contribute sth. (l. 30), tax revenues (l. 30), use up sth. (l. 30), welfare (l. 31), schooling (l. 31), crime (l. 32), deserve a chance in life (l. 37), assimilate (l. 38) *tasks*: deal with an issue, argue one's case, evaluate sth., convert sth. into sth. else
Assimilation, *American-style* *p. 175*	census (l. 1), consciousness (l. 1), have a huge impact (l. 5), assimilate sb. (l. 7), change for the worse (l. 11), multiculturalism (l. 15), diversity (l. 16), dated (l. 16), retain (your) ethnic traditions (l. 18), take pride in your (American) identity (ll. 20–21), self-reliant (l. 22), hardworking (l. 22), morally upright (ll. 22–23), third-generation (Latinos) (l. 30), mirror sth. (l. 30), backlash (l. 36), recession (l. 36), benefit from sth. (l. 37), economic boom (l. 40) *tasks*: cultural diversity, enrich sth., endanger sth.
The Magic of *Baseball* *p. 178*	memories of sb./sth. (l. 3), recall sth. (l. 7), relive sth. (l. 11), permit sb. to do sth. (l. 14), recapture sth. (l. 14), settle into sth. (l. 29), curse sb./sth. (l. 32), cheer sb./sth. (l. 33), break sb.'s heart (l. 34), tease sb. about sth. (l. 37), obsession (l. 37), committed to sth. (l. 39), create a bond between sb. (l. 40), in deep conversation (l. 41), share sth. with sb. (l. 45), in the presence of sb. (l. 53), a bond between sb. (l. 56), link sb./sth. to (l. 57)

A Sedentary
Nation
p. 180

sedentary (title, l. 11), have sb. round for dinner (l. 2), blank look (l. 5), make a study of sth. (l. 9), barely (l. 12), be no stranger to sth. (l. 12), within walking distance of sth. (l. 16), insist (l. 30), leave the scene of an accident (l. 34), occur to sb. (l. 36), ludicrous (l. 37), leave the motor/engine running (ll. 40, 43), an acquaintance of (mine/ours) (l. 46), adjust sth. (l. 52), urban planners (l. 65), suburban malls (l. 68), thrive (l. 72)

Chapter X: Who Am I?

Lead-in:
Statements
p. 184

a) assume sth.
b) withdrawn, outgoing, overcome sth.
c) have a fit, bring sb. home with you, dating
e) show an interest in sth.
g) faith
k) self-confident, assertive
m) easy-going, get upset, go with the flow
n) earn money, fulfilment
o) lack of sth., socialist

Origami
p. 186

follow directions (l. 9), be lost (l. 11), confusion (l. 15), persevere (l. 18), give up (l. 19), impostor (l. 23), fuss over sb. (l. 30), minimum wage (l. 34), smell of sth. (l. 40), party (of people) (l. 43), greet sb. (l. 45), hand sb. sth. (l. 47), moist (l. 55), blush (l. 65), tainted (l. 68), scoff (l. 71), not have a clue (l. 73), freckles (l. 87), feel guilty (l. 92), awkward (l. 105)
tasks: refer to sth., attitude, achieve sth., self-confidence

Beckham
Is the Best
p. 190

don't mind sb. (l. 3), fancy sb. (l. 8), nod (one's head) (ll. 17, 31), fall for sb. (l. 22), the penny drops (l. 29), shrug one's shoulders (l. 35), marry sb. (l. 37), punch sb. (l. 38)
tasks: reveal sth., issue, leave sth. unsaid, indication, according to sb./sth.

A Question
of Accent
p. 192

posh (l. 4), snobby (l. 4), admittedly (l. 5), cruelty (l. 7), be doomed (l. 11), unrelenting (l. 11), grief (l. 11), pariah (l. 25), giggle (l. 32), feel humiliated (l. 33), distingush between sth. (l. 39), womb (l. 41), be obsessed by sth. (l. 42)
tasks: refer to sth., be associated with sth.

Aim Higher
p. 195

so what if ..., photographer, editor, be brilliant at sth., loads of sth., have a say in sth., higher education

I Have
an Ambition ...
p. 196

extraordinary (l. 1), be affected by sth. (l. 4), fame (l. 5), have the fortune/misfortune to be sth.(l. 7), swotty (l. 15), true to oneself (l. 17), be fooling yourself (l. 21), make the grade (ll. 21–22), decade (l. 23), academic (l. 24), map out your future (l. 25), read up about sth. (ll. 25–26), ambition (l. 31), strive for sth. (l. 35)
tasks: celebrity, distinction, goal, achieve sth.

Find
Your Hidden
Strengths
p. 197

dream job (l. 1), obvious (l. 2), talent (l. 2), hidden strengths (l. 3), be great at sth. (l. 9), point sb. toward(s) sth. (l. 10), have a knack for sth. (l. 14), fix sth. (l. 15), endure sth. (l. 19), device (l. 25), struggle with sth. (l. 26)

'The Road
Not Taken'
and 'Ships?'
p. 198

'The Road Not Taken': diverge (l. 1), undergrowth (l. 5), sigh (l. 16), make all the difference (l. 20)
'Ships?': sail (a ship) (l. 1), float (l. 4), breath (l. 13), failure (l. 16), (not) be ashamed to do sth. (l. 17)
tasks: experience, message, outlook on sth., appropriate, content

Chapter XI: Moving Out

The Road to London p. 202
discover sth. (l. 3), farewell (l. 4), blessing (l. 4), make up your mind (l. 10), belongings (l. 12), appeal (l. 13), persuasion (l. 13), settle down (l. 25), unease (l. 26), inevitable (l. 26), vigour (l. 36), reluctance (l. 37), indifference (l. 39), solitary (l. 41), be on your own (ll. 45–46)
tasks: relationship, mood, be intended to, comparable, account

Running Away p. 204
run away from home (l. 2), malcontent (l. 3), underwear (l. 5), waterproof (l. 5), sleeping bag (l. 6), wits (l. 8), abduct sb. (l. 10), pervert (l. 11), binliner (l. 12), rubbish tip (l. 12), get fed up with sb. (l. 13), leave of your own accord (l. 14), leave home (l. 17), no hard feelings (l. 20), unbearable (l. 22), beware (l. 23), undermine sth. (l. 24), credibility (l. 24), book sth. (l. 25)

Free! p. 205
good riddance (l. 3), have time on your hands (l. 5), convertible (l. 7), all day long (l. 8), rape sb. (l. 14), murder sb. (l. 14), resent sth. (l. 16), waste sth. (l. 21), plan for sth. (l. 22), retirement (l. 22), prepare for sth. (l. 26), retire (l. 28), refuse to do sth. (l. 29), look back on sth. (l. 29), responsibility (l. 33), drudgery (l. 33), tedium (l. 33), pretentious (l. 35), catch sb.'s drift (l. 38), ultimately (l. 38), raise a family (l. 44), have a point (l. 48), die of sth. (l. 48)

So I Have a New Name – Refugee p. 207
personality (l. 3), refugee (l. 4), share sth. (l. 5), comfort (l. 8), restore sth. (l. 9), offer sth. (l. 11), borrow sth. (l. 12), seek sth. (l. 13)
tasks: association, preference, contrast sth. with sth. else

Career Plan p. 209
available (l. 2), make a decision (l. 2), determine sth. (l. 7), evaluate (l. 10), challenging (l. 11), be employed (l. 14), activities (l. 17), volunteer (l. 19), intern (l. 26), internship (l. 26), gain ex-perience (l. 27), network (l. 28), assess sth. (l. 29), work experience (l. 33), focus on sth. (l. 34)

Doomsday p. 211
apply for sth. (l. 6), course (l. 6), reconsider sth. (l. 7), reapply (l. 7), refer to sth. as sth. (l. 8), doomsday (l. 8), scared (l. 9), revise (l. 10), social life (l. 10), expectations (l. 14), a degree in (a subject) (l. 16), retake (an exam) (l. 17), dread (doing) sth. (l. 17), tension (l. 18), take a gap year (l. 19)
tasks: in particular, consider sth., rigorous

Applying to a US University p. 212
vital (l. 2), apply to (a university) (l. 3), evaluate sth. (l. 4), academic record (l. 5), accomplishment(s) (l. 7), activity (l. 7), gain insight into sth. (l. 7), evident (l. 10), a frame of reference (l. 14), initiative (l. 16), motivation (l. 16), leadership (l. 16), persistence (l. 17), overcome sth. (l. 18), challenge (l. 18), internship (l. 21), establish a goal (l. 24), effective (l. 30), allow time for sth. (l. 33), contribute to sth. (l. 35)

Victoria, Not Vicky p. 214
make an entrance (ll. 3–4), smile at sb. (l. 11), introduce yourself (l. 12), turn to sb. (l. 12), titter (ll. 13–14), inhale deeply (l. 38), wash your hair (l. 42), look a fright (l. 42), tell sb. the truth (l. 42), stink of sth. (l. 43), move away from sb./sth. (l. 44), delicate (l. 50)

Eveline p. 217
odour (l. 2), where on earth (l. 21), familiar (l. 22), casual (l. 28), consent to do sth. (l. 30), run away with sb. (l. 34), elated (l. 72), forbid sb. to do sth. (l. 83), quarrel with sb. (l. 85), lap (l. 87), indistinct (l. 88), remind sb. of sth. (l. 98), catch a glimpse of sth. (l. 117), distress (l. 123), grip sth. (l. 128), railing (l. 128), clutch sth. (l. 130), frenzy (l. 130), anguish (l. 131), farewell (l. 135), recognition (l. 135)
tasks: trace sth., justify sth., play a major role, achieve an effect

Acknowledgements: CD, Video/DVD

CD

I/All in the Family
'Sex Columnist': © WGN Radio, Kathy and Judy Show (1.3.2003).

II/Youth Culture
'Everybody's Free (to Wear Sunscreen)': © EMI Music Australia Pty. Ltd.
'A Whiter Shade of Pale': *Procul Harum*, P and © 1967 Cube Records.
'Because I Got High': P 2001 Universal Records. © 2001 Universerval Records, a Division of UMG Recordings.

III/Science and Technology
'Wernher von Braun': *The Remains of Tom Lehrer*, P and © Warner Bros Records Inc. & Rhino Entertainment Company.

IV/Our Fragile Planet
'It Was a Lover and His Lass': Published by Peter Maurice Music Co Ltd. P 1978 Mercury Records Ltd.
'Country of Our Time': *Country of Our Time*, © BBC, Radio Four, (12.8.2002).

V/A Global Marketplace
'Interviews with Braj Kachru and David Crystal': *The Routes of English*, © BBC, Radio 4 (11.10.2001).
'NPWA': *England, Half English*
P and © Billy Bragg, BMG Music Publishing Ltd.

VII/Turning Conflict into Art
'Extracts from the Resurrection Symphony': *Mahler's Symphony No. 2*, P and © EMI records, 1987.

IX/ We the People
'Car Culture and the Shopping Mall': *The American Century*, © BBC, World Service, (4.2003).
'America the Beautiful': *God Bless America*, Mormon Tabernacle Choir; P © Sony Music Entertainment, 1965.

X/Who Am I?
'Why Can't the English?': *My Fair Lady: The Original Soundtrack Recording*, © Sony Music Entertainment, 1964,

VIDEO

I/All in the Family
'Taking Responsibility': *My Family*, A BBC Production, 2003, Footage from My Family courtesy of DLT Entertainment Ltd

III/Science and Technology
'Oppenheimer: Extract 1': *The Day after Trinity*, © 1980 Jon Else
'Oppenheimer: Extract 2': *Oppenheimer*, A BBC Production, © 1981

IV/Our Fragile Planet
'The Destruction of Habitats': *State of the Planet*, A BBC/Discovery Co-Production, © BBC Worldwide Ltd 2000

VI/Inform, Educate and Entertain
'How to Get on TV: Extract 1': *Popstars,*: A London Weekend Television Production, © 2001 London Weekend Television Ltd
'How to Get on TV: Extract 2': *The Weakest Link (Insults and Exits),* A BBC Production, © BBC Worldwide Ltd 2001
'How to Get on TV: Extract 3': *Big Brother Uncut 2*, © Channel 4 Television Corporation MM 2000, Endemol Entertainment International B.V.
'How to Get on TV: Extract 4': *Survivor – Unseen*, A Planet 24 Production for the ITV Network, © Planet 24 Productions Ltd 2001

VII/Turning Conflict into Art
'A Shakespearian Performance': *Shakespeare in Love*, Miramax Film / Universal Pictures / The Bedford Falls Company © 1998 Miramax Film Corp. and Universal Studios
'Henry V: Prologue': *Henry V*: The Rank Collection, © 1945 Rank Film Distributors Ltd
'Two Performances of Henry V: Extract 1': *Henry V*, Produced by BBC and Time-Life Films, © 1979
'Two Performances of Henry V: Extract 2': *Henry V*, The Samuel Goldwyn Company and Renaissance Films PLC in association with the BBC, © 2001
'Conventry: Destruction and Reconciliation': *Coventry: Rising from the Ashes*, A Video-Ex Production, © 1994

VIII/The UK – Redefining a Nation?
'Those Wild and Crazy English: Task 2': *Monty Python's Flying Circus – DVD 9*, © 1972, 1973 Python (Monty) Pictures Ltd

IX/ We the People
'Inaugural Speech': *George W. Bush – Election and Inauguration,* CBS News Productions, © 2001 CBS Worldwide Inc.
'The American Way of Life as Reflected on TV': *The Sopranos*, Brillstein-Grey Entertainment/Chase Films Production in association with HBO Original Programming, © 1999 Brillstein-Grey Entertainment Inc. / HBO Original Programming

X/Who Am I?
'Beckham is the Best: Task 2b': *Bend It Like Beckham*, A Kintop Pictures Production, © 2002 Kintop Films

XI/Moving Out
'Off to College': *College Girls,*A Channel 4 Production, © 2001